Humanism
Y1

AN INTRODUCTION
TO THE
STUDY OF MAN

AN INTRODUCTION
TO THE
STUDY OF MAN

BY

J. Z. YOUNG

M.A., F.R.S.

PROFESSOR OF ANATOMY IN THE UNIVERSITY
OF LONDON AT UNIVERSITY COLLEGE

NEW YORK AND OXFORD
OXFORD UNIVERSITY PRESS

PREFACE

THIS book arose out of lectures given to medical and dental students at the beginning of their studies. It is therefore literally an introduction to the possibility of studying man in a scientific manner. To do this is not 'natural' for most people, and indeed may seem actually repellent to some. Yet doctors and dentists have found that by approaching our problems in a scientific way they have been increasingly able to help us. Indeed it is almost true to say that it is only since medicine became scientific that it has been able to be of any real help in curing human ills. It may be that there are still large areas of man's activity in which we can be helped by more detailed study. Many people fear that in some way this threatens an invasion of the individual personality. It is important to respect this apprehension and at all times to emphasize that the aim of all scientific studies is to assist in the improvement of the quality of human life and to enlarge its capacities.

This book is the record of the search for a method by which this can be done. Indeed it can be read as a sort of detective story in which we are searching for an answer to the question 'What is man?' or, more subtly, for the answer to 'What are good ways to study men?' We begin by asking some conceptually rather simple and obviously 'scientific' questions such as 'What are men made of?' This gives an opportunity to look at some of the spectacular recent information that biochemistry has provided about the large molecules in the body, and especially about the information-carrying properties of the nucleic acids. Such knowledge provides completely new ways of talking about the old questions of the nature and origin of life. These serve as preludes to the more specific questions we are interested in about man himself. His life, like that of other creatures, is organized by the information that is received from the past, so that he takes actions that are likely to preserve his life and that of his species in the future. An understanding of the origin and nature of this mechanism for ensuring continued maintenance or homeostasis would go far to give us that basic knowledge of the principles of life for which we are looking. Certainly we have not achieved it yet, but there have been large advances recently, and they revolutionize our knowledge of ourselves. To many people this will seem a necessarily imperfect framework because, they would say, the essential feature of a man is his difference from other creatures in that he possesses a soul, in some sense valuable in itself.

Anyone proposing to study man must face this problem, and we shall indeed attempt to do so. The answers will probably be found inadequate in many respects. Indeed many thoughtful people perhaps feel that we do not know enough to be able to solve this or indeed any other of the fundamental problems of the origin of the world or the meaning of life, and should frankly admit our ignorance. One of our recurrent themes will be that human intelligence, for all its ability, is still very imperfect, but is improving fast. We shall try to look for new light on some of the problems that have worried mankind for centuries.

I am very conscious that such consideration as is given to these great questions is very superficial compared to that of theologians and philosophers who devote their lives to them. Certainly there is no substitute for study of the works of those who have investigated man in all his many aspects. Nevertheless the biologist has at least one special contribution to make in that he studies the agent of study itself—the brain. The possibilities and difficulties that this brings are major themes of the book. As the investigation develops we shall meet repeatedly the particular paradox of human biology, that we are trying to find methods for studying the student himself. Does this involve circular reasoning and if so how does it affect our whole endeavour? These are very old and deep questions of the theory and nature of knowledge (epistemology). Although the biologist is not trained to deal with such problems of logic and philosophy he finds it impossible to avoid doing so. This is perhaps the most serious of the many ways in which the reader must be suspicious of this book. The intention, however, is that he shall at least be stimulated to see some of the philosophical problems that are involved in his ordinary scientific and everyday ways of speech, even though the treatment is too superficial to provide really satisfying answers.

Certainly no one discipline has a monopoly of the right to say what men should do. The body of human knowledge is now so vast that no one set of people trained in a particular discipline can provide the guidance that we need. We have to depend upon artists as much as priests, physicists as well as philosophers, engineers and lawyers, historians, economists, doctors, and politicians, to mention only a few. The course of human life today depends upon the knowledge of all of these and a host more.

I hope that the facts and attitudes recorded here will be found to be useful and will give some satisfaction and help to different sorts of people. What I have aimed to do is to provide enough information to evoke the inspiring spectacle of the vast range of controlled activities that constitutes the life of men and of the living world. With sufficient knowledge we can now just begin to imagine all the tens of thousands of chemical processes that go on in an orderly way as one individual man or woman sits and thinks. We can begin to see the wonderful complexity of the instrument in which the thought is taking place, calling upon a great range of remembered past events, stored in the memory. We now know a little about the origin of the emotional urges that keep us alive and thinking and acting, almost in spite of ourselves and often without even considering the consummations that sometimes satisfy our desires.

Knowledge about the population and its growth will help us to think of our more than three thousand million fellow humans and of all their genetic and cultural differences. Yet they are all working together every minute to make the changing, evolving patterns of man's life. Knowledge again can give us the means to think about all the men who have gone before, gradually emerging from their rough beginnings, acquiring language and laws, clothes and civilization. Was this really a slow continuous process? Have we in any real sense separated from the rest of creation?

Even if man is very different it is fundamentally important to recognize how deeply he is part of the one great living world. In spite of all his artificiality and civilization he depends utterly on plants and animals and is both assisted and menaced by the bacteria and viruses. The preparation of a proper future for man depends upon thinking of the whole life-system as one. Recent discoveries have indeed emphasized the unity of life. All organisms are directed by instructions written in the same genetic code; all are made of almost similar elements and compounds and their cells are made up of similar units. With all the deep similarities as well as endless differences the animals, plants, and bacteria act together to produce one world, of which man is as much a part as the rest, whatever his special features.

In particular what the neurobiologist finds out about the brain must surely be relevant to fundamental views of the nature of all this knowledge. The interpretations of recent findings that are given here may be wrong in parts but they suggest that the whole structure of our language and thought is limited by a pre-programme in the organization of the brain. Our knowledge of this is yet really too meagre to provide sure foundations, but I have tried to show how it may influence not only our understanding of child development but the very way that we speak of our own thinking selves.

Such difficult and fascinating questions keep on intruding and some people would say that in trying to answer them the biologist is stepping outside his field. Certainly much of human biology can be pursued in a more mundane and less philosophical fashion. Many aspects of human life such as sex differences, reproduction, growth, and ageing are greatly illuminated by exact study. Some aspects of the problems of aggression can be studied by 'biological' methods, though here as elsewhere we have to be cautious about analogies between animals and men. The growth of population is certainly another matter that concerns us all, but about which few are properly informed. The assessment of the importance of hereditary factors, again, whether in medicine or education, requires very careful evaluation of evidence.

In order to try to weave the facts about such matters into a coherent science I have concentrated on the fact that human beings use their brains in a characteristic way to produce language. Of course we are almost wholly ignorant of how this is done, but as more is found out it should lead us to increasing understanding of the basis of human individuality and society. The attempt here has been to construct with what is known about early human history and our rudimentary knowledge of cerebral physiology a scheme or model that 'explains' why we behave as we do. In particular I have stressed the importance of the idea that human brain operations revolve around a cerebral model that interprets much of the input in terms of persons. Our first explanation for all happenings is that they are due to the actions of entities like people. And this is natural because the child's first lessons are about the characteristics of people and how to communicate with them. His brain may indeed be pre-programmed to operate in this way. In any case he continues to do so for all except his most sophisticated activities. In this way he thinks about God and the ultimate order of the world and in this way also about himself and his own precious personality.

There is as yet no physiological evidence about how the brain produces this programme. It may be unwise to use it so widely as the framework of human biology. But for this purpose it has the unique advantage that it unifies the approaches of the biologist, psychologist, and indeed of the philosopher. It enables us to speak systematically about many aspects of the human way of life. It shows the basis of many of our anthropomorphic interpretations. Above all it enables us to say something about the most fundamental problem of the study of man—his disposition to distinguish between mind and body.

These may seem to be absurd pretensions for an unsystematic presentation by one who is inexpert in many of the fields of study that are involved. I am only too conscious of its imperfections and shall not be surprised if it fails to convince. But the search for a system has been invigorating and has taught me much that I wished to know. The facts discovered on the way should, at least, be useful to some people.

But the search for principles has been the main aim, principles that shall organize our knowledge of ourselves and help us to organize our lives. Of course no one in their senses would suppose that such principles can provide a primer for life. I hope that this excuses the quite ridiculous imbalance and omissions in the book. It contains little about aesthetics, emotions, or spiritual life; nothing of humour, acting, music, or literature; nothing of architecture or invention, economics, sociology, or law; little of human joys and sorrows, of how to keep well or why we get ill. The psychiatrist will feel the treatment to be very dry and barren, and so may many others.

It is true that these things are of the essence of human life, and in fact I have at no point been unmindful of them. Any proper introduction to the study of man would include them all. But this would be quite impossible. All these features of human life presumably have their significance for survival. Here we have been concerned to discuss the survival value for some features, for instance language. Perhaps this may help to consider the place of others.

With all these excuses the fact remains that this is an absurdly superficial book, both in principles and in detail. We know so much about man and yet understand so little. I shall be satisfied if the book does anything to encourage others to try to understand more.

These are some of the thoughts that have occupied me as I inquired into the many factual and practical matters involved. They have taken me into many fields where I am not expert and the treatment is nowhere as thorough as I would wish. Every specialist will recognize the imperfections of the information in his subject. Therefore every student should be aware that this is not the work of an expert—no one could possibly be that in so many fields. In each of them serious inquiry must involve consultation of the references given and many others.

I have had the advantage of checking facts and opinions with the many colleagues listed at the top of page xi. I am exceedingly grateful to them, not only for their help and criticism, but for the pleasure I have had in following the leads they have given.

I should like to thank the generations of students who have listened to my lectures and commented upon them. Their difficulties have made me aware that many of the points of view are unfamiliar and not easy to accept. Perhaps they are none the worse for the novelty—goodness knows we need new methods.

I am most grateful to the research assistants who have helped in the preparation of the book over several years, including J. S. Altman, C. C. Wood, and E. A. Bradley. M. J. Hobbs has given most valuable help in the later stages and in preparation of the index, in which task R. M. and K. F. Young also assisted. M. Nixon has played an especially large part in organizing the material and references and making corrections. Moreover she has made many suggestions for helping the reader where there might be obscurity, as by the addition of a glossary, conversion tables, and the like.

I am deeply grateful to Mrs. J. Astafiev for continuous help in the difficult work of preparing new figures and the adaptation of those of others.

Mrs. N. Finney and Miss M. Dickens have patiently prepared the long series of revised drafts of the chapters.

It is a great pleasure to thank all at the Clarendon Press for their care in preparation of the book.

A work of this sort is only possible by the collaboration of many brains and hands and I should like finally to thank all my colleagues on the academic and technical staff of the Anatomy Department of University College London, for their help over so many years.

J. Z. Y.

January 1970

ACKNOWLEDGEMENTS

THE following have given great assistance by reading and commenting on parts of the book or providing data.

N. A. Barnicot	E. D. R. Honderich	K. P. Oakley
G. Belyavin	D. W. James	R. Quirk
E. H. S. Burhop	A. R. Jonckheere	A. Rosenfeld
E. Clarke	H. Kalmus	J. Rotblat
A. Comfort	R. M. Kempson	P. J. Ucko
D. T. Donovan	Norma McArthur	C. A. Vernon
M. J. Evans	A. I. Matus	P. D. Wall
E. G. Gray	W. R. Mead	R. A. Weiss
W. F. Grimes	J. R. Napier	D. R. Wilkie
C. M. Harrison		

Thanks are also due to the authors, editors, and publishers of the following works and journals for permission to use figures and tables. The appropriate reference is given in each caption.

Acta psychologica; Adey (ed.), *Progress in brain research*, Vol. 27 (Elsevier, Amsterdam); Aerofilms Ltd.; *American Anthropologist*; *American Journal of Physical Anthropology*; American Museum of Natural History; *American Psychologist*; *Annals of Eugenics*; *Archives of Disease in Childhood*; Assali (ed.), *Biology of gestation* (Academic Press, New York); Barclay, *Techniques of population analysis* (Wiley, New York); Biasutti, *Le razze e i popoli della terra*, Vol. 1 (Editrice Torinese, Turin); *Biochimica et biophysica acta*; Blinkov and Glezer, *The human brain in figures and tables* (Plenum Press, New York); Brachet and Mirsky (eds.), *The cell* (Academic Press, New York); Brace and Ashley Montagu, *Man's evolution* (Macmillan, New York); Brazier, *The electrical activity of the nervous system* (Pitman, London); Bresler (ed.), *Human ecology* (Addison-Wesley, Massachusetts); *British Journal of Educational Psychology*; *British Journal of Psychology*; *British Medical Bulletin*; Buettner-Janusch, *Origins of man* (Wiley, New York); Buettner-Janusch (ed.), *Evolutionary and genetic biology of primates*, Vol. 1 (Academic Press, New York); *Bulletin of the American Museum of Natural History*; Bullough, *The evolution of differentiation* (Academic Press, New York); Burkitt, *Prehistory* (Cambridge University Press); Campbell, *Human evolution: An introduction to man's adaptations* (Aldine Press, Chicago); *Carnegie Institution Yearbook*; Carrington, *A million years of man* (Weidenfeld and Nicolson, London); Carter, *Human heredity* (Penguin, London); Cherry, *On human communication* (M.I.T. Press); Clark, *Population growth and land use* (Macmillan, London); Clark, *World prehistory* (Cambridge University Press); *Clinical Science*; Colbert, *Evolution of the vertebrates* (Wiley, New York; Chapman Hall, London); *Cold Spring Harbor Symposia on Quantitative Biology*; Comfort, *Ageing. The biology of senescence* (Routledge and Kegan Paul, London); *Comparative Psychology Monographs*; Darwin, *The expression of the emotions in man and animals* (Murray, London); Day, *Guide to fossil man* (Cassell, London); Dean and Hinshelwood, *Growth, function, and regulation in bacterial cells* (Clarendon Press, Oxford); Dickinson, *A topographical hand atlas. Human sex anatomy* (Baillière, Tindall, and Cox, London); Dobzhansky, Hecht, and Steere (eds.), *Evolutionary biology* (Meredith, New York); Eccles (ed.), *Brain and conscious experience* (Springer, Berlin); *Eugenics Review*; *Evolution*; *Experimental Cell Research*; *Experimenta Gerontologia*; Fairbridge (ed.), *The encyclopedia of atmospheric sciences and astrogeology* (Reinhold, New York); Falkner (ed.), *Human development* (Saunders, Philadelphia); Fawcett, *An atlas of fine structure. The cell, its inclusions and organelles* (Saunders, London); Flavell, *The developmental psychology of Jean Piaget* (Van Nostrand, New York); *Gerontologia*; Goss, *Adaptive growth* (Logos Press); Grassé (ed.), *Mammifères: Traité de zoologie*, Vol. 17, pt. 2 (Masson, Paris); Gregory, *Evolution emerging*, Vols. 1 and 2 (Macmillan, London); Haggis (ed.), *Introduction to molecular biology* (Longmans, London); Hamilton, Boyd, and Mossman, *Human embryology* (Heffer, Cambridge); Harlow, in *Roots of behavior* (ed. Bliss) (Harper, New York); Harrison (ed.), *Genetical variation in human populations*, Vol. 4 (Pergamon Press, Oxford); Harrison, Weiner, Tanner, and Barnicot, *Human biology* (Clarendon Press, Oxford); *Human Biology*; International Union of Pure and Applied Chemistry; Jacob, in *Les Prix Nobel en 1965* (Imprimerie Royale P.A. Norstedt & Söner, Stockholm); Jarvik, *Théories de l'evolution des vertébrés* (Masson, Paris); *Journal of Anatomy*; *Journal of Biological Chemistry*; *Journal of Bone and Joint Surgery*; *Journal of Gerontology*; *Journal of Heredity*; *Journal of Molecular Biology*; *Journal of Physiology*; *Journal of Ultrastructure Research*; Kendrew, *The thread of life, an introduction to molecular biology* (Bell, London); King, *A dictionary of genetics* (Oxford University Press); Kinsey *et al.*, *Sexual behavior in the human female* (Saunders, Philadelphia); Kinsey *et al.*, *Sexual behavior in the human male* (Saunders, Philadelphia); Kit, in *Information storage and neural control* (eds. Field and Abbott) (Thomas, Springfield); Kodak Ltd.; *Lancet*; Le Gros Clark, *The antecedents of man* (Edinburgh University Press); *Le Medical*; Lenneberg, *Biological foundations of language* (Wiley, New York); Lerman, in *Neurosciences Research* (eds. Ehrenpreis and Solnitzky) (Academic Press, New York); Maringer, *The gods of prehistoric man* (Weidenfeld and Nicolson, London); Mather, *Human diversity* (Oliver and Boyd, London); *Meddelelser om Grønland*; *Mémoires du Muséum nationale d'histoire naturelle*, Série C; Montagna and Ellis (eds.), *The biology of hair growth* (Academic Press, New York); Morowitz, *Energy flow in biology* (Academic Press, New York); Mourant, Kopeć, and Domaniewska-Sobczak, *The ABO blood groups* (Blackwell's Scientific Publications, Oxford); Napier and Napier, *A handbook of living primates* (Academic Press, London); *Nature*; Nature Conservancy Unit of Grouse and Moorland Ecology, Seventh Progress Report; Needham, *Chemical embryology* (Cambridge University Press); Needham, *The growth process in animals* (Pitman, London); Norman, *A history of fishes* (Benn, London); Oakley, *Frameworks for dating fossil man* (Weidenfeld and Nicolson, London); Oakley, *Man the tool-maker* (British Museum); Oparin, *The chemical origin of life* (Thomas, Springfield, Illinois); Pearl, *Introduction to medical biometry and statistics* (Saunders, Philadelphia); *Pediatrics*; Penfield and Roberts, *Speech and brain mechanisms* (Princeton University Press); Penrose, *The biology of mental defect* (Sidgwick and Jackson, London); *Postilla*; *Proceedings of the American Philosophical Society*; *Proceedings of the Malacological Society of London*; *Proceedings of the National Academy of Science of the United States of America*; *Proceedings of the Royal Society*, Series A and B; *Proceedings of the Royal Society of Medicine*; *Quarterly Journal of the Geological Society of London*; *Quarterly Review of Biology*; *Registrar-General's Report 1900 and 1968*; *Registrar-General's Statistical Review 1966*; *Revue Scientifique*; Rogers, *Techniques of autoradiography* (Elsevier, Amsterdam); Romer, *Osteology of the reptiles* (University of Chicago Press); Romer, *The vertebrate body* (Saunders, Philadelphia); Romer, *Vertebrate paleontology* (University of Chicago Press); Sandars, *Prehistoric art in Europe* (Penguin, London); Scammon and Calkins, *The development and growth of the external dimensions of the human body in the fetal period* (University of Minnesota Press, Minneapolis); Schütte, *The biology of trace elements. Their role in nutrition* (Crosby Lockwood, London); Schweigart, *Vitalstoff-lehre Vitalstoff-Tabellarium* (Verlag Hans Zauner jr., Dachau-München); *Science*; *Scientific American*; *Smithsonian Miscellaneous Collections*; Speyer, in *Molecular genetics* (ed. Taylor) (Academic Press, New York); Stamp, *Our developing world* (Faber and Faber, London); Stern, *Principles of human genetics* (Freeman, San Francisco); *Symposia of the Society for Experimental Biology*; Tanner, *Growth at adolescence* (Blackwell's Scientific Publications, Oxford); Trustees of the British Museum (Natural History); Ucko and Rosenfeld, *Palaeolithic cave art* (Weidenfeld and Nicolson, London); *United Nations Demographic Yearbook*; *United Nations population studies*;

Vickerman and Cox, *The Protozoa* (Murray, London); de Vore (ed.), *Primate behavior : field studies of monkeys and apes* (Holt, Rinehart, and Winston, New York); Walker, *Mammals of the world* (Johns Hopkins, Baltimore); Washburn (ed.), *Classification and human evolution* (Aldine Press, Chicago; Methuen, London); Waterman, in *Systems theory and biology* (ed. Mesarović) (Springer-Verlag, New York); Waterman and Morowitz (eds.), *Theoretical and mathematical biology* (Blaisdell, New York); Watson, *Molecular biology of the gene* (Benjamin, New York); Wolstenholme and O'Connor (eds.), *CIBA Foundation Colloquia on Ageing. 5. The life-span of animals* (Churchill, London); Zoological Society of London.

CONTENTS

'We are like sailors who must repair their ship on the open sea without ever being able to bring it into dock to be dismantled and rebuilt with the best materials' (NEURATH 1932)

'The philosopher and the scientist are in the same boat' (QUINE 1960)

AN INTRODUCTION
TO THE
STUDY OF MAN

1

POSSIBILITIES AND DIFFICULTIES FOR A SCIENCE OF MAN

1. The general study of man

THE object of this book is to discover whether we can provide a general scheme within which to arrange knowledge about the lives of ourselves and others. Everyone is interested in the subject and most of us feel that we should be greatly helped in our life and work if we knew more about ourselves and our fellow men and women, what they do and why they do it. In our daily life and reading we pick up isolated facts that provide promising scraps of information on the subject, for instance about intelligence, sex or heredity, diet, disease, ageing, social relations, aggression, religion, race or population problems, but we feel the lack of a general scheme that shall show us how all these facts are related. If the study of man claims to be a science it should be able to provide this general point of view, to give us answers to the rather rhetorical questions 'What is life?' and 'What is man?' in a form that is not rhetorical, but shows how any particular event in the life of an individual, any birth or illness, pleasure or distaste, joy or sorrow, growth or death can be placed in its context, ceasing to be seen as an unrelated thing, but rather as part of a larger scheme.

Of course it is not obvious that we shall be able to see any such general relations between special happenings, but it has been one of the great achievements of humanity to do so, in part at least, in relation to the physical universe, and there is no reason to suppose it impossible in the biological. We no longer regard each star or mineral or mountain as a separate unrelated thing, but have been able to detect attributes and modes of behaviour that all of these have in common, so that we can say for instance that all these physical objects contain combinations of certain fundamental particles (though we might find it difficult to stand up to examination as to the meaning of that statement). It should be possible similarly to make our statements about life and especially human life in a *general* way, so that seeing ourselves or other people eating or reproducing, writing books or dancing, recovering from disease or growing old we shall see instances of general law in somewhat the same way as Newton recognized a community of behaviour, which he called gravity, between the movements of the planets and his apples, or Clark Maxwell saw that light and electromagnetic waves could be treated together.

We have to be careful from the start to recognize that the 'laws' that we find in nature are in fact partly a product of ourselves. 'The world is not made up of empirical facts with the addition of the laws of nature: what we call the laws of nature are conceptual devices by which we organize our empirical knowledge and predict the future' (Braithwaite 1953). Our thesis will be that biology can make a fundamental contribution to the theory of knowledge by showing how and why we organize and predict as we do.

2. Deduction, induction, and other methods of thought

The attempt to find general schemes to include particular things or events is evidently a rather common human tendency. Every human society has its ways of 'understanding' particular natural events as 'caused by' some member of a system of spirits. In this sense there are of course countless and ancient sciences for the study of man. A part of all religions consists indeed in the formulation of just such general schemes for explaining human life. Attempts of this sort mostly fail for lack of economy and efficiency rather than of consistency or generality. It is easy to make up a theory that all the activities of man are caused by the operations of a series of entities, called say angels and devils, under the control of a hierarchy of more powerful spirits of which one, called God, is the strongest. The scheme has great generality and can be made perfectly consistent by postulating spirits where required.

Indeed we shall see presently that there is reason to suppose that the human brain may be so constituted that it is natural for us to think in such ways. The brain must be so planned as to store its information according to *some* set of principles. There are suggestions from the way children develop that these principles may include attributing the causes of all phenomena firstly to entities like people (Chapter 19). Only later in development does the concept of causation acquire the very complex character that it has in adult scientific discourse (Chapter 21).

We know as yet almost nothing precise about the actions of the brain in such matters. Certainly the attribution of causes to entities like persons comes naturally and comfortably to nearly everyone. For many it provides an explanation that they find a necessity for their lives. Great steps have been made by theology in simplifying and clarifying such concepts. It may be that such systems of thought are useful for organizing discourse about life and mankind, if used with sufficient care and restraint to allow forecasts of behaviour to be made. But the efficiency of any such scheme depends upon the postulation of a strictly limited number of variables, and accurate information as to how they interact. The system must be general and yet able to explain and forecast particulars.

Yet of course the methods of speech and thought that we use are built up only in small part logically or systematically. All such methods, from those of the pagan to the physicist, are determined by the customs and language of the society in which he lives. The child inherits the capacity to learn to utter sounds in sequences that are agreeable to other people. Ultimately he learns to make propositions that are considered true. Our suggestion will be that all this is achieved because the brain is so organized as to make it possible for us to pay special attention to the shades of expression of others. We learn to arrange our whole store of information around what we shall call a model in the brain, which makes useful forecasts. This is still a vague conception, but it suggests that the whole system by which we remember centres on the features and words of people and the places and events of the daily life that they lead. So each of us tries to obtain satisfaction by agreement with others, and indeed to fulfil his bodily needs by the aid of the social system around.

The ways in which the brain works to achieve these ends are very varied, and yet perhaps all closely related. Conceptions of what is right and true are linked with fundamental beliefs about ultimates. These in turn are derived partly from childhood experiences and surroundings and may be directly influenced by genetic heredity. In this sense we deduce our conclusions from fundamental factors and influences over which we have little control. In this sense too responses and decisions of the sort that are called intuitive or instinctive may indeed often be correct, in that they produce effective action. They are the products of genetic and social systems that have been selected for thousands of years because they have ensured survival.

Languages have evolved to convey the effects that each society requires. The use of words for general philosophical or scientific reasoning therefore cannot be divorced from their daily use. Methods of thinking and criteria of truth differ, for instance, between Western European and Asiatic cultures. Nevertheless it is possible to reach some degree of agreement as to the classification of the modes of reasoning that provide sure conclusions. It would probably be generally recognized that, granted proper definitions, such deductions as $1+1 = 2$ are valid and general (but in binary reckoning $1+1 = 10$). Uncovering the truths that lie behind our words is another matter, and of course has puzzled men at least since Aristotle. Incidentally it is no accident that he, the inventor of the syllogism, was a great classifier. Deduction works well if the entities referred to are sharply defined. However, ultimately all words are related to shared experience, and in this sense all truths are inductive. The discovery that words allow communication is itself an empirical one. Yet the capacity to make that discovery is dependent upon the inborn workings of the brain. The powers of observation, of speech, and of reasoning are indeed interwoven in most complex ways.

The information that makes exact forecasting possible has, of course, to be collected by individuals and generalized by the process we call induction. From the observation of numerous and special instances we conclude that certain sequences of events that have been followed are likely to occur again. The human brain has great powers of accumulating information in this way from special instances. It may be that its inherited construction provides on the one hand tendencies to operate deductively in certain set ways and on the other to accumulate instances and to forecast from these by induction. Human operations have probably been controlled in both ways ever since we were like apes, but in recent centuries the inductive way has been growing in importance through the activities that we call those of science, though we must hasten to add that of course scientific method is not to be so simply described.

A major danger is to suppose that any one method of thought is paramount. There are endless ways in which we can speak about ourselves, ranging from those of the poet to the priest, from the psychoanalyst to the physicist. In this book we use the approach of the biologist and try to show how it can illuminate phenomena revealed by other methods. There is no need or intention to try to 'reduce' all human studies to those of biology. Every discipline should recognize its own limitations. Psychoanalysis, for example, has revealed some startling features of our lives, but 'man is more than his Oedipus complex'. Each method of study can be judged in the last analysis only by whether it is used, and found to help people in organizing their lives. The biologist hopes that he can do this by trying to show how the various things that men do contribute to the maintenance of human life.

There is no doubt that the inductive and predictive powers of the brain have become exceptionally enlarged in the course of the evolution of man. They have led him to his greatest discoveries about the regularities in the operations of nature and of men themselves. These habits of enquiry are the fruit of the anxious need for the security of knowledge, which is a characteristic and sometimes painful human trait. The anthropologist Malinowski called it 'The curse of forethought and imagination' (see Dobzhansky 1969). It has led man to perhaps the two greatest discoveries of all, on the one hand that each individual will die and on the other hand that there was a time when no human beings existed. Such knowledge still dazzles us and leaves many people unsatisfied and unsure, so that they seek for security in the inventions of myth, as Mankind has probably done ever since he began to talk and reason. Can we contribute anything to the solution of these great problems?

3. By what methods can the student study himself?

Our aim might thus be said to be to discuss the principles of the science of man. But 'scientific method', like theology, is a procedure adopted by men, involving collection of information, making hypotheses about future events, testing these by experiment, and reporting the results in a form that allows others to verify the facts and apply them in their lives. Can these same scientific methods be used to study those who have devised them? There is here a problem of circular definition that will plague us throughout our search. What methods can be used to obtain information about the gatherer of information? All knowledge is the product of brains, therefore in principle the study of the brain should be the most fundamental of all the sciences. But what method can the scientist use to study brains and in what terms can he describe them? He must use the methods and language that have been acquired not from the study of brains, but from the experience of the physical world, and the terms available are those used to describe it in his society. The study of man and his brain are in this sense not the first but the last to be developed, and so it has proved historically.

Clearly these are complicated matters and we must not expect that the principles for a science of man will emerge altogether readily and obviously. Indeed it would be vain to expect them to do so for *us*, remembering the countless attempts that have been made by philosophers, theologians, and indeed scientists already. Nevertheless we need not be too greatly awed by the past, or ashamed to try again now. Many of our predecessors were very wise men and we do well to study them, but their sources of information were so slight compared with those available now that their conclusions on many subjects could not possibly approach those that we can make, even if we are less clever. Men who had no knowledge of the facts now available about, say, the genetic code, the actions of the brain, or the origin of man obviously could not possibly produce a scheme for a science of man such as we can have today. Moreover, besides this great increase in knowledge of relevant facts there have been great improvements in our understanding of methods of communication, by studies of logic, grammar, statistics, set theories, and other mathematical devices, and of course there are computers to help us to make calculations that were unimaginable before.

4. Advantages and limitations of physical science

Our task then is to present the facts of human life that interest us in such a way as to relate them to a scheme that is as general as possible, with a maximum of explanatory and predictive powers. Needless to say we shall not be altogether successful. We are but men and women, and still very ignorant. Our effort is but a striving for understanding. No doubt within a few years it will seem absurdly primitive. Meanwhile can we construct something that is of help in our lives and above all can we enjoy the search and learn wisdom from it? In general we shall find that the methods and concepts provided by the natural sciences in their classical forms of physics and chemistry provide the best available basis for the study of man. This statement will be considered by many people as an absurd extreme of materialism. Since all concepts are produced by men there is a sense in which the science of man takes precedence over all others. But the physical sciences include the most fully developed system of concepts to describe events in the world around us. What we propose is to discuss how far these concepts can also satisfactorily describe the world within. It is indeed true that we cannot, with the principles of physical science as we know them today, fully describe, say, the origin of life (Chapter 26) or the nature of consciousness (Chapter 10). But there are now facts available about these and many other such obscure matters that make it possible to see the outlines of solutions to problems that have baffled even the wisest. At least we can see how our understanding is limited by the imperfections of language in dealing with them. We soon learn that 'common sense' is nonsense when applied to matters that are outside common experience. Indeed part of our difficulty is that physical science itself becomes uncertain when it deals with such great problems as those of infinity and of origins. To repeat, we must not expect complete and perfectly satisfactory answers to all our questions. To expect them is one of the characteristics of the primitive systems of thought and language of the child and the unsophisticated (Chapter 21). They must have 'certainty' for their life systems. But the adult modern man lives by doubt (see *Doubt and certainty in science* 1951).

Of course it is difficult to define the appropriate limits of doubting. A language system in which no one agreed about anything would be of little use. We all need some certainties and many people feel the need to follow quite rigid absolute systems. Possibly, even, this need may be a result of their inborn nature as well as of their training, but we know little about this. In any case each person must find an action system that allows him to maintain stability or homeostasis, in fact to remain alive (Chapter 6). The studies of Piaget and others have shown how the modern child in a western environment develops such an action system (Chapter 21). But although we can see the same general outlines in all normal development yet it is a truism that the final system by which people operate differs considerably according to their heredity and the culture in which they are raised. Many find themselves unable to live their lives without a system of allegedly comprehensive and ultimate 'explanation' such as is embodied in religious belief. It may be that it is natural for the human brain to function in this way, ascribing all action to the operations of some entity like a person (Chapter 10). Nevertheless this is not the mode of operation that is characteristic of the final stages of development of the brain, which proceeds by inquiry, collection of data, and the framing and testing of hypotheses. These are the methods that have led man in the last few hundred years not only to be able to support greatly increased numbers but also, in parts of the world, to produce much better conditions of life, though no doubt with many attendant disadvantages (see Popper 1965).

5. The scientific view of man

We shall therefore begin our search by seeing how far we can go in making a study of the fundamental physical and chemical features of man. This may seem a boring and even banal prospect to any who wish to leap forward to what they might call the higher things of the mind. But it is a great mistake to suppose that the facts of life lose their beauty and interest when they are described and explained in physical terms. People who believe this have probably never tried to see the intricate web of relations that emerges, or lack the imagination to grasp that this knowledge is an obvious advance on the descriptions of the behaviour of whole men or animals without attention to the component parts. The view of the world given by modern methods is essentially detailed and intricate. It reveals an immense richness of facts that were completely unsuspected before, for instance those shown by biochemical methods or the electron microscope (Chapters 2 and 3). This detail is full of beauty both of form and of logical relations. In order to understand and appreciate life and man today it is necessary to see something of the intricacy of the systems by which life is controlled, and we shall not hesitate to plunge into these details. The principles that they involve should be apparent to those with only slight knowledge of science, though of course more is better.

6. Living activities. Homeostasis

Of course, study of the components in simple physical terms will leave us only with a knowledge of the anatomy of organisms. Looking for the characteristic features of life we shall find them in the activity that goes on continually within the organized substance, beginning with the activity of copying or replication. All this activity is directed towards the end of preservation of the individual, during his life span, and ultimately of the species. This capacity for maintenance of continuity, or *homeostasis*, is the central, characteristic, feature of life. More specifically, the characteristics of human life are the activities by which human continuity is maintained. Here we begin to meet with facts that are rather hard to understand in terms of classical physics and chemistry. Living organisms do not disobey such fundamental laws as those of thermodynamics. They do not create matter or energy (first law) and they resist the tendency to dissolution, by appropriate expenditure of energy which, not being closed systems, they obtain from their surroundings (second law). Nevertheless they maintain themselves by virtue of a degree of organization that is greater than that found in any other systems on earth (Chapter 26). In this sense they are 'improbable' systems and man is the most improbable of all. Astrophysicists are beginning to study the question whether similar steady state systems occur elsewhere in the universe. The synthesis of elements in the stars by rapid neutron absorption may be followed by fission, and repeated over and over again. Such comparisons have led to further thinking about how best to define the characters of living things in physical terms (Fong 1968).

We shall explore in detail the mechanisms by which life and especially human life is maintained. This involves studying not only the daily activities of eating and breathing but many others, such as those of healing, by which life is defended or repaired (Chapter 12). Such repair cannot go on indefinitely and ultimately the body ages and dies (Chapter 23). Obviously one of our central problems is to explain the significance of this fate, and studies of ageing have at least shown many facts that throw light on its significance and give some help in its amelioration (Chapter 22).

7. Reproduction as the guarantee of continuity and of change

The continued life of the species is of course dependent upon reproduction (Chapter 15) and the consequent formation and growth of new individuals. We shall follow these processes in detail, especially in man, and show how the power of replication and addition of new material is perhaps the most characteristic feature of living organization (Chapters 16–21).

The more general question, however, is 'Where does the information necessary for all this organization come from?' This involves us in the problem of the origin of life, about which we can now say something, though not nearly as much as we should like (Chapter 26). The striking feature about living creatures is that they are continually becoming more complex, and in this sense more improbable, if this concept has any meaning. During the process of evolution living things have collected more and more information about ways of keeping alive (Chapter 27). Details of evolution have been discussed elsewhere (*The life of vertebrates* 1962). Here we shall follow human evolution from the stage when we were like shrews, until today (Chapters 29–33). There have been many attempts to pin-point the particular environmental or other features responsible for the appearance of man. We shall join in this discussion, but, in anticipation, it must be admitted that we do not know the full answer—yet.

8. Exosomatic inheritance. Brain and mind

The later stages of human evolution include the extraordinary events of the emergence of the use of tools and of language. It is exact to use the word 'extraordinary', because these methods of operating have enabled man to develop a new method of storing and transmitting information, supplementary to that of heredity by which evolution has operated for thousands of millions of years (Chapter 34). These methods involve the use of the brain in ways that allow processing of quantities of information that are orders of magnitude greater than those achieved by any other creature. We do not yet know how this is done or how these powers arose, but facts about the brain are crowding in every day. There is hope that we may soon understand how its memory operates (see *A model of the brain* 1964).

This extraordinary capacity for information storage undoubtedly gives the human brain its power to mediate what we call consciousness and thinking. The description of these in terms of physical science constitutes for many people the major difficulty in framing a science of man (see Sherrington 1940, Eccles 1953). The very suggestion of such a possibility constitutes for many people a linguistic absurdity. They will tell us that brain and mind are 'obviously different'. Of course they are, but it is not wise to be dogmatic about how we use such words. It is encouraging that there are now some facts that throw light on the question of the relation of the brain to conscious thought (Chapter 10). It would be quite wrong to say that this fundamental problem of the dualism of mind and matter has been solved, but there are signs that the reasons for its apparent central importance are beginning to be understood. *Cogito ergo sum* is not the only possible basis for the theory of knowledge. Language was presumably invented for speaking, not for thinking.

Language today is still a primitive instrument, based largely on dualistic assumptions, insisting on statements about subject and object, unable to relate external 'facts' to our self-orientated 'feelings'. It is no wonder therefore that we find it very difficult to relate sober facts about the brain to our emotions. How can we discuss the wild dramatic feelings that are so important to the individual, fear, hope, anxiety, ecstasy, agony, ambition, and the like? And is a description in any language now known which would correlate them with 'bodily' physiological and biochemical processes? (see Cannon 1929). The reply is that a beginning can be made. The answers may not seem as satisfactory as the ordinary individual would wish, nor yet very useful, say, to the psychoanalyst or for his patient. But we do begin to understand these matters better. Knowledge of the brain often seems strange and even slightly alarming to those brought up in a classical tradition of mind and matter. Yet there is nothing more derogatory to the independence of the individual in the study of his 'brain' than of his 'mind'. Indeed the manipulators of mankind have operated all too successfully on 'minds'. Anything found out scientifically about the springs of human behaviour should indeed serve to *liberate* us from the uncertainties and fears produced by ignorance. It may seem unromantic, but the injunction 'Know thyself' really comes down largely to 'Know thy brain'. Understanding of the sources of human love and creativity as well as of hate and destruction should surely provide a basis for better ways of life.

Whatever status we may decide to ascribe to the mind there is no question that the individual human being with his capacity for collection, storage, and transmission of information is a unit of exceptional biological importance. After all it is by individuals that the decisions are made that regulate human life. It is true that each can (in practice) survive only as a member of a society, but this is the corollary of the fact that he lives by acquiring and transmitting information. We can begin to see the answer to the paradox of the roles of the individual and society (Chapter 9), though this unfortunately does not mean that the relationship will easily be made satisfactory in all parts of the world, or indeed in any part. The relation of the individual to the collectivity of men is one of the greatest problems of our time.

9. Human variety. Its advantages and disadvantages

Man's especial powers of information transfer have led to his explosive evolution, in both numbers and techniques, especially in the last few hundred years. Yet he remains divided into the sub-groups that we loosely call races. The biologist cannot offer solutions to the personal and political problems that are produced by this division, but he can make a special contribution by the study of genetics (Chapters 38–41). The conflicts engendered between groups do not seem to have any positive homeostatic significance at the present time. Different groups have different habits as well as different languages and genes, but there seems to be no biological reason why they should remain distinct indefinitely (Chapter 41).

It is presumed that each characteristic of every population at some time represented an adaptation to particular environmental conditions. But it is typical of modern man that he has great powers to control his environment. At present he uses them only sporadically, often prevented by reasons of individual greed. There are signs that these powers will be increasingly used to improve the conditions of life everywhere, though the pace is tragically unequal in different regions. Forecasting is dangerous, but, in spite of the prevalence of nationalism, it may be that the tendency for racial divisions will diminish, if its biological relevance has disappeared. It is not obvious that selfishness, whether national or personal, is the most successful way of life for man.

The need for genetic diversity remains. Various sets of people are needed to make a rich human community (but see p. 575). Populations that are genetically homogeneous are at risk for many reasons. They may be overcome by infection, they may fail to adapt to new conditions set up from outside or within their own population. The study of genetic diversity and its effects on, for instance, health and intelligence is a major duty for the human biologist (Chapters 38–41). In some fields he can give definite advice, for instance of the risks of consanguineous marriages, and perhaps of the effects of patterns of distribution of educational and other resources (Chapter 18).

10. Man's current problems

The increase in numbers that is resulting from man's special abilities is now followed with anxious attention. Demographers, biologists, and sociologists have given it very much study, but the chief lesson one learns from their results is that forecasting human numbers is hazardous (Chapters 22–5). Moreover the effects of the increase in population on welfare cannot be predicted, as the falsification of Malthus's forecasts showed. This is one of the fields where most conspicuously 'common sense is nonsense'. There is certainly cause for concern at the rapid increase of mankind, but not cause for panic. Surveys of resources show that many more people could be maintained upon the earth, and methods of food production are improving continually both in theory and practice (see Rockefeller Foundation 1967). However, there is certainly a danger that the delay in social implementation of scientific knowledge will produce acute shortages as a result of rapid increases in population during the next few years (Chapter 25). Some large increases seem already certain to take place, though again we must beware of forecasts. The hard lesson that demographers have learned is that human reproductive habits change rapidly. Thirty years ago some of them were forecasting the twilight of parenthood. There is need for all the attention we can give to study of these matters, to help us to discover optima for human life and how to achieve them (Sauvy 1969).

It is a paradox that although we are still ignorant and feeble our chief problem is to learn to live with our power. We have learned how to destroy each other and even perhaps the whole earth. We have begun to understand our brains, so that we can no longer rely on old beliefs to organize society, but we have not learned how to do it afresh. In spite of the urgency of this situation it seems likely that man will solve these problems piecemeal, as in the past, rather than by global planning. In any case he needs to find out all that he can about himself and the world if he is to survive.

11. Summary

Our theme then is that living things act as they do because they are so organized as to take actions that prevent their dissolution into the surroundings. They maintain this organization by virtue of a system that may be called the transfer of information from the past. Human living organization is maintained and transmitted by its own special operations, among which the most characteristic are the use of language and of tools or artefacts to assist with bodily functions. We shall try to reach an understanding of the significance of the events of human life by examining how they contribute to this process of maintenance of continuity or homeostasis. We shall find that a surprising range of actions can be understood in this way. Many simpler ones such as breathing and eating or the healing of wounds are necessary to preserve the individual, other obvious ones perpetuate the species. But man's particular genius is for the transfer of information between individuals and many subtle features are involved in his homeostasis. Communication by symbols is improved by all the agencies that we include as art, literature, and aesthetics, and these, far from being 'impractical', *are major contributors to human homeostasis* (Chapters 36 and 37). So are, of course, all the actions that contribute to social organization, religion, politics, law, and education.

Human homeostasis therefore depends upon an infinitely complex set of factors, which no one author or book could possibly cover. Our attempt is only to make an introduction to the study of man.

2

WHAT ARE MEN MADE OF?

1. Historical and non-historical sciences

How then are we to begin our study of homeostasis? Since living things are 'improbable' systems, it might seem that we should not be very likely to find the principles that we require by the use of the methods of the physical sciences. These are based, in general, on study of selected samples of matter, purified for purposes of experiment, so that their history can be ignored. If we wish to study the atomic weight of silver we hope to do it on pure samples into whose distant history we need not inquire. It is true that such sciences as geology and astronomy are historical, but they meet the same difficulties as biology in that they depend upon fundamental concepts derived from physics. Yet the history of the materials studied in physics belongs to geology and astronomy and the methods of study belong to biology. This is the circular paradox noted in the first chapter. We cannot overcome it and shall in the end decide that for our study of man we should try to proceed as far as we can with the use of principles of physics and chemistry. But we may first inquire briefly whether we should do better by beginning with historical studies such as those of evolution or genetics.

2. The search for an adequate approach to man

One approach, with which some people might say we should start, is that *evolution* is the fundamental principle of biology. But life cannot be understood by looking at evolution alone. Evolutionary study tells us only that animals and plants changed in the past, but not how they live. It is true that study of evolution suggests that in some sense organisms gradually become 'higher' or 'better'. The earlier fossil records in the rocks contain no remains of vertebrates. When vertebrates first appear it is as fishes, followed by amphibians, reptiles, and finally birds and mammals. We are inclined to think that we are the 'highest', as we are among the latest, arrivals on the planet, but one of our chief problems is to find out what we really mean by such a scale. The point is that study of evolutionary change alone cannot provide us with the set of general principles of the operation of living things for which we are looking. It does not show us the significant features of each life and each type of life when in action.

Yet another starting-point that might be suggested is from genetics, which studies not only the similarities and differences between parents and offspring but, more recently, the actual code of instructions by which living activities are controlled. The concept of control brings us closer to the heart of the matter, but study of the mechanism of a control system implies a previous understanding of what is controlled, of what the system is *for*. For our fundamental principles, be it repeated, we must try to find an understanding of living things in action. Moreover, if our system is to be applicable to man, it must use concepts capable of covering the sorts of activities that men engage in. It is not enough to base our biology only on familiar concepts with which we describe the non-living world. We must find ways of explaining concisely and with the maximum of generality all those phenomena that are characteristic of life in general and human life in particular. We say that human beings work, think, and make conscious choices; experience pains and pleasures; have beliefs and memories, love and hate; reproduce, age, and die. We must somehow manage to find statements about these if we wish for a truly general science of man.

3. What do we understand by the principles of physical science?

Obviously it will not be easy to find any such system. The very attempt will seem to many people ridiculous, perhaps even impious. Indeed, we shall be wise not to try to formulate a complete logical system, but simply to see how far we can go with the types of information that we can acquire with the principles of physical science about human and other life. The information should prove interesting and useful in itself, and we can then see in what respects it succeeds and where it fails to allow adequate description of life.

The subject is so near to our hearts and yet so complicated and difficult that it is especially necessary to ask carefully what it is that we hope from the study of man. The subject-matter of the physical sciences is fairly easily defined, at least in a superficial way. We can say that chemistry and physics deal with the properties of matter, astronomy with the behaviour of the stars, and so on. Even here, difficulties will begin to appear when we ask what are the 'properties' that we choose to discern in the objects around us. Are all 'properties' of the same kind? For instance, are we to classify the colour of sulphur, its smell, and combining power or valency as all 'properties' of the same sort? And what are the 'properties' of the stars that have defined their movements in the heavens? It may be that by thinking of such examples we shall discover that we are less certain than we should wish about the procedure that we use in the study of the physical world around us. The whole apparatus of physical science is an attempt to define some parts, at least, of the behaviour of the phenomena that we find, and it allows us to forecast their future. Our systematic study cannot, however, go indefinitely beyond our senses. No system, however general, tells us *all* about any object; it only shows us what observations have been made and how they may be related to each other. Most of us, especially Anglo-Saxons, have a strong desire to ask of any object 'What really is it?' When we look closely, however, we find that we cannot even know what we hope to achieve by answering such a question. We should not know when we had reached the 'true essence' of any matter, and all our endeavours are but descriptions of how any object appears and how it behaves.

Of course we cannot hope to examine all possible physical approaches to man in an elementary study. All we can do is to examine some of them, discuss their adequacy and limitations, and suggest how they may be supplemented to provide the fundamental principles that are needed for a science of life and of man. (Table 2.1, Figs. 2.1 and 2.2 give some data.)

TABLE 2.1

Some approximate dimensions of the universe. The universe appears to vary with time so the information in the table is given for an observer on earth at the present time
(after Fairbridge 1967)

1. *Time-scale associated with the universe*

Human heartbeat	1 s
1 day	10^5 s
1 year	3×10^7 s
Life of man	10^9 s
Existence of man (3 million years)	10^{13} s
Period of rotation of the Milky Way	10^{16} s
Age of the earth	$11 \cdot 1 \times 10^{16}$ s
Time since the universe exploded	3×10^{17} s

2. *Dimensions associated with the universe*

Height of a man	2×10^2 cm, 10^{-8} light-second
Diameter of earth	10^9 cm, 10^{-1} light-second
Distance to sun	10^{13} cm, 8 light-minutes
Distance to nearest other star	10^{18} cm, 4 light-years
Distance to centre of Milky Way (Milky Way=our own galaxy)	10^{22} cm, 10^4 light-years
Distance to nearest galaxy like ours	10^{24} cm, 10^6 light-years
Distance to centre of local cluster of galaxies	10^{25} cm, 10^7 light-years
Distance to farthest object for which detailed astronomical observations exist	10^{28} cm, 10^{10} light-years

3. *Masses associated with the universe*

Mass of a man	10^5 g
Mass of a large mountain	10^{17} g
Mass of earth	6×10^{27} g
Mass of sun	2×10^{33} g
Mass of our galaxy	10^{45} g
Mass of local cluster of galaxies	10^{48} g
Mass of 'well-observed' part of universe	10^{53} g

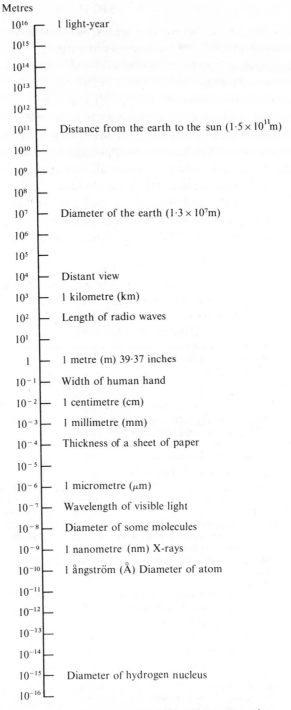

FIG. 2.1. Some distances and sizes expressed in powers of 10.
(After Fairbridge 1967.)

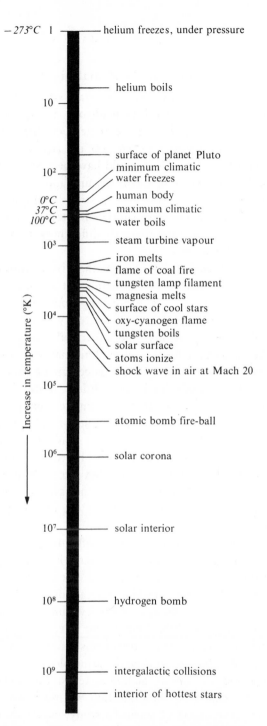

FIG. 2.2. The range of temperature encountered in the universe. The temperatures are given in K (Kelvin), an absolute scale with the same units as the centigrade scale. The freezing-point of water is 273 K and the boiling-point is 373 K; the temperature of man is 310 K on this scale. (After Dyson 1954.)

4. Advantages and disadvantages of analysis

It might seem that one of the most important simple scientific questions we can ask about a man is 'What is he made of?' The question is not really simple, as immediately appears if we remember that the answer given would have changed remarkably even over the last two centuries. In the seventeenth century and earlier it would have been said that living things were composed of a mixture of earth, air, fire, and water, like all the rest of the world. There would have been a strong addition of 'spirits' and 'humours', whose status, whether material or not, is an interesting question that will remind us at once that there are differences in the use of the concepts of 'spirit' and 'matter'.

Nowadays we are used to the concept that living things, like all other 'material' bodies, are made of combinations of the ninety-two naturally occurring elements, themselves formed by combinations of still more fundamental elementary particles. All matter, we may say, is composed of protons, electrons, neutrons, and other subatomic particles; living matter like the rest (see Galbraith 1967). This may seem to be a very great and far-reaching discovery of which science can be proud. A moment's thought will show us that, valuable though it is, it also *discovers too much*. By removing the complications that differentiate the types of matter from each other we have removed the very subject-matter that we set out to study. No one but a physical monomaniac could feel satisfied with the statement that 'A man and an atomic bomb are the same, because they contain the same particles'. To say that they are made of 'the same sort of unit' is, in a sense, to admit that we have not said of what each consists besides. We must continue the search for the characteristic features in other directions.

We meet here, at the very beginning, a difficulty that will often recur in our study. By comparison of different systems it is often possible to find features that they have in common, and the scientist feels that in the discovery of such similarity he is making a great advance, because he is substituting general principles for special observations. This is indeed an aim with which we can sympathize. Perhaps the attempt to find general principles is the scientist's version of the religious instinct—an attempt to unify all knowledge, to discover the underlying principles that govern all. Perhaps we may even see signs in this of the human fear of the unknown. Whatever the origin of this desire for simplification we must, while approving it, assert again that the object of scientific study, especially that of man, is to see the material from as many aspects as are necessary to describe man in all his complexity. There may be some forms of exact science that are content to discover a few very general principles, perhaps of a mathematical nature. We shall indeed find some quite splendid and startling generalizations about man, but we shall try not to forget that he has many aspects. Besides being composed of protons and electrons he also sings for joy on a spring morning, like the birds in his garden. Can we make a study of all this?

5. Levels of discourse

To return to the study of man's composition. We must also beware of another danger; namely, using words we do not understand or, more particularly, applying to words ideas that should not belong to them. This sounds difficult, but is easily illustrated by thinking what we mean by 'elementary particles'. What are these units that are found to be the basic components of all matter? Certainly no one but a good physicist would like to attempt an exact answer. We speak of them as 'particles' and they have properties akin to mass, but they are not little pieces of stuff like grains of dust only smaller. We know of them because under suitable circumstances they can be made to produce changes on a photographic plate. All our knowledge about them comes by indirect means, from quite elaborate experiments. The knowledge is not the less valuable because of this, but it needs to be used with more caution. Statements such as 'This man is made of protons and electrons' are not altogether similar to 'This house is made of red bricks'. The word brick is the name of an object about which we can all receive agreed information by touch and sight. We can all forecast a number of things about bricks. Physicists can also make forecasts about protons, but these forecasts involve a different and more complicated background of information from that involved in dealing with bricks. For example, it may be helpful to consider that the idea of a proton is more closely related to that of an 'activity' than of a 'piece of matter'. To assert that the world is made of entities with certain 'activities' or 'powers' is very different from saying that it is made of numerous small pieces of stuff. In this, as in many other ways, science is now much less 'materialist' than is commonly supposed.

Furthermore, we learn from these thoughts the very important lesson that different methods of statement may be needed for phenomena at different levels. The most exact form of mathematical treatment, as used by physicists to describe the behaviour of their 'particles', is, at present, quantum mechanics. But only rarely can we use quantum mechanics to assist us to understand the behaviour of even small molecules. This is because the more exact terminology applies only to certain limited conditions. It is not yet generally useful for forecasting the behaviour of the great aggregates of these particles that form the larger molecules. However, the use of quantum mechanics is continually being extended and now reaches to some biochemical problems (Pullman and Pullman 1962).

Consider that our ancestors only 50 000 generations ago probably used, at most, a very simple ape-like language (Chapter 35). The point is that, as mankind evolves, new ways of discussing and describing phenomena gradually emerge and spread. There never has been any one definitive 'study of man' and presumably there never will be. There are men with technologies and languages of varying complexities. In this introduction to the study of man we analyse only some of the various types of approach that are used and try to bring out some of the characteristics of those that are adopted today and perhaps show how they may be modified in the future.

It is especially important for the human biologist to appreciate and use this general principle, which we might call 'the significance of levels of discourse'. It appears to be a property of human beings that they devise systems to describe their discoveries as they make them. As they examine the world more and more minutely with instruments of ever higher resolution they come upon phenomena not previously described. Yet, to talk about these phenomena, terms must be used that have some relation to the grammar and logic of previous discourse. For example, we speak of the ultimate entities of physics as 'particles' or 'waves', but we only say this in order to state that in some aspects of their behaviour they are a little like bullets and in others the best mathematics for describing them is that which is also applicable to ripples upon water.

As science advances, the relation between the phenomena and language of the various levels becomes continually less direct. There is a kind of scientific faith that a continuity exists between the causes of events at all levels. But in practice the descriptive methods used for subatomic physics are of only limited use in chemistry, very little as yet in molecular biology, and none at all in sociology.

This is a 'fact' of human communication. To enunciate it may seem almost blasphemous to some scientists and one can join them in regretting that it is true. Probably there is much still to be done to explore the basis for the concepts of causation in our language by study of the brains that produce them.

For the human biologist it means that he will not be ashamed if he finds that the principles he needs in order to describe his material adequately may include some that are not to be found, say, in atomic physics. The language used of the finest division of matter is 'fundamental' only in that it describes the behaviour of these 'particles' when in isolation, or under certain controlled conditions. It does not *follow* that studies of the same sort will enable us to forecast the behaviour of large aggregates. The unitarian scientist may hope that it will do so and strive to show that it does. The practical scientist will not only do this but will also use all the information he can gather to obtain the widest possible generality for the predictions he can make *about the aggregates as he finds them.*

The state of our knowledge is therefore 'imperfect', and perhaps it will always remain so. But to emphasize this by treating the sciences dealing with large aggregates (say man) as poor relatives of those dealing with smaller ones (say physics) is an illogical mistake of what we may call scientific snobbery. The true scientist is surely the one who strives to give the best possible description of all phenomena. He will seek for generality and prediction and be especially pleased if he can improve them in fields such as human biology, where they are more difficult to find and have previously been lacking.

6. The elements present in the body

We are content, then, to find that living things are made of elements identical with those outside the body. Indeed, we should be astounded and dismayed if anyone claimed that it were not so. Nevertheless, we shall not be satisfied that living things are therefore 'just the same' as non-living ones. We shall not be surprised to find that there is something different and even 'special' about them and particularly about their 'behaviour'. We shall hope that this difference will be somehow related to their material composition. This does indeed appear, even from examination of the elements that are present. Out of a total of ninety-two naturally occurring elements, only sixteen are found in nearly all organisms and eight others in a few (Fig. 2.3 and Table 2.2).

This is a very small selection, and certainly neither a random one nor one based upon the relative frequency of the elements outside the living world. Hydrogen, carbon, oxygen, and nitrogen are, it is true, among the commonest elements of the universe, but they are present on earth in proportions very different from those in living things. Oxygen is the most abundant element by weight in the universe and it and hydrogen make up large proportions of the elements in the atmosphere, hydrosphere, and lithosphere. Oxygen forms 23·02 per cent and hydrogen 0·02 per cent of the atmosphere. In the hydrosphere oxygen forms 85·79 per cent and hydrogen 10·67 per cent, while in the lithosphere there is 47·33 per cent oxygen and 0·22 per cent hydrogen (Needham 1965). There is, therefore, plenty of these elements for organisms to use. But the other elements abundant in organisms are relatively rare on earth (carbon 0·03 per cent, phosphorus 0·12 per cent, and sulphur 0·05 per cent). On the other hand, some very common elements in the earth's crust are found only in small

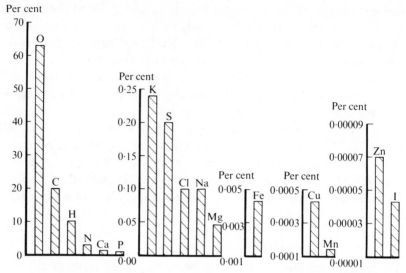

F IG. 2.3. The percentage composition by weight of a human being of 70 kg body weight. Over 98 per cent of the total weight consists of oxygen, carbon, hydrogen, nitrogen, calcium, and phosphorus. The other elements, although present in small quantities, play an important part in the life of man. (Data from Schweigart 1962; figure after Schütte 1964.)

TABLE 2.2

An alphabet of organisms. Living organisms are composed almost entirely of sixteen elements, listed below, while eight other elements, within parentheses, have a more restricted distribution in some groups (after Wald 1964)

Elementary particles	Bioelements	Unit molecules
Protons	water: H, O	glucose, ribose
Electrons	organic: H, C, N, O, P, S	fat, phosphatide
Neutrons	ions: Na$^+$, K$^+$, Mg^{++}, Ca^{++}, Cl$^-$	20 amino-acids
Photons	trace elements: Mn, Fe, Cu, Zn, I, (Co, Si, Se, Cr, Ga, B, V, Mo)	5 nucleotide bases

amounts or not at all in living things (silicon forms 27·74 per cent and aluminium 7·85 per cent of the lithosphere but they are absent from many living organisms).

So we meet at once one of the most characteristic features of life— it is selective. And this carries the important implication that only some materials are 'suited' for life and have been 'chosen' for their particular

TABLE 2.2A

Ubiquitous compounds found in all organisms. Macromolecules and ions not included (from Morowitz 1968)

Vitamins, coenzymes, and precursors	
Biotin (oxybiotin)	Thiamine
Flavine mononucleotide	Pantothenic acid
Flavine adenine dinucleotide	Riboflavin
Diphosphopyridine nucleotide	Vitamin B_6 (pyridoxine, pyridoxal,
Triphosphopyridine nucleotide	pyridoxamine)
Coenzyme A, acetyl coenzyme A,	Nicotinic acid precursor to
malonyl coenzyme A	diphosphopyridine nucleotide
Adenosine triphosphate,	Tetrahydrofolic acid
adenosine diphosphate,	Vitamin B_{12} (cyanocobalamin)
adenosine monophosphate	

Amino-acids			
Alanine	Glutamine	Leucine	Serine
Arginine	Glutamic acid	Lysine	Threonine
Asparagine	Glycine	Methionine	Tryptophan
Aspartic acid	Histidine	Phenylalanine	Tyrosine
Cysteine	Isoleucine	Proline	Valine
Cystine			

Sugars and derivatives	
Glucose	2-Phosphoglyceric acid
Glucose-6-phosphate	Phosphopyruvic acid
Fructose-6-phosphate	Pyruvic acid
Fructose-1,6-diphosphate	Lactic acid
Glyceraldehyde-3-phosphate	5-Phosphoribosyl-1-pyrophosphate
Dihydroxyacetone phosphate	D-Ribose
1,3-Diphosphoglyceric acid	D-2-Deoxyribose
3-Phosphoglyceric acid	Ribose-5-phosphate

Lipids and precursors	
Glycerol	α-Glycerol phosphate
Fatty acids	Ethanolamine

Purines, pyrimidines, and derivatives	
Uracil	
Cytosine	Nucleosides, nucleotides including monophosphates,
Thymine	diphosphates, and triphosphates
Adenine	
Guanine	

Miscellaneous			
Water	Glutathione	Phosphoric acid	Fumaric acid
Carbon dioxide	Carbamyl phosphate	Succinic acid	Acetic acid
Ammonia			

properties. Even at this early stage of inquiry we begin, therefore, to find some signs that properties comparable to those such as choice, originally attributed uniquely to man, are to be found in some degree throughout the living world.

By examining the characteristics of the elements that are found in living matter we can see some of the reasons for their fitness or, to put it the other way round, we can see some at least of the characteristic features of life (which it may be noticed we have not yet attempted to define).

Hydrogen, oxygen, nitrogen, and carbon make up 95·5 per cent by weight of living material and chemically they are an extraordinarily clearly defined and compact class (Needham 1965). They are the four smallest elements in the Periodic System that make stable electronic configurations, by accepting, respectively, 1, 2, 3, and 4 electrons. Moreover, carbon, nitrogen, and oxygen are the only elements that regularly form double and triple bonds. The four common bioelements are thus peculiarly 'suited' to form molecules, and since they are small elements the molecules are particularly stable. We may at once suppose that we shall find the characteristics of life in its molecules and particularly in the stability of some of them. Indeed we shall find that organisms contain what we shall call accumulations of stored information, retained for many, many million years. For this alone they must have very stable molecules whose information they perpetuate by very accurate replication.

7. Hydrogen, oxygen, and water

These enter so fundamentally into living things that it may seem hardly sensible to ask what is their 'significance'. But it is obvious that life-like systems depend essentially on their properties. Hydrogen is not only much the most abundant element in the universe but is probably the fundamental component of solar systems at stages when they might form complex systems (Chapter 26). Life on earth probably arose in a reducing medium, and we can imagine a sort of semi-life without oxygen. Nevertheless, today oxygen (produced by organisms) has come to make up 23·02 per cent of the atmosphere. Being one of the elements most readily able to accept electrons, oxygen has become the centre of the processes of life, combining, directly or indirectly, with hydrogen to yield energy. Thus respiration has become the main source upon which organisms depend for the energy they need to keep themselves intact when sunlight is not available. The direct method of 'burning' carbon (or carbohydrate) by combining with oxygen is replaced by the more efficient technique of glycolysis, producing reducing substances that combine with the oxygen to form water (see

TABLE 2.3

Alternative pathways of burning carbon. The first examples are of industrial methods. Biological oxidations, with rare exceptions, are performed by removing hydrogen (from Wald 1964)

Aerobic:	$C+O_2 \rightarrow CO_2$ (combustion of coal)
Anaerobic–aerobic:	$C+H_2O \rightarrow CO+H_2$ (water gas)
	$CO+H_2O \rightarrow CO_2+H_2$ (industrial production of hydrogen)
	$2H_2+O_2 \rightarrow 2H_2O$ (combustion of hydrogen)
Metabolism:	$(CH_2O)n =$ carbohydrate ($=$n equivalents of water gas)
	$(CH_2O)+H_2O \rightarrow CO_2+2H_2$ (glycolysis)
	$2H_2+O_2 \rightarrow 2H_2O$ (respiration)

Table 2.3). As Wald points out, this is essentially similar to the industrial production of water gas.

The two main elements in living matter, carbon and hydrogen, in the oxidizing condition of our atmosphere, are found as carbon dioxide and water. Carbon dioxide is readily soluble in water and hence well suited to circulate carbon in nature.

Water makes up more than 50 per cent by weight of many living bodies (often much more: man 59 per cent, jelly-fish 96 per cent). It provides the solvent for a vast range of substances and reactions and the means of transport of many materials. It enters into the composition of many organic molecules, fundamentally influencing their physical and chemical properties. It has been suggested that ammonia might substitute for water in life-like systems elsewhere in the universe. But ammonia is liquid only between -77 °C and -33 °C. Wald (1964) believes that this would mean a much slower evolution of life. A further serious disadvantage is that solid ammonia is denser than the liquid, whereas ice floats. Furthermore, if ammonia was split by organisms as water is by photosynthesis, it would presumably produce nitrogen, which could never have filled the place that oxygen has in making energy available for life.

Enough has been said to show that even hydrogen and oxygen and their simple compounds have special features that make it possible for living organisms to be as they are today. It is for such reasons that they were 'selected' at the origin of life by a process akin to natural selection as we see it in more complex organisms today (Chapter 27). This is even more true of carbon, but before we deal with that we can see how far it is true also of the less abundant elements in the body.

8. Sulphur and phosphorus

These elements also have properties that 'fit' them for life. They are especially prominent in compounds acting as links between oxidation and cellular activities, such as adenosine triphosphate (ATP) found in all organisms. This property is due to the facts that: (1) phosphorus and sulphur have very long bond radii; (2) they are atoms able to receive electrons in the orbitals of their outer shell; (3) they are also able to form multiple bonds and hence to take part in a variety of exchange reactions in which energy changes can occur. These exchanges are, of course, furthered by the reactivity of the compounds of these elements owing to the first two of the above characteristics. Such compounds are thus readily attacked by molecules with lone pairs of electrons, such as water, and are suitable for energy-transfer reactions. But why do organisms 'need' such reactions? This brings us at once to another of the fundamental characteristics of life. Organisms are not stable systems in thermodynamic equilibrium with their surroundings, but 'open' systems maintained in a steady state by continual expenditure of energy. We shall have to inquire much further into this condition later—it clearly necessitates the presence of materials suitable for large energy transfers. Sulphur and phosphorus are elements with characteristics suited to this purpose (though they have other interesting features as well).

9. Monatomic ions

These elements differ from all the others in the body in that they occur in proportions that have some relationship to those outside. They are the ions that are commonest in the sea, and are present in the blood of invertebrate animals in proportions similar to sea-water, though not quite identical. In vertebrates the proportion of ions in the blood is also similar to that in the sea, but as if diluted between three and four times (Table 2.4).

This has suggested to some workers that vertebrate blood represents the composition of the sea as it was when the circulation became a closed one, perhaps in the Silurian period, 400 million years ago. There is other evidence that the sea has become more concentrated since Paleozoic times by the addition of salts washed off the land. It is therefore suggested that the composition of the internal medium today is about what it was when our ancestors came to be able to maintain a fixed concentration of their blood. It is interesting that the hag-fish, a living survivor of the very earliest vertebrates, has blood resembling modern sea-water. The ionic concentration of its blood has perhaps increased in parallel with that of the ionic concentration of the sea, presumably because it has not developed a means of preventing ionic equilibrium with sea-water.

TABLE 2.4

The concentration of ions in sea-water and in the blood of various animals and man. The values are of mM/l of sea-water or blood

	Na	K	Ca	Mg	Cl	SO$_4$
Sea-water (average)	459·0	9·78	10·05	52·5	538·0	26·5
Sepia (cephalopod) Cuttlefish	460·0	23·7	10·75	56·9	589·0	4·7
Myxine (cyclostome) Marine hag-fish	558·0	9·6	6·25	19·4	576·0	6·6
Muraena (teleost) Marine conger eel	211·8	1·95	3·86	2·42	188·4	5·67
Man	145·0	5·1	2·5	1·2	103	2·5

There is undoubtedly something significant in this similarity of blood and sea-water. However, we certainly cannot say that organisms acquired these ions just 'by accident'. They are also specially suited for certain activities that are characteristic of life. We have been speaking of them so far in the blood, but one of their most characteristic features is that they occur in very different proportions inside and outside the cells. Whereas the blood and body fluids, like the sea, are rich in sodium and chloride and poor in potassium, the opposite is true inside the cells. Here there is much more potassium than sodium, and only a little chloride (see Table 2.5). This state of affairs has almost certainly been arrived at

TABLE 2.5

The concentration of ions in (1) *the sea-water and* (2) *the blood of* Loligo forbesi *(cephalopod); the concentration of ions in both cases is given as mM/l.* (3) *The extruded axoplasm from a resting nerve of the same species of squid, given in mM/kg* (from Lerman *et al.* 1969)

	Na	K	P	Cl	Ca	Mg
(1) Sea-water (mM/l)	459·0	9·7		535·3	10·7	52·3
(2) Blood of squid (mM/l)	429·7	21·1	..	560·0	11·6	53·0
(3) Extruded axoplasm from squid nerve fibres (mM/kg extruded axoplasm)	46·0	323·0	25·3	72·0	00·4	10·0

by selection in the way that we shall try to show for all other parts of the living system.

Many biochemists find this sort of reasoning altogether too simple-minded. They would rather say that the composition of blood at present is a 'fundamental need for the cell that bases its metabolic processes on the organic esters of phosphoric acid and has as its main composition negatively charged protein. If a marine composition of the internal medium in this restricted sense did not exist, then it would seem necessary for the organism to invent it' (Conway 1943). But presumably the argument could be used the other way round to show that given the ionic composition that was available a living system could develop only with phosphoric esters or negatively charged protein.

This question of the inorganic ionic composition provides a useful example of some of the considerations that arise as we try to investigate the reasons why organisms are as they are. Clearly such inquiries are very hard, but should play a part in developing a system for the study of man. It may be noticed that among the requirements for such study is information not only about the composition and metabolism of organisms and the environment today but also about the history of these in the past (Chapter 26).

A much more practically interesting thing about the differences between the sodium and potassium levels inside and outside cells is that it is the basis of some of the changes at the surface membranes by means of which signals are transmitted. This is best known for nerve cells, whose signals, the nerve impulses (action potentials) are propagated by serial breakdown of the charged surface membrane, allowing sodium to enter and potassium to escape. During recovery of the nerve cell membrane, after the passage of impulses, these ions are pumped back, readying the system for further signalling. This provides an efficient system for propagating signals without decrement. Such communication is an essential feature of the organization of a large and complicated system such as a metazoan body. But communication is a feature of all life and it may be that this has been one of the main reasons for the assimilation of these inorganic ions. With the associated membranes they provide for communication both within cells and between cells.

10. Calcium

Calcium is also involved in maintaining the stability of membranes, and in changing it. Indeed this element is found at the centre of many processes that 'go off suddenly' in the body, for example, muscular contraction. Triggered systems of this sort provide the body with the agents by which it acts upon the environment, changing it to suit its own needs. This again is one of the features that we recognize as so characteristic of human life— the power to modify the environment. It is yet another of the main differences between the living and the non-living. The former 'do things' in order to keep themselves alive. These directed actions are not, of course, simply a property of calcium, but some of them exist in the form we know them only because of that element. Calcium has, in many different sorts of organism, the further functions of providing support, both as a framework as in bone and as a protective covering.

11. Trace elements

The elements present as traces also have their special significance. All of them except zinc are transition elements and therefore readily form complex molecules (as also can zinc, though not so easily). They also have variable valencies and so can take up electrons and yield them again. Linked with appropriate organic molecules they thus provide the possibility of taking up materials in one place, or at one potential level, and depositing them at another. For example, the vertebrate pigment haemoglobin contains iron in the ferrous form; this combines loosely with oxygen which is thus taken up where it is plentiful and released where the oxygen tension is low. But these metals can work in the opposite direction. They make it possible for many enzymes, if provided with suitable energy sources, to build up the energy-rich or complex compounds that are so characteristic of the body (p. 64).

12. The alphabet of bioelements and molecules

We reach the very important conclusion that the elements that support life are a highly selected set. Living bodies are formed by incorporating the correct quantities of each element. An understanding of the process of control by choice from a predetermined set has been one of the achievements of mathematical and engineering science in the last few decades. The fact that all living bodies consist of such sets encourages us to hope that by application of suitable theories we shall greatly improve our understanding of life. We can now extend the treatment to consider sets of molecules.

Wald (1964), in his 'biochemical alphabet', lists the relatively few sets of organic molecules that provide the basic units of all living systems (Tables 2.2 and 2.2A). Glucose is the chief product of photosynthesis and hence the provider of energy. Fats are the main form of storage of energy. The phosphatides are a set of molecules in which fatty chains are combined with a radical containing nitrogen and phosphorus. This end of the molecule is soluble in water, whereas the fatty end is not. These phosphatides thus tend to line up and orientate themselves at interfaces and are prime constituents of the membranes that form so important a part of the structure of cells (Chapter 4).

The most characteristic sets of molecules of all, proteins and polynucleotides, are enormously folded chains known as polymers, each molecule sometimes containing several million atoms. They are considered in detail later. Another set of large molecules are the chlorophylls. This family is fundamental for plant tissues and hence also for all animal life, because by the property of photosynthesis they give the power of building up carbohydrate under the influence of sunlight,

$$CO_2 + H_2O \xrightarrow{h\nu} (CH_2O) + O_2,$$

and hence transforming electromagnetic energy (shown by the quantum ($h\nu$) above), into chemical potential in the form of carbon and hydrogen at the oxidation level of carbohydrate.

Rather similar metal-containing haem pigments play a central part in animal respiration. Sensitivity to light by animals (i.e. vision) is mediated by some members of the similar sets of carotenoids and vitamin A.

The members of each of these sets do not differ very greatly from each other. For us the important point is that living organisms are made up by selection from a rather limited set of such sets. For example, oxygen transport in octopuses and other molluscs is by means of haemocyanin, similar to haemoglobin but containing copper instead of iron. Other haem pigments contain different metals, including vanadium, found in sea squirts.

Similarly, there are slight differences among the haemoglobins themselves, and indeed something is known of the details of the genetic mechanisms by which particular haemoglobins are controlled (p. 551). In most cases it is not yet known why any particular member of a family is chosen in any given class or species of organisms. We do not know why molluscs use haemocyanin. Presumably that was a 'decision' made long ago and thereafter necessarily adhered to.

13. Carbon compounds

All the elements in the body are there for what we might call special purposes, but it is not too much to say that the properties of life are quite peculiarly related to those of carbon. By its capacity to accept four electrons to make stable configurations and to form double bonds it makes an immense variety of compounds. Especially significant for the present discussion is the fact that carbon compounds exist in families, forming complex chains and rings. The familiar homologous series of organic chemistry provide the basis for the sets of molecules out of which living things are built (Table 2.6). In each family the members have similar general properties but differ in detail.

The fact that living molecules are built up by selection among such series may be a very important, indeed fundamental, feature. One of the most typical and puzzling properties of living things is that their actions can take one of two or more different courses under circumstances that are identical or only very slightly different. In ourselves we express this by saying that we have 'choice' or 'free will'. We do not usually ascribe quite the same powers to animals and still less to plants but we recognize that they are all to some extent 'adaptable' (Chapter 8). That is to say, there are alternative states in which they can continue to live. (See Chapter 42 for more about choice and free will.)

The properties of carbon may be responsible for the existence of these slightly different states, between which there can be 'choice' and hence 'control'. The presence of these properties in living systems leads us at first to suspect that there may be some difference between the 'determinate' behaviour of the inorganic and the 'freedom' of organic life. It may be possible to make some progress in analysing this very real problem by studying the implications of the fact that living things are made by selection within the families of organic compounds. Selection between alternatives is the essence of choice and is also a means of control and hence of balance. If the organism is a system that can exist in several states, differing only slightly, it may be possible to discover how mechanisms have evolved to 'choose' the right one for survival.

This is a very loose and general formulation. Biochemistry is concerned to describe precisely these families of carbon-containing molecules and the macromolecules that they form (Fig. 2.4). Our aim here is to show the concepts that are available for the description of man and other living things. For this purpose it may be useful to list some of the chief sets of organic molecules that are involved.

14. Proteins

Next in the list of sets come the amino-acids, the main constituents of proteins. They are simply organic acids with an NH_2^- group attached ($R \cdot CH(NH_2) \cdot CO_2H$). This gives them power to act both as acids and bases. A protein is built of sequences of them linked together to form a chain, there being several hundreds or thousands in one molecule. There is obviously an immense variety of possible amino-acids, but it is a startling fact that only some twenty are found in proteins, *and these are similar in all known organisms*. The particular properties of the protein depend upon

TABLE 2.6

The interrelations of alcohols, aldehydes, and fatty acids

ALIPHATIC (CHAIN) COMPOUNDS

Alcohol series		Aldehyde series		Fatty acid series

Alcohol series

```
    H  H
    |  |
H—C—C—OH
    |  |
    H  H
```
ethyl alcohol
(made by yeast during fermentation)

⟶ oxidation (removal of electrons)
reduction (addition of electrons) ⟵

Aldehyde series

```
    H  O
    |  ‖
H—C—C—H
    |
    H
```
acetaldehyde

⟶ oxidation
reduction ⟵

Fatty acid series

```
    H  O
    |  ‖
H—C—C—OH
    |
    H
```
acetic acid

```
    H  H  H  H
    |  |  |  |
H—C—C—C—C—OH
    |  |  |  |
    H  H  H  H
```
n–butyl alcohol
(obtained on fermenting starch or molasses with the micro-organism *Clostridium acetobutylicum*)

⟶ oxidation
reduction ⟵

```
    H  H  H  O
    |  |  |  ‖
H—C—C—C—C—H
    |  |  |
    H  H  H
```
butyraldehyde

⟶ oxidation
reduction ⟵

```
    H  H  H  O
    |  |  |  ‖
H—C—C—C—C—OH
    |  |  |
    H  H  H
```
n–butyric acid
(constituent of fats, particularly in milk triglycerides)

$CH_3 \cdot [CH_2]_{16} \cdot CH_2OH$

stearyl alcohol
(constituent of naturally occurring waxes)

⟶ oxidation
reduction ⟵

$CH_3 \cdot [CH_2]_{16} \cdot CHO$

stearylaldehyde

⟶ oxidation
reduction ⟵

$CH_3 \cdot [CH_2]_{16} \cdot CO_2H$

stearic acid
(one of the major constituent fatty acids of fats in most animals)

AROMATIC (CYCLIC) COMPOUNDS

Alcohol series

CH_2OH

benzyl alcohol

⟶ oxidation
reduction ⟵

Aldehyde series

CHO

benzaldehyde
'oil of bitter almonds' found in the glucoside called amygdalin which occurs in bitter almonds

⟶ oxidation
reduction ⟵

Acid series

CO_2H

benzoic acid
found as hippuric acid (benzoyl glycine) in the urine (of horses particularly). Also present in gum resins and balsams

---

MORE COMPLEX AROMATIC COMPOUNDS

e.g. a phenol (alcohol)

CH_3

HO   OH

orcinol (occurs in many lichens)

Biological oxidations are usually designated as removal of electrons. Sometimes this is written as removal of H (i.e. removal of electron proton) or as the addition of O atoms.

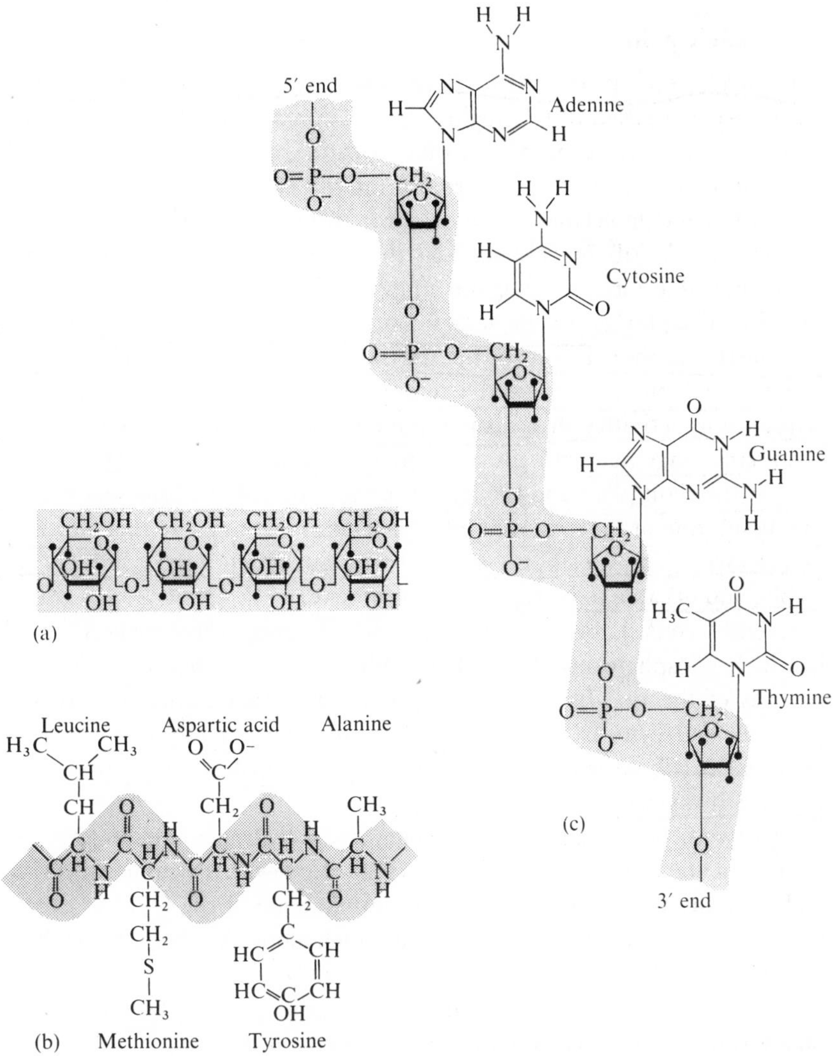

FIG. 2.4. Biological macromolecules. (a) Part of a glycogen chain made up of glucose subunits. (b) Part of a polypeptide chain of a protein, composed of amino-acid subunits. (c) Part of the polynucleotide chain of deoxyribonucleic acid. (After Watson 1965.)

the order in which these twenty acids are arranged and repeated in the chain. Other elements may, of course, contribute their special properties, for instance, iron in haemoglobin. So are built up the proteins, which form a major part of the molecules of the body, including all the enzymes, which make possible the remarkable reactions that go on even at relatively low temperatures (p. 64).

15. Nucleic acids

Finally, there are the instructional or information-carrying molecules. These are composed of five main nitrogen-containing purine and pyrimidine bases, adenine, guanine, cytosine, thymine, and uracil, combined with phosphoric acid and the sugar ribose (or the related deoxyribose). They make the giant molecules of DNA (deoxyribonucleic acid) mainly of the nucleus, RNA (ribonucleic acid) of the nucleolus and cytoplasm, which are responsible for arranging the amino-acids in proper sequences in the proteins (Chapter 3). In the actual condition in the cells the nucleic acids are mostly combined to form neutral salts, known as polynucleotides.

These polynucleotides are the central factor in maintaining the ordered sequence of activities that ensures the continuity of life. They do this by producing, together with the appropriate enzymes, proteins of the right sort, at the right place and the right time to produce reactions that prevent the dissolution of the organism into the environment. To do this they must be (1) varied, and specifically selected to control each type of life, (2) very stable, and (3) able to be reproduced precisely.

1. DNA consists of very large molecules formed of two helical strands in which phosphate and deoxyribose radicles form the backbone and hold a series of the ring-like purine and pyrimidine bases, adenine, thymine, guanine, and cytosine (Fig. 2.5). RNA differs from DNA in the sugar component (ribose instead of deoxyribose), and in having the base uracil in place of thymine.

The two helical strands are held together by hydrogen bonding between complementary pairs of bases, always adenine with thymine (or uracil) and guanine with cytosine. The controlling action of the DNA is exerted by the sequence of bases, each three of which along the chain, through the agency of RNA, add a particular amino-acid to a growing protein chain (Chapter 3). There are some thousands of base pairs in bacterial DNA, enough to code for the formation of hundreds of different proteins. Each sequence of three bases serves to organize the addition of one out of the twenty amino-acids that are used in proteins.

Moreover, each triplet codes for the same amino-acid in all organisms (so far as is known). The instructions for living are thus always written in the same 'language'.

2. These DNA molecules are folded, but enormously long, 52 μm in the T2 bacteriophage, 2 mm in the bacterium *Escherichia coli* and 1 m in man. Nevertheless, they are very stable. The precise chemical reasons for their stability are complicated and not yet fully clear. The base adenine has an electronic configuration that makes it particularly stable towards

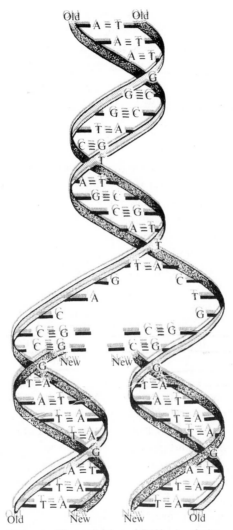

FIG. 2.5. The replication of DNA. A, adenine;
C, cytosine; G, guanine; T, thymine. (After Watson
1965.)

external agents. This may be the reason why it has come to play a key part
in the nucleic acids (see Pullman and Pullman 1962).

     3. The continuation of each type of life depends upon the fact that the
DNA molecules under appropriate conditions replicate others with the
same sequences as themselves (p. 50).

     The fact that the polynucleotides can be said to carry the information
necessary for the continued maintenance of ordered life should not lead

us to think that they contain some 'secret of life', in the sense that they can support it alone. The transmission of order or information involves a channel, in which a sender selects the items to be sent and a receiver decodes them. The continuity of life involves much more than DNA alone. In particular, it requires the polymerase enzymes that decide which part of the DNA information shall be read out into an RNA message, according to the prevailing conditions. The enzymes responsible for protein synthesis are an equally fundamental feature of the system, translating the message into particular proteins.

Enormous advances have been made in the last ten years in giving precise chemical knowledge on these matters. This allows us to begin to formulate a picture that is very much more exact than was possible by naïve observation of life, or even by study of 'protoplasm' with the microscope. Like all important new information it is transmitted in a complex language. Anyone who wants to understand life as fully as is possible today must learn a lot of chemistry and especially biochemistry.

16. Summary

The general concept that has emerged from study of what living things are made of is that although only ordinary materials enter into them yet some extraordinarily rigid selection has been at work to give the sets of elements and compounds involved.

Moreover, we begin to see certain general features that are common to all life. Out of the 92 natural elements there are 16 that occur in most organisms while there are a few that occur in some organisms but not others. This is an amazing fact and perhaps even more amazing is that only about 20 amino-acids, out of the many possible, occur in proteins, and further, the *same* 20 in all organisms from bacteria to mammals. Most amazing of all, the instructions that direct the synthesis of proteins depend in every organism on sequences of three of the four nucleotide bases and any given triplet always serves to incorporate the same amino-acid. The instructions for all life forms are written in similar languages. Such facts tell us at once that life is a 'peculiar', 'improbable' condition, and that all surviving life must have a common origin. We shall find this conclusion reinforced when we examine more fully the still more complex units into which the molecules of living systems are organized within the cells.

3

LIVING ORGANIZATION

1. Molecular order

STUDY of the outlines of the elementary molecular composition of living things in the previous chapter has already shown some of the characteristic features of organisms. But analysis only at that level can never provide the full basis that we require for forecasting their behaviour. In every known organism the molecules are organized into systems of a higher order of complexity, the cells. This is as true of the simple bacteria (Fig. 3.1) as of the most complicated plant or animal (Figs. 3.2 and 3.3), though the organization differs somewhat among them. The viruses (Figs. 3.4 and 3.5) are not cells but are composed of a core of complex ordered molecules, the nucleic acids, and a structured 'body' of protein. The virus is not itself a self-replicating unit but becomes so by injecting the nucleic acid into a true cell, whose own polynucleotide is destroyed and the remaining machinery captured and turned to making more virus. Although the viruses are therefore not independent living entities they show us a great deal about the nature of living organization. The ordering or patterning of molecules that is so characteristic of life evidently comes specifically from the nature of the nucleic acids. These can do nothing alone, but they can direct an appropriate synthetic enzymatic system so that it produces both more nucleic acids and proteins of the particular sorts that build a body suitable to ensure continuity.

All this can now be shown in detail for the T4 bacteriophage, a virus that infects the bacterium *Escherichia coli*. The virus has a rather complicated structure, with the DNA in a 'head', attached to a base plate, a neck with a spiral contractile thread, and six legs, which attach to the bacterial 'prey'. The neck then shortens and injects the DNA into the victim. The genetic machinery has been studied by using mutant strains which make viruses imperfect in different ways (Fig. 3.6). There are several hundred genes in the virus, of which some fifty regulate the bacterial enzymes to allow the production of the proteins.

Apparently the bulk of the protein of the virus is of one type, whose production is controlled by a single gene (number 23 on the map of the

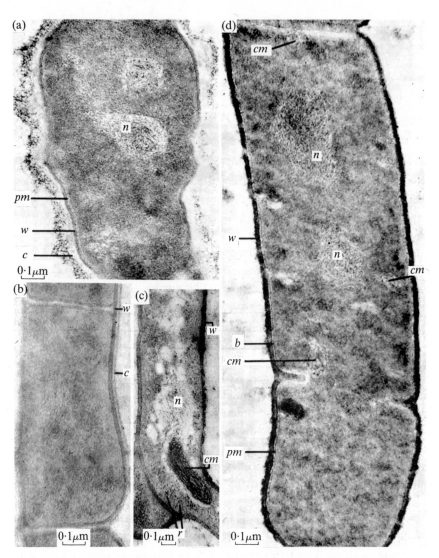

FIG. 3.1. Electron micrographs of thin sections of bacteria. (a) *Corynebacterium fascians*, (b) *Nocardia calcarea*, (c) *Streptomyces coelicolor*, (d) *Bacillus subtilis*. *b*, thin bridges between the wall (*w*) and plasma membrane; *c*, capsular material; *cm*, membranous bodies; *n*, nuclear material; *pm*, plasma membrane; *r*, cytoplasmic granules; *w*, cell wall. (From Glauert 1962.)

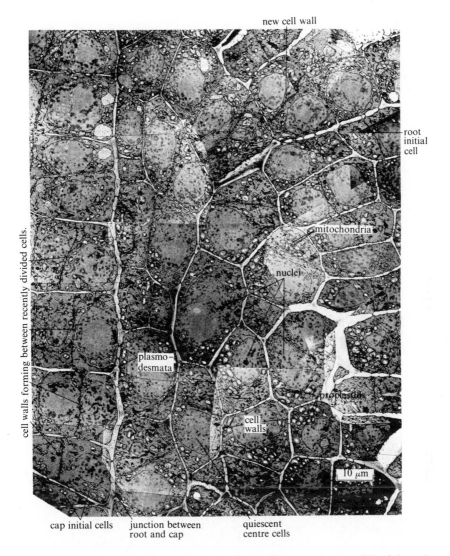

new cell wall

root initial cell

mitochondria

nuclei

cell walls forming between recently divided cells.

plasmo-desmata

proplastid

cell walls

10 μm

cap initial cells   junction between root and cap   quiescent centre cells

FIG. 3.2. Electron micrograph of cells of the root tip of maize. The vacuoles characteristic of plant cells have not yet been formed in these cells. Most of the cells are surrounded by very thick walls, except in the left of the photograph where the early stages of cell wall formation can be seen. (By permission of Dr. B. E. Juniper.)

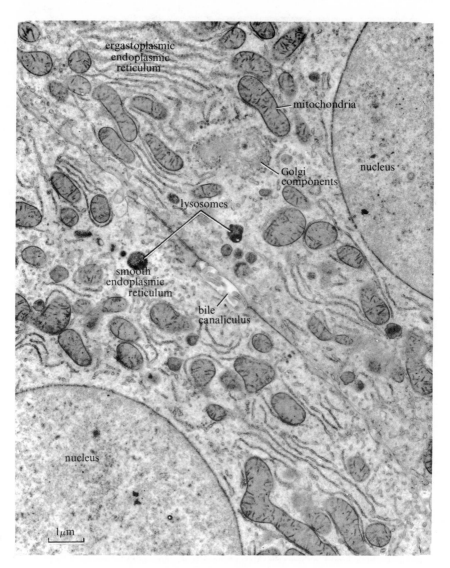

FIG. 3.3. Electron micrograph of portions of two cells from rat liver, showing the various types of organelle that are found in all cells. (From Porter 1961.)

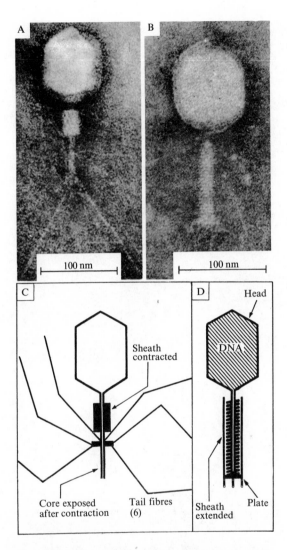

A | B

100 nm | 100 nm

C

Sheath
contracted

Core exposed
after contraction

Tail fibres
(6)

D

Head

DNA

Sheath
extended

Plate

FIG. 3.4. The fine structure of viruses. (A) shows a negatively
stained contracted particle of T2 bacteriophage, the components
of which are shown diagrammatically in (C). (B) An intact T2
particle with fully extended sheaths, which is shown below (D)
diagrammatically. (From Horne and Wildy 1962.)

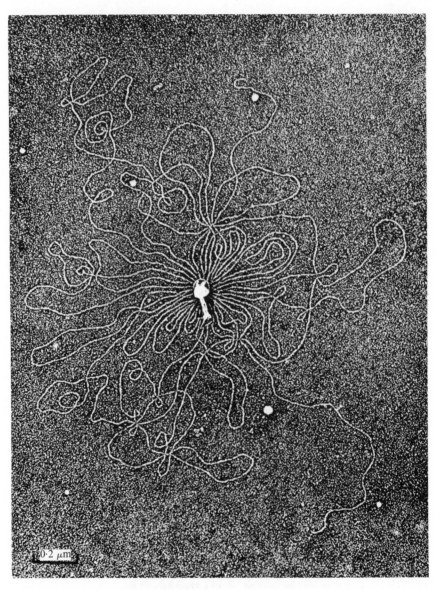

FIG. 3.5. A bacteriophage that has burst, allowing the nucleic acid to emerge as a very long single molecule. (From Kleinschmidt *et al.* 1962.)

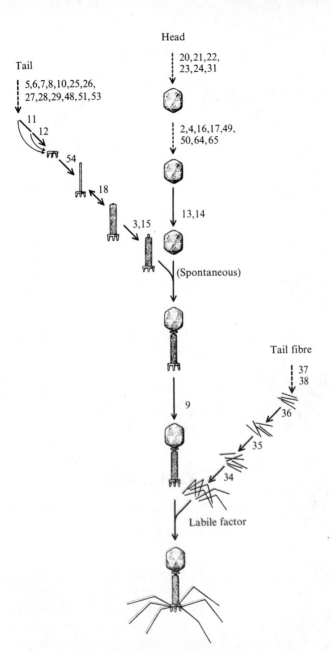

Head

Tail

20,21,22,
23,24,31

5,6,7,8,10,25,26,
27,28,29,48,51,53

11
12

54

2,4,16,17,49,
50,64,65

18

3,15

13,14

(Spontaneous)

Tail fibre

37
38

9

36

35

34

Labile factor

FIG. 3.6. Steps in the pathway to the assembly of T4 bacteriophage. The steps can be made to occur *in vitro* in cultures of phage DNA with bacterial extract. Each step involves a number of genes. There are three principal branches leading independently to the formation of heads, tails, and tail fibres. Thus the primary structure of the head depends on genes listed to the right of the arrows. In the absence of these genes the culture makes only tails and fibres. Union of the finished heads and tails is spontaneous and does not need genetic material. The numbers refer to the genes involved at each step. The solid portions of the arrows indicate the steps that have been shown to occur in extracts. (After Wood and Edgar 1967.)

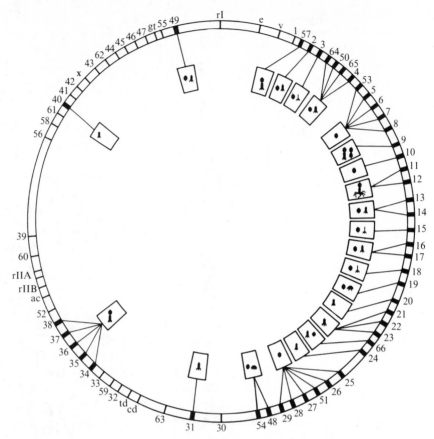

FIG. 3.7. Genetic map of T4 virus. Boxes show components seen in electron micrographs when morphogenetic genes are defective, e.g. with 31, only tails are seen, showing that the gene is required for head production. For clarity tail fibres are omitted; 34-8 and 57 are required for their production. A defect in 11 or 12 produces a complete but fragile virus. (After J. King 1968.)

strand of DNA of Fig. 3.7). The other genes are concerned with producing the various parts and also in making small proteins that are the 'hinges, joints, and bolts' of the virus, joining the parts together. Each part is made by a set of genes. Thirty go to make the head, twelve the hexagonal base plates, three the centre of the tail, others the contractile part, and still others the legs. In the absence of any of the genes imperfect viruses are formed. The putting together of the parts is beginning to be understood and involves various subassembly lines. Some of the manufacture can be made to occur *in vitro*, by adding extracts of *E. coli* to bacteriophage DNA.

For this one case, therefore, we begin to be able to see in detail how the ordering of the life form (if we can call the virus that) derives from the polynucleotide order, working with the complex cellular machinery. No doubt further details will soon be known of this and other examples of morphogenesis. It is important that, while welcoming the relatively clear view we are obtaining, we should recognize the complexity of the system. The order is basically in the DNA, but it is manifested only when this works with the cell enzymes. It is true that the two need not be of the same species. Apart from the virus example, DNA from one animal species can produce protein with the enzymes from quite a different one. At present we do not know the details of the system that is involved in the processes, but there is little doubt that before long we shall do so.

It remains true, however, that there is no instance where life exists in any homogeneous mixture of various types of molecule. It is always in the form of cellular units, each physically bounded and distinct, and with a heterogeneous internal organization. We obviously have, therefore, a further task beyond study of the molecular species before we can say that we have described what living things are made of. Indeed, to speak of 'molecular species' at all is already partly to beg the question of living organization. There are, of course, many relatively simple molecules, such as glucose, that are in true solution in cells. Some of the simpler peptides and even proteins may exist as single molecules in solution. Most are in the form of organelles, immense, heterogeneous aggregates, strictly defined, but formed of major parts, each the size of a protein, only loosely bound together. The weight of such aggregates is determined as that of the units that move by diffusion or sedimentation or by the osmotic pressure exerted. The unit of sedimentation is named after Svedberg, the inventor of the ultracentrifuge; thus, 32s particles move twice as fast as 16s ones. But these measurements can, of course, be made only after applying a given method of isolation, which may often have broken up the originally larger aggregates. In life many protein molecules are united to form the fibres, particles, or membranes that we ordinarily consider as parts of the cell structure. There is, in fact, no precise point at which what may be called 'chemical structure' ends and 'cellular morphology' begins. Both are characterized by a high degree of order.

2. Ordering by the information of the DNA code

If there is order at a supramolecular level, we have immediately to consider the question 'Where does this order come from?' Isolated molecular systems in the non-living world in general show, over a period of time, an average *increase* of entropy, that is, decrease of order. That this tendency to disorder does not operate in a living organism implies that the system is not isolated and somehow has access to a store of order upon which it draws. Such a transfer of order is the process that we commonly call the transmission of information. The 'information' in a system is its degree of order, which is obviously a relative concept. Quantity of information (order) can be measured only against some other ordered system, arbitrarily chosen (Chapter 7).

In living systems the information is mainly carried in special molecules, the polynucleotides. These serve to maintain the particular order of cellular life that is characteristic of each species of organism. They are very stable molecules and have the capacity to copy (replicate) themselves, under suitable conditions and with the assistance of appropriate enzymes. These two properties, of stability and replication, are the basis of the order that is maintained by living systems. But of course these molecules, like any others, cannot keep and transmit their order indefinitely. In the study of the communication of information it is a fundamental principle that the quantity of it cannot spontaneously increase and with time must decrease, the process being known as the intrusion of 'noise'. The fact that living organisms none the less continue seems to imply that they must have access to some other source of information or order. This formulation, however, contains both an error and a mystery. The error is that organisms do not maintain their order. In fact, they are not truly 'self-maintaining' because they are continually changing into something slightly different. The paradox or mystery is that this change, which we call adaptation and evolution, is not in the direction of greater disorder, but of greater order.

There must therefore be some source of information upon which organisms draw and have drawn throughout the years. It is probably fair to say that we do not fully understand what this source of order is. This is partly because we have not yet solved the problem of how life began (Chapter 26). We can, however, see that the source of the information depends somehow on the processes of differential death and selection, which serve to adjust organisms so as to keep them in a steady state of exchange with the environment. Continual receipt by cells of the instruction 'live' or 'don't live' over the centuries has led to the accumulation of increasing order within organisms, culminating in the remarkable information-gathering powers of man (see Chapter 27 and p. 515).

The solution of this problem of how the continuity of life is maintained is somehow connected with the fact that the polynucleotide molecules serve to arrange the parts and actions of organisms so that they correspond to, or *represent*, their environment. This correspondence allows the matching of actions to 'needs' and thus ensures the continuation of the self-maintaining homeostatic activities that are characteristic of life (Chapter 6).

Here we are concerned to notice that the process by which the nucleotides transmit information can be called, by analogy with human communication, selection from a set or code. The practice of considering living processes in terms of representation by means of a code of symbols has many advantages but may lead to confusion, since the status of the analogy is not easy to clarify. The hereditary code is biologically more fundamental than the human speech code. But we use the language and terms of the latter to discuss the former, which has generated it! This obviously involves severe problems about the nature of knowledge.

The essence of the operation that we call coding is that events patterned in one medium are made to correspond to events patterned in another. For example, in human speech particular sound patterns have been made, by convention, to correspond to particular objects or actions in the world. The sound patterns can be re-coded, as when they are passed along a telephone wire or other communication channel, and then are finally decoded in some receiver, in which they *produce a response that is appropriate to the event that was originally represented.*

The concepts of representation and communication are thus related to the action of ordering. The order in one system is so transmitted as to produce some corresponding order in another. The concept of order or pattern is also in turn related to the very difficult concept of choice, as already mentioned in the previous chapter. The information in the channel produces one pattern of response in the receiver, but with different information another pattern could have been produced. Communication of information is thus essentially a matter of selection among a set of possible patterns. The carriers of information are technically called 'elements of discourse'. The elements of discourse are known as *symbols* and the set of them is an *alphabet.* The symbols may be grouped into units such as words, sentences, or books.

Human communication depends upon representing whatever 'news' or 'intelligence' is to be sent in a form that can be conveniently transmitted. The mathematical operations of information theory have revealed many of the principles that govern efficient coding and transmission (see Quastler 1965). The genetic code serves essentially to transmit information about the environment. It does this because (1) only those cells or organisms that have survived transmit; (2) the message they transmit is decoded to produce a new cell or organism with particular characteristics; (3) with these features it may or may not survive and transmit in its turn.

The symbols of the genetic code, reduced to the simplest terms, are the nucleotides arranged in the helical DNA molecules in an order that dictates the sequence in which amino-acids are arranged along proteins. Each sequence of three nucleotide bases determines which particular amino-acid shall be inserted at that point on the chain. Thus one of the first 'breaks in the code' was the discovery in 1961 by Nirenberg and Matthei that an artificial polynucleotide, containing only the base uridine, when provided with appropriate enzymes and raw materials, caused the synthesis of large polypeptide molecules all of whose side chains were the amino-acid phenylalanine. Assuming that three bases code for each amino-acid, then the sequence UUU is the 'word' meaning phenylalanine.

Since there are twenty amino-acids in proteins, 2 bases would not be enough, as they would allow only 16 combinations even if the ordering of the pairs was different. If 3 bases code for each amino-acid, however, there are 64 possible triplets (4^3), which is more than enough. In fact, coding triplets for all the acids have now been found: most have more than 1, some as many as 4, which is technically expressed by saying that the code is 'degenerate' (Table 3.1). Some triplets code for the initiation of a chain (AUG and GUG) or its termination (UAA and UAG and perhaps UGA). The termination symbols were unfortunately given the absurd arbitrary names 'ochre' and 'amber'. The code has no other punctuation marks, but is read triplet after triplet along the molecule. In summary, then, 'the code is triplet, commaless, non-overlapping, and degenerate' (Speyer 1967).

The alphabet thus consists of four letters, A, G, C, and T (or U), each sequence of the three of them being the 'word', or *codon*, for a particular amino-acid. Each sequence of words makes a meaningful 'sentence', being the gene that specifies a particular protein.

It is a very interesting question how it has come about that a particular triplet codes for a given amino-acid, especially as the twenty amino-acids are not distributed at random among the sixty-four triplets (Crick 1968, Orgel 1968). There are roughly two views about this. According to the stereochemical theory each amino-acid is somehow specifically related to its codons (or perhaps to the anti-codons of the tRNA, p. 57). There is some evidence that this may be so for some amino-acids. The alternative 'frozen accident' theory is that the code began by chance and thereafter any change would be lethal. Probably the earliest codes involved few amino-acids, perhaps selected because of some stereochemical relation to a codon. Early ones perhaps included glycine, alanine, serine, and aspartic acid. There is some evidence that tryptophan and methionine were later additions. The primitive system may have used classes of amino-acids, perhaps with only the middle base of a triplet recognized, thus U standing for one of the hydrophobic amino-acids, A for an acidic one. This would explain the rules that restrict the randomness of the distribution today.

These are only the outlines of the problem of the origin of the genetic code. Thinking about it helps us to focus on the fact that any code must somehow be so framed as to *represent* that about which it carries information.

TABLE 3.1

The genetic code

The nucleotide bases are shown as:
U, uracil; C, cytosine; A, adenine; G, guanine.

SECOND LETTER

		U		C		A		G		
U	Phe	UUU UUC	Ser	UCU UCC	Tyr	UAU UAC	Cys	UGU UGC	U C	
	Leu	UUA UUG		UCA UCG	Ochre Amber	UAA (End) UAG (End)	?Cys Try	UGA (?End) UGG	A G	
C	Leu	CUU CUC CUA CUG	Pro	CCU CCC CCA CCG	His Gln	CAU CAC CAA CAG	Arg	CGU CGC CGA CGG	U C A G	
A	Ile Met	AUU AUC AUA AUG (Start)	Thr	ACU ACC ACA ACG	Asn Lys	AAU AAC AAA AAG	Ser Arg	AGU AGC AGA AGG	U C A G	
G	Val	GUU GUC GUA GUG (Start)	Ala	GCU GCC GCA GCG	Asp Glu	GAU GAC GAA GAG	Gly	GGU GGC GGA GGG	U C A G	THIRD LETTER

Amino acids: Ala=alanine; Arg=arginine; Asn=asparagine; Asp=aspartic acid; Cys=cysteine; Gln=glutamine; Glu=glutamic acid; Gly=glycine; His=histidine; Ile=isoleucine; Leu=leucine; Lys=lysine; Met=methionine; Phe=phenylalanine; Pro=proline; Ser=serine; Thr=threonine; Try=tryptophan; Tyr=tyrosine; Val=valine. (From Speyer 1967.)

UGA may code for cysteine in vertebrates; in *E. coli* it may be a signal for chain termination, as are the triplets UAA and UAG, which are given the arbitrary names 'ochre' and 'amber'. AUG and GUG act as signals for chain initiation by coding for N-formylmethionine, because the transfer RNA for this is the only one that can occupy the peptide-donating site of a ribosome to which no peptide chain is attached.

It can do this most obviously if it has features that are in some sense iso-morphic with what it represents as by the above stereochemical similarity, or in a Chinese ideogram (冗 = house). The genetic code may have begun in this way, but, like language, it has probably been immensely compli-cated by later additions, possibly often 'accidental' (whatever that means!).

Since there are two chains in each DNA molecule, with strings of com-plementary base pairs, there must be two alternative sets of proteins that could be produced. Only one of the two nucleotide sequences is used when the DNA is 'read' to produce messenger RNA (p. 54).

Each nucleic acid polymer molecule consists of a sequence of hundreds of thousands of triplets, containing the information for the building of thousands of proteins, each with, say, 100–200 amino-acids. The same triplets code for each amino-acid in all organisms from viruses to man. In this sense we can read the code, but we cannot yet really be said to under-stand the genetic instructions. The function of each protein depends largely upon its folding structure (p. 60), which is determined by the amino-acid sequence, though we only partly know how in one protein, myoglobin. At present, therefore, we have only a partial view of how the sequence of nucleotides is related to the actions by which the organism survives. If we are to understand how the code ensures the ordering of life in cells we have to inquire how the information is 'read out' from the store by 'transcrip-tion' and then 'translated' in the cytoplasm into proteins suitable to allow life to continue.

This is, of course, largely the theme of our whole inquiry. If we under-stood the operations of human DNA today, and how they have come to be as they are, we should have the basis for a truly exact science of life and of man. The fact that we can even approach this end shows that our search is not likely to be wholly in vain.

3. Replication of DNA

The continuity of life requires the provision at appropriate intervals of new DNA with base sequence exactly the same as the old. This is most easily studied in viruses or bacteria, where the DNA forms a single paired strand (Figs. 3.8 and 3.9). The chromosome forms a complete ring and has one replication point. The precise mechanism by which new strands are added alongside the old is not known. Probably there is a weakening of the attachment of the strands to each other at the replication point (as there is also in transcription). This involves a spinning of the DNA threads, probably about their own axis, since spinning of the whole DNA mole-cule about its axis is considered unlikely in view of the viscosity of its surroundings.

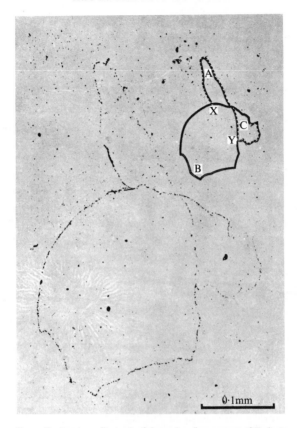

F IG. 3.8. An autoradiograph of the entire chromosome of *Escherichia coli*, labelled with tritiated thymidine for two generations. It constitutes a continuous circular structure. The length is 1110 μm, and this can account for the amount of DNA per nucleus estimated chemically. The inset is of the same structure shown diagrammatically and divided into three sections, A, B, and C, that arise at the two forks X and Y; see Fig. 3.9. (From Cairns 1963.)

The formation of the new chain involves the uptake of the four deoxyribonucleotide triphosphates from the metabolic pool under the influence of DNA polymerase. This enzyme has been isolated from *E. coli* and has a molecular weight of about 100 000 (Richardson *et al.* 1964). There are about 400 molecules per bacterium. The reaction can be made to occur *in vitro* with an optimum at pH 7·4, magnesium being required (Sueoka 1967).

4. The unit of inherited information

The means for carrying information from the past has long been a central problem of biology. It is no accident that this inquiry in its modern form

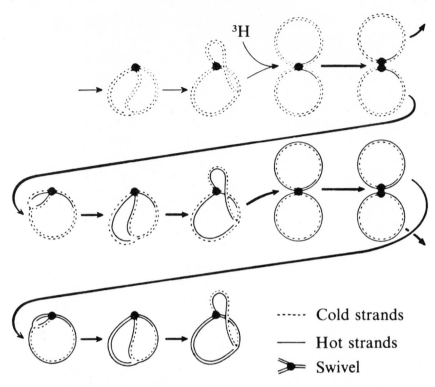

³H

----- Cold strands

——— Hot strands

➤═ Swivel

FIG. 3.9. The mode of chromosome replication in *Escherichia coli* is shown diagrammatically after [³H] thymidine has been applied from the point shown onwards. The parent strands are shown separating and each acquiring a complementary strand. They swivel about the origin and the two new chromosomes then separate. There is only one replication, or growing-point in the chromosome. The two daughter origins and the terminus are connected to form a circular chromosome. The origin should be at the same position in successive rounds of replication. (From Cairns 1963.)

(genetics) has provided the basis for the remarkable discoveries outlined above about the control of order. The laws discovered by Gregor Mendel showed the fundamental relations of parent and offspring, namely, that inheritance was by particulate units, two for each diploid organism, one derived from each of the parents. Cytology revealed that nuclei contain pairs of chromosomes and that one member of each pair passes to each haploid gamete, allowing recombination in the zygote. During the preparation of the gametes (meiosis) the chromosomes twist and may break and rejoin, so that we do not inherit whole grandparental chromosomes. Study of this crossing-over enabled definition of the unit of heredity, the gene, as the minimum piece that hangs together. Another unit is defined by mutation, the change of bases produced by radiation or chemical means, leading to change in some outward characteristic. The classical study of genetics has mainly been the investigation of the inheritance of differences, say between tall and short pea plants or people with blue or brown eyes. In this sense a 'gene' is the part of the chromosome that is responsible for the difference, which may be a single nucleotide triplet. But clearly the unit that codes for one amino-acid side chain cannot operate alone or in isolation. It is best, therefore, to use the term gene for a sequence of nucleotides with a specific function. Various types of gene can be recognized. A *structural gene* is one that determines the sequence of amino-acids in a particular polypeptide. A *regulator gene* is a nucleotide sequence that mediates the activity of structural genes. Other sequences, the *architectural genes*, control the integration of protein into the structure of the cell or the synthesis of transfer RNA or ribosomal RNA. Still other parts probably control the timing of the programme of differentiation of the cell, but little is known about these *temporal genes*.

Mutation may occur by the change of any single base and these are thus the letters of the genetic language (also known as *mutons*). Each triplet specifies one amino-acid and may be called a word of the language. A sequence of say 500 triplets is a *gene* and it specifies a single polypeptide, if it is a structural gene, and is thus a sentence of the language. Genes regulating the production of the enzymes concerned with a single synthetic process usually lie close together on a chromosome and constitute an *operon*, being a paragraph of the DNA language, concerned with a single functional topic (p. 59). The identification of the sequence that constitutes a gene is made by a method called the *cis-trans* or complementation test. The name *cistron* is therefore often used for the sequence that constitutes a structural gene.

The DNA of the nuclei is mainly inside the chromosomes. Its exact disposition and mode of operation have not been seen with the electron microscope but can be deduced in suitable cases biochemically. The finest analysis has been of the viruses known as bacteriophages (Figs. 3.4–3.7). Here genetic experiments have shown that the smallest unit of crossing-over corresponds approximately to one nucleotide pair. This is as would be expected and will doubtless be shown true also for other organisms.

5. Reading the information in DNA

The method of 'reading' or transcription of the information has been investigated thoroughly in bacteria, using the fact that following a change in the medium the organisms are induced to produce enzymes that they need. Thus the intestinal bacteria *Escherichia coli*, if deprived of glucose and provided only with lactose sugar, begin within minutes to produce the enzyme β-galactosidase, which splits lactose into glucose and galactose.

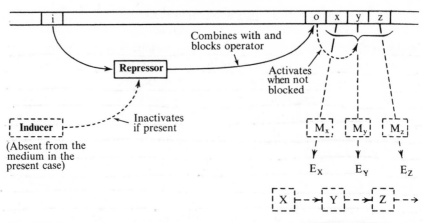

FIG. 3.10. The intracellular repressors are considered to be proteins with two different active sites, one specific for the inducer and the other specific for the operator (Jacob and Monod 1961). The figure shows enzyme repression. The regulator gene is indicated by i. The structural genes x, y, and z, together with the operator o, constitute the operon, and their products M_x, M_y, and M_z are the messenger RNA molecules coding for the amino-acid sequences of the enzymes E_x, E_y, and E_z, controlling sequential conversion of x through z. The broken lines indicate the parts of the system that are 'switched off' and remain latent in the absence of inducer. (After Michie 1964.)

By study of this system Jacob and Monod (1961) have proposed that the cistron necessary to produce the enzyme is present in the normal bacteria but repressed. This repression acts by blocking a single site in the operon, known as the *operator gene*, without which the remainder (structural genes) cannot operate. The repressor is produced by a *regulator gene*, which comes from a near-by site. The action of the inducer (lactose) is to inactivate the repressor, which is specifically sensitive to it. This releases the operator gene, which activates the structural genes (Fig. 3.10).

The transcription of the information of the genes of bacteria is by production of a stream of molecules of messenger RNA (mRNA) (Figs. 3.11 and 3.12). These are relatively short stretches of nucleotide with chains of 1000–2000 bases and molecular weights of 300 000–600 000. Each molecule corresponds to one or several structural genes, that is to say carries the specification for one or more proteins. The DNA produces the mRNA under the influence of the ubiquitous enzyme RNA polymerase. The molecules of this enzyme have a molecular weight estimated at nearly 1 million and may therefore be up to 10 nm in diameter. It is uncertain how they gain access to the rods of DNA. One suggestion is that the DNA template itself spins, the polymerase moving along it 'reading' one base after another. It does this by taking a molecule of the appropriate one of the four nucleotide triphosphates (the parent molecules of the bases) and adding it to the growing polynucleotide. Probably the DNA is unwound

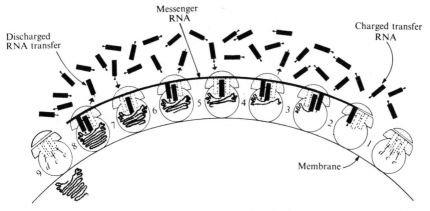

Messenger
RNA

Discharged
RNA transfer

Charged transfer
RNA

Membrane

F IG. 3.11. During protein synthesis the genetic information of messenger RNA is translated into specific amino-acid sequences. Ribosomes (1–9) provide the primary amino-acid polymerization sites and move along the mRNA exposing sequentially attachment sites for amino-acid tRNA molecules. The initial bond between charged tRNA and mRNA is made at the entrance or decoding site *d* (2). At the condensing site, *c*, the tRNA adds its amino-acid to the growing polypeptide chain (3). The exit site *e* is occupied briefly by the discharged tRNA before its release (4). The completed polypeptide-chain is shed after the last amino-acid has been added (9). (After R. C. King 1968.)

at the point where the mRNA is produced, and it is held that in higher animals this is shown in certain regions of chromosomes that become expanded as 'puffs' when synthesis of a particular protein is initiated. There are, however, various difficulties in this view of the 'puffs' and we really do not understand what regulates transcription of the DNA in higher forms (Harris 1968). It may be that the new mRNA is synthesized stepwise in the nucleus, as the stretch of DNA uncoils, in such a way that the triplets are copied. The mRNA then detaches and leaves the nucleus for the region of the ribosome granules of the cytoplasm. The mRNA of bacteria is characterized by being rapidly labelled and metabolically unstable (decay constant 5 min). However, very little mRNA has been found in nuclei of higher organisms and it has recently been claimed that genetic information is carried from the nucleus by a different nucleic acid—informational DNA (Bell 1969). This is said to be a rapidly labelled 7s fraction found in large amounts in the cytoplasm of muscle cells, where it is associated with protein as 16s 'I-somes'. These are also associated with RNA, which may be transcribed from them and may be informational.

The ribosomes are the seat of translation of the message of the mRNA into protein. Each ribosome is formed of a large and a small subunit, one approximately twice the size of the other as recognized by their behaviour in the centrifuge. Both parts consist of about equal amounts of a second species, ribosomal RNA (rRNA) and protein. In the larger part the growing protein chain is stored until release (Fig. 3.11). The ribosomes are

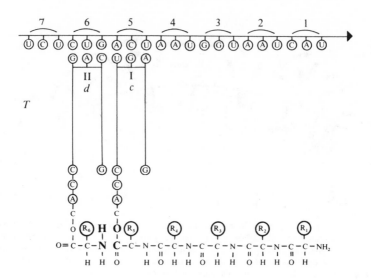

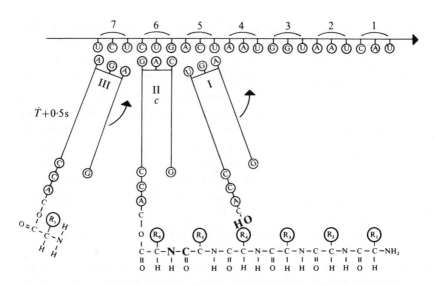

FIG. 3.12. Stages in the translation of the mRNA message into a protein. At time T the codon 6 of the messenger tape occupies the decoding site d of a ribosome. The CUG pairs with the anti-codon GAC of a tRNA molecule, which carries the amino-acid R_6. The condensing site c is occupied by the preceding tRNA molecule bearing a UGA anticodon tRNA whose amino-acid R_5 is being attached to the growing chain R_1, R_2. . . .

In the lower figure, at time $T+0·5$ s, the mRNA has advanced by one codon. The fifth amino-acid has been attached by changes in the bonds of the atoms shown in bold face. The UGA tRNA is being released and a new one AGA is attaching to the decoding site. (After R. C. King 1968.)

often lined up in rows along the sacks of the endoplasmic reticulum and it is postulated that the molecules of mRNA pass through each ribosome much as a tape goes through a tape recorder. This process has never been convincingly revealed, but it may be that as each triplet of nucleotides comes into line on the ribosome it attracts from the surrounding pool the appropriate member of a third sort of nucleotide, which is known to occur, transfer RNA (tRNA). These are still smaller molecules than those of mRNA, containing usually less than 100 nucleotides. Each carries an 'anticodon' of three nucleotides, capable of attaching to the appropriate triplet of mRNA. At the end of the tRNA molecule is a grouping that picks up the appropriate amino-acid from the surrounding pool. Thus an alanine transfer RNA molecule might have the anticodon CGA, which is the complement of GCU, one of the triplets that code for alanine (p. 49).

As the mRNA tape moves through each ribosome it passes first an entrance or decoding site, where the appropriate tRNA is picked up. This then goes to a middle or condensing site, where the amino-acid is attached to the chain, and then to an exit site where the now empty tRNA is released. When the whole molecule of mRNA has run through, the finished protein is released. Since the ribosomes are lined up on the endoplasmic reticulum it may be that a single molecule of mRNA can be read by several ribosomes successively (Figs. 3.11 and 3.14). The actual rates of transcription and

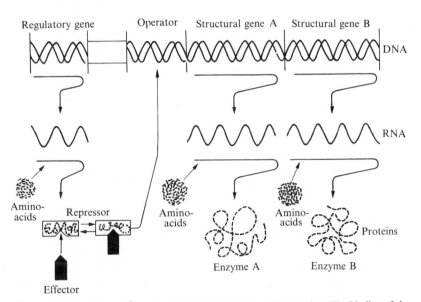

FIG. 3.13. Control of enzyme synthesis by gene activation and repression. The binding of the effector to the repressor produced by the regulatory gene allows it either to activate or inactivate the operator, according to the type of system. (From Bullough 1967.)

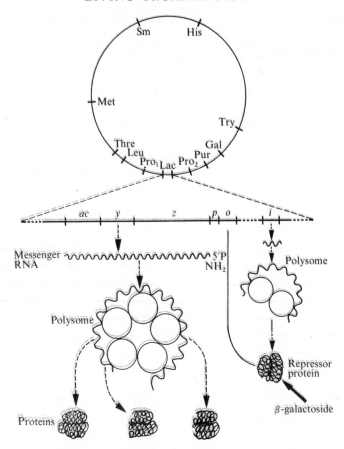

FIG. 3.14. The lactose region of the bacteria *Escherichia coli*. The chromosome of *E. coli* is circular. The position of the lactose region is indicated (amongst other genetic markers). An enlargement of the lactose region is shown below. Each structural gene synthesizes a single messenger, which associates with ribosomes to form a polysome, where different polypeptide chains are assembled. *i*, regulator gene; *o*, operator; *p*, promotor; *z*, gene for the structure of galactosidase, *y*, gene for the structure of β-galactoside-permease; *ac*, gene for the structure of β-galactoside transacetylase (these are enzymes used in the splitting of lactose). (From Jacob 1966.)

translation have been estimated in suitable bacteria. The genes for four enzymes of a certain operon of *E. coli* are transcribed in 7 min. Translation of the relevant mRNA proceeds at 1200 nucleotides/min (i.e. 400 amino-acids are added each minute) (Morse, Baker, and Yanofsky 1968).

It is clear that the nucleotide pairs are the fundamental units of heredity, strung together in functionally significant sets, the genes (or more strictly cistrons). If the Jacob and Monod scheme is correct these are of two sorts, structural genes, coding for proteins, and operator genes near by, which control these, the whole constituting an operon. Each operon is controlled by one or more regulator genes, acting by producing an extra-chromosomal product. The substance acting as the repressor of the lactose cistron has now been isolated and proved to be a protein that binds specifically to the DNA molecules of the lactose operon and is released from it by the galactosidase inducers as described on p. 53 (Gilbert and Müller-Hill 1967, Bretscher 1968). The explanation for the regulation of gene action by the removal of suppression has therefore been well substantiated for bacteria. It has never been proved, however, for truly cellular (eukaryote) organisms.

An alternative hypothesis to explain the regulation of gene actions for higher organisms has been put forward by Harris (1968), as a result of fusion of cells of different types, which can be made to take place if cultures of them are treated with a virus. These experiments show that the regulation of transcription is by some influence of the cytoplasm on the nucleus. Thus in the nucleated red cells of birds only a small fraction of the DNA is active and only very small amounts of RNA are produced. But if their nuclei are introduced into actively synthesizing human cells many genes become active and much RNA is produced. Moreover, these nuclei begin to incorporate tritiated thymidine, showing that they are now synthesizing DNA, which they never do in the adult bird, being 'end-cells', doomed to be removed from the circulation.

Harris summarizes these results as follows. 'The regulation of nucleic acid synthesis in the heterokaryon is thus essentially unilateral: whenever a cell which synthesizes a particular nucleic acid is fused with one which does not, the active cell initiates this synthesis in the inactive partner. In no case does the inactive cell suppress synthesis in the active partner . . .' (Harris 1968).

These experiments suggest that regulation of DNA transcription is not a matter only for regulator genes, but is controlled from the cytoplasm. Of course in any case it is clear that the specific information upon which differentiation of an animal cell into one type rather than another is based must come from outside the nucleus. Evidently the relations of nucleus and cytoplasm are complex and not yet properly understood.

6. The inheritance of order

The information about the primary source of living order, though still incomplete, forms a central theme of modern biology. We have known for a long time that the order exists, that it is a fundamental feature, and that in some way it differentiates living from non-living systems. Biologists have often emphasized the theme that their science is 'morphological' rather than purely 'chemical'. Also, of course, that there is more in a living organism than 'just chemistry'. We can now bring these vague ideas together by showing at the centre of living things molecules that carry an *inherited* order. Moreover, the order is in the form of a code, that is, a set of symbols whose significance appears only when they are passed through an appropriate communication channel and decoded. All of this is based on firm knowledge of the chemical composition of DNA.

In this sense the discoveries have truly revolutionized our approach to general biological problems. They have not, however, as yet led to particular advances that have great practical importance, though undoubtedly they will do so. The relevance of such a system of ideas to a human problem can be illustrated, however, by the classic case of sickle-cell disease, which is inherited as a simple recessive. Pauling and his colleagues (1949) showed that the red blood corpuscles of persons suffering from this condition contain an abnormal haemoglobin. It has now been shown that the difference is the substitution of the amino-acid valine for glutamic acid at one point in the protein chain. This makes the molecule less soluble and therefore liable to precipitate. Homozygotes usually die as children, and the gene would seem to be highly disadvantageous. Yet it is widely spread, especially in populations that are subject to malaria. Apparently the heterozygotes have an increased resistance, perhaps because the parasite suffers from the abnormal haemoglobin, which is present in a heterozygote, though in reduced amounts (pp. 551 and 595).

In populations in which the malaria risk is reduced the gene seems to be dying out. It is rare now in Curaçao, whereas it remains common in Surinam; the inhabitants of both are from Ghana but only the latter still suffer from malaria. Such changes of gene frequency by selection take time. In principle it may be possible in future to accelerate them through knowledge of the DNA code.

7. The folded structure of proteins

The DNA thus controls the sequence of amino-acids along the proteins. To understand how this results in the control of living activities we must examine how the protein composition regulates the various structures and functions of the cell. The first aspect to be considered is the configurations adopted by the protein molecules themselves. The protein chains are mostly not simply long loose threads, but are often elaborately folded, with interactions between their side chains. As a result, irregular globular structures are formed, in which not all parts of the chain are presented equally to the surroundings. This tertiary structure determines their reactions as

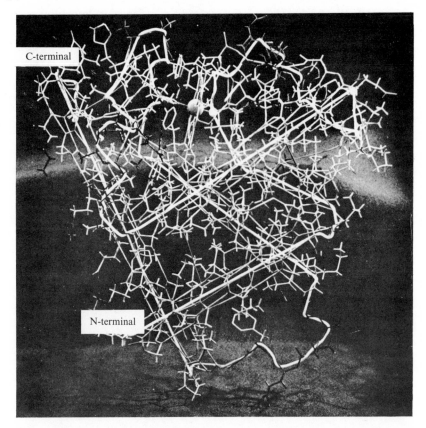

FIG. 3.15. A model of the myoglobin molecule showing the location of all the atoms. The cord indicates the polypeptide chain and its two ends are indicated N-terminal and C-terminal. The larger sphere in the molecule indicates the atom of iron, while the small sphere marks the position of the molecule of water. This would be replaced by oxygen when the myoglobin is oxygenated. (From Kendrew 1966.)

enzymes (Figs. 3.15 and 3.16). The details of the folding are determined by the amino-acid sequence and this is therefore the next sense in which we must consider how the DNA controls the organization of the cell. Clearly it will dictate which groups are presented to the outside (Fig. 3.17). It is this that largely specifies the activity of the protein as an enzyme. So even at this level we see how the DNA code controls the life of the cell by deciding the form of its parts and hence their activity.

The bonds between the peptide groups of the protein chains allow considerable flexibility, and in many proteins this results in the chain being rather tightly folded in a regular way. A common form is a helix in which there are about eleven residues for every three turns. This structure is maintained by the affinities of each positively charged hydrogen atom along

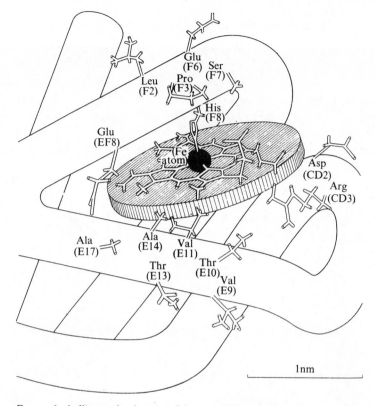

Glu
(F6) Ser
(F7)
Leu Pro
(F2) (F3)
His
(F8)
Glu
(EF8)
Fe
atom
Asp
(CD2)
Arg
(CD3)

Ala
(E17) Ala Val
(E14) (E11)
Thr Thr
(E13) (E10) Val
(E9)

1nm

FIG. 3.16. A diagram showing part of the myoglobin molecule of Fig. 3.17, much
enlarged to show the positions of the atoms in some of the amino-acid side chains
round and within the haem group. (From Haggis 1964.)

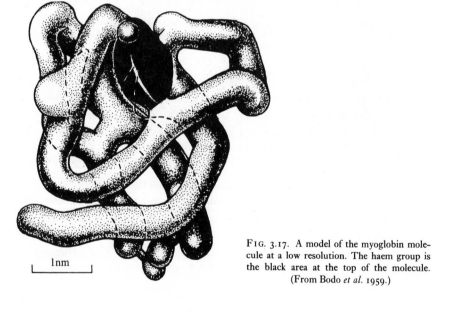

1nm

FIG. 3.17. A model of the myoglobin molecule at a low resolution. The haem group is
the black area at the top of the molecule.
(From Bodo *et al.* 1959.)

the backbone for its neighbouring oxygen atom in the next turn. Such hydrogen bonding is relatively weak and can be broken by mild treatments such as heating to about 70-100 °C. This results in a change in the protein known as *denaturation*, depriving it of its characteristic enzymic and other properties. Interactions between the neighbouring amino-acid residues of the chain serve to strengthen the coils of some proteins. According to the degree of such effects, different proteins vary in the extent to which they show helical coiling. Haemoglobin molecules are 60-80 per cent coiled, egg albumin 30-45 per cent, pepsin 20-30 per cent, and casein hardly at all.

The protein structure is further complicated by the fact that each molecule is made up of several subunits, that is, peptide chains with differing sequences and hence different coiling. Perutz and his colleagues (1960) have shown that in the haemoglobin molecule there are four subunits, two each of α and β chains, differing slightly (Fig. 3.18). This association of

FIG. 3.18. A model of the haemoglobin molecule. Two of the four haem groups are indicated by grey discs. (From Cullis *et al.* 1962.)

parts may be called the *quarternary structure* of the protein and it shows us a further stage by which the cell structure is controlled through the sequences of the peptide chains.

A particularly important feature of the structure of proteins is that it may be readily changed by combination with small molecules such as lactose or amino-acids. Such 'allosteric' proteins may, according to Monod, Changeux, and Jacob (1963), be the basis of regulation of gene action. Regulation involves the transmission of signals from the cytoplasm to the DNA and this may be achieved by specific repressor molecules that are allosteric proteins, with at least two distinct receptor sites, which cannot both be active at once. One of these binds to the operon. The other site is normally empty but if it becomes activated by the presence of a specific metabolite known as the *co-repressor* or *inducer* (say lactose in the example on p. 59) then the repressor molecule changes its structure, the site joining it to the DNA becomes inactive, the operon is de-repressed, and synthesis, say of β-galactosidase, begins.

8. Enzymes

As has already become apparent, many of the characteristic and 'improbable' actions of living systems are the work of enzymes. These may be defined as catalysts, and this at once helps us to think more clearly about some of the more puzzling problems that life presents. A catalyst is a substance that increases the rate at which a chemical system achieves equilibrium, without itself undergoing any ultimate chemical change. Nevertheless, the catalyst may play a part in deciding which of several possible reactions takes place. Thus, depending upon which catalyst is used, alcohol can be decomposed to make either acetaldehyde or ethylene or ether.

Catalysts make reactions proceed as they would not otherwise do at a given temperature and pressure. A reaction that proceeds with a drop in free energy may do so only very slowly because too few of the molecules reach the activation energy necessary to react. This can be increased in various ways; for example, the chemist usually does it by heating the mixture, so that the internal energy of the molecules is increased and they are more likely to collide and react. A catalyst produces the same effect by allowing a greater proportion of the molecules to interact. It usually does this by forming complexes with the substrates, which then separate off to form the product. Catalysts produce 'improbable' results, namely actions that would not happen in free solutions. Often, this is simply because of some particular feature of the structure of the catalyst such as the large extent of surface presented, at which reagents can meet. Thus with many metallic catalysts the reagents become physically adsorbed, raising their local concentration and increasing the chances of encounters. In other catalysts the reagents are chemically attached to the surface, involving quite profound changes in the bonding within their molecules. Such altered molecules or molecule fragments undergo reactions very different from those that take place in molecules in simple gas or liquid phases. When they are at such a surface they react at lower activation energies. The details of such mechanisms are imperfectly understood even in simple inorganic catalysts. It is not surprising that we cannot give precise physico-chemical explanations for the reactions catalysed by the immense folded protein molecules. However, as physical chemistry develops, no doubt we shall come to understand living as well as inorganic catalytic reactions. The mechanism of action of the enzyme lysozyme is already quite well understood (Dingle and Fell 1969).

The surface activity of metals such as platinum in inorganic catalysis may be compared with the secondary, tertiary, and quarternary structures of proteins. These provide surfaces, the active sites, at which the molecules of the material to be acted upon (substrate) become attached. While there, they are in some way activated and the electrons redistributed to produce changes that would not otherwise take place at that temperature.

Knowledge of enzymes grew originally from the study of the fermentation of sugar by yeast to form alcohol (*en-zyme*, literally 'in yeast'). Buchner first showed in 1897 that it is possible to prepare from yeast a cell-free extract that will ferment sugar; therefore the reaction is essentially a chemical one, not something inseparable from life. In fact, there are more than ten separate enzymes in a yeast extract, each responsible for one stage in the breaking down of sugar to alcohol.

A very familiar example of an enzyme is the amylase (= 'starch splitter') of the saliva. Starch $(C_6H_{10}O_5)_x$ can be split into two molecules of the sugar maltose by a change that proceeds with a drop in free energy—but only very slowly at 37 °C (body temperature). In the presence of amylase, however, the reaction goes so fast that a sweet taste can be detected in the mouth soon after a piece of starch is chewed. We need no elaborate chemical apparatus to tell us that in the mouth there is an enzyme able to allow starch to turn to sugar.

With slightly more trouble it can be shown that extracts of the stomach, acting in acid solution, break up proteins into shorter chains, the peptides —the enzyme being pepsin. In the duodenum and intestine further enzymes, derived from the pancreas, continue the process and break up other molecules too. These extra-cellular digestive enzymes of the mouth, stomach, and small intestine are destructive, and therefore in a sense less typical than those within the cell. There may be many hundreds, of the latter perhaps only a few molecules of each. They accelerate not only the breakdown of materials submitted to the cell but, much more important, the reactions by which materials are combined to *produce* the cellular components. Many enzymes can work in either direction, producing splitting or synthesis according to the concentration of reagents and other conditions. However, to ensure adequate regulation the most important pathways employ different mechanisms for synthesis and breakdown.

Many enzymes are extremely specific and will act upon only one particular type of molecule. Others act upon all members of a class. Unfortunately, little is known either about the basis of the specificity or of the means by which the electron redistributions are produced. However, it is known that activity is often lost by the relatively mild treatments that destroy the tertiary and quarternary structure (denaturation by heat or pH change). This suggests that the particular side-chains presented at the outside of the molecule are significant. It is now known that binding of a substrate or inhibitor causes considerable conformational changes round the active site of the enzyme (Blake *et al.* 1967).

The number of enzymes is very large, even in a simple bacterium; for example, in *Escherichia coli* there may be between 1000 and 2000 present (Luria 1960). Furthermore, the possible variations in the combinations of side-chains presented are enormous and are still further increased by the incorporation into many enzyme molecules of other atoms, called *prosthetic groups*, such as the iron-containing haem radical of haemoglobin. Such groups usually confer some specific property. In this case the formation of particular complexes with the electronic shell of the transition metal allows that oxygen is taken up under one set of conditions and then given up again elsewhere.

Many enzymes function only with the co-operation of other molecules, the co-enzymes, which are not specific but remarkably uniform throughout bacteria, animals, and plants. Thus nicotinamide adenine dinucleotide (NAD) serves as a hydrogen carrier in oxidation reactions of many organisms, by accepting hydrogen atoms presented by one enzyme, and then giving them up subsequently on the operation of another enzyme.

$$NAD \underset{-2H}{\overset{+2H}{\rightleftharpoons}} NADH_2$$

Other co-enzymes are thiamine (vitamin B_1), riboflavin (B_2), and co-enzyme A (pantothenate). Like NAD (nicotinate), all of these are 'vitamins', that is to say, cannot be synthesized by man (or by most mammals) and must therefore be supplied in the diet.

9. Control of enzyme action

Enzymes often operate in chains, each using as substrate the product of the one before. Obviously, anything that changes the rate of one reaction may alter that of the whole sequence. The velocity of any reaction is controlled both by the amount of enzyme and by the concentration of substrate. So if in a series

$$A \xrightarrow{a} B \qquad B \xrightarrow{b} C \rightarrow$$

the reaction velocity V_a increases then so does V_b to the maximum extent that the system allows. Regulation of the rates of enzymatic reactions is one of the fundamental methods of control of the complicated actions that constitute living. The concentration of the substrates is one of the controlling factors. Another is the effect of the products of reaction in inhibiting their further operation. This 'product inhibition' may operate directly on the preceding reaction, or by a feedback action on some more distant member of the chain of enzymes, or upon the operon that produces a critical enzyme. Thus an excess of the amino-acid L-isoleucine added to a culture of *Escherichia coli* immediately inhibits the action of L-threonine deaminase, which is the first enzyme in the pathway by which leucine is synthesized from threonine. Not only this, but the leucine *also* inhibits the operon that induces the formation of L-threonine deaminase, by activating its repressor gene.

A third means of regulation is that the presence of a substrate induces the formation of the enzyme. The genetic constitution of the cell must of course be such as to allow this; in other words, selection during the previous history of the race has ensured that the appropriate codons occur in the DNA. Repression of synthesis of enzyme by the product, as mentioned above, is a fourth means of control, also acting through the operon.

We can thus begin to understand how in these various ways the rates of all the reactions in the cell are adjusted. But the total number of them is very large and the complexity of interaction almost unimaginable. It is a great tribute to the ingenuity of microbiologists that the outlines of the plan have been revealed in bacteria. Even for these we know only some features, and for the cells of higher organisms almost nothing. In order to control living reactions we shall need a great deal more detailed information of the same sort.

4

CELLS, ORGANS, AND ORGANISMS

1. Individuals

No single enzymatic protein is able to carry on the business of life alone. As our inquiry proceeds it will become increasingly clear how very complex this business is, and it requires the co-operation of many, many parts. We have next, therefore, to try to see how the instructions of the DNA regulate the ordered interaction of all these parts. This is in itself a gigantic task, hardly yet begun by biology. To initiate the study we note that the units within which all the parts necessary for the continuation of one type of life are found are the integrated individual organisms. They vary from a bacterium weighing 2×10^{-12} g to a blue whale of 1.3×10^7 g or a giant redwood tree of 6.3×10^8 g. They remain as coherent units for times varying from a few minutes (say 10 for bacteria) to several thousand years (say 10^9 min for a redwood tree). The 'individual' is certainly a genuine unit of biological action, but we shall increasingly learn that the life of the species is not wholly epitomized in any one individual and that, moreover, the lives of all the various species are related.

However, it is clear enough that from bacteria to man we can recognize an individual that is a unit of function. It is bounded-off from the surroundings, integrated within itself in its homeostatic reactions, provided with mechanisms for defence and repair of parts and of the whole (within limits), able to replicate itself, and destined to die as a whole (again with exceptions). We shall later return to many of these features and especially to discuss the individual as the unit of replication and hence of selection. Here we are discussing living organization, and it is important to emphasize the obvious but fundamental fact that living matter is always found as one of a myriad types of individual bacteria, plants, or animals.

2. Cells

All types of organism are composed of cells, though the cells of bacteria are rather different from the rest. Plant and animal cells have a nucleus containing most of the DNA together with other materials, separated by a nuclear membrane from the cytoplasm (Figs. 4.1 and 4.2). The cytoplasm is bounded externally by a cell membrane (see Fig. 4.4), which may be

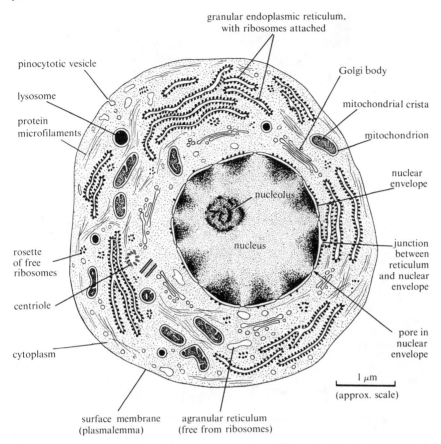

granular endoplasmic reticulum,
with ribosomes attached

pinocytotic vesicle

lysosome

protein
microfilaments

rosette
of free
ribosomes

centriole

cytoplasm

Golgi body

mitochondrial crista

mitochondrion

nuclear
envelope

nucleolus

nucleus

junction
between
reticulum
and nuclear
envelope

pore in
nuclear
envelope

1 μm
(approx. scale)

surface membrane   agranular reticulum
(plasmalemma)   (free from ribosomes)

FIG. 4.1. Diagram of a cell reconstructed from electron micrographs.
(Professor E. G. Gray kindly made the drawing.)

supported by further structures, the cell walls, especially prominent in
plants (see Fig. 3.2). Plant cells also often contain a very large watery
space, the vacuole, the cytoplasm being restricted to a narrow film around
this.

The cytoplasm is highly heterogeneous. Within a general watery phase
are suspended particles of all sizes from ribosomes of 20 nm to mitochondria
up to 400 μm long. These cell organelles will be discussed later (p. 71).
Here we are concerned to notice simply the fact of the complexity of cell
organization. The ribosomes and microsomes are concerned with protein
synthesis. The mitochondria carry the respiratory enzymes, and are hence
called the power packs of the cell. There is a whole system of membranous
reticulum acting as the sites of synthesis. The granular endoplasmic reticulum carries ribosomes and perhaps passes their products to the smooth

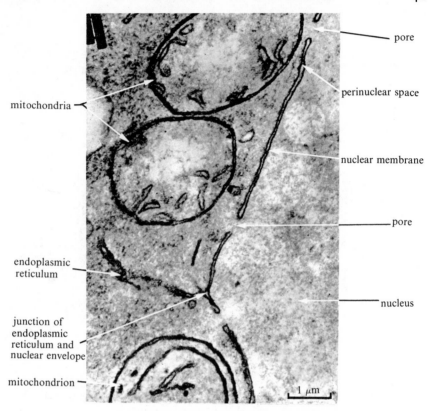

FIG. 4.2. The nuclear membrane of a cell of the plant *Oxalis*. (From Marinos 1960.)

Golgi membranes. In plant cells, of course, there are the plastids (chloroplasts, see Figs. 4.3 and 4.4), carriers of the chlorophyll by which the energy
of sunlight is made to synthesize organic compounds from carbon dioxide.

This crude list gives no idea of the highly complex structure that the
electron microscope shows in any cell (Fig. 4.5). In addition, there are
many special organelles, such as the centrioles, concerned in cell divisions,
or the basal granules of the motile flagella. Many cells contain reserve
materials, granules of fat or carbohydrate. Each particular type of cell
usually has its own characteristic cell inclusion. Thus, muscle fibres contain contractile myofibrils; connective tissue cells produce the strong fibres
of collagen and elastin; the various glands produce their characteristic
secretions.

Each of these cellular materials must be formed in the right quantity,
at the proper time and place, basically under the control of the DNA.
There is very little information as to how the synthesis of cell organelles is achieved. There is no reason to doubt that, as we understand the

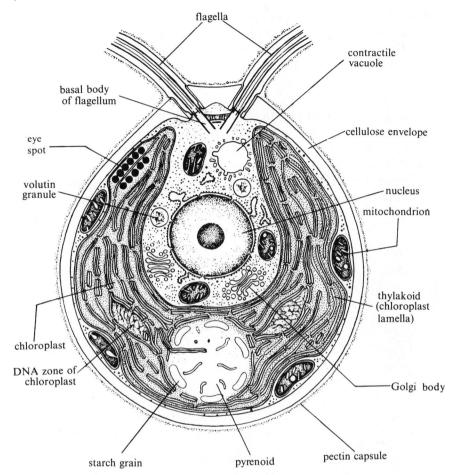

flagella

contractile
vacuole

basal body
of flagellum

cellulose envelope

eye
spot

volutin
granule

nucleus

mitochondrion

chloroplast

thylakoid
(chloroplast
lamella)

DNA zone of
chloroplast

Golgi body

starch grain   pyrenoid   pectin capsule

F IG. 4.3. A diagram of a green flagellate *Chlamydomonas* reconstructed from electron micrographs.
(After Vickerman and Cox 1967.)

higher-order foldings of the proteins better, the control of many of these
cell organelles will become apparent. Some of them have astonishing regularity and constancy of structure. Thus the basal granules of motile cilia
and flagella have rings of nine fibres, usually with two at the centre. This
organization is found from protozoa to mammals. It depends upon the
arrangement of the proteins that produce the movements.

As information accumulates, further similarities of the tissues throughout nature are becoming apparent. Thus the ribosomes of all bacteria have
components sedimenting at 23s and 16s, with molecular weights of 1·1 and
0·56 million. In higher plants the rRNA is 25s and 18s with molecular
weights of 1·3 and 0·7 million. In animals the smaller component of the

RNA is 18s (0·7 million) as in plants, but the larger component ('28s') has changed during evolution from 1·40 million molecular weight in sea urchins and *Drosophila* to 1·58 in chick and 1·75 in mammals. It is suggested that these differences are related to the fact that whereas plant cells remain totipotent those of animals can become differentiated to produce each a narrow range of proteins (Loening 1968, Noll 1970).

But the similarities remain striking and further data within classes of animals should be most interesting. A curious point is that the rRNA of chloroplasts resembles that of bacteria, suggesting that they are symbionts, and this may also be true of mitochondria (see Dawid 1970).

Even more striking is the fact that competitive hybridization experiments by which nucleic acids are compared show that considerable base sequences are the same in all eukaryote organisms. Presumably the corresponding

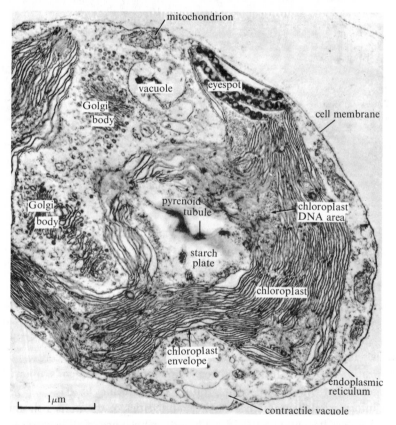

FIG. 4.4. Electron micrograph of a cell from the colonial green alga *Eudorina illinoiensis*. The intense staining of the Golgi bodies is characteristic of the young cell and probably reflects high activity. The pyrenoid complex is sectioned tangentially, thus only the tubular chloroplast thylakoids penetrating the spaces between the starch plates are to be seen.
(By permission of Dr. M. J. Hobbs.)

DNA stretches are also homologous. There are known to be about 450 genes responsible for the 28s and 18s RNA of *Xenopus* and they are clustered together on one of the 16 chromosomes of the haploid set (Brown, Dawid, and Reeder 1969).

The similarity of so many of the organelles in all animals (and often also in plants) helps enormously in our task of obtaining a unified view of the living process—indeed it demonstrates that there *is* such a process, available for study. Yet we must admit that our knowledge and methods of analysis are so feeble that no one can yet truly say which features of these various parts of the cell are significant for its functions, still less how they are regulated. We can look, of course, only at fixed and dehydrated specimens, but the problem is not only that what we see are artefacts. It is that

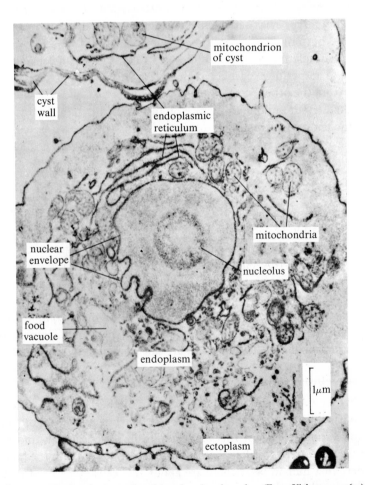

FIG. 4.5. The fine structure of a soil amoeba, *Acanthamoeba*. (From Vickerman 1962.)

we have no proper ways of thinking about the organization at all. It is usually not highly geometric or regular. Nor can we generally see any comprehensible plan, with supply lines or communication channels. Yet the cell must have such features, and in our electron microscope preparations perhaps they are already staring us in the face—but we have not learned to see them.

It is difficult to emphasize sufficiently the need for imagination in such matters. We have been describing the various components of the cell, what it is 'made of'. But in life they are continually undergoing change, as the next chapter will show. Moreover, many of the changes are interrelated and the whole system must be an intense whirl of controlled activity. It is particularly unfortunate that some of our most powerful techniques deprive us of the possibility of seeing this organization *while it is at work*. The electron microscope has sufficient resolution to show the protein and other molecules, but only when they have been dried. What we see with it is at best like a single frame of a ciné film. The centrifuge can separate for us fractions that perform particular chemical activities—but then they are isolated from the others.

We shall try to build up a picture of all this cellular activity by emphasizing the end to which it is all directed. In this chapter we are concerned to emphasize that a great variety of different subsystems is to be found even within a single cell.

3. Unicells

Some organisms are composed only of a single cell and in them we see the differentiation of parts especially clearly (Fig. 4.3). Thus within a green flagellate we find the usual nucleus, mitochondria, Golgi vesicles, endoplasmic reticulum, ribosomes, and chloroplasts (Figs. 4.3–4.5); also a flagellum for movement, with an elaborate basal apparatus and a light-sensitive spot, for orientation.

Ciliates such as *Paramecium* have an equally or more complex organization and this is found also in the sporozoa, in which some parts are specialized for somatic life only, and are not passed on in reproduction.

4. Multicellular animals

All higher animals and plants possess a still higher level of organization: they consist of many different types of cell. We obviously cannot consider here the various stages of this organization in lower animals and plants. But it is impressive to realize that it introduces a new level in the hierarchy of order. In a human body there are about 10^{15} cells (3×10^{13} of them are red blood cells) and we may estimate that these belong to at least 1000 different cell types. Of course what constitutes a cell type is arguable. All skin has common characteristics but the skin of the face is not the same as that of the chest or of the sole of the foot. Transplanted skin retains its original character, so this must be specific, and not determined locally or by function. We might say there is a genus 'skin', with some hundred species (face skin, hair skin, neck skin, etc.). Here again, divisions would be arbitrary and there is no special point in making enumerations. But we are concerned to discover what a man is made of. We have found that he is made of very complex cells and now we find that these cells may be of numerous different sorts. We have to seek for the origin and significance of these differences. The DNA of the nuclei, once again, must be the ultimate source of the order; it must serve to control systems that produce differentiation. Each type of cell must appear in the correct numbers and in proper relation to others. The studies of embryologists have shown something of the factors by which the formation of particular cell types is 'induced'. We shall see something of this from time to time in our study, both during embryonic development and in the adult.

5. Control of cell differentiation

The different sorts of cells are produced by mechanisms that select from all the instructions in the DNA only certain ones for each type of cell. Thus cells of the salivary glands produce the enzyme salivary amylase, which splits up starch; cells of the skin produce keratin, the protective, insoluble protein of skin and hair; and so on for all the many thousands of different enzymes. The over-all regulatory processes must ensure that each protein is produced at the right place, in the right amounts, and at the right time. As yet we know only little about the control of such differentiations. When we understand them we should be much better able to control life in ourselves and other organisms (see Britten and Davidson 1969).

The principles of the regulation may be that most of the operons of the DNA of any cell are repressed, only certain relevant ones being allowed to act. In bacteria the active ones can be changed to suit the environmental conditions. In multicellular animals it seems that often each cell in the adult is 'differentiated'; only certain operons are active, and most of the others are firmly repressed perhaps irreversibly. There are, however, some lightly repressed operons, which can become active under certain conditions, allowing the cell some range of action, for example to repair itself. The question of how and when the operons become suppressed during development is still unsolved. Nuclei from intestinal cells from the swimming tadpoles of frogs can be put into enucleated eggs and cause them to develop into mature fertile adults (Gurdon 1962). So the genes at that stage are still intact. On the other hand, under some circumstances nuclear transplantation experiments show that the nuclei of differentiated cells seem to have undergone a stable change. When put into enucleated eggs they produce embryos with special features, which will be reproduced if their nuclei are used for a further transplant. Their DNA has been permanently changed. The problem of the control of the read-out of the information in DNA during development is further discussed on pp. 59, 177.

One mechanism for transcription is to produce a large number of copies of part of the DNA itself. Thus oocytes of the toad *Xenopus* contain 1000 times as many genes for the 28s and 18s RNAs, which make ribosomes, as are found in a somatic cell. These extra copies are synthesized during a short period soon after the tadpole metamorphoses—that is to say, long before they will be needed. Only about 0·1–0·2 per cent of the DNA is copied and it is not known how it is selected. There may be specific DNA polymerases that recognize the rRNA sites (Brown, Dawid, and Reeder 1969).

Moreover, something is known about the initiation of RNA synthesis during cleavage. At first none is produced; then some heterogeneous nuclear RNA; then transfer RNA; and finally rRNA. Nuclei from this late stage put back into enucleated eggs stop synthesis and then start again at the right time. The cytoplasm can thus both repress synthesis and later on initiate it (Gurdon and Woodland 1969, Gurdon 1970).

Other evidence that the nuclei of differentiated tissues may retain their full information content is that very small pieces from a non-growing region of a plant, say a carrot root, can be made to give rise to a new plant (Steward 1970). In some animals regeneration from small fragments is common (sea-squirts). It is possible that even in adult mammals there are many cells that are 'undifferentiated', perhaps, for example, those that give rise to new blood cells. There is continual controlled production of various types of new cells during normal replacement, let alone in regeneration and repair. Understanding of how to control this production should provide some of the most powerful new techniques for the medicine of the future.

6. Organs and tissues

The question of the supracellular organization of the body is less simple than merely defining the various types of cell. Most parts of the body are not made of one single sort of cell, but of many sorts combined. For example, the skin is particularly complex. Besides the layers that produce the outer covering of the body there are blood vessels, lymph vessels, muscles, nerves, sweat glands, sebaceous glands, pigment cells, and other special features. Even a relatively simple tissue such as the liver is not all liver cells. It has the arteries, veins, and lymphatics with their muscles, connective tissue, and nerves. Moreover, the liver cells are not all alike; some are for chemical transformation, others to take up waste particles, and several different sorts synthesize various substances.

The production of each of these types of cell must be strictly regulated and controlled to make each organ. Here are further tasks for the DNA, operating, of course, through the cells and their interactions, though we have little evidence how this is achieved. One suggestion is that various cellular activities may be oscillatory and that neighbours may influence each other (Goodwin 1964). Complicated field effects could thus be produced and perhaps control the differentiation of the various mutually interacting cells. The level of the complexity of the organization is obviously vastly greater than in a bacterium or protozoan. Moreover, the complexity of the tissues is greater in what we commonly call the higher animals than the lower. There are few actual measurements of such differences. It is easy to underestimate the complexity of the tissues of, say, a fish, which is certainly already formidable, but perhaps marginally less so than that of a mammal. According to our thesis the increase that has occurred during evolution has been in the variety of devices used by the species to keep alive in face of an unhelpful environment (*The life of vertebrates*). Life has been continually invading less and less propitious situations, for which ever more complex machinery is required. The instructions have become correspondingly more complex and the total amount of DNA has increased. Table 4.1 and Fig. 4.6 show that the amounts of DNA per cell are about a

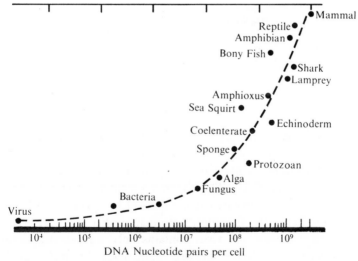

FIG. 4.6. Minimum haploid amounts of DNA observed for species at various levels of organization. The ordinate is not numerical and the shape of the curve has little significance. (After Britten and Davidson 1969.)

TABLE 4.1

The DNA content per cell is shown for various species. The values are expressed as picograms of DNA per cell, or virus particle (from Kit 1963)

ϕX174 phage	$2 \cdot 6 \times 10^{-6}$
T2 phage	2×10^{-4}
Rabbit papilloma virus (Shope)	$6 \cdot 6 \times 10^{-6}$
Vaccinia virus	3×10^{-4}
E. coli B (log phase)	0·0137
Clostridium	0·0245
Yeast (diploid)	0·05
Neurospora	0·017
Fish	
Shark	5·46
Sturgeon	3·2
Carp	3·49
Perch	1·9
Catfish	1·89
Barracuda	1·37
Amphibians	
Frog	15·0
Toad	7·33
Reptiles	
Green turtle	5·27
Wood turtle	4·92
Alligator	4·98
Birds	
Domestic fowl	2·34
Guinea hen	2·27
Mammals	
Man	6·8
Rabbit	6·5
Rat	5·7
Mouse	5·0

million times greater in higher animals than in the simplest viruses. However, the bacteria have only 100 times less than the higher organisms and this at once suggests that much of the organization of living matter is similar from bacteria to mammals. There is much further evidence that this is so.

It is interesting to consider the numbers of base pairs in such quantities of DNA and hence the amount of information that they carry (Kit 1963). The tobacco necrosis coat virus contains only $1 \cdot 2 \times 10^3$ nucleotide base pairs, sufficient to code for the 367 amino-acids that make up the coat, which is all that this virus can make (molecular weight 39 000). The rabbit papilloma virus has about $6 \cdot 6 \times 10^3$ nucleotide base pairs, perhaps coding for a single protein. Vaccinia virus, with 3×10^5, is more complex. Bacteria have 2×10^7 pairs and mammalian cells 7×10^9.

There is thus a general correspondence between the level of complexity of an organism and its DNA content. Yet there are obvious aberrations. All vertebrates have haploid amounts of the same order, but it is unexpectedly high in some of the cells of a frog (and even higher in some other amphibians). The DNA strands may be replicated in somatic cells to provide working material from which RNA can be synthesized (Chapter 22). DNA, like any other material, runs a risk of becoming altered with use. The astonishing continuity of life depends upon its stability, but this is partly achieved by devices that keep a master sample of DNA exempt from the risks of a working life. The quantity of DNA in a nucleus is not therefore necessarily the minimum (diploid) amount, but may be some multiple of this. There is also the further point that there is a considerable amount of DNA in the cytoplasm, for example in mitochondria. Again this is probably an arrangement to put apart the working DNA of a very active cell region so that damage to it does not affect functioning of the whole cell. Indeed these organelles can replicate themselves. The mitochondrial DNA probably organizes the structure of the organelles, the enzymes they contain being coded for by nuclear DNA (see Kroon 1969, Dawid 1970).

5

LIVING ACTIVITIES, TURNOVER

THERE are cells of many different types in the body, and cells of several sorts join together to make the various organs, which in turn compose the whole body. Before we could conclude our account of what the body is made of, we should have to describe all the different structures that are found there; the subject-matter of the whole science of anatomy. There is no escape in biology from the study of a whole complicated organization. We cannot know about the body by knowing the structure of a few types of cell, any more than we can by knowing about a few types of molecule. The essence of any higher organism is that it is organized, that it has many parts, and unless we know about these parts we do not know the organism.

However, by beginning our account with the various elements that go to make up a man and ending with a description of his organs we have been able to give some answer to the question 'What is man made of?' The answer has been given in terms of what may be called a hierarchical organization, like that of an army. There are certain elements in the body; these are organized into certain types of molecules, such as proteins, fats, and the rest. These molecules in turn are not all mixed up uniformly inside the body, but are arranged in particular ways, the unit of organization being the cell, with its various parts. The cells themselves are not all alike but are organized into the tissues and these in turn into the organs, which make up the body.

Such an account gives us, in some ways, a satisfactory idea of the composition of the body, and yet we recognize immediately that it fails as a description of a living man. We set out originally to answer the question 'What is man made of?', because this seemed to be a scientific question to ask; it seemed that in this way we might begin to give some exact answer to the question 'What is man?' by examining him just as physicists and chemists have examined the inorganic world. It is time now to retrace our steps and to consider whether we should not do better in our attempt by some addition of this point of view, or whether some change of it would give us a more satisfactory insight to our subject.

The question 'What is man made of?' assumes immediately that he is made of something for a duration of time long enough to allow analysis, in fact it assumes that the essence of any animal is a substance or substances

that can be submitted to analysis. The account that we have given is a very
good account of the parody of a man that is a corpse. What we have done
is to describe something that is like a man, yet definitely not a *living* man.
One way of expressing the difference is to say that in a living man the substance is never the same: the man is always changing, substances are being
added and others subtracted, maintaining a steady state of balance, so that
there is no single mass of stuff of which we can say for more than a moment
'This is the same man'. The difference may not be very precisely stated
in exact physical terms, and may seem a quibble, but to recognize it alters
our whole attitude to the study of life. We must certainly examine more
closely how these changes go on in the body and how the living organism
differs from a system in equilibrium, such as a mountain or a piece of metal
that is available for chemical examination.

That matter continually enters and leaves the human frame is obvious
enough from the numerous entrances and exits provided. Food goes in at
the mouth and its residue out at the anus. The Frenchman, Lavoisier,
showed at the end of the eighteenth century that the gases breathed out
of the nose and mouth differed from those breathed in, containing less
oxygen and more carbon dioxide. Besides the output of the urine there is
also that of sweat all over the body. Scientific study of these interchanges
of the body has shown with continually increasing emphasis that change
is going on all the time, so that few parts remain the same for very long.

We can follow this very well by tracing the history of an atom of carbon
taken in with the food, say as part of a lump of sugar dissolved in a cup of
tea. After being acted on by various enzymes the sugar passes through the
wall of the intestine and into the blood-stream. By this it is carried, say, to
the biceps muscle of an arm that has been hard at work, and is then taken
into the muscle substance. Here it may be oxidized giving energy to the
compound concerned in the contraction of muscle, adenosine triphosphate
(ATP). This substance is formed in muscles at rest and breaks down when
they contract, releasing the energy that makes it possible for the muscle to
work. Our carbon atom helps to provide ATP and is thus essentially used
for fuel. It is oxidized by various indirect stages, giving bicarbonate, which
is carried in the blood to the lungs and there breathed out as carbon dioxide.

If the muscle is in active use the whole cycle may be quite rapidly completed, so that the atom of carbon in the lump of sugar leaves the body again
within a few minutes of entering. Can we say that it has ever formed part
of the living tissue of the body? Many people when asked this question
quickly answer 'No', but before giving the answer it would be well to trace
the history of another atom in the same way. This time let it be an atom of
nitrogen contained, shall we say, in the protein of a steak. The protein is

broken down by the pepsin of the stomach into peptides (parts of proteins), and these in turn are reduced by the trypsin of the intestine to amino-acids. As such they pass through the intestinal wall and are probably then quickly combined again to tripeptides and thus circulate to the tissues. We may imagine that our particular atom of nitrogen is part of an amino-acid taken up by a cell of the cerebral cortex of the brain, into which it therefore enters and is there built up into a protein by the process described in Chapter 3. We may suppose that it will stay there for some time, form-ing part of the fabric of the brain, but there is now good evidence that even in such parts of the body many of the molecules remain only for a relatively short time. The protein containing our atom ultimately breaks down again, the amino-acid travels to the liver and is perhaps there de-aminated, that is, the nitrogen is set aside as urea to be removed by the kidney.

Much further evidence of the rapid interchange, even in parts of the body previously supposed to be stable, has come from the use of labelled atoms of radioactive material. The American Rudolf Schoenheimer, who unfortunately died young, pioneered in this field by injecting compounds labelled by isotopes (e.g. deuterium) and seeing how long they remained within the body. He expressed the general idea in the title of his book *The dynamic state of body constituents* (1946).

One of the benefits that has come from the active pursuit of atomic and nuclear physics has been the making available to biologists of a large range of radioactive isotopes. By their use, our knowledge of these fundamental changes in living matter has been enormously extended. Many of the elements exist in isotopic forms, which break down spontaneously. These isotopes can be introduced into the body and used to 'label' a particular compound and discover for how long it remains in the tissues. The isotope differs in nuclear mass from the normally occurring form (having a dif-ferent number of neutrons) but this does not, in general, make it behave chemically in any markedly different way.

Thus ordinary carbon (^{12}C) has a nuclear mass of 12 and is stable, while the isotope ^{14}C is unstable and by radioactive decay breaks down slowly into the stable ^{12}C (it has a half-life of 5000 years). In order to study the permanence of the waxy substance cholesterol in the nervous system cholesterol labelled with ^{14}C has been injected into the yolk sack of day-old chicks (Wright 1961). The chicks absorb this material and, since cholesterol is a constituent of all cells, a chick killed a day or two later will have radioactive cholesterol in all its organs. The amount can be estimated by dissolving it out from an organ and measuring the β-radia-tion emitted, as the carbon breaks down, with a Geiger counter. Alter-natively, if it is wished to see exactly where the radioactive material is in

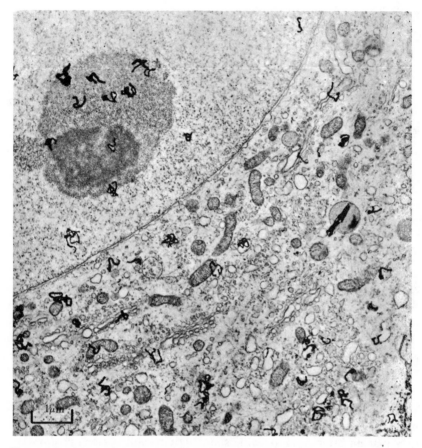

FIG. 5.1. An electron microscope autoradiograph of part of a neuron from a sensory ganglion of a newt after the injection of tritiated histidine, which has been taken up in various parts of the nucleus and cytoplasm. The dense black tracks mark emissions of radiation and hence presence of the amino-acid. (From Rogers 1967.)

the tissue, a section is prepared and laid upon a photographic plate. When the plate is developed the radioactive sites are revealed (autoradiography, Fig. 5.1).

By study of a series of chickens killed after increasing times it is seen that the radioactivity of the liver declines rapidly and reaches zero (Fig. 5.2). We express this by saying that the rate of turnover of cholesterol in the liver is such that it has a half-life of $5\frac{1}{2}$ days.

Many constituents have similar or shorter half-lives—but not all (Table 5.1). Some materials remain in the body for a long time, perhaps throughout life. Thus in the above study the radioactivity in the brain was found to decline, not to zero, but to a plateau (Fig. 5.2) and this was also found in

TABLE 5.1

The magnitude and biological half-life of tissue components of the
rat (from Thompson and Ballou 1956)

| Tissue | Long-lived components | | Shorter-lived components |
	Magnitude (% of total tissue)	Biological half-life (days)	Biological half-life (days)
Carcass	47	130	22
Liver	3	140	12, 4·5†
Kidney	8	180	11
Muscle	40	100	16
Brain	54	150	16
Bone	72	240	16
Collagen	72	1000	15

† In the liver the shorter-lived components were divisible into two parts.

rabbits in a similar experiment (Fig. 5.3). Further investigation showed that it is the myelin sheaths of the nerve fibres that retain their activity. Cholesterol is one of their chief constituents and the experiment thus shows that once these lamellated fatty sheaths have been laid down they are not replaced. The radioactivity of the nerve cells themselves, however, declined like that of liver or kidney cells.

Indeed study of some brain-specific proteins shows that the maximum specific activity of incorporated leucine may occur within 30 min after injection of a sample labelled with ^{3}H. The activity then declines rapidly to a plateau after 6–12 h, with some activity still remaining days later (McEwen and Hydén 1966).

Other studies have confirmed that while many of the materials in the body turn over rapidly, others do so little if at all. Thus the protein collagen, the substance of the connective tissue fibres and tendons, may remain in the body indefinitely. Many cells have partly stable and partly 'dynamic' constituents, even among their proteins. Thus in muscle, carbon-labelling of proteins shows a long-lasting component perhaps residing in the contractile actomyosin system. The crystals of calcium salts in bone may remain unchanged for years. This is not because they are inaccessible; on the contrary, they may be quickly broken down and used for some other purpose if the situation requires it (for example in pregnancy or calcium deficiency).

There is, therefore, in some sense a 'fabric' of the body, enduring from childhood to old age, with slow changes. Nevertheless, this framework is a much less interesting and active part of the system than the dynamic

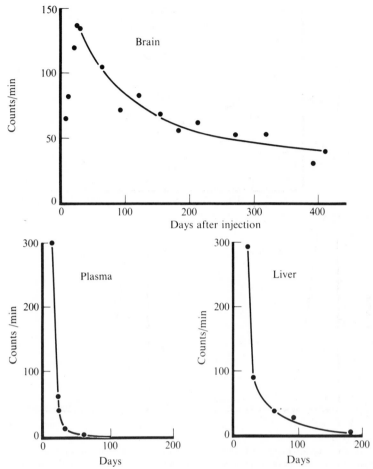

FIG. 5.2. Examination of the brain, liver, and plasma at intervals after the injection of ^{14}C-cholesterol into the yolk sacks of 1-day-old chicks indicates the differences in the persistence of the substance in these tissues. (After Wright 1961.)

part. Indeed, it provides only some of the structural support and is not the main organizing factor of the whole system, most of which is in a continual state of change.

There is, however, one fundamentally important type of molecule that shows remarkable stability, namely the DNA of the nuclei. After tritium-labelling of embryo rats' brains and then later separating the parts of the cells by centrifugation, 20·6 per cent of the material of the nuclei retained its activity undiminished for 215 days. This is about the proportion of the nucleus that is made up of DNA. By contrast, the mitochondria of the nerve cells had a half-life of 16·4 days and the microsomes one component with a half-life of 15 days and another one of 120 days (Kahn and Wilson 1965).

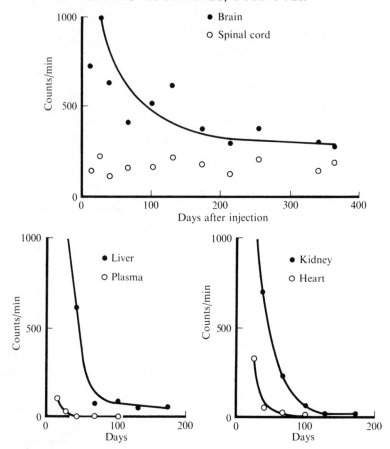

F IG. 5.3. The persistence of labelled cholesterol in the brain, spinal cord, liver, kidney, heart, and plasma was followed after the injection of ^{14}C-cholesterol into the circulation of 18-day-old rabbits. (After Wright 1961.)

The permanence of the DNA is presumed to be the central feature of the organization. From the sequence of the nucleotides in its helical molecules is derived the appropriate sequences of the amino-acids in the proteins. Part of these instructions must, of course, include items that regulate the times and quantities in which the various enzymes that regulate DNA synthesis are themselves made.

Life depends on a certain background of permanent components, but is, nevertheless, in a perpetual state of change. Not only are molecules continually coming in and going out but they may move from one part of the body to another.

In fact, the essence of a living thing is that it consists of atoms of the ordinary chemical elements we have listed, caught up into the living system and made part of it for a while. The living activity takes them up and organizes them in its characteristic way. The life of a man consists essentially in the activity he imposes upon that stuff. If we try to keep this point firmly fixed before us we may find that it is not difficult to frame a biological science that is both exact and complete, in the sense that it provides information about men and animals as we know them in our daily life. We experience our own life as an activity, and we see the results of this activity all around us; it is therefore natural to make the concept of activity the central point of any system of ideas about life. To take one example, in trying to decide what constitutes the ageing of a man we need to think, not of a gradual change of the substance of the body, but of some change in the activity of the individual and all his parts. The substance is indeed changing, much faster than we see, and it is because the activity producing this change is itself modified that we notice the slow alteration of the appearance of the man that we call senescence.

6

THE DIRECTION OF LIVING ACTIVITY.
HOMEOSTASIS

1. Activity

IF the characteristics of life are to be described as the manifestations of an activity, we must think very carefully what we mean by this word and be sure that we do not use it as a catchword to hide our ignorance as so many other words have been used in the attempt to define the nature of life. We used the word 'activity' to describe life first of all because it was not possible by analysis of the composition of the body to give a satisfactory account of the typical features of a living system. There is no single substance that is constantly present and characteristically living; rather, the atoms in the body are involved in a characteristic activity. It is true that the molecules of DNA are found only in living things and each individual has his own DNA. But DNA alone is not living. A living system involves DNA plus much else and is engaged in active interchange with the environment (except in cryptobiosis, p. 287). The DNA regulates the exchanges so that they follow a pattern selected in the past. It functions as the information store, which contains a permanent record of the individual's organizational potential. However, the characteristic activity of the individual, and furthermore his specific activity at a given time, depends upon which sections of the information encoded in the DNA are being expressed and also the relative rates at which the information contained in the various sections is being transcribed. Thus the activity that we hold to be characteristic of life is not expressed by describing DNA alone, since the interchanges between the organism and its environment are the factors that determine what sections of DNA are to be transcribed at a particular time and the rates of transcription.

The state of being active, implies the movement or change of one or many things, and we commonly use the word to suggest that the movement in some way comes from within the entity or entities; they may be said to act, they are initiators. It is true that we sometimes speak of the surface of the sea, for instance, as active, without meaning to imply that the waves are themselves the moving agents, but the characteristic use of the word is to describe action springing from within. A living man is the prototype of activity in this sense; he is essentially a being who does things and does them because of something in himself, not merely because he is being pushed around by the happenings near to him. Probably, historically, the study of activity began with man's observation of this characteristic in himself. The word 'energy' was thus used by Aristotle to describe the activity of man, his power to move and do work. It was indeed in a technical philosophical sense the word for man's very existence. However the modern physicist's idea of energy as a power to do work only arose in the nineteenth century, with the development of the steam engine. Previous to this the concept was confused with that of a force, considered as an agent producing acceleration of a body. In modern terms force is defined (for low speeds) as

$F = ma$, where m is the mass and a the acceleration.

Its unit is the newton, the force required to accelerate 1 kilogramme by 1 metre per second per second (1 dyne $= 10^{-5}N = g$ cm s^{-2}).

The concept of forces has become progressively refined, so that they are no longer considered as agents, and essentially are no more than logical terms used in the description of physical phenomena. When early scientists were describing the actions of bodies upon each other they said that they were drawn by forces, just as we ourselves pull with our arms upon other objects. But the important part of Newton's discovery was that the motion of the earth and of an apple can be described by the same mathematical rules. Yet this discovery probably still remains associated, especially in the non-mathematical mind, with vague non-material entities called 'forces', which are really only relics of an earlier way of thinking.

Physics has indeed shown that four types of interaction between particles can be recognized, and these are still called forces. The weakest interactions are gravitational forces, still relatively little understood. All the interactions between atoms that bind them together to form molecules, are members of the class known as electromagnetic forces and it is therefore these that are mainly at work in the body. Within atoms there are two other types of force known as weak and strong interactions.

The important point for us is that physicists have been able to recognize a certain rather small number of ways in which particles interact. The world is as it is because these types of action have presumably been proceeding throughout the evolution of the universe. Of course since we know so little about that evolution this discovery of forces does not really tell us why the world is as it is (see Chapter 26). But it does tell us that the matter in living bodies is likely to operate with the same rules of electromagnetic force as all the rest of the known universe. We are not likely to find that the solution to the problem of what is life is that it contains or uses some special type of force. For the idea of forces as in any sense separate entities has been abandoned for our treatment of all the rest of the universe.

2. Energy

Thus, when non-living bodies act, the strength with which they do so was compared by early science with the power that we feel ourselves able to put out. In modern terms the energy in a body is, as the name implies, literally the work that is in it and can therefore be expressed by it. The analogy is not always very easy to follow and evidently differs somewhat in various contexts. The scientific unit of work is the joule, which is the amount of work (or activity) necessary to overcome a resisting force of 1 newton for 1 m (1 joule = 10^7 erg). It can be shown by quite simple devices that other sorts of energy can be considered equivalent to this mechanical energy. For instance, the energy in a hot body can be measured as the amount of work it can be made to do in a suitable engine. So we can also estimate the energy present in a lump of coal or in a lightning flash. The concept is that each entity is able to produce only a certain amount of change, that is to say, has a given amount of potential activity or energy in it, just as each person feels himself to have.

From this it is not a very long step to the idea that all change involves something that can be considered as an expenditure of energy. Without the application of activity there will be no change. Somewhat more surprising is the notion that even in being so used the energy is not destroyed, but is only converted into other forms. For this, however, there is very good evidence, and this law of the conservation of energy is one of the greatest of scientific generalizations. Whenever the power of activity (or energy) is lost by one body it is gained somewhere else. Thus a stone falling from a high cliff has lost a certain part of its potential for motion by approaching the surface of the earth but, as it hits the rocks below, heat is generated to an amount exactly equivalent to the gravitational energy lost by the stone. These are the principles with which physical science describes the behaviour of the world around us. It is interesting that, having borrowed the concepts of activity, force, and energy from the simple biological observations of everyday life, science is now laboriously reintroducing them into biology as if they were great discoveries made by physical science. This borrowing of words from the language used to describe man's activities for use in describing those of other bodies is one of the oldest and most constantly used devices of speech. Having made the use of the word more exact by application to the simpler man-made systems, we then reintroduce it back again to produce more exact statements in biology.

3. Living activities

Our present object is to show that a man's life is best described by saying that it is an activity, and we are trying to ensure that we understand something clearly by the word. We have seen that all material objects may be said to possess some possibilities of activity and that this is expressed as the energy that is in them. Let us now look at some other aspects suggested by the word.

Activity has, no doubt, different connotations for different people but perhaps recalls some such scene as a number of men and women coming and going, moving about in a crowd, say, in a market. A disturbed nest of ants presents a picture of activity. By contrast, rows of children asleep in a dormitory or rows of boats drawn up on the shore are 'passive'. The essence of the concept of activity is movement and change and we are certainly justified in applying this to the process of life. But is activity by itself sufficiently expressive of what we see going on? A set of active agents may show many signs of movement and change, but none of a common direction or objective in their actions. Thus the movements of people in a crowded square of an evening may be aimless, as are the movements of wavelets in a light breeze. Yet in most cases, and indeed even in those two mentioned, we recognize something that can be called the direction or aim of active agents. By this we may mean either the direction of the individual parts, as of the wavelets or of individuals on a holiday heath tending homewards. Or we may see the movements, even in different directions, of individuals as parts of some achievement of the whole that they compose, as when the ants scattering in different directions gradually carry their eggs underground.

4. Stability of life

The activity of a living organism is most certainly of this sort. It tends towards a goal, namely the preservation of the organization of the whole system. The individual molecules comprising an organism change continually, but the manner of proceeding, which is its life, is preserved intact. The best evidence of this tendency of living activities is the fact that living organisms have remained in approximately the same state for a very long time. The study of fossils has shown that organisms not very different from those alive today were present on the earth at least 500 million years ago and probably much earlier. It is true that organisms do change gradually, by the process that we call evolution, but this process of slow change is itself part of the means by which the *main features* of the living organization are maintained intact, in spite of the changes of environment (p. 382).

Although living matter is very complicated and most of its atoms are continually changing, yet the pattern of living activities remains more stable than that of the non-living materials around. Ocean levels rise and fall quite rapidly, by geological standards, so that large parts of the earth become submerged and may emerge again within a few million years. Mountain ranges are raised up and then worn away by frost, wind, and rain. Meanwhile, living systems go on with their complicated activities with only such relatively small changes as convert, say, a fish into an amphibian, this to a reptile, and then to a mammal. Some types of living matter do not show even this change—the Australian lung fishes, *Neoceratodus*, are almost identical with their ancestors (*Ceratodus*) of 300 million years ago. The population of shrews alive today is a little changed remainder of the population of the early mammals that gave rise to all of us some 70 million years ago (Chapter 29).

5. The sources of directed action

If living activities are directed towards the ends of self-maintenance we obviously have to ask how this has come about. Could systems operating in this way have arisen from systems with equilibria of the more usual sort? (Chapter 26). Whatever the origin of life may have been there can be little doubt that living things once started have continued to maintain themselves and to evolve without the intervention of any outside forces or *élan vitale*. This view has been greatly reinforced by the discovery of the chemical nature of DNA and the means by which it carries the instructions that make self-maintenance possible. We therefore have to ask the further difficult question whether the directed actions of man himself can also be understood as the operation of the same principles. This whole problem of direction or purpose has mostly been considered by philosophers the other way round. Since human directed action is usually spoken of as the outcome of men's 'desires' or 'intentions' it is presumed that 'intentionality' is the characteristic of the directed actions of living things (see e.g. Taylor 1964, Dennett 1969). This of course involves us in the difficult task of looking for the intentionality of beetles and bacteria. It cannot be claimed that approach from either end has produced a generally satisfactory solution, but this book makes various tentative suggestions about it (Chapters 10 and 42).

6. Homeostasis

The problem, then, is to find an adequate description for these living activities that maintain such a remarkable constancy of general pattern, though with certain gradual changes. We give to the maintenance of living organization the name *homeostasis*, which was first used by the physiologist Cannon (1932) to describe the tendency noticed by Claude Bernard in mammals to maintain constant composition of the blood in spite of changes in surroundings. Bernard's famous expression was 'La fixité du milieu intérieur c'est la condition de la vie libre.' By 'internal environment' physiologists mean the blood, but the principle applies to living matter in general, which shows the property of homeostasis and tends to maintain its pattern of activities. The various actions that it undertakes—feeding, breathing, moving, reproducing—are all parts of its system for ensuring this maintenance of continuity. The key to understanding the significance of the activities of plants, mammals, and men is the recognition of their homeostatic nature, and the fact that they tend to preserve the continuity of life. This is obvious enough for many actions, for example, breathing and feeding. The difficulty is to recognize the significance for homeostasis of other activities such as the complicated operations of mating or the apparently self-destructive activities of growing old. In order to do this it is necessary to focus attention on the fact that the stability of the organization is maintained not merely for short periods but for hundreds, thousands, and millions of years. *The entity that is maintained intact, and of which we all form a part, is not the life of any one of us, but in the end the whole of life upon the planet* (Chapter 27).

7. Equilibria and steady states

The various activities that go on in the body are thus directed to provide such materials as are necessary for further maintenance of its particular type of organization. We have seen already that a living creature differs from a stone in that it is not a system in equilibrium with its environment; we must take some time to see what is meant by this not being in equilibrium.

In all closed physical systems there is a tendency for the molecules to distribute themselves uniformly by diffusion, so that the residual energy is reduced towards a minimum. We recognize this tendency in many forms, such as the falling of bodies under gravity, the flow of electric current along conductors, the diffusion of a gas, such as escaping coal gas, or the mixing of some liquids by diffusion. The general statement of this fact is that in any closed physical system the amount of order can either stay constant or decrease. It never increases. More technically, the entropy of such a system tends to increase (p. 45).

These tendencies towards randomization of all the matter on the earth (we cannot here speak of the heavens) are, however, delayed by the interactions upon each other of the various bodies that exist. Thus the hardness of the substance of the earth 'resists' the force of gravity so that a falling stone cannot penetrate to its centre. A property of oil and water, which we can call immiscibility, delays their mutual diffusion to form a homogeneous system. Thus a stone resting upon another one will not change position further on account of gravity or diffusion alone, even though the substances of the two are highly different. No energy expenditure is needed to maintain this condition; the energy is inherent in the bodies themselves. Actually, it is not strictly true that they do not mix. Atoms of one metal may diffuse into another, but only *very* slowly.

Living organisms differ markedly from their surroundings. We have seen already that a man is a very watery system, yet he lives in air that even in the wettest climates seldom contains more than 1 per cent of water. Similarly, in his body there are found elements, some of which occur only in minute quantities in the surroundings; they have been concentrated very highly in the body. If all these substances were shut off from the surroundings there would be nothing very remarkable in all this. On the shelves of any chemist's shop there are substances at far higher concentrations than in the world around. But they are in containers, shut off from their surroundings. Everyone knows what happens when such goods are not well packed. The powder escapes over everything, the scent bottle soon upsets and leaks, and the substances become uniformly distributed. In an organism the substances are not packed in closed containers *but yet they do not diffuse away*.

The fact that the whole organism does not fade away into its surroundings is due to continual expenditure of energy serving to keep the various materials in place and to renew them from the surroundings. Since the materials of the body are not shut in closed boxes the body can be kept as it is only if they are continually replaced by others of the same kind. This is what is meant by saying that the living thing is not in static equilibrium. Its substance is not at rest like a stone on the ground, but is in continual activity, and it is only by virtue of this activity that the shape and organization of the whole thing is maintained. Such a system, which remains the same although matter flows in and out, is said to be a 'steady state' (see Morowitz 1968).

8. Maintenance of a steady state by expenditure of energy

The means by which the living organism prevents itself from dissolution are as varied as life itself. In the very simplest animals and plants the difference between an organism and its surroundings is less marked than in the organisms that appeared later. For example, some of the early animals may have been protozoan creatures rather like *Amoeba*, living in the sea, and such are still found there today. They are, like ourselves, systems containing

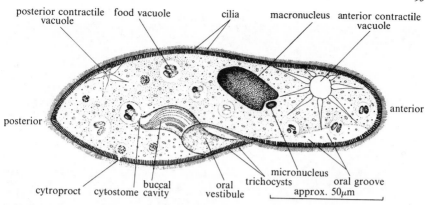

posterior contractile   food vacuole   cilia   macronucleus   anterior contractile

vacuole   vacuole

posterior   anterior

cytoproct   cytostome   buccal cavity   oral vestibule   micronucleus trichocysts   oral groove

approx. 50μm

FIG. 6.1. A diagram of *Paramecium caudatum*, a protozoan found in ponds, to show the two contractile vacuoles by means of which osmoregulation is carried out. They are permanent structures into which lead a number of canals. (After Vickerman and Cox 1967.)

much water and much salt. However, the sea around them also contains water and salt; so no work is necessary to prevent these substances diffusing away. A man, on the other hand, is a watery salty system living in a medium containing very little water and most of that lacking in salt. He must therefore first of all economize water as far as possible, by covering much of his body with a waterproof skin; and then, since he cannot avoid losing some water, he must replace it. To do this his body has available a whole set of activities that we call the mechanism of thirst. When the system becomes short of water, or dehydrated, an elaborate set of actions follows so that the whole man walks around expending energy in order to obtain water.

A simpler and easier example is provided if we return to the protozoans and consider the difference between the work necessary for an animal in the sea and in fresh water. Since, as we have seen, all living systems must contain inorganic salts (p. 26) it follows that an *Amoeba*, *Paramecium*, or other protozoan in *fresh* water will contain more salt than is to be found in the surroundings. It cannot, therefore, like its marine cousin, come to an equilibrium as regards water and salt. On the contrary, by the process of osmosis water will tend to flow in from the outside, dilute the animal, and blow it up till it bursts. In order to survive in fresh water it must have some means of pumping this water out again, and in fact protozoans living in fresh water have a pumping organ, the contractile vacuole, with just this function (Figs. 6.1 and 6.2). We do not know exactly how it does its work, but it certainly removes water from the protozoan's body, and Kitching (1951) has shown that the rate at which it contracts and the volume of fluid removed is proportional to the difference between the concentration of salt inside and outside the cell.

macro nucleus   food vacuole   cilia

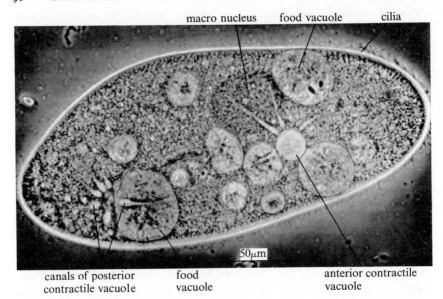

50μm

canals of posterior   food   anterior contractile
contractile vacuole   vacuole   vacuole

FIG. 6.2. A phase-contrast photomicrograph of a living *Paramecium aurelia* seen from the dorsal surface to show the anterior and posterior contractile vacuoles. The anterior vacuole is in the act of filling. The posterior one has just emptied its contents to the exterior. The swollen ends of the radial canals, which empty into the vacuole, indicate its position. (From Vickerman and Cox 1967.)

Now of course this removal of excess water is achieved only by the performance of work, and it can be shown that protozoa and other animals living in fresh water expend more energy than their marine relatives. This example thus gives us an idea of the sort of process for which energy is needed by the body. An activity has to be maintained and this involves energy expenditure; in order to allow this expenditure, further activities must go on to collect the food for fuel and the oxygen to burn it with, to provide the energy.

7

THE CONTROL OF LIVING ACTIVITIES

1. The concepts of structure and function

IT will now perhaps be becoming more clear what we mean by the activities that are life. They are those usually called metabolism, the whole set of changes that enable the living system to remain what it is. These metabolic changes can be subdivided and classified in various ways. For instance, one often speaks of anabolic or synthetic activities, which build up the organism, as distinct from the catabolic ones in which there is a breaking-down. But the boundaries of these are by no means clear and such division into two categories obscures the fact that all metabolism is a set of changes directed to maintenance of the whole organization.

We need a terminology that will enable us to describe all these changes and show how they are controlled so as to ensure continuity of life from day to day and through the centuries. The currently accepted method for describing these activities is to speak of them as the 'functions' of the various parts. The concept of a function as the proper activity of anything is very old. In a sense it can be applied to any action or activity, but as used for living beings it implies that the action has purpose—'Dark night, that from the eye his function takes, . . .' (Shakespeare 1600). The term acquired new shades of meaning as machines were made to imitate and assist the functions of the body, a practice that became common in the sixteenth and seventeenth centuries. Machines are made to effect certain purposes; they have therefore 'structures', which have particular 'functions' to perform. It is implied in the comparison that the body has been made for certain ends or objects and that the activities of the parts tend to fulfil these objects. In the sixteenth and seventeenth centuries this method of speaking was more satis-factory than it is today, for it was possible then to complete the analogy by saying that the body had been made as it is by God and that its 'functions' were to fulfil his purposes. It may still be possible to say this in a more general way, but the difficulty is that we now know in detail how the bodies of the various plants and animals have *come to* their present state by the operation of evolutionary processes over many millions of years. Whatever may be meant by saying that God made the bodies of animals and plants it is certain that he did not immediately and arbitrarily fashion them in the form that they have today. The discoveries of evolutionary studies make it necessary to take a wider view than is given by comparing the body with the pumps, clocks, and windmills that were available to Harvey, Descartes, and their successors, who founded the science of physiology on the comparison of living bodies with these simple machines.

Much more satisfactory comparisons can be made by utilizing the advances that have occurred recently in engineering science. We can repeat the process of describing man in the language used for his artefacts, comparing him with the modern machines that control themselves. Primitive machines mostly provided substitutes for the muscular work of men and animals, for example, wind- and water-mills and steam-engines. The control of this work was still in the hands and brains of men. Therefore the concept that was central for physics and engineering up to the end of the nineteenth century was that of *energy*, and an elaborate language and mathematics for the exact study of energy grew up. Correspondingly, the more exact parts of physiology dealt with the energy exchanges of the body, measuring the amount of work performed by muscles, the amount of food needed daily for fuel and so on. This science of physiology, based upon the comparison of the living organism with machines for doing work, was of the greatest value, but it remained incomplete because it said little about the *control* of work done. Something was known about the operations of the nervous system in producing the simpler 'reflex' actions, but there was no language for speaking about the more complicated activities of the brain. In the last resort the control could only be spoken of as the property of an entity, the mind, which was postulated as something distinct from the body. This dualist approach has puzzled generations of philosophers and scientists and still leads to serious imperfections in our methods for dealing with perhaps the most important part of our lives. It will be maintained here that the dualism is a linguistic result of the fact that we have hitherto possessed no artefacts whose actions imitate those of the brain, and have therefore had no exact language for speaking of its functions as we can speak about other parts of the body, say the stomach or muscles. This is a very dogmatic statement of a position that has many implications. We shall try to deal with these in Chapter 10, though still inadequately.

2. Machines that control themselves

During the present century the position has changed because of the development by physicists and engineers of more elaborate methods for controlling machines, and of theoretical techniques for describing this control. This development has, of course, gone hand in hand with the evolution of machines that assist man not only with the work that he does but with the transmission of information from one person or machine to another person or machine. With the inventions of telegraphy, the telephone, radio, and television the study of communication of information is being made exact in the same way as the study of energy was treated in the last century. By making machines that imitate and assist one of our most important functions we have once again learned how to speak more precisely about that function in ourselves. This is a part of the science known as cybernetics or the study of control, from the Greek word for a steersman (Wiener 1949).

The importance of this for our present purpose is that we can improve our description of the nature of living activities by speaking of the methods by which living organization is controlled. The essential feature of that organization is that it maintains itself intact in spite of changes in the surroundings. This homeostasis is made possible because the organism receives information about the changes in its environment and this information controls the course of its actions. We can therefore speak of the whole process by comparing the body with machines whose course of action is controlled by information received from some outside source.

Such machines are now undergoing rapid development. A well-known example is the guided missile provided with receiving apparatus that detects the effects upon it of the wind or other surrounding features. Its 'brain' then makes calculations that produce appropriate adjustments to keep the missile on its course. There are also devices by which such missiles can detect their 'prey' and follow its course until they meet it. These warlike self-controlling machines are only one example of the widespread tendency to make machines or factories that control their own operations. Once started they proceed to regulate the flow of various materials to suit the course of the chemical or other processes going on in the machine or factory. For this purpose it is obviously necessary for the 'brain' of the machine to receive information not only about the flow of supplies from the outside but also about the 'need' of the machine for particular types of material. Similarly the body is provided not only with eyes and other organs to supply information about the outside world but also with internal receiving organs. For example there are sense organs in the stomach that tell about the need for food, others in the arteries report the pressure there, and still others in the muscles record the tension that is exerted.

3. Information theory

No machine has yet been made that approaches the body in the number of adjustments that can be made, though some machines regulate individual operations with great delicacy. What is important is not to compare the body with particular machines, but to use the machine language to enable us to investigate and describe living processes more exactly. The mathematical and logical methods of the theoretical engineer and physicist are more important for our purposes than the particular machines that are devised.

In a certain sense the 'information' in a system is its degree of order, and can be measured with reference to some other systems (Chapter 3). Conversely, the information is related to the degree of possible disorder. For example, a message that specifies the positions and velocities of the molecules in a gas contains far more information than one that specifies the positions in the crystal lattice when the gas becomes solid at low temperatures. The number of possible states is then less. It is important, however, to realize that there can never be any generally agreed statement about the number of possible states in a complex system and hence no absolute measure of amount of information is possible. To show this consider a dice. It has six possible states of orientation on a flat surface, where angle is neglected. But if we consider angle as a continuous variable the dice can be in an infinite number of states. If, however, angle is measured to the nearest degree then there are 360 states for each face. Similarly, we can get any number we choose for the possible states of a man or machine and hence for the information needed to define them. Information theory does not tell us how many states to choose, this must be arbitrarily decided. Then the theory gives us a measure, as a ruler does with any other arbitrary units. We are concerned here with the concept that the information in any channel leading to a system is that feature of the physical changes in it that decides that one course shall be pursued rather than another. Thus the information of a speaker is in the form of the sound waves he emits. This can be re-coded into the pattern of electrical changes transmitted along a telephone wire. The final effect of the information when received by another person may be to make him select one out of several possible courses of action, as a result of what he had heard from his informant.

We have seen already that it is a characteristic feature of organisms that they select particular elements from their environment and organize them in special patterns (Chapter 2). Such selection and organization implies the receipt of 'information' from another organized source. The amount of information that a given organism or machine receives per unit time is therefore measured as the number of decisions made between alternative courses. A useful unit of information is one *bit*, the binary choice that decides between two equiprobable courses, as measured with a given degree of accuracy.

Information theory is the science that studies the whole subject of the relation of events to their antecedents. It is, therefore, a special branch of statistics, dealing among other things with the problems of communication, instruction, and control. Its methods are of great interest to biologists who have to face continually the problem of finding ways for describing the sequences of events in living organisms and the way in which they are controlled so as to ensure continued maintenance (see Quastler 1965).

The amount of information contained in the selection or transmission of any message is obviously related to the number of binary choices required to pick that message from the set of possible messages in that particular ensemble (or language). If there are n equally probable choices the information content of one choice is

$$H = \log_2 n.$$

Such a calculation may not seem to be especially useful for us. It was indeed devised for the purpose of specifying the rate at which information can be sent along telephone wires or other communication channels. It has, however, application in several fields of biology, where control consists in making choices from sets of possible alternative actions. For instance, we can in such ways make estimates with which to compare the amount of information that is contained in the DNA of different species (p. 77) or the rate at which speech can be transmitted.

Where n choices are not equally probable (as among the words of a language) the average information per message (weighted) is given in bits (binary digits) as

$$H = \sum_{i=1}^{n} p_i \log_2 \frac{1}{p_i} = -\sum_{i=1}^{n} p_i \log_2 p_i,$$

where p_i is the probability of message i occurring and $\log_2 1/p_i$ is the information associated with that particular alternative. This is the measure of information defined by Shannon and Weaver (1949) as a measure of uncertainty or freedom of choice, applicable independent of the message or physical system concerned. In a sense it is the opposite of the everyday use of the word *information*, which is concerned with certainty rather than uncertainty (see Waterman (1968) for discussion). It is clear that the information built into a biological system, as in a gene or in impulse patterns in the nervous system, results from choices already made.

4. The information flow through organisms

The information that an organism receives is responsible for initiating the actions that prevent it from merging into its surroundings. The amounts of information involved may be very large. Thus a single bacterial cell has been estimated to contain 10^{12} bits of bound information, using a particular definition of number of possible states (Lehninger 1965). A typical growth rate representing one cell division every 20 min would require a developmental rate of 10^9 bits/s.

The sum of the sensory inflow from all exteroceptor (i.e. sensory) organs to the central nervous system in man has been estimated at 10^7 bits/s; in a lifetime of 10^9 s this would amount to 10^{16} bits. The rate of motor response is less—by about 6 log units—but would, nevertheless, add up to a very large lifetime number. The maximum likely storage capacity of the human brain, which has approximately 10^{10} nerve cells in the cerebral cortex, has been estimated at around $10^{10}-10^{11}$ bits. Even though most of these numerical estimates are subject to substantial errors, the astronomical nature of the information-processing task for a living organism is clearly indicated (Waterman 1968).

The information transfer from the genes is the basic source of the regulatory system of the whole organism (Fig. 7.1). The genetic controls are inherited from the parents P_1, and passed to the offspring F_1. Using them, other polynucleotides are produced, including messengers to control production of appropriate enzymes. These reactions, of course, themselves require energy and draw it from the existing metabolic system, to which they in turn contribute fresh components.

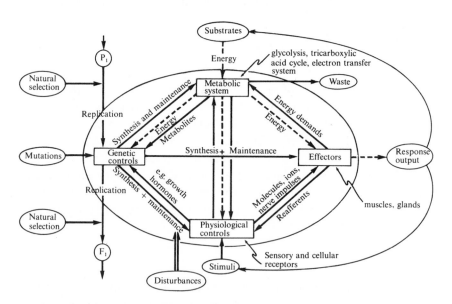

FIG. 7.1. Diagram to show the flow of information and energy by which homeostatis is achieved. (After Waterman 1968.)

In order to obtain the necessary raw materials the organism has effectors, also produced under genetic guidance. These in turn expend metabolic energy to bring the organism into situations where it can acquire more sources of energy and other raw materials. In order to do this effectively it receives further information about the environment from the receptors, which are of course also produced under the influence of the genetic system.

Such an analysis gives us the basis for a study of the intricate flows of information and energy by which the steady state of a living organism is maintained. We have already seen that it is a characteristic feature of organisms that they select particular substances from their surroundings and organize them in special patterns (Chapter 2). Such selection and organization implies the receipt of information from another organized source.

The earliest regulators to appear during development are intrinsic pace-makers, such as that of the heart, genetically programmed. Extrinsic influences are then gradually added, set points change, and the extent of regulated variation increases. Tolerance limits change and feedback arrangements are added. In general, regulations change from early fixed limits to later plasticity as the capacity to adapt to environment develops (Adolph 1968).

5. The principles of control

Machines perform their operations because they have been appropriately constructed. More elaborate machines are also provided with instructions as to how they shall operate, perhaps in the form of a set of punched cards or tape. Indeed, the very constructional details of the machine may be con-sidered as part of its instruction what to do. The essential feature of effective construction and instruction is obviously that it shall provide a machine that is able to operate in the circumstances in which it finds itself. We may speak of this by saying that such a machine contains *representations* of those features of the environment to which it is expected to respond. To take a simple example, the regulator of a water-bath (thermostat) contains a reference voltage indicating the temperature it is to keep (Fig. 7.2). It is able to receive information about a change in the temperature and to operate the mechanism in such a way that the water-bath is kept at whatever temperature has been specified.

The concept of a representation involves that of *coding*, another word that we can usefully borrow from the language of communication. Informa-tion can be carried by *signals* in a variety of forms, and can be transferred from one form to another by the process of re-coding. Indeed, the informa-tion in any system may be defined as the entity in it that remains intact in

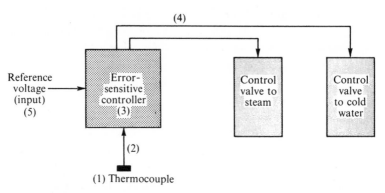

F I G. 7.2. Diagram of a thermostatic control system. A thermocouple (1) responds to changes in temperature and the consequent changes in current flow in the channel (2) leading to the controller (3) constitute 'signals' in a 'code' because the system has been so designed that particular changes in current produce particular effects in the controller. Similarly the reference voltage (5) constitutes a further signal in a code 'recognized' by the controller and telling it what to do on receipt of signals from (1). The result of the computations in the controller is to produce 'decisions', as a result of which further signals pass in the efferent channels (4), having the effect of turning on either cold water or steam as required.

spite of re-coding. Information thus obviously implies a certain relationship between the parts of any system. In a representation of any sort the parts are arranged in a manner that is in some way similar to that which is represented (or is conventionally regarded as being so). Information can thus be carried in coded form and can be stored in a memory, which provides a representation of the past occurrence (see Chapter 3).

Any machine that is to keep a constant course in relation to particular features of its surroundings must contain some representation of these features. The receiving apparatus then records the conditions from moment to moment and transmits this information to the seat of the representation, where a comparison is made. If there is any deviation, appropriate corrective action is taken to keep the machine on its course.

To ensure effective and steady control a series of decisions has to be made; for example, as to how closely the system is to follow its instructions, how fast it is to be made to change when it deviates, and how much it is to be allowed to oscillate. The science of cybernetics (or 'steering') is largely concerned with theories about such decisions. This can be illustrated in the case of a thermostat—say for regulating the temperature T °C, of a hothouse (Fig. 7.3) that is subject to fluctuations of outside temperature. A thermometer measures temperature T °C $= t$. Experience has shown what temperature is needed (say, for growing mushrooms), and the relevant information is used in the choice box, C_1, to choose the temperature setting,

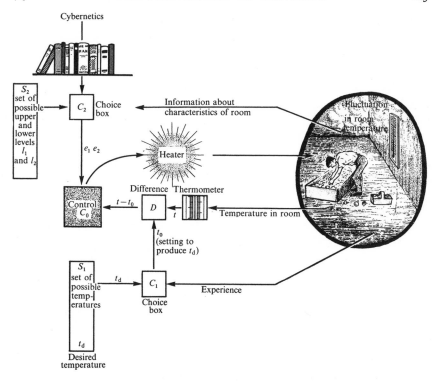

FIG. 7.3. Some principles of a thermostatic control system (see text). The figure illustrates, among other things: (1) feedback, i.e. steering by sensing of results; (2) regulation depends on choice, i.e. selection from sets of possibilities by information; (3) information is the feature of physical changes that produces choices. (After Quastler 1965.)

t_d, out of the possible set, S_1. To produce this t_d the thermostat setting t_0 is decided by experience in the box C_1, since imperfections of the thermostat and its instruments usually ensure that t_d and t_0 are not equal.

The control box C_0 now decides how to actuate the heater to correct the difference between t and t_0, determined by subtraction in box D. But this is not simply a matter of subtraction. A further decision has to be made. How small should the difference be between t and t_0 before it is corrected, and how frequently shall the heater go on and off? How much oscillation shall be allowed? These are the really essential features of cybernetic regulation. They require that in each case experience shall select the appropriate values of the excess e_1 and deficit e_2 at which the heater is turned on and off and with what intensity (speed). These values are chosen from a further set S_2 by a second choice box C_2, using the experience of the conditions, such as volume and insulation of the space, and the general instructions that are provided by cybernetics.

The values e_1 and e_2 are used by the control box C_0 to switch the heater, H, on and off at appropriate values of $t-t_0$. In a control system there is therefore comparison of the course that the machine is taking with the representation that constitutes the instruction to act in a particular way in relation to certain environmental features. If the instruction is correct, then by making adjustments according to it the machine achieves its aim. In man-made machines the forecast that the machine will be effective is made by human brains, but we now have to consider the possibility of making machines that do their own forecasting, that is to say, modify their instructions in the light of information they receive about the course of events around them. The development of calculating machines makes it not very difficult to imagine the construction of such a self-modifying control system. An essential requirement is obviously that the machine should have a memory of past events and that it should be able to compare current information with this memory. Physical embodiments of the past are familiar in the form of books, pictures, punched cards, magnetic tapes, and other systems. We are not so familiar with memories that change gradually with the information they receive, but it is not difficult to imagine them and they can be constructed by engineers.

6. Living control systems

A control system that does its own forecasting will thus use the information it receives to improve the correspondence between its representation of the environment and the actual conditions there. The representation will be thus kept up to date, and by comparing current events with it the machine will be more likely to take actions that are effective than if it merely bases its actions upon fixed instructions laid down in the past.

We may now proceed to see whether we can give an adequate account of living organisms as machines whose actions ensure continued maintenance. The various operations of the organism are controlled by the information it receives from three sources. The central controlling factor is the set of instructions embodied in the organization it has inherited from its ancestors. This organization, and in particular that of the DNA, constitutes a coded representation of events that are likely to occur in the environment, in the sense that it makes it possible for the organism to do appropriate things according to the events that happen around it. The particular sequences of bases in the nucleotides ensure that the right proteins are made to provide adjustments that will keep the organism alive in its characteristic environment.

As an example we may take the regulation of the body temperature of a mammal. Certain cells in the hypothalamus (p. 612) are very sensitive to slight rises in temperature above the normal (37 °C). They then discharge nerve impulses that set in action the mechanisms that cool the body, such as sweating. This cools the blood and switches off the hypothalamus. In order to study such closed-loop feedback systems engineers use the device of 'opening' the loop. This has been done in the rabbit by putting heating electrodes in the hypothalamus and arranging that they keep it at a constant temperature a few tenths of a degree above normal in spite of the cooling blood. As a result the temperature measured in the rectum can be made to fall, by cooling, to as much as eight times more than the level of the hypothalamus is above normal (Euler 1964). This gives a measure of what the engineer calls the open loop gain of the system. Incidentally, this experiment shows that the detectors of temperature-change in the skin and elsewhere are only of minor importance in regulating temperature, compared to the hypothalamus. They probably serve more to protect the body against heavy temperature loads by initiating movement when the skin becomes uncomfortably hot or cold.

This example shows only the outlines of the complexity of the control systems that maintain homeostasis in the body. We have to consider how such an organization can have arisen. It represents the environment in the sense of re-presenting appropriate responses to it.

The representation of the environment is not necessarily included in any one individual only; it is a property of all the members of the species jointly. In many organisms maintenance of the similarity between the environmental representation and that of the species is ensured by the simple fact that those individuals that do not fit their surroundings die. To take one example, among bacteria there are individuals with slightly differing powers of chemical action, acquired by heredity. In a given environment containing certain raw materials, only those of the population who are able to utilize these materials will survive. It is thus ensured that the phenotype of the population appropriately represents the condition of the environment. The individual receives the simple piece of information 'live' or 'not live' from the environment, enabling the species to continue to survive if the future is like the past (see Chapter 3).

7. Natural selection

This is, of course, the principle of natural selection enunciated by Darwin in 1859. The clue to the question 'How is it that organisms are so marvellously suited to their environments?' is essentially simple. Those that are not suited die. This would of course mean that *all* die but for the fact that the genetic systems contain vast sources of variety. The mechanisms of mutation and reproduction, and especially of sex, are largely directed towards ensuring that a constant supply of slightly differing individuals appears (Chapter 28). Some of these may be able to meet each new condition that the environment presents. The genes controlling these 'favourable' characters will rapidly spread through the population of the species.

Careful mathematical analysis has been made of this process of selection, especially by Fisher (1930), Haldane (1932), and Wright (1949). The conditions of selective advantage under which a gene will spread have been rigidly defined. In most circumstances one gene will replace another if it provides an advantage over the latter such that individuals carrying the first leave 1 per cent more offspring. For recent discussions see Ford (1964) and Mettler and Gregg (1969).

This definition of success is often criticized as suggesting that evolution and adaptation result in nothing but improved reproductive efficiency. Of course the capacity to continue is precisely the central characteristic of life. It is in this power to delay the tendency of organization to pass over to homeogeneity that living things differ from non-living ones. The point is that the essence of the power resides in the presence of a reservoir of variety out of which selection can be made to achieve a given end. Such concepts of 'selection' and 'end' seem to be very different from those concepts of reversibility upon which physics is built. We shall have to inquire how this capacity may have arisen (Chapter 26).

The essence of living organizations, then, is that they contain memory systems that represent the environment with very great reliability. The stability of the giant DNA molecules is one of the 'surprising' but characteristic features of life (see Schrödinger 1944). The continued existence of organisms is ensured by producing large excesses of materials with slightly differing characteristics and rejecting those that are not suitable. This process is not limited to a natural selection between individuals as Darwin understood it. There is selection going on *within* each of us, every day, especially in the tissues that continually produce new cells (Chapter 11). The very fact of growth, that is of continual addition, is itself the guarantee that there will be competition, those materials that are unsuitable being rejected.

It may seem that this principle of fashioning a system for an end by rejection of the unfit is the very negation of intention and planning as humans understand them. In fact the achievement of very precise results may be done better by such random methods than by a plan. Even the engineer finds that for the production of very perfect plane or spherical surfaces for optical purposes a mass of raw material is made to work against tools with *random* motions (Platt 1958). One can see that, in principle, greater refinements are sometimes possible in this way than by *planning* the operation of a tool, which can obviously be done only within the limits of specification of the measuring instruments involved. In fact we can say that with nature's system the limit is set by the degree to which randomness is allowed to operate (for instance the degrees of variability provided by the genetic material). The fineness of the result is shown not only by the survival of species but by the exactness of specification of such organs as eyeballs and joints, which are fabricated precisely under such conditions of random movement. Yet all such moulding by random action can operate only given the striving of individuals. Indeed the constant efforts of organisms to continue are the very driving-force of life. In man these efforts take many subtle forms, especially by intentional laying of plans for the future. This must be done by individuals, alone or in co-operation with others. Natural selection depends upon the will to survive and to continue to make such efforts as we can is the contribution that each of us makes to life through the ages.

8

PERSONAL ADAPTATION. IMPROVEMENT OF THE REPRESENTATION ON DIFFERENT TIME-SCALES

1. Adaptation of the phenotype and genotype

IN the last analysis all populations maintain their correspondence with the surroundings by natural selection within and among the organisms, as described at the end of the last chapter. There are, however, other ways in which this same end is achieved. Individual organisms are able to adjust their activities to suit those of the surroundings, by processes of 'adaptation' or, more specifically, 'phenotypic modification', to distinguish it from adaptation of the genotype as a result of natural selection. In the language we are suggesting we recognize that individual cells or organisms are able to adapt in this way when they are capable of receiving from the environment more information than the simple message 'live' or 'die'. One way of defining information is as 'the feature of physical change in a communication channel that improves the correspondence between a representation and that which it represents'. We have seen already that the simple elimination of unfit individuals improves the representation that is provided by the whole population. The process of phenotypic adaptation by the individual consists in receiving information that modifies its structure or functioning in such a way that it provides a better representation of environmental conditions.

2. Mechanisms of phenotypic adaptation

Examples of this adaptation are found in all organisms. Bacteria are able to adjust their enzyme systems to make them capable of using the particular substances that are present in the environment (p. 53). Plants show many adjustments of the same sort; they may, for example, grow long roots when water is scarce. Among animals nearly all the organs of the body are able to adjust in this way, and we shall deal with these changes in detail later. To give familiar examples, muscles become stronger if they are used, blood carries more oxygen in people living at high altitude, and the structure of bones is arranged to meet the strains that fall upon them. All these are examples of tissues receiving information from the environment and altering their structure so as to provide a representation that is appropriate to present conditions and therefore will enable the organism to survive if the future is similar.

Each of these processes of adaptation involves a specific mechanism, controlled by genetic instructions, and laid down during development. The mechanisms must include some kind of receptor system capable of sensing the need for change in the operation of the tissue concerned. The relevant information must then be transmitted along a communication channel to a control system, basically DNA, which allows for the performance of appropriate compensatory actions when necessary. From the control centre further signals must proceed to whatever regions are responsible for making the adjustments, for instance by synthesis of the necessary new proteins.

3. Erythropoietin

Some information is available about these mechanisms, for example that by which the production of red cells is regulated in mammals. The serum of animals that have suffered a loss of blood, when injected into others, causes increased red-cell production by the red bone marrow. This is not directly due to the dilution of the blood or absence of oxygen-carrying power, but to the presence of a substance erythropoietin, not detectable in normal serum. This is probably a glycoprotein, not species-specific, and produced by the kidney. After removal of both kidneys loss of blood is not followed by increased red-cell production, but the marrow of these animals is still able to respond if erythropoietin is introduced with the serum of others (see Krantz and Jacobson 1970).

Unfortunately, the features that would interest us most remain obscure. What stimulates the kidney to produce erythropoietin? Is it the absence of sufficient oxygen or the accumulation of some product that results from that lack? What is the receptor system involved and how does it activate whatever cells produce the stimulating substance? Finally, how does the latter act upon the bone marrow to increase the uptake of iron and production of haemoglobin? Is it by directly activating a particular enzymatic system for synthesis or by de-inhibiting such a system?

Studies of adaptive enzymes in bacteria have provided us with clues as to how to set about thinking of such matters. It is easier to study such questions using standard cultures of bacteria than in the heterogeneous tissues of a mammal. Nevertheless, studies of the adaptive systems of mammals and man are urgently needed and hold very great promise both for understanding of life and for control of ailments. Providing assistance for these natural adaptive responses of the body is obviously likely to be one of the most effective forms of medicine. To do this we need to analyse the communication channels by which the needs of the body are sensed and transmitted to the organs that are able to meet them. Part of the problem is to relate these adaptive processes to those of normal growth and replacement and these in turn to those of healing and repair. The basic need is for understanding of the control systems that maintain the homeostasis of the individual.

4. Memory. Phenotypic adaptation in the brain

It is, of course, in the nervous system that the higher animals carry the most detailed representation of their environments. The receptor systems of the sense organs are able to collect information much more rapidly than, say, the muscles or the blood. The information in the brain is then used to make rapid adjustments of the organism's behaviour. This is the controlling system that is most obviously similar to that of machines such as guided missiles. The receptor organs send information about the course of events in the world around, and the significance of this for the organism is assessed by comparing it with the representation within the nervous system, enabling the animal to take appropriate action. The nervous actions take place at many different levels, which cannot be fully considered here. The simple 'reflex' mechanisms of the spinal cord provide representations that are laid down by heredity. Thus, when we touch a hot object, information in the form of nerve impulses in certain nerve fibres is used to activate a simple system by which the hand is withdrawn. The nervous pathways involved represent the action that has been found suitable when traumatic events occur, and this system has become embodied by natural selection in all normal members of the species.

The nervous mechanisms of the brain provide coded representations that constitute instructions as to how to proceed in much more complicated situations. Moreover, it is their special characteristic that they differ from individual to individual, having been laid down not by heredity but in the memory of the brain during the lifetime. Little is known of the means by which memories are built up in the brain, but at least we can realize that there is some sort of physical trace embodying the past history of the individual (Young 1964). As life proceeds, each new situation is compared with this representation of the past and a forecast is made of the action that is most likely to ensure homeostasis. Meanwhile, the memory system itself continually becomes modified so that it shall continue to be an up-to-date representation of the environment, able to make accurate forecasts for the future (see Chapter 42).

5. Summary. Adaptation on different time-scales

Our method of description of living systems, including man, is thus to say that their very elaborate internal organization constitutes a machine that maintains itself in a steady state. It does this by a system of control leading it to take actions that are likely to ensure survival. The controlling instructions constitute a coded representation of environmental conditions. They are kept up to date by repeated comparisons with the surroundings and by the presence of mechanisms that ensure that only effective instructions survive. The control operates with many different time-scales. Information received from the environment may influence the course of action very quickly, especially through the nervous system of higher animals. Slower adjustments of the representation within the animal take place by the process of adaptation of the individual, which we know of most clearly in the case of the building up of memories within the nervous system, but memories not essentially dissimilar are found in the condition of the blood, muscles, and even bones. Finally, on a still slower time-scale, the activities of life are controlled by the process of natural selection, matching the basic hereditary instructions of the nuclei against the environment, and ensuring that only those that provide adequate representations shall survive.

To put it in a slightly different way, we may say that the information that constitutes the controlling system of the body comes from three sources. (1) Much of it is provided by the immediate changes in the surroundings, especially such as influence organs of the nervous system. (2) Instructions are also provided by the memories that have been laid down during the lifetime of the individual, especially in the brain. (3) The main controlling system of all animals and plants is the hereditary instruction of the genetic system, maintained in an adequate state by natural selection.

This method of description of living will perhaps seem to many people strange and unduly laboured. Its advantages appear only with practice and, indeed, we are not yet in a position to exploit them fully for lack of development of the method, lack of knowledge about the signals and coding systems involved, and lack of means for specifying the nature of representations and the control that they exert. Whatever modifications and developments the treatment may undergo we can be sure that in some form it will be widely adopted. It is inevitable that the language acquired in this way from artefacts that assist human memory, computation, and communication shall be applied again to man himself and other organisms. For the present we shall be content to exploit the great advantage that is offered by having a single system for treating biological control at all levels, from that of daily life to evolution throughout the millennia. To see our own actions and memories as parts of a wider scheme is one of the main aims of a unified study of man and we can do it best by considering together in one scheme all the various ways in which life is controlled.

6. Living matter as a single homeostatic system

It will not have escaped attention that all the machines with which we have suggested comparison are made by man for particular purposes and therefore do not help us with the problem of describing living bodies, which are *self*-perpetuating homeostatic machines. In the last analysis we are certainly left with the question of how life first arose and we shall consider this in Chapter 26. But by thinking sufficiently boldly we can proceed a considerable distance by using as our unit of comparison not individual animals or plants but whole populations of them. Indeed, it is not too much to say that we can consider the whole living system as one vast homeostatic machine, whose operations serve to keep living matter in existence on the earth and to maximize the amount of it in existence at any one time. Let us not condemn this as too ambitious a project until it has been examined. If successful, it clearly has great possibilities for showing us the proper place of man and of individual men in the scheme of life.

Just as no individual is typical of his species, so there is no one species at any time or place that can be called particularly characteristic of life, or even of any type of life. The very concept of a population of creatures as constituting a distinct species inevitably breaks up if we consider its evolution in time (Chapter 27). A systematist provided with all the fossils of a lineage that ends in two distinct populations would not be able to find any natural way of dividing it into the original and the two final groups. It is not simply that the task would be difficult—it would be literally not possible.

This makes difficulties for those who like to deal with clear-cut categories. But it is the beginning of wisdom for the biologist. Life is embodied neither in particular single individuals nor even in particular populations of these, but in sets of populations, often scattered throughout the world. We are familiar with the various forms of cat, from lynx to lion, but the biologist recognizes the same phenomenon, in much more marked form, in relation to almost every type of life. Thus in the cephalopod molluscs there are about 150 species of octopods, scattered around the world today, 350 species of squids (though this category is harder to define), and some 100 species of cuttle-fishes (Sepiidae). In smaller and more abundant creatures such as insects, the same phenomenon is even more marked. There are not less than 1000 species in the genus of fruit-flies (*Drosophila*), and more than a million species of insects altogether.

We can sometimes readily see that particular variants are suited to different modes of life. In other situations species differing in minor particulars seem to occupy the same habitat (sympatric species), but this may well be due only to our blindness and ignorance. In general, each type of animal is well suited for one type of life (allopatric species). But of course the niches that are open to life are continually varying and the creatures change with them. This is indeed what we mean by evolution, and is a large part of the secret of successful maintenance (Chapter 28).

The essence of living is thus not to be found in any one population or species but is dispersed throughout all the different types of life in existence on the earth. We are just able to recognize that all men are brothers. Should we not go much further and proceed on the assumption that we are of one flesh, not only with all animals but with all plants, fungi, and bacteria as well? This is no mere emotional statement or metaphorical figure of speech. One of the most startling revelations of molecular biology is that the same code of triplets of bases is used to define the proteins of all organisms (p. 49). We are indeed one flesh and we depend upon the information in a set of books, written not in a babel of tongues but in a *single common language*.

The more one thinks about it the more clearly it appears that this concept is the sober scientific truth. It is difficult perhaps to see that it has wide practical applications, because it appears so grand, and indeed grandiose, that it may seem to have little beyond literary content. Yet were it not that we all contain the same amino-acids we could not feed upon the plants. In a sense we parasitize them. The forms of life that we call intelligent would presumably not be possible if they also had to perform the work of photosynthesis. It may be the similarities of genetic codes that make it possible for viruses to invade us and pervert our enzyme systems (and this suggests possible ways of frustrating them). There is an endless web of interactions between organisms, and our future well-being depends largely on understanding it.

One way of seeing the point is to ask how an observer from another planet would regard life upon earth. He would certainly record the presence of systems with quite surprising chemical and structural uniformity, although some of them stayed in one place, were green and brown, often had coloured tops, and sometimes grew to upwards of 100 ft high, others moved through the air, over the ground or through the water. He would, of course, record all the variants of the populations, but he might pay more attention than we commonly do to the underlying *similarities* of composition and structure. Above all, he would emphasize that the whole mass constitutes one single self-maintaining system. Every part is related to every other (though obviously communication is more direct between neighbouring than between distant parts).

The Martian would, I think, be able in this way to describe the characteristic composition and structure of life. He would do it in terms of a hierarchy of levels. Thus only certain elements of the ninety-odd possible are included, and these group to form a certain range of molecular compounds, rather restricted compared with the number of possibilities. These compounds are collected to make cellular organelles and cells of quite surprisingly limited forms, considering how many might be made from such molecules. Among cells there is again variety, and whole creatures are built by selection among this set of cells to form the organs and tissues. But the selection is made differently for each individual so that a population is generated with varying characteristics suited for particular environments. The variety of species of animals and plants is but an extension of the same process of selection among the sets available. The only proper description of life is, therefore, of the whole hierarchical assemblage of sets, from which selection is constantly being made to transmit the continuity to the future.

9

THE INDIVIDUAL MAN

IN the earlier chapters we have tried to describe the nature of the activity that constitutes life. It can be seen to consist of a series of interchanges between the organism and its environment such that the organization of the former is maintained in spite of continuous change of its actual materials. Like Parliament or the Catholic Church, its members come and go, yet it remains approximately the same thing. The purpose of this chapter is to inquire further about this entity or thing, the organism (and particularly a human being), which is maintained by the activity of life. Evidently it is not any particular piece of material that is in some way continually patched up and mended. We have seen abundantly already that change goes on rapidly in all parts of a man. No doubt it is faster in some tissues than in others. Whereas the molecules of many proteins and other soft parts of the body are replaced every few hours or days, some molecules of the bones, tendons, and hair may remain for months or years. Nevertheless, in the end they all change, and it cannot be emphasized too strongly that what continues is not any particular body but an organization of processes, a way of acting, of living.

In order to make life possible in such conditions as those inhabited by man, these processes must be very intricate and varied. Besides respiration, feeding, excretion, and so on, there must be delicately adjusted movements of the whole body, calculated to keep it in a place suitable for its life. A place not too hot nor too cold, too dry or too damp; not too near to other organisms likely to destroy the man, nor too far from others with whom he can collaborate. The activities necessary to ensure all this involve the drawing-in to the body of large amounts of stuff and the building of them temporarily into the elaborate structures that make up the muscles, nerves, glands and the rest, by whose actions the steady state is maintained. The body and all its organs are manifestations of the activity that constitutes life; they are the materials collected together by this activity and, as it were, made part of that entity towards whose maintenance the life is directed. For this maintenance to be ensured, then, an elaborate organization operating according to suitably chosen instructions is necessary. The complete system of life that endures is, strictly, the unit that should be called an 'individual'. Yet clearly a single man or woman is not an individual in this sense, for he or she can maintain the human characteristics only for a limited period. The organization that carries the instructions that make survival nearly permanent is not that of any single creature, but is embodied in all the members of a given sort. These, by the various combinations that they make through sexual reproduction and biparental inheritance, provide all the varied types that are necessary for life to be preserved under changing conditions. In this sense, therefore, the 'individual' is made up of all the members of any one species. Taken together they can be considered to make one single homeostatic machine. The whole population carries the instructions that ensure continuity of life; these are not to be found in any single member or individual as the term is commonly used.

This, however, is only the first turn of the paradox. The individual man does not survive, yet he is the fundamental biological unit. Neglect of the importance of the individual man in the face of society as a whole is not only liable to lead to monstrous political tyranny but is also a biological absurdity. *Each man, woman, or child, in his skin and with his brain, is a very real unit of homeostatic control.* In particular, in man as opposed to other species, the instructions by which life is lived are largely built up in the memories of individual brains. Each of us recognizes and refers to this fundamental fact of our biology by centring his system of world description on his conscious self. We shall therefore have to give special attention at this stage in our inquiry to the nature of the concept of consciousness (Chapter 10).

Of course, the status of the individual is an old question for moralists and theologians, but looked at as a biological problem it assumes a new aspect. In this way, we should be able to find a method of speaking that enables us to see in proper proportions the contribution that each single man or other organism makes to the whole system of life of which it is a part. Emphasis on the fact that no single creature is 'individual' in the sense of being able by itself to carry on life does not by any means reduce the importance of the contribution that each singly must make. On the contrary, we shall now be able to see much more clearly the *essential* part that each single creature plays in the business of providing the race, not only with a set of instructions that shall lead to actions that are effective forecasts of the future, but in actually *taking* these actions. Although the continuity of the race is in the genotype, it is only when the instructions are read out to produce phenotypes that their effectiveness for homeostasis is tested. The 'race' is a totality, an abstraction; only the individuals are real.

The role of each single member of the species differs greatly in different types of living system. In many of the simpler organisms such as bacteria the single units are very small, and each remains in being only for a period of a few minutes. Accuracy of forecasting is ensured by the pressure of great numbers of such units, differing slightly from each other, so that strains suited to various conditions are always available. A notorious example of this process of adjustment has been the development of strains of bacteria resistant to penicillin and other antibiotics. This means of keeping the race alive by continual revision of the hereditary instructions can evidently be very efficient if the units are small and breed rapidly. Granted the possibility of mutation (p. 392), the method may be effective in haploid organisms even in the absence of any typical sexual processes. The revision is even faster with the recombination that is possible in diploid species. Perhaps it is no accident that the malaria parasites, which possess a sexual mechanism, continue to plague mankind and other species of animal.

Even in bacteria there is a process of 'phenotypic adaptation' by which the single units change their metabolism to suit particular environmental conditions (Chapter 8). As we have seen, this process of building up personal memories within the single units of a population is further developed in higher animals and plants. In these more complicated or 'higher' organisms, with their elaborate means of maintaining homeostasis, reproduction is less rapid, so that the hereditary instructions are less frequently revised. The race is able to keep alive because each unit becomes adapted, its new organization comes to represent the particular conditions in which it finds itself. The actions that it takes are therefore likely to be effective for survival so long as the conditions continue to resemble those of the past. This capacity to acquire memories from the environment is particularly well marked within the nervous system and is, of course, the special distinguishing feature of mammals and man.

Evidently there is a certain conflict between the two methods by which the instructions of the organism are kept up to date. The building-up of a large store of personal memories by each unit is incompatible with frequent change of units to ensure revision of the hereditary instructions. In a general way we shall find that the greater the use that is made of the memories acquired by the individuals the longer are their lives (Chapter 23).

This process reaches an extreme in the larger mammals and man, and in man it is further complicated by the great development of means of communication between the units. This ensures that the memories built by each person may be added to a general store, common to the whole population. The presence of this common stock of information, handed on by representations in the form of signs and symbols and not by the genes, is perhaps man's most peculiar feature (Chapter 35). So much of our life is controlled by this social information that we have to be very careful in trying to apply to ourselves biological principles common to animals that have no such social information. Neglect of this aspect has spoiled the attempts of many biologists to provide a general view of human life.

The central feature of the system that is proposed here is to pay attention all the time to the way in which the various activities of living organisms contribute to their continued maintenance. If we do this we shall not be confused by the problem of trying to recognize some special value in single unit members of the species or in any one of their parts, but shall learn to look for the importance that any part or activity plays in the maintenance of the organization that we call life.

The importance of individuals, defined in the usual way, is not so much that nothing can be subtracted from the unit without it losing its characteristics, as that the individual man or animal is the unit that goes forward, adjusting itself as best it can to its surroundings. Although it may be able to suffer some loss without ceasing to exist, the life resides for the time being in this whole that maintains itself. Because some parts change less than others we are apt to think that they are in some way less alive than the matter in the protoplasm of the cells. For instance, the material of the hair, nails, bones, and teeth might be considered by some people as 'non-living'. The danger of this view appears if we consider some of the other intercellular substances, for instance the fibres of connective tissues, which weave all the organs together, or even the liquid plasma of the blood, which contains protein but is not presumably to be regarded as protoplasm. Are we to say that these are not parts of the living body? Evidently we are in danger here of repeating the fallacy we had learned to avoid of looking for the characteristics of life in some special stuff. The life of a creature does not lie especially in its heart or its brain or any other part, as primitive biological thought would suggest. Nor is there any mysterious living substance in the protoplasm of the cells, as the slightly more sophisticated biology of the last century believed. The life of a man or woman is in the whole activity of the body and all its parts, keeping the individual alive or helping the race to continue. Any woman knows that her hair is a part of her life as is any other organ. It may not be quite so important as her heart, but ask her to face the prospect of having it all shaved off and continuing life as before!

Any small part of the body may affect the life of the person to quite a disproportionate extent. A man limping with a painful corn, or lying awake with toothache, will soon tell you that the hard skin of his foot or the dentine of his tooth are as much part of his living substance as are the cells of his liver, heart, or stomach. It is especially important for those who have to care for the sick and injured to appreciate this integrity of the organization, to realize that the body is a whole and represents the life of the person, and that all parts of it may be important. Failing to understand this, doctors and nurses may give their attention only to parts of the body that seem to them especially important, considering, reasonably enough, that their first duty is to keep their patients alive as long as possible. Especially in 'minor' illnesses, however, they are apt to ignore the aspects of the treatment that may be of outstanding importance to the unfortunate patient. To lose a finger or a tooth or to show a scar may seem of slight importance to the doctor, but yet constitute a permanent impairment of the power of life for the patient. Similarly, to have to feed, excrete, or dress in a particular way, perhaps in public, may be for the patient the hardest part of a major operation, and the nurse is wrong to regard such difficulties as stupid idiosyncrasies.

Fortunately, there is a growing understanding of the way in which small features of the bodily structure and physiology play a part in the life of everyone. The clue to this is the point stressed so often before. Life is not something mysterious residing in the heart or the brain or some other secret centre, but is *all* the activity of *all* the parts of the bodily system and, indeed, extends beyond the confines of any one body. Therefore in treating, say, an infected finger or an ugly tooth we are not dealing with merely a mass of matter to be prevented from decay, but with organs that form important parts of the life of a human being. Loss even of a small part may impair that life to an extent difficult for anyone to realize who has not fully studied the life of that particular person.

In any social species such as man the activity that constitutes the life of the individual might be said to reach out beyond his single physical body and to include those of others around. There is certainly a sense in which the unit of human life lies in the family or even in large groupings such as the city or nation. If any demonstration of this were needed, it is given by the effort that individuals make to return to their homes, even for short visits, when separated from them, for instance during war.

The larger social individualities can easily be exaggerated and made the basis of pompous philosophy and power politics. Yet anyone who deals with people will do well to recognize that social and political units are realities. Moving people away from their accustomed place, habits, family, friends, and society is, in a sense, a surgical operation, disturbing the pattern of activity that constitutes their life.

In order to understand this, which may seem to be something of a mystery, we have evidently to abandon narrow habits of scientific thought, which teach us continually to try to 'isolate' substances and properties.

Instead, we must look for the whole system of organization that regulates the actions of individuals and their interactions with each other, and try to feel and understand the underlying blueprint or set of instructions that their activity continually expresses. If we can succeed in visualizing the plan of regulation of all this activity, even dimly, we shall be far more likely to succeed in treatment of our fellow men than by regarding them as if they were masses of matter, subjects only for chemical analysis. But this leads us to the most difficult of all biological problems, namely, whether there is some special organizing entity, the mind, present at least in humans, perhaps in other creatures. We shall attack it here at the centre of our study by inquiring what, as biologists, we can say about consciousness.

10

CONSCIOUSNESS

1. Mind and matter

ANY study of man must take account of the fact that many people regard the starting-point of all inquiry as the existence in themselves of a central feature, the conscious ego, which is somehow not identical with the body. The practice of speaking of distinct entities, body and mind, is so deeply embedded in our linguistic traditions that to many people it seems absurd to question its fundamental validity. But this problem, like many others, has complexities that are not apparent to common sense. Moreover, careful scientific study of consciousness has revealed many relevant but unexpected facts, and will no doubt produce many more. We do not need to rely upon mere argument and common experience, but can appeal to the detailed knowledge about the manifestations of consciousness collected by neurologists, psychiatrists, and even surgeons. Yet the central problem is to consider how it comes about that each of us believes that he has some peculiarly personal, direct, and precise source of information about the world, or at least of the sensations, pains, and satisfactions that it gives him. Is it true that these 'feelings' are in any sense more real than, or indeed different from, events in the physical world?

To illustrate the opposite points of view that have to be considered we may quote two very distinguished scientists, both past Presidents of the Royal Society. For the late Sir Cyril Hinshelwood: 'I have to begin logically with the, to me, indisputable fact that I have a wide range of conscious experiences (which are indeed more important to me than anything else)' (1959). On the other hand, for Lord Adrian: 'I used to regard the gulf between mind and matter as an innate belief. I am quite ready now to admit that I may have acquired it at school or later. But I find it more difficult to regard my ego as having such a second-hand basis. I am much more certain that I exist than that mind and matter are different' (1966).

Both statements would bear much discussion. Hinshelwood's has a frankly metaphysical flavour, and he would have defended this. It speaks of a beginning. Adrian's sounds more scientific, and seems at first to make no contribution to the metaphysical problem of ends. But then his second part speaks of certainty!

Professional philosophers can do better than these scientists, but clearly the issue is very complicated. It is an issue that worries many people and they reach different conclusions, which often influence their way of life. We may make an approach by asking whether this is really the right order for considering the problem. Perhaps people's way of life determines their belief and statements in this matter, rather than the reverse. Some are committed by their upbringing, religion, and language to dualism; others, perhaps by their revolt from these patterns, and their addiction to a monistic science, try to find a system that avoids the separation of mind and matter. At least we may agree that upbringing and conventional usage have a great deal of influence on attitudes to the problem. As scientific students of humanity, therefore, we may look at some of the criteria that are used to establish the category of consciousness. Even more important, we may try to find how they are manifested during development of the individual. This approach may not only go some way to solving the problem but will give a basis for a study of aberrations and deviations of consciousness.

2. Some semantic problems

Even if the question of mind and body is not just one of words it certainly requires careful use of them. We are apt to ask such questions as 'What is mind?' or 'Do minds exist?', without first settling what is to be meant by 'is' or 'exist'. One useful approach is to recognize that nouns are not all the names of 'things' and therefore cannot all be used in the same way. An extreme case is words that are used only in very limited contexts, like 'sake' in 'I did it for his sake', or 'behalf' in 'On his behalf'. It is no use asking to see a sake, or whether a man's behalf continues after death (Quine 1960). Such nouns are degenerate or vestigial, they can be used only in certain contexts, they are locked-in to certain phrases. But can such words as 'mind' be dismissed in this way? Pains seem to have a more real existence than behalfs. Consider 'voice'. Do 'voices' exist? Are they sound waves? Is a man's voice part of his larynx? Clearly nouns like voice are most useful and indeed precise, and are somehow related to matter, but yet do not quite refer to things.

Indeed we may begin to worry further 'What is existence, what are things?' How do we recognize a thing? By touch, or by sight? We can be deceived by these. Are things known by sound, or by smell? The more we think the less sure we are about it. And when we ask, are electrons 'things' we realize that we are not at all sure what we mean by 'matter'. A further worry is that most of our modern information about matter comes from measuring, but do measures 'exist'? Does a mile exist, or a second, or a gram? (see Quine 1960, Braithwaite 1953).

What such an interrogation surely teaches us is that we no longer want to continue to ask questions about 'What really, truly exists?', deeply though the search for it is rooted in our habits of thought and language. As members of a communicating species what we seek is to make statements that shall interest our fellow-men, and with which they will find they can agree. These in the last analysis are the only sanctions for acceptability of usage.

As it applies to our problem this means that we must be careful to use words only in the contexts in which they properly apply. To ask whether minds exist is to use together two words that belong to different vocabularies, it is a category mistake (Ryle 1949). One plan for classifying categories is into those that do and do not refer to what are generally agreed to be things. Thus all the words of the mental language are said to be 'non-referential' and should not be used in referential contexts. To ask 'do minds exist?' is thus as stupid as asking 'do sakes exist?', it is a question that should not be asked (Dennett 1969). But this classification into referential and non-referential is not by any means easy to apply. It means that we must only use non-referential words in their proper contexts. For example if 'voice' is non-referential we must not conclude from 'John strained his voice' that 'John was doing something excessive'. If we did we should be open to the confusion

'John strained his voice,
John strained his vocal cords,
therefore,   John's voice is his vocal cords.'

At first the refusal to take words like mind and pain only in certain non-referential contexts may seem evasive. But it not only helps with many of our difficulties, much more important, it leads us to expand our views about what we *do* mean by 'reality' and 'existence'. We all know that there is some sense in saying that we have both mind and brain. With careful exploration and use we can enlarge the study of both of them.

3. The problem of a private language

This subject is particularly full of linguistic traps. We have to be careful that we do not invent a 'problem of consciousness' simply by the way that we talk about it. Wittgenstein (1953) expresses this when he asks 'Does the use of this word consciousness present any problems in ordinary life?' Someone asserts 'Human beings agree that they see, hear, feel and so on. . . . So they are their own witnesses that they have *consciousness*.' Wittgenstein replies 'But how strange this is! Whom do I really inform if I say "I have consciousness"? . . . Now expressions like "I see", "I hear",

"I am conscious" really have their uses. I tell a doctor "How I am hearing with this ear again", or I tell someone who believes I am in a faint "I am conscious again".'

The point he is making is that we do not as part of ordinary talk assert that we have consciousness—though I may say that on a certain occasion I lost consciousness. This may seem over-subtle, but there is a real danger that we invent difficulties by using words out of their appropriate context.

Consciousness is not a word we use much in ordinary life anyway. It is certainly not the name of an observable entity or thing. Because we attach meaning to the words 'He is conscious', it does not follow that we are adding anything by changing the form to 'He has consciousness'.

Many of the difficulties that we experience about 'mind' and 'matter' arise because the form of our language suggests that bodily and mental states are in some way comparable entities. 'The mistaken analogy that lies behind the sceptical absurdities of dualism is that between "I see a tree" or "I touch this stone" on the one hand and "I feel pain" and "I understand this calculation" on the other. Just as the first two sentences report perception of and action on physical things so, it is supposed, the other two report mental perception and action. The world is then conceived as containing, alongside material objects and acts of manipulating them, mental objects like pains and mental acts or processes like understanding, meaning and thinking' (Quinton 1968).

Wittgenstein tried to show that whatever private experiences may be there can be no possibility of describing them by a sort of special private language. The language we have is by its very nature a public one, used for describing, among other things, the states of ourselves. But we can only do this by applying to ourselves the same rules of language as we apply in talking about others, that is about their outward behaviour. The words we use when we try to describe 'mental' phenomena are therefore necessarily connected with features that anyone can observe. 'Every inner process must have its outward criteria.' Even when we say 'it hurts' we are not really describing the pain but are giving the conventionalized response to the situation.

Other philosophers have not been entirely convinced by such arguments (see Strawson 1968). It has been claimed that one could of course invent a private language (Ayer 1963). To which there is the reply that simply to invent new names for, say, sensations is only possible to someone who speaks a language in which there are names for sensations, that is one who knows what the name of a sensation is. '. . . it is a different question whether anyone could have invented language' (Rhees 1968). The biologist will remind us here that of course language has been 'invented' at least once

(Chapter 35) and that the problem may take on new aspects as we learn more about how it was invented and the brain structures and activities by which it is produced (see Lenneberg 1967 and Chapter 20).

One of the difficulties of such discussions is that they involve the question of how we can speak about the private sensations that are in question since we cannot, as it were, point to them. '. . . no amount of gesturing on my part can direct their attention to a private sensation of mind, which *ex hypothesi* they cannot observe, assuming further that this sensation has no "natural expression"' (Ayer 1963). The biologist may call attention to the last two words. Would it make a difference if by means of recording electrodes we could examine a 'natural expression' of private thoughts? Or would such electrical patterns merely serve as another natural expression such as those of speech or gesture? Additional information obtained in this way certainly seems to affect some of these arguments. Wittgenstein would say that in the statement 'I know I am in pain' the word 'know' does not have the same meaning as 'I know it is raining' because the former cannot be falsified. The sense of the word 'know' about the rain is that I can explain the evidence by which I know it, and I might be wrong. Is there any such sense about the pain? Suppose an appropriately placed electrode shows signs of activity in my brain of a type similar to that always shown in your brain when you feel pain. Is this evidence in any way different from my telling you when I am in pain?

Clearly the whole question of a private language is very difficult and confused, perhaps beyond remedy. It may be that there are certain fundamental difficulties that will obstruct any attempt to penetrate this mystery. The scientist will probably be unwilling to admit defeat by words in this way. For the present we must admit that we are still puzzled, but the recent careful linguistic and philosophical investigations, as well as physiological findings, at least suggest new approaches to the problem (Castañeda 1967).

4. The criteria of consciousness

We can probably all agree that consciousness is not the name of a thing but of a state or condition. It is a state that we ordinarily associate with life and in particular with life in man and perhaps also animals. The problems of defining the conditions to which the word can best be applied arise from our apparent power to recognize who is conscious, either by looking outwards at others or inwards at ourselves. Should we best start with the one approach or the other? Let us try the harder task of looking in both directions. This should not be impossible, for each of us after all is an organism and sees himself only at a somewhat different angle from that with which he views others. It is a truism that the way we talk about our inner consciousness must have close relationship to the way we talk about it in others. Of course that is not to say that there may not be something unique in the individual's view of himself, but it must surely be in his *point of view*, rather than what is viewed. It could possibly be maintained that there is in each of us a state (or entity) that can *only* be discerned by the individual himself, but then we should have to examine what we mean by 'discerned' as referring to something that could not possibly be described to others. Evidently the whole question is closely tied up with the very nature of language and description (see Quine 1969).

When asking whether other people or animals are conscious we often ask merely for signs that they are alive or active. Thus we speak in physiology of 'the conscious cat', simply in contrast to one that is anaesthetized or asleep. But in asking more subtly whether animals are conscious we look for something more. As Hinshelwood said, 'Nobody intimately acquainted with individuals among the higher animals can seriously doubt that they possess some inner life, perhaps not entirely unlike our own' (1959, p. 443). This puts it more frankly than the professional ethologist would dare to do. But what exactly does it mean in terms of observation? Surely it is that cats and dogs and monkeys show signs of communication, both among themselves and with us. Communication as we have seen implies a sharing of homeostatic equipment and of codes for signalling. We are sufficiently like these other mammals to be able to exchange rather detailed signals with them. Moreover, this implies that their communication system, like ours, is based on an elaborate information store encoded in the form summarized by calling it a model of the world (Craik 1943, Young 1964). The method of operating of mammalian brains is to build this model as they develop and to match the input that comes along in daily life against it (p. 619, Miller 1965). Further, like ourselves these higher animals can continue to compute relationships in time and space without the stimulus being available in the environment (for evidence see Holloway 1966 and, better, Osgood 1964). To put it more simply, they seem to 'think'.

Creatures that operate in this way have 'individuality'. Each carries the record of his own life and operates accordingly. It is no accident that we find signs of 'consciousness' in these higher animals. The inner life whose status puzzles us corresponds in some sense to whatever entity continually consults the inner record or model and compares the input with it.

Animals that learn and communicate by means of simpler models do not seem to us to show any real signs of awareness or consciousness. We may be doubtful about a fish and even perhaps an octopus, and the line gets fainter as we go from bees to wasps, to ants, to flies, to fleas and so to worms and simpler invertebrates such as sea anemones, jelly-fishes, and corals.

If anyone wishes to ascribe consciousness to sponges or plants or atoms or volcanoes we are entitled to ask to which manifestations of the behaviour of these systems he is referring. The blanket assertion that 'all matter must contain an element of consciousness' simply makes all the linguistic mistakes we have been considering. We claim to say something clear when we state whether a given human is conscious or not. What are the signs by which we make the distinction? Can they be detected in a given animal, or plant or volcano or atom? The honest answer for the simpler systems is 'No'! There may be doubtful cases, but the creatures we ordinarily regard as perhaps showing some signs of what we call consciousness are complicated ones, mainly mammals and birds.

5. Can computers think?

This leaves us with the question whether if we made a suitably complex artefact we should call it conscious. Perhaps this really only brings up again the problem of what criterion we are to use to define that state. Some people would say that the computers we have already 'think', because they solve problems as well as we do. Others might say 'obviously not. They can't feel, they are made of metal and are not living.' The similarities of man and machine have been often discussed by mathematicians such as Turing (1950) and Ashby (1960). In spite of their ingenious proofs the biologist retains a suspicion that there is more to designing a brain than mathematical reasoning about ideal tape machines. It is too early yet to say whether a machine to store and manipulate information on the scale of the brain can be put together by planned engineering methods and materials. It may be that it needs carbon compounds and selection on an evolutionary time scale. We can imagine a machine showing knowledge of the external world. But could it have the inner information needed to show our signs of self-awareness? It has been said that there is a fruitful analogy between logical states of a Turing machine (computer) and mental states of a human being on the one hand, and structural states of the machine and physical states of the brain on the other (Broadbent 1970). This is indeed a useful comparison, but there is a danger that it be used to conceal fundamental differences. In a computer there is a sharp distinction between the machine and its contents. The machine can be cleared completely of its logical content ('mind') and given another one. In brains this is not so. The logical content is built up, from childhood, continually and *largely irreversibly* (Chapter 42). Moreover the instructions (logic) to proceed in certain ways have been built up by a selection of appropriate DNA over thousands of years. Human brains operate as they do because of their fundamental organization. Only as we come to know more about this organization do we understand how fully the phenomena that we call mental can be described as states of the brain. To try to define them as the operations of any single system ('the mind') is a primitive oversimplification anyway. As knowledge improves it becomes increasingly satisfactory to use 'brain' wherever we ordinarily use 'mind'. But this is only useful if 'my brain' is used to mean all that material *and its organization and activities.* To put it in another way, the software and hardware are not distinct as they are in a computer. We have to learn that matter and its actions are not conceptually separable. It is those who wish to understand the activity of matter who have learned not to be materialists. It is a hard lesson, conflicting with much daily use, and can only be learned by detailed study of brain processes, *and these are very complicated.*

6. Problems of the identification of consciousness in man. Divided brains

This may lead us to think about some of the difficulties in saying, even of a human being, whether he be conscious or not. After a cerebral vascular accident (a stroke) it is not uncommon for a man to be paralysed and unable to speak, or indeed to move. It may be quite difficult to say whether he is conscious even if his eyes are open. Probably we would accept that he was conscious if he gave some signs of communication—say with his eyes. But can we be sure of the opposite?

Then there is the intractable problem of whether consciousness implies the capacity to verbalize. Obviously we often seem to have experiences that are not verbal, but equally, being verbalizers we characterize much of our stream of consciousness in verbal symbols. The case of people with split brains presents this problem dramatically. The corpus callosum uniting the two cerebral hemispheres has been severed in a few patients in the attempt to control severe epilepsy. The result is summarized by Sperry (1966) as that 'the surgery has left these people with two separate minds, that is two separate spheres of consciousness . . . the left, dominant hemisphere has speech . . . the other, the minor hemisphere, however, is mute or dumb, being able to express itself only through non-verbal reactions.' We may compare this formulation with what would be said of a person with a spinal-cord injury. The part above the lesion cannot report what goes on below, but no one would say that there are now two separate minds. This is presumably because spinal-cord behaviour is of a type for which we do not use such words as 'mind' or 'consciousness'. Why not? Clearly it is not because of lack of speech, which is equally characteristic of the dumb hemisphere of the split-brain people. When some familiar object such as a pencil or comb is placed in the left hand of one of these blindfolded subjects the right hemisphere cannot say what it is, but it 'appears to know quite well what the object is. Though it cannot express this knowledge in speech or in writing, it can manipulate the object correctly, it can demonstrate how the object is supposed to be used, and it can remember the object and go out and retrieve it with the same hand from among an array of other objects either by touch or by sight. While all this is going on the other hemisphere meanwhile has no conception of what the object is and, if asked, says so.'

Although the right side cannot speak 'it is not entirely stupid or illiterate; it reads a word like *cup*, *fork*, or *apple* flashed to the left visual field and then picks up the corresponding object with the left hand'. This surely gives the clue as to why we may wish to say that there are two minds here—because there are two entities, *each independently capable of communicating with us in our rather elaborate symbolic ways*. Incidentally, they can also communicate between themselves in this way, but in no other. 'If a familiar object is placed in the right hand, while the subject is blindfolded, the left hand is unable to pick out by palpation the same or a matching object from among others. However, if the subject is allowed to name out loud the sample object in the right hand, then the left hand does find the correct object.' As Sperry remarks, if extrasensory perception truly operates surely we should find it here, where the two 'minds' are in one head. But the fact is that they can communicate only by sounds or other physical symbols. What does this tell us about their 'minds'?

These fascinating surgical cases pose, in extreme form, questions that arise from various 'dissociations of personality' from injury or disease. Indeed, we are perhaps not infrequently divided personalities in this sense. MacKay gives as an example an occasion when he was in his bedroom changing his shirt while talking to someone else and found himself putting on his pyjamas. It is a truism of psychiatrists that we are often 'unconsciously' compelled in such ways, which only illustrates a further difficulty in our attempt to discover what we mean by 'conscious'. The problem raised by the split-brain people is not that they perform acts 'unconsciously'. Precisely the reverse, they show some of the signs by which we identify consciousness, but these are as if localized in two separate 'minds'. Thus 'we have seen a few indications of emotional feeling generated in the minor hemisphere, like a broad smile following the completion of a test task with the left hand, a smile which the subject was unable to explain verbally. Or the reverse, frowning at an incorrect verbal response or an inept performance by the right hand when only the minor hemisphere knew the correct answer'. Moreover, one of the patients, a modest lady, would blush when a picture of a naked woman was 'seen' by the right hemisphere, though she could not say why she blushed.

There were even signs of a division of the will, especially in the early days after these operations. 'The patient and his wife used to refer to the "sinister left hand" that sometimes tried to push the wife away aggressively at the same time that the hemisphere of the right hand was trying to get her to come and help him with something' (Sperry 1966).

We are forced by these cases to conclude that many of the actions of people that we classify as characteristics of the mind can be divided by the surgeon's knife. It may be that this does no more than emphasize that 'mind' depends on brain, but even fully to establish this is an advance. Probably those without preconceived ideas would agree that these cases emphasize that our language for discussing cerebral activities needs revision.

7. Identification of events in consciousness

We have been looking at the evidence by which we identify consciousness in others. The really intractable problems arise from our attempts to characterize what we call consciousness in ourselves. It may not be irrelevant to notice here the asymmetry. I can ask 'Is he conscious?' but it is nonsense to ask 'Am I conscious?' More specifically, however, I can of course ask 'Am I conscious of any pain in my finger?' Indeed one of the experimental approaches to the problem of consciousness is to study its 'threshold' by providing stimuli of various intensities, i.e. brightness, and duration and asking subjects to record whether they have experienced them. But this does not get us any nearer to understanding the situation that we call being conscious. What we are in search of is a way of talking about the peculiar 'me-ness' of our conscious life, this quality of personal experience, which somehow seems to be of a nature distinct from the events of the material world, even of our bodies. Yet it is a commonplace fact that our experiences are at least often preceded by physical events in our eyes, ears, nose, and other sense organs. Conscious events are continually being evoked by particular external events. Conversely, it is also true that we cannot find the immediate antecedents for much of our conscious life in sensory changes around us but there is good reason to think that the brain itself generates much of it. Electrical stimulation of a particular point in the 'experiential cortex' will arouse a particular complex of events reported as the conscious re-evocation of previously experienced situations, 'experiential response' (p. 489, Penfield and Perot 1963; Libet 1966). What the electrode can do, without any input from the senses, is presumably done daily by whatever consulting system there is that activates particular portions of the memory (see Chapter 42).

The reticular activating system is clearly involved in the phenomenon of consciousness (Moruzzi and Magoun 1949). This is a set of nerve cells and tracts running up and down near the centre of the axis of the nervous system. Suitable electrical stimulations of it will make an animal either wake or sleep. Its functions in arousal are very close to what we might call the initiation or closure of episodes of consciousness. Unfortunately, we know very little of whether or how this arousal system searches the memory, or how similar its actions may be to those of direct cortical stimulation. There are curious differences between the sensitivities of the peripheral and central equipment. Under suitable conditions of electrical stimulation of a small isolated nerve trunk, a human being can indicate correctly the presence of one nerve impulse in a single nerve fibre (Hensel and Boman 1960, McIntyre *et al.* 1967). Yet electrical stimulation of the post-central cortex arouses sensation only after repeated pulses have been applied for 0·5 s or more.

There is further evidence that the arousal of 'conscious' sensation requires a long period. A flash of light of intensity that can only just be seen is made 'invisible' if a second brighter flash follows up to 0·2 s later (see Libet 1966). Yet motor reactions to stimuli can be performed within delays as much as four times shorter than this (0·05 s), even when some element of decision has to be made. Evidently, therefore, arousal of events in consciousness implies some quite elaborate central activities. This would be in agreement with the idea that what is involved is some system of matching of the input with the model in the brain, and that it is this arousing of some part of the activity of our cerebral system that we report as an event peculiarly within ourselves.

8. Sleep

One powerful clue to the nature of the state of consciousness is that we periodically lose it in sleep. Moreover, although we cannot be sure about the consciousness of other animals we can be sure that they sleep, and the growls of a sleeping dog suggest that he dreams.

Yet the definition of the state of sleeping is not easy (see Akert, Bally, and Schadé 1965, Oswald 1962). The eyes are not always closed (e.g. in cattle) or the reflexes absent (in perching birds). We do not require sleep to allow recuperation of the muscles but rather, in some way, of the brain. Yet not all nerve cells can rest; those of the respiratory centre are active from the cradle to the grave. Indeed the state of sleep in the cerebral cortex is certainly not one of rest. The electroencephalogram shows that for much of the time the cells lose alpha rhythm and are synchronized in a slow periodicity (p. 609). In the cat these times of slow-rhythm sleep are interrupted by periods in which there is desynchronization, and some alpha rhythm, with fast (20-30 c/s) low-voltage changes. This so-called paradoxical sleep occupies some 15 per cent of the total time. As the cortical cells are not at rest in sleep it may be that we should look for some special activity that goes on at this time. Evidently the functioning of more complex brain systems requires that they pass some part of every day in these particular states of activity. The fact that the physiologist must admit that he does not know what is happening in these periods, or indeed why we sleep, is another sign of the depth of our ignorance of brain functioning.

Probably both slow-rhythm sleep and paradoxical sleep are important functional states. During paradoxical sleep various signs of activity appear, such as rapid eye-movement, twitching of the body, limbs and whiskers of a cat. There is evidence that this condition is essential for the therapeutic effect of sleep. For if cats are deprived of sleep for some days then the succeeding sleep will consist of up to 60 per cent of paradoxical periods, with movements so violent that they seem almost epileptic.

In man phases of sleep somewhat similar to the paradoxical ones of the cat are accompanied by rapid eye movements (hence R.E.M. phases). These phases are recognized by an EEG of the light sleep type and alpha rhythm appears briefly from time to time. These REM phases are associated with dreaming, whose onset can thus be forecast by watching the EEG. Such dream episodes occur some four to six times every night, but usually nothing is remembered of them on waking. Probably everyone dreams for as much as two hours a night, though he may say that he never dreams.

Not only do we forget our dreams but probably we cannot learn while asleep. If it is arranged that a list of words is played all night but switched off whenever the subject's brain waves show alpha rhythm, then he will show no memory of the words in the morning (Emmons and Simon 1956). Some experimenters have claimed to be able to teach by presenting repetitive auditory material to sleepers. But more critical observation suggests that the occurrence of short waking periods was not excluded as it was by Emmons and Simon (see Oswald 1962).

During the last few decades it has been discovered that arousal can be induced in animals by electrical stimulation of the reticular formation of the brain, and that after bilateral lesions in this system attention and vigilance are reduced (Sprague et al. 1963). There is no single 'sleep centre' but a complete system extending from the caudal part of the medulla to the preoptic region (Fig. 42.2). This reticular activating system depends upon excitation both by impulses from peripheral receptors and by humoral factors. It not only arouses the cortex, but is itself influenced by impulses from the latter. Moreover there are regions in the thalamus and hypothalamus whose stimulation produces the opposite effect, namely sleep. The normal rhythm of sleep and wakefulness is therefore produced by an elaborate system of interaction of nervous and hormonal factors. We are so accustomed to these changes in our state of alertness that perhaps we do not sufficiently consider how strange it is that the 'consciousness' that we like to regard as the very essence of our personality is suspended altogether for a third of our lives, whose continuity is then maintained only by the bodily processes that we are apt to relegate to a lower category of being. And yet the paradox is that there is now evidence that even during sleep the brain is working for much of the time in ways similar to its waking state. Yet only fragments of this activity are recalled as dreams. This suggests that what is suspended during sleep may be the mechanism for recording in the memory. During sleep information that gets through to the brain may be recalled in distorted form. Thus Berger (1963) played a word over and over again during periods of rapid eye movement and found that it could sometimes be identified in the dreams. Thus after 'Robert' a girl reported a dream of a rabbit, which 'looked distorted'. Such data have been considered to show that 'mental life may continue during all stages of sleep' (see Oswald 1965). But such a statement ignores the complications hidden in the words 'mental life'. The phenomena of sleep offer us one of the possible ways of dissecting out this complicated concept and reaching further understanding of our consciousness. The importance of the study of dreams as a means of understanding conscious life has of course been considered since the earliest human cultures. The modern form of such study is an integral part of psychoanalysis (see Freud 1927). It is likely that further knowledge about what goes on during sleep will be an important contribution to our understanding of the models in the brain and how they are used to find the addresses necessary to recall information about past events.

9. The body image

The phenomena of consciousness are somehow concerned with a person's identification of his whole being, his bodily image, and its relation to the outside world. The concept of a bodily image has been explored both by neurologists and psychiatrists. Studies such as those of Schilder (1935) show that what we call our ego or awareness is closely related to bodily events. Consciousness consists in 'trying to see the context of our experiences by comparing those we find in our outer and our inner world'. This may not sound very explicit, but clinicians have long been collecting evidence that there is truly a body image somehow located in the brain and subject to partial damage in cerebral lesions. Thus Head (1920) reports a case where the phantom limb remaining after amputation disappeared following a stroke involving the frontal cortex. There is evidence that the tactile and visual images are separate. The image has the function of relating external events to internal ones centred around the oral, anal, and genital apertures and their receptors. Paul Schilder puts it in this way: the 'I' of the internal sensations is related to the 'thou' of the outside world. He repeatedly emphasizes that the internal and external categories cannot be separated in the sharp manner that is usually assumed in talking about mind and body. 'There is no sense in "ego" where there is no "thou".' Or again, 'Which do we know first, our own body or that of others? Our own body is not really any "nearer" to us than is the rest of the world, as naïve adult introspection at first suggests.'

As a neurologist who was also a psychoanalyst, Schilder was able to develop this theme to show how the personality and its libido develops, as it were, around and with the body image. The individual bases all his actions on an anticipatory plan, which is based on the image. This concept is remarkably similar to that of a model in the brain developed later and independently by Craik (1943) and used throughout this book. The clinical neurologist develops and validates it from the effects of different lesions in subtracting from the normal gamut of human capacity. An aphasic person cannot speak but can write, while the agraphic can speak, but not write. The apractic 'knows what to do but cannot do it'. He can talk about the matchbox, but not light the candle from it. And so on. It is true that we do not understand how the brain produces the capacities in question, and our language of model and image is but a primitive first attempt. But perhaps it is better than none at all. And in some parts of the nervous system we begin to understand a little more. Thus Schilder's interpretation of the limbic system is as 'a mechanism for emotion, compelling selfishness but tempered by forecasting in a social setting'. We can read this as the role of the reward systems in the use of inductive mechanisms for the control of behaviour in the manner to be discussed (Chapters 42 and 44).

As Adrian (1966) says of such work, even though one cannot exactly follow what the author means, 'at least he makes it clear that our ego and our awareness have many features which are related to bodily events. He makes it very difficult to maintain the belief in an impassable gulf between mind and body.'

Once again we see that this problem shows signs of yielding better to further experiment and observation than to studies involving only logical manipulation of accepted facts and their symbols. Investigation of the type that may be called 'scientific' is possible even into the nature of that which investigates.

10. Development of consciousness

One line of investigation that is open to us is to study so far as we are able the growth of awareness in the child. There is abundant evidence that even up to about the age of 7 the child does not make the distinction between itself and the world that is so characteristic of the adult. We shall see something of the study by Piaget of the growth of concepts by which the child learns to operate (Chapter 21). It is relatively late before he has ideas of space, size, and direction that are adequate to describe the relationship of objects in the world to each other and of himself to them. Indeed at first the child is in the stage characterized as 'absolute realism', where it confuses itself with the world. When it comes to use words and names, these are considered, as it were, to be resident in the things they describe.

Clearly all this shows once again that what we call awareness has more to do with communication and indeed with social situations than naïve adult analysis implies. There is a story told by Edmund Gosse that he only began to think of himself as a person when he lied to his father and was not found out. Thus he learned that there was a secret belonging to Edmund Gosse and to someone who lived in the same body with him. 'There were two of us and we could talk together . . . the sense of my individuality now suddenly descended upon me' (Gosse 1907).

11. The growth of the model in the brain

The brain of the new-born child has, presumably, particular capacities for learning certain sorts of things, although it is as yet in the main a blank sheet. Upon it, therefore, will quickly be written the records of those experiences that have been useful to it in continuing its life. Helpless as it is, the child depends utterly on others to meet its needs. The things that it first learns to do, therefore, are to evoke in others responses that satisfy its wants. It learns to recognize the signs of their response, whether positive as smiling, or the reverse. It learns which of the noises and actions that it makes promote its welfare. In short, it learns to communicate. Indeed, it may well be that the structure of its brain is such that it learns the lessons of communication more readily than any others (Chapter 19).

If it be true that learning in brains consists in forming something that could be called a model of the outside world, then the basic model of the child's brain will be of communicating entities—or let us say simply—of people. As it comes later to name things and events around it and to describe their actions, it will do so most readily by considering them all as hypothetical people and their actions. Piaget's studies showed once again that concepts of cause, for example, are considered to be the properties of person-like entities resident within such objects as clouds or waves, and responsible for their actions (p. 285).

The brain of every one of us is framed in this way by the earliest events of upbringing. It is for this reason that even as adults we *all* tend to speak 'anthropomorphically' for much of the time, and the simpler of us do so all the time. It is literally the first way of expression and for many purposes always remains the most direct. But it is not the most exact means of communication. To describe the causes of events in terms of human emotions may be adequately effective for simple description. But when used as a means of changing events it fails. Placation of the supposed spirits within things is a poor tool with which to manipulate the world. The scientific and technical language that has been developed during the last few millenia is also related to human needs, but especially by comparisons with the means of their satisfaction by tools and artefacts. It is through this exact language that we make our fullest mastery of the world around.

But what is the best language for mastery within? This still remains something hidden from us. We can see dimly how we have this model in the brain and that it is a reflection of the image of others around us. Just as the brain is apt naïvely to describe all other things as acting like people, so each of us describes himself as if occupied by another person—me. It is the same 'natural' way for the brain to think. But, using the language of science, we can learn more of the properties of this brain and of its model. We can describe them in what we please to call the objective language of science. But who has made this language but ourselves? And we have made it to help with our own homeostasis. The 'world' as we describe it certainly has a 'reality' outside of ourselves, but how could we ever describe it wholly from without?

12. Is there really a problem of mind and matter?

All these observations about consciousness do not solve the dilemma of mind and matter, but they show that the question is full of complications. It involves the whole problem of the nature and powers of language. This in turn involves us in discussion of the ancestry of man and so of the origin and progress of life (Chapter 26). The problem of mind and matter is not simple but very elusive. If anyone doubts this let them ask precisely what the question is. What sort of 'answer' could there be to it? The psychologist Lashley, at the end of his life, expressed it thus, after considering various views. 'I am not ready to accept these doctrines of scientific despair and Christian hope. The problem requires a thorough analysis of the phenomena of consciousness, oriented with reference to the phenomena of neural activity. . . . The correlation may eventually show a complete identity of the two organisations' (see Penfield 1968). But would this really be an answer?

Observations of the relation of activities of the brain to consciousness have given us much information that is obviously relevant. They suggest that the problem arises because of the particular way that the brain's model of the world grows, is structured, and used as a chief instrument of the life of the individual. In the light of these discoveries it is not evasive of the biologist to hope that with further knowledge of the growth of the model in the brain and its homeostatic actions the 'problem' of the mind will simply disappear. Those whose homeostatic system demands dualist language will continue to find this approach wholly unsatisfactory. They will remain where they are. Let us, however, try to advance by study of growth and differentiation of parts as the basis of survival. In particular, we shall follow the growth and development of man and of the brain during each lifetime. Then a look at the evolutionary history of the brain should provide further data before we finally return to try to synthesize a satisfactory view of man as a whole.

11

GROWTH, TURNOVER, AND THE
RISKS OF DAMAGE

1. Growth as the guarantee of homeostasis in spite of wear

THE tendency to increase in size is, in a sense, the most fundamental feature of living things. We are all familiar with it, and take it for granted as a 'natural' process. Yet even slight study will show that growth is very far from simple and that we do not properly understand it. Moreover, it is very 'unnatural', since it is unusual among physical phenomena. It involves incorporation of less-ordered material into the highly ordered living systems, contrary to the general tendency for increase of entropy. It is indeed worth while to study growth closely, and we may expect to have surprises when we do so.

There are many ambiguities even in attempting to define growth. It has been called 'the net balance of mass produced and retained over mass destroyed and otherwise lost' (Weiss and Kavanau 1957). But is all increase of mass to be called growth? Is addition of storage fat or carbohydrate as much 'growth' as addition of protein? And what about the addition of water? How are we to define the mass of any organism? It fluctuates from moment to moment.

Features other than mass may serve to define growth. Height would be regarded as a good criterion by many children. Increase in cell number is obviously linked in some way with the concept of growth, but individual cells may grow, so the increase of number of cells alone cannot define the process of growing. From this point of view we might distinguish between (a) the addition of material to cells, (b) increase in their number, and (c) increase of intercellular material.

It would be satisfactory to be able to put forward some concept that would unify these various aspects of growth. The differences between them are semantically puzzling but trivial. A true measure of growth might be related to the rate of increase of order that is implied by the incorporation of non-living into living matter. The increase of DNA in a population might serve as the basis for an assessment of the degree of order, which would evade these difficulties about fat, water, etc. This statistic (amount of DNA) is indeed very useful for some purposes, but we may also have to be content to measure growth by whichever of the parameters discussed above is most readily available to us. If a general phrase is wanted we can perhaps say that growth is 'the addition of material to that which is already organized into a living pattern' (Young 1950).

We shall be concerned here not so much with definitions or even with finding quantitative expressions for growth (though this will follow). It is more important to try to see the relation of growth to the processes of self-maintenance. In fact we begin by asking why should there be growth in order to ensure homeostasis? This may seem a very large question. And indeed so it is, for it touches the very nature of living organization. A system of steady-state interchange is able to continue only because it is provided with 'instructions' that ensure correct responses in the situations that are likely to arise. To put it in another way, an organism can continue to live only because it has been provided with the necessary organs. The instructions thus constitute a system for forecasting the situations and risks that the creature is likely to meet. But by the very nature of the randomness of events, something will happen sooner or later that destroys part of, and eventually the whole, organism. Continued survival in a steady state by any one given set of materials is therefore impossible. Survival of the organization can, however, be ensured by a suitably arranged system of replacement. This is, therefore, the 'function' of growth. It operates at a whole series of levels, from the continuous replacement by turnover within cells, to continuous replacement of cells, to replacement of whole individuals by others, in the processes we ordinarily call reproduction, and in the replacement of one species by another in evolution. All these are a single series of phenomena by which the power of replication and of incorporation into the living system serves to ensure the maintenance of life.

2. Exponential growth

One of the most unexpected findings for the layman is that growth, if it is not restricted, continues without limit. What grows is itself capable of growing. This is well illustrated by bacteria. When bacterial cells are isolated in a culture medium there is first a lag period and then exponential growth begins (Fig. 11.1). Each bacterium divides about once every 30 to 40 minutes and the products then 'grow' until they reach the size of the original. This process continues until the supply of nutrients is exhausted, after which special conditions set in, which do not interest us here. If the culture medium is renewed, growth continues indefinitely. Use is made of this for continuous cultivation methods. If all the growing organisms were to be supplied with the required nutrients there would have to be an exponential increase of the size of the vessel and the amount of inflow. This

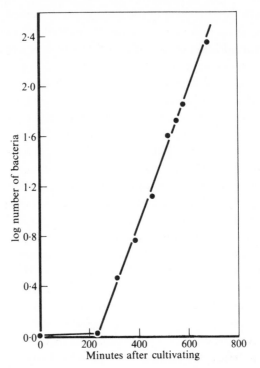

FIG. 11.1. Growth of bacterial cells in culture after explantation. (After Dean and Hinshelwood 1966.)

is obviously not possible, but if part of the volume of multiplied micro-organisms is withdrawn at the same rate as nutrient medium is supplied, then a steady state can be maintained in which all the materials are utilized (see Málek and Fencl 1966).

More penetrating observations have shown that we must think more carefully about continuous growth. Does each individual grow at an in-creasing rate per unit of mass, as would be required if what grows is capable of growing? Mitchison studied the growth of single cells of yeast, using interference microscopy to determine the 'dry weight' of single cells con-tinuously. He kept the yeast in a sterile medium so that there was no ques-tion of interference by the growth processes of other organisms. Each yeast cell grew at a constant rate independent of mass, until late in the process of division, which occurred every four hours, and then the rate doubled and remained the same throughout the next generation (Mitchison 1957). The rate of synthesis therefore depends upon a group of components, perhaps the ribosomes, which may double their numbers before cell division.

The whole process of division must obviously be related to the replication of DNA and this, in many organisms, occurs at about the middle of the period between divisions. The determination of the DNA cycle probably depends upon a complex relation between the replicating material and the associated polymerase enzymes, but the system is not fully understood.

The whole question of the basic cycles that regulate cell division is still obscure. The cell does not divide because it has reached a certain size. By various means the growth can be stopped prematurely, but division will take place, though delayed. Addition of material is therefore one factor influencing division, but not the only one. Probably replication of the DNA is a second, and perhaps cycles of the RNA and ribosomes a third. A fourth may be a rhythmic change in the energy-yielding mechanisms and other enzymatic processes of the cell, perhaps related to the cycle of reducing sulphur-containing compounds (e.g. glutathione).

In examining the fundamental process of control of increase we find, therefore, many facts that are interesting and sometimes paradoxical, but difficult to reduce to any single system of control. Life may perhaps once have been simple, but today even the lower organisms maintain their balance through a web of interacting control mechanisms.

We have, however, the important conclusion that the general condition is to continue growth indefinitely, at least in these simple organisms. The situation with which we as humans are familiar, namely, decline and cessation of growth, followed later by death, thus appears as a limitation of the general condition. Our thesis will revolve around the concept that our life cycle indeed includes special sets of limitations upon continuous growth, serving to ensure that the population as a whole can continue to survive by means of a particular way of life.

3. Differentiation and growth control

Perhaps it should not surprise us to find that continuous growth is the general condition. Since continuous replacement is the absolutely necessary condition of self-maintenance we should expect to find it everywhere in living processes. The growth must of course be regulated, especially in the higher organisms, where survival depends upon the presence of a most complicated system of tissues, differentiated for particular functions. Differentiation is in this sense the inverse of growth; indeed, it often follows growth. We shall expect to find, then, that the study of growth consists largely in the study of the control and limitation of growth, especially in the higher organisms.

4. Intermittent growth

When we look more closely, it thus appears that even in bacteria growth is not continuous. Addition to the mass of a whole culture masks the cycles in the growth of each individual. Replication of the DNA occurs at set intervals, and something is known of the means for regulating this (see Mandelstam and McQuillen 1968). In the absence of limitation by lack of raw materials, it seems that the single strand of DNA in each bacterium is replicated by the attendant polymerases at intervals that are not closely related to the total increase in mass. The factor that regulates this cycle thus serves to control the whole growth potential of the species. Presumably, however, this cycle is itself genetically controlled.

This question of the power of increase of a set of cells comes very close to the heart of all biological problems. Unfortunately, we have only a glimpse of it in bacteria and viruses and know almost nothing of it in higher animals and plants. It is difficult to conceive of the process of growth as a wholly continuous phenomenon, for the simple reason that organisms themselves are essentially heterogeneous. We can think about the continuous synthesis, say, of a given protein. But the more interesting proteins do not simply accumulate, they associate with other substances to form membranes, organelles, fibres, and so on. When any one of these has been formed the continuity is in a sense broken as the building of another organelle is begun.

The point is not trivial, for organisms are assemblies of such units. Higher organisms are assemblies of assemblies of them (cells, tissues, colonies, populations). Since the components of such systems do not increase together and continuously we have to think of them separately and individually. The origin and fate of each mitochondrion or man is therefore inevitably a large part of the study of biology. Investigation of the cycles of their multiplication and growth may reveal some general principles, but is also likely to show that there is a *great diversity of rules of growth*.

5. Turnover and growth

A further complication is that addition to living systems is not a one-way traffic. We must also include the subtraction that is involved in breakdown, and then compute the growth as the net gain. It seems so obvious that growth is the resultant of anabolism and catabolism that we do not pause to ask 'Why should there be breakdown at all?' More practically, we may seek an answer by looking at lower organisms to see whether turnover is always present. Perhaps it is a necessary feature for the maintenance of a steady state.

Viruses cannot be said to show turnover, but they are not capable of independent self-maintenance. In bacteria there is turnover, but at a simple level that can hardly be distinguished from reproduction.

In the more familiar situation of multicellular organisms, it has been clear since the time of Bizzozero (1894) that some parts of the body become changed much faster than others (Chapter 5). Whether we are considering cells alone or their components (fibres, organelles, etc.) it is convenient to think of three types.

1. Labile populations, multiplying throughout life (vegetative intermitotic cells of Cowdry (1952)).
2. Stable populations, usually multiplying only during development, but capable of doing so in the adult after damage (reversible postmitotics).
3. Permanent populations, never multiplying once formed (fixed postmitotics).

As applied to cell populations in mammals this would produce the following classification.

Labile (renewing) populations

Epidermis and its derivatives
Endodermal epithelium
Transitional epithelium of ducts
Blood-forming tissues (in part)
Endometrium of uterus
Germ cells of the testis

Stable populations (able to expand when necessary)

Liver
Kidney
Exocrine glands
Lens
Connective tissues
Skeletal tissues (in part)

Permanent populations

Striated muscle
Neurons
Germ cells of the ovary

6. Turnover and the anticipation of risks

In spite of our considerable understanding of the functions of the various tissues in the economy of the body it is not always clear why some tissues should remain intact and others be regularly replaced. Moreover, little is known about the important question of what determines the rate of production of the labile tissues or stops the stable ones from further expansion.

The products of the epidermal line are ultimately keratinized. Thus removed from metabolic sustenance, they are subject to the cruder forms of wear and must be replaced. This simple situation may serve as an example of the principles that we may search for. The body as a self-maintaining system inevitably suffers the physical hazards imposed by a more or less tempestuous environment. Some of these risks are of simple physical nature (like the wearing away of the skin), others are chemical changes or fluctuations of temperature. No portion of the body can be regarded as permanently immune from risks. However strong the bones, in some individuals one or another of them will ultimately be broken. To make them still stronger would involve not only collecting much material but, worse, carrying it around. The tortoise provides himself with a house of inert material that is hard to break. Within it he lives longer than, perhaps, any other creature, but tortoises are not among the most widespread animals and have not been able to colonize many habitats, for example the trees or the air. Such massive over-insurance has not proved to be the ideal policy for life.

In general, the best protection seems to be provided, not by excessively strong or inert materials, but by a system of turnover that allows for replacement. Cell replacement may proceed continuously, as in the skin, or be called into play when needed, as in the repair processes of the connective tissues or skeleton.

In this sense the continuous change of the renewing populations is an aspect of homeostasis. It provides a permanent insurance against the inevitable damage to the components that is imposed by the environment. That this is likely to be an efficient policy is clear, for example, in the skin, whose material is directly subject to wear. It is also easy to understand for the lining of the alimentary canal, which must deal with all the chemical influences that are introduced with the food, including the products of the bacteria that thrive there. In other tissues it is less clear why continuous cell-replacement is needed. There is no obvious need for rapid renewal of the red corpuscles of the blood. Possibly the limiting factor here is the energy needed to pump them round the body. It is cheaper to pump sacks of almost pure haemoglobin then to destroy them after a while, and replace them from a factory, than to pump also the instructions, machinery, and materials for their renewal. Incidentally, birds find the latter course better. Their red cells, though they are still end cells, have nuclei, and this enables them to manage with a small factory and so to lighten their bones with air sacks, while haemopoiesis on a much reduced scale proceeds in the liver, spleen, and elsewhere.

Cell replacement is obviously not the only possible means of renewal. In some tissues replacement is probably undesirable for functional reasons. Thus the activities of the nervous system depend upon an elaborate system of connectivity between the cells. To renew this would need complicated instructions and in fact regeneration can be achieved only in simpler animals and simpler parts of the nervous system. No effective regeneration takes place in the brains of mammals (or of cephalopods). Where the brains contain memories, capable of holding records of the experiences of the individual, it may obviously be difficult to provide also instructions to replicate these records if cells are destroyed. Correspondingly the neurons lose all power of cell division. They do not, however, lose their powers of synthesis. On the contrary, protein turnover is especially active in the nervous system. Nerve cells are characterized by a large amount of ribonucleic acid in their cytoplasm—the basophilic Nissl bodies. Probably there is a continuous flow of material down the nerve fibres from the cell bodies (see Ochs 1966). What happens to it at the peripheral end is uncertain (Chapter 13).

It is clear, therefore, that these static 'post-mitotic' cells are not really different from the rest. Indeed it may be that they are provided with especially active mechanisms for self-renewal. For, unlike the other populations, they cannot be replaced if damaged, and must therefore continuously repair themselves. This presumably applies to striated muscle as well as to nerve. The very large number of nuclei in each syncytial muscle fibre suggest the operation of continuous processes of replacement (though myosin itself turns over little if at all).

It becomes clear, therefore, that the phenomenon of growth, that is to say, synthesis of new material, is much more than the production of a new individual, as we commonly regard it. Growth is one of the fundamental features of homeostasis; growth provides the means of replacement of what will inevitably sooner or later be damaged—a guarantee, so far as possible, against the risks of destruction. The growth with which we are familiar, that of the child, after the act of reproduction, we shall find to be the special form of this guarantee, since it allows survival *in face of almost all risks*, a promise for the future that would seem impossible to give, but which has so far served to ensure life for 3000 million years or more.

For the purpose of a general study of growth, then, our conclusion is that addition to the existing mass of living material is a fundamental property, presumably existing since life began (Chapter 26). The numerous special forms of life that exist today have been arrived at partly by limiting this general power of growth. Thus all the higher organisms are colonies of different types of cells, serving different functions in the homeostatic system. The number and position of each type is regulated to produce a smoothly working whole. The study of growth thus becomes, in effect, the study of what limits growth in each tissue, during development and in the adult.

12

REPAIR OF THE INDIVIDUAL

1. Maintenance, repair, replacement, and regeneration

THESE are a series of similar processes, linked both in their significance for continued maintenance and through the methods by which they operate. All are processes by which the individual life is enabled to persist in spite of actual wear or damage. As we have seen in the last chapter, in most tissues there is continual turnover and in some the cells are regularly replaced. These maintenance operations anticipate the damage or destruction of the parts in question, and they are found particularly in such vulnerable areas as the outer skin and lining of the gut.

Other parts of the body, though liable to damage, may suffer it only 'accidentally', that is, occasionally or not at all. For these the genetic system provides processes of healing, repair and replacement that are set into action only when called for as a result of trauma. 'Regeneration' is usually kept as the name of a similar process but on a larger scale, leading to the production of a whole new part such as a limb.

These powers are therefore, as it were, a second line of defence when the forecasting mechanisms that avoid damage have failed. For example, the mechanisms of heredity and development provide a mammal with bones of strength adequate to meet most of the stresses likely to fall upon them. If greater stresses are met and a bone breaks, then a specific mechanism of regeneration is available to mend it.

All these processes involve growth, and are linked with the daily turnover within the tissues. They also involve cell migration and differentiation, and in this are linked with normal development from the egg. All of these repair operations that we usually separate conceptually for convenience under the headings given above form a series running from those more closely related to turnover to those that partake more nearly of reproduction and development. Each uses specific mechanisms to contribute to the homeostasis of the system. In this sense all are 'normal' processes. They differ in the regularity and timing of the wear or accidental events that they are designed to correct. Processes of 'maintenance' are designed to meet the damage that occurs in certain tissues regularly every day, for example in the skin of man, or the incisor teeth of a rodent. 'Repair', 'replacement', and 'regeneration' are processes that come into operation only intermittently, when the organism has suffered one of the various hazards that are likely to befall it. In this sense they approach nearer to the mechanism of reproduction, which is the act that initiates the replacement of the whole creature before eventually something happens by which it is destroyed.

The earlier categories, maintenance and repair, are thus more directly concerned with minor, recurrent, and temporary damages; the last two, especially regeneration, constitute major acts of differentiation, approaching reproduction. Indeed, in some organisms it is hard to distinguish between regeneration and reproduction by budding (e.g. sea squirts (tunicates) or tapeworms).

Since the processes of repair, replacement, and regeneration are characteristically brought into operation after accidents or unusual events in the life cycle, they are obviously of particular concern for the medical man. He is, for many people, the specialist who is called in to help with the results of such untoward stresses, rather than the guardian of longer-term homeostasis (though he may well play a great part in this too, and will perhaps do so even more in the future). In order to be able to assist the repair processes of the body effectively, the doctor must obviously know about their means of operation. It is to some extent the function of pathology to provide this understanding. Here, however, we meet with the complication that, as a prelude to the study of repair, the pathologist also investigates the processes of damage themselves, especially as inflicted by invasive agents such as bacteria and viruses. We shall not attempt to study pathological conditions here but shall try to investigate the nature of the healing processes as exemplified in a few examples in which they have been set into action by controlled surgical experiment. Elementary principles can be illustrated in this way, but while the reactions to particular pathogens are alike in the early stages, later the picture may change specifically for each disease condition.

2. Maintenance

Of the four categories that we are considering this approaches most closely to the normal turnover processes. The concept of maintenance, as borrowed from engineering and household management, implies the repair of wear and tear that is normal in the sense perhaps of 'expected'. We have to paint our houses and renew electric light bulbs or motor-car tyres or brake-linings, because the designers of these items were not able to make them more permanent. A similar distinction can be made for the body, though it is not perhaps altogether appropriate. The body has no permanent components (unless it be the instructions in the DNA), but it has some parts that turn over very little (e.g. the collagen of tendons, acto-myosin of muscles, or antibodies), while others turn over so efficiently that we do not ordinarily think of them as suffering wear (e.g. the continual replacement of red cells or intestinal epithelia). Perhaps, however, this is indeed a wrong attitude and we should recognize that it is exactly because of the inevitable molecular wear and degradation that the turnover of these tissues is so active. In addition, of course, it allows the continual adjustment of the level of their functioning by adaptation (Chapter 8).

The conceptions of maintenance and repair should be extended for living organisms to the molecular level. Some enzyme molecules persist only for a few minutes (Haldane 1954). It is not clear in what sense this is due to wear, but in muscle there is an increased turnover after activity.

The replacement of the surface of the skin or nails from deeper layers is more obviously an act of maintenance. We find it easy to conceptualize this process because we can literally *see* it at work on our own bodies. There is no reason to doubt that with sufficient insight we should equally recognize that the replacement of our red corpuscles and all the other replacing tissues shows the operation of specific mechanisms under the control of the DNA, ensuring maintenance of the integrity of the system in spite of wear.

As a steady-state open system, the organism is continually subject to stresses resulting from the tendency to merge with its surroundings. These knocks provide the stimuli for the operation of the synthetic growth pro-cesses, which are made possible by the replicative powers of the instruc-tional molecules within. Each tissue is thus maintained at the appropriate level of functioning by a *double dependence*, on stresses from without and synthetic forces from within (Young 1946). The problem for the student of growth is to learn to identify and measure these forces so that he can estimate the probability of successful continuance and show how to in-crease it by appropriate action. To take a simple example, in managing the healing of bone the physician needs to know how the effect of mechanical stress will influence the process at each stage (specifically, when and how much to let the patient with a broken leg walk). On the other hand, he needs to know whether the bone-growth potential needs the assistance of par-ticular dietary factors; say, vitamin C (for collagen), vitamin D, or extra calcium. It would also, of course, be of great importance to know of any specific agents that stimulate or retard healing, a question to which we shall return.

3. Nerve repair as an example of healing

Healing, repair, replacement, and regeneration are so closely related that there is no sense in trying to distinguish sharply between them. All are distinguished from maintenance in that they are processes initiated by the occurrence of some incident that is likely to happen but does not recur regularly. The instructions of the organism nevertheless contain provisions to meet such accidents, the occurrence of which is in this sense predicted and expected, although arhythmic. We may use the names as headings under which to describe the repair of damage of increasing severity, by operations ranging from simple clotting of the blood to replacement of a whole limb.

Healing has many meanings, but refers especially to such processes as the closure of wounds in the skin or of other organs, where the damage is due not so much to the loss of substance, which may be minimal, as to the interruption of the continuity of the tissues. The effect of severing a nerve provides an interesting example. The physical break in the nerve trunk damages simply when it interrupts, not because of loss of tissue, but because the contained nerve fibres are dependent for their trophic maintenance on continuity with the nerve-cell body. After severance, therefore, only the central part remains alive. The peripheral axons undergo degeneration and if the two stumps are close together the old axons are then replaced by outgrowth from the central end. We can therefore regard the activities that reunite the stumps as an example of healing and the function of the new fibres as replacement or regeneration (Fig. 12.3).

After any wound (in a mammal) the repair can be considered to proceed in three phases (Ross 1968): (1) inflammatory, the first-aid operations of closure and removal of debris; (2) proliferative, the advent of fibroblasts, able to lay down new structural materials, and perhaps of specific types of cell; (3) remodelling, such as the maturation of scar tissue or, in nerve repair, the growth to maturity of some nerve fibres and the atrophy and disappearance of others.

The first aid is provided by clotting of the blood (*The life of mammals*, Chapter 13). This is produced by a special set of enzymes and other proteins provided for the purpose. The inactive enzyme prothrombin of the blood is activated by an enzyme thrombokinase, liberated by the damaged tissue, which, in the presence of calcium, converts prothrombin to the active enzyme thrombin. The latter then turns the protein fibrinogen, circulating in the plasma, into threads of fibrin. These help to close the openings of the vessels, stopping the loss of blood. Contraction of the vessels themselves assists this. The fibrin clot serves also immediately to meet the first need of repair, which is to fill up the space left by the wound. But the clot is not itself strong enough to resist any great compression or tension and must be replaced by stronger tissues. Almost at once, therefore, it becomes infiltrated by white blood corpuscles. The first are small microphages (polymorphs), able to remove debris and infective agents; later, larger macrophages move in. Together these cells remove the fibrin clot, probably by fibrinolytic enzymes, made available by breakdown of the neutrophil white blood corpuscles and release of their lysosomes. These enzymes work differentially on the fibrin molecules, attacking first those that are not under tension. The clot thus comes to present orientated strands. Along these migrate the fibroblasts, which then proceed to produce collagen to unite the severed surfaces more firmly.

When a nerve trunk has been cleanly severed, without other damage, the process of healing varies according to whether the two severed ends remain close together. Let us assume that they do so, or that, having been separated, they have been sewn together by a surgeon. Such clean interruptions may occur when a nerve is cut by glass, say in the wrist when a hand is pushed through a window. There may often be complications from damage to tendons, and nerves may be equally or more seriously damaged by being pulled, as when a humerus is broken and the radial nerve is bruised by contusion. However, if the severed ends of the nerve are together, a blood clot forms between them. After three or four days the fibrin will be dissolving away and fibroblasts will move in from both the central and distal stumps. Peripheral nerve normally contains much connective tissue, and the fibroblasts presumably come from this, though what activates them will have to be discussed below (Figs. 12.3 and 12.4).

The fibroblasts, moving along the strands of fibrin, soon begin to lay down their characteristic protein, collagen, and mucopolysaccharides. If the two joined ends of the nerve are under light tension, then the new collagen fibres will run longitudinally between the ends, in the direction that is most calculated to join them firmly. It is probably desirable, therefore, that nerve stumps should be left under slight tension, rather than pressed together, which would produce a scar of collagen fibres not all orientated along the line of the nerve. A similar argument applies even more strongly to the union of the severed ends of a tendon.

The strands of fibrin and new strands of collagen serve a further function besides this resistance to stretch. They also guide the course of the outgrowing nerve fibres, or rather of the satellite Schwann cells, which precede the latter. Vertebrate nerve fibres are surrounded by these Schwann cells, which in some make an insulating myelin sheath (Fig. 12.1) that greatly increases the speed of nervous conduction. Even those peripheral nerve fibres that have no myelin all have some form of Schwann cell. In regeneration

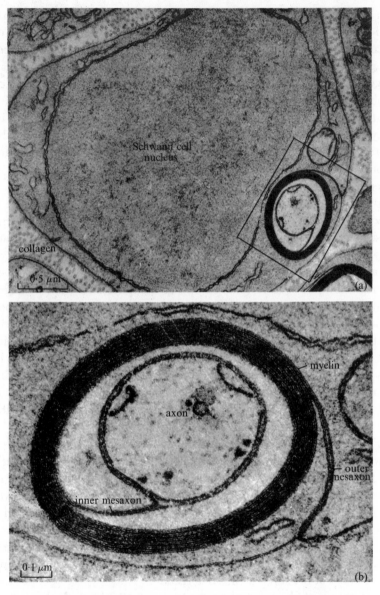

FIG. 12.1. Electron micrographs to show the Schwann cell nucleus (a) and the myelin sheath around the axon (b). (J. D. Robertson in D. Fawcett 1966.)

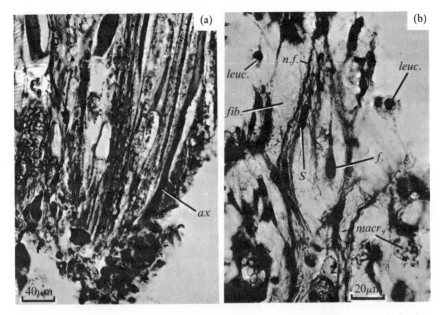

FIG. 12.2. (a) Material emerging at the central end of an axon (*ax.*) of a rabbit's nerve severed 2 days previously. (b) Portion of the tissue between the two ends of a nerve severed 5 days previously. The central end is above. From it there proceeds a nerve fibre (*n.f.*) which has attached itself to the surface of a column of Schwann cells (*S*) that have emerged from the peripheral stump (below). The tissue contains the remains of the fibrin clot (*fib.*) and several types of cell including white corpuscles (*leuc.*) and fibroblasts (*f*). Large phagocytic cells (macrophages) are seen in the peripheral stump (*macr.*).

these satellites have a special function. They cease to be ensheathing cells and move out into the site of the wound by active amoeboid movement (Fig. 12.2). They creep along the threads of fibrin and collagen, forming a web of nucleated tissue between the two stumps. They emerge mainly (perhaps wholly) from the lower (distal) stump, where they are released from their ensheathing function by the gradual breakdown and dissolution of the axons, which have been separated from their cell bodies and are therefore degenerating (Fig. 12.3). A piece of protoplasm separated from its nucleus sooner or later dies. Nerve fibres, being very elongated, are especially vulnerable to this hazard. The nuclei of the nerve fibres that run to the toes are in the spinal cord and must therefore sustain the protoplasm of threads about a metre long, but only 10 μm in diameter. It is not known what influence passes along to do this, but there is evidence of an actual transport of material down the fibre.

Therefore, 2–3 days after a nerve fibre in a mammal has been interrupted, the isolated part breaks up, first at a few widely separated points and then into a string of ovoids and ultimately spheres. The process is not complete for many days; indeed, some pieces of axon remain for several weeks (or longer in a cold-blooded animal).

Meanwhile the Schwann cells of the peripheral stump divide mitotically, forming strands within the tubes of the supporting tissues of the distal stump (Fig. 12.3). The strands emerge from the cut end and grow up to join the central stump. Here they may make contact with the severed central ends of the nerve fibres. These have formed swollen amoeboid tips, putting out 'feelers' into the tissues between the stumps (Fig. 12.4). When one such feeler touches a strand of Schwann cells it makes some specific form of union and the tip moves away down into the distal stump, spinning a fine thread, the new axon, behind it. We shall discuss its further course later on as an example of regeneration.

4. The nerve-growth factor

Some information is available about chemical factors that stimulate the growth of nerve fibres in the embryo, and these may be related to those of the adult. If tumour cells of mice are implanted in place of the limb bud of a 3-day-old chick the nerve fibres of the latter wander around among the cancer cells. The sensory or sympathetic cells from which the fibres originate are stimulated to increase in number several times so that their nerve fibres invade all the tissues of the host embryo. They even enter the blood-vessels in such numbers as to interrupt the circulation (Levi-Montalcini 1964, Levi-Montalcini and Angeletti 1968). In the search for the chemical nature of the 'nerve growth factor' (NGF) responsible for the increase it was found that snake venom has a great power to produce the phenomenon, and that an even more potent source of NGF is the salivary glands of a male mouse. The substances are both proteins but not identical. That from snake venom has a molecular weight of about 40 000 (Vernon *et al.* 1969). The effect of the factor isolated from the male mouse salivary glands and injected into young mice is to produce a specific hypertrophy only of the sympathetic system. All the rest of the nervous system remains unaffected, even the parasympathetic ganglia.

A further development was the preparation of an antiserum that *suppressed* growth of the sympathetic cells. The purified NGF protein was injected into the foot-pad of a rabbit. Serum from the rabbit injected into new-born mice then caused the latter to develop with as little as 3 per cent of their normal quota of sympathetic cells, the growth of the rest being suppressed by the antibodies.

We cannot yet relate these findings to the processes of normal growth and development of nerve, but they provide further valuable evidence of the existence of specific chemical factors able to stimulate or suppress the growth

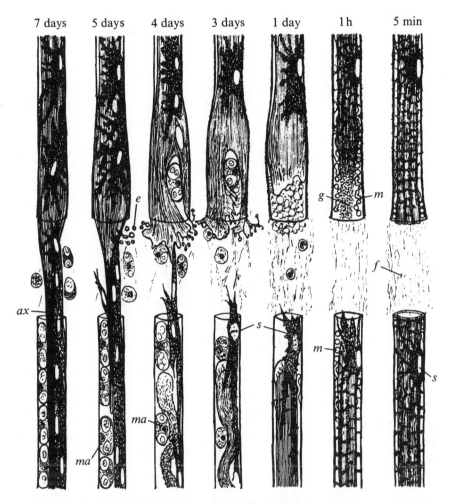

7 days   5 days   4 days   3 days   1 day   1 h   5 min

FIG. 12.3. Diagram of changes following severance and suture of a nerve in the rabbit, the stumps being joined by a fibrin clot (*f*). During the first hour after severance the myelin breaks into droplets (*m*) for a short distance in both stumps, and the axon also breaks into granules (*g*). The Schwann cells of the peripheral stump (*s*) begin to form migratory fibrous structures, and this process continues, with division of the nuclei, forming columns of cells growing out into the scar. Meanwhile, the axons and myelin of the distal stump break up and the tubes are invaded by macrophages (*ma*). The central stump axon swells, and the material pours from the end of the tube until some of it makes contact with the Schwann cell columns and is led back as a new axon (*ax*) into the peripheral stump. Unconnected portions break off to form spheres and loops (*e*). The Schwann cells of the central stump first draw in their processes and then advance again over the outflowing axoplasm. The migratory Schwann cells of the peripheral stump also put out processes over the surfaces of the new fibre. (From Young 1949.)

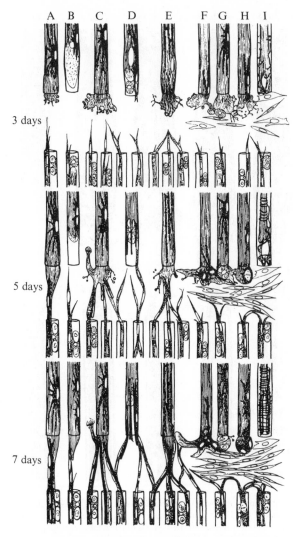

FIG. 12.4. Diagram of several nerve stumps of the rabbit on the third, fifth, and seventh days after union, to show some of the variations that occur. A, a direct union, as Fig. 12.3. B, some retrograde degeneration in the central stump. C, the axoplasm divides into various streams in the scar and these make union with several distal tubes. The same result is achieved in D by branching within the central tube, and in E by branching at entrance to the distal stump. All these unions are satisfactory, but in those shown in F–I there is a lateral invasion of fibrocytes, preventing union of the stump, with resultant formation of giant clubs (H), or spirals (I).
(From Young 1949.)

of particular types of nervous tissue. With further knowledge of such factors it should eventually be possible to understand how the nervous system becomes provided with the many types of channel that constitute the essential feature of its system of coding and signalling.

5. The processes of healing

The union of two nerve stumps provides a typical example of the basic processes of wound healing. We might list the following as the components.

1. Quickly filling the defect, achieved by the fibrin clot—as it were, a provisional emergency repair.
2. Next, filling the defect with cells, first polymorphs, then macrophages, fibroblasts, and Schwann cells, and finally the characteristic cells of the tissue, nerve fibres.
3. Giving physical strength to the new tissue by collagen, making good the mechanical damage.
4. Repairing also the vascular defect, by ingrowth of new vessels.
5. Finally, repairing the actual functional defect, in this case by maturation of the nerve fibres to make effective lines of nerve conduction (p. 167).

It is obvious that many specific growth processes are concerned. A few of them are simple enough for us to be able to see the reactions in some detail. Thus, the clotting of the fibrinogen and formation of the new collagen are the results of change or synthesis of relatively simple proteins. It is much harder to understand how the orderly sequence of so many processes is achieved. In particular, we should like to know what activates the cells to divide and to migrate after wounding and what stops them when their aim has been achieved.

6. Theories of wound healing

The various theories of the stimulus to wound healing offer different levels of explanation.

1. The simplest is that there are wound hormones produced by the damage to the cells. There are two versions of this,
   (a) that the substances stimulate the cells to divide and migrate,
   (b) that they remove an inhibition on these activities.
2. A second group of theories suggests that as the repair process serves to fill up the defect left by the injury, it is this deficiency or lack that somehow sets in motion the actions of repair.
3. The third theory is that it is the functional lack that is sensed by a suitable system and thus initiates repair.

The second and third approaches seem at first sight much vaguer than the first, but may have more value than appears. In particular, we have to study not only what initiates repair but also what ends it at the correct point. The fact that the defect has been filled or the function restored may provide the relevant information that stops the tissue growing.

It is unfortunately true that at present we do not know what initiates or controls repair mechanisms. This is indeed a great weakness, but biological and medical science are faced here with a fundamental difficulty of method. One cannot distinguish between theories of the three types outlined above because one cannot produce a loss of tissue without producing traumatized cells. Conversely, one cannot do damage without causing some form of deficit (see Abercrombie 1964).

In plants it has been established that injured cells release a substance, traumatic acid $(HOOC(CH_2)_8CH{=}COOH)$, which stimulates cell division near by. No similar relatively simple wound hormones have been identified in animals. Indeed, the whole question of growth-promoting substances is highly complicated. From the earliest days of tissue culture it was found that growth is stimulated by extracts, especially by extracts of embryos, but also of other tissues. But such extracts are very complex mixtures and it is still not clear to what extent their effects are due to the nutrients they supply or to specific growth stimulants. There is, however, a considerable body of scattered evidence that the growth of each tissue can be stimulated or inhibited by specific substances produced within that tissue. Examples of these substances are the epidermal growth factor in the skin (p. 161), nerve growth factor (p. 156), and erythropoietin (p. 111), which stimulates the bone marrow. Extracts of various adult and embryonic tissues have been shown to stimulate growth in tissue culture under carefully controlled conditions (Kutsky 1959, Abercrombie 1964). The stimulating power is associated with protein.

7. Wound-healing in the skin

Repair of damage to the surface has perhaps a special human interest since we all observe it so often in ourselves (see Schilling 1968). Moreover, its superficial position makes the skin especially easy to study. After damage to the epidermis and underlying dermis there is first the formation of a fibrin clot and then its dissolution after a few days. Cells of the neighbouring epidermis are stimulated to division. They are normally, of course, in a cycle of continuous division, and presumably the mechanism for ensuring the increase is related to this. After 12 to 24 hours the cells move in such a way as to cover the damaged area (Odland and Ross 1968). Meanwhile the cells of the underlying dermis also proliferate, and polymorphs, macrophages, and fibroblasts proceed to operate as in the nerve regeneration already mentioned.

The response of the epidermis is especially interesting. In a small wound its cells continue to proliferate and to migrate until they form a complete covering. The migration is apparently triggered by the absence of contact between the cells and stops when the space is filled by contact inhibition which stops the fibroblasts. The cells then proceed to contract, drawing the separated edges of the wound together (James 1964). This process of wound contraction is distinguished from the 'wound contracture' by which collagen fibres may draw together the edges, at a much later stage, in a large, poorly healing wound leaving a bad scar.

The mechanism of skin-healing thus shows all the factors we have seen before: filling the space, adding new cells, and restoration of function. Here, however, there is some information about the stimulating factors. The stimulus to cell division is specific to the cells that are damaged. If a flap of mouse skin is cut beneath the dermis, then the overlying epidermis shows no increase in mitosis (Bullough and Laurence 1960). Conversely, damage to the epidermis causes mitosis only there and not in the dermis.

There is some evidence that the stimulation is produced by an extractable *epidermal growth factor*. Extracts of epidermis have been reported to increase the rate of epidermal wound healing when applied either locally or by intraperitoneal injection. Particularly convincing evidence has been obtained in the bug *Rhodnius*. A small skin wound is surrounded by a zone of mitotic cells and this area is increased by the application of an autolysed epidermal cell extract (Wigglesworth 1937). However, the effect is not specific and is produced by a variety of degraded protein extracts. It may be due simply to damage of the cells of the recipient by the extract. So we have again the same problem that the healing response appears only when tissues have been removed.

A somewhat similar phenomenon is found in mouse skin. After an epidermal wound the hair follicles at some distance away show mitotic stimulation (Argyris and Argyris 1959). This again suggests a chemical effect, but brings up the question of whether this is the production of a stimulant ('promotor', Abercrombie (1964)) or the depletion of an inhibitor ('depressor') due to loss of tissue. The theory that removal of depressors is involved has many attractions, since it explains the otherwise puzzling phenomenon that the tissues respond to a *loss* in their neighbourhood, and also suggests the negative feedback by which growth is stopped as the defect is repaired.

Evidence that the stimulus is in fact removal of an inhibition has been obtained by Bullough and Laurence (1960). They found that mitosis

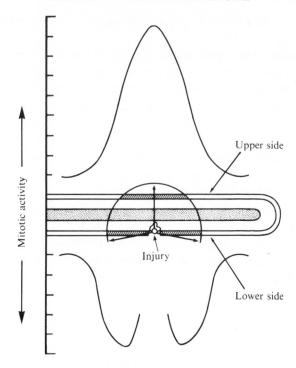

FIG. 12.5. The relation of epidermal hyperplasia to a wound.
An injury inflicted on one side of a mouse ear causes proliferation
in adjacent epidermis as well as in that on the opposite side of
the ear, within a radius of 1 mm. The patterns of mitotic activity
are therefore bimodal and unimodal respectively. (After Bullough
and Laurence 1960.)

extends for about 1 mm around a small wound and will occur even on the
opposite side of the thin ear of a mouse (Fig. 12.5). But the response of,
say, the upper side of the ear occurs only if the epidermis of the under side
is *completely* removed. It is not, therefore, a reaction to damaged epidermal
cells but to removal of some influence previously inhibiting mitosis.

The concept is that the cells are prevented from mitosis by the inhibitory
action of substances they themselves produce ('chalones'). Further support has come from the study of wounds of the lens epithelium of the rabbit.
Twelve hours after wounding, cells in the neighbourhood of the injury
begin to synthesize DNA (as shown with tritiated thymidine). Shortly
afterwards they divide. The region of DNA activation and division then
spreads peripherally away from the wound (Fig. 12.6). The explanation
seems to be that after injury cells migrate into the wound. This depletes
the neighbouring zone, reducing the concentration of inhibitor and setting
in motion the procedure of DNA replication (p. 50). Meanwhile cells

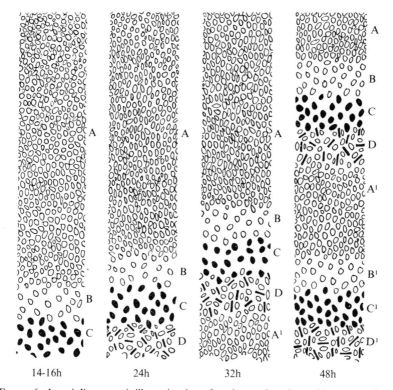

14-16h   24h   32h   48h

FIG. 12.6. A semi-diagrammatic illustration, in surface view, to show the spatial sequence of events in rabbit lens epithelium after infliction of a wound at the region shown at the lower side of the figure. Zone A, unaffected epithelium. Zone B, area of diffuse cell population density. Zone C, region of DNA synthesis; cells labelled with tritiated thymidine are black. Zone D, mitotic proliferation. Zones A¹, B¹, C¹, D¹ represent a second wave of reaction, 2 days after injury. (From Goss 1964, after Harding and Srinivasan 1961.)

further out have moved in, leading to a wave of depletion and hence to a wave of mitosis that is propagated outwards at about 17 μm/h. Twenty-four hours later the cells near the wound again incorporate DNA and a second wave passes outwards. This is indeed a possible interpretation, but there is no direct evidence of a chemical inhibitor. Another possibility is that the cells begin to synthesize DNA only when they have lost contact with their neighbours, as happens in some tissue cultures (R. Weiss, personal communication).

We thus have the outlines of a hypothesis about the control of repair in epidermal structures. Once again, the replication of DNA is seen to be the central phenomenon. The process of repair appears to be triggered by the most obvious stimulus, namely the absence of a component previously present in the neighbourhood. If this is due to the absence of a substance normally produced by the cells themselves, then we have a mechanism by which the repair is terminated when the appropriate concentration has been restored. It is unfortunate, however, that the specific substances concerned have not been isolated or identified. But there is enough evidence to make it well worth while to continue the search for suitable sources of them. We now have to inquire whether similar principles apply to replacement of larger quantities of material and to regeneration of whole organs.

13

REPLACEMENT AND REGENERATION OF PARTS AFTER LOSS

1. Regeneration of the liver and other glands

THE replacement of a single mass of a tissue such as liver is easy to study experimentally, although perhaps a not very common event in nature, except through disease. In tissues that renew by cell multiplication (such as the epidermis) the increased production needed for regeneration is presumably started off by acceleration of whatever system controls daily replacement. In the so-called 'expanding' tissues, however, such as the liver, where mitotic activity in the adult is normally very low, special mechanisms must be brought into play to produce replacement after loss of a large mass. These mechanisms are indeed exceedingly powerful. After reduction of the liver of a mouse to as little as 30 per cent of its mass it will return to normal within 6-8 days. A kidney will enlarge if its fellow is removed, and a host of similar compensatory responses can occur throughout the body.

We may perhaps distinguish situations in which the loss affects a systemic function, and produces hypertrophy elsewhere in the body, from purely local losses. Thus, after removal of the salivary glands of a rat on one side those of the other side hypertrophy.

Such examples are numerous and suggest that the response to removal is basically governed by functional considerations (Goss 1964). This, however, does not give us an insight into the mechanisms concerned, except to suggest that they are specific to each tissue and have been highly selected. Indeed, there is really no general body of information available as to the means of action of these compensatory processes.

The liver of rats has been especially well investigated (Bucher 1963). After partial hepatectomy the cells and nuclei enlarge and at about 18 hours after removal mitosis begins. It quickly reaches a maximum of nearly 3 per cent of the cells (normal 0·01 per cent) and then after about 30 hours begins to decline towards normal. The original weight is recovered within a week. The functions of the liver are so varied that it has been impossible to decide which of them it is whose deficiency triggers the cell multiplication (see Teir and Rytömaa 1967). It is probably partly the lowering of the plasma protein and the induction of specific protein synthesis. Other factors may be the failure of the digestive functions, or simply a result of the distortion of the pattern of vascular flow.

Similarly, after kidney removal there are many physiological repercussions, any of which may trigger the hypertrophy of the remaining kidney. This is not due simply to the need for the single kidney to produce more urine. One ureter can be diverted to enter the peritoneal cavity or the gut. Its secretion is absorbed and makes more work for the other kidney, but the latter does not hypertrophy.

Similar unexplained discrepancies are abundant in the literature of replacement. Thus one effective way of producing hypertrophy of the salivary gland of the rat is repeated amputation of the lower incisor and the effect is unilateral on the salivary gland only of the same side. Here some very special mechanism (presumably nervous) must be involved to relate the secretion to the wear on the tooth. The wear would usually be symmetrical and it is an accident that the mechanism has remained unilateral.

Compensatory growth of the endocrine organs is very marked and is normally produced by stimulation from other endocrines. Thus the pituitary stimulates the thyroid, adrenal cortex, sex glands, and others. In each case any deficiency produced by removal stimulates the stimulator, but the details of how it does so are obscure.

Increased activity alone does not necessarily produce increase, as is shown by stimulating an exocrine gland repeatedly, say with a drug. Neither the pancreas nor the salivary glands hypertrophy after repeated stimulation by pilocarpine. Curiously enough, another drug that stimulates salivary secretion, isoproterenol, does produce hypertrophy, so that the glands may become five times larger than normal (see Goss 1964). These examples really serve only to emphasize our ignorance of the mechanism that sets off the hypertrophy.

2. Functional regeneration in the nervous system

Special processes are available for repair of some parts of the nervous system in all animals and of major parts in simpler animals. This is the extreme example of repair of a tissue with fixed cell-number. In mammals, defects of the peripheral nervous system are made good by outgrowth from the existing neurons, without any production of new ones (Chapter 12). It should be possible, therefore, to see the factors that are at work initiating and controlling the 'hypertrophy', uncomplicated by cell division. It is indeed true that we can discern the principles of control but there is no detailed knowledge of their chemical basis.

Although nervous tissue is post-mitotic it probably undergoes continual replacement even in the absence of injury (p. 147). As in other tissues, therefore, the regenerative processes are probably an extension of those normally at work. The axons of the central stump swell to make irregular masses of material, probably of amoeboid nature, from which filaments are spun along the bands of Schwann cells to reach the peripheral stump (p. 153). Once within the tubes of the stump they advance at a rate of 5 mm/day (in mammals) and are probably led by the tube all the way to a peripheral organ. However, the question of how correct connections are made is still highly controversial. The nervous system differs from all others in the extent of its division into specifically different units, which must be correctly connected to function properly. Effective regeneration therefore depends upon the outgrowing fibres making connection with the right peripheral tubes. This is assuming that there is no other means of finding the right peripheral organ or alternatively of remodelling the central connections. The latter is improbable, at least in adults of higher organisms. On the other hand, there is strong evidence of special mechanisms for ensuring correct connections at the end of the axon. The optic nerve can regenerate in many vertebrates, from fishes to birds. The new nerve fibres may become much interwoven in the nerve trunk, but each of them ultimately comes to re-make connections with its original partners in the optic lobe of the mid-brain (see Jacobson and Gaze 1965). Unfortunately there is really no satisfactory view as to how this astonishing and very important result is produced, and it would not be profitable to discuss the interesting evidence here. It emphasizes that very precise mechanisms must be at work.

A little is known about the types of factor that operate for the control of the development of new fibres in a regenerating peripheral nerve stump. In a normal nerve the fibres with different functions differ in diameter. Thus the fibres that carry signals to the muscles to make them contract are large, and conduct fast. Afferent fibres that carry signals about the tension on the muscle are also large. Fibres signalling touch are rather smaller. Fibres controlling blood flow (sympathetic) are very small and conduct slowly, presumably because they change the state of the blood-vessels only slowly and maintain them in a given state for relatively long periods.

When new nerve fibres are first laid down they are all very thin, whether in the embryo or in a regenerating nerve. Some remain small, others grow large and acquire sheaths, the process of 'maturation'. There must be specific factors at work to control the growth of each to the correct size. In fact each type of nerve fibre is highly specified from some early embryonic stage, probably by virtue of the connections made at the periphery, though we know little in detail about this. During regeneration the process is at least to some extent repeated. For example, motor fibres that do not reach

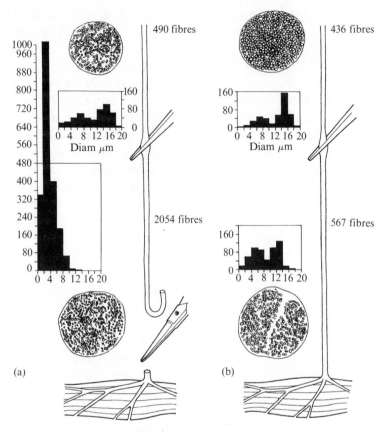

FIG. 13.1. The effect of peripheral connection on regeneration in the rabbit. Both nerves were crushed with forceps above but in (a) the nerve was also cut lower down and turned aside, whereas in (b) it was untouched. The period of recovery was 100 days in both cases. The photographs and histograms at the top show the shrinkage of the fibres of the central stump in (a). Below they show the conditions of the nerves 1 cm below the crush. There are many small fibres in the regenerated nerve of (a), while in (b) the new nerve is more nearly normal. (After Young 1949.)

to their normal periphery do not return to their original size (Fig. 13.1). Some influence must pass *up* the nerve from the muscle or other end organ to control the synthesis of new axoplasm. Unfortunately, once again we must admit to complete ignorance of the nature of this influence. New axoplasm is probably produced mainly in the nerve-cell body. After the axon has been interrupted there are quite explosive changes in the RNA and synthetic mechanism in the cell, as indicated by the process known as retrograde degeneration or chromatolysis. This again shows that some reverse signalling takes place, by which the damaged lower end of the neuron evokes the production of extra supplies of axoplasm. Presumably a further set of signals switches off the synthetic processes when sufficient axoplasm has been produced to return the fibre to its appropriate diameter, large or small (see Watson 1968, Lieberman 1971).

The end result of the nerve regeneration is thus to fill the space left as a result of the injury. However, the effectiveness of the repair lies in the capacity for useful signalling that it confers. Whether a specific mechanism will be present to repair any part of the nervous system therefore depends on whether repair is likely to increase the survival value of the individual and of the species. Regeneration of the peripheral nervous system is no doubt partly associated with a normal wear and tear process, for example at the tips of the nerves in the skin of the fingers. Interruption of a few small peripheral nerve fibres will not be sufficiently incapacitating to make life impossible, and repair processes to make the part useful again are well worth while. On the other hand, damage to the central nervous system is probably such a serious handicap that it is not worth while to attempt to make it good. A mammal or bird with the spinal cord severed is so severely handicapped that in nature it could never stay alive long enough for regeneration to take place. Indeed, it is surprising that it is worth while for many fishes to have the capacity to regenerate the CNS when the spinal cord is severed. Perhaps it is because the swim-bladder and the water provide support that is lacking on land. It is interesting that frogs also lack power to regenerate the spinal cord whereas this is present in newts and tadpoles.

Similarly, the higher nervous centres are so important to the life of a bird or mammal that survival is impossible without them and there is no mechanism for their repair. That the fore-brain and tectum can be regenerated in some fishes and newts thus really shows how little use the animal makes of them, since it can survive for a while without them! It may be asked what form of damage to the brain is likely to leave a fish in a condition in which repair is worth while. Presumably not after mechanical injury, for if the jaws of a predator damaged the brain, they would hopelessly disorganize the skull. It may be that the power of regeneration in these animals has developed to repair the damage of parasites rather than predators. The brains of fishes are often found to be packed with helminth (worm) parasites. The brains of higher vertebrates apparently have methods that prevent the entry of such invaders and it may be for this reason that they have lost the power of regeneration. But of course with increasing complexity and detail of connections the morphogenetic processes needed for regeneration must become exceedingly complex.

The capacity to regenerate the optic nerve in many vertebrates, up to and including birds, shows presumably that one eye can compensate for the missing one for a time, but also that to have both significantly increases the probability of survival. To understand this situation properly we should need to know more of how the animals use their eyes in the normal environment.

3. Regeneration of limbs

The same principle applies to regeneration of limbs and of internal organs. Mechanisms able to produce repair have been evolved for organs that are useful but not indispensable for the life of the individuals. This raises interesting questions about the selective value of carrying whatever load is imposed by processes that are used only intermittently. Of course the rate of loss varies greatly. Ninety-three per cent of individuals of some species of crustaceans have been found to show loss of major parts. Since crabs and lobsters have many limbs they can afford to be without one while it is growing (Needham 1964). There is little doubt, from the fact that the power of regeneration is used so often, that it has survival value. It is sometimes suggested that this capacity is merely a 'casually persisting pristine power of morphogenesis'. It is much more likely that the basic powers of metabolic turnover have been specially selected and improved upon to produce regeneration of the more vulnerable members.

Proof that these are specially selected powers comes from the animals such as lizards that have evolved autotomy mechanisms, regions at which a limb or tail is cast off when it is seized and remains wriggling to distract the attacker. There are special mechanisms to close the wound, and regeneration takes place faster following autotomy than after injury elsewhere. Autotomy may be useful even when not followed by regeneration. The crane-flies ('daddy-longlegs', tipulids) often cast off a leg when captured, but cannot replace it.

4. Regeneration and evolutionary advance

It is widely held that lower organisms have greater regenerative powers than higher ones. The attempt to produce quantitative scales either for evolutionary status or regenerative power is hazardous but has been bravely made by Needham (1964). He concludes that regenerative power is inversely related to evolutionary grade and that the reason is probably that morphological, and particularly histological, differentiation are directly related to the grade, so that if de-differentiation is necessary as a prelude to regeneration it becomes increasingly difficult or uneconomic. He recognizes, however, that the matter is very complicated and many factors may influence the presence or absence of regenerative power. Thus the alertness and nimbleness of the higher animals as potential prey saves them from serious wounds short of capture and total destruction, for which the appropriate biological defence is not regeneration but reproduction.

On the other side there are indications that the regenerative power is not *necessarily* lost in all higher animals. The capacity of stags to regenerate huge antlers each year is a conspicuous example. It seems unreasonable that the skin of a small area should have the power to produce the luxuriant velvet of new hair follicles, much more perfect than the skin that is regenerated over wounds. Yet this beautiful new covering is then 'rubbed off in tatters soon after antler growth is complete' (Needham 1964). It is clear that we are still a long way from understanding the biological significance of many phenomena of growth and regeneration. We think that we can appreciate repair processes that are of value to ourselves, such as healing of wounds or of bones. But we know so little of the significant features of the life system of other species that some of their major repairs seem to us to be simply a waste. It is doubtful if this is a sound judgement.

14

REPRODUCTION AND DEVELOPMENT AS GUARANTEES OF HOMEOSTASIS

1. The significance of reproduction

THE activities of life are directed towards maintaining the organization of every single member of the species intact, but each of us knows that his activities cannot be permanently successful in this, and that in the end he will die. Very many things are mysterious about this ageing and death, but when we have looked at them biologically we may be able to see some solution for the paradox that life, which is defined as a self-maintaining activity, must after a time cease in each separate member of the race. We cannot consider death properly without thinking also of birth, and this is a very fundamental biological platitude. The pattern of activity that we have seen to be so important is continued indefinitely, not in one individual but in the group, race, or species of which he forms a part. In a very real sense the unit of organization that is preserved by life lies in the whole set of possibly interbreeding individuals that constitutes the species. This population is able to change very slowly through the centuries and millenia, producing new types that can survive under changed circumstances. Any single individual can adapt himself considerably to his environment, and it may well be that humans will be able to do so more fully in the future, perhaps setting a longer span to their lives. Yet, in the higher animals at any rate, the slow adjustments that ensure that the race continues to be suited to its surroundings have been made possible by the repeated provision of *new* individuals, each slightly different from the others. This, for obvious reasons, requires the death of some of those that are already there. If all remained there would be overcrowding, but in practice there are specific mechanisms for removal of the excess, at least in some species. However, under the conditions that obtain in the life of many animal species, death usually intervenes by accident or the attacks of enemies or parasites before phenomena comparable to those that we know as ageing become manifest. This was probably also true of our Palaeolithic ancestors, and the life tables of some tribes of hunters still show the same conditions today (p. 331). It is interesting, however, that senescent changes do appear when animals are brought into the safe conditions of domestication. Although aged and decrepit animals are not commonly found in the wild, we can assume that changes similar to those of senescence in man would appear in most if not all higher animals if they were kept alive long enough (Chapter 22).

The processes of adjustment that are made possible under the control of the instructions acquired by heredity cannot maintain the individual indefinitely. This is a statement of fact. We shall have to look further before we can decide whether this ageing process is, as it were, an accident of living, or whether it has a positive value, serving some purpose, like the other changes and activities of life. To some people the possibility that ageing and death are a positive contribution to life may seem paradoxical and absurd. We cannot yet assert that it is so, but before dismissing the possibility we may note first that it would be odd if, when so many actions of organisms are directed towards the long-term maintenance of life, senescence and death alone should not be so directed. Secondly, it is clear that the mechanism of continual change of the hereditary instructions by sexual reproduction could not operate in any species if the already existing individuals remained alive indefinitely. However, once again it must be emphasized that, although some species certainly have a fixed life-span, in many others the individuals are killed by accident before they become senescent.

We may therefore inquire whether there is a reason for the rhythm of sex, birth, and death, which makes such a large part of the structure of our lives. To try to understand it more clearly we shall trace the process of reproduction in some detail, seeking to discover what it is that is reproduced and how this copying is achieved and so to show how each single member of the species comes to its completed state.

The essence of reproduction is the passing of the instructions for organization of the life of the race to a new unit. By reproduction the characteristic activity that is the life of the species is started again. At first, during the activities of the egg, embryonic, and infant stages, the new life is incomplete, simple, and not wholly able to look after itself. These stages finally produce an adult that can make the adjustments that maintain its life for a long time. In order to ensure the survival of the race the new unit must be like the old, *but not exactly like*. Biologically there would usually be no advantage in replacing units by others precisely like them. But if the new differ slightly from the old, and among themselves, a range of types is provided, some of which may be able to meet changes in the state of the world and to allow the race to colonize new parts of it.

2. The importance of variety and its sources

A continual supply of individuals of new types is ensured by the two processes of *mutation* and *genetical recombination*. Mutation is a change in the hereditary instructions, occurring sporadically as a result of agents whose actions are still only partly understood (Chapter 28). In general, the hereditary material is remarkably stable and does not vary, in spite of changes of food or other conditions. However, certain powerful forces, such as X-rays, cosmic radiation, or the action of neutrons or other forms of atomic radiation, alter the codons of the DNA in the nuclei, causing them to produce new types in the next generation. Little is known of these changes chemically. Some genes are more liable to mutate than others, but the effects are random, in the sense that a mutagenic agent may produce mutations that affect a wide variety of features, differing each time the experiment is made. Mutations are thus not 'directed' by information received from the environment but are changes made at random. In this sense they provide the novelties that are the raw material of all evolution. Most of these novelties are probably disadvantageous and fail to survive, but some of them may provide just the type of animal or plant that is needed to meet new conditions. It is probable that the most useful mutations are those that produce only a slight change in some feature of the next generation. In this way they provide the stock of variability. Uniformity is the danger that the race must avoid; for success, the race must contain a wide variety of types so that some are suitable and can survive (Chapter 28).

The maintenance of variability is also ensured by sexual reproduction, the arrangement that each new individual unit begins with an organization derived not from one but two parents. Basically, the significance of sexual reproduction is not simply that it produces new individuals but that it provides for a mixing of the characteristics of the individuals in a population, and hence allows gradual evolutionary change. The controls that regulate the characteristic life of adult men or other animals are immensely complicated and it is obviously not possible to unite those of two fully formed individuals. In reproduction, therefore, there is passed on an outline or 'blueprint' of the instructions of the organization, in coded form, simple enough to be combined with that derived from another person. The first beginnings of each new individual are two relatively simple cells, the gametes, egg and sperm, which fuse to form a single cell, the zygote, or fertilized egg. This then proceeds to divide and its products divide again and again, producing millions of cells, which gradually arrange themselves to form the organs and tissues characteristic of a new human being.

The power of the egg and sperm to make copies in this way depends primarily on their nuclei. We have seen already that the DNA of the nucleus is the part of the cell that controls the exchanges that go on throughout life. The essential feature of sexual reproduction is that nuclear material from male and female together make a single new nucleus. The differences between adult males and females and between the eggs and sperms are largely directed towards producing this fusion of the two nuclei. This is the objective that is achieved by all the structures, habits, and desires that ensure that male and female shall be attractive to each other and shall come together. There are even, in man as in other animals, special provisions to ensure that the process actually mixes different hereditary strains. The provisions against incest have a sound biological basis, though as we shall see, the offspring of an incestuous cross are not necessarily biologically unsatisfactory.

Although the differences between man and woman are first of all concerned with making certain of a cross, these differences have also come to be used in other ways to help to give a proper beginning to the new life. The task of the parents is not restricted to providing the gametes, but also includes nourishing the young, the female first within her body and then with her milk, and the male by caring for the whole family. The different functions of the sexes are therefore very complicated in humans and it is not wise to reduce them to any simple formula. Moreover, they differ at the various stages of reproduction. A woman who has just borne a child is for the time being a very different person from herself a year earlier or later.

3. The reading of the information of the egg and sperm

As in all animals, the mixing of hereditary material is ensured first of all by having two different sorts of gametes, a relatively large and passive egg and a small, active sperm. One of the most astonishing of all biological facts is that the instructions that control the life of so elaborate an organization as a man or woman can be passed on in such minute masses of material. Seeing a child grow, not merely into a human being but into one with characteristic gait, shape, thoughts, and actions, it is almost incredible that the similarity to the mother was acquired through an egg 140 μm in diameter and to the father by a sperm scarcely 10 μm across and 100 μm long. The zygote resulting from the fusion of these bodies weighs about 34 thousandths of a gramme, and yet in this tiny quantity of stuff there resides the power to produce a man, beautiful like his mother, or a woman with a will like that of her father.

In spite of the primitiveness of biology we are beginning to know a little of the organization of activities that makes this material able to perform such wonders. We can begin to see how there are in the gametes nucleic acids and enzymes arranged to work in characteristic ways to produce the whole result. It is clear that the nucleus plays a key part in the control of the characters of the offspring. For the spermatozoon consists of only a nucleus, with a small cap of material on the front end and a swimming tail.

Probably the cap and tail are not used in the zygote (the tail can be centrifuged off in some animals without affecting the result) and the chief contribution of the male to the next generation is therefore the tiny sperm nucleus, some 7×5 μm, weighing perhaps one hundred-thousandth of a gramme. Yet by suitable observations it can be shown that the contribution of male and female to inheritance is equal. A man is not more like his mother than his father. From this it would follow that all the inheritance is by means of the nucleus but we shall beware of pushing this conclusion too far. The egg provides the cytoplasm with which the zygote nucleus works to produce a new person. This cytoplasm is essential for development; not only is it the part of the cell in which the active process of formation of new substance must go forward, it also provides the system that calls from the nucleus the information needed for the proper operation of each cell, according to its place in the embryo.

Crosses can be made between eggs and sperms of sea-urchins belonging to different sub-orders, whose larvae have characteristic differences (Baltzer *et al.* 1958). During early development the hybrid larvae in some aspects show the purely maternal characteristics, although later those of the male are added and the results may then be intermediate. Presumably the RNA liberated from the maternal nucleus is able, with the appropriate enzymes, to organize the events of early cleavage. Later on RNA synthesis involves also the male pronucleus.

Further, enucleated fragments of eggs of one species of echinoderm can be fertilized by sperm of another and they then cleave at a rate characteristic of the mother, again indicating control by the cytoplasm. An interesting aspect of these results is the fact that the cytoplasm of eggs contains large amounts of DNA, probably of rather low molecular weight. The significance of this is not known. It may serve as a precursor for DNA synthesis during development but may also be the source of the signals that control performance of the cytoplasm while the nuclei are actively dividing.

The contributions of the nucleus to developmental processes are initiated by enzymes in the cytoplasm (see Gurdon and Woodland 1968). One of the key events of reproduction is the initiation of DNA synthesis, which starts in frogs and sea-urchins within 20 minutes of fertilization (in both male and female pronuclei). This can be shown to be an effect of the cytoplasm. Nuclei from the brain of the clawed frog (*Xenopus*), which are not synthesizing DNA, begin to do so when injected into activated eggs whose own nuclei have been killed by irradiation. The effect is produced by the action of a single enzyme, DNA polymerase, promoting the incorporation of deoxynucleotide triphosphates into DNA, as can be proved by using tritiated thymidine. The enzyme is not active in the cytoplasm of young

oocytes, but appears after the 'germinal vesicle' (oocyte nucleus) has rup-
tured, as the cell matures. Presumably the production of the enzyme is
ultimately under DNA control but the genes for it may be common, since
the action of the enzymes is non-specific. Adult mouse liver nuclei are
induced to synthesize DNA when placed in frog egg cytoplasm.

The cytoplasm is also responsible for the control of RNA synthesis.
Nuclei of the endoderm of late neurula larvae, which are actively producing
RNA, cease to do so when transplanted to enucleated eggs, at a stage when
the latter are not producing RNA. Again, nuclei of the blastula of *Xenopus*,
which are actively producing DNA, but little RNA, can be injected into
cultured immature oocytes, which produce RNA but no DNA. The transplanted nuclei show no change for 1 hour but then swell, stop producing
DNA and turn to RNA production. Thus the oocyte cytoplasm can
suppress DNA synthesis and promote that of RNA.

The development of the egg into an embryo with all its various parts
probably depends upon the synthesis of different mRNA in the various
regions. There is beginning to be some knowledge about how this process
of reading-out the information of the DNA to make an adult is achieved.
Probably the basic feature is the existence of gradients within the egg
cytoplasm (*The life of mammals*, Chapter 35). The existence of such gradients is one of the most obvious features of eggs. In a frog's egg the increasing amount of yolk and change of pigmentation proceeding from the
animal to vegetal pole can be seen with the naked eye. Such differences
arise during the maturation of the egg, probably because of the fact that
one part obtains more nourishment from its attachment to the ovary. In
other eggs (e.g. those of some fishes) the yolk gradient appears on fertilization. Many authors have suggested that such gradients serve to specify
different levels of activity in the egg and so could be the basis for differentiation. For example, Conklin (1905) gave a magnificent description of the
substances visible in the cytoplasm of the eggs of sea-squirts, and the way
they are redistributed during fertilization and cleavage. Experimental
removal of parts, or alteration, by centrifugation, of the distribution of
the substances visible in the egg shows that some of the substances are
associated with the development of particular tissues. In some species however, centrifugation does not alter the polarity, which must depend upon
factors localized in the relatively rigid cortex of the egg. Experimental
transplantation of pieces of cortex shows that it does in fact have graded
inductive powers (Curtis 1960).

In amphibian and echinoderm eggs there is good evidence of two such
gradients, running at right angles to each other, and these would be sufficient to specify each region of the cytoplasm (Dalcq 1952). Moreover,

these gradients correspond to gradients of nucleic acid synthesis, as shown by autoradiography of embryos treated with tritiated nucleosides. In amphibian eggs gradients of RNA are brought about by distribution of pre-existing groups of ribosomes (polysomes) along the animal–vegetal (i.e. yolk) gradient (Brachet 1967). One interesting possibility is that the metabolic processes in cells show oscillatory changes (Goodwin 1963). The oscillations in the neighbouring cells may interact, producing the graded effects that in turn determine further differentiation. Such fields may well then become subdivided in complex ways.

The process of differentiation involves the specialization of different types of protein synthesis in the various types of cell. On the analogy of the system of repressors present in bacteria, this may involve the switching-off of the bulk of the genes in each cell type, leaving only selected ones operating (see Abercrombie 1967). There is no direct evidence of such repressors in higher organisms, and alternative hypotheses have been suggested for the mechanism by which different genes are put into operation in various differentiating tissues (Harris 1964; see p. 59).

By whatever means, there is a gradual restriction of potencies in the developing embryo, so that as time proceeds the wide range of variety of differentiation that at first is obtained from a given piece of tissue by transplanting it becomes progressively reduced. Once the tissues have been finally determined they cannot in general readily be 'de-differentiated', and some hold that this never occurs (Schmidt 1968). The cells of differentiated tissues, if they continue to divide, propagate their own type. If there is a mechanism for repression of most of the genes it must be able to be replicated, and presumably, therefore, is controlled from the nucleus, even if the substances responsible are produced by the cytoplasm (Gurdon 1970).

We can form a general picture in this way of the processes of cell differentiation, but the means by which the variously differentiating cells associate themselves in the morphogenesis of the parts is almost unknown. The graded 'fields' that have been mentioned may initiate the differentiations but they must soon become subdivided into most complicated sub-fields, presumably interacting with each other, through chemical or other means (Goodwin 1968, Waddington 1966). The progressive division of the material into regions differentiating in distinct directions is obviously a very complex topological problem. It is not even an operation of specifying that each type of cell shall develop in one part of the embryo for, as we have seen, most tissues include various cell types.

These old and new results of embryological research combine to give an outline picture of how a new multicellular organism is built in each generation by reading-out the instructions of the DNA received from the parents.

One suggestion is that, at least in the early stages of development, during each mitosis when the nuclear membrane is absent the chromosomes are exposed to the enzymes of the cytoplasm, whose character depends upon their position in the gradients. At the end of mitosis (telophase) these enzymes associate with the chromosomes and, as it were, reprogramme the genes to determine what mRNA they are to produce until the next division. If this analysis is correct it means that the working machinery of the planning of the process of development is in the polymerase enzymes of the cytoplasm. Their distribution contributes to the orderliness of development, as of course also does the detailed programme of the genes. So far as we understand it, the control of distribution of cytoplasmic enzymes depends first upon such factors as the symmetry within the maternal ovary and the point of sperm entry. At first sight the question of which side of an oocyte is closest to a blood-vessel may seem to be trivial. Nevertheless, the capacity of the oocyte to respond in this way by setting up gradients may be one of the most fundamental forms of inheritance, and no doubt will shortly receive much further study.

15

MATING AND FERTILIZATION

1. The sources of sexual appetites

SINCE reproduction is the process by which long-term homeostasis is ensured, it is not surprising that a large part of the organization of each animal species is given up to it. The mechanisms that ensure reproduction may override all others, the individual dying in the act, or shortly after, like the mayfly or female octopus (p. 312). A large part of the total body-weight of many animals is given up to the production of germ cells. Many parasites such as the tapeworm seem to be little more than machines for producing eggs, so that some may find a new host, who will then do all the work of finding food for them. Vast numbers of eggs are produced by organisms that do not look after the young, say the herring, whose soft roe (testis) and hard roe (ovary) are a large part of the body. In mammals the mass of germ cells produced is much smaller, but to ensure that the young shall be conceived and then properly nourished, elaborate behaviour sequences of stimulus and response have been developed, all activated by a basic sexual driving-mechanism. The biological importance of reproduction produces the situation that in man both the male and female may 'seem to think of nothing but sex'.

In order for reproduction to achieve its aims for the species it is necessary for the ends of the reproductive processes to be linked to the satisfaction of the needs of the individual. The needs of the body for food, warmth, and other conditions are met by the presence of sets of receptor organs and nervous centres that indicate need and its satisfaction. Hunger, for example, is the combined effect of receptors in the stomach and paired nerve centres in the hypothalamus, one centre tending to make the individual eat more, the other less (p. 612, Cross 1964). There are some cells sensitive to the level of sugars and also to other substances in the blood. The centres in the hypothalamus somehow activate both the search for food and its intake and also respond to satiation. Thus on stimulation of a part of the lateral hypothalamus with electrodes, a cat will immediately make movements to kill a rat, catching it by the neck. If only a piece of cotton wool is available the cat does not attack it. Typically, the release of the action requires the operation both of an impetus from within and a stimulus from without. And so it is with sex. In rats, if an electrical stimulus is applied to another centre in the hypothalamus of a male rat, sexual responses are immediately made to females who were ignored before.

The great difference between hunger and reproduction is that sexual acts are not initiated by any simple deficiency or lack, such as that of food. Nor does the consummation of the act of reproduction produce any immediately recognizable material effect upon metabolism, as does the taking of food or water. Nevertheless, the body is provided with a physiological system that sets reproductive processes in action very much as the hunger mechanism does those of eating. This mechanism is operated by receptors in the sex organs and centres in the hypothalamus and elsewhere in the brain, injury of which may make the individual excessively active sexually —or the reverse. In order to ensure the propagation of the species the body is thus provided with powerful mechanisms that produce a strong need for sexual activity in every normal individual. Moreover, the consummation of sexual activity, instead of providing the physical and psychic satisfactions that accompany the taking of food, is provided with its own special satisfaction in orgasm. The pleasure of orgasm is, as it were, Nature's substitute for the cruder satisfactions provided by the intake of food, water, or heat. It provides the immediate consummatory feedback, which cannot be provided by the fact of producing a new creature, because only much later if at all can the reproducing individuals recognize that this has occurred. Of course in man, as in many other animals, there are also mechanisms that operate after the child is born to ensure continuing attention to it.

Social influences and conditioning have very large effects upon the operations of the physiological reproductive processes, but the central fact is that in every normal adult individual there are neural mechanisms peripherally in the sex organs and centrally in the brain that produce a recurrent need for sexual stimulation and release in orgasm. These are as 'natural' as the mechanisms in the stomach and brain that dictate that from time to time we shall eat. The two sorts of system have, indeed, several features in common, and some of the nerve centres involved are close to each other in the hypothalamus. This is not to say that the satisfaction of sexual needs can be considered in any way as simple as those of hunger. Reproduction is absolutely and literally vital to the species, though not to the individual. The mechanisms that create in the individual these overpowering needs to perform reproductive acts are therefore inevitably complicated and their results even perhaps ambiguous. The needs of sex, although so powerful, are yet divergent from the other needs of the individual and in some ways indeed antagonistic to them. The implications of this ambiguity seem not to have even yet been fully explored, but they may provide part of the explanation for the psychological and social complications that surround the subject, and have become particularly acute as man has gained the faculty of insight into his situation.

There is still much to be learned about variation in sexual needs and their fulfilment at different periods of the life cycle and among different societies and parts of society. We are, however, fairly well informed about the situation in the United States and Great Britain (Kinsey *et al.* 1948,

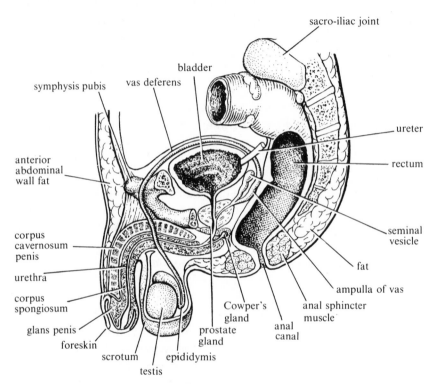

FIG. 15.1. (a) An oblique sagittal section of the human male pelvis to show the reproductive organs. (After Dickinson 1933.)

1953, Ford and Beach 1951, Gorer 1971). There is considerable variation in the character of the physiological manifestations of males and females when mating, and also in the influence of social and other conditioning on the methods appropriate to meeting sexual needs and in the attitudes adopted by individuals towards their own needs. The variety is such that no one should be surprised to find that their own condition, even if somewhat different from those around, is frequent in others elsewhere.

In spite of great variety, we can say that the physiological mechanisms of sex are such as to necessitate for most individuals from time to time stimulation of the sex organs and the production of a climax. This is perhaps universally true of normal males and of most females. The source of the need or tension that demands this outlet is not fully understood. In men there is a continual production of sperm from the testes, which accumulates in the very long coiled epididymis and must be released from time to

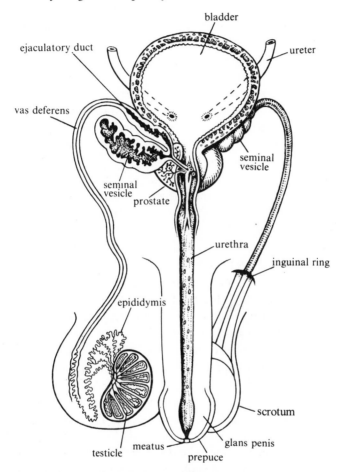

FIG. 15.1. (b) The male reproductive organs seen from the front. The organs have been dissected on one side to show the arrangement of the seminal vesicle, prostate, and testis. (After Dickinson 1933.)

time (Fig. 15.1). But the quantity of sperm is small and there is no evidence that there are receptors to detect its pressure, though they may exist. There is a greater volume of accumulation of secretion in the glands known as the seminal vesicles and prostate, which produce the bulk of the semen. However, it is not known whether there are receptors in these organs, as there are in the urinary bladder, indicating that they are full. Also it is probable that the rate of production is itself accelerated by emptying and indeed is perhaps retarded when there is no emission.

In a woman there is no similar accumulation in any part of the sexual organs and this may possibly mean that her need for sex may be less insistent. But these needs are determined by factors much more subtle than mere pressures. They are products of the brain, under the influence not only of hormones but of many factors of upbringing and culture.

We shall consider later the information that has been collected showing the amount of need, as expressed by the sexual activities of men and women. Whatever the official moral and religious codes of a society there is no doubt that individuals need and find outlets for the basic sex drives. These drives are implanted in us by heredity (though no doubt modified by training and tradition). They are as natural and physiological as the need for food and, indeed, in a sense the fulfilment of them expresses a supreme function, that of long-term maintenance, in contrast to meeting the minor material needs of the individual. There is certainly no reason to be ashamed of them.

The sex drives are often so strong that they cannot be met by the available opportunities for full achievement of copulation and reproduction. In many mammals besides man some part of the outlet takes the form of either self-stimulation or homosexual relations. This is especially so in man, where the delay in reaching maturity and the need to establish stable pairing of adults to rear the family have imposed special restrictions upon the sex drives, which evolutionary changes have perhaps not yet entirely met. Thus the female sex drive is certainly more continuous in humans than in other primates so that copulation can take place at any part of the menstrual cycle (p. 483). However, in a recent study it was found that rates of coitus and orgasm in a sample of forty women investigated rose steadily after menstruation to a peak at mid–cycle. They fell gradually throughout the luteal phase to a steep low 4 days pre–menstrual, rising then sharply to a peak in the last 3 days as high as that at mid–cycle. This pattern was present but not so clear in two other groups studied (Udry and Morris 1968).

It seems that in many women the drive demands fewer outlets than in men, and this is especially so in some young women. Therefore the economic and sexual difficulties of pairing impose upon both sexes the need for special outlets such as petting and masturbation. These and other problems are raised by man's late development and care for the young. We need all the facts we can get in the attempt to find satisfactory solutions for them, but perhaps they are not really such difficult 'problems' as they are made to seem. Mankind has obviously been wrestling with them for a long time, as witness the vast array of prohibitions, taboos, initiation ceremonies, and moral codes that surrounds sex generally. Indeed it is proper that the acts concerned with long-term maintenance should be near the centre of the concern of religious and moral systems. But one cannot feel convinced that any of these systems has yet reached an entirely satisfactory solution. For reproduction to be effective the individual must be so motivated and satisfied as to set aside his or her more immediate material needs. To ensure this, both sexes are endowed with the need for orgasm and the means for reaching it. We know far more about these matters than we did, but there is still more that we need to know before we can produce a really adequate account of how human sex-life can best be lived.

In both men and women the basic drives to sexual activity probably originate in the brain. Unfortunately there is detailed evidence of this only in other mammals. Lesions in the hypothalamus of female rabbits show that there are separate centres for sexual maturation and ovulation (which in the rabbit follows copulation). The first centre controls the long-term processes, under the influence of seasonal changes, especially light; the second, controlling more immediate actions, is itself influenced by oestrogens, which activate it to produce sexual behaviour (Harris 1959, Bastock 1967). There are similar centres in males. Many other parts of the brain besides the hypothalamus promote mating behaviour. There are both excitatory and inhibitory inputs from the limbic system (p. 613) and cerebral cortex. In man, scents, sounds, and tactile stimuli influence the system both directly and by association through learning.

It is not clear just how these centres act and co-operate to produce the drives to sex. Probably the hypothalamic nerve cells are themselves sensitive to sex hormones and have an effect, through the pituitary, in stimulating the production of hormones and of the sperms, and perhaps eggs, themselves. The hypothalamus and sex glands act reciprocally, and it may well be that the sexual urges of adolescence are due to the stimulation of some of these brain cells by the newly developed sex hormones (Chapter 18).

But this does not tell us what the brain centres actually do to make the individual begin to be attentive to the opposite sex and to seek the stimulation of the sexual organs to obtain the satisfaction of orgasm. We do not know enough about the brain to answer this question, or the parallel one of how it is that in many adults the need for sex grows regularly to a point at which it must and does find an outlet. All that we can yet do is to give some account of the actual phenomena of sex and of the times and regularities of their recurrence, so far as these are known. Everyone will recognize that these are the most personal and individual of all human activities. There are certainly great differences in their manifestations, both among individuals and between cultures, and we cannot even survey these variations here.

Fundamentally, sexual activities are physiological responses, as natural as the heart beat, occurring in all men and women, and indeed similar in the two sexes in many respects, though, of course, differing also in others.

2. Sexual stimuli

It is a truism that sexual activity is released by a great range of physical and psychological stimuli. It may be by the visible appearance of male or female and the sex signs with which they are endowed, such as beard or breasts. It may be by scents, whether natural body odours or artificial ones (though perfumes mostly include extracts of the sex glands of mammals). It has been shown that male monkeys are attracted to females at the time of ovulation by some olfactory signal (pheromone) probably produced by the vagina under the influence of oestrogen (Michael and Keverne 1968). There is some evidence that in women the bodily odours produced are under hormonal control, by progesterone. Attraction may be by sounds of music or words of love, or by prospects of marriage and children that these produce. Psychologists tell us that much sexual activity is released by memories of early experiences of desire for continued union with parents. An impressive variety of stimuli and associations can come to have the effect of sexual arousal. Complicated influences control the development of the human brain during its long childhood. Partial suppression of direct sexual activity during this period, together with the complex of attachments to one or both parents are no doubt among the factors that determine the final pattern of stimuli that produce sexual arousal. It is not really very surprising that after such a long-delayed development sexual expression is seldom directed quickly and simply to the opposite sex; at first it may be more readily aroused by autoerotic or homosexual stimuli. Anxiety is often produced in individuals by this fact, but surely it is a consequence to be expected from the special pattern of man's delayed development. To be subject to anxiety is the price we pay for being rather more complicated than other animals, and the cleverest creatures in the world. There is a good scientific case for urging that to understand and sympathize with the varieties of sexual experience is only to recognize a characteristic feature of our human biology. Unfortunately we cannot here follow the intricacies of these variations but shall concentrate on the direct biological phenomena that lead to the culmination of normal sexual action. Human mating is of course much more than a simple physiological process. Falling in love involves mutual responses to the whole range of attributes of the human personality. The full sexual relationship includes much more than the particular physical reactions. It serves not only to produce children but to love and cherish them as they develop.

Both sexes are provided with especially sensitive erogenous zones, particularly the underside of the tip of the penis and the corresponding part of the female clitoris (Figs. 15.1 and 15.2). Stimulation of the nerve endings of these and neighbouring regions produces a series of changes in the distribution of blood, basically by a rather simple reflex pathway through the spinal cord. The most conspicuous of these changes are the stiffening of the penis or clitoris, both of which contain large spaces that become filled with blood to produce the erection. Other comparable vascular changes

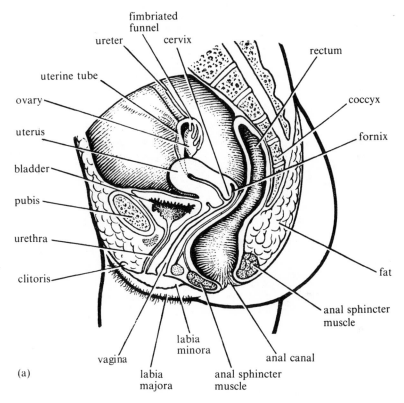

FIG. 15.2. (a) An oblique sagittal section of the human female pelvis to show the reproductive organs. (After Dickinson 1933.)

take place at the same time all over the body, in the breasts (of both sexes) and other parts such as the wings of the nose, ears, the anal area, and even the limbs.

The effect of erection is, of course, to enable the penis to penetrate the vagina. At the same time the erogenous zones of both sexes become still more sensitive and the nerve impulses flowing from them produce a series of further physiological changes throughout the body. The heart rate and

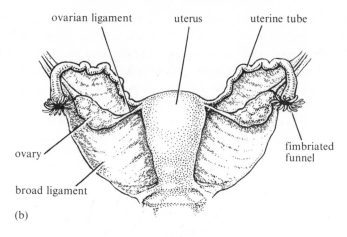

ovarian ligament   uterus   uterine tube

ovary

fimbriated
funnel

broad ligament

(b)

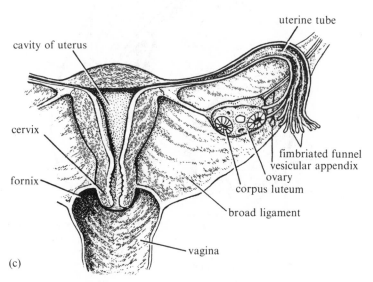

cavity of uterus

uterine tube

cervix

fornix

fimbriated funnel
vesicular appendix
ovary
corpus luteum

broad ligament

vagina

(c)

FIG. 15.2. (b) Human ovaries, uterine tubes, and uterus seen from behind. (c) The same dissected to show the corpora lutea in the ovary and the arrangement of the fimbriated funnel and ligaments. In life the folds of the funnel probably surround the ovary. (After Dickinson 1933.)

breathing accelerate and there are various muscular movements, giving still further stimulation to both sexes.

The final result of the stream of nerve impulses is to produce the reflexes of orgasm. In the male these include contraction of the muscles of the walls of the epididymis and vas deferens, discharging the spermatazoa themselves. The walls of the seminal vesicles and prostate glands also contract; their secretions make up the great part of the fluid (1–3 ml) that is then ejaculated along the urethra. These internal changes are accompanied by others throughout the body. Muscles at the base of the penis move it to assist the ejaculation. There may be rhythmic contraction of muscles of the limbs or face and a series of gasps and other sounds.

In the female there is, of course, no discharge of semen, but the pattern of full sexual response is otherwise strikingly similar to that of the male. The glands of Bartholin, opening near the entrance of the vagina, increase their secretion under erotic stimulation, especially of the clitoris and labia minora, producing lubrication and neutralizing the acidity of the vaginal fluid (this increases the life of the sperm). There is a similar but much smaller gland in the male. Glands around the opening of the uterus to the vagina (cervical glands) also increase their secretion during stimulation. The changes in the woman's internal sex organs at orgasm are not well understood. Contractions take place in the walls of both the vagina and uterus and it may be that these serve to draw the semen into the uterus. This is probably necessary if fertilization is to occur. Sperms in the human female tracts remain able to fertilize for a maximum of only 48 hours after ejaculation, probably for much less, perhaps even for only 28 hours (Restall 1967). Estimates of their rate of swimming vary with the conditions (see Nelson 1967), but $35-50$ μm/s (150 mm/h) is about the range; often they swim in circles, not straight. After copulation sperms appear in the oviducts after something between 30 min and 3h (in woman, much less in some animals). It is clear that the transport is not due to the sperms' own motility. They must be moved by contractions of the female tubes. The function of the movements of the sperms themselves must be mainly to find and enter the ovum (Blandau 1969). Curiously enough sperms cannot fertilize immediately after deposition but only become 'capacitated' to do so after some hours in the female tract (see Mann 1964).

One ovum is discharged at about the middle of each menstrual period and is probably sucked, with the discharged follicular fluid, into the funnel of the oviduct (p. 194). It is then transported along the latter by the beating of the cilia and peristaltic contraction of its muscular wall. Fertilization usually takes place in the ampulla (upper end) of the oviduct and probably can occur only during quite a short period after ovulation, perhaps failing after as little as 6 hours or a maximum of 24 hours (Restall 1967). Thus to reach the ova the semen must certainly be carried by movements of the uterus and Fallopian tube. It is probable that one of the effects of full orgasm is the production of these movements, but there is no certainty of this, and of course fertilization may occur without orgasm by the woman or, indeed, without even penetration by the penis, though this must be rather rare.

The effect of nervous and muscular changes at orgasm common to the male and female as described already, is to produce the release of a tension that has accumulated as a result of the stimulation of the erogenous zones. The physiology of this build-up and discharge is almost wholly obscure. There is nothing exactly like it in the reflex mechanisms with which we are familiar. It can be accomplished at the spinal level alone; for instance, a man with the spinal cord severed can ejaculate. Nevertheless there is obviously a very large cerebral component in orgasm and the phenomena of release are a product of the brain. During arousal and orgasm the whole cerebral activity and consciousness of the individual man and woman are greatly altered. Sensitivity to external stimuli other than sexual is reduced so that the individuals are little aware of events around them. At the same time sensitivity to light may be increased and the eyes closed.

The phenomena of arousal and orgasm are thus such as to change the man and woman considerably from their usual state into another and special one. The discovery of this different and transcendent state is of course surprising and perhaps at first alarming to the adolescent or newly married. It may reveal individuals to each other as different even in features and behaviour from what they had supposed. It is indeed not really strange or unexpected that in the acts of reproduction, in which we prepare for the distant future, we should be creatures different from our daily selves. Not to be ready to understand this is really a form of selfish attachment to the material daily life of the individual.

3. Sexual needs

It remains true that we do not fully understand what awakens sexual needs nor in what manner the culmination of orgasm releases or satisfies them. Certainly there must be hormonal influences by which secretions of the sex glands act upon brain cells, perhaps to sensitize them to nerve impulses coming from the erogenous zones. But some degree of peripheral stimulation is certainly needed for arousal. A woman, in particular, may continue for years after puberty without stimulation to orgasm. Usually even if not married she ultimately discovers self-stimulation and thereafter finds this outlet once every 2 or 3 weeks (Fig. 15.3). However, there may be little regular periodicity of need, with long periods without sex, followed by considerable activity. This suggests that in a woman the brain does not necessarily set up an insistent and regular demand for sex. Yet of course there is no doubt that in many, perhaps most, women it does so, even if unmarried. Fifty-eight per cent of American women reported masturbation at some time (increasingly in the older groups), with an average of once every 2–3 weeks. Some report a periodicity in relation to their menstrual cycle, the highest frequency being in the few days before the onset of menstruation. This is a curious time for maximum sexual need, since the woman is certainly not going to conceive then (p. 194).

Evidently we still do not have all the evidence required to evaluate the basic sexual needs of the female as expressed in the unmarried state. Perhaps indeed this is not really the 'basic' situation, but is an unnatural way to consider the matter, in either sex. However, before looking at the data for married men and women, we may look at those found for men, in an attempt to compare the needs of the two sexes. In the American males the corrected mean reported frequency of total sexual outlet from adolescence to age 30 was 3·27 per week and for the total population up to age 85, 2·34 per week.

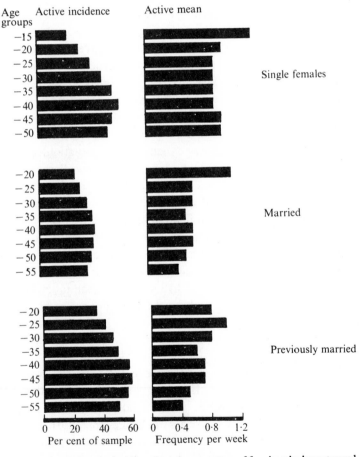

F I G. 15.3. The 'active incidences' are the percentage of females who have engaged in masturbation in each age group. Those who were single, married, or previously married are shown separately. The 'active means' show the mean frequencies per week. (From Kinsey *et al.* 1953.)

These figures, however, cover great variations, some of them correlated with such obvious factors as age and marriage, others with less obvious ones, religion or education. There are individuals who ejaculate only very rarely, and conversely a few maintain average frequencies of 20 or more a week for long periods. This variation between extremes (of several hundred times) is much greater than is found for other biological characteristics, but the significance of this is not understood. However, three-quarters of all males have outlets of between 1 and 6·5 a week (Fig. 15.4). The rates for unmarried males between 16 and 20 were 3·35 and for married 4·83. Probably the average male potentiality is even higher; over 7 per cent of males showed rates above once a day and these rates are also stated for some cultures other than American. There is therefore abundant evidence that in young males there is a considerably greater drive for sex outlet than in females. The outlets by unmarried females of age 25 are perhaps only one-fifth of those of males. In marriage the frequency of coitus seems to represent, as it were, a compromise between the basic needs of male and female. Medians of 2·8/week are reported in their marriages by girls in their late teens, falling to 2·2 at 30, 1·5 at 40, 1·0 at 50, and 0·6 at 60 (Fig. 15.5). Perhaps it is misleading to speak of this as a compromise. Obviously the situation is completely changed by marriage, especially for females. Many of either sex now for the first time are in a sexually normal situation. It is a continual difficulty that we do not fully understand the physiology of the basic sex drive and therefore cannot say to what extent the need for sexual outlet is intrinsic or is a function of the stimulation received from the other sex or other erotic sources. This difficulty pervades all discussions of sexual morality and advice. But we cannot wait for further knowledge before we make our decisions on these matters, for sex is with us all every day, and it is right that it should be so for the future of mankind. If its pressures produce difficulties it is better to learn how to live with them than to try to suppress the drives, which are basically perhaps the most important of all, for the individual and the species.

4. Fertilization

In view of the short life of eggs and sperms the timing of copulation in relation to ovulation is obviously critical for conception. The other relevant variable is the state of the uterus, which in all mammals is prepared to receive the fertilized ovum by the series of changes constituting the oestrus cycle (see Parkes (1965) and *The life of mammals*, chapter 41). In women the oestrus cycle takes the form of the menstrual cycle of 28 days. This is conventionally said to begin with the first day of bleeding, when the uterine lining breaks down, which it continues to do usually for 3 or 4

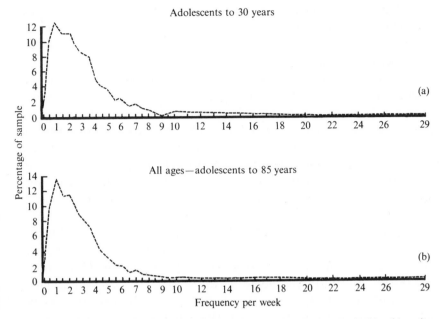

Adolescents to 30 years

(a)

All ages—adolescents to 85 years

(b)

FIG. 15.4. Individual variation in the frequency of total sexual outlet in young males (a) and in males of all ages (b). (After Kinsey *et al.* 1948.)

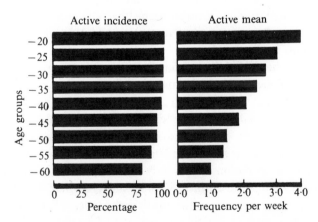

FIG. 15.5. Experience of females in marital coitus arranged in age groups. (After Kinsey *et al.* 1953.) (See Fig. 15.3 for definitions.)

days. For the next 10 days or so the lining rebuilds under the influence of the follicle-stimulating hormone of the pituitary (FSH). This also causes ripening of one or more egg follicles in the ovary, and the production there of the oestrogenic type of steroid hormones.

At about the fourteenth day of the cycle the ovarian follicle bursts and discharges the egg, which is taken up by the funnel of the Fallopian tube (oviduct). It is here, or shortly after in its passage towards the uterus that it must meet active spermatozoa if it is to be fertilized. If this happens the male and female nuclei fuse and the fertilized egg immediately begins to divide as it passes along the tube, moved by the muscles and cilia of the latter. It reaches the uterus about 5 days after ovulation and there becomes attached to the wall, which proceeds to form the placenta, by which the embryo is nourished for its 9-months gestation.

Just prior to and after ovulation the pituitary produces the luteinizing hormone (LH), and this promotes secretion by the cells of the discharged ovarian follicle of the progesterone type of steroid. This hormone has the effect of further building up the uterine wall and maintaining it for the early part of pregnancy. If no fertilization has occurred the secretion of LH and progesterone begins, but falls off after about 28 days and the uterine wall, deprived of stimulus, breaks down, starting the period.

This cycle thus makes elaborate provision for the support of the embryo by the mother. By protecting and nourishing the young in this way mammals have been able to produce creatures equipped with elaborate devices to ensure their survival. This developmental process is perhaps one of the most sophisticated predicting mechanisms that we know. It is not therefore surprising that it requires such elaborate and biologically expensive preparatory events in the female.

To increase the probability of fertilization at the appropriate period of the oestrus cycle the female in the majority of mammals gives special signals that she is on heat at the time of ovulation. Only then is she attractive to a male and only then will she accept him. This is the situation, for instance, in the bitch, mare, cow, and many others, which are thus said to be spontaneous ovulators. It has long been known, however, that in the doe rabbit and domestic cat ovulation occurs only after copulation. In these animals nerve impulses from the clitoris, vagina, and elsewhere reach the hypothalamus, and this stimulates the pituitary to release LH, which causes ovulation. Such animals are therefore said to be reflex ovulators. It has recently been shown that the rat, long considered to be a spontaneous ovulator, can be stimulated by coitus shortly before the expected time of ovulation to ovulate earlier than it would do otherwise (Aron et al. 1966). There is thus no sharp line between spontaneous and reflex ovulation and this raises the interesting question of whether copulation has any effect on the time of ovulation in women.

The situation is different in humans from that of most mammals in that there is no well-defined sexual signal at the time of ovulation, though this can be detected by various signs, including changes of temperature. Copulation is acceptable at all times, and this is part of the basis of the pair formation that is one of many human biological characteristics (Chapter 34). Reports of patterns of frequency of desire and copulation in relation to the menstrual cycle are varied and rather inconsistent. Evidence from the very young embryos recovered at hysterectomy (surgical removal of the uterus) and from statistics following allegedly single copulations show that conception is nearly always near mid-cycle, and there are only very few reported conceptions at other times of the month. It is possible that copulation may have an influence on ovulation near to the spontaneous time, as it does in the rat, but it is not likely that copulation can stimulate ovulation in other parts of the cycle, except perhaps if the cycle is very irregular.

It is not known whether the capacity for fertilization of either eggs or sperms decreases suddenly or gradually. It is possible that fertilization by dying gametes is responsible for the very large number of foetal deaths that are believed to occur, especially during the earliest stages of pregnancy. It is not known whether late fertilization is responsible for any appreciable proportion of congenital malformations.

Obviously it would be most undesirable for there to be a sort of twilight condition of subnormality for either eggs or sperm. There may be special mechanisms to ensure that fertilizing power falls very sharply. There is some evidence that the condition of mongolism, which is the result of abnormalities of the chromosomes, may be made more likely by late fertilization of the ova. The risk of having a mongol child rises sharply with the age of the mother, reaching one in sixty above the age of 45. It has been suggested that this rise may be due to the lower frequency of copulation, and hence greater risk of delayed fertilization. However, the rise of the risk is much greater than the fall in frequency of coitus as shown by the Kinsey report, and some other age-linked factor must be involved (Penrose and Berg 1968, Matsunaga and Maruyama 1969). In any case it is clear that frequent coitus near the middle of the cycle is the way to beget healthy children.

5. Artificial insemination

The Italian biologist Spallanzani showed in 1784 that it was possible to produce conception in a bitch on heat by injection of sperm from a dog. The importance of this technique for stock breeding has been realized only in the last 30 years. Many millions of cows have now been inseminated in this way in all parts of the world. The advantage to the breeder is that sperm from a single bull with an especially desirable pedigree can be used to fertilize many cows. A single ejaculate can be diluted to produce up to fifty fertilizations. Moreover, the sperm can now be stored either for a short time by cooling to just above 0 °C, or for longer if cooled with special precautions to −79 °C in a diluent of egg-yolk, antibiotic, and glycerol. It is obviously much cheaper to transport the sperm than the bull, and again more cows can be fertilized. It is probable that yields of milk and beef have been improved as a result of artificial insemination (AI) though the improvement is not universally recognized (see Parkes 1960).

Artificial insemination has been used in man, mainly to overcome sterility. It is usual to distinguish between fertilization with sperm from the husband (AIH) or from some other donor (AID). The former is used where the couple are unavoidably separated or where it is necessary because of some physical abnormality to obtain sperm directly from the reproductive tract of the man. Artificial insemination by a donor has been used where a child is desired and infertility is shown to be due to the husband. It has met with considerable criticism, but some hundreds of children are probably conceived this way every year in Great Britain.

The use of preserved sperm has so far proved difficult in man, but children have been born as a result of insemination with frozen and thawed semen. It is almost certain that preservation of sperm for long periods is technically possible. Bull sperm has been used effectively after storage for more than 6 years. The prospect of a human begetting his children even after his death seems to some people to be particularly controversial. It violates no biological principles, but they would be 'fatherless'.

6. Cultivation of embryos outside the body

It has been known for a long time that mammalian ova can be fertilized outside the body and that they will there develop up to the stage of a blastocyst. For further development they need a placenta and for this purpose in domestic mammals they can then be placed in the uterus of a female. Many ova can be obtained from a single female (by injection of pituitary hormone) and thus a single female with especially desirable characters can have numerous progeny. This has been done in sheep. Associated with fertilization by a single male this technique gives the possibility of great acceleration of improvement of stocks by breeding. It has even been possible to transplant developing blastocysts by placing them in the uterus of a small mammal (rabbit) for a few days before placing in a sheep. This would make for great economy of transport.

The fertilization of human ova *in vitro* has been reported (Menkin and Rock 1948, Edwards *et al.* 1969), and they have proceeded at least to early cleavage. These attempts at 'ectogenesis' have caused controversy but they are a long way from showing any practical results (Mann 1969). Insemination *in vitro* may help us to study problems of failure of fertilization and development in its early stages. It is possible that it might be used in certain types of sterility where the ovarian tubes are blocked. Rat embryos 11 days old taken from the uterus can be grown outside the body for a while (New 1967). Several workers have tried in other mammals to produce more or less 'artificial' uteri—for example by perfusion *in vitro*. This has not yet been achieved, though there is no reason why the uterus should not be maintained in this way as other organs can be. To nurture a human embryo presumably a human uterus would be a necessity. There is the theoretical possibility that this could be available in a few cases, but it is a very long way indeed from actual realization. The maintenance of an isolated sheep foetus by means of an extracorporeal circulation is under investigation (Alexander *et al.* 1968). It is difficult for a practising biologist to believe that there will soon be a time when any considerable number of babies will be reared in bottles. If mankind did decide to go in for eugenic experiments the practicable limit would seem to be the use of the sperm of selected males to fertilize many females. Perhaps many eggs could be obtained from selected females and reared in others. These are possibilities; this is not to say that they are desirable practices, even from a biological point of view. So little is known about the inheritance of 'valuable' characters in man that even if a geneticist were given full powers to arrange experiments he would not really know what to do. As suggested above it has taken some time by selective breeding to improve the yields of milk and beef in cattle, where we know what we want. Before even thinking about eugenics in man we have greatly to improve our understanding, among other things of the physiological basis of human intelligence and its inheritance. The adoption of special methods of reproduction might possibly allow production of genetically homogeneous human populations in which altruism was very marked, as in bees and ants. Such behaviour would promote the survival of the one group of genes and such a population might be very successful (see p. 576). This does not necessarily mean that this is a desirable aim for mankind. Methods for deciding about the wisdom of such practices may be needed before very long, and it is important to discuss them.

16

HUMAN GROWTH

1. Factors controlling growth

THERE are many features of special interest in human growth, but we shall try to consider it, like other living processes, in its context as one aspect of homeostasis. Growth of the embryo, foetus, and child is the process by which a fresh creature is reconstituted, ensuring the continuance of life in spite of the inevitable toll of accident. Growth in the limited sense of addition of matter is only a part of this reconstitution. Increase proceeds alongside the unfolding of development and differentiation. The addition and the differentiation are not really distinct processes. The fabrication of the appropriate mass of any organelle or tissue, whether a tiny mitochondrion or a whole liver or brain, is obviously achieved by growth. On the other hand, if each organ is to be the right size its growth must be checked when it has reached that size. Similarly, the development of specific differentiated protein systems within cells is itself a form of addition, that is to say, growth, but in many tissues differentiation proceeds only after the cells have ceased to divide.

We see again that the concept of growth is far from simple and may indeed be misleading. It is not enough to look simply at the process of addition. Ideally, we need to study the rate of increase of specific components in the various tissues. Some progress has indeed been made on these lines for single components such as collagen or bone. However, for the present we shall be content to examine the process of growth of the human body as a whole and of some of its main parts.

In so far as we are able to classify the factors controlling the rate of addition to a mass of cells they are:

1. The intrinsic division rate, set presumably by the DNA and its polymerases, under the influence of their cytoplasmic surroundings (Chapter 14);

2. Factors influencing the division rate:

(a) excitatory, both general, such as temperature, and specific, such as hormones or gradients of morphogenetic substances or other influences;

(b) inhibitory, again general or special, the latter including the influence of cells upon each other.

3. Influences on intrinsic growth-rate imposed by quantity or availability of raw materials. In particular, limitation of growth by inadequate diet is obviously of special human interest.

2. Limitations on the study of over-all growth

With these amplifications it is clear that the over-all rate of addition to the whole body has relatively little clear meaning. It is compounded of many different rates of addition to the various organs. Nevertheless, study of growth has played an active part in the understanding of child development and improvement of human health, and will do so more in the future. Apart from all questions of theory, the growth throughout childhood is one of the easiest variables to measure and provides at least some index by which to judge whether development is proceeding adequately. Weight measurements have practical advantages, but they can be misleading as measures of progress. Measurements of height sometimes provide a surer guide. However, there are severe difficulties in establishing standards for comparison. Many of these difficulties are so obvious as to seem trite, yet they are still often overlooked in collecting medical statistical data and using them to assess clinical conditions.

3. Some difficulties in collecting data on growth

(a) *Longitudinal data*. Growth is certainly affected by hereditary factors, and therefore every individual should strictly be treated separately. Data are available in which the growth of individual children has been followed, and these are the only really satisfactory raw material (Fig. 16.1). It is nearly impossible to obtain such data for growth within the uterus. For post-natal growth such longitudinal surveys obviously take a long time and are difficult to carry through successfully. Even when they have been made it is not easy to know how best to use them to establish norms. For one thing, children whose families are ready to ensure that they are measured regularly over a long period are already a highly selected sample. A more fundamental problem is that because of the differences between individual rates of growth, the changes in *average* size of a group of individuals do not adequately indicate the sequence of events that is followed by any single individual (Fig. 16.2).

(b) *Cross-sectional data*. A much quicker way of collecting data is to take a *cross-section* of all the children of different ages, sampled at one time. Reflection will show that curves of this sort have all the disadvantages of

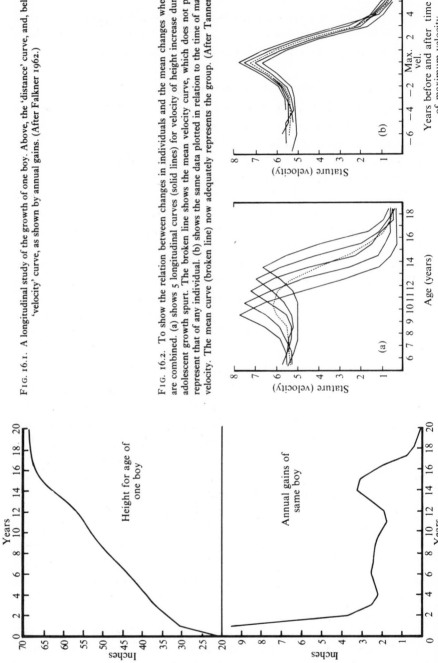

Fig. 16.1. A longitudinal study of the growth of one boy. Above, the 'distance' curve, and, below, the 'velocity' curve, as shown by annual gains. (After Falkner 1962.)

Fig. 16.2. To show the relation between changes in individuals and the mean changes when these are combined. (a) shows 5 longitudinal curves (solid lines) for velocity of height increase during the adolescent growth spurt. The broken line shows the mean velocity curve, which does not properly represent that of any individual. (b) shows the same data plotted in relation to the time of maximum velocity. The mean curve (broken line) now adequately represents the group. (After Tanner 1962.)

the mean curve of Fig. 16.2(a). They do not represent the actual course of growth that will be followed by any one child. However, because they are obtained relatively easily and quickly, they are the usual means of establishing normal standards and the extent of the deviations that are likely to be found. Such standards are very useful, for example, in a school system. Cross-sectional weight and height records are obtained for London schools every 5 years. Even when repeated in this way they contain an element that is difficult to evaluate, because of inevitable changes in the population. For example if there have been any changes either in genetical composition or nutritional circumstances, the children of age 16 in any one area are bound to be a different population from those of, say, 4 years old. Conclusions drawn from any cross-sectional survey may have to take account of such inhomogeneities.

4. The initiation of embryonic growth

In an adult, the growth has not ceased but its rate is such that the amount of catabolic destruction is compensated by an equal amount of anabolic synthesis. The rate of turnover of each tissue is determined, presumably, by specific inhibitions, which have achieved a balanced state. The growth of childhood is the result of a release from this inhibition. The egg and sperm are highly specialized cells, triggered to produce this release from the inhibitions on the growth of adult tissues or at least to set up a new pattern of synthesis. One of the most dramatic changes after fertilization is a tremendous increase in synthesis, first of DNA, then of protein (Chapter 14). The mechanism that controls DNA replication and cell division is activated and the cleavage divisions follow each other rapidly. Even at this very early stage it is not easy to find any meaningful measures of the overall growth of the whole organism. Nucleotides, proteins, and other material are being produced at numerous different rates, probably all specifically controlled. It is really not sensible or useful to ask questions about the rate of growth of the whole at this stage, nor to try to find a measure of over-all changes in rate, whether acceleration or deceleration.

Nevertheless, there is undoubtedly a stimulus to growth after fertilization and then later a gradual decline. It is not clear whether the over-all rate can be regarded as maximal shortly after fertilization, or at some later time.

A study of the decline of 'growth energy' in the cells of the chick's heart was made by Medawar (1940). He estimated how much of a growth inhibitor was needed to check growth at different ages (Fig. 16.3). This ingeniously establishes the change in growth power by a nul method. Presumably a somewhat similar decline proceeds in other tissues, but at different rates. However, it is not easy to be sure what feature of the

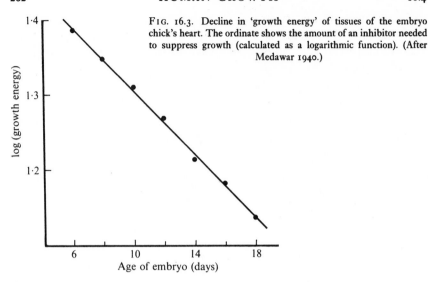

FIG. 16.3. Decline in 'growth energy' of tissues of the embryo chick's heart. The ordinate shows the amount of an inhibitor needed to suppress growth (calculated as a logarithmic function). (After Medawar 1940.)

complex growth process is declining. The change might be simply in the power of the cells to resist inhibition of their movement when cultured. This would in itself be some index of their power of growth.

5. The growth curve of the embryo

The course of growth in the human embryo before birth is inevitably known only approximately. Longitudinal studies are obviously impossible and the material available for cross-sectional studies is abnormal and biased. A great mass of data on embryonic growth in other species has, however, been collected (see Needham 1931). There has been much controversy as to how these data should best be represented and interpreted. One useful method is to plot the logarithm of the weights of the embryos against time (Fig. 16.4). This gives us in effect a view of the changing multiplicational activity of the organism. The logarithm of the weight (or height, etc.) is an especially suitable measure to express this aspect of growth, since it tells us how many times the organism has increased over a given period. This can generally be expressed as

$$\frac{d \log W}{dt} = K.$$

K has been called the *specific growth rate*. In the unrestricted growth considered on p. 141 K is, of course, constant. Growth under those conditions proceeds continuously by compound interest. In all metazoan organisms K gradually declines, though not constantly or at a steady rate. It increases at adolescence in man. There have been many attempts to show

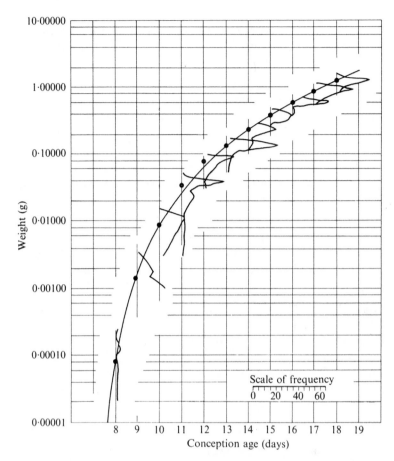

FIG. 16.4. Embryonic growth in the mouse. The ordinates show the $\log_{10}$ of the body weights, the abscissae show the age in days, and the number of individual embryos is indicated by the scale of frequency shown on the right. On each day the frequency distribution of weights is shown. The means, weighted by the number of individuals, are shown as dots. In general they are close to the mode, except early in development. On any day there are some individuals equal in weight to the mode of the day before, perhaps due to differing delays in fertilization. The curve fitted is based on the time at which the embryo acquires an axis.

$$\log W = 3 \cdot 649 \, \log_{10} (T - 7 \cdot 2) + \bar{8} \cdot 6587$$

Where T is the conception age and 7·2 the number of days to primitive streak stage.
(After MacDowell, Allen, and MacDowell from Needham 1931.)

that the rate of this decline follows some regular pattern, indicating a fundamental biological principle. We shall pay little attention to these attempts,
since they are incompatible with the principle we are following, namely
that the whole of development consists of a group of synthetic processes
so arranged as to reconstitute a creature capable of homeostasis in a particular
environment. There is every reason to suppose that these various synthetic
processes must proceed at different rates and change in different ways. It
is this *relative growth* of the parts that eventually makes a new functioning
organism (see below). We are particularly concerned to find out what
controls the rates of these various synthetic activities that proceed during
growth and development. We therefore regard any attempt to discern some
over-all principle of decline in growth potential as not merely doomed to
failure but as positively misleading. The only general principle about
growth is that given suitable conditions it can proceed logarithmically, for
example in bacteria (p. 141). (Even this is not really a very general statement
unless we define 'suitable conditions'.) The particular rates of growth seen
in each part of a metazoan are the result of some specific and differing limitations applied to this power of growth. In order to understand development
we want to know what sets these limitations. Since they are different for
different parts, we cannot expect to find any clear general significance by
the study of the time course of the decline of the rate of growth of the whole.

The description of the shape of any growth curve must therefore be
undertaken, if at all, by finding an empirical equation with as few parameters as possible that gives a reasonable fit. The curve fitted to Fig. 16.4 was

$$\log W = 3 \cdot 649 \log_{10}(T - 7 \cdot 2) + \overline{8} \cdot 6587,$$

calculated by McDowell *et al.* (see Needham 1931) on the assumption that
the age at which growth should properly be considered to start was not
fertilization but the time of acquisition of an axis (where W is weight in g,
and T is time in days). This leaves us of course uncertain whether there is
any moment at which some process occurs that releases an accelerated rate
of growth. It is possible that this release occurs at fertilization but is damped
in the early stages. This might perhaps be the effect of the yolk or of some
feature of the two parent DNAs and their polymerases, newly united. The
surprising fact is that the fall in over-all growth rate should proceed so
steadily. As we have seen already, this must be compounded of falls in
many different areas at different rates.

Data for the embryonic growth of many species are of course known.
Some are shown in Fig. 16.5 plotted as the logarithms of the weight against
the logarithm of age. This method of presentation is given in order that it
may be deprecated. Not surprisingly, many of the figures seem to show

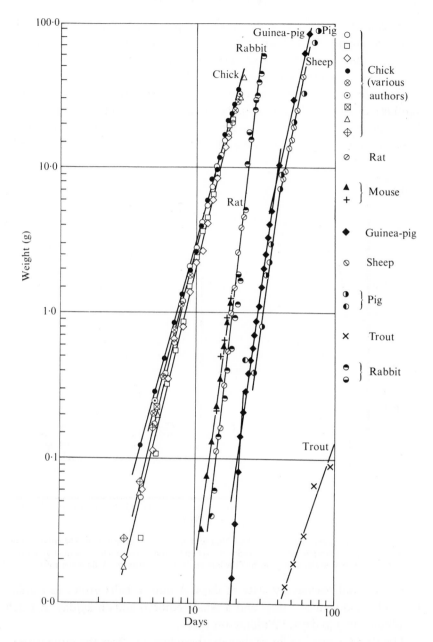

FIG. 16.5. Growth of various species as shown as log weight against log time. (After Needham 1931.)

straight lines. Others, for example for the pig, can be represented only by several straight lines, arbitrarily constructed. This must suggest that something is wrong. Indeed, the shapes can have no real meaning, if only for the reason that time does not increase logarithmically!

The rate of growth varies enormously from one species of mammal to another. In general the rate is higher in animals that reach a larger size at birth, there is a far bigger variation between species in birth weight than in length of gestation. Thus a mouse embryo grows at a mean rate of only

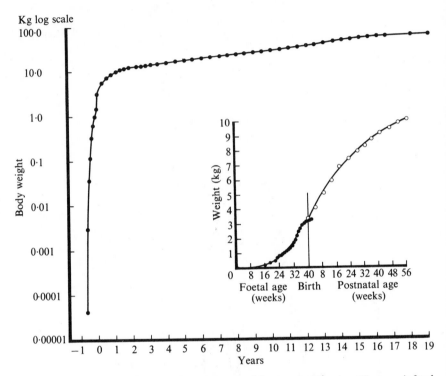

FIG. 16.6. Growth of man shown as the logarithm of weight plotted against time. The curve is fitted by eye. (Data from Johnston 1909; see Needham 1931 and Tanner *et al.* 1966.) The inset graph is an arithmetic plot to show the growth of the human foetus and neonate (Widdowson 1968.)

0·09 g/day and reaches 2 g after 21 days. A human baby grows 12·5 g/day to reach 3500 g in 280 days and a whale embryo adds 9 kg/day to reach 3 million g in 330 days! (Widdowson 1968).

The data for man, so far as they can be relied on, show the same pattern (Fig. 16.6). The points for the earlier stages are obtained from estimates of volume made on the models of human embryos produced by His and Ziegler (see Needham 1931, Tanner, Whitehouse, and Takaishi 1966). The rate of growth is rapid throughout pregnancy. The fall is regular and con-

tinues after birth. There is a suspicion of a slowing before birth and acceleration thereafter. This may reflect the relatively unfavourable conditions for
growth in the uterus at the end of pregnancy. However, the pre-natal
samples differ from the post-natal and the dip and subsequent rise may be
an artefact of this selection. There is evidence that in other mammals a
genetically large embryo in a small mother grows relatively slowly *in utero*,
perhaps due to a specific inhibition, making parturition possible. Thus the

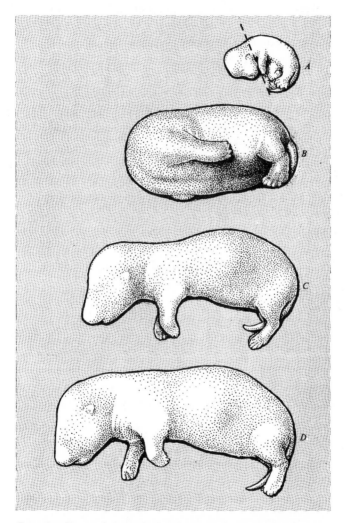

FIG. 16.7. Four rat foetuses, the three lowest (*B*, *C*, and *D*) being 21·5-day-
old litter-mates from a female who was hypophysectomized 12·5 days after
copulation. The foetus *B* was decapitated 16·5 days after copulation (*A*).
The headless foetus was similar in size to the controls, despite the absence
of both maternal and foetal pituitary glands. (After Jost and Picon 1957.)

offspring of a large shire stallion and a Shetland pony is born without difficulty, due to the maternal effect on the foal (Pomeroy 1955). The data for man are inadequate. A chief factor involved seems to be the maternal genotype. Thus the mothers of children with a small birth weight were themselves small at birth.

There are obviously considerable difficulties in estimating the normal course of human growth *in utero* (Gruenwald 1967). It is not known whether the pattern differs in various human populations nor whether a high birth weight at a normal 38 weeks from onset of the last period confers an advantage on the population or the reverse (Widdowson 1968).

The factors controlling growth *in utero* are very little understood. Presumably they produce specifically different changes in rate in the various tissues. It may be that there are over-all humoral influences, but surprisingly enough these do not seem to depend upon the pituitary. Very young embryo rats can be decapitated *in utero*. They may grow normally, even if the mother's pituitary is also removed (Fig. 16.7). Human embryos with the brain seriously damaged or absent (anencephalics) also grow well. However the trophoblast of the placenta itself produces a growth-stimulating hormone (placental lactogen). The extent of trophoblastic growth depends upon the degree of antigenic dissimilarity between mother and foetus. Thus, if the quantity of growth-stimulating hormone produced in early pregnancy is a function of trophoblastic exuberance we see a mechanism capable of regulating foetal growth (Ounstead and Ounstead 1966).

6. The post-natal curve

The rate of increase in weight declines sharply shortly after birth and continues along the same curve for at least the first 4 years of life (Figs. 16.6, 18.1). From here, it remains nearly constant for a while and then slowly increases in the adolescent growth spurt, reaching a maximum at about 13 in boys and 11 in girls (Tanner *et al.* 1966). The plateau is called the mid-growth period and may be interrupted by a small mid-growth spurt.

17

RELATIVE RATES OF GROWTH TEMPORAL AND SPATIAL PATTERNS OF GROWTH

1. Local differences in growth rate

THE final form of the adult body is the result of different rates of addition to the parts of the developing embryo. These differences begin to appear from the start of cleavage, division is more active at one end, the animal pole, than at the other, the vegetal pole. The difference may be due partly to the distribution of yolk, partly to a more subtle control system of gradients. From this initial differential growth there develops, in an amphibian, a complex wave of more active cell proliferation, along the dorsal side, finally producing a centre of growth in the tail bud.

It is not clear to what extent the events that lead to embryo formation, gastrulation, in an amphibian, or formation of the primitive streak of an amniote, are due to differential cell growth (*The life of mammals*, Chapter 38). Movements of cells and of sheets of tissue are very active at this time. The organism is undergoing marked topological changes. Masses of cells that were outside move in, as during invagination over the lips of the blastopore or through the primitive streak. In a sense these movements all involve differential growth, but they are too complicated to allow full analysis yet in terms such as differential rates of cell-division or protein synthesis.

Once the main outlines of the organism have been established a clear pattern of differential rates of cell-division appears. Division is most active in neural ectoderm, then in the ectoderm elsewhere, lower still in the mesoderm, and lowest in the endoderm. In the rabbit by the seventh day there are no longer these marked differences. The rate of mitosis in all tissues then drops rapidly from 18 per 1000 cells at any one moment to 14 on the tenth day and 10 on the thirteenth day. This decrease suggests some over-all, controlled decay of growth energy, as did Medawar's experiments with the chick's heart (p. 201).

From this stage onwards, there develops a progressively more detailed mosaic of differential rates of division and synthesis within the organs. There is little detailed information about this distribution or how it is controlled; probably it is by both systemic and local factors. In a well-known experiment, one part of the eye rudiment, either the lens or eye cup, of a newt, is grafted on to the other part, derived either from an older or younger individual, or to one of a larger or smaller species. There is then adjustment of size by both parts, one upwards, the other downwards, to produce approximately complete eyes (Twitty 1955). There must therefore be local control factors at work and they are mutual and reciprocal, rather than imposed upon the tissues. If a whole developing eye is transplanted it grows at its own rate for a long time, but later shows some degree of regulation, becoming larger or smaller as may be appropriate, perhaps through a systemic influence from the larva as a whole.

Mutual interactions between the cells of tissues take various forms. Mitosis may be synchronous throughout a tissue, as it is in the units of syncytia (see Needham 1964). One tissue may stimulate another. Thus, the epidermal hair-follicle cells stimulate the dermal papilla.

In later stages the nervous system has a considerable influence on differentiation. Limbs grow slowly or not at all if denervated, and multiple innervation produces supernumerary limbs. On the other hand, the growth of hair (mice) or of antlers proceeds if the nerves are absent (Wislocki 1956).

Something is known of the influences that control the growth of nerves. Some degree of atrophy of receptor systems follows if they are not used. In mice reared in darkness from birth, a decrease in the various components occurred in all the visual centres (Gyllensten et al. 1965). Exposure to light of rats reared in darkness was found to promote the formation of new synapses and growth of those already formed (Cragg 1967). If a nervous channel is deprived of its afferent side, degeneration follows transneuronally down the chain, finally leading to atrophy of the muscles involved (Weiss 1941). Conversely, the nerve depends for its growth and maintenance on the integrity of its peripheral connections. After removal of a limb, the corresponding motor neurons fail to develop. During regeneration, nerve fibres reach their proper diameter only if they make connection with their end organs (see p. 168, Aitken, Sharman, and Young 1947).

The mechanisms by which these effects are achieved are not known. A potent stimulator of nerve growth can be extracted from the salivary glands of male mice and other tissues, but it is not clear whether this has any normal morphogenetic significance (Levi-Montalcini 1964). After injection of this nerve-growth factor antibodies to it are produced (p. 156). If these are injected into another animal the sympathetic nervous system fails to develop, showing that NGF is needed for normal development.

There is much evidence that organs produce substances inhibitory to growth of the same sort of tissue, and that these substances circulate in the blood. Thus a grafted organ is destroyed more quickly if the host's own organ is present (Halstead effect). Organ-specific inhibitors are known from many tissues and may be the same substances that act as antibodies (presumably serum globulins). Thus, an inhibitor of spleen growth appears in the embryo at the same time as a spleen antibody, and both are said to be taken up specifically by the spleen (Ebert 1954). Interpretation of these results is, however, controversial.

These are only a few isolated examples, to give hints of the immensely complicated pattern of interactions that must be present to control differential growth. These specific organ factors may act locally or systemically (Abercrombie 1957). There are, in addition, many over-all hormonal influences on growth. The pituitary growth hormone and the thyroid hormones affect the growth of many tissues.

2. The spatial pattern of growth

In some parenchymatous organs the capacity for growth is distributed uniformly, for example, in the later growth of the liver and thyroid. More usually the addition occurs at growth centres, which may be spatially distributed in various ways. One of the smallest units of growth in a metazoan body must be the points at which material is deposited to make microvilli (Figs. 17.1 and 17.2). Of course, we do not know that the protein or other material concerned is produced immediately below the place where the villus forms or whether it is carried there from elsewhere. But the example will remind us that if we are to find satisfactory ways of treating growth phenomena, we shall have to consider in each situation first how the new material is produced and then how it is broken down or redistributed.

The addition of cilia is a somewhat more complex process, but since all cilia are built on a common plan (p. 71), presumably the basic instructions for forming them are also the same. In ciliate protozoans, new cilia may be added within existing rows or new rows may be introduced. It is not clear whether the method of control is that the presence of a cilium and its roots promotes (or inhibits) that of another one near by (see p. 161).

Growth zones are usually patches of active cells distributed in various ways. Considering only those that lie at surfaces, they may occupy only one small point, or be extended along a line, or spread over a larger area. Growth limited nearly to a point clearly produces only a filament, for example, the above microvilli. Many glands develop first by the growth of solid cords (e.g. the thyroid). Growth at right angles to a line or band of cells produces a plate, for example the nail on a finger or toe. A line of growth curved to form a ring can extend itself in its own plane as well as at right angles to this, producing a cone. Such cones are commonly found in molluscan shells, which are produced by the edge of the mantle. The shell

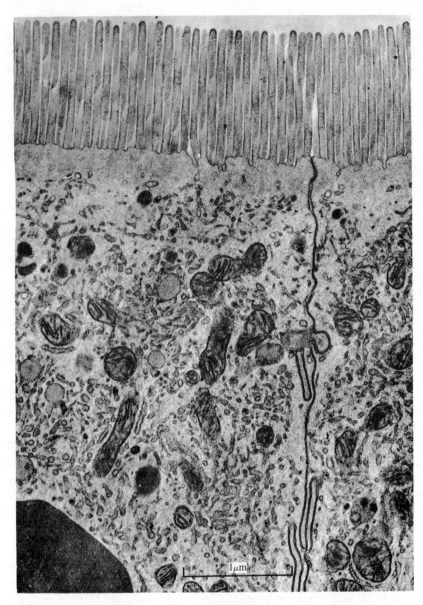

FIG. 17.1. An electron micrograph of cells of the intestinal epithelium of a hamster, showing the microvilli. Where is the material produced by which they grow? The material produced by the machinery of the cell presumably migrates to the base of the microvilli to provide for the growth. (From Fawcett 1966.)

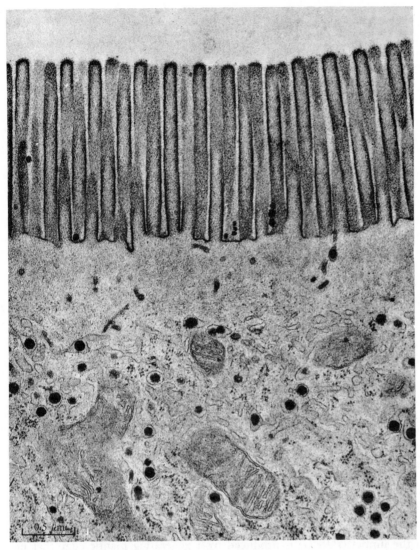

FIG. 17.2 An electron micrograph of an intestinal epithelial cell of a rat; showing the microvilli at a higher magnification than in Fig. 17.1. (From Fawcett 1966.)

FIG. 17.3. The shell of the common limpet (*Patella vulgata*) photographed
from above (a) and side (b) to show the simple form produced by a uniformly
generating mantle edge. (Photograph taken by D. Gunn.)

of the limpet (*Patella*) is produced by a generating mantle edge that increases uniformly in diameter and produces shell behind itself (Fig. 17.3).
More usually, one side of the ring grows faster than the other, producing a
spiral. In *Nautilus* and in the Foraminifera the spiral is in one plane (Figs.
17.4 and 17.5). When there are two high points of growth in the ring the
various helical spirals of snails are produced (Fig. 17.6). The horns of
ruminants provide another example of helical growth. The simpler forms
of teeth are cones, produced first over the surface of a dermal papilla (Fig.
17.7). In constantly growing teeth the addition is produced by a ring at
the base. If this is asymmetrical the tooth will be curved in a spiral, as in

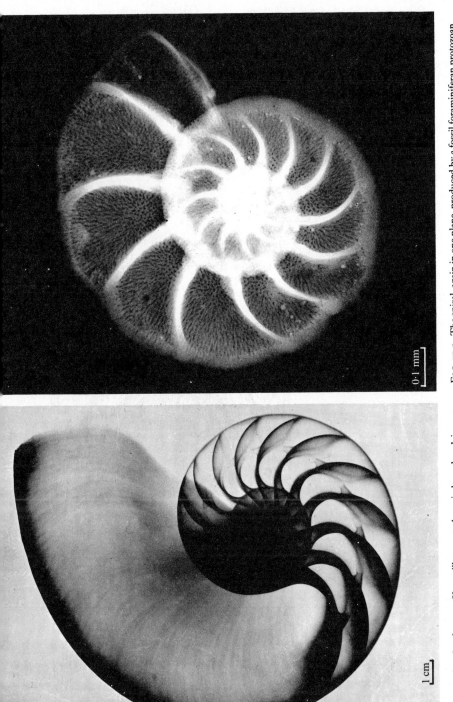

FIG. 17.5. The spiral, again in one plane, produced by a fossil foraminiferan protozoan. (Enlarged radiograph supplied by Kodak Ltd.)

0.1 mm

FIG. 17.4. A print from an X-ray illustrates the spiral produced in one plane by the cephalopod *Nautilus*. (Supplied by P. Venning.)

1 cm

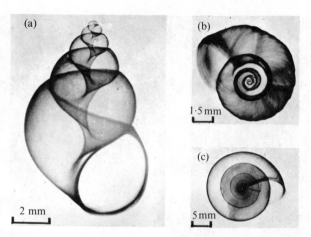

FIG. 17.6. Prints made from radiographs of three molluscs showing helical spirals (a) *Bithynia tentaculata*, (b) *Planorbarius corneus*, (c) *Helix* sp. (Photographs supplied by D. J. Bradley.)

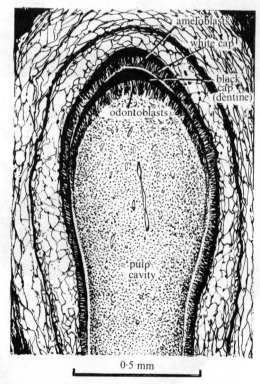

FIG. 17.7. Drawing of a vertical section of a developing tooth of a mammal. The dermal papilla produces a simple cone. (After Needham 1964.)

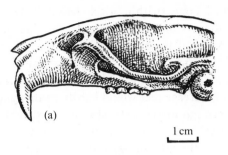

1 cm

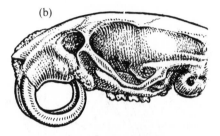

FIG. 17.8. Two skulls of *Rattus*. (a) A normal animal showing the incisors, which grow and are continuously worn by use, and (b) an animal in which the incisors have grown to form a spiral resulting from malformation as the teeth were not worn as in the normal rat.

the rodent incisor (Fig. 17.8). The more complex cusp patterns of many molars must involve further distortions of the simple cone. Little is known of how these morphogenetic patterns are produced, but it is interesting that there is often a serial gradation of structure through incisor, canine, and molar teeth (Fig. 17.15 and *The life of vertebrates*). It should be within human power to understand such growth patterns, and even to influence them if desired, as a part of orthodontic treatment to correct irregular teeth.

When a ring produces tissue only at right angles to its plane, it forms a cylinder. The kidney ducts of vertebrates grow in this way, the pronephric duct proceeding backwards and the ureter forwards from the cloaca. By branching of these tubes, massive tubular glands are produced.

Proliferation from an extended area or lamina of growth produces a solid cylinder, either straight or curved. The shape, of course, depends upon that of the growth zone. Thus antlers are produced from the dermis of the over-lying skin (the velvet). This laminar area branches at intervals. The whole skin over the body of a vertebrate can be considered as a single growth lamina, obviously of very complex form. It produces the cornified epi-dermis with its various specializations such as scales, feathers, and hairs outside, and dermal bones within. Each hair follicle contains a conical lamina continuously producing columns of cells that become keratinized (Fig. 17.9). The bones of the skull can be considered as produced by an extended lamina over the outer surface of the cranial table, bone being resorbed at the inner surface of the table (Baudey and Laval-Jeantet 1963). This is a method of increase that would hardly be thought of as practicable for a human artefact—to increase the size of a box by thickening the wall and removal of material from the inside! Of course, in early stages the skull bones also grow along the lines of separation between them.

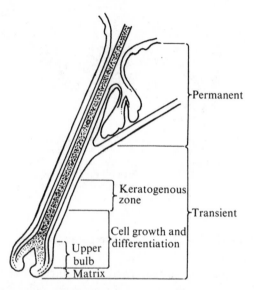

FIG. 17.9. Diagram of a hair follicle to show the area of growth and differentiation. (After Montagna and Scott 1958.)

The periosteal membrane covers the shafts of long bones and is the agent by which they grow in diameter, bone also being removed from the inside around the marrow cavity. The growth in length of bones takes place by the plates near the ends known as epiphyses. These occur at one or both ends of the bone and by continuing their operations only over a given time-span they ensure that the limbs attain the correct proportions. The long bones are thus solid at the ends, and throughout growth they are continually remoulded, being hollowed at the centre, where they are not so highly stressed (*The life of mammals*).

3. Relative growth rates

The attainment of correct proportions obviously requires that various structures shall grow at different rates. Discussion of growth of human parts may serve to illustrate the problems that arise in the course of this study of relative growth rates.

Some organs grow throughout development at about the same rate as the body as a whole, but others diverge widely (Fig. 17.10). The functional

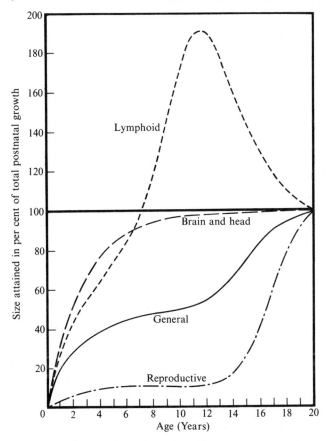

FIG. 17.10. Growth curves of tissues and parts of the body shown as a percentage of the total gain from birth to 20 years. (After Tanner 1962.)

reasons for these divergences are sometimes clear. The lymphatic system presumably develops early because the young organism, freshly exposed to a new world, is then actively acquiring immunity. Conversely, the gonads develop late because early in life the organism is not ready to reproduce (especially in man, see Chapter 34).

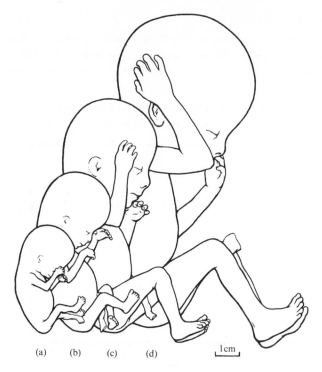

(a)   (b)   (c)   (d)   1 cm

FIG. 17.11. Drawings of foetuses of 3–5 months to show the increase in size of the head. (After Hamilton, Boyd, and Mossman 1964.)

The head and brain develop relatively fast early in life (Figs. 17.11 and 17.12, Table 17.1). This can be vaguely seen to be an action in preparation for the great cerebral development that is man's especial feature. Yet paradoxically much the most important part of the functional development of the brain occurs after birth, namely in learning. Moreover, the delivery of the head is the most critical stage of parturition. It may be efficient that the legs should develop relatively late, since a primate infant remains for a long time within the care of the mother (unlike the foal or young fawn).

There has been much discussion of the various rates of growth by means of which such differences of proportion are achieved. The rates of growth of some parts relative to the whole are stable over the greater part of growth. Thus in man the legs, arms, and jaws grow in a linear manner with the body, but each at its own rate. The size of each part (y) relative to the body height (x) can be expressed as a linear regression (Fig. 17.13),

$$y = a+bx,$$

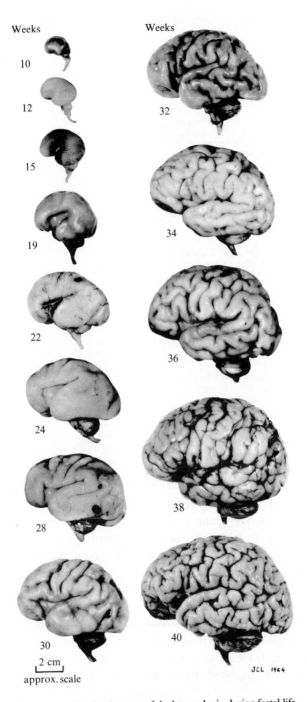

FIG. 17.12. The development of the human brain during foetal life to show the increase in size and development of the gyri. (Larroche 1968.)

TABLE 17.1

Some estimates of the weight of the human brain and body, before and after birth (foetal data from G. Ya. Mikhailets 1952; remaining data from Mühlman 1957; both cited by Blinkov and Glezer 1968)

Age (gestation age in lunar months)	Body weight (g)		Weight of brain (g)		Weight of brain as % of body weight	
2	6		2·6		43·3	
3	31		12·0		38·7	
4	121		29·0		23·9	
5	320		50·8		15·9	
6	650		87·4		13·4	
7	1420		138·0		9·8	
8	1660		189·0		11·5	
9	2360		247·0		10·4	
New-born	3365		378·2		11·2	
Age (years)	**Males**	**Females**	**Males**	**Females**	**Males**	**Females**
New-born	3100	3000	380·0	384·2	12·29	12·81
1	9000	7780	944·7	872·0	10·50	11·21
2	11 000	9740	1025·0	960·8	9·32	9·86
3	12 500	11 880	1108·1	1040·2	8·86	8·76
4	14 000	13 300	1330·1	1138·7	9·50	8·56
5	15 900	14 700	1263·0	1220·9	7·94	8·30
6	17 800	16 000	1359·1	1264·5	7·63	7·90
7	19 700	17 100	1348·4	1295·8	6·84	7·58
10	25 200	22 100	1408·3	1284·2	6·06	5·81
14	37 100	34 800	1289·0	1345·0	3·47	3·86
16	45 900	41 700	1435·1	1272·8	3·16	3·01
18	59 500	51 000	1444·5	1228·4	2·43	2·41

The value of a has no biological significance; b indicates change in length per unit height change. Values of b are: leg, 0·34; arm, 0·27; jaw, 0·045 (Shepherd, Sholl, and Vizoso 1949). These authors showed convincingly that this linear relationship is constant throughout the post-natal period (and see Hiernaux 1968 for other examples of such linear relationships). Also data for intra-uterine life show a similar linear relationship for the arm and leg (Fig. 17.14) (Scammon and Calkins 1929). No comparable data are available for the jaw. If growth rates are constant over long periods in this way it must mean that varying proportions, such as the precocious growth of the head, are initiated very early in life.

It has often been asserted that organs do not grow in this linear fashion but at rates that increase (or decrease) proportionately as the body grows. Such growth is called allometric and (if $a = 0$) would be expressed by

$$y = bx^k.$$

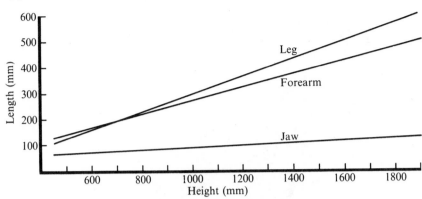

FIG. 17.13. The relationship between the size of the leg, forearm (including hand), jaw, and height during human post-natal life. (Data of Shepherd, Sholl, and Vizoso 1949.)

If k is greater than 1, the organ becomes proportionately larger as the animal gets bigger. If growth follows such a course, then

$$\log y = \log b + k \log x.$$

Allometric relations are often suggested by using double log plots but it would be required to show that these provide a better representation of the data than an arithmetic plot. If a linear regression is statistically adequate, as shown by Shepherd *et al.* for the above data, it should be accepted unless there is some special reason to suppose that a power factor is involved (see Reeve and Huxley 1945).

Thus, by careful measurement of the rates of increase of well-defined regions we can begin to find expressions that show the course by which

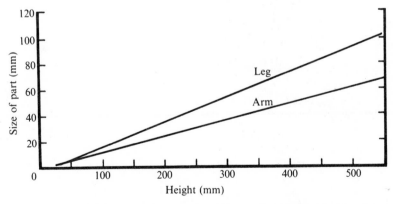

FIG. 17.14. The relationship between the size of the leg and forearm (without hand), and height during human foetal life. (Data of Scammon and Calkins 1929.)

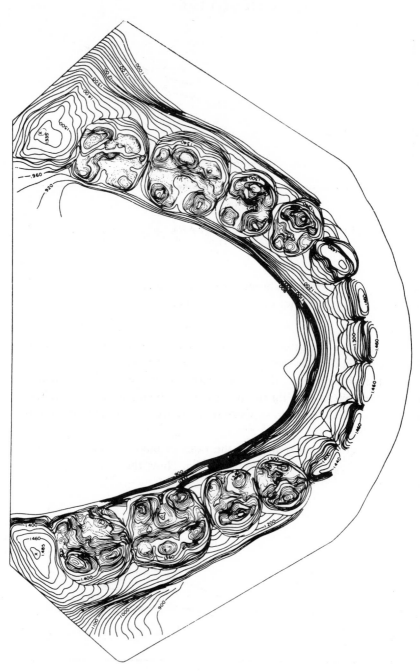

FIG. 17.15. Contour map of teeth in human lower jaw made by use of the methods of photogrammetry. The cusps of incisors, canines, premolars, and molars can be seen to be produced by gradual change in configuration. All along the row there are high cusps on the outer (labial) sides of the teeth. The cusps on the medial (buccal) side become more developed passing backwards down the row. (From Savara 1965.)

the body reaches its final form. This is achieved by an elaborate system of different rates of growth. Some of them are constant over very long periods, others no doubt change at different times of life. There is no general rule by which the rate of growth of organs can be expressed. But there must be most elaborate control systems that produce the correct proportions. We know very little of the detailed mechanism of such local control of growth. Some hint may perhaps be found from analysis of the gradients by which structures of graded form are produced (Fig. 17.15).

18

LATER STAGES OF HUMAN GROWTH

1. Patterns of growth

THE sequence of growth has a very special pattern in man and is an essential feature of his way of life. The cerebral development that is so characteristic of our species is made possible by the existence of a prolonged period of maturation. It is not too much to say that the future progress of mankind depends upon proper use of this early period to improve the capacities of our brains and to learn how to adopt satisfactory behaviour patterns. Understanding of the processes of later human development is essential for proper regulation of educational systems, which are fortunately among the few human institutions that are at least somewhat amenable to change.

In order to help children to develop properly, we need to know first the nature of the changes that occur from birth to complete human maturity. We need to be able to recognize the various stages and to have an estimate of their variation between children. Above all, we need to be able to forecast the likely progress of children with particular developmental characteristics—faster or slower growers. To treat all as 'normal' is to arrange a programme that is ideal only for those few whose development happens to follow the mean course. Fortunately, the importance of the problem has been realized and the means of collecting the data are described (Tanner 1962). The relevant data are still available from only a few areas and will have to be continually extended and revised.

A special feature of the development of man and some other primates is that after growth has proceeded for a long period at a steady rate it suddenly increases (the pubertal growth spurt) before falling to zero as maturity is reached. As with all human characters, we shall try to find what particular biological virtue there is in this pattern of growth. How does it assist with the particular ways of life that have enabled man to survive and multiply?

The increase of growth rate before adolescence seems peculiar to primates (Figs. 18.1–18.3). It is clear in both the macacque and chimpanzee, though less marked in females than in males. It may be significant that at least in the monkey this lesser spurt in the females is associated with a lesser delay

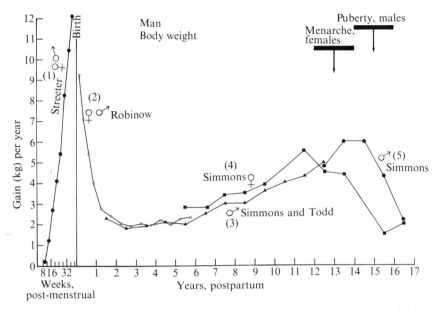

FIG. 18.1. Weight velocity curve for the growth of man calculated from (1) cross-sectional data for sexes combined, on pre-natal weights (after formalin fixation) (Streeter 1920), (2) actual increments for sexes combined (Robinow 1942), (3) longitudinal data for males (Simmons and Todd 1938), (4) and (5) longitudinal data for females and males (Simmons 1944). (Figure after Tanner 1962.)

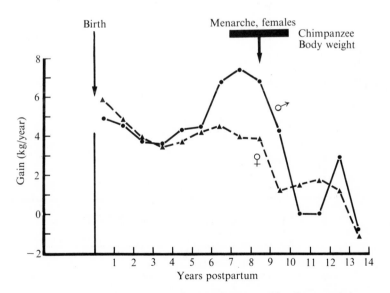

FIG. 18.2. Weight velocity curve for the chimpanzee. (After Tanner 1962.)

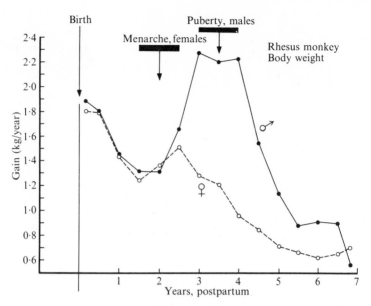

FIG. 18.3. Weight velocity curves for *Macaca mulatta* (Rhesus monkey). (After Tanner 1962.)

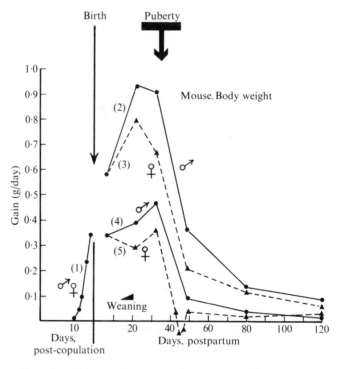

FIG. 18.4. Weight velocity curves for the mouse. (1) Cross-sectional data for sexes combined. Curves (2) and (3) males and females respectively, pure longitudinal. Curves (4) and (5) males and females respectively, from a small strain. (After Tanner 1962.)

between puberty and the end of the original growth curve (Fig. 18.3). In mammals other than primates, sexual maturity occurs either while growth is still proceeding actively (mouse and rat, Fig. 18.4) or shortly thereafter (rabbits, ruminants, Fig. 18.5). It has been suggested that the pre-pubertal spurt is in some way masked in these mammals, but surely it is more revealing to consider rather that the spurt appears only in primates because in them specific factors have been evolved that delay maturation of the gonads. The essence of the primate system of development is that it is advantageous that children should pass through a long period when they are relatively small and weak. During this time they can be kept in order, they are obedient (originally because they are too weak to rebel), and they

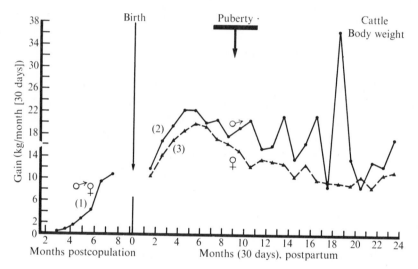

F IG. 18.5. Weight velocity curves for cattle. Curve (1) sexes combined, cross-sectional data. Curves (2) and (3) males and females, longitudinal. (After Tanner 1962.)

can be taught. They can learn by playing, without hurting each other too much. Delayed growth may also produce an important economy in food. If the species is to hold a considerable part of its biomass in a stage when it is learning but not producing, then it is more economical to feed a few kilogrammes of child than greater weights of adults (Chapter 34).

The essential feature of the system is that the growth and maturity' are delayed. Then at puberty the sudden spurt produces adults capable of dominating the young, and caring for them.

All these factors thus tend to make primate societies efficient if they contain genes that retard development of the gonads for a long time and then ensure rapid growth just before final maturity. It is not known how the timing is achieved, but presumably it is by some clock within the hypo-thalamo-hypophysial system (p. 236). This clock ensures that at the appropriate time gonadotropic pituitary hormones are released. The gonads of both sexes secrete oestrogens from birth onwards, but only in small amounts. This is because of a feedback effect of the oestrogen on the cells of the hypothalamus, inhibiting them from stimulating the production of the gonadotropic hormone FSH (p. 194). This is the hormone that stimulates the oestrogen production. Before puberty, the sensitivity of the brain cells to oestrogens changes, more FSH is produced, and the oestrogen level rises —sharply in girls but appreciably also in boys. The setting of the clock is therefore some factor that regulates the time of change of threshold—presumably through the genetic programme. The extent of the growth produced at puberty is probably regulated to suit the particular social system of the species. It is greater in the males, noticeably so in those primates where the dominant male is the centre of the social organization (Chapter 31).

This increase in growth during adolescence emphasizes for us once again that the growth curve does not represent some general decline in growth energy. It is the resultant of a set of different rates of development in each part of the body, so planned as to produce finally an adult who is able to assist the homeostatic maintenance of the species.

2. Developmental age

Children differ greatly in rate of development but they all pass through the same stages in the same order. The degree of development that has been reached can be assessed from a variety of features, which may be classified as:

1. stage of sexual development; every individual passes through the same stages;
2. skeletal age; the ossification of the bones proceeds in general in a regular sequence;
3. dental age; the milk and permanent teeth erupt in a regular sequence;
4. morphological age, determined from measurements of size, height, and various proportions.

Each of these methods of assessment of age has its importance for particular purposes. In general, they give highly correlated readings but the dental age often differs from the others. We can thus specify for any given child what may be called the *developmental age* or *physiological age*. From this it is possible to make certain forecasts, limited but useful. Thus a girl with advanced skeletal development is likely to have an early growth spurt and early menarche. The height that a child is likely to reach ultimately can be predicted with moderate accuracy. Table 18.1 shows such data for children of retarded, advanced, and medium development.

TABLE 18.1

The mean percentage of mature height reached at each age from birth to 18 years. The boys and girls have both been subdivided into (1) children of a skeletal age within a year of their chronological age; (2) children with a skeletal age a year or more advanced from their chronological age; (3) children with a skeletal age a year or more retarded from their chronological age. The standard deviations refer to the spread of an entire group of children round the average mean, and would be considerably less within each of the three classes. The data are based on longitudinal study of approximately 150 children of each sex (see Tanner 1962)

Chronological age		Boys				Girls			
		Average	Ad-vanced	Re-tarded	Overall S.D.	Aver-age	Ad-vanced	Re-tarded	Overall S.D.
Birth		28·6	..	..	..	30·9	..	..	..
Months	3	33·9	..	..	1·0	36·0	..	..	1·3
	6	37·7	..	..	0·9	39·8	..	..	1·2
	9	40·1	..	..	1·1	42·2	..	..	1·2
Years	1	42·2	44·5	40·4	1·0	44·7	48·0	42·2	1·4
	1½	45·6	..	..	1·3	48·8	..	..	1·4
	2	49·5	51·3	47·0	1·4	52·8	54·7	50·0	1·3
	2½	51·6	..	..	1·4	54·8	..	..	1·2
	3	53·8	55·6	51·6	1·3	57·0	60·0	55·0	1·2
	4	58·0	60·0	56·0	1·4	61·8	64·9	59·8	1·5
	5	61·8	64·0	59·7	1·5	66·2	69·3	63·9	1·5
	6	65·2	67·8	63·8	1·6	70·3	73·4	67·8	1·6
	7	69·0	70·5	66·8	1·6	74·0	76·0	71·5	1·6
	8	72·0	73·5	69·8	1·7	77·5	79·5	74·5	1·9
	9	75·0	76·5	73·2	1·7	80·7	83·5	77·7	2·0
	10	78·0	79·7	76·4	1·8	84·4	87·9	81·0	2·4
	11	81·1	83·4	79·5	1·9	88·4	92·9	84·9	2·9
	12	84·2	87·2	82·2	2·2	92·9	96·6	88·2	3·3
	13	87·3	91·3	84·6	3·0	96·5	92·2	91·1	2·2
	14	91·5	95·8	87·6	4·0	98·3	99·1	95·2	1·2
	15	96·1	98·3	91·6	3·7	99·1	99·5	97·8	0·7
	16	98·3	99·4	95·7	2·7	99·6	99·9	98·9	0·4
	17	99·3	99·9	98·2	1·4	100·0	100·0	99·6	0·3
	18	99·8	100·0	99·2	0·6	100·0	100·0	100·0	0·1

3. Characteristics of the changes at adolescence

The central feature of the changes is, of course, in the reproductive organs (Fig. 18.6). These now begin for the first time to produce considerable quantities of sex hormones, and the influence of the latter is felt in the functioning of nearly every organ in the body. Indeed, the immediate manifestations

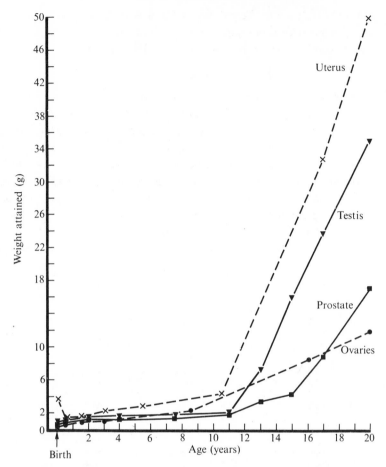

F I G. 18.6. Growth in weight of reproductive organs in man. Autopsy data, cross-sectional. (After Tanner 1962.)

of impending adolescence may be such phenomena as first decrease then increase in rate of deposition of fat, and other changes such as the development of boils and skin infections, which are indirect effects of the endocrine changes. Knowledge of the cause and course of these phenomena, as well as of the direct changes of the sexual apparatus, can assist in devising means of assuring optimum conditions of development.

4. Changes in the sexual organs and secondary sex characters

The weights of the various parts of the reproductive system can be obtained only at autopsy. To assess the development of growing children, therefore, a series of arbitrary ratings of stages has been developed. These

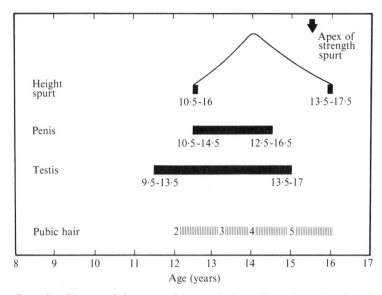

Fig. 18.7. Diagram of changes at adolescence in boys. The periods and stages of change of the various characters are represented for an average English boy. The range of ages within which each event may begin and end is shown by the figures below its start and finish. (After Tanner 1962.)

ratings are mainly made from the stage of development of the testes, pubic hair, and penis in boys, and the breast development and pubic hair in girls. Standards for these features have been made by taking serial photographs at regular intervals, with corresponding weight and height measurements. In boys the first sign is growth of the scrotum and testes and appearance of some pubic hair. The increase in size of the penis begins only about a year later. The sequence of events is plotted in Fig. 18.7 as it might occur in a 'normal' English boy. The reservations that must be placed on this normality are shown by the great extent of the scatter of the beginnings and ends of each phase.

Hair appears in the axilla about 2 years after the first pubic hair, and on the face of boys at about the same time. The amount of hair on the rest of the body is, of course, very variable and may continue to increase long after puberty. Hair distribution is strongly influenced by heredity. There are many changes elsewhere in the body. The shape of the boy's face, jaw, and neck changes, the larynx develops, and the voice deepens. As this breaking of the voice usually happens only gradually, and at the end of adolescence, it is considered unreliable as a means of rating adolescence. There are changes in the breasts during adolescence in boys as well as girls. The areola (area around the nipple) becomes enlarged and darkened.

The full development of the testes and of the prostate gland (which produces a large part of the semen) is completed only at the end of adolescence. The first ejaculation of semen occurs about 1 year after the beginning of the enlargement of the penis. This is at an average age of 13 years 9 months in white American boys, but varies from 11 to 15 (Kinsey *et al.* 1948). The maximum increase in muscular strength also occurs towards the end of adolescence.

The first sign of puberty in a girl is usually the enlargement of the breast bud, with some appearance of pubic hair (Fig. 18.8). This is at about the age of 11 in the 'normal' British girl, but may range from 8 to 13. The increased development of the uterus and vagina probably begins at this

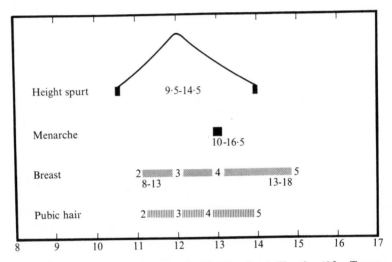

FIG. 18.8. The changes at adolescence in girls, plotted as in Fig. 18.7. (After Tanner 1962.) (Revised.)

time and is evidenced shortly after by a sharp increase in the acidity of the vaginal mucus, due to the appearance of lactic-acid-producing bacteria. The details of ovarian and uterine development are not well known but they result in the initiation of menstrual cycles (the menarche) about 2 years after the first signs of puberty, that is about the age of 13 in the girl considered in Fig. 18.8, but with a very wide range, at least from 10 to 16. The first few menstrual cycles are often irregular and not fully typical of the adult pattern. They often do not include ovulation. Fecundity is relatively low in the first year after the menarche, and does not in fact reach its maximum until much later (after the age of 20) (p. 318).

There are, of course, many other changes in growth pattern in the girl at puberty. Particularly evident is the large increase in width of the hips.

A special ossification centre (os acetabuli) develops between the iliac and pubic bones, perhaps due to direct stimulation by oestrogen. In the boy, on the other hand, the shoulders and chest enlarge much faster than the hips, owing to the appearance of special ossification centres in the clavicle, scapula, and ribs, probably under the influence of androgens.

TABLE 18.2

The mean difference, in months, in age at menarche of related and unrelated women (see Tanner 1962)

Relationship	From Petri (1935)		From Tisserand–Perrier (1953)	
	No. pairs	Diff. (months)	No. pairs	Diff. (months)
Identical twins	51	2·8±0·33†	46	2·2
Non-identical twins	47	12·0±1·62†	39	8·2
Sisters	145	12·9	..	..
Unrelated women	120	18·6	..	..

† Standard error.

5. Relationship of increased growth to other changes

The increased rate of growth begins over a period as widely spread as $10\frac{1}{2}$ to 16 years in boys and $9\frac{1}{2}$ to $14\frac{1}{2}$ years in girls. The rate increases slowly at first and then sharply to a peak, from which it then falls rapidly (Fig. 16.2). The pattern is remarkably similar in all children, whether the spurt begins early or late. The increase begins in boys later than the increase in size of the testes. The control of the growth must be complex, even if the increased rate of growth is produced by circulating sex hormones, and there is no proof of that. Presumably production of sex hormones rises to a peak and stays there. We have therefore to inquire 'Why then does the growth rate first increase and later decline?'

There is no good index of the earliest stages of ovarian development, so we cannot say whether it precedes the growth spurt. The peak velocity for weight and height considerably precedes the menarche (Figs. 18.1 and 18.8). This does not, of course, tell us what are the controlling factors. Like other events at puberty, the peak growth velocity and menarche are very highly correlated (correlation coefficient $r = 0.93$). The events of puberty, once initiated, usually proceed with clock-like regularity in spite of the great variation between individuals in timing of onset, but in some individuals the links between the stages are less close, so that the unfolding of the pattern may be atypical.

6. The control of maturation

The whole course of growth after the earliest embryonic stages is probably regulated by some timing mechanism within the brain. Something can be seen of this most interesting system. The execution of the brain's control is through the hormonal influence exerted by the hypothalamus on the anterior pituitary gland, as already described. The pituitary of a new-born rat grafted near the tuber cinereum of the brain of an adult rat quickly begins to secrete gonadotropic hormone (Harris and Jacobsohn 1952). The basic change before puberty may be the release of a previous inhibition of this power of hypothalamic cells to stimulate the pituitary. There is evidence that oestrogens act in this way to regulate the hypothalamus. It may be that the small amounts of oestrogen secreted before puberty serve to restrain the hypothalamus. The events of puberty would then be set off by a rise in the threshold of the brain cells, so that they are no longer inhibited and begin to secrete substances that release gonadotropins. This would increase the amount of oestrogens, which ultimately restrain the hypothalamus, even at its higher threshold. This mechanism would also explain the termination of the growth spurt, if it could be shown that the latter also depends upon effects of the gonadotropins.

The other pituitary hormones do not seem to vary to the same extent. Adrenocorticotropic and growth hormone are present in the same concentration in glands of infants and adults. Evidence about the actual levels of hormones secreted is very inadequate but suggests that the really large increases at puberty are in oestrogens and androgens (Fig. 18.9). These substances are probably secreted in increased amounts not only by the gonads but also by the adrenal cortex. Corticoids and aldosterone, however, continue to be secreted at a similar relative rate throughout life, *without* showing an adolescent spurt. This must mean that the pituitary effect on the adrenal is mediated by some agent other than ACTH.

These facts suggest that the immediate cause of the growth changes at adolescence is in the androgens, of the testis and adrenal in the male and of the latter in the female. The oestrogens affect growth much less than testosterones. The increase of oestrogens at puberty (Fig. 18.9) may, however, as already explained, be the factor that ultimately inhibits the hypothalamus and ends the growth spurt. This hypothesis thus explains the greater extent of the growth in the male as directly due to testosterone, and the fact that it ends later to the lower oestrogen level in the male, which leaves the hypothalamus uninhibited for a longer period. In any case the details of differences of development as between the sexes have presumably

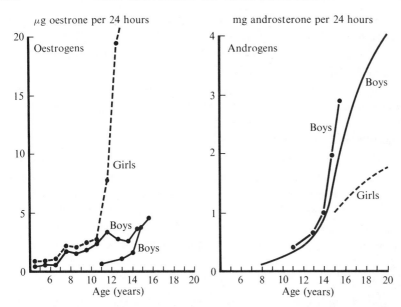

FIG. 18.9. Activity of extracts of urine per 24 h in boys and girls of various ages. Separate
data from various sources for the boys. (After Tanner 1962.)

been of some adaptive significance, which at a higher level constitutes the
'cause' of their appearance (p. 229).

Although many features of the control system remain to be studied there
is little doubt that it operates in man as in other mammals basically under
hypothalamic control. Tumours of the hypothalamus and especially of the
tuber cinereum may cause precocious puberty in either sex. The changes
proceed in their usual sequence, including the production of a fully functional genital apparatus. There is on record the case of a girl who reached
the menarche at 1 year and gave birth at 5 years 8 months to a full-term child
(by Caesarian operation). Such cases show that sexual maturity *can* develop
relatively soon after birth in man as in many other mammals (p. 229). This
brings us again to emphasize that the mechanism producing delay has been
specifically selected to produce maturity only after an interval that is valuable for the species. It is no accident that the mechanism is controlled from
the brain, and from a part of it lying not far below the highest cerebral
centres. A similar control system for the time of maturation is found in
other very different animals. In insects the brain controls glands, the corpora
allata, inhibiting their secretion, which when released activates the gonads
(Wigglesworth 1964). Similarly, in octopuses a nerve centre close to the
parts of the brain that are concerned with memory inhibits the optic gland,
whose secretion activates the gonads (Wells and Wells 1959). Presumably

the basic requirement is that the rate of development should be adjusted to make the optimum use of the equipment of the species. Rapid maturation will suit a species with poor nervous equipment, providing numerous and varied offspring. Conversely, if the individuals have good brains and can learn much, they need a long period to acquire information, which they then use to support themselves and their offspring (p. 313 and Young 1964).

7. Factors influencing the rate of development

A child's rate of development probably depends mainly on hereditary factors, limited by nutritional influences. Temperature and other climatic factors seem to have little influence. There is a high correlation for the age at menarche between mothers and daughters, between sisters, and especially between identical twins (Tables 18.2, 18.3). Presumably the father contributes genes even to this female characteristic. As evidence of a similar

TABLE 18.3

Correlation coefficients between time of appearance of epiphyseal ossification centres in related and unrelated persons (see Tanner 1962)

Number of pairs of persons	Number of pairs of centres	Relationship	Correlation coefficient for centres
6	178	Identical twins	0·71
22	666	Siblings	0·28
8	256	First cousins	0·12
9	274	Unrelated	−0·01

influence on male development there is a rare familial condition of precocious male puberty, apparently produced by a gene with sex-linked manifestation, limited to males.

Evidence of the effect of malnutrition in slowing growth and development is seen in Fig. 18.10. If after a short period of malnutrition conditions become better, growth is accelerated and the child catches up and returns to the developmental curve from which it had been forced to depart. Adolescent changes then take place when the child reaches the appropriate size in other respects. The growth of boys is more readily inhibited, but their catch-up growth proceeds faster than in girls. However, 5 years after the atomic bombing of Hiroshima the girls affected were the less retarded (Greulich, Crismon, and Turner 1953).

There may be special nutritional factors responsible for rapid growth, but the evidence about this is still not entirely clear. Gross deficiency,

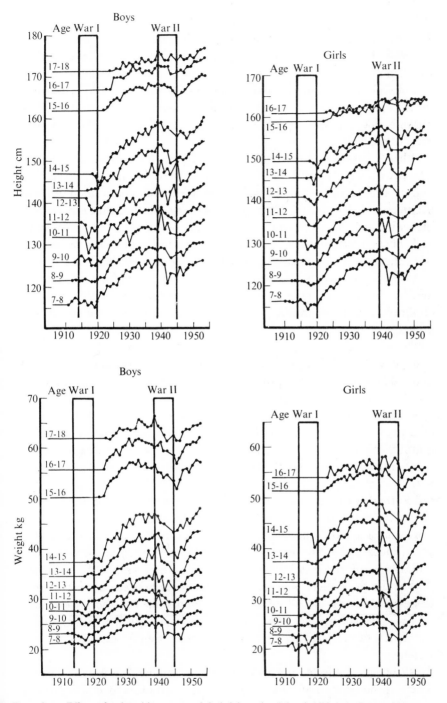

FIG. 18.10. Effects of malnutrition on growth in height and weight of children in Stuttgart between 1911 and 1953. The lines connect points for children of the same age. (After Tanner 1962.)

whether of energy-producing foods, proteins, or vitamins, produces retardation. It is uncertain whether, given an adequate all-round diet, further supplementation can increase growth. The general conclusion is that the diet of children of higher income groups in the western world is adequate for maximal growth and does not ordinarily need supplementation. This certainly does not apply to lower income groups, especially those in other parts of the world.

Other factors often supposed to influence growth are illness and climate. The British Ministry of Health survey of 1959 (covering all classes) could find no differences in gain of weight between babies with good and bad health records (1–3 years). Other surveys have confirmed this, especially in higher income groups, but it is not always true of the poorer. However, here, as Tanner (1966) points out, there may be a confusion produced by children whose hereditary equipment is giving them both bad health and slow growth.

A serious illness delays growth and maturation. Part of the cause of this may be that large amounts of corticosteroids are secreted under the stress of illness and these inhibit growth. Chronic diseases such as malaria probably retard growth.

There is evidence that climate does not influence menarche. Thus, girls in hot dry northern Nigeria reach menarche at about the same age as those in hot damp central India. Boys reach puberty at the same time in Nigeria and England. Factors of race, heredity, and nutrition are usually hopelessly entangled in assessing such data. There is some evidence of distinct racial differences in rates of development; ossification occurs relatively early in negroids, puberty is early in Chinese. Certainly there are wide divergences even within relatively small areas. Thus the age at menarche in Colombo is $12\cdot8\pm0\cdot07$ years, whereas in rural Ceylon it is $14\cdot4\pm0\cdot16$ years (Wilson and Sutherland 1950, 1953). It is not known whether such differences are hereditary, nutritional, or produced by obscure cultural factors. A somewhat similar situation has recently been found in Poland, where the mean age at menarche in the city of Wrocław is $13\cdot21\pm0\cdot027$ years, whereas in a rural area of north-east Poland it is $14\cdot40\pm0\cdot13$ years (Milicer 1968). Within the town there were marked differences between socio-economic classes. Daughters of college-educated parents showed the lowest mean (12·87), those of manual workers the highest (13·43). This difference of 6·7 months is much higher than any previously seen in western European societies.

Psychological effects on growth are often claimed, but seldom proved. There is, however, one classic case where, when extra food was given in a dietary experiment, it was found not to produce the expected growth increase because it was administered by a grossly sadistic person who

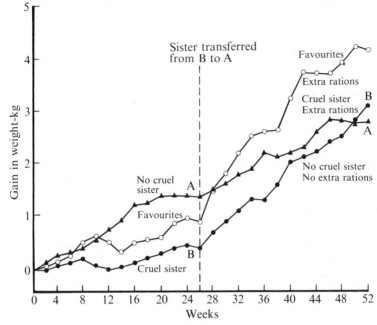

FIG. 18.11. Changes in the weight of children from two German orphanages during 1948. Both groups were given the same diet up to week 26 after which those in orphanage A received supplements of unlimited bread, jam, and orange juice. At the same time a cruel and unpopular sister-in-charge was transferred from orphanage B to orphanage A. The growth curves follow the presence or absence of the sister, not the diet. However, eight children who were favourites of the sister and were transferred with her did benefit from the supplemented diet (Widdowson 1951.)

frightened the recipients (Fig. 18.11). There is some rather unsatisfactory evidence that children grow more slowly in term-time than holidays, whether they are day pupils or boarders living away from home. The effect of psychological stress upon appetite and hence nutrition and also upon the adrenal cortical secretions has to be considered. Further investigation of such matters might be very useful as a guide to how to provide conditions that are better for the child's happiness as well as for his growth.

8. Relation of maturation to social and economic status

There are considerable differences in weight and height between adults of different occupational classes and there are comparable differences in rates of development. Children of members of professional, employer, or salaried classes are more advanced in all stages than those of manual wage-earners. The difference is of about 3 cm and 0·25 kg between the extremes (up to age 12) in England, Canada, and U.S.A. (data collected between 1940 and 1950). Associated with these size differences there are differences in rate of maturation in nearly all other respects. Thus menarche occurs 3 months earlier in girls who are children of upper socio-economic classes than in those of lower classes (Bristol, England 1958; (Tanner 1962)).

Associated with the class differences in size there are also curious differences in intelligence (as judged by standard tests, Chapter 20). With this go differences in proneness to rise or fall in the social scale. It is, of course, difficult to disentangle the effects of higher incomes, better home conditions, and hereditary differences. Yet the differences certainly exist, though they are small and will appear only in large samples. Obviously not all tall men are brilliant, intelligent, and handsome, nor are all small girls stupid and ugly.

Nevertheless, there are these correlations between height and socio-economic matters. For example, people who move from one part of the country to another while still children (or young adults) are taller and more 'intelligent' than those who remain in the same place (Tanner 1966). Women who marry into a social class higher than that of their parents are taller than those who do not (Figs. 18.12 and 18.13) (Thomson 1959). Taller

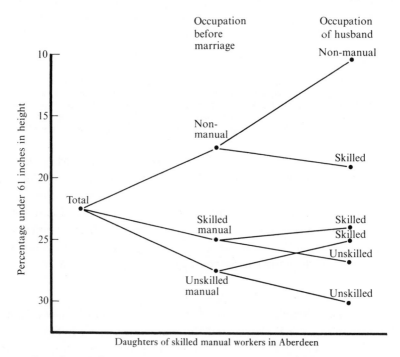

Daughters of skilled manual workers in Aberdeen

FIG. 18.12. Taller women take more skilled jobs and marry men with more skilled work. The first point shows the percentage of women pregnant for the first time who were under 5 ft 1 in tall. The next points show their occupations before marriage Those in unskilled work included more small ones. The third set of points show that in each of the three groups those who married non-manual or skilled workers included fewer small ones.

women tend to take more skilled jobs than smaller ones. Again, boys from state schools who reach Oxford University are considerably taller than the average of those schools, and indeed also taller than boys from private schools (who mainly come from higher-income parents).

Certain sociological and educational considerations seem to follow from these facts (see Medawar 1960 and Tanner 1966). If hereditary weakness in growth potential and intelligence leads people to the lower-income groups, then their children will be thereby further handicapped. We do not know enough to begin to try to eliminate the genes concerned but we do know a little of how to mitigate their deleterious effects on the individuals and upon society. If such handicaps are liable to be present in children of lower-income groups we can take steps to give such priority to their educational and nutritional needs as shall help to offset the handicap. To many people it may seem at first that this assistance to the handicapped is dis-genic, especially if it limits the facilities available for the talented. This is an understandable reaction, especially in view of the widespread if irrational tendency to regard the failures of the unsuccessful as somehow 'their own fault'. Such a judgement is less intelligent than it seems, both sociologically and psychologically. It ignores the fact that *the effectiveness*

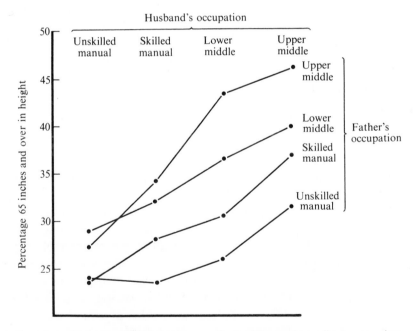

FIG. 18.13. Percentage of British women over 5 ft 5 in tall arranged according to occupations of father and husband. (After Tanner 1966.)

FIG. 18.14. Infant rhesus monkey with cloth and wire mother surrogates. (After Harlow 1962.)

of a community depends upon the net or average level of abilities reached by all its members. Any community is fortunate to have a few members of outstanding ability, but still more so if all its members realize their full potentiality. In any case, we have no detailed data about the relative effects of given amounts of care and training that are likely to produce optimal effects in different people.

Indeed, it may be that special care for the apparently handicapped has socially favourable genetic effects (Tanner 1966). The genetic bases for useful developmental traits may be present but unable to appear for lack of the appropriate environmental stimulus. As a crude example, the retina does not develop properly without light. The power of visual analysis develops only with a suitably complex visual experience (Riesen 1947 and Gregory 1966).

Again, emotional development depends upon suitable cuddling of the child. This has been studied in some detail in monkeys by Harlow (1962). He analyses the patterns as progressing 'through four semi-separable stages —reflex, attachment, security, and independence'. The normal progression was shown to depend at every stage on the presence of appropriate stimuli in the environment. Thus tests were made by rearing eight new-born rhesus monkeys on mother-surrogate objects either of wire or cloth (Fig. 18.14). Milk was obtained from a bottle with the nipple protruding through the wall of wire or cloth. Both types were available to all, but half were

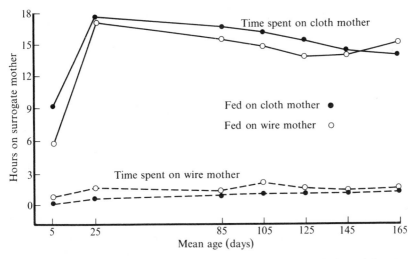

FIG. 18.15. Time spent by the infant rhesus monkeys on the surrogates. Half were fed on the wire and half on the cloth surrogate but all preferred to be on the latter. (After Harlow 1962.)

given the milk only from the wire and half only from the cloth mother-surrogate. Nevertheless, measurement of the time spent on the two types showed that *both* groups became attached to the cloth 'mother' (Fig. 18.15). The tactile stimulus, rather than the food, is the conditioning factor. Pursuing this further, four monkeys were reared on 'mothers', both of cloth, but one green and the other brown. Milk was obtained from one colour only; for a while this colour was preferred, but 'affection' was later given to both equally (Fig. 18.16).

Many other interesting facts appeared. Interest in the surrogate face increased from 45 days onwards. Strong exploratory tendencies began to appear from 20 to 30 days. However, in the early stages the infant monkey will show investigation of objects presented only if the fear reaction is allayed by the presence of the 'mother' (Figs. 18.17 (a), (b), and (c)). With a suitable combination of presence of the mother and of stimulating surroundings the infant passes from attachment to the stage of affectional security. Those raised on wire mothers made this transition later than those raised on cloth. In one variant, the direct path of the mother was blocked by a Plexiglass screen, and the infant had to bypass a fearful monster to attain the cloth mother. The situation induced severe trauma in the infants but they circled the monster to contact the mothers. After obtaining contact, comfort, and security by rubbing against her body they would go out and explore, manipulate, and, in three cases, attack and destroy the frightening beast.

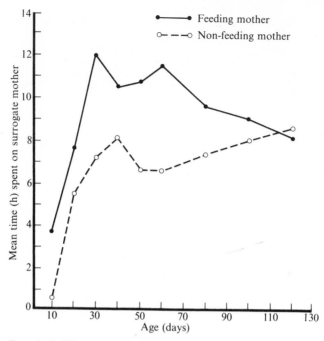

FIG. 18.16. When both surrogates were of cloth but of different colours the infants at first preferred that from which they had been fed but this was not a lasting effect. (After Harlow 1962.)

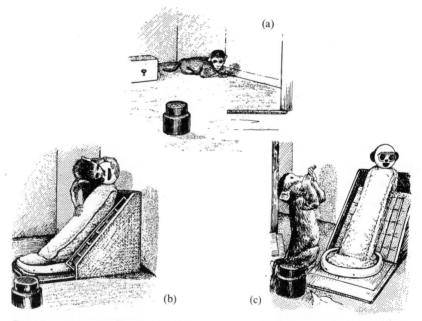

FIG. 18.17. Fear and exploration. (a) Without the mother the infant is disturbed; (b) with it he is relaxed; and (c) can play and explore. (After Harlow 1962.)

The final stage of achieving independence was not thoroughly studied, but perhaps it was more difficult for the monkeys raised on substitute mothers. Even when they had not seen the mother surrogate for 6 months they would reach to it and embrace it, although it was now much smaller than themselves. Some would even carry the mother about with them.

No doubt reactions to other individuals are important in attaining independence. Some experiments are available on this. Two monkeys raised in complete social isolation for 2 years proved to be entirely passive ('catatonic') when introduced to others, who pulled and bit them. They continued to be unable to adjust.

So every stage of development requires its appropriate external stimulus to allow the internal maturation. This conclusion may seem obvious enough as a general proposition—but it is important to know what these stimuli are. It is easy to deride such experiments as those mentioned above as simpleminded. Indeed the very subject of study may well induce a certain revulsion by the intellect. This reaction is itself interesting. We feel we know all about that already. But do we? Who knows what are the stimuli necessary to release the powers of any individual, let alone of say a Shakespeare or Napoleon? Yet it is obvious enough that there are great variations in the stimuli that are given to children. Every parent knows what a problem it is to choose the best conditions for his child's life and play. We may be grateful for the experiments that have been made—and hope for more (see Ambrose 1969).

Extending this concept to later education we find that the gene pool is improved by detecting favourable hereditary characters and allowing them to become assimilated by interaction with suitable other factors, both hereditary and environmental. Waddington has shown how selection can in this way produce an effect that looks at first sight almost like the inheritance of acquired characters (Chapter 28). The whole pool of genes of the population changes if certain of them are allowed to manifest their effects. Tanner gives the example of mathematical symbolism. If children are not taught to use it they cannot show whether they are capable or not. If they are taught, then some will succeed and if the capacity is useful these will be at a selective advantage and the community will benefit.

The points are:

1. That any policy of eugenics can be effective only against an optimal environmental background.
2. We need more data about how to arrange these matters.

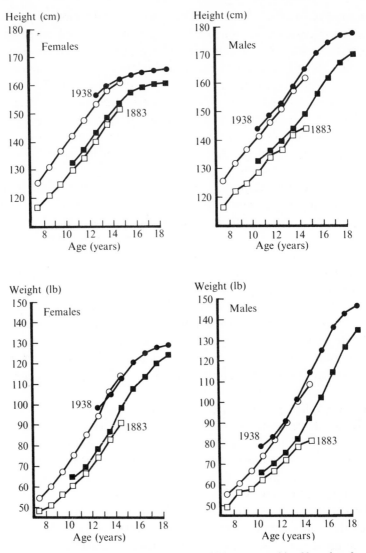

FIG. 18.18. Weights and heights of Swedish children measured in 1883 and 1938. Cross-sectional distance curves. (After Tanner 1962.)

9. Long-term change in growth and adolescence

It is well known that children are now growing very much faster and maturing earlier than formerly. This is a change that has been going on for the last 100 years and at a similar rate in many different countries (Figs. 18.18 and 18.19). The maximum increase between 1880 and 1950 is of about 2·5 cm and 2·0 kg per decade (during adolescence). It is sometimes stated

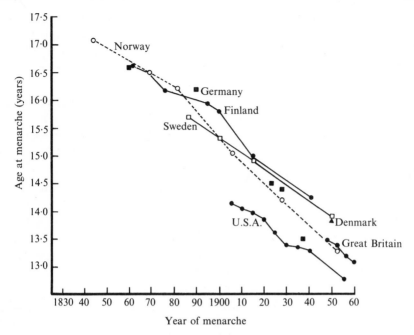

FIG. 18.19. Secular trend of age at menarche from 1830 to 1960. (After Tanner 1962.)

that what is involved is an earlier development, rather than a greater final size. This is only partly true. The final adult height has been increasing at about 1 cm/decade over the period. These figures are similar in British, Swedish, Polish, German, Japanese, and North American data.

The few earlier data available show that the phenomenon began only about 1830. Thus, the heights of Norwegian soldiers from 1760 until 1830 showed little increase. From 1830 until 1875 they increased at 0·3 cm/decade and from 1875 to 1935 at 0·6 cm/decade.

There is a similar change in the time of attainment of maturity, both in boys and girls (Fig. 18.19). Age at menarche has been getting earlier by 4 months/decade over the whole period 1830–1960 in western Europe and is still continuing at the same rate.

These facts of changing patterns of growth and maturation obviously have very large implications, both sociological and educational. If it is true that man has achieved his success by prolonging the period of childhood, then these tendencies could be considered retrogressive. But in any case we have to live with these conditions. In order to reconcile the tendencies for increased length of education and earlier maturity, we presumably need both a permissive attitude to the sexual needs of the teenagers and a greater spread of contraceptive knowledge. There is no reason why the sexually active boy or girl should be any the less able to study. It is a popular superstition that there is some creative value in sexual frustration and anxiety. Actually as good or better a case can be made out for the opposite. On the other hand, it is not easy to see how the very young can be at the same time good parents and good students—but this can be avoided.

The problems produced by this long-term trend are not insuperable. However, it would be satisfactory to have a fuller understanding of its causes and of the probable future. Better nutrition and environment are obviously partly responsible, especially perhaps for the greater growth. But the poorer classes have gained only a little more than the richer. It has been suggested that the acceleration of growth is due to these environmental causes but that the increase in final size is due to heredity. There has been a steady increase in outbreeding, especially since the introduction of easier transport, and the resulting heterosis (hybrid vigour) may be one of the causes of the increases in size. Thus the grown-up sons of Swiss children were 2 cm taller if their parents came from different rather than the same villages (Hulse 1957). But those marrying distant partners have many genetical features not found in the stay-at-homes and interpretation of the data is difficult.

Heterosis can hardly be the whole explanation for the changing developmental pattern (p. 599). Nor can the change be due to selection. It proceeds too fast, even if there were a fertility differential such that large people produce more marriageable offspring. Environmental conditions have been suggested as a possible cause. World temperature was rising from 1850 to 1940 but the rise was not continued between 1940 and 1960, yet the trend to earlier maturity was maintained.

We are left without any single convincing explanation. The phenomenon must be a recent one, since it obviously cannot be extrapolated backwards indefinitely. There is evidence that in Austria in 1610 peasant girls menstruated 'much later than the daughters of the townsfolk or aristocracy, and seldom before their seventeenth, eighteenth, or even twentieth year' (see Tanner 1968). Shakespeare gives the age as 14 (Juliet); this may be a literary convention, but even so it perhaps suggests a widely accepted figure. There was probably a considerable retardation in the early nineteenth century, presumably as a result of the bad conditions produced in the early industrial revolution. Perhaps we could describe the more recent acceleration as one of the fruits of the later phases of invention. The more remote effects of the trend and its effects upon fertility and education are difficult to foresee.

19

MATURATION OF THE BRAIN AND THE STUDY OF THINKING

1. Growth and maturation of the brain

THE growth of the size and weight of the brain can in practice be studied only cross-sectionally (Fig. 17.10 and Table 17.1). The brain is almost complete by the age of 7 or 8, and so far as is known it shows no acceleration at adolescence. But size alone is a poor measure of the efficiency of a computing organ. What we need to know is the growth of the pattern of connectivity, yet only elementary ways of measuring connectivity are available, even in an adult (see Sholl 1956). The number of nerve cells does not increase after the time of birth; nor, probably, does that of glia cells. The branching pattern of the dendrites certainly gradually becomes much more elaborate (Eayrs and Goodhead 1959, Purpura et al. 1964), but we have little understanding of what this signifies, how it is related to the computing power of the brain, or whether the branching is itself influenced by the use that is made of the cell.

The progress of development as the child grows depends partly upon maturation by processes that are a continuation of the morphogenetic operations of the embryo. There is, however, no hard-and-fast line between maturation and the acquisition of skills by a process of learning. Such actions as learning to walk clearly involve maturation, but practice plays a part. Similarly, recent linguistic studies suggest that learning to speak, though certainly dependent upon practice and listening to other people, may also be dependent upon maturation (Lenneberg 1965). Certain basic similarities in all languages (such as the existence of word units, though not of particular ones) and indeed the existence of grammar itself (though not of particular grammars), suggest an anatomical basis. Other actions, such as learning to write or to ride a bicycle, depend upon maturation only in the general sense that they require the presence of an adequate neuro-muscular system.

It would help education very much to know more about the optimal relationship between particular stages of maturation and power to learn. Use assists the development of effective patterns of connectivity (see Sperry 1968). Conversely, it might be that attempting to learn complex patterns precociously actually retards maturation. It may be that learning consists in appropriate training of a system of classification neurons, each recording a particular feature of environmental change (Chapter 42). The time to begin accumulating such units of memory (mnemons) would be as soon as they are ready, and suitable tests should show this.

It is now known that experience during a particular short period is necessary for proper development (Hubel and Wiesel 1970). The receptive fields of cells of the striate cortex of the kitten develop abnormally if one eye is kept closed for as little as three or four days between the fourth and seventh week after birth. The more complex classifiers may develop only after the simple ones, and probably new types of classification can be developed by use. But evidently there are limited critical periods when experience can produce its effects, though as yet we know almost nothing about these in man. The effect of the whole process of learning is to build in the brain a model that can be used to forecast the probable outcome of events. The aim of education is to make this model adequate to meet the situations that the individual is likely to encounter.

In general, the parts of our behaviour-pattern that develop later probably depend more on learning and culture than those that appear earlier. However, it would be unwise to use this as a maxim to prove that a late-appearing trait has been learned and owes little to maturation. To give one obvious example, the multiple activities of sex behaviour reach their full expression only as the gonads develop and the hormones they produce come to act upon the brain. These influences produce changes in the operations of the cerebral computer that may be startling equally to the adolescent and those around him. The primary targets of the sex hormones are presumably in the hypothalamus. Their effect is to make the individual much more sensitive to sexual signs of all sorts, in particular those from the other sex. At the same time, the tendency to act in such a way as to emit signs and behaviour that lead towards sexual intercourse is increased. These tendencies are undoubtedly the direct result of the operation of hormones on the nerve cells of the brain, and we should expect that they will issue in behaviour as directly related to their ends as do the effects of hunger and thirst upon the hypothalamic centres for eating or drinking. The fact that overt sexual behaviour does *not* always result is one of the most interesting of human biological features. We can relate this to the very late onset of our sexual maturation and to the restraints imposed by social life.

2. Person language and the logical capacities

As a child grows the performance of its cerebral equipment is clearly in some sense improving. It is learning new skills, acquiring more information, and becoming more 'intelligent'. It is natural that we should be interested in this process of change, since we are anxious to assist it towards the end of producing an effective adult. However, for the child, the living of its life is more important than preparing to develop properly into something else. At all times every individual must undertake the actions necessary for homeostasis. We may be better able to help a child to develop by remembering its needs *every day*, than by continually fixing attention upon some goal, as yet unseen by it, and therefore not obviously important. In particular, many of the actions that seem to the adult to be random expressions of emotion, or at best 'play', may serve the child in some way at the time, as well as being necessary steps to a further stage.

Our thesis is that the infant's earliest methods for obtaining what it needs are to elicit appropriate responses from those around it (p. 138). Among the earliest functioning systems in the brain will therefore be those concerned with communication. The first phenomena that the child attends to in the outside world are those provided by other people, especially parents (Fantz 1965). Its responses are directed to obtaining satisfaction of its needs from these people. The child is completely selfish and egocentric. The only features of the world that concern it are those that minister to its wants, and *these are mostly the features and responses of men and women*. It is for this reason that the whole method of observation and communication adopted by all mankind is essentially anthropomorphic. Ways of observing and describing the world other than by human analogies and comparison with people develop only slowly, and are only partially adopted in the speech even of the most sophisticated adults. We all need 'person language' all our days. We may reject primitive animism, or even all theism, but we still need to speak in terms of I and you, self and otherness, subject and object, and a host of such concepts that derive from the model with which we operate as children. How could it be otherwise since this is the way our brains first learned to work?

The task in following the growth of intelligence is to try to see how the homeostatic system changes, so that the child proceeds from helpless dependence on communication with its parents to the ability to use complex symbolism to wrest a living from the earth. For in spite of the pervasiveness of person language that we have been considering, it is by his more complex operations that man today earns his living. In particular, he depends upon his tools and machines and the language and mathematics that go with them. It is right, then, that in trying to measure the growth of intelligence we should use especially tests of logical powers and of information acquired with them. We can do this without denying the importance of aesthetic and emotional reactions, which are, as it were, the expressions of homeostatic capacity and achievement at all stages of life. In this sense emotional reactions are the very stuff of life, expressing the ends for which it is lived, whereas the logical symbolism provides us with tools to achieve those ends. The finding of a good way of life obviously depends upon making a satisfactory linkage between the two.

3. 'Thinking'

The measurement of intelligence is notoriously difficult and there are special problems in studying its growth. We may perhaps gain some help in finding methods by equating it with computing power. This, however, is only a rather superficial formulation if one aspires to describe the development of all the complexity of the thinking of a human being, which is obviously a very hard task. It has been approached in many ways (see Inhelder and Matalon 1960).

Almost any attempt to analyse so complex a system is likely to be open to the criticism either that it is too diffuse and general to be scientifically useful or that it is precise only because of what it omits. As an example of an attempt to meet this challenge, we shall first examine the study by Bartlett of 'Thinking' (1964). It is interesting because it is both thoughtful (sophisticated) and scientific (factual). Bartlett begins with the proposition that what we call thinking is 'a high-level form of skilled behaviour, requiring signs and symbols for its expression, yet still possessing many of the characteristics of the earlier established bodily skills from which it may have developed and which it has supplemented'. Accepting this proposition for the moment, thinking must therefore follow the pattern of all skilled responses in that it is set into the form of a significant sequence in which transition is made with proper timing from one direction to another until a point of no return is reached and the sequence terminated.

If this approach is correct it should be possible to make experiments by which the efficiency of thinking by different people in various situations is measured, just as their bodily skills can be measured. Bartlett devised a number of such experiments. Fundamentally all kinds of thinking start from what we can call factual evidence. This consists of items, simple or complex, laid out in a sequence but leaving a gap. The task of thinking is to fill the gap either by interpolation, to complete the series, or by extrapolation to extend it. Bartlett seeks to demonstrate that this is true of a great variety of tasks described as thinking, whether they be analytical, as in mathematics or science, or creative, as in literary composition or painting. Of course it would take a long time to discuss whether such a system adequately covers the whole of cognitive activity. We can only give examples.

In Bartlett's simplest experiment observers were told: 'Take 1 as the first and 17 as the last number, and fill up the gap between them in any way that seems to be indicated.' The people asked (in Great Britain or America) were found to use one of four ways in the following proportions:

A (43%)   1, 3, 5, 7 · · · · · · · · · · · · · · · 17,
B (36%)   1, 2, 3, 4, 5, · · · · · · · · · · · · 17,
C (14%)   1,   9,   17,
D (7%)   various individual and often
             fanciful responses.

Disregarding the last class, Bartlett points out that the thinking consists in determining the number and order of steps to be taken. These have to be decided from the information available, supplemented, where necessary, in some way by the information stored in the individual. If one item of information as to the number of steps is given, the 'correct' interpolation is more nearly settled as, say, with the odd numbers, by

$$1, 3, \cdots \cdots \cdots 17.$$

Even so, many people will decide to 'break the rule of the steps' as they proceed, for example

1, 3, 5, 9, 13, 17
or 1, 3, 7, 11, 13, 15, 17.

Considering this absurdly simple example begins to make us think about the problem of how to study thinking. Bartlett follows it with an example with words. He tells subjects: 'Look at the terminal words and then fill up the gap in any way that you think to be indicated.'

A, By · · · · · · · · · · · Horrible.

This was given, *after* the above number problem, to over 200 people, but only two made what Bartlett regarded as complete 'transfers', namely:

A, By, Car, Dive, Eager, Fright, Gaskets, Horrible, and
A, By, Can, Door, Every, Floods, Gunners, Horrible.

Three others produced an alphabetical sequence of initial letters without control of the number in the words. All the rest made up 'meaningful' sentences, often very ingenious. If now further information was given as

A, By, Cow · · · · · · · · · · Horrible,

a number of the observers produced series with one or other of the critical features, but the majority still tried to make up a meaningful sentence. Only with a fourth item of information were nearly all 'brought into line'.

These experiments immediately raise the questions that recur in discussions of how we may study thinking and intelligence. It will be objected that the observers who were concerned to make a story out of the words were thinking at least as hard as those who were 'correct'. Further, that correctness is determined by previous experience of this or similar tests or ways of treating data, but if there is no other reason why should it have preference over others? Indeed those who value words will say that to think about them in this ordered, numerical way is outrageous.

The difficulty is that similar objections can be raised against any attempt to analyse the results of human cerebral activities. A common reply to this is that such activities are, by their nature, outside the range of analysis and measurement. We can agree that there are great dangers of over-simplification in such matters without going so far as to deny that further advance is possible.

Somewhat similar experiments have been made by others, with added investigations to follow the course of the thinking of the subject. Thus Wason (1968) told subjects that the series 2, 4, 6 conformed to a simple rule which they had to discover by generating several series of their own. After each series they were told only whether their numbers conformed to the rule, which was 'numbers in increasing order of magnitude'. The subjects were told to announce the rule when they thought they had detected it. If it was wrong they were asked to continue. They could of course test their hypotheses by generating as many series as they wished before announcing a decision.

Out of 29 subjects 22 announced at least one incorrect rule, 9 of these a second one, and 2 a third. Only 6 announced the correct rule without any incorrect ones, and these people *varied and tested their hypotheses much more frequently* than those who announced an incorrect rule. After a mistaken announcement the subjects mostly showed signs of unwillingness to give up the erroneous hypothesis. The tendency to form and adhere tenaciously to hypotheses is evidently very strong, even in intelligent people. Moreover, 'most people are unable to use the procedure of negative proof—it would appear to be a totally alien concept' (Wason 1968). It is no wonder that people who think in closed systems, such as many of those of religion and politics, and indeed science, are unable to entertain the possibilities of alternatives, and so easily fall into error. The framing of hypotheses on a basis of the apparent fit of the evidence to previous ideas is probably one of the brain's chief ways of operating. It has great advantages in economy of storage, but also very great weaknesses and indeed dangers (see Popper 1965).

The strategies that people adopt in solving various classes of logical problems can now be studied by on-line computer control. The computer is programmed to display the problem to a subject, and records his efforts. Models of various possible means of solution are then developed and compared with the actual behaviour. In this way a General Problem Solver that learns has been developed. Such approaches may lead to great improvement in teaching people how best to go about solving problems (Newell, Shaw, and Simon 1963, Norman 1970).

4. Adventurous and creative thinking

Bartlett proceeds with his method to discuss 'adventurous thinking', including the activities of the creative scientist and artist. His experiments suggest that 'Thinking, as a mental process, likes, so to speak, to go on in closed systems.' By this he means sequences of the relatively easy and fixed interpolative kind that we have been considering. However, there are 'those forces which lie behind the human zest for adventure and are continually revolting against and breaking out of the closed system'. It is these that produce what he calls adventurous thinking. It is because of this preparedness to consider them that his approach provides a valuable introduction to the question of finding methods of measuring intelligence.

The broad objectives of thinking he holds to be nearly always the same. The thinker tries to use the information available to reach some terminus, based upon the information but not identical with it. In making this passage the thinker tries to go through a series of stages such that any normal person will agree with his conclusions. In closed-system thinking, such as, say, that of logic or arithmetic, the aim is to compel others to agree. As thinking becomes more 'open' or 'adventurous' the thinker's hope becomes more that others will approve of his steps and conclusions rather than be compelled to the latter.

One very important difference between open and closed thinking obviously lies in the completeness of the information available. All thinking must start from some information, and both the scientist and the artist are, in a sense, trying to complete something, either by filling gaps or by extending the limits that the information allows. The scientific thinker in a closed system is searching for something that is 'there', or should be, in the system. The open experimenter is 'in the position of somebody who must use whatever tools may be available for adding to some structure that is not yet finished'. He is trying to find something but does not yet know what it is. This is the truly creative situation that can also be described as scientific doubt (see *Doubt and certainty in science*). We find it difficult to analyse the procedures that it adopts, but, taking Bartlett's point of view, one can discuss whether it is a 'skill'. Undoubtedly some people are better at it than others. Some have a 'natural', perhaps inherited, gift for it, but equally it is possible to train people to think adventurously, and this produces a different result from training to think only *within* a system.

This may well be denied by some people, who will hold that the capacity to think creatively is in some sense a 'gift'. They would perhaps hold that it can be allowed to develop but not that it can be taught. Indeed, the comparison with a skill may seem odious. The fact is that we do not understand how the brain produces these original conclusions, which are based on so little evidence. But it is defeatist to assume that we never shall know anything about it. However much 'true artists' may cherish their gift, it is unbecoming of them not to recognize that 'true scientists', by wanting to study them, show only their great admiration of these gifts.

We can then agree that in the study of thinking and in the testing of intelligence it should be possible to devise ways both of measuring adventurousness of thinking and, more important, of increasing it.

Even the thinking of the artist begins with information, but he has his own particular way of selecting it. He chooses not just what is presented to him but the selection that he feels is for him the most suitable. His aim is to produce some work that shall be convincing and satisfying to himself and to others. His choice must be dictated partly by the insight that he has consciously or unconsciously acquired into the way that others perceive or feel. Thus a painter may use spots of colour (the pointillistes), or a series of stripes with the brush (van Gogh), or a series of rectangular coloured forms (cubists), or follow the curves and other outlines to indicate the nature of objects. The eye and brain make use of these and other transformations of the flux of light around. What the artist is doing might be described as breaking the code by which other people see or hear. He can then communicate with them directly by his pictures, his musical sounds, or his written words. Of course the purposes of communication are very varied and the artist will use that part of the 'language' that arouses in himself some desired emotional or intellectual response.

We have hardly any understanding of what provides some people with the capacity to select certain among all the data around us and combine elements of them in satisfying ways. The process is undoubtedly one of extrapolation and the product grows as the artist works at it. Its final form may only become apparent gradually, as, for example, when a novelist's characters take charge of his story. Much of the artist's capacity may be innate, but much obviously depends upon his experiences and at least in this sense can be learned, even though it may be that at its best it cannot be 'taught'. The mechanisms for selection and for composition of a whole must stand in some relation to what we have called the model in the brain.

We may admit, then, that we find it difficult to know how to analyse 'open' scientific or artistic thinking, but not that the concept of doing so is impossible. Many people will perhaps protest that they still think that to try to do so is undesirable, because it restricts creative genius. But it is only by extending our capacity for study of the higher powers of the human brain that we can correct the tendency to assess only the lower powers. This, unfortunately, has been in the main the limit of 'intelligence tests', to which we must now turn.

20

THE MEASUREMENT OF INTELLIGENCE

1. The difficulties and dangers of measuring brain power

A LARGE range of methods of testing human cerebral capacities has been
devised and the search still continues. The classical system of testing that
was originated by the Frenchman Binet, together with Simon, in 1905 has
been brought up to date and is still widely used. Many other tests have
been devised, both of 'general intelligence' and of special capacities, emotional responses, or social gifts. Classification of personality was already
practised by the Greeks. Immanuel Kant (1798) summarized the history
of the four temperaments: sanguine, melancholic, choleric, and phleg-
matic. Medical psychologists such as Kretschmer and Jung elaborated
such classes but without systematic testing. Galton and Spearman were
largely responsible for the initiation of testing in England, and it was
developed there by Burt, and by Guilford, Cattell, and many others in
America (see Eysenck and Eysenck 1969). These studies have produced
a whole system of assessment, mainly devised and controlled by psychologists. However, the tests are used in education, alongside other examination techniques, mainly controlled by teachers and other academics, who
have little knowledge of psychology. It is difficult to make a general judgement of the value of these techniques of assessment (see Vernon 1966).
Indeed, they vary in their efficacy and in their effects, not only between
nations and communities, but even between sections of one community.
The effect of an examination may be quite different on the students in
different departments of the same university or school—according to the
attitudes of the staff and of the students themselves.

It is important, therefore, to approach this subject with consideration
of some of the facts of human interaction, especially in situations that
involve dominance and dependence, such as those between teacher and
pupil or employer and employed (see Hudson 1966).

2. Test performance depends on the relations of the tested and tester

The cerebral capacities of a human being cannot be measured like his
height without influencing what is measured. Into all intelligence tests

there enters the question of why the test is being given, by whom, and with what probable effects of success upon the testee. Human beings live in social systems, with which their individual homeostatic systems are closely bound up. Tests are nearly always part of the social system, and this will determine the sort of results that they give. It has been argued that the function of intelligence tests in British education has been to justify the system and then to perpetuate it (Pidgeon 1966). There is evidence that the standard reached by pupils depends partly upon the standard expected, at least for achievement tests. Thus in Britain the proportion of children obtaining good certificate examination results varies greatly in schools in different areas—perhaps because the expectations differ. As an absurd example, there is the belief of some teachers that only abler children can be taught French. In fact some children are better at languages than other subjects.

This factor of the social influences and expectations with which the question of intelligence is approached can never be ignored in the application of any testing procedure to large numbers of individuals.

3. All tests are empirical

The second fundamental difficulty is that all attempts to test intelligence are at present empirical, in the sense that we have almost no idea of the nature of the cerebral processes involved. We do not know how the brain operates to allow each individual to maintain himself satisfactorily by adjustment to his circumstances. For example, capacity to use language freely is obviously of the first importance, but we have no hypothesis, even, about the changes in brain activity by which language capability increases in the child nor upon what particular stimuli it depends. The capacity to make comparisons and to recognize sets is often used in intelligence tests. We do not know what it depends upon, but psychologists have shown that such tests correlate with school performance and success in life.

Such considerations compel one to the conclusion that until we have more basic knowledge we should try to avoid depending upon tests, wherever we possibly can. Above all, we should greatly increase our efforts to understand the higher cerebral capacities. The best reason for assessment of different people is to help them, and especially to find how they can use their capacities to the utmost for the benefit of themselves and others.

4. Is there a general factor of intellectual capacity?

We know so little of cerebral function that it is impossible either to assert or deny that there is a single scalar quantity called intelligence, perhaps with a largely inherited factor. It has been widely debated both whether there is such a factor and whether it is hereditary (see Chapter 38). The question is partly the technical one of statistical techniques for extracting a common factor from tests of different abilities (see Burt 1955, Eysenck and Eysenck 1969). British psychologists have tended to believe that a single factor, Spearman's *g*, forms a large part of intellectual capacity (p. 268). On the other hand American psychometrists recognize 'a number of distinctive, even if overlapping, faculties or factors' (Vernon 1964). Burt summarizes his view as that 'These converging lines of enquiry, therefore, furnished strong presumptive evidence for a mental trait of fundamental importance defined by three variable attributes: first, it is a *general* quality; it enters into every form of mental ability; secondly, it is . . . an *intellectual* quality—that is, it characterizes the cognitive rather than the affective or conative aspects of conscious behaviour; thirdly, it is inherited or at least *innate*. . . . We thus arrive at the concept of an *innate, general, cognitive* ability (for which) what better label can be found than the traditional term "intelligence"?' For an opposite view see p. 267.

Burt himself recognizes that 'each of the three propositions that I have just laid down has been vigorously challenged'. A useful distinction was made by Hebb (1949) when he wrote 'the word "intelligence" has two valuable meanings. One is (A) an *innate potential*, the capacity for development, a fully innate property that amounts to the possession of a good brain and a good neural metabolism. The second is (B) the functioning of a brain in which development has gone on, determining *an average level of performance or comprehension* by the partly grown or mature person. Neither of course is observed directly; but *intelligence B*, a hypothetical level of development in brain function, is a much more direct inference from behaviour than *intelligence A*, the original potential.'

5. Multiple factor analysis

These are useful theoretical clarifications but the real problem is the difficulty of defining and measuring human capacities; which, fortunately, are extremely varied.

Individuals differ widely in the cerebral operations by which they adjust to their surroundings. For example, some are 'outgoing' and also prepared to take risks. Others are 'reserved' and also cautious. Some use verbal language more readily than quantitative and yet others use visual imagery. Some have a good memory and are conformist, others with the same memory capacity are 'creative', and some are creative but have a poor memory. And so on through all the possible combinations of ability and character.

The multiplicity of components of the human intelligence is recognized by the intensive development of *factor analysis* by Burt, and by Thurstone and others in America. In such tests 'each intellectual component or factor is a unique ability that is needed to do well in a certain class of tasks or tests' (Guilford 1959). The factors or intellectual abilities may be grouped in two different ways—first according to the kind of operation performed and secondly according to the material or content involved. The first classification gives five groups of intellectual activities: cognition, memory, convergent thinking, divergent thinking, and evaluation. Each of these may operate differently (in any individual) on material whose nature may be found in one of three classes: figural (i.e. things we see or hear), symbolic (i.e. letters, digits, or other signs), or semantic (i.e. verbal meanings or ideas). It is questionable whether such batteries of tests are better predictors than tests of general intelligence (McNemar 1964).

Factor analysis produces a system that indeed includes a wide variety of human capacities. It meets many of the objections to testing, though perhaps at the cost of producing an unusably cumbrous system. But inevitably an adequate system will be complex. If we are to allow individuals to develop optimally we must recognize these differences and encourage them in educational and vocational procedures. Society needs to develop these distinct qualities as much as does the individual. The danger of many test procedures of the 'intelligence test' type is that they tend to ignore differences and to reduce them. There is a 'right' answer to the test, determined by the tester and the society that he represents. Inevitably, conformity is rewarded. As Liam Hudson (1966) puts it, we should not make assumptions about the potentialities of a child (or any individual) until we have exhausted every possible means of eliciting them. This is a hard saying for the educational administrator, but it should be the motto of every teacher—and tester.

6. Correlation of test results and careers

Finally, there is the growing suspicion that many tests do not in fact predict performance of the abilities they are supposed to measure. Thus MacKinnon (1962) showed that in America the level of IQ (Terman Concept Mastery Test) correlates only -0.08 with creative achievement. Hudson (1966) in Britain found that successful scientists, judges, and politicians had not achieved better university degrees than less successful men. Twenty-three per cent of Cambridge Fellows of the Royal Society got second- or third-class degrees, against 21 per cent of the control group. Forty-three per cent of D.Sc.s got 'seconds' or less against 31 per cent controls. Fifty-four per cent of High Court Judges and 66 per cent of Cabinet Ministers (1945–59) had 'seconds' or less. This is only a small sample, but 'success' evidently depends on more than ability in examinations. However the study by

Terman and Oden (1962) of 1528 children of high IQ showed that they were consistently successful in their careers for 40 years.

Certainly pessimistic assessments have not weakened the hold of examinations and tests upon western educational systems. The British Psychological Society has a large grant from the Department of Education to devise a new intelligence scale (5-12 yrs). An estimated 150 million tests were applied in American schools and colleges in 1964. It would be an unrealistic Canute who tried to reverse this flood, but there are more useful things to do with a tide than to defy it. Best of all would be to enlist its power for the release of useful energies. Examinations and tests should be themselves a creative part of education. They should be judged by the positive contribution they make to individuals and societies and by the information they provide about the underlying homeostatic processes.

7. Types of test and examination

It is not our purpose to provide a comprehensive exposition of the large variety of tests (see Meade and Parkes 1966). It is important, however, that any student of mankind should have some notion of their nature. The classification used here is ambitious but amateur.

1. *Verbal tests* depend upon capacity to state accepted meanings and to reason. They provide a good index of a person's capacity to operate in many parts of society. They are highly influenced by family, social, and other environmental factors. They are difficult to compare across cultures.

2. *Non-verbal tests* often involve recognition of similarities, irregularities, or omissions in sets—often visually presented. They are, perhaps, especially valid for mathematical and scientific attainments. They are easier to apply across cultures than verbal tests, though the variations in difficulty with culture may be hard to anticipate (Vernon 1969).

3. *'Intelligence tests'* (*Stanford-Binet*). The tests stemming from Binet in 1905 through their revision by Terman at Stanford, and since by many others, provide for each age a short series of tests involving both vocabulary and verbal facility and factual knowledge. Within limits, they can be modified across cultures. They remain the most widely used tests of 'general intelligence' (see p. 267).

4. *Tests of knowledge*, verbal or otherwise, are useful in relation to particular cultures, especially where conformity is at a premium. They are greatly influenced by cultural factors.

5. *Tests of special abilities.* These are so numerous as to make a subject of their own. They include assessments of capacities such as numerical manipulation, clerical manipulation, musical power, creativity, spatial orientation, and a host of others.

6. *Tests of attainment and information.* These are put in a special class to include what might be called conventional examinations. They range from the earliest tests of reading, writing, and arithmetic to examinations for final honours and Ph.D.s and a host of professional examinations. They are an integral part of our educational and social system. It is difficult to see how we could do without them, but it is also difficult to feel sure that their effects are what they are supposed to be, either for the individual or for society.

7. *Tests of personality.* 'Personality' has been studied for centuries by many different types of psychologist and psychometrist, clinical, experimental, and plain venal, and new techniques are constantly appearing. The models developed range from those of Freudian psychoanalysts to behaviourists. The former are expressed in a person language (the mind is said to contain entities such as the 'ego', 'id', and 'superego'). The behaviourist's model attempts to describe the human behaviour in terms of the actions of the brain, nerve impulses, synapses, and conditioning. Each school has, of course, its own methods of 'testing', if only for the purpose of assigning to each individual the labels appropriate in terms of the model. Indeed the pre-scientific language of all societies does this with such concepts as good and bad, saint and sinner. We all make such classifications in the operations of daily life with our fellows, whether or not we use the labels (see Vernon 1964, Eysenck 1962). Personality tests include series of questions that elicit the characteristic traits of a person, such as sociability, impulsiveness, activity, and liveliness. It is claimed that responses to such tests are correlated in a manner that enables one to define a limited number of types of personality—in particular those tending to extraversion on the one hand or neuroticism on the other. Moreover, these are held to carry a large inherited factor and to be the product of recognizable physiological variables, especially in the ascending reticular and autonomic nervous systems (Eysenck and Eysenck 1969). It is doubtful whether we know enough to make more than preliminary correlations of this sort.

In spite of all the difficulties that have been discussed (and there are many others), tests at present form an integral and inescapable feature of advanced societies, though some movements would try to free us from them. Systematically administered under standard conditions, they allow performance to be compared with norms arrived at from tests of large groups. The great variety of tests available allows for some estimate to be made of different human capacities, and indeed also emotional responses and manifestations of 'character'.

Inevitably, any test only measures the response of the individual to an examiner, who proposes to compare him with some standard. In whatever way the test is designed it is orientated by the examiner, rather than by responses initiated by the child. The investigations of the Swiss psychologist J. Piaget (to be described later) partly overcame this difficulty, since the observer, while beginning with standard questions, then pursued the investigation with subsidiary ones. Moreover in this way the complexities of the brain's operations are also, perhaps, more fully revealed, though no numerical rating on a scale is achieved. Some measures, such as the Stanford-Binet Intelligence Test, have been arranged to provide a continuous measure of ability at all ages from 2 years to maturity. Even when such a nominally homogeneous scale is applied, it is certain that different powers are being tested at different ages. Indeed, it may be that when we ask whether 'intelligence' has increased, we really mean to inquire whether *new* modes of brain functioning have appeared, which by definition, could not be measured earlier because they were not yet there.

Investigation of intelligence at least does not meet the difficulty that it cannot be the subject of longitudinal studies. It is only too easy to give repeated tests. There is, however, the problem of the error introduced by the practice effect on the tests. Longitudinal studies have certainly shown largely consistent performance by children over long periods. This seems, at least, often to be true for school-age children, and it may increase our confidence that what is measured includes a body of coherent capacities. That is not of course to say that these are the most relevant capacities for all purposes of assessment. Different forms of testing may serve to measure different qualities.

8. Measures of intelligence in infancy

It is fundamentally important that we should realize that we have not yet achieved any real understanding of the cerebral processes underlying intelligence, nor how to measure them. This appears when we try to extend measurement back to birth. The Berkeley Growth Study has followed sixty-one Californian children from birth to 25 years (Bayley 1955). For the infants, they used tests based upon the work of Gesell at Yale and found that their estimates of the children oscillated strikingly. 'There was no relation between relative performance in the first few months of life and scores earned at the end of the first year.'

It is easy to say that the tests must have been inadequate. But, as Nancy Bayley puts it, 'efforts to devise other more adequate scales invariably run into the hard fact that infants exhibit a very limited range of behaviours that can be observed and recorded. . . . At first there is little to note beyond evidences of sensory functioning in reacting to appropriate stimuli. One can observe that the 1-month-old looks momentarily at a dangling ring, or at a rattle. . . . A little later the responses are evidenced in motor coordinations: the 6-month-old may pick up a 1-inch cube or a teaspoon placed in easy reach. There are some early evidences of adaptation to the presented stimuli, of memory from a past experience: the 7-month-old, for example, looks "aware" that a fallen toy is no longer there, and when a little older he may turn to look for it on the floor. One can note the progression of vocalizations as they become more complex and then as they are used meaningfully. . . . The question is: Which, if any, among these is the forerunner of later intellectual functions? Which, if any, will predict the individual differences found in school-age children?'

In order to try to find an answer to this question Bayley and her colleagues took six children at each extreme of intelligence as measured at 14–16 years and went back over their scores on various tests when they were infants. They found 31 items in which those scoring high as teenagers had seemed to be 2 months or more advanced over the other six as infants. Perhaps these, though an odd lot of items, somehow served to reveal intelligence. Alas, when this method was applied to the whole available group of Berkeley children, the intelligence scores at 16–18 years were found to correlate with the thirty-one-item infant scale only 0·09 for 6 months, 0·32 at 9 months, and 0·30 at 12 months.

More recently, in a re-examination of the data, a correlation has been found in girls, but not boys, between later intelligence test scores and the time of appearance of certain items of vocalization (e.g. 'says da-da', 'says two words') (Cameron, Livson, and Bayley 1967). This slightly modifies Bayley's earlier pessimistic conclusion that there is 'little hope of ever being able to measure a stable and predictable intellectual factor in the very young'. Perhaps the reason for this difficulty 'rests in the nature of intelligence itself. I see no reason why we should continue to think of intelligence as an integrated (or simple) entity or capacity which grows through childhood by steady accretions.' This contrasts with Burt's view, p. 262.

These are arresting if sobering facts and ideas. Yet it is unlikely that they represent the last word in the matter. They show the type of conclusion that is reached by trying to study the capacity of a system without attention to its actual operations. This 'black-box' approach is relatively easy and may have advantages, but if we are to understand our capacities more fully we must learn more of what goes on inside our heads. There is no other really satisfactory method. (For recent work on infants see Ambrose 1969.)

9. Development of intelligence in the schoolchild

After the age of 2 or 3 years the correlations between scores on tests of the Binet type become much more consistent, and correlate positively with later test scores. By about 5 or 6 years of age children can be reliably classified into normal, defective, or bright. It has therefore been suggested that three distinct factors are involved influencing performance in different proportions at the different ages. The first is sensory-motor alertness, the second persistence, and the third manipulation of symbols (Hofstaetter 1954). Over the later periods it is alleged to be possible to isolate several factors contributing to the performance and even a single factor, g, representative of all the capacities (see p. 262 and Spearman 1932, Burt 1940).

A usual method of representing the intelligence of a child is by estimating what is known as his IQ (intelligence quotient). This figure is arrived at after a procedure that has the effect of measuring the child's performance by comparing it with that of the average of children of the same age (Wechsler 1958, Terman and Merril 1961). For the Stanford–Binet scale the standard population has been derived from various types of communities in different parts of the United States. The 1960 revision was based on 4498 subjects, largely from California.

To determine the IQ each child is given a series of tests and achieves a score that represents his proportion of correct answers. This raw score is then adjusted to the appropriate point on a scale produced by reference to the standard population. A usual system is for 100 to be the mean score for each age and 16 to represent a departure of one standard deviation in either direction. Thus an IQ of 116 means that the child gave more correct answers than 84 per cent of those of his age in the standard population. Another method of scoring is to use the child's mental age, which is obtained by awarding a certain period, usually two months, for each test passed. Obviously before interpreting any statement about IQs it is important to know by which means they have been calculated. It is a much more difficult problem to measure the growth of intelligence. For this we need some absolute measure which has been looked for by various devices (see Bayley 1955). The technical problems involved are formidable but the result suggests a declining rate of growth of intelligence over the first 5 years (Fig. 20.1). This is constructed from a group of longitudinal curves and has the defects we have already considered (p. 200). The individual curves given show a generally similar pattern, however, and consistent differences.

Applied over a longer period this method has still greater difficulties (Figs. 20.2–20.4). Neither the group curve nor that of individuals show clear signs of an adolescent spurt. But it would be hard to deny that one occurs. The general shape of the curve suggests an increase that continues up to the age of 20, but at a declining rate. It seems probable that this does indeed provide a reasonable estimate of the growth of some aspect of cerebral capacity. It is obvious enough, however, that it does not really map the

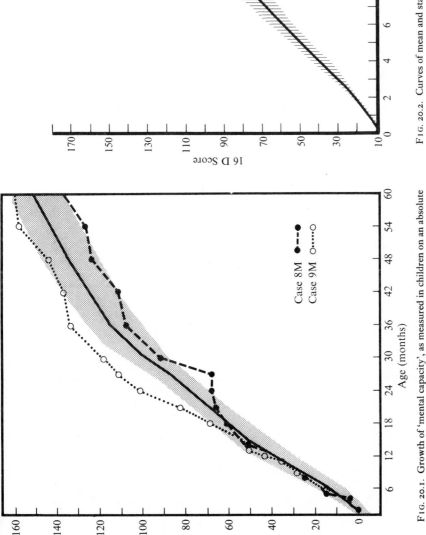

FIG. 20.2. Curves of mean and standard deviation of intelligence as measured by '16 D' units. The units were chosen to allow results of tests made earlier and later than 16 years to be compared. The mean score at age 16 is taken arbitrarily at 140 and the standard deviations appropriately adjusted. (Bayley 1955.)

FIG. 20.1. Growth of 'mental capacity', as measured in children on an absolute scale, during the first 5 years of life. The mean is indicated by —— and the dotted area indicates the standard deviation. Two individual cases are shown (After Bayley 1955.)

Case 8M ●––●
Case 9M ○····○

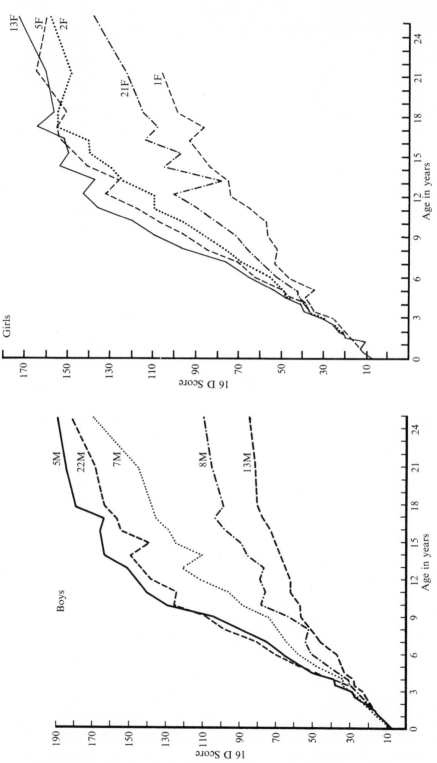

FIG. 20.3. Individual curves of intelligence growth (16 D units) for five boys from 1 month to 25 years of age. (Bayley 1955.)

FIG. 20.4. Individual curves of intelligence growth (16 D units) for five girls from 1 month to 25 years of age. (Bayley 1955.)

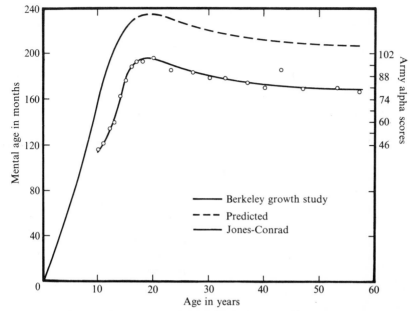

F IG. 20.5. Curves of intelligence in relation to age. The scores from the longitudinal Berkeley
Growth Study are expressed in a scale of mental age and compared with data by Jones and
Conrad (1933), which showed a lower level from a cross-sectional study up to 60 years. Other
data do not show the fall after adolescence (see Fig. 20.7). (Bayley 1955.)

development of the brain as a useful agent. For example, many people
begin to understand and use abstract symbolization only in the late teens.
This represents, perhaps, the biggest leap of the brain—to inquire into its
own processes—but is unrepresented in the graph.

10. Changes in adult intelligence

It is often held that intelligence as measured by usual tests is at a maximum at about the age of 20 and then declines (Fig. 20.5). But careful longitudinal studies suggest that there is a further small gain, perhaps continuing
even to the age of 70 (Figs. 20.6 and 20.7). This is not a conclusion that can
be considered as firmly established, but the increases registered can hardly
all be attributed to practice effects, since the tests were separated by many
years. The increase seems to occur among those scoring low, as well as
among the more intelligent.

11. Studies of social and emotional development

The Berkeley Growth Study included a periodic assessment of a number
of items that together indicate what may be called 'the dimensions of extraversion and introversion, love versus hostility' or positive versus negative
social responses (Schaefer and Bayley 1963). These are rather general

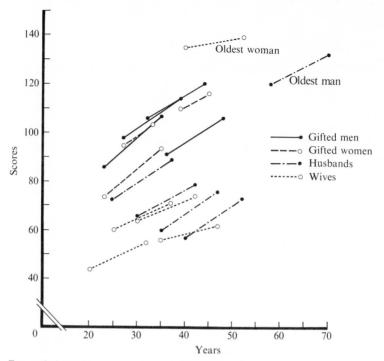

FIG. 20.6. Scores on a concept mastery test given twice, about 10 years apart, to especially gifted men and women and to their spouses. The first and second tests are connected. Even the oldest showed some improvement, the 'gifted' more than their spouses. (After Bayley and Oden 1955.)

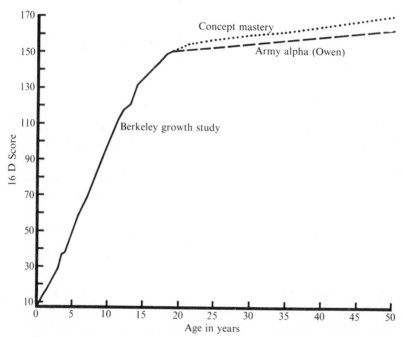

FIG. 20.7. A proposed age-curve of intelligence based on the Berkeley Growth Study, the Terman Gifted and Concept Mastery tests (Fig. 20.6), and Owen's study with the Army Alpha Test. (After Bayley 1955.)

('molar') terms used to express the results of very careful and objective ratings. Especially important for our purpose were the consistency of the findings for individual children, and their predictive value.

Ratings were made in early infancy of what may be called rapidity and activity (extroversion). These were found to be significantly *negatively* correlated with ratings of positive task-orientated behaviour up to 12 years old, in both boys and girls. However, 'positive and negative social adjustment during the first 2 years of life show very little correlation with later behaviour for either sex. More enduring patterns of adjustment develop at later ages since both social and task-orientated behaviours are relatively consistent for both boys and girls from about 4 to 12 years.' This stability of development during the latency period is thus similar for emotional and intellectual traits. However, unlike intellectual development, the emotional factors show rapid changes during adolescence.

This summary can do little more than indicate the possibility of such study. The Berkeley investigators actually combined the investigation of the children with that of their mothers, elucidating further factors that influence development. Obviously, it will be a long time before we have enough data to provide a proper analysis of all the many influences that affect the growth of human cerebral capacity, whether emotional or intellectual. Moreover, these will probably be found to differ greatly within different sections of a given culture and still more between cultures. The task of investigating these matters is indeed intimidating. But it is also challenging and can be undertaken in the hope that a truly scientific understanding of brain action is possible. Its value for the improvement of the human condition would be immense, though no doubt safeguards against abuse of knowledge of how to control people are necessary and should indeed have been applied long ago to the many who exploit us already.

12. The development of speech in the child

Study of the fundamental nature of language and grammar has recently allowed considerable advances in understanding of the stages by which the child acquires the characteristic human capacity to communicate (Chomsky 1957, Lenneberg 1967). This process is often called 'learning to talk', but the evidence suggests that this is not a skill that is 'taught', as is reading or writing, but is largely arrived at by maturation, like the capacity to walk.

'Why do children normally begin to speak between their eighteenth and twenty-eighth month? Surely it is not because all mothers on earth initiate language training at that time. There is, in fact, no evidence whatever that any conscious and systematic teaching of language takes place, just as there is no special training for stance or gait' (Lenneberg 1967).

If speech emerges as there develops in the brain those particular human features that allow communication, then it should develop similarly in all children. In fact, 'important speech milestones are reached in a fixed sequence and at a relatively constant age' (Lenneberg 1967).

Lenneberg has listed a series, with some counterparts in motor development.

Time, end of	Motor development	Vocalization and language
12 weeks	Lifts head. No grasp.	Smiles, coos, vowel-like sounds.
20 weeks	Grasps, sits with props.	Consonantal sounds, labial fricatives, spirants, and nasals.
6 months	Sits. Stands only with support.	Babbling. One syllable utterances, 'ma', 'da', 'di'.
10 months	Creeps, pulls to standing position.	Sound play, gurgling, imitates. Differentiated responses to words heard.
12 months	Walks when hand held. Crawls on feet and hands. Sits on floor.	Definite single words, 'mamma', 'dadda'. Definite understanding of simple commands.
18 months	Walks alone. Sits on chair. Builds tower with 3 cubes (hard).	Has repertoire of 3–50 word items, used singly. No frustration if not understood.
24 months	Runs, walks up and down stairs.	Vocabulary more than 50 words. Two-word phrases.
30 months	Jumps, stands on one foot. Builds tower of 6 cubes.	Vocabulary increasing very fast. Utterances of 2, 3, and even 5 words. Grammar not always understandable. Seems to understand everything said to him. Frustrated if not understood.
3 years	Runs, operates tricycle.	Vocabulary of 1000 words. Grammar complex essentially adult and understandable.
4 years	Jumps over rope, catches ball, walks a line.	Language differs from adult only in style rather than grammar.

This sequence is very regularly followed and cannot easily be broken. At one stage the child can say 'daddy' or 'bye-bye' but not combine these into a two-word sentence. The difficulty is cerebral, not in motor competence. The child at this age can babble long sentences with complex intonation patterns. Indeed the capacity to produce the fine movements of the larynx, tongue, and lips appears spontaneously long before the main period of acquisition of motor skills with the hands.

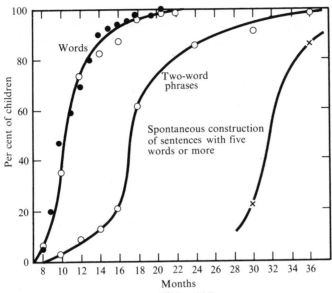

- ● 49 Austrian children (Bühler 1931)
- ○ 114 British children (Morley 1957)
- ✗ 500 American children (Boston, author's observation)

FIG. 20.8. Emergence of various developmental milestones in the acquisition of language. (After Lenneberg 1967.)

The rapidity with which the thresholds of speech capacity are passed is illustrated in Fig. 20.8, which also shows one example of the similarity of timing that is found in different cultures. Of course the child needs the appropriate environment to develop speech and, in particular, needs to hear the words of himself as well as others. Speech may mature remarkably well, however, with quite extreme deprivations, for example, when both parents are completely deaf. Again, deaf children go through the earlier stages of speech maturation as do normal ones, cooing at 3 months and babbling at 6 months. They never develop words but they become adept at communication by signs, conveying not only needs and ideas but opinions. The conclusion seems to be that human beings are endowed by heredity with certain cerebral powers that allow communication. We have no idea what features of brain organization are involved (see Chapter 42). Discovery about this will no doubt proceed rapidly in the next few decades and should provide knowledge that will help us to improve our education. The early stages of acquisition of speech seem to proceed satisfactorily in most children under the safe guidance of heredity. Perhaps there is not much to be done to assist them (in the normal child). For the next stages in the development of the power of thinking the situation is very different.

How do we pass from the first simple communications of the 2- or 3-year-old to the power to use the concepts that the child will acquire slowly over the next two decades of its life? Knowledge about these years is mostly unsystematic and yet it is here that a sound theory for teaching is most needed. As a basis for discussion we may use the penetrating investigations of the Swiss child psychologist Piaget, described in the next chapter.

21

THE DEVELOPMENT OF THE CHILD
AS SEEN BY PIAGET

1. The schema or action sequence

THE approaches that are used to frame intelligence tests have, as we have seen, put the need for quantification as their first aim. Piaget has tried rather to discover something of the steps by which a developing child approaches the full human reasoning powers. He recognizes a number of stages and sub-stages, but his work does not provide norms. The intelligence-test method depends upon the answers of children to a series of fixed questions or problems. Piaget gives the child a task or question, designed to test, say, his power to classify, then, after the reply or solution of a problem, the investigator proceeds to follow up with questions concerning the child's own reasons for the answer he has given. In such ways Piaget and his collaborators have succeeded in throwing some light on the gradual development of the capacities of the brain. The method is one for research rather than for practical application in the assessment of capacities (though it can be used for the latter; see Vernon 1965). The richness of the analysis makes the results difficult to summarize (see Flavell 1963). Indeed, part of its value is that it prevents us from falling into the dangerous trap of assuming that human affairs are simple.

The numerous works of Piaget constitute more than simply a study of developmental psychology. They are really a treatise on the nature of human thinking, including epistemology, or the study of how we think about the world. Whatever may be the place of Piaget's thesis among those of the many philosophers and psychologists who have studied these problems, he has certainly performed at least a preliminary analysis of the stages of development of the use of symbols. The treatment throughout involves much subjectivism, discussion of 'cognition', and so on, producing a system that is perhaps not ideal for describing the growth of cerebral capacities. Some of the concepts used for descriptive purposes are complex and may seem to the ordinary scientific reader to be burdened with unnecessarily difficult names. Many, however, are very useful, especially the concept of a 'schema'. In Piagetian language this is described as a 'cognitive structure which has reference to a class of similar action sequences . . .'

(Flavell 1963). Though we are warned that the concept is vague, rich, subtle, and full of shifting nuances, we can recognize that it is an attempt to isolate elements of behaviour. For each schema presumably there is a corresponding item of cerebral organization. Thus, at a simple level, the sucking sequence of a child is a schema. So, at the other extreme, is a problem-solving logical strategy of the adult.

The concept of the use of schemata is connected with that of 'assimilation'. 'No cognition (*connaissance*), even perceptual, is simply a copy of the real, because it always includes (*comporte*) a process of *assimilation* to anterior structures.' These structures are the schemata, which thus serve as inescapable filters, organizing the input in such a manner as to serve the needs of the individual for homeostasis. 'All cognition is tied (*liée*) to an action and to know (*connaître*) an object or an event is to utilize them by assimilating them to action schemes' (Piaget 1967).

'Knowledge (*les connaissances*) does not constitute a copy of the surroundings but a system of real interactions, which reflect the self-regulatory system of life rather than things themselves.'

These ideas are obviously close to many of those we have been trying to develop. They emphasize the position that the biologist feels bound to take over the ancient problem of our knowledge of the world.

2. The stages of development

It is easy to criticize Piaget, but few indeed have his immense range of experience and experiment to support them. It is not clear how far his system will provide the basis for analysis of behaviour and symbolism in the future. It is worth following today as a pioneer effort to categorize human behaviour, without undue over-simplification. Of course there have been very many other studies of children, and many systems for describing human behaviour, cognition, development, and cerebral capacities. Freud, for example, has much to say on all questions of symbolism. So, at another pole, have students and teachers of linguistics. Any introduction to the study of man should really attend to the contributions of these and many others. We shall limit ourselves in the present chapter to Piaget.

For purposes of description Piaget often identifies a number of stages and sub-stages. This device is obviously dangerous as well as useful. Children do not arrive at a stage and stay there until moving to the next. No stage is independent of those before or after, nor sharply marked off from them. Moreover, children's cerebral capacities develop at different rates, though rather closely in the same sequence, just as they do in other physical respects (Chapter 18).

The whole time of development may conveniently be divided into four main sections, each with subdivisions.

1. The period of sensory-motor intelligence (0–2 years).
2. The period of pre-operational thought (2–7 years).
3. The period of concrete operations (7–11+ years).
4. The period of formal operations (11 years onwards).

3. The period of sensory-motor intelligence (0–2 years)

During the first part of its life the child is a reactor, responding to the stimuli that fall upon it. It shows little sign that its actions are influenced by the presence in the brain of any representations of the objects or events around it; or at least, if such representations are forming, they do not yet allow the performance of delayed responses or solutions to the problems such as would be characterized as the results of 'thought' or 'reasoning'.

During this time the child is changing rapidly and Piaget recognizes six subdivisions:

1. In the first part of its life the child operates mostly by reflexes (0–1 month), then
2. these become interrelated (1–4 months).
3. The child begins to undertake actions towards objects outside its body, with the beginnings of aim (intentionality) or goal-directedness (4–8 months).
4. Such intentional sequences become a major part of the pattern from 8–12 months, when it is characteristic that particular behaviour patterns become habitual and are used rather indiscriminately in each new situation.
5. In the following stage new means of action are discovered by experiment, as if novelty were pursued for its own sake (12–18 months).
6. Only now do there begin to be signs of internal symbolic representations of problems, allowing the production of solutions implicitly rather than by trial and error. This is characterized as the stage of pre-operational thought ($1\frac{1}{2}$–2 years).

As a very rough indication of the sort of progression that is involved, we could take the response of the child to an object in its visual field. In the first stage it gives some response and it will fixate (see Fantz 1965), but probably not follow an object if it moves from the field. In the fourth stage the object seen will be grasped with the hand. Even so, no effort is made to retrieve an object when it leaves the visual field: it then ceases to exist for the child. A few months later the child will recover it when it is put under a pillow. If the child then sees the observer put his hand under the pillow and move the (concealed) object to another pillow he will at first not seek for it. Only at about 2 years is he able to retain some representation of it and to act accordingly.

These various 'stages' succeed each other in a rather regular sequence in all children, but with great differences in timing. Moreover, each stage does not displace the one before but new behaviours are added to the old ones to complete, correct, or combine with them.

Throughout this period the child shows little evidence of distinguishing things or events in the world around as apart from their action upon him or his upon them. In the first two periods he may be regarded as completely egocentric. In the third by his hand movements he begins to explore the world at least in its relation to himself. In the fourth period objects are seen in relation to each other, though still only in the context of their effect upon the child. In the fifth and sixth periods, at the end of the second year, the objects in the world are reacted to increasingly as independent of the child. They are introduced into play habits, related to each other spatially and temporally and with signs of the beginning of symbolization.

4. The period of pre-operational thought (2-7 years)

The development of the capacity for representation is, indeed, a chief characteristic of the period called that of pre-operational thought, from 2 to 7 years. In representational intelligence the child is 'able to differentiate signifiers from significates and thereby to become capable of evoking the one to call forth or refer to the other. The generalized capacity to perform this differentiation and thus to be able to make the act of reference Piaget designates as the *symbolic function*' (Flavell 1963). The development of this capacity continues throughout this period but is only fully put to use subsequently in the third main period, that of *'concrete operations'* (7-11 years).

The period of pre-operational thought is that in which the child develops his use of language. This involves far more than merely acquiring a set of capacities to produce sounds. The general task is to learn the substitution of symbols for direct stimulus–response situations. Symbols ultimately achieve more, but immediately may be poor substitutes as means of obtaining the satisfaction of needs. It is not too much to speak of 'the extreme and long-enduring hardship the child encounters in trying to cognize the world symbolically' (Flavell 1963).

The first words used probably still operate mainly as private signs, releasing particular pieces of behaviour. Just as the beloved blanket is the sign for going to sleep, so 'Mummy' refers not so much even to the person as to the child's needs. It would be ridiculous to try to give in a short space an adequate account of the elaborate process of the development of symbolization and concept formation. We here can only recognize the problem and its interest in our search for the essentials of human homeostasis.

A large part of the essence of learning to use symbols is to detach them from their particular relevance to ourselves. This is one of the hardest tasks for the egocentric child. He finds it hard to use reciprocal concepts such as 'brother' or 'foreigner' in the same sense in relation to himself and to others.

A further task is to learn to dissociate the symbol from what it represents. The study of the child's 'nominalism' indeed illuminates many stages of mental development. Questions asked of the child can revolve around the themes:

1. What is a name?
2. How did names start?
3. Did the sun always have its name?
4. How did we know the sun's name?
5. Can names change?

The answers show that for the child who is beginning to speak, names have an enduring reality attached to what they signify. Names have always been part of things and things know their names. Later this last will be recognized not to be true; then, later again, that names were given by men, though still considered as unalterable attributes, 'You know it is the sun by looking at it'. Only finally will it be recognized that the name is arbitrary and can be changed.

Such a sequence illustrates the gradual dissociation of a concept from its concrete attachments. Such processes must occur, but linguists disagree as to the particular sequences by which the use of conceptual symbolization is achieved. The fact is that we have no adequate model by means of which to discuss the processes that are involved. It should be a main aim of human biology and neurology to achieve some such model, so that we may understand and regulate ourselves better. All that we are doing here, however, is to call attention to the existence of the problem and to some of the heroic pioneer studies that attempt to find a solution. In our thinking on these problems we are, as it were, not far from the stage of the pre-operational child whom we are considering. He is only gradually acquiring a system that will adequately use all the information that is available.

If the child is shown two identical tall thin jars, A and A^1, full of liquid to the same level, he will agree that they contain the same amount. But if the liquid in A^1 is now poured into a broad jar B he will not agree that the amounts in A and B are equal. He cannot see that the extra height in A is compensated by the breadth in B. Children at these ages often seem to contradict themselves, 'they have no stable, enduring and internally consistent cognitive organization. His cognitive life, like his affective life, tends to be an unstable, discontinuous, moment-to-moment one.'

All these characteristics come from the fact that the symbolism is separating only gradually from its direct sensori-motor origins. The symbols are still used directly and concretely, in contexts determined by the more obvious characteristics rather than in actions requiring attention to underlying significations and references. Moreover, the child's transactions do not deal in proof or logical justification and are unconcerned about the effects of its communications upon others.

5. The period of concrete operations (7-11 years)

During the period of about 7-11 years the child learns how to use the capacity that it has acquired for symbolic representation. But the fact that it has begun to use symbols does not mean that it can quickly proceed to use all the various types of symbolism that are available in language. For most children, the techniques of abstraction necessary for operating such processes as those of science, logic, mathematics, historical assessments, practical forecasts, or moral judgements all have to be learned by patient acquisition of the details. It is true that in all children to some extent, and in some conspicuously, there develops at this time a coherence of capacity to use symbols of all sorts. It is as if the model developing in the brain includes overriding equipment, varying in power, that can be brought to bear on all logical problems. Nevertheless, many children remain able only to learn to operate individual symbols and their transforms, seriatim, one after the other. Looking at the problem in this way emphasizes the urgency of the need for deeper understanding of the nature of the computing processes that are involved.

Even the most gifted must learn how to use words and operations individually. Piaget has made elaborate studies of the steps by which this is done for a whole range of concepts dealing with matters as varied as space, number, quantity, geometry, causation, and moral judgement. These studies are pioneer efforts to provide a scheme by which we can understand the operations of the human brain. It is only possible here to give some examples, illustrative of the method.

In spite of revealing details of these various operations, it is interesting that Piaget picks on the over-all capacity to use symbolism as the chief characteristic of the period. The pre-operational child uses representations, it is true, but individually and with characteristic confusion, as if incapable of generalizing. This is the new power that was found to grow during the period of about 7-11 years in the Swiss children studied. The child becomes able to 'structure the present in terms of the past without undue strain and dislocation, that is, without the ever-present tendency to tumble into the perplexity and contradiction which mark the pre-schooler' (Flavell 1963).

The essence of the analysis is the study of the child's method of grouping, using a variety of logical operations such as those concerned with relationships of distance and position, parts and wholes, and indeed in non-cognitive operations such as interpersonal relationships. Piaget believes that he has discovered a set of nine personal properties that the groupings of a child's logic system comes to possess. To discuss these would involve an assessment of the extent to which Piaget has succeeded in 'anatomizing' the human system of logical operations—a task that has an ancient history. His first 'grouping', for example, specifies the essential operations involved in the manipulation of the symbolism of a hierarchy of classes. Spaniels, Pekinese, etc. are a class of domestic dogs; there is a class of non-domestic dogs (wolves, etc.). All dogs are members of the class Carnivora; there are other members (bears, cats, etc.). All Carnivora are mammals, etc. . . . Obviously the processes by which use of such hierarchal classification is achieved are among the fundamental features of our logical system. How far Piaget has succeeded in describing its growth by means of his nine groupings is partly a question for logicians, but for us more a question of observation of children and its interpretation. We cannot discuss the other groupings here, interesting though they are.

6. The period of formal operations (11 years onwards)

The final stage of development may be called the period of formal operations (11-15 years). This grows from the previous one, differing in that the possibilities of symbolic operation acquired are now themselves the subject for manipulation. 'Representational thought has . . . become hypotheticodeductive, orientated towards possibility as the supraordinate term and towards reality as the subordinate term' (Flavell 1963). This formulation may seem ponderous, like many of those of Piaget and his expositors (and indeed what philosopher is free of such language?). But perhaps the words give a suggestion of the final stage of liberation of the cerebral apparatus from the immediate concern of its user. It is by adopting the 'hypotheticodeductive' system that men have been able to make forecasts much more far-reaching and reliable than those of any animal. And this is the essential secret of man's success. Looked at in another way, it is the freeing of the brain from concern only with immediate details. This enables it to use the words and other symbols that it has learned in ways that produce new groupings, which are the essence of creative art and of science. They provide the hypotheses with which further search for significant patterns in the world is conducted.

7. Examples of Piaget's experiments

We can unfortunately select only a few from the great range of experiments and observations that have been conducted, largely at the Institut J. J. Rousseau, in Geneva. Many of them deal with speech; in others, experimental situations are presented to the child, either as practical problems for solution or puzzles demanding explanation. In the study of early speech, Piaget was struck by the fact that in its first stages speech lacks truly communicative intent. It is stimulated by others but has no relevance to them. Talks between children at this stage are egocentric non-conversations or 'collective monologues'. Even as late as the age of 6, half the utterances are egocentric speech rather than socialized speech. Only very gradually does the child try to use the latter to inform the listener or to persuade him to give help.

Learning the free use of word symbols involves a large range of acquisitions. The child must learn new attitudes to the relationship of himself to others. We can use his difficulties to show how much is involved in the use of verbal symbols.

A simple illustration is to ask a child what is absurd about the statement 'I have three brothers; Paul, Ernest, and myself'. Out of forty boys of 9-12 years only one-third found the absurdity. The difficulty is to distinguish between 'brother' as a class and being a brother to someone else. Following this up with questions asking in effect for a definition of 'brother', Piaget found in the first stage 'brother' is simply a boy, then it is used with the implication that it has to do with a family of two or more children, but only much later is it correctly used fully to verify the relationship. It is alleged that only 60 per cent of 7-year-olds and 75 per cent of 9-year-olds achieve this definition. This may seem hard to believe, and perhaps there may have been some special factors involved either in the subjects or the methods of questioning. Thus the definition of 'brother' given by Hal (age 9) was '*When there is a boy and another boy, when there are two of them.* Has your father got a brother? *Yes.* Why? *Because he was born second.* Then what is a brother? *It is the second brother that comes.* Then the first is not a brother? *Oh No! The second brother that comes is called brother.*' It is true that Hal proved himself unable to clarify the relationship when discussed in this context. Is it relevant that he might have done so in a more helpful one? Probably not, if we are searching for signs of the stages of use of language that have been reached. In this, as in many such situations, one has the impression that what is being studied is the range of contexts within which the child has had experience of the use of symbols. In a sense he knows how to use 'brother', for instance in relation to his own sib. He has not had occasion to explore the details or subtleties of the concept and falters when made to do so. The point surely is that such mistakes and inadequacies gradually disappear as the child's experiences produce adequate schemata for the use of symbols in more and more abstract contexts.

Many problems of the growth of the use of symbols are explored in Piaget's books such as 'The child's conception of the world', and 'The child's conception of physical causality'. He distinguishes three attitudes developing successively as 'realism', 'animism', and 'artificiality'. In the first the child confuses symbols about human thoughts, feelings, and wishes with happenings in the outside world. Piaget believes that out of this confusion arises animism, the tendency to endow physical objects and events with attributes of life such as consciousness and will. There has, however, been no detailed exploration of the early sources of this confusion (see Russell and Dennis 1939). It may be found more simply in the attention to human attributes as the earliest conditioning factor in the development of the brain (see Chapter 19).

Certainly the tendency to provide animistic causal explanations is very strong and persistent. It may perhaps better be called magico-animistic or bipolar, implying that someone is issuing commands to sun, moon, and clouds and that these willingly follow them. Thus up to age 5 years clouds move by our magic, '*We make them move by walking*'. Even as late as age 8 years the explanation is '*When we move along they move along too*'. This is complemented to explain what happens when everyone is asleep by '*They always move. The cats, when they walk, and then the dogs, they make the clouds move along.*'

A little later it is God or men who make clouds move (usually about age 6 years). Then they are said to move without human agency but as a result of interaction between sun, wind, etc., but these operate not as one might say by physical cause but as one man commands another—and the clouds obey.

Frequently the actions of objects are attributed to their own volition. Thus, of a box suspended from two strings and twisted, 'Why does it turn? *Because the string is twisted*. Why does the string turn too? *Because it wants to unwind itself*. Does the string know it is twisted? *Yes*. Why? *Because it wants to untwist itself, it knows it's twisted!* Does it really know it is twisted? *Yes . . . I am not sure*. How do you think it knows? *Because it feels it is all twisted*' (age 4 years).

Even as the animism recedes the action of physical events upon each other is not understood. '*It's the sun makes the clouds move*. How? *With its rays. It pushes the clouds*. Or *They move along by the wind*. Where does the wind come from? *From the sky*. And how is the wind made? *Don't know*.'

Here once again we are really dealing quite simply with ignorance. The child has not yet acquired the information needed to use the symbols in their full modern connotation. What would be interesting would be to learn how the general framework of ideas about causality comes to an end-point in the adult. Probably it is by various routes and the end-product would be found to vary surprisingly. Piaget himself claims to have discovered no less than seventeen types of causal explanation at various stages. Certainly some remains of these are to be found in the symbolism that is used by adults. It is indeed only in the later stages of development that concepts of what we may call mechanical causality are used satisfactorily and animism disappears. As we have seen, the whole fabric of concepts that is used in modern scientific exposition has grown up largely around the artefacts invented by man and the words used to describe them (p. 98). The child (or adult) must have at least some familiarity with the operations of the artefacts if he is to use the language correctly. The concept of a memory as used in this book can be properly applied only by someone who has at least an acquaintance with computers. It is not easy to say how far the sophisticated modern usages of science have really penetrated the language and symbolism even of westernized countries. The forms of person language and animism are the first to develop and the brain continues to operate partly with them even in the most sophisticated of us. Such forms still constitute the major types of symbolism used by those who have not been exposed to the artefacts of modern civilization.

22

AGEING AND SENESCENCE

1. Suspended animation. Cryptobiosis

ONE of the principal generalizations of biology is that living organisms depend on active expenditure of energy to maintain a steady state. In certain exceptional conditions, however, living organization can continue for a long time in a resting state of equilibrium. The exceptions prove the rule, because such arrested life has no repair mechanisms and its order is progressively eroded by random changes.

During active life the turnover of materials involves incorporation or anabolism, which is a form of growth, and catabolism and elimination, which is a sort of death, in that matter returns to the inorganic world whence it came. In the exceptions to this state of change all metabolic processes come reversibly to a standstill (Hinton 1968). Dehydrated bacterial spores, algae, moulds, lichens, and even some multicellular animals, such as rotifers and nematode worms, can revive and grow normally after being reduced to temperatures as low as 0·008 °K. Moreover, seeds of the sacred lotus plant (*Nelumbium nuciferum*), shown by ^{14}C-dating to be over 2000 years old, can germinate well. Seeds frozen in permafrost for 10 000 years have also grown (Porsild, Harington, and Mulligan 1967).

There is therefore no doubt that the organization responsible for the processes of life can be maintained when reduced to a condition requiring no interchanges, but only certain spatial molecular dispositions.

In this cryptobiotic state most of the changes that make death more likely with passage of time do not occur, but begin again when it is revived. We can therefore enormously increase the calendar life-span by a period of cryptobiosis, but not the total duration of active life. There is no reason why this should not be possible for mammals, although, so far, the maximum period of freezing seems to be 45 min at − 5 °C for a hamster (Smith 1961).

Physiological ageing is thus evidently due to the actual operations of the cells and can be avoided in cryptobiosis. Nevertheless, the viability of the organism decreases even in that state. This is due to adventitious oxidations, reductions, and other changes, as can be shown by their dependence on temperature. Thus dehydrated eggs of the brine shrimp, *Artemia*, showed a steep fall in viability according to the time for which they were kept at a high temperature (103 °C). The injuries sustained in this inactive state are thus strictly cumulative. A normal organism in the active state effects repair, so that it can sustain a series of injuries over a span of time that would have caused death if simultaneous. In 'cryptobiosis only the total amount of damage is of concern and not the rate at which it is inflicted' (Hinton 1968).

2. Changes in homeostatic capacity with time

These facts serve as an introduction to the study of senescence. They show that the proteins of the organism and the instructions incorporated in the DNA can remain intact (apart from adventitious changes), *provided that they are not used*. In the active state of organisms the instructions are used to produce controlled metabolism, and for this or other reasons the instructional molecules become damaged and the information is lost. Some of the damage may be repaired (see later), but any repair mechanisms are themselves subject to error, and the general conclusion is that any operating organism must inevitably gradually become impaired by use and by accident. The gradual accumulation of defects constitutes senescence. As mistakes become more numerous, homeostatic mechanisms are progressively impaired and the probability of death increases. The defects may occur in any part of the organism. Many workers have ascribed senescence to changes in the synthetic mechanisms of the cell, or alternatively to the accumulation of mutations in the DNA of somatic cells (p. 392). These may take many forms, perhaps by derepression of operons (Medvedev 1967). They may lead to a decay of various parts of the mechanism of protein synthesis (Maynard Smith 1962) and this may also occur owing to defects other than those of the DNA. In particular, the accumulation of errors in the systems of enzymes ensuring transcription and translation is more likely than errors in the DNA itself (Speyer 1965). Indeed, the DNA is presumably selected to operate without damage to itself. Perhaps there are also mechanisms for repair if damage occurs (Orgel 1963 and see p. 300). Errors in the hereditary instructions and their transcription may be of especial importance in post-mitotic cells, such as those of muscle and nerve, where they cannot be corrected or eliminated by cell division. Degeneration of post-mitotic cells has also been widely considered as characteristic of senescence (see Alexander 1967), leading especially to the increasing probability of degenerative and autoimmune diseases (see p. 297). These diseases may, of course, be produced by factors other than errors in protein synthesis. Defects due to cross-linkage of the chains of collagen molecules are particularly important in producing failure of skeletal and other structural organs of mammals.

There have been many attempts to define senescence, and to relate it to particular molecular species or organs. Perhaps the only general statement that can be made is that senescence consists of time-dependent changes tending to produce failure of some part of the homeostatic system so that death becomes more probable. As Strehler (1967) puts it, the changes of senescence are:

1. gradual,
2. harmful, and
3. universal (at least in all Metazoans except those that are clones, e.g. *Hydra*, sea anemones).

We must immediately emphasize that all these statements apply to the 'individual' as a unit of survival. There is no evidence that populations as a whole undergo senescence. Indeed, life goes on indefinitely in spite of the ageing of the individuals, and it may be even that life goes on *because* individuals age and die, leaving place for others. In fact, we have to inquire whether some manifestations of senescence, far from being harmful, are actually beneficial to the race. Some phenomena of death of whole organisms or parts of them are undoubtedly of value to the species. In all animals and plants there are specific mechanisms that terminate the life of the individual or parts of it at some stage in the life-cycle. It does not follow that all ageing changes are of this specific sort. In particular, it may well be that the changes we call senescence in man are not part of a programme, and, indeed, occur because there is no selective force to prevent them. All this we shall discuss.

Estimates of the force of mortality have often been accepted as measures of 'ageing'. But liability to die is not necessarily a measure of senescence. Fig. 22.1 shows that dogs kept by private owners are more liable to die

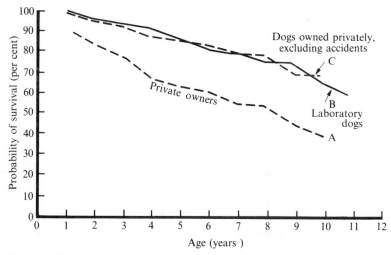

F IG. 22.1. Comparison of survival of two matched groups of dogs: A, kept by private owners; B, kept in laboratories; C survival in the privately kept animals *excluding accidental death*. (After Anderson and Rosenblatt 1965.)

than those in laboratories, but this is due to accidents, not to premature senescence. Again, heavy smokers die on average $7\frac{1}{2}$ years younger than non-smokers, but this is mainly because they contract lung cancer and bronchitis, not because they age faster (Alexander 1967). However, smoking may also accelerate senescence by reducing cellular homeostasis in the lung.

To state that senescence is the accumulation of defects is no very original doctrine. What we need is understanding of the details of those defects that are the more common in man and how their effects may be ameliorated, if not avoided. From the general point of view, many questions can be asked. They mostly centre round problems about the selective effects of different rates of accumulation of defects leading to the characteristic life-spans for each species. It is not merely a question of what deficiencies each homeo-static system can stand, but of whether there is a genetically programmed rate of accumulation of them and hence a specific life-span, correlated with other characteristics of the species. In particular, we are interested in whether the human life-span is in some way related to other features of human life and what might be the effects of lengthening or shortening it.

3. Senescence and differentiation

There is obviously some connection between the phenomena of develop-ment and those of senescence. Some people have maintained that these constitute one continuous set of events, the later changes being the con-tinuation and completion of the earlier, all selected to occur in a manner advantageous to the species. This may be so in some species of animals and plants, but the relationship is usually more complicated, and is so in man. Throughout life every organism operates mechanisms for homeostasis on many time-scales simultaneously. It makes forecasts continuously for both short and long periods; it manifests not only homeostasis but also homeorhesis (Waddington 1968). For example, a growing foetus is mainly constructing equipment for a distant future, but its tissues must also make the short-term forecasts to produce correct levels of cellular respiration, metabolism, and repair processes. Conversely, a grown man may be mainly engaged in nervous and muscular work to find food for the immediate needs of himself and his family, but his tissues are also constructing new materials as medium-term forecasts (for instance in the bone marrow) or long-term ones in the testes.

Thus the processes of differentiation are directed towards producing a homeostatic individual, capable of maintaining the life of the species in its appropriate environment. Any such system is subject to errors, for which there cannot be an indefinite set of repair mechanisms. The most powerful system for securing correction is cell division, which involves abandoning the working parts and starting again from the instructions, eliminating cells that are incorrect. Cell division does, indeed, continue throughout life in many tissues, but it is not possible in the most highly differentiated cells, such as those of the nervous and muscular systems. Failure of the operations of these post-mitotic cells is one of the most characteristic features of senescence. They have their own repair systems, but these depend ultimately upon use of the DNA, and there are liable to be errors during transcription, and especially in RNA in translation, as well as by mutation induced by radiation and other agents. Indeed in a sense the DNA must be especially vulnerable to damage, since each part may exist only as two molecules in each cell. Presumably it is in order to minimize this risk that nuclei undergo various forms of multiplication such as polyploidy and polyteny, by which extra 'working DNA' is provided as a template when a great deal of RNA has to be produced for cells that are engaged in active synthesis. Indeed some of the most active parts of cells have their own DNA (e.g. mitochondria, chloroplasts). This avoids coding from the nucleus when there is rapid enzyme turnover.

There are probably other such devices for avoiding the possible effects of damage to the instruction system. It may be that in differentiated tissues there is a reduction of the information available, to avoid side-effects of damage to the unused parts of it. This may be by repression (though this leaves the danger of de-repression by mutation or in other ways) or perhaps by limitation of the transcription so that it will operate only for particular combinations of the various codons for each amino-acid. Each tissue, if it thus 'interprets' the DNA code only in its own way, will reduce its risk of confusion by changes in other parts of the script (see Gurdon and Woodland 1968).

Unfortunately, at present we understand rather little about these fundamental changes during differentiation (see p. 75). Hence we cannot say whether differentiation inevitably involves the ultimate failure of the cell, nor whether there are mechanisms by which such failure is delayed. It seems probable that many of the phenomena of senescence are attributable to the imperfections and errors inevitable in the functioning of any system. Ageing is thus the ultimate fate of all organized individuals. Selection will ensure the provision of such repair devices as prevent the imperfections from interrupting life before the programme appropriate to a given environment has been run. Selection may also in some cases arrange for 'imperfections' to kill the whole individual at a certain time, as it ensures the fall of the leaves from a tree in autumn.

4. Ageing in plants

Plants show especially clearly that some phenomena akin to senescence are adaptive and are arranged for in the genetic programme of the species. We regard the death of annual plants in the autumn as so natural a phenomenon that we fail to recognize the implication that death may be an essential part of the life system of a species. Further, the fact that in many perennials of temperate regions a large part of the body, the foliage, dies every year, should remind us of the danger of equating death with annihilation of the whole individual as we are apt to do for mammals, though unreasonably. We should be in no danger of making this error if we think of the continual changes of metabolism, or of the death of many cells during development of the embryo, or in the continually replacing tissues. But the fall of the leaves in autumn is visible, while the death of thousands of red cells is not, although the latter is occurring in every one of us every minute.

In any case neither leaf-fall nor the death of red cells indicates the phenomenon we ordinarily call senescence. They show us that death, in the sense of degradation of differentiated material and its return to the non-living, is not by itself a sign of senescence. The mark of the latter is the increased probability of degradation of the whole homeostatic unit, where such can be recognized.

In plants, therefore, we have to consider two kinds of longevity and two kinds of senescence (see Woolhouse 1967), namely those of the whole plant and of its parts. Thus the leaves of woody deciduous perennials show senescence each year. The whole tree gradually becomes old and decrepit from wear of its unreplaced or infected parts, and shows a reduced growth rate. Its chances of being destroyed are thereby increased. But conversely there is probably no long-term senescence at the cellular level, and cuttings from old trees will resume the growth rate of the parent tree when it was young. However, the question of whether there is a progressive decline in homeostatic capacities in long-lived plants seems to be still undecided. Many factors complicate the assessment of experiments in which there seems to be renewed vitality on transfer to new conditions. For one thing, new opportunities may be provided for growth and cell division and hence elimination of aberrant cells.

5. Senescence in Protozoa

The fact is that a great many different patterns of development and senescence are present and we cannot possibly survey them all here. Not all metabolizing organisms show the signs of deterioration that we call senescence. There are some strains of *Paramecium* that continue indefinitely, dividing without conjugation, and without the nuclear reorganization, called autogamy or endomixis, that substitutes for it. In other protozoa indefinite survival requires periodic meiosis, cross-fertilization, or endomixis. Moreover, many bacteria, yeast cells, and clones of plants propagated vegetatively do not show senescence. Furthermore, there are great variations in the effects of ageing among higher animals.

The case of *Amoeba* has been investigated in detail (Danielli and Muggleton 1959, Muggleton and Danielli 1968). Under normal culture conditions *A. proteus* forms a clone that continues to divide indefinitely. However, by protracted treatment (with reduced nutrition, 3·5 weeks at 17 °C) growth can be prevented and the clones ultimately die out. Injections were made of nuclear or cytoplasmic material from such 'spanned' amoebae into normal cytoplasm, and vice versa. Transfer of a normal nucleus into spanned cytoplasm produced resumed logarithmic growth, and a spanned nucleus in normal cytoplasm produced the spanned condition. It was also shown, however, that small amounts of spanned cytoplasm (or a homogenate of it) would produce the spanned condition in normal amoebae.

The transplanted nuclei would of course carry some cytoplasm and it is impossible to say that either part of the cell is exclusively involved. It is clear, however, that the conversion of one type to the other involves the intracellular control mechanisms. Since changes in the DNA are not readily produced, it seems likely that the main factor involved in the 'spanned' condition is either the mRNA or the mechanism for its translation into proteins in the cytoplasm.

6. Is senescence a product of selection or of its absence?

Evidently senescence is not the universal fate of living matter, as it appears to be for us humans. However, all these creatures show cell division, even if they do not need periodic sexual reproduction. We shall have to inquire whether there is a connection between methods of cell replacement and senescence, the failure of homeostasis, and the mechanisms by which the integrity of the instructions is preserved. There would be perhaps some satisfaction in thus finding a 'cause' for senescence. A more intellectually complete reason for believing it to be true would be found if the different patterns of ageing of different species could be explained as adaptations to particular ways of life. Unfortunately, further analysis shows reason for thinking that a main reason for senescence in higher animals and man is both simpler and less interesting. The essential point is as follows. Obviously genes that manifest their effects late in life escape partly or wholly from the force of natural selection (Medawar 1952). There is every reason to think that such genes exist, for example genes producing cancer, and that they have not

been eliminated because the individuals who bear them have already reproduced before the bad effects occur.

More generally, it is demonstrable that any genes that confer reproductive
advantage relatively early in life will be selected, even if they are pleiotropic
and have ill-effects later. Senescence may thus even be an inevitable consequence of natural selection (Hamilton 1966).

It is important to realize that this analysis involves many assumptions
about the incidence of the force of mortality. This must be so since we have
to reconcile the facts that

(*a*) organisms have very different life-spans, and

(*b*) 'in wild populations generally, it probably seldom happens that
senescence has more than a slight modifying influence on mortality'
(Williams 1957).

Animals fall a prey to some natural accident before they become senescent.
But this is only to say that the selective forces operate so as to produce a
developmental programme of a length appropriate to the circumstances of
the species. There are, indeed, indications that low adult death-rates are
associated with low rate of senescence (p. 312 and Williams 1957).

It is very difficult to make reliable inferences in such matters. It is certainly demonstrated that genes giving an early reproductive advantage are
likely to be selected. But there remain all the influences that must counteract
this effect, since lifetimes vary. In man, in particular, selection has obviously
not chosen those genes that ensure maximum fertility at the earliest possible
age (Chapter 18). It may be that a process of natural selection inevitably
implies senescence, yet the rate of senescence of each species must be
individually determined by particular selective factors. It seems likely that
these differences are somehow connected with the means adopted by the
species to maintain its integrity.

7. Programmed cell death

Just as there is constructive synthesis on all time-scales, so there is programmed death at all times throughout the life-cycle. Statisticians like to
study only the death of the whole organism, and are happy that each dies
only once. But there is death of cells at all ages. And certainly often this is
not simply a degenerative phenomenon of senescent failure but a part of the
constructive actions of morphogenesis (Glucksmann 1964). Thus, waves
of cell death occur as the brain is formed (Källen 1955). Certainly, therefore,
there are systems in the developing organism that ensure the death of a
proportion of the cells, as part of the programme that is to lead to the continued life of the whole.

Thus the periodic rejection of material in catabolism and of whole cells and organisms by death is a universal feature of living things. Death is as universal as life, and in this sense is essential to life. Like other phenomena manifested by organisms, it somehow serves to assist in the homeostasis of the species. Of course we must recognize the possibility that death, being the negation of life, is not 'adapted' as are all other aspects of living systems. It is sometimes said to be 'outside the programme' of the genetic instructions. It is even denied that phenomena of wear or failure of repair are involved in senescence. Williams (1957) considers that the concept of wear is inappropriately borrowed from static man-made machines and should not be applied to self-replacing living systems. But the difficulty of avoiding the effects of random influences on an organized system does not depend on calling it a 'machine'. Nor are self-replacing systems made invulnerable to the inevitability of random errors by the fact that in our language they are not 'machines' in quite the usual sense. Our task is to define the changes that take place with time in living systems and to show how they are connected with the outstanding fact about life—that it continues.

Living organisms maintain their lives in many diverse ways, and the usual biological principle is that their differences have been tailored by natural selection to allow continuance in varied environments. We shall ask whether this is so also of the pattern of ageing. Curiously enough, this is not a popular question for gerontologists, who perhaps feel that it over-simplifies the problem. Certainly a first task must be to define more clearly what changes with age we are considering. No one would deny that the age changes by which an embryo builds its enzymes are 'adapted', nor would this be denied of the waves of cell death in neurogenesis, discussed above (Källen 1955). But are the deaths of the nerve cells during senescence properly to be compared with those in the early embryo? Evidently we are in the danger that words like *ageing*, *senescence*, and even *death* are inexact and carried over from everyday speech. We must define more precisely the phenomena that are to be included.

8. General definition of senescent changes

The changes of old age affect so many parts of the body and are superficially so familiar that it is not easy to classify them in a biologically meaningful manner. What is the connection between the facts that old men and women have wrinkled skin, are foolish, pant when they exert themselves, are no longer able to reproduce, and are increasingly prone to die? It is not our purpose to present a detailed catalogue of all the aspects of the misfortune that we call senescence. In order to try to bring out the essential features of the process we have to see whether it is possible to go behind all these particular manifestations and to classify them all into a few categories. It would presumably be the view of Williams, and perhaps Medawar, that no such classification is possible. According to them, the changes of senescence are a mixed bag of side-effects of genes that happen to have favourable effects in younger stages. On the contrary, Comfort (1966) provides a very concise classification of senescent changes divided into three categories:

1. changes in dividing cell quality ("faulty copying");
2. loss or damage among fixed post-mitotic cells; and
3. colloidal change in molecules, including extra-cellular structural molecules (such as collagen) and the intra-cellular information store.

Comfort goes so far as to say that all the changes that we associate with senescence can be placed under one or several of these headings. Thus, collagen and elastin, which are molecules with a small rate of turnover in the adult, become increasingly changed with old age. New combinations appear in the molecules, serving to cross-link the polypeptide chains and alter the strength and elasticity that are their valuable properties for the body. Many of the more obvious changes in old age are due to alterations in the connective tissue, for example some of those in the arteries and the skin.

The fixed (post-mitotic) cells, such as those of muscle and nerve, seem to show especially severe effects of senescence. Rate of change of psychological capacities is said to provide the best index of expectation of life (see Jarvik and Falek 1963). Neurons are probably lost steadily in the later decades of life. A figure of 100 000 dying per day is often mentioned, but there are no good data, or information as to whether the rate of loss increases. The nervous system depends upon the redundancy of its numerous channels, with which it can make adequate predictions and communicate them to the effectors, in spite of the high noise-level and relatively slow speed of operation and conduction. Reduction in the number of channels would have the effect of reducing the reliability of prediction. This may be especially important in such key regions as the hypothalamus, whose neurons influence so many homeostatic processes, including several systems that operate as clocks. The hypothalamus and other lower centres contain relatively few neurons (but there are no exact data about their loss in senescence).

The post-mitotic cells are presumably especially vulnerable to the probability of damage by use and by mutation. Indeed many biologists believe that somatic mutations (in the widest sense of any genetic injury) alone provide a sufficient explanation for senescent change (see Curtis 1966). For example, in old mice 70 per cent of liver cells have gross chromosome abnormalities. Evidence has recently appeared that chromosome abnormalities, especially in the X and Y, are increasingly evident in man after age 45 (Hamerton *et al.* 1965). There is evidence, therefore, of declining mitotic efficiency. Further, radiation, which increases the mutation rate, also shortens life, in a manner that some hold to be similar to senescence (radiation ageing). However, a careful study of the effects of radiation on the population of Hiroshima showed no correlation between senescent changes, measured in various ways, and closeness to the centre of the atomic explosion. Moreover, there are other reasons for supposing that somatic mutation is not by itself the cause of all senescent changes.

On the other hand, as we have seen, degenerative diseases play a prominent part in the increasing probability of death with age. It is suggested that they may be due to stepwise changes, each produced by a mutation with its own ageing probability (Fig. 22.2) (Curtis 1966, Burnet 1965). If

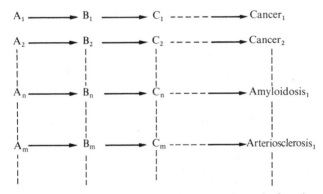

F IG. 22.2. Representation of the ageing process as the result of a series of step changes. Each of the degenerative diseases is the result of a series of processes each with its own rate constant. One or more of the steps from one process to the next is almost certainly a mutation, but equally not all are mutations. (After Curtis 1967.)

this were so the relation between death-rate for any disease and time should be a power function, the power depending upon the number of steps.

$$\frac{dN}{dt} = Kt^{(n-1)},$$

where N is the percentage of persons contracting the disease, t the time, n the number of steps in the process, and K a constant depending upon the mutation rate, the environment, and other factors. This equation fits the facts very well (Fig. 22.3). The chief exceptions are diseases strongly influenced by environment, such as cancer of the lung, or by hormones, as cancer of the breast. Somatic mutation, then, probably plays a large part in the causation of diseases of the old, but these do not in themselves constitute senescence, or at least certainly not the whole of it.

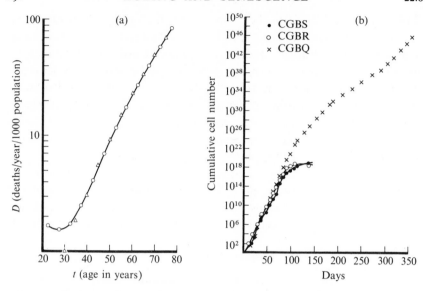

FIG. 22.3. (a) Log of the age-specific death rate of males in the United States from all causes in 1963 plotted against age is shown by open circles. The triangles show the theoretical curve suggested by the hypothesis of Fig. 22.2 and derived from the equation (after Curtis 1967)

$$\frac{dD}{dt} = 3 \cdot 0 \times 10^{-8} t^5$$

FIG. 22.3. (b) An established cell line of goose fibroblasts. Cumulative growth curves of cells of three geese grown in tissue culture. Two of the cultures, CGBS and CGBR, were typical cell strains and became senescent after 65 generations, but the third has continued to grow as a line for more than 150 cell generations. The chromosomes of these birds are difficult to study, but so far as can be seen those of the line CGBQ are normal, although they may perhaps be polyploid. (From Coon, H. G., and Williams, I., *Carnegie Institution Year Book* 67, 1967–8.)

But of course radiation mutation, presumably damage to the DNA, is only a conspicuous example of the hazards that affect all parts of the system from the operation of random influences. We are assuming that any system in continued operation will be subject to such hazards and therefore be in need of repair or correction (Chapter 12). This can be achieved only by one of the two methods we have discussed, namely comparison with some standard to effect a repair, or rejection of the damaged part. There are specific repair mechanisms in the post-mitotic cells, including synthesis of new DNA, but these mechanisms must themselves ultimately be subject to wear, and so on. The regress can only be evaded by some special procedure, which seems to be connected with cell division, and perhaps involves simply elimination of errors by rejection of the unfit.

9. Ageing in dividing cell populations

It is therefore especially important to find that the dividing cell populations also show signs of ageing. It is probable that cells growing in tissue culture survive for only a limited number of generations, *unless they undergo chromosome changes and become cancer cells* (Hayflick 1965). It has been very widely held in the past that cells in tissue culture multiply indefinitely, a view first proposed by Carrel (1924), one of the pioneers of this technique. The secret of such apparently immortal cultures may be either that new cells were unwittingly introduced with the embryo extract that was used in the medium for the repeated subcultures, or it may be simply that the cells had mutated and become cancerous. It has become the practice to discriminate between *cell strains*, which are of limited life, and *cell lines*, which are unlimited but abnormal. The cells in cell strains keep their normal morphological and immunological properties and normal diploid chromosome number. They can divide only a finite number of times. Cell lines will multiply and produce tumours when inoculated into members of their parent species, which cell strains will not. The cells of cell lines have abnormal chromosome numbers. They will continue to multiply indefinitely —some have lasted more than 20 years, dividing every day. There are, however, a few cell lines known whose cells, though abnormal in karyotype and in other ways, are not cancerous (e.g. the 3T3 strain of fibroblasts of mice, Todaro and Green 1963, and the line shown in Fig. 22.3(b)).

The cells of different animals vary in their capacity to produce cell lines. Thus, cultures of mouse cells almost always become changed and malignant, whereas those of chicks do not do so. It is not known why some clones are stable and others not.

Human embryonic somatic cells (fibroblasts) cultured *in vitro* survive for about fifty cell generations; those from adults for less, usually about twenty generations. It has not been possible to establish an exact correlation between the age of the donor and length of life of the strain. The strain can be preserved in an arrested state at sub-zero temperatures indefinitely. When warmed it will recommence division, but finally this ceases after a total of about fifty divisions before and after cooling. Cultures of human cells are longer-lived than those of most mammals, and this is presumably correlated with man's longer life-span.

These facts suggest that mammalian somatic cells have a fixed life-span, in terms of cell divisions. This is confirmed by the facts of heterochronic grafts between inbred hosts (Krohn 1962). The grafted tissue survives for a time that is set by its own life-span, not that of its surroundings.

Other evidence of a finite life-span for cultured tissues is that the latent period before migration of cells from chick-heart cultures increases with age (Lefford 1964). The decline in 'growth energy' of cells of the chick has already been mentioned and a similar phenomenon has been shown for explanted liver of the rat (Glinos and Bartlett 1951).

However, some plants show indefinite asexual reproduction, and we have used these examples to suggest that there is no inherent principle of senescence (p. 292). Presumably cell division and cell death may be able to supply the corrective measures that repair inevitable damage, particularly to the DNA (see below). The existence of such instances supports the view suggesting that senescence is an unfavourable feature (in relation to homeostasis) *inevitably incorporated into organisms that develop a soma that is not passed on in reproduction* (p. 312).

The fact that there is a finite life-span even among dividing cells of a metazoan agrees with the view that there is a species-specific age determined by the genotype. It is not difficult to understand that in post-mitotic cells the metabolic processes must ultimately go out of control. Individual enzyme systems may be repaired or renewed, but the mechanism for reading-out the instructions must also be liable to damage by use. Even the DNA instructions themselves cannot be immune from the liability to wear as they are used to produce messenger RNA. These molecules are very stable but they have no magical inherent property that insures them against all possible damage. However, they must be capable of repair when damaged, for we know that the DNA is passed on from generation to generation by the germ cells, unchanged except by mutation.

10. Damage and repair of instructional molecules

There is still no clear agreement on changes in DNA itself with age. DNA prepared from the thymus of old cows is more resistant to heat than that from calves (Hahn and Verzár 1963). This has been compared to the structural ageing of collagen by cross-linking (p. 288). This protection of the DNA from heat may be due to increased binding of the DNA to protein (probably histone, Hahn 1966), which interferes with its power to act as a template for RNA-polymerase action (Devi *et al.* 1966). It remains to be discovered whether this cross-linking is a result of the use of DNA for manufacture of messenger RNA.

The interpretation of all such observations is still uncertain since the changes may be in any of various cell components. Thus the difference in thermal stability of cow and calf nucleo-protein disappears if the preparation is made in such a way as to reduce the amount of non-histone protein and RNA in the preparation (Pyhtilä and Sherman 1968). The age-change in template action also disappears, and in fact no change in the DNA itself could be detected.

On the other hand, in rats, the amount of ^{3}H thymidine incorporated into liver is said to increase linearly from 154 to 881 days and thereafter still faster to 1007 days *without increase in net DNA per nucleus or in mitotic index*

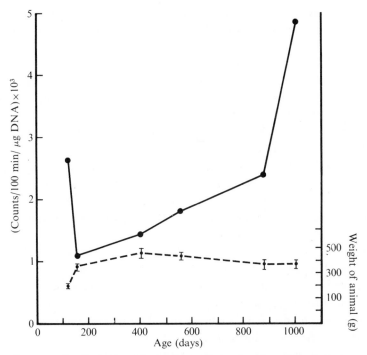

F IG. 22.4. Specific DNA activity (continuous line) and weights of animals (broken line) after ³H-thymidine uptake by rats, as a function of age. Each point is from one animal only. The youngest shows a high specific activity, presumably associated with growth. There is a striking increase at the end of life. (After Samis *et al.* 1966.)

(Fig. 22.4, Samis *et al.* 1966). The suggestion is that the RNA polymerase system is able to detect a nonsense sequence and that degradation of the damaged segment by DNAase and repair by DNA polymerase follows, using the information in the unaltered homologue. This is as yet a rather vague and untested hypothesis, but DNAase and DNA polymerase certainly exist in tissues that have a low mitotic activity. In any case increased DNA synthesis might well result from causes other than degradation of DNA itself. Thus it may well be that the cytoplasmic systems for RNA translation and protein synthesis function less well with age and this produces a demand for greater DNA template activity.

A further suggestion is that there is in the chromosomes working DNA, distinct from the master copy, which is not used to produce RNA but only to make the working DNA (Callan 1967).

11. Cell division and cell death as guarantors of the instructions

If our general view is correct there is a tendency for faults to occur in all parts of a living system. They occur as the result of random operating errors, but their frequency may well be greater in certain parts that are especially liable to wear. Many of these effects will be small and they will affect homeostasis only if they accumulate.

In order to remain alive the system must somehow compensate such errors. In order to do this it must have a mechanism for detecting them, and we have already considered possible means by which defects in the DNA are detected and repaired.

It is suggested that further important mechanisms for eliminating errors are provided by mitosis and perhaps by meiosis. During the period when a cell is dividing its DNA is unable to produce RNA and its enzyme systems must function without renewal. This is therefore a time of stress, which may serve to test the adequacy of the cell machinery. Cells are known to be especially susceptible to radiation while they are dividing (though this may be due to the state of the nucleic acid molecules at the time). The point is that mitosis provides a filter by which altered cells are detected and destroyed.

Filters of some sort are evidently important mechanisms that protect the integrity of the information store. An essential part of the process is reduction of the organism or part of it to a minimal state in which selection can operate. The necessity for this periodic reduction and selection might be said to be the reason for senescence and death, but does not explain to us the factors that control the pattern of senescence as it operates in different species.

Although this selective action during cell division is important there may also be other factors at work. With the breakdown of the nuclear membrane the chromosomes are placed in contact with the enzymes and other contents of the cytoplasm. These may serve to alter the pattern of repression of the genes, suppressing some that have been operating and releasing others. This reprogramming of the read-out of the DNA may serve to bring into play a new complex of enzyme systems, appropriate to changed circumstances (Gurdon and Woodland 1968, and Chapter 14).

These suggestions are all relevant to the basic problem of how the information store is preserved and whether there is a connection between the failure of the mechanisms that ensure this and the ultimate death of the individual. It seems certain that repair mechanisms such as the above exist, and that they are developed to different extents in organisms with different life-spans. It is equally certain that they cannot be ultimately successful, for this would involve the regress of the repairers that we have considered so often. The only ultimate guarantee of homeostasis is to allow for the failure and elimination of the incorrect. This is the function of death, whether of cells or organisms.

23

LIFE TABLES AND THE PATTERN
OF SENESCENCE

1. Changes with age in the expectation of life

IN order to study patterns of senescence we must have means of measuring it. Obviously many aspects of old age could be measured, but the most useful one has been found to be the liability to die. When we say 'he looks older' we do not mean only 'we think his chances of dying have increased', but the remark carries this implication. Biological statisticians find it easier to measure the expectation of life than the wrinkles, inanity, and other features by which we judge old age. Their studies of death-rates have provided a means of measuring the rate of senescence and they thus provide some basis for a scientific approach.

The rate of mortality is expressed as the number per 1000 of a given population living at time x, who will have died by time $x+1$, from which we can derive an expression for the force of mortality (Fig. 23.1). Senescence is measured as the progressive increase in the probability that the individual will die during the next interval of time. Each organism dies only once,

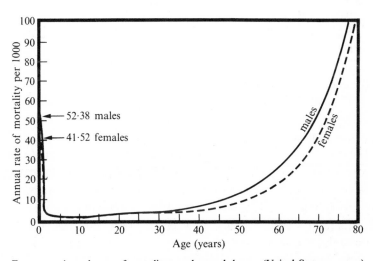

FIG. 23.1. Annual rates of mortality per thousand, by sex (United States 1939-41).
(After Comfort 1964.)

therefore a quantitative estimate can only be determined statistically in a population (but see p. 294).

Living organisms are highly complex systems, which are so controlled as to maintain their steady state by use of information received from the past. If the efficiency of the control and the amount of information available to an individual remained constant throughout its life, the chances of its dying would be the same at all ages. If it acquires more information (or better control) its chance of life improves, and if it loses information or control they decrease. All three conditions can be found. We ordinarily call the increase of information 'learning', or becoming wiser, but it also includes acquiring immunity, growing suitable muscles and bones, and the many other sorts of information storage we have discussed.

2. Life tables

If the chance of death is independent of age the proportion of survivors will decrease steadily, as shown in the logarithmic curve of Fig. 23.2(a).

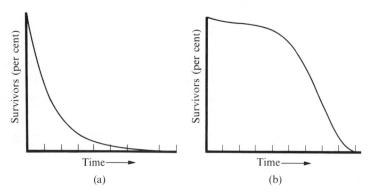

FIG. 23.2. (a) Survival curve at a constant rate of mortality (50 per cent per unit of time). (b) Survival curve of a population that shows senescence.
(After Comfort 1964.)

If they die only because of senescence the curve will approach the 'rectangular' form of Fig. 23.2(b). In this case as life proceeds individuals die from causes that would not have killed them before, the exact shape of the curve depending upon the rate of senescence. Fortunately, it is relatively easy in man to record life tables. It is also possible for animals kept in the laboratory, especially if their lives are short. But it is very hard to get life tables for animals in the wild state, which are the ones we most need to study since they are exposed to natural risks. The life tables available show the above possibilities and various mixtures of them. Thus

the slug and *Hydra* of Fig. 23.3(b) showed death-rates almost independent of age. In other species, such as the minute rotifers that live in ponds,
the onset of senescence is sudden and death comes to the majority of the
population at the same age (Fig. 23.4). When it is more gradual we get
the curves of Fig. 23.3(a) and this is the general form of human life tables
(Fig. 23.5).

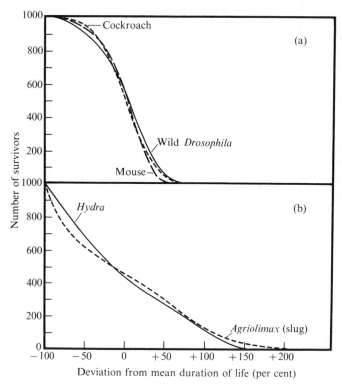

F I G. 23.3. Types of survival curves illustrated by different organisms.
(After Pearl and Miner 1935.)

When death occurs in most individuals at about the same age this is
called the specific age, and it is presumably determined by selection. For
the rotifers it is probably an advantage to kill off all the individuals when
they have reproduced, in order to allow for several generations during the
short persistence of the pond. In other animals there may be different reasons
for terminating life abruptly (p. 312). The life-span, like so many other
features, is determined for each species, not by any general factors. In man
the shape of the life table is obviously the result of the operation of several
influences. The chance of survival with age neither decreases nor increases

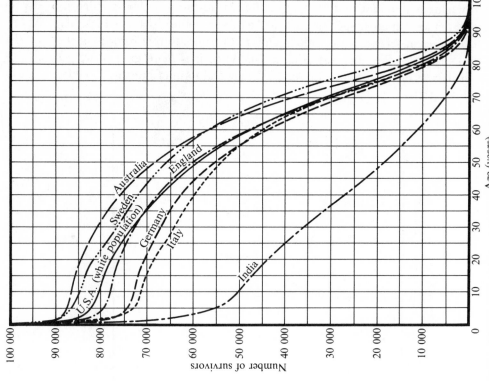

FIG. 23.5. Survivors of 100 000 males born alive in various countries, 1901–10. (After Pearl 1940.)

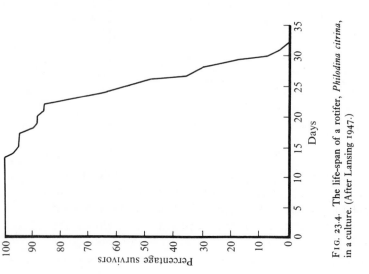

FIG. 23.4. The life-span of a rotifer, *Philodina citrina*, in a culture. (After Lansing 1947.)

steadily and we have to try to identify the overlapping influences that affect
the death-rate at each part of the curve.

1. Young children are very liable to die, largely from infectious diseases,
   for which they have not yet acquired immunity.
2. The greatest expectation of life is at about 10 years (Fig. 23.6) after
   much immunity has been acquired, the full reproductive period is
   ahead, and there is maximum selection against deleterious genes.
3. There follows a long period of uniform or slowly rising mortality up
   to the age of about 50.
4. Thereafter death-rates rise sharply to peaks at 76 years for men and
   80 for women. These peaks have moved forward by 3-4 years for men
   and 7 years for women in 100 years.
5. Most of the remaining deaths take place before about 100 and the total
   life-span has not changed in 100 years (the oldest person living in
   Great Britain in 1968 was 112).

An interesting analysis of the data is to assume that deaths during period
(3) are due to accident and that only after this does senescence begin. Assuming that its onset is symmetrically distributed about the time of maximum
mortality (76 years for men in 1950-2) and that all deaths after that age are
due to senescence, we can separate the two causes of death over the period
50-76 years (Fig. 23.6) (Benjamin 1959). This method of analysis makes
many assumptions, but its conclusion is that there is a *specific age* for man in
a good climate, and that this has changed little over recorded human history.

The life tables of many human populations have been changed greatly
as a result of medical and other social advances (Fig. 23.5). Before these
changes populations approach the logarithmic curves of constant death-
rate. With better conditions the rectangular shape becomes increasingly
apparent, emphasizing that there is a specific age for man.

There are no accepted hypotheses as to how this situation has come about.
One explanation may be that the limit is related to the time of menopause in
women. It is suggested that this may have been determined at about 45 as
the time at which she and her mate would have produced the maximum of
offspring that could be properly cared for (p. 314). If the maximum age of
reproduction is thus fixed, deleterious genes manifesting later will only be
selected against as long as they seriously prejudice the upbringing of the
younger members of the family. This would put the time of the specific age
at about 60. Obviously no such simple single influence has been at work.
It is even just possible that the brains of the longer-lived people have helped
the survival of their descendants in social communities!

It emerges clearly that the phenomena of senescence are not simply a

TABLE 23.1

Expectation of life, that is the average number of years of life that would remain for males and females reaching the ages specified if they continued to be subjected to the same mortality conditions as obtainable in the period mentioned (from *U.N. Demographic Yearbook* 1966)

Age		0	1	2	3	4	5
United Kingdom†	Males	66·42	67·66	66·82	65·91	64·98	64·04
1950-2	Females	71·54	72·38	71·53	70·61	69·67	68·72
1963-5	Males	68·3	..	..	..	..	65·1
	Females	74·4	..	..	..	..	71·0
Albania	Males	63·69	68·2	68·58	68·24	67·56	66·74
1960-1	Females	66·00	71·13	71·99	71·93	71·34	70·54
Africa	Males	34·3	40·0	..	..	..	42·0
West Cameroon	Females	37·2	41·0	..	..	..	44·0
African popu-lation 1964-5							

Age		10	15	20	25	30	35
United Kingdom†	Males	59·24	54·40	49·64	44·96	40·27	35·60
1950-2	Females	63·87	58·99	54·17	49·41	44·68	39·97
1963-5	Males	60·3	55·4	50·6	45·9	41·1	36·3
	Females	66·1	61·2	56·3	51·4	46·5	41·7
Albania	Males	62·27	57·54	52·82	48·15	43·51	38·90
1960-1	Females	66·19	61·43	56·66	51·99	47·40	42·83
Africa	Males	41·0	38·0	35·0	31·0	28·0	24·0
West Cameroon	Females	41·0	39·0	35·0	32·0	28·0	24·0
African popu-lation 1964-5							

Age		40	45	50	55	60	65
United Kingdom†	Males	30·98	26·49	22·23	18·31	14·79	11·69
1950-2	Females	35·32	30·76	26·34	22·10	18·07	14·43
1963-5	Males	31·6	27·1	22·8	18·7	15·1	12·0
	Females	37·0	32·4	27·9	23·6	19·4	15·6
Albania	Males	34·33	29·83	25·56	21·64	18·09	14·74
1960-1	Females	38·26	33·73	29·21	24·81	20·67	16·82
Africa	Males	21·0	18·0	15·0	13·0	12·0	9·0
West Cameroon	Females	20·0	17·0	15·0	13·0	12·0	10·0
African popu-lation 1964-5							

Age		70	75	80	85
United Kingdom†	Males	9·00	6·70	4·86	3·48
1950-2	Females	10·97	8·10	5·83	4·20
1963-5	Males	9·4	7·1	5·3	4·0
	Females	12·1	9·1	6·7	4·9
Albania	Males	11·65	8·94	6·63	4·73
1960-1	Females	13·34	10·19	7·56	5·43
Africa	Males	8·0	..	..	..
West Cameroon	Females	8·0	..	..	..
African popu-lation 1964-5					

† England and Wales only.

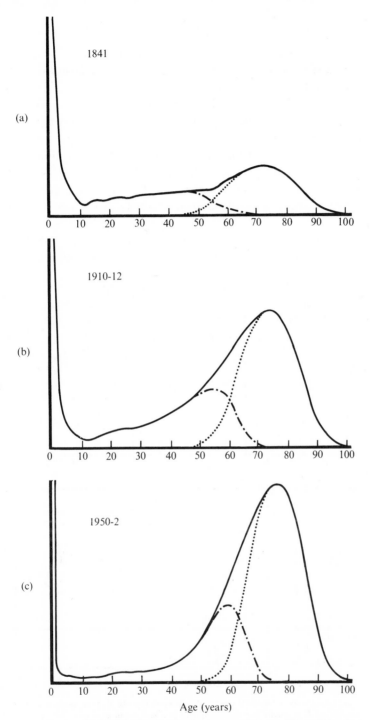

FIG. 23.6. English life tables, males (curves of deaths). The ordinate for (a) based on 51 000 births, those for (b) and (c) on 100 000. The senescent deaths and anticipated deaths are calculated as described in the text. (——— total deaths; ········ senescent deaths; —·—·—·— anticipated deaths). (After Benjamin 1959.)

matter of wearing out, but bear a complicated relationship to the pattern of life of each species. We can see only vaguely what this pattern has been for man and are not yet able to forecast what it will be. Probably our successors with greater knowledge will see the future more clearly. Meanwhile, we can only look for situations in which it is possible to study the expectation of life under various conditions.

As life tables become available, using new methods for determining the age of animals (for example by weighing the lens of the eye or studying the tooth structure, see Linhart and Knowlton 1967, Sikes 1966), it is possible that wide differences may be found between longevity in laboratory and wild populations.

Survival curves are available for various species of fish, whose age can be determined from their scales (Fig. 23.7) (Beverton and Holt 1959). The

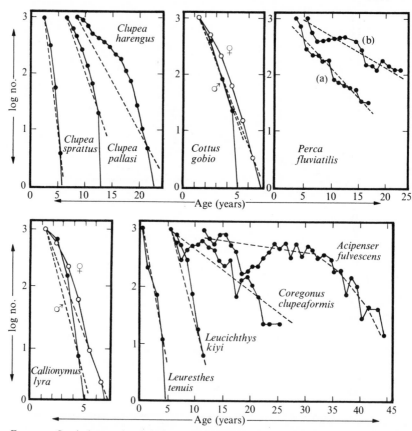

FIG. 23.7. Survival curves in relatively unexploited fish populations. The curves begin at the sizes at which the fish are first caught, but all are adjusted to a peak number of 1000. The scale is logarithmic: a straight line shows constant mortality; a downward curve shows increasing mortality with age. The dotted lines are to help the eye. (After Beverton and Holt 1959.)

shorter-lived species mostly show clear signs of departure from constant mortality, that is, they have specific ages. The longer-lived forms (sturgeon, whitefish, and perch) seem to show constant mortality rates at least over long periods, though in the oldest of all (sturgeons) the death-rate increases in the end. Many other factors enter into the question (i.e. growth and size, p. 312, and reproduction) but it seems that in some fishes life is not terminated at any specific age. On the other hand, some have a definite maximum age, though even this may be influenced by external factors, such as temperature, which affect the metabolism (Fig. 23.8).

Again, wild mice are killed off so early that the effect of senescence never appears, but it is very evident in laboratory animals (whose curve, as Comfort observes, resembles that of western Europeans in 1900 (see also Haldane 1953)). It thus seems that we can distinguish between an ecological longevity found in the wild state and a physiological longevity that can be achieved under better (? optimal) conditions (Bodenheimer 1938). Obviously the former is the entity in which we are, in general, more interested, in determining the relationship of age to risk. The fact that the latter condition more nearly approaches that of human populations emphasizes that in matters of ageing man is unusual—as a result of his exceptional capacities for obtaining and storing information and exerting control.

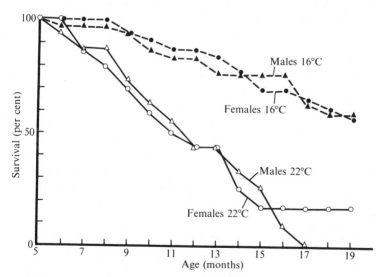

F IG. 23.8. Percentage of survivors of the fish *Cynolebias adloffi* kept at different temperatures. (After Liu and Walford 1966.)

3. The pattern of senescence

If the pattern of senescence is determined by the adverse secondary late manifestation of genes there should be some correlation between senescence and the age distribution of reproductive potentiality in relation to the period of differentiation of the body. The following indications of this are given by Williams (1957).

1. Unicellular organisms, having no soma, may show no senescence (p. 293). This is not of course to say that individuals are immortal. The fact that some clones die out while related ones survive shows that selection is at work.

2. Animals with a relatively low adult mortality show a slow rate of senescence (p. 311). The tortoises and turtles show further examples. Their shells give them a special protection and they have a longer life-span than any other vertebrate. Conversely, animals that have a very high mortality before maturity also do not show especial manifestations of senility (e.g. marine lamellibranchs or crustaceans).

3. Organisms that increase in fecundity after maturity should not show rapid senescence. This is markedly true for those animals that continue to grow after maturity and hence produce more and more eggs, notably many molluscs, crustacea, and aquatic vertebrates. An old carp produces ten times as many eggs as one just mature. This increased fecundity *increases* the reproductive probability for later ages and hence produces selection against senescent changes. Perhaps when we have means for measuring the various senescent changes in these animals it will be possible to make quantitative correlations.

Such continual size increase is much more easily achieved by aquatic and especially by marine animals because their growth is not limited by gravity considerations. Indeed, since the resistance to movement in the water is mainly the skin friction, a large animal (or ship) is more efficient than a small one, because area increases only as the square of the linear dimensions. Conversely, land animals must be provided with mechanisms that limit their growth if their limbs are to carry their weight. It was noticed by Bidder (1932) that this size limitation is accompanied by senescence. The association may be dependent on the different patterns of fecundity that are correlated with the dimensional factors.

4. If senescence results from a failure of selection then it should supervene very rapidly in animal species that breed only once. Certainly this is true of some of them. Conspicuous examples are the octopus and some other cephalopods. The female, after laying her eggs, guards and aerates them, but when they have hatched she stops eating, and dies soon after (see Vevers 1961, Wood 1965). A classic instance among insects is the imago

of the mayfly. Among vertebrates we could name the lamprey and other anadromous migrants. They return to the rivers to breed and die immediately thereafter. Such a pattern would tend to evolve from one with several breeding seasons (Williams 1957). Individuals that returned to the sea would suffer further risks and their reduced fecundity would accelerate the development of faster senescent changes in the population.

In all these species we recognize immediately that the timing of the sequence of the life-cycle is specifically determined by the genotype. Indeed, in some cases we know the mechanism by which this is achieved. In *Octopus* it is hormonal; there is an optic gland that stimulates the ovary (or perhaps releases it from inhibition—see Wells and Wells 1959). The optic gland is itself controlled by changes in illumination (Richard 1967), which, as in so many animals, play a central part in determining the onset of reproduction, presumably because appropriate timing in relation to the seasons is essential in many environments. If the optic gland of the octopus is denervated the female at once begins to mature rapidly and she produces fertile eggs when she is one-tenth of the normal weight. She will then lay her eggs and usually dies, though occasionally such artificially stimulated females survive for a while.

Many similar mechanisms are known in arthropods and vertebrates. They tend to be controlled from a centre that lies relatively high up in the nervous system (e.g. supraoesophageal ganglion and hypothalamus respectively). This is presumably an indication of some connection both with the other control centres in these regions and with the mechanisms for storing information in the neural memory. There are evidently complicated interrelations between the length of life and the means of collecting information by the individual and the species. Where the genetic mechanism is particularly important, lifetimes tend to be short. On the other hand, it is no use having a good brain and filling it with a lot of information if this is then lost by an early death. In *Octopus* the memory-storing centre develops relatively early and with the information acquired the individual then proceeds to grow rapidly and at the right time produces its numerous offspring.

5. The view that senescence is the result of failure of selection seems at first incompatible with the continued existence of individuals after reproduction. Selection should, one might think, always produce a programme that ends with reproduction, as it does in the octopus or mayfly. Obviously this is not so in man or in domestic animals. This may be partly because 'reproduction' in man includes the period of bringing up the young. As Williams (1957) puts it, 'No one is post-reproductive until his youngest child is self-sufficient'. This prolonging of the usefulness of the individual within the family may have led to continued selection for longer life because

of the value of the information store to a larger group. Probably such survival is a recent development (see p. 497).

The sudden cessation of human reproduction at the menopause at about 45 years of age is one of the striking features of human biology. As noted above it must surely have arisen under some special selective influence. Williams (1957) suggests that this was the advantage produced by devoting the woman's care to her (already numerous) children, rather than to be interrupted by further, increasingly hazardous, pregnancies. This concept is in agreement with the fact that a woman's capacity for orgasm does not stop at menopause, but continues into old age.

The theory we have been considering predicts that there must be a declining effectiveness of homeostasis because of the selective advantage of genes that manifest their effects in the young. Any change causing prolongation of the life-span must be produced by some selective advantage that accrues in spite of this effect.

6. Many other aspects of the human and other patterns of senescence can be understood on this theory. Males have shorter lives than females in many animals, as in man. This would result from their increased mortality owing to such factors as more conspicuous colour, more or less ritual social fighting, defence of territory, and repelling of enemies. These factors, by decreasing the fecundity of males at later ages, emphasize the failure to select against any deleterious genes that then appear.

4. External influences on ageing

Environmental conditions certainly affect the rate of senescence. Thus lizards in Florida live for only 1 year whereas in Maryland, where they are less active, they live for 4 years. Of course, without experiment one cannot be sure that such differences are not due to different genotypes (see Bourlière 1957). Possibly similar effects are responsible for the facts that bats live for up to 15 years (they are asleep and cold for much of the time) whereas shrews are very active and short-lived. Such effects are related by some people to the concept that 'Most organisms seem unable to transform more than a certain fixed quantity of energy during their specific lifetime and the rate of energy turnover appears to determine the rate of ageing' (Bourlière 1957). This, of course, assumes that there is a specific lifetime. The life-span of fruit flies (*Drosophila*) is ten times greater at 10 °C than at 30 °C. On the other hand in mammals the increased metabolism produces shorter lives at lower temperatures (in rats). This agrees with the suggestion that the life-span is proportional to the total metabolism per gramme. Thus in man the surface-volume ratio is lower than the mouse and he lives some thirty times longer. But both expend about 700 calories/gramme/lifetime.

Nutrition is the external factor that is most obviously related to senescence. Well-authenticated experiments show that longevity can be increased by reduction of diet (McCay *et al.* 1939). Young rats were given a diet containing all essential nutritional elements but lacking in calories. They remained immature for up to 900 days. Growth could then be restarted by increased feeding. The animals matured and had a life-span up to 200 days longer than controls. There was retardation of such specific senescent changes as collagen-ageing.

These experiments are often interpreted as supporting the view given above that the life-span allows for a fixed energy expenditure, but the lowering in McCay's experiments was much less than the nearly doubled lifetime. There are, however, other interpretations. Domesticated rats probably store more fat than is appropriate, and the starved rats might have avoided this.

The effects of qualitative differences in diet are even less well understood. It is generally assumed that old people require a lower calorie intake, but it has not been shown in general that they require combinations of amino-acids different from those needed by young people. Nor are patterns of excretion different enough to provide clues as to metabolic differences. Although information is very scarce we can certainly assume that many human diets are far from optimal. Thus if they contain adequate amounts of the rarer amino-acids diets must often contain toxic amounts of the commoner ones (e.g. tyrosine, phenylalanine, or tryptophan). These are, however, general questions of diet; such imbalances can hardly be the reason for senescence.

There have been reports of a few particular differences in amino-acid requirements. Thus old people are said to require more methionine than young (see Schlettwein-Gsell 1966). All sorts of possible influences of diet on ageing have been reported. Many of them are obvious rationalizations of local customs (but not therefore by any means to be neglected). The most famous was perhaps the suggestion of Metchnikoff (1907) that drinking yoghurt was the secret of long life. He associated this with a theory of auto-intoxication by products of the intestinal bacterial flora. More 'scientific' is the suggestion that senescence may be accelerated by tanning agents such as tea, which increase cross-linkage between molecules. But this was proved to be false by McCay in rat experiments where only coffee was given as drink.

Other possible dietary influences on ageing are those that influence calcification, especially in the vascular system, thus the physician Osler's famous dictum was 'a man is as old as his arteries'. Selye (1962) recognizes a condition of 'calciphylaxis' in which tissues respond to certain 'sensitizers' in the diet by calcification. Some of the D vitamins act as sensitizers and they operate especially strongly in the presence of 'challengers' in the diet, such as those found, for example, in eggs.

Study of particular factors may be of great value in understanding particular phenomena of senescence, among which calcification is certainly conspicuous. It does not seem, however, that we can find the 'causes' of ageing in the environment. Our view is that there is no one cause, but environmental stresses are certainly the source of both the wear and of some of the random errors that characterize senescence.

5. Genetic basis of ageing

Whatever the basis of senescence may be, it certainly includes a large heritable factor. The best way to attain old age is to have old parents. Conversely, strains of mice have been bred in which all individuals die of leukaemia at the age of 9 months, as against the normal 36-month lifetime of mice. Here of course artificial selection has operated to produce a particular pattern of death. It may be that natural selection has operated in a similar way to determine the life-span of each species. However, as we have seen, this is only part of the 'explanation' of senescence—much of it is due to random influences, but even the liability to somatic mutation and capacity to tolerate and repair it have themselves genetic backgrounds.

24

HUMAN FERTILITY AND MORTALITY

1. The importance of numbers

ONE of man's many paradoxes is that although with him each individual organism is more important than in other animals as an information-gatherer for the species, yet his manner of life is largely controlled by his fellows, and particularly by how numerous they are. It can be argued that as men became more clever in avoiding death the crude pressure of population has been an increasing determinant dictating the changes in human technology. Today many people believe that the problem posed by our capacity for reproduction is even greater than that generated by our potential for mutual destruction. Certainly the pressure of population is great and is growing.

The study of human population change must therefore be one of the central themes of a study of human homeostasis. We all have the closest possible interest in understanding the changes that have occurred and especially forecasting numbers for the future. The provision of our daily bread depends on knowing for how many we have to provide. Everyone can gain from learning where the needs of the future will lie. Plans can be made by politicians, farmers, fishermen, business men, engineers, civil servants, soldiers, hospital authorities, medical men, and the rest of us only if we know the numbers and characteristics of the populations to be expected. Indeed plans are essential to meet the multitudes who are coming.

In this chapter we shall consider simply the question of number and we shall raise the suspicion that this alone is a feature of human life that is almost as important as the characteristics of the individuals. It is not that the contributions of individuals are irrelevant: on the contrary, single brains and the inventions that they make have been essential features of man's astonishing progress. But are individuals able to produce the changes as a result of the pressure of population growth? Or is it the other way round?

These are huge historical questions and we shall not presume to reach final answers. But we can look at least at some biological aspects of the problem and discuss some of the methods for studying population numbers and the facts that have been revealed about the past.

It is by no means a law that all human populations steadily increase. They have often declined, and by looking at the various periods we may be able to obtain some ideas about how population changes themselves influence human life.

It is important to emphasize that the subject is so vast that it is quite certain that a superficial study such as the present will remain inadequate and subject to revision. Perhaps the most important lesson we can learn from it is that nothing about population growth is self-evident. On this as so much else in human biology common sense is no guide. The numbers and scale of the events are outside the usual daily experience for which the simple models in our brains have been framed. If we are to talk sense about population we must start from the beginning and learn some facts. Because the numbers of human beings have recently increased rapidly it *does not follow* that mankind is going to starve or that our successors will stand packed solid on the earth in 300 years' time. But it may be that they will do either or both. There is not enough understanding of the problems yet to make reliable forecasts even for a few decades ahead. But at least we know that we must be cautious and not blindly either 'Malthusian' or 'anti-Malthusian'. There are beginning to be really useful methods of study and accumulations of fact.

2. Human fertility

What is it then that determines how many people live on any area? The number is almost certain to be continually changing and we ought to look for some method of expressing the rate of change. The basic facts we need to know are how fast people are born and how fast they die. Let us therefore examine methods for study of these separately.

The number of people born is limited by the facts of human reproduction, especially in the female. The power of a woman to reproduce is known as her *fecundity* or *fecundibility*, to be distinguished from her *fertility*, which is the number of live children she has actually produced at the end of her reproductive period. Fecundity is defined as the probability that a woman will conceive in any given menstrual cycle, granted that she is living with a man (or men) fully capable of reproduction and not restricting conception in any way (Clark 1967). The definition is not free of ambiguity (expecially in its later phrases!) and fecundity is not easy to measure. The basic data would obviously be the number of children born under some optimal conditions, plus the number of abortions. But the number born depends upon length of lactation and other matters, and the number aborted in the early stages of pregnancy is impossible to determine. Even to estimate reliably the number of children born to a group of women under the conditions that their husbands are freely available and that they are not using contraceptives or lactating is nearly impossible. These conditions are approached for the early years of marriage and for couples discontinuing contraception in order to have a child. But fecundity measured in this way seems to be only about 0·2 for first conceptions and then 0·1 for subsequent ones (rather higher in couples that have just discontinued contraception). Certainly the probability of conception per cycle can be higher than this. Numbers of children born do not give the estimate required, unless we also have estimates of abortions (see below). But many studies have nevertheless depended basically upon numbers born, especially for the important question of variations of fecundity with age. Fecundity is perhaps lower in very young girls directly after menarche, but it rises shortly thereafter and there is little evidence about its later decline towards the end of the reproductive period. Some women may become infecund before the usual age of menopause. A widely held view is that fecundity may vary between populations but for an individual woman remains approximately constant, and is probably much higher than the figures for numbers of children born indicate.

3. The probability of conception

It seems likely that frequency of coitus influences fecundity and this is one of the ambiguities in defining it as above. Some data indeed show such an effect (Table 24.1), but evidence on coital frequency is highly suspect.

TABLE 24.1

*Fecundity estimated by births or known
conceptions, and coital frequency*
(after Clark 1967)

Reported coital frequency per menstrual cycle	Fecundity	% conceiving within 5 months
under 8	0·110	29
10		46
12	0·134	
14		52
16	0·180	
over 18	0·206	83

4. The human reproductive potential

Given certain assumptions one can calculate the maximum human reproductive potential (Bourgeois-Pichat, cited by Clark 1967). The fertilizable life of the ovum is between 6 and 24 h. Sperms certainly do not remain fertile for more than 28–48 h; in the female tract probably much less (Restall 1967). Assuming ovulation during each menstrual cycle, this would give much higher conception rates than the above for given coital rates. But of course no allowance has been made for abortions. It may be that the probability of conception (fecundity) is as high as 0·5 or even higher for young women with a high copulation frequency.

Fecundity is greatly reduced during lactation, owing to direct hormonal influences on ovulation. (It is not lowered after a stillbirth.) The duration of the reduction varies, in general increasing with the age of the mother. It may last as much as 2 years, but perhaps fifteen menstrual cycles is a useful figure for average full lactation. Using this and a set of data for foetal mortality from Hawaii, Bourgeois-Pichat has calculated a model of fecundity and actual reproduction (Table 24.2).

TABLE 24.2

A theoretical model of human reproduction per year of marriage. The average number of expected live births is 0·433 per year of marriage (after Clark 1967)

Age of mother	15–19	20–4	25–9	30–4	35–9	40–4	45–9
Fecundity	0·62	0·52	0·47	0·43	0·39	0·33	0·28
Expected live births/year	0·471	0·474	0·463	0·441	0·420	0·392	0·371

The average expected births per year is 0·433, and there is much evidence that this is near the actual figure achieved by unrestrained human reproduction. The Hutterites are a religious sect in America who believe that it is a duty to have as many children as possible: they average 0·4 a year. There are other data from various parts of the world showing that this figure is near the maximum. Table 24.3 is an example from applicants of

TABLE 24.3

Births per year of married life in different communities (after Clark 1967)

Urban areas		Rural areas	
Nashville whites	0·41	W. Virginian whites	0·44
Nashville negroes	0·46	Tennessee whites	0·41
Puerto Ricans	0·41	Kentucky whites	0·40
		Puerto Ricans	0·47

various communities to birth-control clinics in the 1930s (the estimates are probably biased on the side of high fecundity).

5. Male fertilizing power

There are presumably variations in the basic reproductive power in the male that correspond to fecundity. Less seems to be known about this. Sometimes it is assumed that these variations are not very important reproductive parameters, but data show that husbands younger than their wives produce relatively few children. Only where the husband is much older than the wife do the older men beget fewer children (Table 24.4).

TABLE 24.4

The legitimate live births, from 1962 to 1966, in relation to the ages of the parents in combination. The effect of the difference of age between husband and wife on the frequency of births. The data refer to the population of England and Wales (from the *Registrar General's Report 1968*)

1962-6	Age of mother at birth								
Age of father at birth	All ages	Under 20	20-4	25-9	30-4	35-9	40-4	45-9	50 and over
All ages	3 970 186	297 284	1 268 137	1 248 941	707 177	344 000	98 752	5881	14
Under 20	74 933	61 325	13 044	480	65	18	1	..	..
20-4	787 021	190 110	534 244	57 838	4112	597	106	14	..
25-9	1 303 280	38 562	574 518	616 916	66 075	6465	710	34	..
30-4	948 832	5572	115 648	445 887	338 510	39 822	3277	116	..
35-9	521 121	1247	22 416	98 218	223 432	160 175	15 240	393	..
40-4	232 655	292	5833	21 492	56 883	100 875	46 185	1095	..
45-9	71 689	115	1611	5489	12 542	25 791	23 520	2620	1
50-4	22 291	42	549	1862	4045	7379	7225	1176	13
55-9	5965	12	194	534	1070	2054	1792	309	..
60-4	1754	4	62	156	328	596	509	99	..
65-9	476	3	16	53	78	168	136	22	..
70-4	129	..	1	10	27	45	43	3	..
75 and over	40	..	1	6	10	15	8	..	..

6. Total fertility

If the productivity per year for each woman were about 0·4 we can calculate that the total fertility, the number of live children per woman, should be rather over 10. This would be, of course, the average for the community. The maximum number of children recorded for any one woman is 25 (from Brazil). The total fertility in the Hutterite community was found to be 10·6 (1905). From a large study of data on total fertilities none greater than this has emerged. Some data for Canada for women married under 20 years of age gave 9·9 live children per woman. In England and Wales the comparable figure was 8·4 for those married between 1861 and 1871. From here the data range down to 6·4 in India, for all women married but not widowed

(1951). Asian fertilities are mostly lower than European (China about 6). In many African countries the figure is 4 or even lower. However, the average fertility for tropical Africa has recently been estimated to be 6·5/1000 (Brass *et al.* 1968).

Differences in total fertility are obviously of the greatest importance for population studies but our knowledge about them is still only fragmentary. The influence of fecundity on the growth of the population will depend upon such factors as age at marriage and proportion of totally infecund women, which may be 8 per cent or more. Such factors as opportunity for remarriage of widows, or polygamy, may have important effects on the total number of children.

There are certainly wide differences in the total fertility in different areas. No one knows whether these are due mainly to genetic or to social factors. It is held that they are unlikely to be due to climate or diet, since communities living side by side may show differences.

7. Methods for estimating birth-rates

A considerable variety of methods, of varying subtlety, has been devised to compare the fertility of different populations and to forecast their growth (see Beaujeu-Garnier 1966). The simplest is the crude birth-rate, that is the total number of children born, say, in 1 year per 1000 people in the population. This method is still widely used, but though useful for geographers has many dangers for demographers, who wish to compare the vitality of populations. The crude birth-rate takes no account of the age- or sex-composition of the population, so that a country with many old people may have a low birth-rate, even though those of reproductive age are producing many children. Similarly a colony with few women will show a low birth-rate.

One rather arbitrary way to avoid these difficulties is to relate the actual composition of the population to an idealized standard model population and multiply the crude birth-rate by the coefficient obtained, giving a so-called '*standardized birth-rate*'. A better way is to relate births (or children under 5 years) to the number of women of reproductive age (15-44 years). This figure is sometimes called the *fertility rate*; it can, of course, be obtained only for the 5 years preceding a census. Thus in France the crude birth-rate for 1932-6 was 16 and in Hungary for 1935-9 it was 20, but the fertility rates were 319 and 300 respectively; the French women were actually more productive, but there were more old people in the population.

Another figure is the *gross reproduction rate*, the number of female children born per 1000 women during their reproductive period. It thus indicates whether they are replacing themselves. In the U.S.A. this figure was 1101 before 1940, 1443 in 1946. In England and Wales the figures were 850 and 1210. This shows the rise in births that we have to consider for forecasting, but the reproduction rate is seldom available and can lead to erroneous forecasts if marriage habits change. This also applies to the somewhat more subtle version, the *net reproduction rate*, namely the number of female children born to each woman and surviving to their mother's age when they were born.

8. Age-specific fertility rates

Much of the difficulty in forecasting population changes is due to the differences in fertility of women at different ages. The future numbers thus depend largely on the age-structure of the population. An even larger difficulty is the uncertainty about changes in patterns of marriage and childbearing. The *age-specific birth-rate* is usually calculated as the number of births per 1000 women in each 5-year age group (Fig. 24.1). This is a most

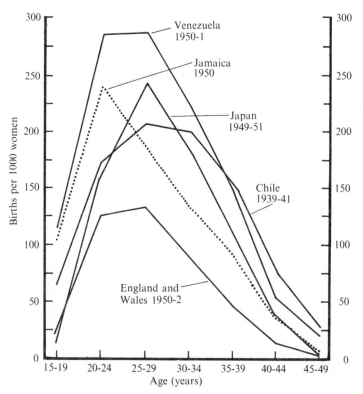

FIG. 24.1. The age-specific birth-rates (that is the ratios of births by age of mother to number of women) are shown in 5-year age intervals for a number of countries in different parts of the world. (After Barclay 1958.)

useful figure, since it shows the characteristic performance of women at seven stages of their reproductive careers, from which other figures can be calculated. For example, an estimate of the total fertility at any date can be obtained, as that of a hypothetical woman who has been through all the age groups, showing the fertility of those groups at the given date. This suggests the sort of statistic to use in estimating the condition of populations at the present time.

What we need is an estimate of the age-specific birth-rate that is based, not on the completed reproductive lives, but on current reproductive practices. This is provided by the method of the French statistician Henry for estimating the *probability of enlargement of families* (see Clark 1967). For each group of children, first, second, third . . . in the family that are born each year he estimates the probable additions to the families, assuming the rates of addition that have been found in the population in previous years. Thus if, say, there are 20 000 third children born, then from the figures of the past 5 years he would find how many of them would be followed by a fourth child, how many of these by a fifth, and so on. The method is obviously difficult, but can be used in various ways to forecast the probable fertility of each cohort in the population *in the light only of recent fertility*, instead of depending on that of completed families, whose history began long ago. The method in fact re-analyses reproductivity afresh each year. A very important conclusion from using it is that parents change their reproductive practices quite drastically, and that forecasting is therefore likely to be most difficult. This can be illustrated by the errors in the forecasts made in the 1930s, when there were about 46 million people in the U.K. It was then supposed that in 1970 there would be less than 44 million there, more of them over 65 than under 15. Actually there are 55 million, twice as many under 15 as over 65 (Eversley 1970). The mistake was made because although fertility had begun to increase in the 1930s no one detected this because of the failure to observe that the statistics used, mainly the net reproduction rate (p. 323), varied with changes in the age of marriage. Estimates of the probability of enlargement avoid this error, and with this, and other methods, forecasts will no doubt improve, but they will always remain subject to uncertainty about the changes that humans, rightly, make as to the best course of action for homeostasis.

9. Some differences in birth-rates

Statistical weaknesses still make it very difficult to give reliable data about many questions we should like to answer; for example, are there inherent differences in fertility between different populations? Are these influenced by climate, diet, economic factors, and so on? Apart from the statistical difficulties there are those that spring from the variation between human beings even within one area. For example, fertility varies with class and with occupation. Country people are often more fertile than town people and those in the suburbs more fertile than those in the city centres. Over-all figures for a region must be interpreted with such factors in mind.

Comparisons of populations living in the same area are particularly liable to be influenced by such social factors, but at least they go some way to eliminating effects of climate. Thus in Brazil the number of children produced per 100 women is given as 311 for whites, 332 for 'coloureds', 302 for blacks, and 313 for yellows (mostly Japanese). In Trinidad, Asian women over 45 had had 5·36 children each, blacks 3·45. In South Africa we have birth rates of 38/1000 for Bantu, 37 Indians, and 43 'coloureds'. There are thus some suggestions that mixtures are the most prolific, followed by Asians and then Africans with whites the least prolific (but not always less so than black). But such generalizations must be taken with great caution (Beaujeu-Garnier 1966).

10. The 'evolution' of the birth-rate

In spite of all the difficulties it is possible to see a general pattern of change in birth-rates. Beginning first in France at the end of the eighteenth century, there has been a general tendency to diminution from the very highest birth-rates. This change is still proceeding in many countries, even where the rate is still high. On the other hand, in countries where the rate fell to very low levels it now shows a distinct but small rise. We can therefore see different parts of the world in various stages of this pattern of evolution, from a high birth-rate. The initial 'natural' crude birth-rate may be as much as 60 per 1000, which was the rate in French Canada at the end of the eighteenth century and perhaps still occurs in parts of tropical America and Asia. In England the rate was 37 per 1000 in 1800, 33 in 1850, 30 in 1900, 16 in 1930, and 15·5 in 1950. This fall in fertility has been seen in every country of Europe over the past 150 years (Fig. 24.2). It began earliest in France, much later in Germany and Italy. It seems to go with a general increase in standard of living and intellectual and educational development, and is roughly paralleled by the decline in the death-rate (p. 328). In recent years the fall in the birth-rate has in Europe been arrested or reversed (Figs. 24.2 and 24.4). This is largely due to younger marriages and has falsified the prophecies of declining population in Europe, given by demographers in the 1930s (p. 324).

This pattern of evolution has been followed with variations in all the industrial countries. In France, where the birth-rate fell to 15·1 per 1000 in 1935-9, it reached 18 by 1966, assisted by active government tax support

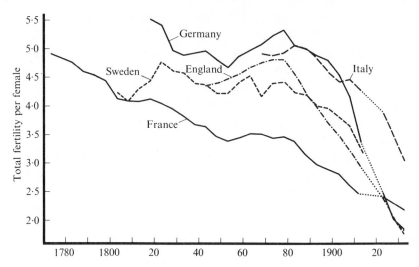

FIG. 24.2. The curves from different countries show the trend of total fertility in Europe since birth registration was begun in these countries (After Clark 1967.)

since 1938. It is interesting that the effect has been an increase of 2 per cent in one-child families and of 22 per cent for those with two children, but of only 6 per cent for three-child families, and there is a reduction of 2 per cent in families of four children.

In countries populated relatively recently by white people, the recent rise has been marked, without any special government measures. Thus in the U.S.A. the crude rate has risen from 17·4 (1930–9) to 24 (1950), and there are similar changes in Canada, Australia, and New Zealand. Japan

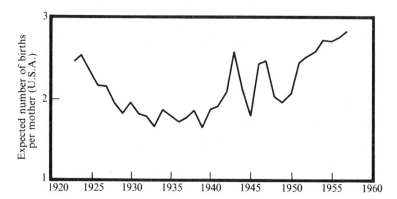

FIG. 24.3. The curve shows the changes that have occurred in the estimated average number of children per marriage in the U.S.A. (among the white native women) from the early 1920s to the late 1950s (After Clark 1967.)

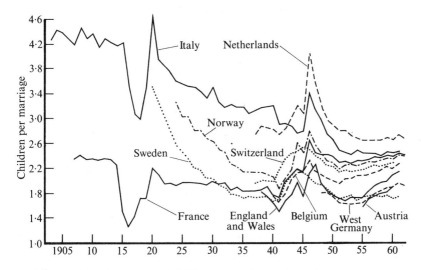

FIG. 24.4. The average number of children per marriage is shown for western European
countries, from the beginning of the century until the present time. (After Clark 1967.)

has shown a dramatic fall in birth-rate from 30·1 in 1945–9 to 17·1 in 1960
as a result of active support of contraception and spread of abortion. It is
not clear whether a rise will follow.

The tendency for the birth-rate to fall from its initial very high values
can be detected even in countries such as Brazil, where the rate is high and
even rising! This apparent absurdity depends on the fact that registration
of births is continually improving, giving a spurious over-all rise in birth-
rate. Study of restricted areas that have a longer history of registration
shows the tendency to fall. Thus in the whole of Brazil the rate is 43, but
in Rio de Janeiro and the state capitals it is only 30. In some parts of South
America and in some Moslem countries of North Africa and the Middle
East the indications of a fall are only very slight. In other places they are
marked; for instance, in Taiwan the rate fell from 46 per 1000 in 1950–4
to 40 in 1958–60, and Puerto Rico from 39 per 1000 in 1940 to 36·6 in 1950–4
and 32 in 1958–60.

Looking at the whole world we can divide countries into three groups.

(A) *Countries with birth-rate under 20 per 1000.* These include the
majority of those in Europe, and Japan. The eastern European countries,
Czechoslovakia, Rumania, Hungary, and Bulgaria all have birth-rates less
than 20, as have Greece and Italy (though with great internal variation).

(B) *Birth-rates 20–30 per 1000.* Here there are two groups. First, in
some Mediterranean countries rates are still falling: Spain, Portugal, and

Yugoslavia, and also Poland. Secondly, there are the U.S.A. and other white-colonized countries mentioned above.

(C) *Birth-rates above 30 per 1000*. Here there are all the countries of Africa, Latin America, and southern and eastern Asia, though the data for these are poor. As we have seen, there are reasons to believe that even in these areas the rates are beginning to fall, but they will show great growth in population for many years to come.

11. Death-rates

In order to estimate the changing number in a population we need to know the rate at which people die. This will of course vary with the age composition of the population, even more than does the specific fertility rate. Crude death-rates can be as misleading as crude birth-rates—but often they are the only data available. In order to obtain an estimate we need the age of each individual at death and the number of people of each age in the population. From these figures we can estimate the expected number of each cohort of births (say 10 000) who will survive to each age. Some details of such life tables have already been considered (Chapter 23). Here we are concerned with finding a single figure to express the whole mortality of the community and for this we may use the *average expectation of life at birth*. Another useful figure is the *proportion of females surviving to their mother's age*. This net reproduction rate gives us the number available to produce the next generation.

Unfortunately these figures can be obtained only when there is a good system of registration of births and deaths. This is a very recent practice, beginning in Sweden about 1750, and in Britain in 1834; in the U.S.A. it was not complete (in Texas) until 1933. In Asia, Africa, and South America very few countries have proper statistics yet. For the greater part of human history and for most of the world today, we have to use various imperfect samples or other evidence.

Our earliest estimates come from study of the teeth and other features of fossils, or Palaeolithic or Bronze Age burials, from which Table 24.5 has been compiled. For details of 'Palaeopathology', see Janssons 1970.

The figures have been corrected on the assumption that young children were often not buried; the infantile mortality rates for the Samburu tribe have been used. Palaeolithic men presumably had survival rates as low or lower than the Samburu, a pastoral people living in very dry country in East Africa, who have the lowest known contemporary survival rates. They keep records of the age groups as part of their ceremonies and we can see that the age structure has changed little in 30 years (Fig. 24.5). Only about half the children of each cohort reach the age of 14 and only one-fifth exceed

TABLE 24.5

The mortality by age in different epochs (after Clark 1967)

	Number of cases	Deaths % at age of				
		< 14	14–20	21–40	41–60	Over 60
H. erectus (Pekin)	22	68	14	14	4	..
H.s. neanderthalensis	20	55	11	30	4	..
H.s. sapiens (U. Palaeolithic)	102	55	6	32	7	..
H.s. sapiens (Mesolithic)	65	55	4	38	2	1
H.s. sapiens (Early Bronze Age)	273	50	9	22	15	4

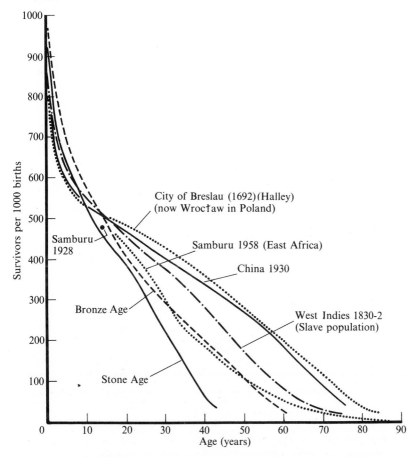

FIG. 24.5. The curves are of low survival-rates in different populations. The lowest contemporary rate is that for the Samburu, a pastoral tribe inhabiting arid country in East Africa. (After Clark 1967.)

the age of 40. This pattern is approximately the same as we derive from the Bronze Age burials.

Fig. 24.5 also shows three other populations whose survival curves have similar shapes. That for Breslau (now Wrocław in Poland) was calculated by the Astronomer Royal, Halley, in 1692 and shows that European populations were then not far removed from the primitive condition. In the subsequent three centuries there has been a steady change towards the 'rectangular' survival curve that we have already discussed in Chapter 23 (Figs. 24.6 and 24.7). Today more than 95 per cent may survive to the age of 40, but very few beyond 100.

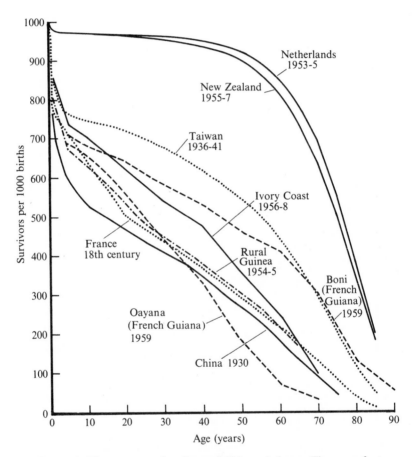

FIG. 24.6. The curves are of medium and high survival rates. The curves for two indigenous tribes living side by side in French Guiana are shown (Boni and Oayana). There is a large difference in their mortality; immunity of the Boni to malaria may play some part in this; there is also a difference in their reproductivity.

(After Clark 1967.)

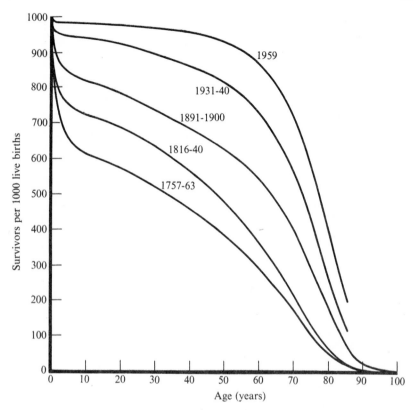

FIG. 24.7. The change in the shape of the survival curve from the middle of the eigh-teenth century until the present time is shown in the series of curves, all from Sweden. The shapes of the curves change as they pass from a low-survival community where half of each generation is lost by the age of 15, to a high-survival community, where 95 per cent of a generation may survive to the age of 40 years. (After Clark 1967.)

A large part of this change has been due to the fall in infant mortality, which proceeded steadily up to 1900 and continued dramatically thereafter (Fig. 24.8). The figures from Catalonia come from records of a single parish in a district where smallpox vaccination was introduced much earlier than in most of Spain.

12. Replacement of the population

We can now put the figures for additions and subtractions to the popu-lation together and examine the conditions under which the population maintains itself, or increases or falls. Using the fertility data for Guinea (a 'primitive' community) and death-rates of the Samburu, we find that the population only just maintains itself (Table 24.6). The total number of children born to the cohort of 1000 female births is 2060, namely 2·06 each,

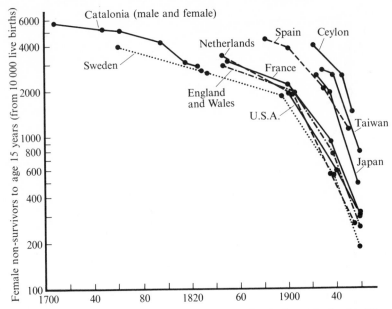

FIG. 24.8. The improvement in survival rate through time is shown, for females. The graph includes a study of a single parish in Catalonia for a long period of time; these figures refer to both male and female survival until 14 years of age. The rate of improvement has accelerated greatly in the present century. (After Clark 1967.)

which is the *net total fertility* or gross reproduction rate. Since the sex ratio at birth is 1·06 males to 1 female this means that exactly 1000 females are produced by their 1000 mothers. The net total fertility divided by 2·06 is the *net reproduction rate*, in this case 1·0.

TABLE 24.6

A model of the net reproduction at lowest fertility and survival rates (after Clark 1967)

Age of mother	Estimated survivors of 1000 female births	Births per year of married life	Total fertility. Estimated annual births
15–19	414	0·18	75
20–4	355	0·42	149
25–9	288	0·30	86
30–4	233	0·25	58
35–9	187	0·20	37
40–4	150	0·05	7
			412
		× 5 years =	2060
		÷ 2·06 =	1000

The net reproduction rate thus expresses the ratio of numbers of surviving females to their mothers and has been widely used as a measure of whether a population is steady or changing (p. 323). Unfortunately it has led to erroneous forecasts because it takes no account of the possibility of changes in age at marriage. This age has become lower in many western countries recently, producing far more babies than were forecast from the net re-production rate. Thus, in England and Wales the proportion of girls marry-ing for the first time who were under 25 was 58 per cent in 1931, 66 per cent in 1939–50, and 81 per cent in 1963 (see Glass 1967). The net reproduction rate is, however, still widely used and Table 24.7 shows the rates of popula-tion increase that it forecasts. If 25 years is assumed as the average length of a generation, then the correspondence between the net reproduction rate and the population increase per annum can be calculated and is shown in the table.

To give a few examples, the net reproduction rate was 1·5 in Ghana in 1956 and below 1·0 in some regions of Africa. It was 1·4–1·5 in Jamaica 1879–1923 but 1·85 in 1955. We shall discuss it again later in relation to various populations.

TABLE 24.7

Correspondence between net reproduction rate and annual increases (Clark 1967)

Net reproduction rate	1·2	1·4	1·6	1·8	2·0	2·2	2·4
% per annum popula- tion increase	0·7	1·4	1·9	2·3	2·8	3·2	3·5

13. Reasons for the fall in mortality

It is commonly supposed that the rise in population in the last centuries is somehow connected with the industrial revolution. Connections there may be, but perhaps more in the sense that the population explosion caused the revolution, or at least that both were caused by human inventiveness. It is unfortunately almost impossible to discover precise causal connections even about such important matters as population changes. For example, it has also been suggested that it was the *relief* from surplus population by emigration to America that made English and European prosperity and fertility possible.

It is probable that the great increase in population in the west in the late eighteenth and nineteenth centuries was related to falling mortality from disease. The connection is by no means certain and many serious diseases persisted throughout the period (e.g. cholera, variola, typhus, typhoid fever). However, one of the worst, bubonic plague, did become rare in Europe, apparently as a result of war among the rats. During the eighteenth century brown rats (field rats) moved from their home in temperate Asia into western Europe, perhaps because the climate became colder. They were reported in England in 1728. Field rats are stronger, more cunning, and more fecund than the black rats (house rats) then living in Europe, which were therefore nearly exterminated.

But black rats only, and not brown, carry the particular species of flea (*Xenopsylla cheopsis*) that transmits the bacillus of plague when it bites a man. Episodes of bubonic and pneumonic plague beginning in 1348 with the Great Mortality or Great Pestilence (later known as the Black Death) had played a large part in restricting population, perhaps following the introduction of the black rat to Europe from India (Shrewsbury 1970). At least one quarter of the population of Europe died during the three years of the Black Death, perhaps 'the worst disaster that has ever befallen mankind'. Certainly from the thirteenth to the late seventeenth century Europe was more disease-ridden than ever before or since. It may be that the relief after this was due to the arrival of the brown rat, but others point out that the decline had already begun earlier, and in any case the black rats were not wholly replaced. It is nearly always impossible to find proof of the causes of the origins and ends of epidemics. The end of the plague may have been partly due to the rats, partly to changes in the fleas or, indeed, in the humans, so many of whom had died that perhaps only those more nearly immune remained. In any case it is certain that the effect of the great reduction in population was a long economic recession both in agriculture and in the towns. There was probably a connection between the disappearance of the plague and the increases during the eighteenth century of both population and prosperity (see Burnet 1953 and Langer 1964). In Norway increases resulted from vaccination and potatoes (Drake 1969).

It is only in the last two centuries that human beings have acquired any large measure of control over their chances of death (Table 24.8). It is difficult to remember that even 100 years ago there was very little that a doctor could do to help his patient. The change has been brought about by the application of the methods of science to the problems of disease and illness. This has enabled us to have a better understanding both of the nature of disorders within ourselves and of the chemical and other agents that we can use to restore health.

Probably the extent and importance of this revolution in knowledge is still not sufficiently appreciated either by academics or by politicians who have responsibility for the human condition. We are used to thinking of 'science' as something that has to do chiefly with 'matter', in the sense of non-living

TABLE 24.8

Some developments in prophylaxis

Disease or condition	Agency	Prevention or remedy	Main responsible discoverer	Approximate date
Plague	Bacteria (*Pasteurella pestis*)	Death of black rat	Brown rat	1700
Smallpox	Virus	Vaccination	E. Jenner (1749–1823)	1798
Bleeding as a remedy	Doctors	Medical statistics	P. C. A. Louis (1787–1872)	1835
Surgery	Pain	Anaesthesia	W. T. G. Morton (1819–68)	1846
Infection	Bacteria	Antisepsis	J. Lister (1827–1912)	1867
Infectious diseases	Bacteria	Germ theory of disease	L. Pasteur (1822–95) R. Koch (1843–1910)	1876
Uncertainty of diagnosis		X-rays	W. C. Röntgen (1845–1923)	1895
Loss of blood	Accidents	Blood groups	K. Landsteiner (1868–1943)	1900
Inborn errors	Inheritance	Laws of heredity (1865)	G. J. Mendel (1822–84)	1900
Deficiency diseases	Wrong diet	Vitamins	F. G. Hopkins (1861–1947)	1906
Syphilis	*Spirochaeta pallida*	Chemotherapy	P. Ehrlich (1854–1915) S. Hata (1873–1938)	1910
Septicaemia, etc.	*Streptococci*	Sulpha drugs	G. Domagk (1895–1964)	1935
Tuberculosis	*Mycobacterium tuberculosis*	Isonicotinic acid	Squibb, Hofman-Laroche, and Bayer Laboratories	1952
Many diseases	Bacteria incl. *Staphylococci*	Antibiotics Penicillin	A. Fleming (1881–1955) H. Florey (1898–1968) E. B. Chain (1906–)	1929 1940

things. It was indeed developed first in relation to these and produced the industrial revolution of the last century. Similar methods of precise thought and experiment applied now to living things are producing a revolution that affects even more people. It has already changed the whole age-distribution of the population in western countries and is rapidly changing the rest. Moreover, the revolution is so fresh that its future is quite uncertain. So far it has not succeeded in prolonging the maximum period of life. What will happen if it does so? Again, scientific thought is only beginning to provide us with ways of assisting our brains; as it does so the whole of our methods of thinking are likely to change.

As these revolutions proceed it becomes increasingly important for the medical profession to watch and help to guide them, as part of the personal care that it gives to its patients.

The main continuing enemies of man, medically speaking, are infectious disease, accident, mental disease, degenerative diseases such as heart disease, and cancer. The pattern in which these agents operate varies greatly between different cultures and at different times (Table 24.9). A first aim of medical care, in the widest sense, is to discover the pattern for a particular community, to try to forecast its changes, and to plan medical services that will improve the condition of the population and assist its members when they fall ill.

TABLE 24.9

The causes of death in England and Wales, per million of the population

Cause of death	1900†	1956‡	1966‡
Heart diseases	2350	4333	4327
Cancer	829	2112	2279
Diseases of nervous system	1271	1792	1764
Gastric and duodenal ulcers	47	120	85
Typhoid fever	173	0	0
Diphtheria	292	0	0
Scarlet fever	117	0	0
Measles	391	1	2
Whooping cough	356	2	0
Pneumonia	1374	520	750
Bronchitis	1692	670	663
Tuberculosis	1902	120	49
Poliomyelitis	..	3	0
Childbirth	42·8§	0·42	0·20
Accidents	214§	490	508
Other causes		1509	1297
		11 672	11 724

The information has been taken from Stamp, †, the *Registrar General's Statistical Review for 1966*, ‡, and the *Annual Report of the Registrar General*, 1900, §.

The result of improved medical knowledge and care has been to change the pattern of disease dramatically. Chiefly, of course, there has been an enormous decrease in infant mortality. Queen Anne (1665–1714) presumably had the best medical care but only one of her seventeen children survived infancy (and he died at the age of 11). Infectious diseases, especially of the young, have largely lost their terrors.

14. The control of population by contraception

Tribes such as the pastoral Samburu, like their Palaeolithic predecessors, need their full reproductive powers for continued maintenance (p. 331). With increased food production and decreased mortality many communities have been faced with the prospect of an unwanted increase in population. It was shown long ago by Carr-Saunders (1936) that population limitation is very widespread among peoples of all stages of development. Abortion and infanticide have been and are practised in most parts of the world.

The conscious limitation of conception has also no doubt long been practised, for example by *coitus interruptus*, withdrawal to prevent the arrival of sperms in the vagina (see Suitters 1967). The use of sheaths for this purpose was certainly prevalent in the eighteenth century in western countries. They were made from the caeca of sheep and the swim-bladders of fishes and were said to have been invented by a Colonel Cundum. Boswell tells us that such 'armour' was used as much to prevent infection as pregnancy. It is impossible to say whether such practices produced any effective population control.

The invention of rubber contraceptives during the present century has undoubtedly been one of the factors limiting population growth in western countries. The male sheath is a development from the sheep's caecum condom, and the female 'dutch cap' can be used in conjunction with a chemical spermicide. Such methods of contraception, mainly by physical means, have their obvious disadvantages. These are largely overcome by the intra-uterine devices (I.U.D.), which are loops, bows, or spirals of polyethylene plastic. They are inserted in the uterus by a trained person, and can be left there until conception is desired. It is uncertain how they operate. Since they need no attention once fitted and do not interfere with copulation, they obviously have great advantages. They reduce the pregnancy rate to 2–3 per cent per annum or less.

The understanding of the significance of the menstrual cycle and its hormonal control has opened the way to more biological methods of contraception. The knowledge that ovulation occurs at about the fourteenth day after the beginning of the last period provides a simple natural means of contraception by the 'rhythm' method. Ova and sperms both usually survive only a short time (see p. 189). Avoidance of copulation during the 2 or 3 days around the middle of the cycle provides a method that is secure except for those whose ovulation is very irregular.

Substances that resemble the hormones that control the menstrual cycle are effective contraceptives if given by mouth (the 'pill'). Oestrogens are normally preponderant in the blood in the first half of the cycle, and progesterones in the second (Chapter 5). It was discovered by Pincus (1965) that progesterone inhibits ovulation. He tested a large series of steroids that have progesterone-like actions. Eventually he found some that were effective when taken by mouth and produced the minimum of side-effects.

This is the basis of oral contraception by the pill, introduced in 1950. Usually a mixture of hormones is taken every day from the fifth to the twenty-sixth day of the cycle. Various doses and combinations have been tried and improvements in the method are still possible and likely. The method is said to be now used by 10 million people, with a pregnancy rate of 0·1 per cent per year. Various side-effects have been noted but are said to be avoidable by changing the hormones. There has been much talk of an increased risk of blood clotting but this is very slight, and is no greater than the risk of thrombosis through pregnancy.

With the coming of improved and simpler methods it seems likely that contraception will spread widely and perhaps rapidly, as it has in Japan, Taiwan, and India (see Berelson and Freedman 1964). Programmes or policies for population control exist in many countries and the list grows longer every year. Of countries with populations of over 25 million only Nigeria, Brazil, and Burma have no such policies. Of course to have a population control policy does not mean the actual reduction in rate of growth of population, which has been achieved in Japan, Hong Kong, Singapore, Taiwan, and perhaps S. Korea. The great numbers of young men and women in the countries with 'young' populations will certainly produce a greatly increased population in the next few years. It is unlikely that the 'population explosion' will continue precisely along the lines shown by the curves even of the recent past. Many people already know how to limit their families and more and more will soon know. It is probable that contraception will become much more general, but no one knows just what effect this will have on population numbers.

PAST AND FUTURE GROWTH OF THE HUMAN POPULATION

1. Early population growth

THE first population that might be considered human was perhaps something like Australopithecines, living over a million years ago (Chapter 32). No one has estimated how many individuals there were, but almost certainly there were few, yet with genetical diversity greater than the biblical pair. Let us say, as a speculative guess, at least 100 000.

Our first real (though scanty) evidence about populations is from burial grounds, from which in late Palaeolithic times estimates of a population of only 10 000 are given for the whole of France and even less in Britain—perhaps only a few hundred temporary migrants in the Thames valley. There seems to have been a slow increase as populations became more settled. Maximum figures for England and Wales, and Scotland are given in Table 25.1.

TABLE 25.1

Approximate population of England, Wales, and Scotland at different times (partly after Clark 1967)

	Estimated population	Years B.P. (say A.D. 2000)	A.D.
Late Palaeolithic	2000	15 000	
Mesolithic	4000	10 000	
Neolithic	20 000	5500	
Middle Bronze Age	40 000	3500	
Iron Age	400 000	2500	
Roman Britain	1 750 000	2000	0
Norman Britain 1086	1 320 000		1000
Before Black Death	3 700 000		1300
After Black Death	2 800 000		1400
	3 250 000		1450
	5 400 000		1600
	6 000 000		1650
	6 800 000		1700
	7 300 000		1750
	10 700 000		1800
Figures obtained from population censuses	20 800 000		1850
	37 000 000		1900
	48 800 000		1950
	51 300 000		1960

A more detailed account of the changes that have occurred since 1800 in the population of England, Wales, Scotland, and Northern Ireland is given in Table 25.2.

TABLE 25.2

The populations from 1801 to 1966 of England, Wales, Scotland, and Northern Ireland. The total area of each country in acres is given. The population numbers are in thousands (from the *Registrar General's Statistical Review for 1968*)

Year	England and Wales 37 344 948 acres	Scotland 19 463 784 acres	Northern Ireland 3 495 608 acres
1801	8892·5	1608·4	..
1811	10 164·3	1805·9	..
1821	12 000·2	2091·5	1380·5
1831	13 896·8	2364·4	1574·0
1841	15 914·1	2620·2	1648·9
1851	17 927·6	2888·7	1442·5
1861	20 066·2	3062·3	1396·5
1871	22 712·3	3360·0	1359·2
1881	25 974·4	3735·6	1304·8
1891	29 002·5	4025·6	1236·1
1901	32 527·8	4472·1	1237·0
1911	36 070·5	4760·9	1250·5
1921	37 886·7	4882·5	1258·0
1931	39 952·4	4843·0	1242·6
1951	43 757·9	5096·4	1370·9
1961	46 104·5	5179·3	1425·0

The total world population before the introduction of agriculture (say 12 000 years B.P.) has been estimated at 5 to 10×10^6. By 2000 B.P. it was about 256×10^6, and the subsequent growth is shown in Fig. 25.1. The most continuous records for any one country are from China (Fig. 25.2).

Two things are clear from these figures. First, the population of any one area does not constantly increase; this is probably true for the world as a whole. Secondly, there has been an over-all increase through the millenia. For most of human history any such net increase has been at a very low rate. Even between 2000 B.P. and 350 B.P. (A.D. 1650) the population only doubled, i.e. increased at 0·04 per cent per annum. Since then there has been a very rapid increase, first in western countries, then over much of the world. The over-all rate of increase is now 2 per cent per year and in some countries is as high as 4 per cent. Moreover the increase has been fastest in the past 50 years.

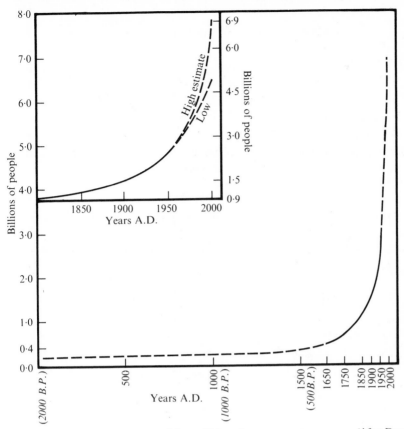

FIG. 25.1. The estimated population of the world from the year A.D. 1 to A.D. 2000. (After Dorn 1966.)

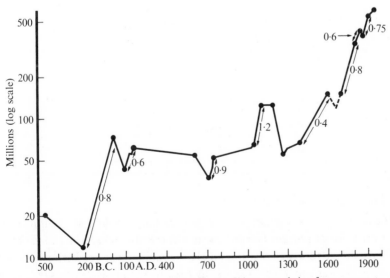

FIG. 25.2. Graph showing the best estimates for the Chinese population from 500 B.C. to A.D. 1953. Some of the slopes look steep, but the highest rate of growth was 1·2 per cent per year. The rate of growth, as a percentage per year, is indicated between the arrows on the steep slopes of the graph. (After Clark 1967.)

2. The population explosion

This explosive increase is clearly one of the most striking and important of all facts about modern man, whether viewed with extreme alarm or with complacency or even pleasure, as by some Roman Catholic, Communist, and Chinese groups. It is not easy to see the situation in perspective or to forecast its outcome. The extraordinary recency and steepness of the rise is seen in Fig. 25.1 and Tables 25.3 and 25.4.

TABLE 25.3

Summary of the population, area, and population density for the major areas of the world (from the *Demographic Yearbook* 1967)

Major areas	Population (millions)					Area km² (000's)	Population density per km²
	1930	1940	1950	1960	1967		1967
Africa	164	191	222	278	328	30 313	11
America	242	274	329	412	479	42 089	11
Asia	1120	1244	1381	1660	1907	27 530	69
Europe	355	380	392	425	452	4929	92
Oceania	10	11	13	16	18	8511	2
U.S.S.R.	179	195	180	214	236	22 402	11
World total/average	2070	2295	2517	3005	3420	135 774	25

TABLE 25.4

Number of years required to double the population of the world (after Dorn 1966)

Year (A.D.)	World population ($\times 10^6$)	Number of years to double
1	250	1650
1650	545	200
1850	1171	80
1930	1608	45
1975	?4000	?35
2010	?8000	?

3. Forecast of future population

In view of the urgency of the population problem it is unfortunate that the most important fact to bear in mind is the uncertainty of estimates. Whereas in 1930 it was possible to claim (vainly) that prediction was accurate for even as much as 50 years, in 1949 it was necessary to say '. . . it is disheartening to have to assert that the best population forecasts deserve little credence even for 5 years ahead, and none at all for 20–50 years ahead' (Davis 1949). The situation is a little better in 1970 because of the new methods of study of changes in fertility year by year such as those discussed in the previous chapter. The United Nations *Population Study No. 28* (1958) provides us with a complete set of data and forecasts, using carefully constructed models and providing low, medium, and high estimates. Even so we must be cautious and may expect that human beings may change their reproductive and health practices quite drastically over a short time. For example, the birth-rate in Japan fell by 46 per cent between 1948 and 1958, this being greater than the fall in mortality and hence leading to an actual reduction in number of births. There are, however, few signs of similar falls in other areas of high fertility. Indeed, the structure of these populations is such as to make an increase of births over the next years almost certain (Fig. 25.3). Thus in Algeria, as in many other countries of Africa, Asia, and Latin America, a very large part of the population (43 per cent) is under 15 years of age, whereas in Sweden the proportion is 24 per cent. Besides providing an immense reproductive potential such population structures have many very important economic and political implications. In the countries with an 'aged' population structure a few

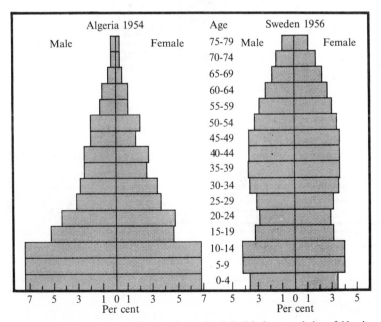

FIG. 25.3. The population of Sweden in 1956 and the Moslem population of Algeria in 1954 shown as a percentage distribution by age. (After Dorn 1966.)

young people must support many old ones. With a 'young' population it is the reverse.

The structure of populations can be illustrated by population pyramids such as Figs. 25.4 and 25.5. Thus in 1891 Great Britain showed the characteristics of a 'young' or expanding population, with the largest number of

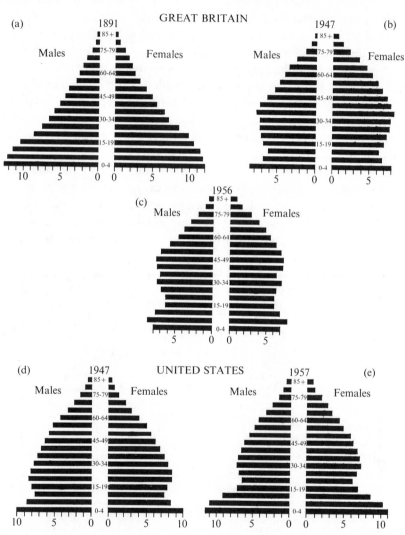

FIG. 25.4. The changing age-structure of a population is strikingly shown in these population pyramids. (a)-(c) The change in the structure of the population of Britain over a period of 65 years. The jump in birth-rate immediately after the Second World War can be seen in (b) and, in (c), this bulge was reflected in the age groups 5-9 and 10-14 years. (d) and (e) show the effect of the great depression of the 1930s in the United States, and then return to prosperity. (After Stamp 1960.)

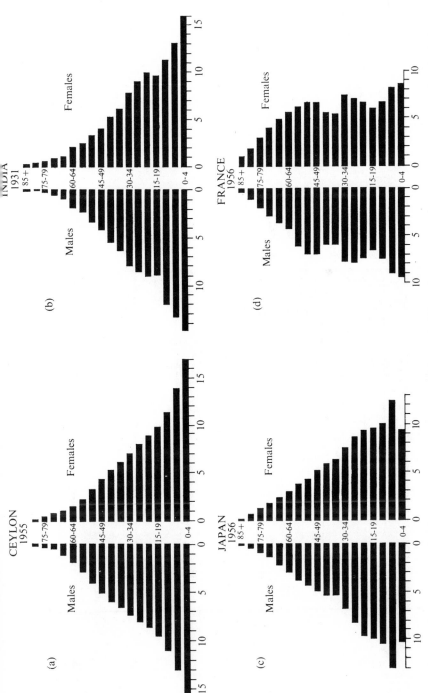

FIG. 25.5. (a) and (b) Population pyramids for Ceylon and India showing the high birth-rates. (c) The structure of the population of Japan is of interest because of recent changes in birth-rate. (d) The age-composition of the French population shows the effects of a series of changes in the birth-rate that have occurred in the first half of the twentieth century. (After Stamp 1960.)

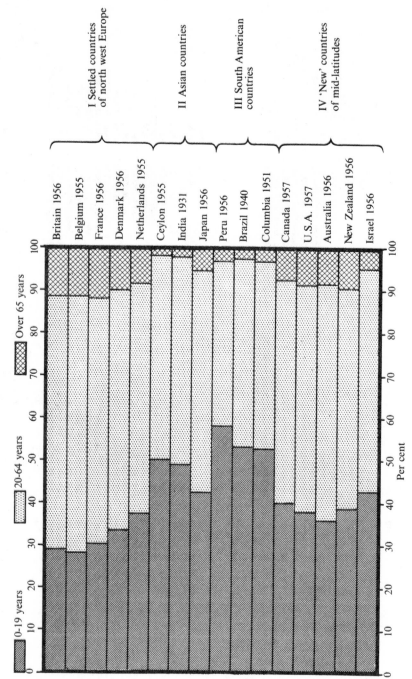

I Settled countries
of north west Europe

II Asian countries

III South American
countries

IV 'New' countries
of mid-latitudes

Britain 1956
Belgium 1955
France 1956
Denmark 1956
Netherlands 1955
Ceylon 1955
India 1931
Japan 1956
Peru 1956
Brazil 1940
Columbia 1951
Canada 1957
U.S.A. 1957
Australia 1956
New Zealand 1956
Israel 1956

Over 65 years

20-64 years

0-19 years

Per cent

FIG. 25.6. The age-composition of the population of selected countries chosen from four groups. I, old settled countries of north-western Europe;
II, countries of Asia and Africa; III, the Latin-American countries; and IV, new countries of mid-latitudes. (From data in Stamp 1960.)

people in the youngest age group. By 1947, with increased expectation of life and lower birth-rate, there was a bulge about the 35–9 age group, there was also a large post-war rise in birth-rate. By 1956 the first bulge had passed up to 45–9 and the second one to 5–10 (Fig. 25.4). The facts summarized in such figures are obviously very important for those planning for education, medical care, and many other matters, as well as for making further population forecasts.

Comparable figures for the U.S.A. show the effect of the depression of the thirties and a post-war bulge (Fig. 25.4). The population of Japan shows the striking recent contraction in birth-rate and that of France a series of oscillations suggesting several changes in national mood and hence parental aims (Fig. 25.5).

The facts about the relative age-compositions of various populations are summarized in Fig. 25.6. Another way of looking at the world situation is shown in Fig. 25.7.

Obviously there are large differences between the demographic structures

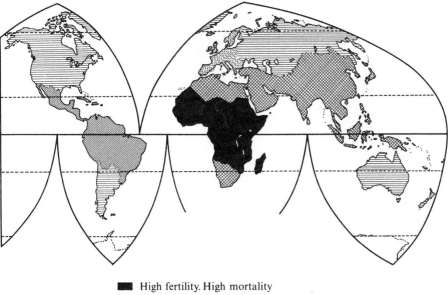

▓ High fertility. High mortality
▒ High fertility. Mortality high but declining
▨ High fertility. Moderate mortality
▥ Fairly high fertility. Moderate mortality
▤ Moderate fertility. Low mortality
▦ Low fertility. Low mortality

FIG. 25.7. The world regions classified by types of demographic situation, 1950–5.
(After Stamp 1960.)

of various parts of the world. These differences may perhaps be diminishing; in particular, there is a widespread tendency for mortality to fall. How fast this will proceed and whether there will be an accompanying fall in birth-rate is very hard to foretell.

For the present study it is useful to mention some of the major assumptions made in the forecast of the United Nations *Population Study No. 28* (1958) (see Table 25.5). They refer chiefly to the populations of relatively

TABLE 25.5

Estimates of world population on three assumptions.
All figures $\times 10^6$ (from United Nations *Population Study No. 28* (1958)

Estimates	1975	1980	1985	1990	1995	2000
High	3860	4280	4770	5360	6060	6900
Medium	3830	4220	4660	5140	5680	6280
Low	3590	3850	4110	4370	4620	4880

high fertility. The western nations of low fertility are unlikely to change either their birth- or death-rates very drastically. In the countries of high fertility this may either (*a*) remain at its high level until 2000 (producing the high population assumptions), (*b*) decline after 1975 at rates similar to those found in some less fertile areas, or (*c*) decline from 1958 onwards at those rates (low assumptions). It is assumed that mortality will continue to decline at present rates.

In order to put these figures into a wider perspective we give some populations from 1900 onwards, in numbers and by continents (Tables 25.6 and 25.6a). It is useful to supplement these figures with the percentage population increases that they represent (Table 25.7).

TABLE 25.6

Population past and future estimated, medium assumption. All figures are
$\times 10^6$ (from United Nations *Population Study No. 28* (1958)

	World	Africa	Northern America	Latin America	Asia	Europe incl. U.S.S.R.	Oceania
1900	1550	120	81	63	857	423	6
1925	1907	147	126	99	1020	505	10
1950	2497	199	168	163	1380	574	13
1975	3828	303	240	303	2210	751	21
2000	6267	517	312	592	3870	947	29

TABLE 25.6a

Estimated future population of the United Kingdom (in thou-sands). These population projections are based on estimates by the Registrars General of the total population at mid-1967. (Annual Abstract of Statistics, No. 105 (1968))

1967	1970	1980	2000
55 202	55 989	59 548	70 339

TABLE 25.7

Increases in various populations that have occurred and may occur in intervals of 25 years. The estimates of percentage increase have been made using the data in Table 25.6 (from United Nations *Population Study No. 28* (1958)

	World	Africa	Northern America	Latin America	Asia	Europe incl. U.S.S.R.	Oceania
1900–25	23	22	56	57	19	19	57
1925–50	31	35	33	65	35	14	36
1950–75	53	52	43	86	60	31	59
1975–2000	64	71	30	95	75	26	40

Finally we may examine how such changes have affected and may in future affect the proportion of people in the various parts of the world, and this is perhaps the most interesting comparison of all (Table 25.8).

TABLE 25.8

People in various continents as percentages of the world population (from United Nations *Population Study No. 28* (1958)

	Africa	Northern America	Latin America	Asia	Europe incl. U.S.S.R.	Oceania
1900	7·7	5·2	4·1	55·3	27·3	0·4
1925	7·7	6·6	5·2	53·5	26·5	0·5
1950	8·0	6·7	6·5	55·2	23·0	0·5
1975	7·9	6·3	7·9	57·7	19·6	0·5
2000	8·2	5·0	9·4	61·8	15·1	0·5

4. Patterns of population growth today

To obtain a picture of the changes that are taking place in world population we may divide the countries of the world into three types (Beaujeu-Garnier 1966).

1. *Primitive populations*

In these there are still both high birth-rates and high death-rates; say, an infant mortality of 200 per 1000 and half of the remainder of the children dying before the age of 15. These populations only just maintain themselves and are to be found today only in a few very backward areas: some in the Andean countries (part of Bolivia), and some areas in central Africa and south-east Asia. It is interesting to think that Europe was in this condition only 200 years ago. Perhaps 100 million people are still in this state, but with the spread of medical care their death-rates are rapidly falling.

2. *Young populations*

In these the birth-rate is much higher than the death rate, so that the population is increasing rapidly. A majority of the world's population is in this condition, though with considerable variations. Among the fastest-growing types the birth- and death-rates are both high, but the latter is already declining. The natural increase in this group is 20-25 per 1000. Thus in 1965 in Brazil the birth-rate was about 43 per 1000 and the death rate 20 per 1000. Countries of this type include over half the world's population, mainly in Latin America, Africa, and Asia (including China). This is where the greatest increase in population will occur in the near future.

Some countries have an even higher rate of increase because there has already been a large fall in the death-rate. Thus in Taiwan the natural increase is 34 per 1000 and the population will double in 25 years. The countries mentioned above with increases of 20-30 per 1000 will pass through this stage unless birth-rates fall markedly as they have in Japan. Another set of countries with a relatively high birth-rate (15-25 per 1000) have in addition to this relatively low death-rates. Thus in the U.S.S.R. the birth-rate is 25 per 1000 and the death-rate 7 per 1000 giving a natural growth rate of 18. All the North American countries are in this class, with the difference that they have reached it as a result of the recent rise in birth-rate after a previously lower growth rate (10 per 1000 or less). Perhaps 500 million people belong to countries in this subclass.

3. *Mature populations*

In these the birth-rate is low and the population increase slight. It must immediately be emphasized that this is not necessarily the 'terminal' or 'stable' condition of a population, since the birth-rate may rise dramatically, and so of course may the death-rate.

In most European countries the mature population condition has been reached gradually by decline in both birth- and death-rates over the last century. Thus in Sweden the growth rate is only 5 per 1000. In France between 1934 and 1938 the birth-rate was 14·5 per 1000 and the death rate 15·3 per 1000. Japan is an especially interesting member of this group, having reached a low population increase by an active policy of birth control over less than 20 years. Altogether some 400 million people belong in populations of the mature type.

5. Distribution of population

It is a truism that people are not distributed uniformly over the earth but it is difficult to realize how very great the inequalities are (Beaujeu-Garnier 1966). There are twenty-four people per square kilometre over the habitable surface of the world, but some variations by continents are:

Oceania	2,
Africa	9,
America	10,
Asia	67,
Europe (except U.S.S.R.)	89.

By countries Java is the most densely populated with 426 people/km², but Indonesia as a whole has only 66/km². In Britain the figure is 218/km², but in England and Wales alone it is 306/km². There are very large variations within countries. Thus for China as a whole there are 75/km² but in the Yang-tse Kiang valley there are 500 and in Tibet only 1·2. Differences between town and country are, of course, even greater. In Victoria Town, part of Hong Kong, there are 290 000/km².

Countries also differ quite fundamentally in the occupational and age distribution of their populations. Thus in England and Wales 5 per cent of the population is engaged in agricultural activities and 22 per cent are under the age of 15, whereas in Java the figures are 80 and 40 per cent respectively.

One could recite such differences indefinitely and they emphasize that one of man's most characteristic and curious features is this very great variety in density of population. Though a commonplace, it needs to be continually kept in mind as a major factor determining the course of affairs. Not only is there this great variety, but also a very rapid change. In many parts of the world an increasing proportion of the population lives in towns. Technical and industrial progress is very rapid in some parts of the world, but hardly occurs in others. Even with improved statistics and methods of calculation it is very difficult to make forecasts where there are so many variables.

6. Population and prosperity

The whole study tells us that there is very likely to be by the end of the century a human population twice the size of that at present. The United Nations high estimates of 1958 had already in 1968 been exceeded in some places. It is therefore probable that the world will have a human population above 7000 million in the year A.D. 2000. This is, of course, a rate of increase very much greater than has ever been known before. It will certainly put great pressures upon mankind to increase the production and distribution of wealth. But it is possible that in many ways larger populations serve actually to stimulate and assist the production of wealth, including food. This is not a popular view today but there is evidence that it has happened in the past, in spite of predictions to the contrary, such as those of Malthus. When he published his essay on *Principles of population* in 1798 the British population was about 11 millions. It would have seemed to him quite impossible that the British Isles should support five times that number, as it does only 170 years later, *and that the standard of living should have enormously increased over the same period.* We cannot look too often at this cautionary tale of Malthus. He was very careful and did indeed estimate that 'this country . . . might, in the course of some centuries, contain two or three times its present population and yet every man in the kingdom be much better fed and clothed than he is at present'. The difficulty was that in spite of his extensive researches the data were not adequate for precise forecasting. And that is still our problem to-day. This is not to say that the increase in population can go on indefinitely or that it will necessarily bring prosperity. It is to say that in this field nothing is obvious and constant thought and study are needed.

There are almost certainly some parts of the world that are under-populated today, using this word to mean that the people living in those regions would be happier if there were more of them. Of course some parts are also overpopulated by any standards. But the number that can comfortably be carried *is determined by factors that are not known or controllable at present.* This is not to say that we should not study how to control them —indeed, it is exceedingly important that we should do so. But we must not take big decisions, or rashly adopt attitudes, as a result of particular episodes of malaise. Everyone sometimes deplores the crowding and rush of modern urban life, but would they really wish to return to the widespread poverty of the mid nineteenth century, when the population was much smaller? Taking purchasing power in France as 100 in 1800 it was 108 in 1850 and 466 in 1965 (Sauvy 1969). What is needed is the application of taste and intelligence to the problem of how man can best further the interests of the living world of which he is a part.

7. Is there an optimum population?

The conception of an optimum population is itself very difficult to define (Taylor 1970). In a very thorough discussion the French demographer Sauvy lists nine different aims for society, such as maximization of individual welfare, or wealth, or employment, or national power, or culture (1969). These aims are often irreconcilable and there are no agreed means for determining population goals, or methods for achieving them. Some people therefore regard the population problem as a 'non-question' in Britain (Boreham 1970). Yet even if the setting of optima is difficult there is no doubt that policy can influence population, as has been shown recently by Japan and France—in opposite directions.

A useful definition of overpopulation in a country might be that there is too little food and too few jobs. Yet in spite of rapidly increasing populations all the major Western countries had much larger working forces and greater prosperity in 1970 than 1939. Most of them, like Britain, are actively importing labour.

8. The population problem in Britain

In this sense therefore there are no signs of overpopulation in the Western countries. It is difficult to believe that the increase at present forecast for Britain to 70 million in A.D. 2000 could not be accommodated, provided that the world trade situation is such that manufactured goods continue to be exchangeable for imports. We need to arrange all our policies to seek to ensure this continuance of trade. This is much more important than trying to grow all our own food, which we cannot easily do anyway (at least with present techniques). It would be better to concentrate on improving the country as a place to live in, while providing goods and techniques for the neighbours who supply us with food and raw materials. We have every reason to make the way we use our green and pleasant land an example for all the world. We can show how man must keep his place as part of Nature if he is not to destroy both it and himself (Fairbrother 1970). It is not possible to say definitely what number of people would ensure this in Britain. Probably the best we can do is to make arrangements to study the various pressures continuously and for the government to take powers to control their effects on the environment. There will inevitably have to be limitation of people's freedom of action if we are to avoid being swept thoughtlessly on by technological progress. If we truly want an improved environment we must be ready to think and plan and to accept controls. It is encouraging to learn that 'Government and Local Authorities can plan with some success. . . . It is likely that there will be no more than just over seven million people in the capital by the early eighties, or nearly two million less than there would have been had London retained its natural increase, and perhaps four million less had there not been policies to re-distribute industry and offices, and fairly tough administration of the Green Belt.' So policy *can* influence large numbers (Eversley 1970).

9. The pressure of the young populations

Table 25.8 shows that the changes to be expected in distribution of the population over the face of the earth are not quite so drastic as the changes in total numbers. Yet probably the political effects of the spread of com-munication will produce greater pressures than are indicated by the rela-tive numbers in the table. Accompanying the increase of population there will almost certainly be a demand for improvement in the standard of living in the poorer parts of the world. People all over the world are now made aware of the possibilities of attaining the higher standard of living of the wealthier. Many advanced societies such as the U.S.A. and Britain can only continue as they are by trade and importation of food and raw materials. Yet already they consume far more than their share of many things, including petroleum, iron, copper, tungsten, and other minerals, as well as fertilizers such as phosphates and potash. The countries at present poorer are going to demand far more of these goods. At the best this is likely to produce difficulties in the richer countries, leading to need for change in many ways, and perhaps to a poorer standard of life. At the worst the pressures may well produce conflicts and the nuclear wars that are our chief dread.

These fears are real and should not be suppressed, but kept in front of us in all policy-making. There is no reason to despair. Techniques of economic assessment and planning are improving rapidly. The difficulties of applying them are the social and political changes that are necessary. Perhaps a chief requirement is to devise new means of political communica-tion that will promote without undue conflict the social and economic changes that are in the interests of rich as well as poor. This is obviously difficult, perhaps utopian, and the situation will certainly present problems for everyone, but the effects of such pressures *need* not be unfavourable to anyone. The poorer countries require the techniques of the rich, and by giving them these techniques the rich can grow richer. Whether and how they will do so is difficult to forecast. But there is no reason to assume that it is impossible. *Perhaps one of the chief requirements is an understanding of the interdependence of men and that welfare can only be generally increased by co-operation and is reduced by greed.*

10. Some fantastic forecasts

The question of how many people can be supported without lowering the present standard of living continues to be debated and to produce casualties among forecasters. In 1945 a figure of 2800×10^6 people was thought by some to be a maximum that grain supplies could maintain, even at an Asian standard of consumption (Pearson and Harper 1945). But this number has already been exceeded and living standards in much of the world continue to improve. One estimate for the distant future is for $50\ 000 \times 10^6$ people 150 years from now, which gives us a picture of real crowding, compared to the mere 7000×10^6 expected in the year A.D. 2000! Indeed, if the population continues to double every 35 years, then before A.D. 2350 it will have reached three million millions (3×10^{12}). If men wished to build multi-storey structures all over both the sea and land far more even than this could be accommodated and a population that continued to double every 35 years might still be fed with new methods of food production. It is suggested that the final limiting factor might be the need to remove the heat that so many people would produce packed at one per square metre of floor space in buildings 2000 storeys high. It is less certain that human beings could adjust to each other as they became so closely packed, but it would be unwise to assume that they would not do so—*H. sapiens* has produced many entirely novel behaviour patterns already.

There is little sense in trying to look so far ahead. We have enough to do to solve the problems that are likely to be raised by the more immediate increases, which are almost certain to happen, barring nuclear catastrophe. The problems that are likely to be most insistent are those of competition, space, and, of course, food. All of these demand biological study, though political and economic studies outside our present range are perhaps mainly needed.

11. Control of use of resources and pollution

Of course there are serious risks in the interference that we inflict upon the earth's surface. In spite of possessing some capacity to predict the consequences of our actions, often we become aware of them too late, as in the production of erosion, deforestation, or excessive extraction of minerals. The dangers of further damage of the same sort are very clear (see Nicholson 1970). Pollution by pesticides and other chemicals has already done harm, though it is uncertain how much. Excessive growth of algae in waters, fostered by nutrients resulting from agriculture and partly treated waste is perhaps a greater danger (eutrophication). Yet there are signs that such risks are beginning to be understood and met.

Pollution by sewage and the risk of diseases such as typhoid is now controlled in many areas; air pollution has been reduced in some cities (London). There is no reason for complacency, but perhaps we are beginning to realize that plans made by single individuals or groups for their own life-times are at best inadequate and may be very dangerous. We are learning to extend the time and area of our plans, allowing them to assist much larger groups of people. Of course this involves unwelcome restrictions upon individuals in some respects, as the price for continued or increased access to resources by everyone.

12. Population and food

Estimates can be made of the areas that have been required to maintain an individual at different periods and with various methods of production. In general, the tendency ever since the Palaeolithic period has been for the amount of food needed per head to be raised on smaller and smaller areas of land. This is the result of continuous technical evolution, itself perhaps stimulated by the growth of population, creating the demand for food.

Men living only by hunting require very large areas for survival. Thus the food-gatherers of Australia required 30 km^2 person (before the whites came in 1788) in a dry climate, the same order as the population density estimated for Palaeolithic France (55 km^2/person).

The first beginnings of settlement in Mesolithic times, and of true agriculture about 9000 B.P., were perhaps induced by population pressure as the climate became warmer, together with drying up of grasslands. Even domestication of animals such as reindeer can reduce the land requirements to as little as 0·5 km^2/person (under good conditions). In forest country pigs are useful, but on the other hand some types of domesticated animals can neither be fed nor watched in this terrain and cultivation is necessary. This involves cutting the trees and stimulates both the invention of tools and perhaps also the growth of population, since the processes of clearing and cultivation by hand are laborious and children's hands to help are at a premium. If draught animals are used they must be fed for part of the year, also requiring labour.

The method of agriculture in forest areas that is still used in much of Africa is to cut the scrub and fertilize the land by burning it and then to cultivate for a few years until the fertility is exhausted. It is then left fallow for many years to regrow before cutting again. Even with this very crude agriculture the productivity per person can be increased to allow perhaps as many as 8 people/km^2 under optimal conditions. Beyond this the next resource is to abandon the cut-and-burn method for settled agriculture and cultivation every year or, for example, 1 year fallow or some other method of crop rotation. But this *requires much higher densities* of population, essentially for the reasons explained above. Because of the limitations imposed by a short rainy season in Africa and the need to curtail the growth of weeds, and other factors, each person can cultivate only a small area. It has been estimated that a minimum of 125 are needed for each square kilometre actually cultivated. This sort of situation may then have stimulated the relatively rapid growth of population following the invention of agriculture.

Subsequent technical developments in agriculture and later in industry have continually reduced the area of land needed to support one person. In fact the density of people on the land is still falling steadily and yet productivity rises. It is now so great that at its maximum, in New Zealand (1966), one man can produce enough to feed no less than thirty-seven families at the highest American standard, and the productivity is still increasing at 4 per cent per annum. Of course, these extremely high figures are achieved under favourable conditions, but the tendency to increased productivity is proceeding in many parts of the world, for example in parts of India. Very great improvements in yield have already been made quite rapidly there by use of fertilizers and insecticides, and especially by improved varieties of crops produced by geneticists. A scheme for this has been operated by the Rockefeller Foundation (1967).

Different parts of the world's surface provide unequally favourable conditions for growing food, but geographers have means of estimating these in terms of 'standard land'. In calculating this they take into account the fact that in some climates two, or even more, crops can be raised each year. There are at present 1.43×10^7 km² of arable and 2.58×10^7 km² of grazing land in the world. Clark (1967) estimates that using methods essentially already possible standard land of 10.8×10^7 km² could be obtained as shown in Table 25.9.

It will be seen that much of the possible increase is in South America, Africa, and Asia, and would thus depend upon very large political and economic adjustments.

The area of standard land required to produce the components of a full American-type diet (including cereals, meat, milk, etc.) can be calculated at 2000 m²/person (half an acre). Therefore a population of no less than 47 thousand million people could be supported even at this standard. This includes allowance for forest land for wood pulp. The American diet is many times above the subsistence level, but if we assume a standard only one-third lower, at a conservative estimate (with use mainly of cereals, etc.) this land could support 157×10^9 people!

These estimates assume only standard or possible modern agricultural practices and no really revolutionary techniques such as watering deserts by use, for example, of nuclear power. The Russian Malin, making some

TABLE 25.9

*Potential agricultural area of the world expressed in terms of
equivalents of standard farm land, million hectares* (Clark 1967)

	By current standards (including two crops in tropical areas)	If more than two crops in tropical areas, add—	If cold climate areas are used, add—
U.S.A. and Canada	1006	4	367
Central and South America	1835	736	29
Europe (excluding U.S.S.R.)	403	..	47
U.S.S.R.	1109	..	539
Africa	1555	732	..
China	409	..	88
India and Pakistan	305	43	13
Rest of Asia	791	464	7
Oceania	268	60	..
World	7681	2039	1090

such radical assumptions, reached a figure of $9 \cdot 33 \times 10^7$ km^2 of cultivable land, much of it able to carry two or more crops as above. This estimate is therefore of the same order of magnitude as that of Clark (1967). Clark includes, however, $3 \cdot 84 \times 10^9$ usable only as a result of 'large additional capital expenditure and new methods'.

Such optimistic predictions are greatly deplored by many practical men, who see clearly the difficulties that are likely to be raised by population increase. It may be true that suitably 'efficient' agricultural methods are available to sustain foreseeable populations. But they depend upon expensive items such as fertilizers, irrigation, and transport, as well as suitable price incentives (Hutchinson 1969). Social factors such as high rents and large discrepancies between rich and poor often stand in the way of development. These are the factors that are likely to limit the application of the techniques that science allows. They can be removed only by political action, often implying serious upheaval.

An objective assessment of the situation is possible by study of the FAO's reports on the *State of Food and Agriculture*. In the report for 1969 the Director-General states: 'In over-all terms 1968 was about an average year, with food production keeping slightly ahead of population growth. Several elements in the current situation, however, continue to justify the hope that a growing number of developing countries can now increase their production a good deal faster than in the past, provided—and this is crucial—that appropriate policies are pursued.'

On the other hand for the medium-term view he shows that more is required. 'Our first estimate of the growth of demand for food in developing countries up to 1985 is 3·9 per cent a year. A really major acceleration in food production beyond the current rate of 2·7 per cent a year will be needed to obtain this target. A long, arduous and expensive struggle will be required if success is to be achieved.' It is greatly in the interests of the richer countries to find ways of assisting in this struggle by 'more vigorous national and international action to step up the flow of external resources to the poor countries'. Those who are seriously worried about the population problem can best contribute to a solution by working hard in support of all sensible means to accelerate this flow.

The poorer countries have perhaps an even greater need for skilled men than for physical resources. It is the men that matter, and yet they do not appear in national balance sheets (Sauvy 1969). The national incomes of the future will depend on the quality of the active populations and especially on their education. The key to development is training, and perhaps the richer countries can help the poorer more in this way than any other.

13. Man and nature

The problems of population growth are really more of politics and space than of food production. To discuss this would lead us into fields beyond the scope of this book, though they are very important. The fact of crowding itself has very large effects on man, as it has on other animals. It is not clear whether human behaviour would be at all the same as at present if each human being was constrained to live only in some small area, confined among his fellows (Chapter 43). Where this condition is approached there are signs that capacity for altruistic behaviour is reduced. Yet apparently life in Hong Kong is not found intolerable. It is impossible to foresee whether population will increase to a point where human relations are grossly altered. Equally it is impossible to tell whether selection would then produce quite a different type of person.

Men have changed their way of life so fast in recent centuries that it is difficult to say what is the 'best' or 'proper' human environment. People are very adaptable and will and do live under extremely unfavourable conditions. It is characteristic of *Homo sapiens* that he makes his own micro-climate and to some extent controls his immediate environment. Indeed he is having a far greater effect than any other species on the whole surface of the earth. Yet individually and collectively we remain tied to nature, as we become all too well aware whenever we are deprived of food, comfort, or health. The conclusions of modern biology all reinforce the lesson that we cannot separate ourselves from nature. Molecular biology has shown that all life is of one construction and kin. Only because of this can we live upon animal and plant food. At the other end of biological studies ecology shows how every organism depends upon a whole chain of others—and this applies to us as much as to all the rest (Fraser Darling 1970).

14. The need for beauty

But man's special feature is the power to make plans that will alter his surroundings. He often does this in ways that allow only the barest survival, in the crudest shacks or the harshest concrete blocks of apartments. Yet since Palaeolithic times he has decorated his homes and meeting-places, and loves to do so still. There is some connection that we do not understand between our power to think symbolically and the urge to have symbolic structures around us. From very early history there are signs that men decorated the artefacts that they made (Chapter 37). Sometimes the symbolism is obviously sexual, but often there is a strong element of creative art, in design, rhythm, lines, or colours. Symbolism of the person and of super-persons, leaders, or gods has been a feature of decoration from the beginning and so it is still today. It is clear that the creation of beautiful and symbolic objects is a characteristic feature of the human way of life. They are as necessary to us as food or sex. Of course individuals *can* and do live without them for a while. But some forms of symbolism and decoration are features of all societies. Not only do we individually need and want the arts, but as a group we neglect them at our peril. It is not too much to say that the search for beauty lies near the source of the highest cerebral capacities.

If we are to ensure a satisfactory survival we need to pay deep attention to the provision of an environment that is adequate both in its architectural design and symbolism and in relation to nature. There is a danger in a self-propagating technology that takes over the whole earth without considering either the men or the other creatures on it. The arts can provide our defence against this if we will allow them to do so. They have the most central of all biological functions—of insisting that life be worth while, which, after all, is the final guarantee of its continuance.

15. Man's future

With all our talk about predicting we really cannot see the future clearly. The only forecast one can make is that there are certainly surprises in store. No rule ensures that our own or any other particular form of life shall continue. Homeostasis will require the making of appropriate new adjustments in the future, as it has in the past. One way of putting it is that man can, if he wishes, populate the earth even more fully. To do so he would certainly have to destroy many other types of organism, perhaps increasing the risk that life would become extinct altogether.

But the important point to remember is that 'man' is an unreal abstraction. No such entity exists. Instead we have millions of individuals, grouped into more or less compact societies, whose interests are often opposed, at least in the short term. These groups and their members are the entities whose behaviour will determine the future. We shall be wise to study them well.

Perhaps the most objective and useful way to look at the population problem is that men are increasing in number very rapidly at present and will probably continue to do so in the near future. This will produce great problems, but is unlikely to prove disastrous. It may well be that the pressure of increasing populations will liberate further creativity in arts, sciences, and technology as it has done during periods of population growth in the past. There is certainly little evidence that a search only for limitation in population is likely to release the best in men. Society needs adjustments and these will be made only if there are pressures. 'Expansion is the only way to adjust proportions. A body can only improve through growth' (Sauvy 1969). It is reasonable to fear *excessive* expansion, but important also to remember the advantages of growth. As Sauvy, again, points out, 'A population without children does not believe in the future and can hardly be expected to have the pioneering spirit.' But if there are too many they will starve.

If there is to be increase we certainly need to know by how much and when and where. Difficulties of adjustment will be maximized by ignorance and uncertainty. We need to improve both the collection of vital statistics and methods of forecasting. This is not to say that such knowledge will easily protect us against every possibility. But all homeostasis depends on predicting which actions are likely to be effective in the future. Mankind has a very rapid and efficient predicting system and should be able to discover ways to forecast how many humans there are likely to be, perhaps even to regulate that number somewhat more rationally than in the past.

26

THE ORIGIN OF LIFE

1. The study of origins

PROBLEMS of origin carry a peculiar intellectual status. They are of quite outstanding interest and yet in a sense they are insoluble. It can be argued that as the past will never be repeated it will never be known what it contained. Yet this is one of those anthropocentric attitudes that seem self-evident but may be only a manifestation of our limited view of nature. We insist on our uniqueness, but if nature is full of recurrences then in time it will repeat us.

Interest in origins has increased in recent decades among a wide range of scientists, from astronomers to biochemists. We can here deal only in a very general way with the origin of galaxies and solar systems, though a view about these can hardly be avoided by anyone who attempts to understand man. The subject has expanded vastly, for, among other reasons, widely increased astronomical data and the knowledge of the nature of matter that has come from recent advances in physics. The origin of life has been increasingly closely examined since it was first discussed in its modern form by the biochemists Oparin in 1924 and Haldane in 1929. Understanding of the nature of living processes has made study of their possible origins conceptually more precise, though not necessarily more easy. Knowledge of the possible sequence of events in the early history of the earth, while still very inadequate, gives us new ideas about the conditions in which life may have arisen. At the same time a new range of experiments by chemists has explored the conditions under which organic molecules can be formed.

These studies give us no certain answer as to how life arose, but they make a serious scientific discipline of the subject. As to their practical importance we only have to think of their relevance to the question of the artificial production of life on the one hand and of the possible discovery of life in other worlds on the other. These may perhaps rank as the greatest of all scientific problems. Moreover our knowledge about origins determines our modes of thought and reasoning, and hence all other inquiries. Clearly we cannot fully explore these great matters here but can only try to give an indication of some of the ways in which they are being considered.

2. The origin of the galaxy

If we were to pursue the programme of search for understanding to its limit we should be compelled to consider the origin of the universe. This majestic subject is indeed the concern not only of astronomers but of all of us, and widely differing views are held about it. Astronomers are making important new discoveries every year. Previously unsuspected types of celestial body are being found, for example the quasars and pulsars. Views about the universe are therefore likely to change very much in the future. It may well be that signs of order that we cannot yet discern will revolutionize all knowledge, so that to our descendants it may seem that our thoughts must have been extremely primitive since they lacked appreciation of the fundamental principles of the cosmos. 'The universe is enormous, strange and untouchable; man's technical means and intellect are small and short-lived. Discussing stellar or galactic evolution is a large task made no easier by the lack of astronomical meaning in such commonly used words as history, evolution, birth, life and death of atoms and stars' (Greenstein 1964).

Modern cosmologies assume that the distribution of matter in the universe is statistically homogeneous for a 'sufficiently large sample', but the galaxies form local clusters. The universe has no centre and no axis. The spectral lines of distant galaxies show a red shift, which is supposed to be a Doppler effect due to the fact that they are all receding from each other. From such facts Einstein and de Sitter developed a model of the universe as expanding from an infinitely condensed state. In the version of Friedmann the expansion reaches a state of maximum distension and minimum density, and then contracts back to the original state, and so the cycle repeats. The apparent 'age of the universe' would then be the time since the last expansion began. It is interesting that the data suggest an approximately similar age for the earth, for meteorites, and for star-clusters— namely $\sim 10^{10}$ years. It may be that this is the age of the current expansive phase of this stupendous cycle. But these are, of course, very complicated matters and there are other versions of steady-state cosmologies according to which new galaxies are continuously being formed by newly created matter.

Recent measurements of the intense cosmic black-body radiation discovered in 1965 provide further evidence that the universe is evolving, rather than steady. The expansion is the same in all directions, confirming that the universe is homogeneous (isotropic) and that there was a singularity at its space–time origin. In other words it began with one big bang (Gamow). Physics has no 'explanation' for such a singular event. It is suggested that during the initial 100 seconds there was an extremely high temperature ($\sim 10^9$ K) in which the primordial nucleons were 'produced' and there was thermonuclear fusion to give helium.

Something can be said from modern physics and astronomy about the later processes of evolution of the heavier elements. Stars on the 'main sequence' are born, pass through a series of stages, and die. They are probably first differentiated from clouds of hydrogen in which some non-uniformity develops, producing gravitational forces leading to contraction. The consequent angular momentum and magnetic field stresses produce intense heating until nuclear reactions begin and the hydrogen fuses to form more helium (^{4}He), carbon (^{12}C), oxygen (^{16}O), and neon (^{20}Ne), and then still heavier elements at higher temperatures. At about 5×10^8 K there is a catastrophic gravitational collapse and the star first implodes and then explodes as a brilliant supernova. Alternatively if there is no explosion the star burns off, becoming a red giant, which grows gradually fainter. The ultimate fate of these is not known but probably they collapse to form the white dwarf stars, which continue to cool for a very long time. In the recently discovered pulsars, emitting pulses of radiation with periods of a fraction of a second, the gravitational collapse is believed to proceed so far that the electrons have sufficient energy for the inverse beta reaction, electron+proton $\rightarrow$ neutron+neutrino, to be important. The electrons disappear and the protons are converted to neutrons. With the disappearance of the kinetic pressure of the electrons there is no force to restrain further gravitational collapse. The pulsars are believed to be neutron stars with the incredible density of 10^{14} g/cm^3.

There is also some evidence about the evolution of galaxies. They have various different forms, which can be classified in a way consistent with the hypothesis of an 'evolution from nearly amorphous irregular galaxies to the very open spirals, through progressive stages where the arms become thinner, more nearly circular and tightly wound' (Greenstein 1964). However it is not clear how these changes begin or end, nor what they signify.

Besides stars and galaxies there are objects in the universe that are even less understood. Radio telescopes have identified enormously strong centres emitting 10^{44}–10^{45} erg/s in radio wavelengths alone. Photographs show that associated with some of these there are quasi-stellar images (quasars) with very peculiar spectra including much ultra-violet and emitting 100 times more light than any galaxy. They have large red-shifts and must be very distant, as much as 2×10^9 light years away, that is approaching the limits of observability. Some of them change their light over a period of a few years or less and these must be very small objects. There is no explanation of what they are or how their enormous energies are generated.

Truly we are ignorant of the pattern of the universe. Yet we learn more every year. At least we now know that some of its parts are undergoing continual change, possibly with cycles of evolution. But we have no unified view of the ordering of events in the universe as a whole (if indeed these concepts have any meaning). We do not know whether they all tend towards increased randomness and disorder or whether in any sense it could be said there is a hierarchy of open systems in a steady state.

Our desire for uniformity compels us to ask whether there is any connection between the rules governing universal events and those on earth, including our own origins. As we shall see, the chief problem of the origin of life is to find the source of the order that allows the continued maintenance of steady states. It is reasonable therefore to ask whether any such order can be discerned in the universe. Up to the present time human inquiry has not proceeded sufficiently to allow physics to provide any clear answer.

3. The origin of the earth

Currently the most acceptable theory for the origin of planets seems to be that as the sun condensed from a nebular cloud it rotated with increasing speed. This would produce magnetic fields in the ionized gas, canalized along spiral lines as the plasma 'particles' moved outwards. This would produce small solid bodies, planetesimals, later aggregated into planets.

The age of the earth can be estimated fairly precisely from the rate of decay of thorium and uranium to lead to be about $4 \cdot 5 \times 10^9$ years. This radioactive decay is the end phase of the process of breakdown of the heaviest elements that were formed during the sun's explosion. In this sense the earth, like the sun, is active and gives out heat, but at a rate 100 million times less than that of the sun. Moreover the earth is becoming less active; that is, it gives out only perhaps one-tenth as much heat as when it was formed.

4. Composition of the earth

Curiously enough there seems to be less agreement about how the earth reached its present distribution of materials than as to how they were first formed. Indeed, there is considerable uncertainty about the distribution itself at the present day. The earth has a metallic *core* of iron and nickel, mostly molten, but solid at the centre. The diameter of the core is about 6000 km and around it is a shell, the *mantle*, 3000 km thick. This is composed mainly of silicates of iron and magnesium and is 'solid' enough to transmit transverse waves, but plastic enough to permit slow deformation.

The only part of the earth with which we are directly in contact is a thin *crust*. This consists of lighter silicates and many other elements. It is not a uniform shell, but is much thicker under the continents (20–50 km) than the oceans (7 km).

The uneven distribution of land and ocean is one of the most conspicuous features that have dominated the history of life. There are various theories as to the origin and evolution of the continents, and knowledge of the subject is developing rapidly. It has been hard to acquire information even about the modern conditions inside our planet, let alone their history. It is also hard for the imagination to grasp the implications of geophysical changes, certainly for the layman. We have to school ourselves to think of such processes as the raising of mountains in the same way as we think of the wrinkling of the peel of a dried orange. Perhaps still harder, we must believe that the continents float and drift in the mantle below the crust, breaking up like icefloes into smaller pieces (see McKenzie 1970).

Leaving aside questions of the origin of the crust, its uneven distribution must presumably be a result of the strains produced by movements within. The continents are formed of lighter matter, floating in the denser mantle. It is likely that there was originally only one land mass, which then split into fragments, the continents, which have since drifted apart. Geophysicists and geologists now mostly agree that some such process of continental drift is at work. One question is the energy source for such vast movements. Presumably the heat production from decay of the radioactive elements in the mantle provides the motor. This is supported by the fact that heat transfer is uneven at different parts of the surface of the earth, being greatest along the central parts of the mid-ocean ridges. This suggests that the rocks are turning over, rising at the ridges in the ocean floors, and carried by convection currents in the mantle, passing along the ocean floors to be pressed into trenches at the edges of the continents (Fisher and Hess 1963). Magnetic anomalies and the pattern of earthquakes suggest that material spreading eastwards from the East Pacific Rise has produced oceanic crust material that is now close to the coast of Chile. This would have been generated 60×10^6 years ago and have moved at 4·6 cm/year. Spreading rates from 1·5 to 6·5 cm/year have been computed. Mountain ranges are formed where the ocean floor is being forced under continents, as around the Pacific, or where continental masses are being driven against one another (Alps, Himalayas).

The important point for the present discussion is the concept of change in the earth's surface. Geologists have long been aware that there have been periodic movements upwards and downwards of the continents (isostasy), and that these have been of first importance in their influence on the history of life (*The life of vertebrates*, p. 12).

5. The age of the earth

If life originated upon the earth it must have been within 4.5×10^9 years ago, which is not very long by astronomical standards. The light now reaching us from some of the more distant objects known left them at about the time the earth was formed. It is estimated that at that time they must have been a million million times brighter than our sun. Perhaps they still are; or possibly they ceased to exist long before we see them. In all these questions of origin, however, it is well to remember how recently our knowledge has increased. Estimates of the age of the earth have grown continually since Archbishop Usher's 4004 B.C. in the seventeenth century. However, 4500 million years is not likely to be far wrong as an estimate of the age of the earth; this figure is based on radioactive decay of thorium and uranium. But of course we may possibly be deceived about this process, just as Kelvin was when he said the earth could not be more than a million years old, an estimate based on what seemed then to be completely sound physical principles of cooling. And that was only in 1890. Kelvin could not anticipate the discovery of radioactive sources of heat within the earth. Incidentally, current estimates of the age of the sun are about 5×10^9 years and of the galaxy, as we have said, $\sim 1.5 \times 10^{10}$ years.

The age determined from the rates of decay of radioactive elements is of course that at which the earth was formed as a spheroidal mass, including the heaviest elements. This must have been the result of some process of condensation such as that already discussed. None of the actual rocks found are as old as this. The oldest are some 3×10^9 years and they are at the centres of the continents. The edges are much younger, some indeed only a few years old, and still growing. In the ocean basins the oldest rocks found are all quite young ($< 10^8$ years) because all the present-day ocean floor has been formed in geologically recent time, by spreading from the mid-ocean ridges.

6. The origin of life

The first question on this subject should perhaps be 'Did life originate at all or has it in some sense always existed?' This unfortunately is one of those great questions, like the origin of the universe, that we cannot handle yet. Looking at the problem from the point of view of terrestial life we may ask four questions.

1. Did life arrive on the planet by migration from some other body?
2. Was life produced on earth by some 'life force' operating outside the laws controlling matter as defined by physics?
3. Do the laws that control the matter of the universe contain factors,

besides the known laws of physics, which dictated the necessity for life to begin (and presumably also to evolve)?

4. Can we show that life may have arisen by the operation of forces known to operate in the terrestrial physical world?

Over all of these there also of course lies the question whether life originated once only and on the earth, or once, or more often, elsewhere.

In the present state of knowledge none of these possibilities can be excluded (see Calvin 1969). It has been alleged that micro-organisms are found in meteorites arriving from space. The possibility that these are in fact the result of terrestrial contamination has not been excluded and some hold it impossible that organisms could survive within a meteorite. This question remains to be resolved. The answer to the problem of the origin of life on earth may still be that it came from outer space, but probably most scientists regard this as unlikely.

Similarly it is not excluded that God or some vital force so manipulated the materials of the early earth that they acquired the property we have called information storage and that controlled systems thus began. Once they had begun, it is easier to see how they proceeded to evolve and there is nowadays little doubt that the processes of homeostasis have continued since then without further intervention. The laws of the physical world will adequately account for the behaviour of organisms, provided that their conduct is controlled by the pre-existing order in an information store. It is the origin of the latter that is in question, and it cannot at present be excluded that it was the result of the operation of an outside agency. The uniformitarian assumptions of science would of course be opposed to such an explanation, but this is not enough to disprove it. The fact that the operation of the agency would seem to be limited in time somehow suggests that some other solution is correct. It certainly alters the emotional appeal of a deity to consider him as intervening only to make the first DNA. Indeed, such an interventionist view may well be thought blasphemous by those who would wish to understand more of the Deity than is possible by thinking only of a being who was simply an initiator.

This brings us to the third possibility, perhaps the most elusive. Since physics has been revolutionized several times in the last few centuries it can hardly be held that we yet 'know its laws'. But we do know something about the operation of some of them, at least within certain limits. The qualification is important because we are not yet able to apply even the laws that we do know to complex systems such as organisms. The question whether other laws that are yet beyond our ken are in operation has not therefore much meaning.

The view that it is possible to understand the origin and subsequent course of life by the operation of what may be called well-tried physical laws is therefore the only one that can be fully submitted to rational examination. As we shall see, this does not by any means imply that we have sufficient knowledge to compel its complete acceptance. In these matters it is important that we should both humbly acknowledge our ignorance *and* firmly assert our knowledge. The latter is much greater today than even 10 years ago and this provides a further warning that any conclusions reached are provisional and are likely to be changed before long.

7. The origin of organic molecules

It is very widely supposed that life originated in the sea, whose composition in early stages of the earth's history is therefore of prime importance. Some, however, have argued that life may have originated on the land surface which 'provides innumerable environmental niches, such as crevices in dust particles and rocks' which 'may have provided ideal conditions for the abiogenic synthesis of organic compounds. Drying in such niches would permit high concentrations of chemicals to occur, and would thus favour chemical reactions when they were wet' (Hinton 1968). The fact that life can be reduced to a purely morphological state by drying (p. 287) certainly removes some difficulties to this view. But it seems more likely that only a fluid medium could provide the continuity necessary to reach the present level of metabolic sophistication in a reasonable time. 'Equally only large moving bodies of water could meet the spatial requirement that materials of all kinds should be continuously available and brought together for interaction' (Needham in Hinton 1968). In any case biogenesis must have taken place in water and made use of materials dissolved in it from the atmosphere. Probably some concentrating mechanism for bringing the substances together must be assumed (p. 371).

The question of the origin of life is clearly closely related to that of the origin of organic materials. Until relatively recently it was generally held that all the more complex organic molecules were products of life itself. Deposits of hydrocarbons such as oil and coal, for example, which are known to be formed from plant decay, are still often held to be wholly so formed. There is, however, some evidence that such substances are quite widespread in the universe and are of abiogenic origin. The evidence is of two sorts. First, the analysis of meteorites shows that some may contain much more organic matter than can be explained by contamination. Secondly, numerous studies have now shown that a whole range of organic molecules can be produced from quite simple carbon- and nitrogen-containing compounds, given a suitable supply of energy, say, by electrical sparking or ultraviolet radiation.

The question of the probable composition of the earth's early atmosphere is therefore crucial. Fortunately there is in the main agreement that there was no oxygen and that reducing conditions prevailed. This is fundamental, because in the presence of oxygen electrical discharges, for example, will produce combustion, whereas reducing conditions allow synthesis. In the early atmosphere there was probably methane, ammonia, water, carbon monoxide, and carbon dioxide. The first three, incidentally, make up the atmosphere of Jupiter.

Oxygen probably appeared only as a result of the action of organisms. The earliest photosynthesis may have served simply as an excretory process. Further developments then made it into the prime synthetic process that it is today. But in the meantime the oxygen produced revolutionized life. Some of it, converted to ozone, shielded the earth from ultraviolet radiation. This radiation may previously have been essential as a source of energy and then of mutation, but complex systems could develop only when their instructional systems were not disturbed by ultraviolet radiation. It is not clear whether it is anything but chance that the nucleotide molecules absorb very strongly in this region of the spectrum.

The other equally important influence of oxygen was of course to allow organisms to obtain large concentrations of energy by respiration. It is calculated that warm-blooded animals produce 10 000 times more energy per gramme than the sun (Revelle 1964). If this figure is correct it does indeed suggest one of the main features that allow organisms to maintain such fantastically complex steady states. But we must remember that these are only the late products of evolution. The earlier syntheses must have obtained their energy directly from outside sources or by some anaerobic process.

We have thus some reason to believe that the early atmosphere of reducing gases later became changed, as a result of the influence of life itself. The time-scale of these events is, however, very speculative. Oparin suggests that the ocean and primitive (presumably reducing) atmosphere were formed 3×10^9 years ago and that oxygen began to accumulate at about $2-1 \cdot 8 \times 10^9$ years, giving the present atmosphere only at 1×10^9 years ago. These figures will doubtless eventually be made more precise. We still have almost no data from records in the rocks of the earliest stages of the origin of life. The earliest known organisms lived about 3×10^9 years ago (p. 406). But we can say much more about it than was possible even 20 years ago, because laboratory experiments have shown that quite complex organic molecules can be produced from the simple gases that are likely to have been present in the early atmosphere.

Miller has shown that mixtures of methane, ammonia, hydrogen, and water vapour subjected to silent electric discharge produce a wide variety of amino-acids (Bernal 1967). Pavlovskaya and Pasynskiĭ (1959) produced these from water, formaldehyde, and ammonium chloride under the influence of ultraviolet light. Other compounds that have been made by Oró and Kimball (1961 and 1962) include phosphocreatine, porphyrins, and purines and pyrimidines, bases that are similar to those found in nucleic acids. Oró has also synthesized the pentoses (ribose and desoxyribose). By electron bombardment a wide variety is obtained, including adenine and hydrogen cyanide, which is a possible agent for polymerization (Calvin 1969). Schramm (1965) has obtained high-molecular-weight peptides and polynucleotides. It is therefore probable that protein-like and nucleic acid-like polymers were formed under the conditions of the early earth. But as Schramm himself points out, they would have had a random arrangement of monomers in their chains. The problem is to discover how the *specific* sequences, with their adaptive properties, arose.

Another interesting feature of these artificial products is that they include both the right- and left-handed optically rotating isomers. It has long been recognized that one of the striking features of living chemistry has been the preponderance of one or other forms, never of both. Thus amino-acids are all of the *l*-rotatory form, as are the amino-acids in the earliest bacterial remains of 3000 million years ago. But sugars are all of the *d*-form. It is clear that this uniformity is an important, perhaps essential, feature, if large molecules are to be built, for example spirals such as DNA. Moreover, the various parts of the biosphere all 'feed' upon each other, in a manner that would be impossible if different species had different symmetry.

This perhaps provides evidence that life on this planet began only once —or at least that the descendants of all lines but one have failed to survive. But this still does not tell us how this particular selection of isomers, one of the most fundamental of all the selections, was accomplished. One suggestion is that these early molecules were formed not in a random environment but in one already occupied by asymmetric quartz and other crystals. Bernal suggested many years ago that some form of absorption on to clays or other minerals would provide for the concentration of the early organic products, preventing reverse reactions.

In any case there is little doubt that given the composition of the early atmosphere and the availability of energy from ultraviolet sources, radioactivity, or electrical sparking, many of the simpler molecules necessary for life would have been produced. We have some direct evidence from finding such molecules in extraterrestrial bodies that this did actually occur. Thus Calvin and Vaughn (1960) found a substance like cytosine in a meteorite.

This raises the further controversial question of the possible presence of bacteria and other forms of life on meteorites. The compounds found in carbonaceous meteorites are similar to those formed by synthetic processes from ammonia and other gases as described above. This suggests that such early stages of biopoiesis were not confined to the earth. Indeed, there is reason on statistical grounds to think that the conditions necessary for life must occur not infrequently in planetary systems throughout the universe. There appears, however, to be no other suitable planet in our own solar system. The difficulty of establishing 'communication' with inhabitants of other solar systems is obviously enormous because of the times involved for signalling, but attempts are being made.

8. The origin of a self-maintaining system

The presence on the early earth of types of molecules essential for life, in some form of fundamental broth, is thus not difficult to accept. A much greater problem is to understand how, even given these substances, the *specific* giant molecules such as information-carrying nucleotides and enzymatic proteins were formed. It is still more difficult to imagine how their actions became so adjusted as to produce self-maintaining and self-replicating systems.

Haldane (1965) focused the problem by considering what might have been the probability of formation of the simplest self-replicating system. He considered four stages.

1. A probiotic soup of amino-acids, ribose, four purine and pyrimidine bases, and a source of high-energy phosphate.
2. Formation of nucleotides, probably at first RNA.
3. Combination of amino-acids with ATP.
4. Coupling of these to make a peptide.

Haldane therefore suggested that the first organism included only one enzyme, a non-specific phosphokinase, able to organize the various energy transfers needed for such a sequence of changes to the materials of the probiotic soup. This one protein would be specified by one 'gene' of RNA. Haldane noted that ribonuclease is the smallest known enzyme, containing 124 amino-acid residues (Chapter 2). This would require 540 bits of information to be specified (assuming equal base-frequencies) and it could certainly not appear spontaneously like the compounds already considered in the experiments of Miller and others. Haldane therefore considered a simpler protoenzyme requiring, say, 100 bits of information. But this is still one of $1 \cdot 3 \times 10^{30}$ chances. That is to say, if one 'trial' were made each minute for 10^8 years there would have to be 10^{17} simultaneous trials. The earth simply is not big enough to house them! By reducing the number to 60 bits and using only 15 amino-acids the probability becomes perhaps just conceivable, but even so, would such a molecule be 'adequate'? We have not really faced the question of how it would control itself.

In his last discussion of the subject, shortly before his death, Haldane seemed not to be able to see a solution to this problem. It is indeed most formidable and must be attacked if we are not to be simply lulled by the evidence of the synthesis of molecules of moderate complexity.

Dixon and Webb (1958), in a similar discussion, calculate that even if the earth had been wholly made of amino-acids and these rearranged themselves at random ten times a second there would have been little chance of forming one molecule of the simple protein insulin.

It may be, however, that we take rather too rigorous a view of the problem by considering enzymes as we know them today. The properties of an enzyme seem to depend largely on features of a small part of it, the active site (Chapter 3). Much of the rest of the protein may be irrelevant for the performance of crude syntheses. There is some evidence that early enzymes were simpler because they did not need to be very effective to 'compete' with what was there before (Bernal 1960).

One kind of solution to this problem is that already mentioned by Bernal, namely in effect that the probabilities of certain configurations were increased by the crystal lattices in clays with which they were associated. This is an appealing argument, but it requires more particular suggestions so that the probabilities can be calculated.

An extension of this view suggests that the clay particles were not simply sites where organic molecules could interact but were actually the first organisms. Crystals can be said to contain information in their defects, specifically in silicates by the substitution of silicon atoms by others, such as aluminium. Such crystals are very stable and might have an information content, by weight, half that of DNA. Moreover, in growth they replicate their defects. Conditions can be imagined in which certain patterns would be selected. In particular, any configuration that tended to keep the clay particle in a clay-synthesizing environment would survive. This suggests how the first 'inorganic' organisms may have provided the templates for carbon-containing organisms, as it were a second origin of life. Organic materials may have made mixed two-dimensional crystals with the clays, by which the probability of growth of the latter was increased. The information in the silicate layers could be imposed upon the organic layers and so simple polymers, proteins, and nucleotides be produced. Such mixed organisms can be imagined to have evolved gradually into the carbon-containing ones that we know. This hypothesis cannot perhaps be taken very literally, but it shows how calculations that claim to demonstrate the improbability of the spontaneous origin of life omit known natural processes that may have been decisive.

Another useful line of reasoning on this problem stems from the possibility that after a long period of non-biological syntheses a very abundant supply of organic materials was available. Simple instruction-controlled systems could therefore readily be built up but would then proceed to deplete the raw materials. As these disappeared those systems with instructional molecules adequate to replace them by synthesis would continue (Horowicz in Bryson and Vogel 1965). The genome would thus gradually have grown in complexity. This would explain the present situation in which many genes must work together to produce an enzyme. It is difficult to see how each separate mutation could have come to have value unless the final product was available throughout.

This 'Garden of Eden' hypothesis has considerable attraction, but it still leaves vague the question of the origin of the first instructional molecules, unless the non-biological syntheses had in effect already produced them, which begs the question. The problem of the possible nature of the first genetic codes has been dealt with in Chapter 3.

9. The origin of individuals

One of the characteristic features of living matter is that it occurs in distinct individuals, each maintaining a steady state of interchange with the environment. Recent work on the origin of life, especially in Russia, has drawn attention to possible ways in which discrete individuals may have been formed from the primeval nutrient broth. In a mixed solution of high polymers molecules of different sorts are liable to join together and separate as droplets. This process, known as *coacervation*, has been especially studied by Bungenberg de Jong (Fig. 26.1). It leads to much greater concentrations of the polymers in the drops than in the outside liquid. The materials are not necessarily homogeneously distributed within the droplet (Fig. 26.1). If lipids are present they may form a membrane. The droplets may extract materials from the environment; this can easily be shown with dyes, which will accumulate within the drops. However, ultimately each drop reaches a state of stable equilibrium with its surroundings and they thus do not serve to provide a model of the steady state balance of living things.

Oparin and his colleagues have made further progress in building up coacervates forming open systems; that is to say, ones interchanging with the environment. Thus, if gum arabic is mixed with histone (at pH 6·0–6·2), and potato phosphorylase is added, the enzyme concentrates in the droplets. If glucose-1-phosphate is now added, starch is formed in the droplets and

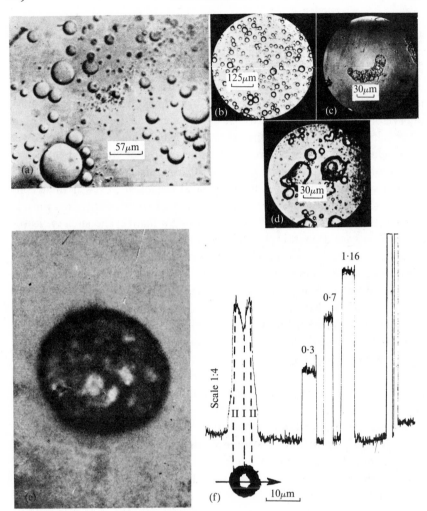

FIG. 26.1. Coacervate droplets of (a) gelatin and gum arabic; (b) gelatin, gum arabic, and RNA; (c) histone and DNA; (d) gelatine, gum arabic, and RNA; (e) serum albumin and gum arabic (electron micrograph); (f) clupein and DNA; determination by ultraviolet microscope of the nucleic acids in various parts of a droplet, showing it to be heterogeneous. (After Oparin 1964.)

they grow in volume and weight. If β-amylase is added as well, the starch is broken down into maltose and this is given off into the medium. The synthetic process occurring in the coacervate may be represented:

Glucose-1-phosphate $\longrightarrow$ | Glucose-1-phosphate $\rightarrow$ Starch $\rightarrow$ Maltose | $\rightarrow$ Maltose

Inorganic phosphate

In this model there is therefore a flow through the system. But we have already seen how improbable it is that even a single simple enzyme could have originated by chance, and the system as suggested is of course very far from self-maintaining or self-replicating.

However, there have lately been further developments of coacervates, in which, for example, oxido-reductive reactions are linked with phosphorylation to produce ATP, whose energy could be used for syntheses or other self-maintaining reactions. Models in which this occurs have not yet been achieved 'but it has already become clear that the construction of such a model is only a matter of time' (Oparin 1964).

Such systems will be in a sense artificial organisms, even if their construction involves the use of enzymes obtained from existing organisms. For practical biochemical purposes this may not matter, and such creatures might have great economic possibilities. In this sense we are within striking distance of being able to make life artificially. Such models will, however, advance our understanding of the origin of life only if they can be shown to arise under conditions similar to those of the primeval nutrient broth. Oparin considers that it is likely that this was the way that the first 'protobionts' were formed, but as this experiment has not yet been done no estimate of its probability can be made. Oparin makes the point that since the earliest polymer coacervates would be frequently broken (by waves, etc.) the daughters would have many differing compositions. Those that failed to continue as open systems would of course be eliminated. It is not, however, clear whether such 'Darwinian' selection can really be postulated to increase the probability of the formation of specific polymers.

Selective accumulation of substances that increase catalytic activity has been suggested as a further mechanism. Langenbeck showed that salts of iron and copper, which cause an increased rate of transfer of electrons, can do so thousands of times more effectively when incorporated in systems containing methylamine and some relatively simple chains. Such 'artificial enzymes' may well point to the way in which the probability of synthesis of the specific systems that we now know was increased. If combined into 'protobionts' they would be preserved by selection. The co-enzymes, which are of universal occurrence today, may be the survivors of those early stages. Thus nicotinamide-adenine dinucleotide (NAD) is the carrier of hydrogen in all cells from those of bacteria to man or the oak tree. Riboflavine, porphyrins, co-enzyme A, and ATP are similarly universal compounds (p. 66).

This stage of the origin of the first stable open system is perhaps the most difficult of all to understand. We cannot say that we can really see clearly and scientifically how it was passed. The studies of coacervates help considerably by giving us the possibility of obtaining further information. They do not yet provide a solution.

We must assume the presence of some polynucleotides with a rudimentary structure, able to organize the production of simple enzymes and to replicate themselves, at least approximately. It is best to admit that we do not know how they were formed, but the great advances of knowledge in recent years encourage the hope that we shall soon know. Granted such rudimentary 'bionts', we can see how selection would favour those whose nucleotides produced proteins with greater catalytic activity, but it is still a long way from such simple systems to fully formed organisms as we know them today.

27

THE EVOLUTION OF POPULATIONS

1. The impact of the discovery of evolution

THE fact that all animals and plants have arrived at their present state by gradual change is now accepted by all biologists. There is no longer any need to prove the fact of evolution, but there is still much to be done to discover the paths that evolution has followed. We are particularly curious to know about our own ancestry in as much detail as possible. This interest can easily be dismissed as of no great practical value; we learn only marginally better how to conduct our lives by looking at those of our predecessors. But the really compelling reason for studying them is that we alone of all creatures have discovered that we had ancestors that were once utterly unlike ourselves. Even 100 years after Darwin it is still too soon to see the end of the fundamental reorientation of individual and social life that is flowing from this discovery. Essentially it amounts to the gift of the knowledge of our origin.

We shall certainly not be wasting our time as human biologists if we look closely at the principal facts of evolutionary change, especially as they affect higher primates and man.

2. Are there directional forces of evolutionary change?

The fact that evolutionary change occurs between generations makes the process seem to be in a sense abstract and even mysterious. It is important not to be misled by this appearance. Evolution is a change in a mass of matter, just like any other change. But the mass involved is the whole inter-breeding population or 'deme' and cannot be localized to any of the individuals composing it. Nevertheless, it is basically a chemical change, and we must try to define its general characteristics and to discover what are the conditions that have led these complex sets of molecules to behave in this way.

Lacking proper understanding of how life began, we find that this is a very difficult task. There is a strong tendency to assume that living things are endowed with some special property that produces their tendency to 'try' to survive. Certainly at the present time the actions of living systems have this characteristic, and we do not know precisely how it began (see Chapter 26). But when we look closely we see that the 'tendency' is not the result of any guiding principle beyond the fact that the atoms, molecules, cells, or organisms that fail to become incorporated are rejected from the living system. It is true that this result follows only because the organism consists of a very complicated chemical system with special properties, of whose origins, to repeat, we are still largely ignorant.

We cannot therefore solve this problem of the origin and nature of directional living activities. But we can at least begin to see where our ignorance lies. It is not that we must look for some special directive force or agent, guiding organisms in their life and evolution. What we need to know are the particular features of the organization of the chemical events in the body that lead to differentiation, replication, and the addition of like to like. Granted these, we can begin to understand how the chemical systems have developed the characteristics that we have called programmes, regulating not only self-maintenance of the individual but provision of others to replace him. Just as mechanisms for quick adjustment of the actions of the individuals developed, so on a longer time-scale the reproductive process and natural selection have gradually adjusted the programmes of instructions that are dispersed through whole populations. This adjustment has produced the whole panorama of evolution, which we can follow, at least in outline, over 500 million years. Whatever the agencies responsible for it may be, they have produced in some sense a directional change, in that more and more complex forms have appeared, culminating in man (*The life of vertebrates*, Chapter 32).

What questions, then, can we usefully ask about this evolutionary change, apart from how it began? First and foremost we can assure ourselves that it has occurred. This was of course the most fundamental feature revealed by the Darwinian concept of evolution. We now take it for granted that there was a time when there were no men; that earlier there were no mammals; earlier still no vertebrates, and so on (Fig. 27.1). Similarly with the evolution of plants (Fig. 27.2). Nevertheless the fact is so remarkable that it may well rank as perhaps the most fundamental of all human discoveries. It is true that we do not know enough to understand fully the origins of life, or the processes that ensure that its actions lead to survival and even to increasing complexity of interaction with the environment. But we humans do know that we *have* originated: that there was a time when we did not exist, at least in anything like our present form. This is in a sense the discovery of the act of our creation, and it produces a compelling need to know more about the actual course that was taken. This course was investigated by a vast amount of biological study following

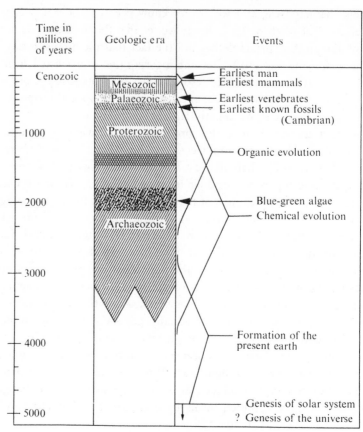

FIG. 27.1. A scheme showing some stages of evolution.
(Modified after Calvin 1967.)

Darwin, though for the last 30 years it has been somewhat out of favour: 'We do not need', it has been said, 'further proof of the fact of evolution. We need only to know *how* it has occurred.' This attitude is now itself beginning to look old-fashioned. We *do* need to know as much as possible about the details of these changes, the rates at which they occur, whether they are continuous or rhythmical, and whether they can be said to follow any consistent pattern or direction. It is therefore no accident that some of the acutest studies of evolution in recent years have been made by paleontologists, such as Simpson (1953) and Romer (1966). From their knowledge of the fossils they are in possession of the relevant facts. Geneticists also have much to say about evolution, but in the nature of their subject they can follow it precisely over only a relatively short period. Some genetical studies have been pursued for long enough to show evolutionary changes

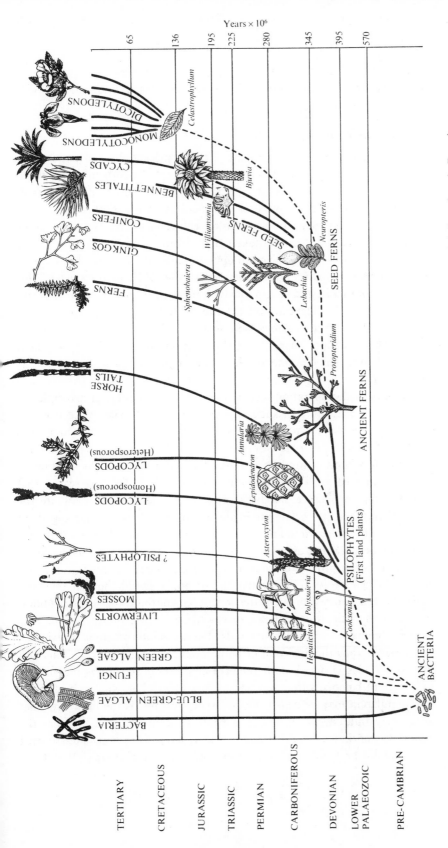

FIG. 27.2. A tentative scheme showing the evolutionary relationships of the principal plant groups. The time scale is linear from the Devonian. Lower Palaeozoic comprises Silurian, Ordovician, and Cambrian. (Drawn with the assistance of Dr. W. G. Chaloner.)

(Ford and Ford 1930) but it would require an impossibly long period of genetic study to tell us many of the things we want to know about evolutionary processes.

3. The change of populations

Evolution is the slow adjustment of the living activities of populations so as to meet varying conditions. All homeostasis depends upon regulated adjustment or change of activity, because conditions are hardly ever stable enough to allow such a complicated system as an organism to act in the same way for very long. The particular feature of the adjustment that we call evolution is that it cannot take place within any one organism. Living systems have become organized to operate under the process that we have called control by instructions contained in the DNA of the nuclei. This control is not manifested continuously in the same way, but consists of two parts. First, at the beginning of the life of each single organism there is control of the way it develops, setting up the homeostatic machinery by which relatively rapid changes in the conditions are met. Then, secondly, after the body has developed, the instructions continue to control its operations.

Changes in the operating instructions obviously could, in principle, be made during life. Indeed, such changes certainly do take place (somatic mutations) but they are usually either trivial (for example leading to patches of hair of colour different from the rest) or lethal (as perhaps in some cancers). Revisions of fundamental developmental instructions must occur at some time before the development begins. It is for this reason that evolutionary changes cannot be a property of individuals. They are the small alterations that occur gradually within populations, adapting them to changes in the surroundings. The development and life of each individual can be regarded as a decoding of the instructions it has received. Evolution is the process of altering the instructions. In this sense, as we have seen in Chapter 9, the individual organism is not the unit that survives. Each is doomed to fail in the end. What continue are the nucleotides, which, with their attendant polymerases, ensure the production of new proteins, enzymes, and other materials. The set of interbreeding individuals (a 'deme') is thus the final unit of homeostatic self-maintenance. This unit only, and no lesser one, has the remarkable power of remaining indefinitely in a state of balance with a varying environment. The whole set of genes in a population may be called the genotype, and this is the basic unit that alters in evolution. Nevertheless it must be emphasized again that the genotype continues only because its instructions are translated during development and differentiation into functioning individuals. It is these that actually 'live', by interchange with the environment. Both the individuals (phenotypes) and the population of genotypes are thus the essential units of survival and continuity. It is perhaps only through an accident of our language that we feel a paradox in this. Yet the relative positions of the individual and the society to which he belongs are still matters of controversy among us.

The changes by which evolution occurs must in most cases eventually affect not single genes but whole sets of them. Each individual is able to function in a given environment because the instructions are such as to give him coherent and effective form and actions. Thus, in order to survive each individual must be of the right size and have the right brain, bones, and, of course, enzymes. Each of these characters is acted upon by many genes and each gene influences many characters. Each animal or plant population is thus a delicately integrated genetic system, selected to fit a particular habitat or niche.

It does not follow that all the individuals of a species constitute one evolutionary unit. Many species contain subspecies, populations adapted to particular niches. Each of these subspecies may have its own balanced genotype, maintained distinct from others by geographical or other factors (p. 397).

4. The efficiency of selective death for adaptation

The activities of the body proceed in an orderly way, guided by the enzymes produced under control of the DNA. Changes in the activities that are to be effective must therefore also be limited to those that are tolerable within a system so delicately adjusted. This would seem to make necessary an elaborate method for monitoring prospective genetic changes in order to determine their viability. There is indeed such a monitoring device, but it is of supreme simplicity. Any detailed plan for testing the probable effects of changes in instructions would surely run into immense complications. But a perfect and simple test is always available—viability. All that is required is to submit large numbers of slightly different types to the environment. Any that are unsuitable will die. This is the procedure that has in fact appeared. We do not know how far back in the history of life it began, nor how it was initiated. It has proved to be capable of producing the most elaborate material systems that we know of in the universe, delicately balanced and yet remarkably able to adjust to change. Moreover, it is a mechanism that leads not only to the maintenance of complex systems but to the *increase* in the complexity and delicacy of their balance. We recognize that evolution is in some sense progressive, and indeed that we are privileged to be at its present apex.

The mechanism of controlling adjustment by the challenge of death is so different from the methods of planning that we adopt in human affairs that it is not easy to believe that it is the main effective agent of evolution. In fact we shall find when we look into it that there is a functionally significant contrast between the method of inductive planning that we individuals adopt, using what we shall call a model in the brain to make predictions, and the random methods of evolution. The planning or model-making method is efficient for short-term forecasting, within a limited range of variables. We like to think that we are expanding this method with our wisdom, but it is inevitably limited in power to exploit the completely new and original. By contrast, the method of random trial and error is indeed extravagant. It operates by the production of a large excess of germ cells, especially in the male. In all species there is an excess of offspring, in many a fantastic excess (6 million in a large cod). Moreover there is 'waste' in the fact that these offspring compete with each other, increasing the pressure of the environment on the balance of life. On the other hand, it may be that this intraspecific competition in itself is the mediator of much of the selection and that if the loser is consumed (as often happens) the net loss is reduced.

The system is particularly repugnant to mankind because in addition to our planning by cerebral modelling we have evolved a social system where intraspecific competition is at least formally condemned and cannibalism is forbidden in most societies. We must not conclude from this that the system does not operate in these ways in nature. We should argue, however, that these random ways are evidently not the only ones, and are certainly not wholly applicable to ourselves, provided as we are with good brains and memories. This is not to say that we can opt out of our natural heritage of evolution—far from it. But each species has its own means of maintaining its balance. In some, the successful eat the weaker (e.g. haddock); in others there is close co-operation for feeding (e.g. bees). One of the most dangerous practices for human biology is to draw conclusions about man from any one animal species. We need to examine the whole of nature and try to find its rules, and then decide what our proper part may be.

The general rule is that no single mass of living matter endures for ever and that all are replaced by new ones after some means of changing the instructions (Chapter 14). Some degree of differential death is probably always involved, either among gametes or zygotes or during the divisions of the cells to produce a functioning adult. Such selective deaths, for example among sperms, are certainly at work in the system that ensures maintenance of the life of mankind.

Sexual reproduction is the particular mechanism by which new sets of instructions are produced in most higher animals and many plants. The combination of two sets of chromosomes allows for novelty while maximizing the chance of compatibility, that is to say producing a new version that is not a non-viable freak. Further, increase in variability is introduced by crossing-over between chromosomes, so that the individual does not necessarily inherit whole chromosomes from his grandparents.

5. Populations, subspecies, and species

In order to treat questions of evolution we must have an understanding of the types of grouping of individuals that present themselves in nature. This is by no means easy to do. Through the act of naming we are all vaguely familiar with a considerable number of biological groupings. Most people know something about such categories as, say, oak trees and elm trees, or blackbirds and thrushes. But few could say that they had any real knowledge about the population of oaks or blackbirds in the world. Are they all alike in size and shape, are there subgroups in different regions, do they all interbreed? And so on. Populations are in fact things that are for the most part outside the 'common sense' of mankind, and as a result a great deal of nonsense is talked and written about them.

Perhaps the only population with which most of us are fairly familiar is that of mankind, and exact knowledge about its extent, numbers, and variety is well advanced (Chapters 23-5 and 38-43). Like all populations, ours is composed of many subpopulations, differing from each other not only outwardly but in their gene structure. Yet matings between all are fertile (all equally so, as far as is known) and we therefore say that all belong to one species, *Homo sapiens*. It is more difficult to know what category to use to describe the subdivisions of mankind or any other population. Sometimes they are called subspecies or races, but there is no real reason to name them in any way, because for the most part they *do not constitute clearly identifiable, discrete groups* (Chapter 41).

The population of *Homo sapiens* stands today clearly apart from all other living populations. Our nearest relatives, the gorilla and chimpanzee (*Gorilla gorilla* and *Pan troglodytes*), are so unlike us that the relationship causes only slight embarrassment. But as we look back in time we can see traces of populations that perhaps included our ancestors, for example the australopithecines (Chapter 32). But were they of the same species as ourselves? Clearly the concept of a species has no simple meaning when we examine populations extending through time. Neither is this a mere historical question about unimportant events long ago: all species are at this moment changing; evolution is occurring continuously. All species, whether of animals, plants, or men, are at least slightly different now from what they were five minutes ago, but it would be quite impossible to say whether any new species had arisen in that time. Our concept of species must obviously somehow be made to take account of the difficulty of identifying their beginnings and ends in time.

Biologists give a great deal of attention to this problem (see Mayr 1963). They distinguish species broadly either (1) by classifying together a group of individuals that look alike, or (2) by finding a group the members of which can breed with each other but not with related groups. The first way of definition is arbitrary (who is to say what is 'alike'?) and may be called the 'typological' method of definition. It is implicit in the very word 'species', derived from the Latin *specere*, to look at. The second method identifies a natural group and may be called the biological concept of a species. This method has obvious scientific advantages, but also many complications. Moreover it is exceedingly difficult to apply it in practice even to existing populations, and is impossible for extinct ones. In order to give names to the various groups of animals and plants that live and have lived we are bound therefore to use arbitrary typological groupings, that is to say to put together those that we think seem most alike in appearance or some other character. This group is then called a species if it is judged sufficiently different from some rather similar group. If the differences are slight the two are called subspecies. Groups of species are called genera and these in turn are grouped into families, orders, classes, and phyla, with as many further subdivisions as desired (e.g. suborders or super-classes). Thus the classification of modern man is the subspecies *sapiens* of the species *sapiens*, i.e. *Homo sapiens sapiens*. A full classification would be

Subspecies	*sapiens*
Species	*sapiens*
Genus	*Homo*
Family	Hominidae
Superfamily	Hominoidea
Suborder	Anthropoidea
Order	Primates
Infra-class	Eutheria
Subclass	Theria
Class	Mammalia
Subphylum	Vertebrata
Phylum	Chordata

The whole process of classification is in practice quite arbitrary, but in principle the species constitutes a real biological unit in the sense of an interbreeding population *over any given stretch of time*. Using the biological concept as a starting-point it is perhaps possible to operate the system with reasonably strict criteria, at least for the lower categories. Good systematists agree fairly well in what they mean by subspecies, species, and genera. The higher categories are mainly arbitrary matters of convenience.

6. The origin of species

Populations living under differing conditions, if the flow of genes is sufficiently restricted, gradually divide, by the changes of their gene pools, into distinct species that can no longer interbreed. There are known to be stages when the capacity to interbreed is reduced but not absent. For example leopard frogs (*Rana pipiens*) from the north and south of the United States are only partially interfertile when they are crossed; most of the embryos die. Presumably as populations diverge more and become adapted to different habitats matings between members of them eventually become unable to produce any fertile offspring (as for example the horse and the donkey). The situation is different according to whether the two populations live in the same area (sympatric) or different areas (allopatric) (see Ford 1964 and Mayr 1963). In the latter case, and especially if separated by geographical barriers, they may become divergent by adaptations to small differences in the environment or perhaps in small populations, simply by chance variations in the genotype. Geographical isolation is a great originator of species (see p. 394). Sympatric species, on the other hand, are often separated by isolating mechanisms, which seem to have been evolved for the purpose after very powerful selection pressures have caused an initial genetic divergence to create a polymorphic population, allowing it to penetrate a variety of niches. If the hybrid resulting from a mating between the divergent types is intermediate in character and suitable for neither habitat it will die. There will then be a powerful selective force for an isolating mechanism. These isolating mechanisms are not simply such as to make the results of mating sterile, and many distinct populations exist in spite of the fact that under suitable circumstances they *can* be interfertile. Thus the mallard duck (*Anas platyrhynchos*) and pintail (*Anas acuta*) are quite distinct animals, extremely common throughout the northern hemisphere, living and nesting side by side on the same waters; they hardly ever cross in nature, but can do so freely in captivity and the offspring are themselves fertile.

Isolating mechanisms may function either before or after mating. Among pre-mating mechanisms are differences of habit or breeding season, preventing meeting, differences of behaviour if the sexes do meet, or mechanical prevention of sperm transfer. Post-mating isolation mechanisms include death of the gametes or of zygotes or reduced viability of the F_1 or of F_2 (hybrid sterility).

These mechanisms are emphasized here because they are an essential part of the elaborate system by which the earth is populated. This involves the presence of numerous slightly different populations, each suited to a slightly different habitat (Ford 1965). The existence of this variety is not obvious to the layman and, indeed, is constantly a surprise to the naturalist. Thus for a long time it was supposed that there was one species of malaria mosquito, *Anopheles maculipennis*, in Europe. It was a mystery why even in parts where it was quite common there was often no malaria. Finally it was found that there is not one but no less than *six* species, differing slightly in various characteristics, including swarming habits, egg shape, temperature preferences, and hibernation. Such groups of superficially similar species are called sibling species, but the name should not be taken to suggest that they are species in course of development any more than any other species are. They are populations as stable and independent as any others.

The existence of such populations with basically the same characters but slightly different adaptations suggests that there is a strong tendency to preserve a given type of organization. The genes that produce a successful organism constitute a delicately integrated genetic system and are kept together by isolating mechanisms and selection, a conservative process that can be called genetic homeostasis or homeostasis of the deme. On the other hand, all the variations of the main type allow adaptation to various habitats. When we try to think about the evolution of man it is important to have in mind this tendency to preserve the genotype but to vary the minutest details. Human populations today differ in many hereditary characters and some of these affect secondary sexual features concerned in mating. Although all human matings are probably equally fertile it is possible (but not proved) that the divisions of mankind have in the past been promoted by isolating mechanisms tending to separate people with different adaptive features (for example to climate) (Chapter 39). The significance of our genetic diversity is one of the unsolved problems of the origin of the human condition. There is no reason to suppose that continuation of isolating mechanisms has any useful contribution to make to future human evolution, provided that environmental conditions, or at least their effects upon us, can be largely controlled.

28

VARIATION AND SELECTION AS THE AGENTS OF EVOLUTION

1. Long-term homeostasis

WE have seen that animals and plants continue to exist because their homeostatic systems take actions that oppose tendencies in the environment to disintegrate them. The need for these actions and the capacity to make them are thus anticipated by what we are calling the predictive powers of forecasting (Chapter 6). These adaptive powers reside partly in the individual; he can change to meet changed conditions, he can learn, get stronger muscles, and so on. But the basic forecasting system is a property of the species, in the form of its DNA, which has been so acted upon by selection as to contain the right combinations of nucleotides to produce the enzymes that will meet the circumstances in which the individuals are likely to find themselves. The process of change of the DNA of the population is what we know as evolution. It is made possible by the fact that individuals produced by the DNA vary and selection can work by eliminating those whose operations are less effective.

2. Non-genetic variation. Acquired characters are not inherited

Of course, some of the variation is due to the different effects of various environments on the phenotypes produced. To take a very simple example, plants vary in size according to the quality of the soil and according to other conditions of their environment. The particular state reached by the phenotype is not, however, transmitted to the next generation. Seeds from plants dwarfed by drought will not produce dwarfed plants (unless perhaps the drought has damaged them). To suppose the contrary was the fallacy of Lamarckism. Many people seem to wish to believe that they can hand on their acquired characteristics to their children (which is rather odd since most people have a sense of guilt about much of what they have done). There has therefore been an intensive study of the question, but of the many experiments suggested and tried none has produced evidence that changes induced in any bodily characters produce corresponding changes in the DNA, as would be needed if acquired characters were to be inherited.

It would nevertheless be a great mistake to think that non-genetic variation is unimportant. On the contrary, it is by trying out the effect of given combinations of nucleotides in different environments that the organisms find those that are capable of allowing the species to survive in particular conditions. This was shown very clearly by Waddington (1953) by submitting the pupae of fruit flies to a heat shock (40 °C), which among other effects produced about 40 per cent of animals with a 'cross-veinless' condition of the wings. If these were used to breed, then in each next generation more and more cross-veinless ones appeared and eventually after some generations the condition appeared without the heat. This did not mean that heat had changed the DNA. It had provided the condition in which those flies that had some polygenes tending to allow the 'cross-veinless' to become manifest could be selected.

3. Genetic variation

All characteristics of living organisms are affected by their DNA, since this controls the enzymes by which they have been produced. Most characters are influenced by many enzymes and hence by many genes, and will vary continuously between individuals. Thus height in man is affected by many factors: by the amount of growth in length of the bones, by the actions of the pituitary, the effectiveness of digestion, and many other things, and it varies continuously (Fig. 39.2). A few character differences are the result of the operation of only one or a few enzymes, and are therefore distributed discontinuously by Mendelian segregation. Thus, whether people have blue or brown eyes depends on the amount of melanin produced, which is influenced by a fairly simple Mendelian genetic system, so that eyes are usually brown or blue, not intermediate. This is not because blue eyes are produced by just one enzyme. Obviously hundreds of enzymes are concerned in making an iris and all its parts, but one (or few) are involved in the critical terminal enzyme that determines the colour.

The only difference between continuous and discontinuous variation is in the number of enzymes and hence genes that are concerned. Continuous variation is much the more common condition. Genetic factors may interact in a variety of ways. Most genes seem to have multiple effects (pleiotropy). Thus, nearly every gene that influences the coat colour of mice also affects the size of the animal (Grüneberg 1952). Important examples in man are that the gene producing the blood group A increases the liability of the individual to cancer of the stomach, whereas people of group O are more liable to duodenal ulcer (Chapter 41). It is usually not clear how these pleiotropic effects are produced because it is not obvious how one enzyme would be involved in such different actions. It must be remembered that the gene recognized by the mammalian geneticist, though partly localized by its cross-over conditions, is by no means the perfect entity specified by the refinements of knowledge and technique that are available for a few genes in bacteria. Although the genetic code has been broken we still have before us the immense task of reading what is written in the genetic books of *Homo sapiens* and other species.

4. Extent of variation and its maintenance

The extent of genetic variation and of the phenotypic effects of genes are themselves varied. Birds, for some reason, vary rather little (coefficient of variability in linear measurements 1–2·5), mammals much more (coefficient 5 or more). This presumably includes variation, not only of the phenotype, but also of the underlying genotype. Presumably the amount of both sorts of variation is itself one of the characteristics of a species, according to its habitat. For some populations it is an advantage to be able to exist in a large variety of forms. Clearly extreme variations would be non-viable and it is not hard to imagine that the specifications of bird life are rigorous. Engineering tolerances for survival are less in an aeroplane than in a motor car or a bicycle.

Obviously, then, it is advantageous for the individuals of a species to vary, but they must not vary too much. Our experience of the differences between people gives us some idea of the extent of the variability, and our experience of family likeness tells us that much of the difference is inherited. How many hereditary points of difference are there between two people? No one knows, but it must surely involve differences at more than 100 genes, perhaps more than 1000. Think, then, what an enormous number of genes there must be in the whole human population. Where does all this variety come from and how is it maintained? Why are we not all alike? These are among the most important questions to ask of human biology, and fortunately we can now begin to answer them.

The factors influencing the amount of genetic variation in a population are listed as follows by Mayr (1963).

1. Sources of genetic variation
    1.1. Particulate inheritance
    1.2. Occurrence of new genetic factors
        1.2.1. By mutation
        1.2.2. By gene flow from other populations
    1.3. Recombination in sexual reproduction
2. Factors eroding variation
    2.1. Natural selection
    2.2. Chance and accident

3. Protection of variation against elimination by selection
  3.1. Cytophysiological devices
  3.2. Ecological factors.

5. Genes and their mutations. Particulate inheritance

The basic reason for the maintenance of variety is that genetic factors acquired from the father and mother do not blend. Until the rediscovery of Mendel's work in 1900 it was almost universally assumed that they did blend. This was believed because in many characters offspring are intermediate between their parents. This we now know is the result of the operation of the many distinct pairs of genes that affect a character such as height in man. Only after it was realized that the basic control of life is by discrete units could biology really begin the scientific analysis that has achieved our knowledge of the nature and replicating power of DNA, the breaking of the genetic code, and study of the enzymes it controls. Genes do not blend but they may change by mutation. This is usually the process of substituting one nucleotide base for another, thus altering one letter of a genetic word. Most of such changes will produce 'nonsense', that is, a protein that either will not work at all in the cell or works only imperfectly. Occasionally the result will be an improvement, and the individuals to which it is passed will survive preferentially. Other forms of mutation involve changes in stretches of DNA longer than one triplet, or deletions or duplications of lengths of it. Many of these may produce non-viable results. However, there is evidence that whole classes of enzymes may have developed by the duplication of primitive genes, followed by divergent mutation. Originally there may have been only very few genes, for fundamental processes (Chapter 26).

The cause of mutation is some faulty copying during replication of the DNA. This may occur at any cell division, but will be inherited only if it occurs in the line of the germ cells. Mutations elsewhere in the body are called *somatic mutations*, and may produce some local patchy effect, for example a white lock in an otherwise dark head of hair. The accumulation of somatic mutations may produce some of the diseases of old age (perhaps some cancers); indeed, faults in the DNA are claimed as one of the major 'causes' of senescence (Chapter 22).

Reasons for faulty copying are probably numerous. The surprising thing about DNA is that it usually replicates so accurately; presumably it has survived because of this very property (see Chapter 3). The agents that are known to promote mutation are rather violent, physically or chemically. The main one is high-energy radiation, whether received from the normal influx of cosmic rays, or from an atomic explosion, or from X-rays administered for medical purposes (Chapter 38). Chemicals known to increase mutability include mustard gas and formaldehyde. Little is known of how these agents act, and the effects they produce are 'random' in the sense that one cannot irradiate an animal and guarantee to produce any particular effect (say change of coat colour). Another implication of the randomness of the effects of mutagens is that no amount of them is too small to be biologically irrelevant, since the chance of mutation is proportional to the dose. There is therefore no minimum dose that is 'safe'. The minimum dose of radiation that will produce a doubling of the spontaneous mutation rate is likely to be in the region of 10 rad per 30 years (estimates vary from 3 to 150 rad). The lethal dose for man is 600 rad (if given to the whole body).

The dosages that modern man is likely to receive in his first 30 years (those in which damage to the gonads is most deleterious to the next generation) from all sources are quite high (Dubinin 1964, Purdom 1963). Medical practice now advises that the total dose given for medical purposes should not exceed 3 rad/30 years. The natural environmental radiation in 30 years is approximately 3–4 rad, of which cosmic radiation accounts for 0·9 rad. The artificial radiation resulting from thermonuclear tests fluctuates wildly from year to year. Estimates for gonad dosage (bone-cell dosage is higher) have been as high as 4·2 mrad/year (for 1959), but estimates for the current 30-year period rarely exceed 70 mrad/30 years for fall-out, assuming no further testing. This is quite a small amount compared with that resulting from natural phenomena and medical practice (X-rays).

6. Frequency of mutation

Some genes are known to be more mutable than others. Moreover, there are some that actually influence the mutability of distinct loci. The frequency of mutation in higher vertebrates is often given as around 1 in 100 000 individuals per locus per generation, otherwise expressed as a frequency of 10^{-5} but it may be as low as 10^{-8} or even less. It is probably lower in bacteria and certainly varies greatly between loci. If we assume a figure of 1 to 5×10^5 mutational sites in man (based on the chemical structure of DNA), a rate of 10^{-5} means that probably every individual carries at least one mutated gene in the germ cells, and of course he has or will come to have far more in his body cells.

It should be emphasized that the effect of most mutations is probably small. Although most are harmful, it is well established that even those induced by X-rays include good effects. The yield of plants has been increased by X-raying seeds and then selecting and cross-breeding to get rid of the deleterious effects that usually accompany the higher yields. Bacteria exposed to antibiotics all too soon acquire resistance by mutation, and so do insects exposed to DDT.

7. Gene flow from neighbouring populations

This is considered by Mayr as distinct from simple recombination, to emphasize that the deme as a distinct breeding community adapted to its surroundings is the unit of evolution. A population tends to maintain itself separate from its neighbours, and yet more or less continuously receives a supply of new genes from them. It seems likely that this has been the situation for man. The recognition of the creative value of new influxes of this sort by migration and conquest has indeed been widespread in discussion of human progress.

The advantages of division of a species into partly isolated groups has been specially stressed by Wright (1950). A subdivided population maintains more alleles at each locus, and more at moderately high frequencies than an undivided (panmictic) species. In the latter, selection tends to operate to leave one type of allele at each locus. The subdivided condition favours adaptability of the species as a whole. Obviously such factors may have been operative in the evolution of man. The whole question of the conditions under which evolution proceeds is, however, complicated, and mathematical treatments have replaced intuitive pronouncements.

8. Recombination by sexual reproduction. The evolution of 'dominance' and 'recessiveness'

Although mutation is the ultimate source of all new heritable variation, yet it is by recombination that new phenotypes are mostly produced. When a new mutant is paired with a previous allele there is a choice of proteins, perhaps conferring an advantage. This may explain heterosis or hybrid vigour (p. 599). The extent of the manifestation of any gene is influenced by many other genes in the gene complex. By the various recombinations produced by sexual reproduction each new gene is therefore manifested to different extents. What then happens is probably that the gene complexes in which its manifestation is optimal survive. For example, if the effects of the proteins it produces are definitely deleterious only combinations in which they are *not* manifested will survive. In other words selection will ensure that its effect will be so reduced as to be not manifest at all when it is heterozygous (recessiveness). Conversely, if it is advantageous it will become 'dominant'.

It is by recombinations that variety is maintained and extended. They include not only those produced by the bringing together of male and female chromosomes in fertilization but also by the crossing-over that occurs during the meiotic divisions in which the haploid gametes are produced.

9. Natural selection

The capacity for homeostasis of an individual depends on the continual addition of new material; growth is the guarantee of self-maintenance by ensuring adaptation to the surroundings (Chapter 11). The capacity of continued maintenance of the whole species is similarly ensured by the production of a great number of individuals of which the best-adapted survive. The principle of overproduction of offspring was first enunciated by Malthus (1798) and applies equally from the fastest-breeding creatures, such as bacteria, to the slower, such as man. The offspring of one bacterium, dividing every 20 minutes, would be $2^{72} = 10^{22}$ individuals in 1 day. We have seen in Chapter 25 how many humans there may soon be on the earth.

Darwin pointed out that all these individuals may differ in countless ways and that the survivors will be those that are best suited to the conditions. In so far as the characters responsible are hereditary they will appear in subsequent generations, and in this sense the 'fitness' of the individual is defined by its probability of leaving offspring. It must be understood that this will of course include its own capacity to survive and also its actual reproductive powers and power to rear offspring to maturity. So it does not follow that mere capacity to produce more gametes or even live offspring makes for fitness. Among birds it has been shown by altering clutch-size experimentally that the number of eggs laid is adjusted to the number of offspring that can be supported: if there are too many young for the parents to look after, then many starve (see Lack 1956).

In trying to appreciate the subtlety of the operations of natural selection it is important to remember that it is working all the time on populations, whose characters vary by minute steps. There is thus a statistical distribution of the manifestation of many characters (as, for example, height in man) and an enormous range of combinations between the different graded characters. People of any one height may have all sorts of digestive capacities, blood pressures, resistance to diseases, or intellectual capacities (see, however, p. 600). There is thus in any population a whole matrix of possible types, available as it were as forecasts, each ready to meet some particular condition if it occurs.

This method of forecasting is in many ways different from that which we adopt with our cerebral forecasting system. This difference makes it difficult to understand and difficult for many people to accept. They feel that a random or hit-or-miss system of this sort could not possibly have produced the wonderfully detailed adaptation that prevails throughout the living world. On the contrary, it is just because the system of natural selection caters for such a wide range of possibilities that it has allowed not only survival but evolutionary change and adaptation to new habitats (see also Chapter 27). A planned system of forecasting presupposes a foreseen end and works towards it. We can do such forecasting well with the models in our brains, but only for a limited time-span. Neither we, nor still less animal life, knows what the future has in store. For the unknown there can be no plan. But nature's method is to provide a whole host of slightly different creatures, out of which vast assembly some may be found to survive.

In thinking about selection it is important to remember the enormous numbers involved, both of individuals and still more of combinations of characters. Once again it may be easier to think of the human population, the only one that most of us know even a little about. Yet can we really imagine 3000 million people? And man is a very large animal. Think how many midges there must be, or bacteria! In any species there may be say 10^5 or 10^6 genetic loci and at each of these among different members of the population there may be perhaps 10 or more alleles. What incredible numbers of combinations are possible in a population of thousands of millions: surely enough to provide the plasticity needed to meet moderate change of conditions.

Yet the population must remain *approximately* true to type. Each character can vary only over a certain range, and extreme variants will die. What happens, therefore, is that characters change gradually if the environment changes. This is mainly by selection of the appropriate genes within the large stock that exists in every population. If all those tending in one required direction had been exhausted, then further change would depend upon mutation. We do not know how far in practice, at times of rapid environmental change, selection may press upon the limits of variation given by the gene pool.

10. Some examples of evolution in progress

Evolution is not something that happens from time to time or only long ago. It has proceeded since you read the last sentence. Populations are altering by differential selection of their DNA. In a few suitable cases it has been possible to show that marked changes have occurred as a result of natural selection over a short time. In most species the changes that are going on are probably in features hard to detect. As we look closely at species, we see more and more signs that they are evolving. But the process is usually very slow. It took 50 million years to convert the little four-toed *Eohippus* into a one-toed modern horse.

Changes in coloration are obviously rather easy to detect, and a classic case of evolution has been the appearance over the last hundred years of black ('melanic') races of moths in areas where the vegetation is blackened by industrial pollution. This has happened independently in England,

Germany, and Japan, and probably also elsewhere. It has been proved that birds tend to eat more of the lighter-coloured animals if these are released in polluted woods and vice versa (Kettlewell 1961).

Similarly it has been proved that birds take more banded snails of colour contrasting with that of their background (Sheppard 1951). The shells of the victims can be counted around the anvils upon which they have been beaten by thrushes. Why then are snails of various different colour combinations found in the population? It is because the background varies with the time of year. The dark ones survive at one time, the yellow ones at another, and the pink at a third. This is an excellent example of the way in which a population survives by virtue of the polymorphism of some of its alleles. Numerous distinct genes may be selected even in the same area, because each confers its own distinct advantage in some situations although it may be disadvantageous in others. The population gains from the polymorphism, even though individuals may suffer.

An example of a very quick change that could be called evolutionary was the effect of the very cold winter of 1946-7 on the population of moles in Europe. When the ground is frozen moles cannot catch worms and many starve. Starvation is hardest upon the larger individuals (in man as well as in moles) and the result was a striking reduction in the size of animals in the population that survived.

The fact that natural selection proceeds rapidly is perhaps most familiar to us in the way deleterious insects or bacteria react to the chemicals that we invent to destroy them. Populations of mosquitoes began to show resistance to DDT within 2 years of its introduction. The evolution of resistance by bacteria is continually eroding the usefulness of antibiotics and is evaded only by the discovery of new ones.

All populations are in fact in a delicate balance with their environment and respond quickly to small changes in it. Quantitative theoretical studies by Fisher (1930) and Haldane (1956) have shown that any gene that is at an advantage of as little as 1 per cent over another (in the sense of leaving 1 per cent more offspring) will spread through the population. It is accordingly unlikely that any inherited feature is of precisely neutral advantage. We cannot safely assume therefore that any conspicuous feature is developed just by chance, nor that an organ is retained simply as a vestige, at least if it imposes a metabolic load to be carried by individuals who show it without any useful return. Thus in man we may be fairly sure that there has been some selective advantage (at least until recently) in the retention of most of the organs of the body. We are better employed trying to find out what such organs as the appendix or the pineal gland do than in speculating about their 'vestigial' nature.

11. Random fixation

There may be some exceptions to the general rule that characters do not arise by chance. In small populations (not more than a few hundreds) isolated from others, one of two alleles may be lost by chance, so that the other reaches 100 per cent. Sewall Wright has called this effect *random fixation*. It has been much discussed as a possible form of evolution, often under the vague heading of 'genetic drift'. Local divergences may indeed arise in very small populations. For example, some religious sects such as the Hutterites in North America (p. 320) constitute very small human communities isolated from those around them (and also often from each other). The gene frequencies of their blood groups differ from those both of the Americans around them and the Germans from whom they originated. Such differences would, indeed, be expected to arise by chance, but they remain only because the populations are tiny and isolated. They would be swamped if crossing with neighbouring populations were resumed. Genetic drift has been alleged to have occurred in small alpine communities, for instance in Switzerland and Chile. A more important case may be the four million Amerindians, all of whom lack the B gene, perhaps because they were founded by only a few hundred migrants. The 300 descendants of the fifteen people shipwrecked on Tristan da Cunha include four homozygotes for the rare condition *retinitis pigmentosa*.

Evidence about this matter comes also from the fauna and flora of small islands. These characteristically differ among themselves and from the near-by mainland, which will itself carry more uniform populations than the islands. Some of the differences between islands are no doubt due to environmental differences, but on very small islands some may be random.

Isolation is a potent factor leading to divergence of population, but it will lead to sustained evolutionary differences only if either the isolates are *very* small and remain separate for a long time, or if the environments have different selective effects (see pp. 394, 593).

12. Rates of evolution

The rate of evolution and its changes are important for man, because there are suggestions that his rate of evolution is faster than that of other species. The problems involved in the measurement of rates of evolution have been fully discussed by Simpson (1944, 1949). One satisfactory method would be to measure the amount of genetic change, but this is largely impractical for obvious reasons. We must therefore fall back upon some measurement of the amount of structural change as measured in fossils. Indeed, this is perhaps really the method of choice, even against the study of genetic change, if that were possible. For in studying the organisms them-selves (or at least their remains) we are examining the form of the actual materials whose change is the subject of selective action. The genetic apparatus is also material, it is true, but it is the material that carries the coded instructions for living. *How* lives are lived can be understood only if the instructions are decoded and this is done for us if we study the pheno-types and their means of homeostasis. The test of whether a given set of instructions is 'good' is simply 'does it develop into an organism whose activities enable it to survive?' In this sense, therefore, study of the changes in the characteristics of the developed organisms in successive generations is a more direct study of evolution than would be study of the changes in the DNA that produced them.

Of course, a major difficulty is to know what features of the phenotypes to examine, granted especially the imperfections of the fossil record. How-ever, in suitable cases where significant characters have been studied the full complexity of the problem becomes apparent. A good example is the characteristics of the teeth of horses, which make them efficient for browsing on tough grasses. These teeth may be assessed by the length of the outer ridge (ectoloph) and height of a main cusp (paracone), both being parts of the grinding surface. These measurements can be made from comparable specimens (unworn third molars) of a series of genera. They show that the two dimensions changed at different rates. Therefore, although both are related to the eating habits of the animals they must have been differently affected by selection. Moreover, the rate of change was not constant.

Obviously much can be learned by following the history of single features in this way. The course of change of each feature is, however, likely to be different and not comparable even in related lineages, still less in widely distinct ones. We could not, with such data about the horses' teeth, answer such questions as 'Has man evolved faster than the horse since the Oligo-cene?' Indeed, even these simple thoughts show us that there really is no answer to such a question. We could decide whether teeth or legs became longer more rapidly in one group than the other, but this would probably be interesting only if the animals used them in similar ways and their environments were the same. At first the question 'Which brain evolved faster, that of man or horse?' seems to have more meaning. But how do we measure the level of evolution of a brain? It clearly cannot be only by size (though this is an important feature). In fact here we meet again with evidence of the primitiveness of biology. We cannot yet define the variables that need to be studied. Even if we could, we should still need to face the problem of how to evaluate rates of change in organs in relation to each other and to the environment.

One neat way of avoiding the difficulty is to relate rate of change to the variance of characters. Haldane proposed that the time required for a change in a population mean of one standard deviation be regarded as the basis. But the variance of different characters is itself variable and is probably one of the factors controlling evolution (p. 391). A more arbitrary unit suggested by Haldane (1949) is 'e' per million years or, what is practically equivalent, an increase or decrease of 10^{-3} per 1000 years—to be known as a darwin. In order to measure the rates of evolution of a large number of organisms it would be necessary to make a fantastically large number of measurements. Moreover, it would always be hard to decide which were the relevant features to measure. A partial substitute for this direct method is to use the classificatory procedure of the taxonomists as estimates of the rate of change. If the number of new species or genera or families that are recognized in a group increases progressively over a given period we can assume that the rate of evolution is also increasing. The systematist bases his identification of a new taxonomic unit upon a set of morphological features. He therefore gives us some sort of average estimate of the amount of differentiation within a group. There are, of course, obvious and even severe dangers. There is no fixed typological criterion of an extinct species, genus, family, or any other taxon. Conventions vary from group to group in the animal kingdom, and there is a great range of systematists from 'splitters' to 'lumpers'. These difficulties are so great that they might seem to reduce the method to absurdity, yet in practice it works rather well and is in any case the only one possible for most animals. The systematist is a scientist who is maligned mostly by those who do not know his work or its value.

It must however be stressed that study of rates of appearance of taxonomic groups suffers from the arbitrary and artificial procedures by which a continuum is broken up into parts. Evolution is a continuous process of change of populations. If we had records of all the individuals involved in evolution, say, from an Oligocene monkey-ape creature to man it would be impossible to place them into 'natural' species, genera, or families. This fact, that continuity implies the impossibility of classification, produces difficulties not only for systematists but for many who feel the need to think in terms of categories. For some people categories such as 'species' are a necessary instrument of thought. We shall take the opposite view that arbitrary division of continuous sets is liable to obstruct search for important features, such as the kinetics of the change that is proceeding. This of course is not to say that 'species' are always equally arbitrary. Populations of individuals are continually becoming divided into distinct groups, separated perhaps at first geographically and then later genetically, so that they can no longer merge again. But in a study of rates of evolution there are obvious dangers in using named units, that is to say, assuming discontinuities although it is known that they are arbitrary (see Mayr 1963). This problem must be continually borne in mind when we try to describe the stages through which man has passed in his evolution (Chapter 32). When we speak of a possible series of stages such as *Ramapithecus*, *Australopithecus*, *Homo erectus*, *Homo sapiens*, it is essential to remember that these are attempts to label populations that changed continuously. If we knew the whole story it would be impossible to isolate any 'stages', or to give them names. Evolution is a continuous process of change.

29

MAN'S PREMAMMALIAN ANCESTORS

1. The nature of the geological record

EVEN 100 years after Darwin many people indeed still find it difficult tc believe that it is really true that their ancestors 4000 generations ago were probably hairy half-human creatures, and at 40 000 generations back they certainly were. It is harder still to realize that our ancestry goes on back in a direct and continuous father-and-son line to a shrew, and from there to a sort of newt, to a fish, and perhaps to a kind of sea-lily. Can it really be that I am *directly* descended from newts? No children's fable or religious reincarnation myth has ever suggested any transformation more strange than this one, which biologists ask us to believe has actually occurred. It is important that we should have some notion of the evidence upon which this belief is based, though obviously we cannot pursue the details here. Further evidence is being continually added year by year as expeditions carefully search for fossils and palaeontologists find new ways of chipping away the rock, revealing the remains of the bones, and learning how to draw from the remains correct conclusions about the life and ancestry of the animals to whom the bones belonged.

The dating of the fossil record has been greatly improved by the use of measurements of decay of radioactive isotopes (Fig. 29.1). Yet it is still seldom possible to give the precise age of any fossil or even of any particular stratum in the layered deposits that make up the fossil record. The palaeontologist has therefore to use the classical divisions of the record into periods named arbitrarily, usually from the place where the rocks were first described (e.g. 'Devonian'). The evidence for evolution rarely consists in discovering a complete series of fossils, presenting a gradual change. Indeed if *all* the bones of an evolving series of animals were available it would be a difficult matter to map the evolution, even if every specimen were dated. The changes that go on in evolution are gradual alterations in the frequency of genes by selective elimination, at different rates in different parts of the population. The phenotype (i.e. the actual structure of the bones, etc.) gradually changes, but it would be an enormous task to map the changing shapes and their variability in an extended population.

Perhaps fortunately, we are presented with the possibility of doing this

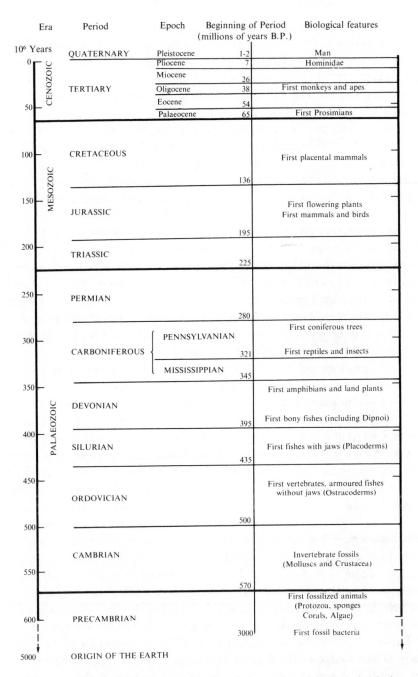

Era	Period	Epoch	Beginning of Period (millions of years B.P.)	Biological features
CENOZOIC	QUATERNARY	Pleistocene	1-2	Man
		Pliocene	7	Hominidae
	TERTIARY	Miocene	26	
		Oligocene	38	First monkeys and apes
		Eocene	54	
		Palaeocene	65	First Prosimians
MESOZOIC	CRETACEOUS		136	First placental mammals
	JURASSIC		195	First flowering plants First mammals and birds
	TRIASSIC		225	
PALAEOZOIC	PERMIAN		280	
	CARBONIFEROUS	PENNSYLVANIAN	321	First coniferous trees First reptiles and insects
		MISSISSIPPIAN	345	
	DEVONIAN		395	First amphibians and land plants First bony fishes (including Dipnoi)
	SILURIAN		435	First fishes with jaws (Placoderms)
	ORDOVICIAN		500	First vertebrates, armoured fishes without jaws (Ostracoderms)
	CAMBRIAN		570	Invertebrate fossils (Molluscs and Crustacea)
	PRECAMBRIAN		3000	First fossilized animals (Protozoa, sponges Corals, Algae) First fossil bacteria

10^6 Years scale: 0, 50, 100, 150, 200, 250, 300, 350, 400, 450, 500, 550, 600, 5000 ORIGIN OF THE EARTH

FIG. 29.1. Geological time. The time-scale follows the conventions of the Geological Society Phanerozoic time-scale 1964 (*Q. Jl geol. Soc. Lond.* **120**, s, 260–2).

only when the fossils are very small and numerous. The geologists who search for oil identify the strata largely on a basis of the minute fossil protozoans in them (Fig. 29.2). Each level is characterized by a particular collection of types, but it rarely seems to be possible to follow linear evolutionary sequences. Paradoxically we know less about the course of evolution of the minute Foraminifera, of which countless millions of fossils are available, than we do of the horses, whose fossil remains are counted only in hundreds. Because of the rather small number of specimens the horses can be grouped into a small number of lineages, defined as distinct 'genera' and 'species'. Every fossil found can be put into one of these categories (genus and species, e.g. *Equus caballus*, etc.). If we had more specimens we should see that they all grade into each other and classification would be impossible. It is important to realize that given a full evolutionary series it would not merely be *difficult* to define species, it would be *impossible*. In a time series there is no natural division into 'species'. Only when one has grasped this can one be said to begin to realize the nature of evolutionary change within a population. There may, however, be differences in rate of evolutionary change, and these can be exploited to give a new name when the rate of change speeds up. This may be especially easy since it is obviously then likely that there will be apparent discontinuities in the record.

We have to approach the geological evidence of evolution with an understanding of such limitations in mind. We have no precise knowledge of detailed evolutionary change over even a short period of time. All we have is a fragmentary record, giving us an incomplete sample of what animals were like at a series of dates in the past, approximately known. From this record we can be sure of some facts; for instance, that great changes have occurred. Many types of creature alive now were not there before, and others once alive are extinct. In making such assertions we must remember that it is impossible to prove a negative. We cannot *prove* that there is no brontosaurus alive today, or that men have not always been alive somewhere, but that until recently they left no fossil remains. Indeed, such discoveries as that of the living coelacanth fish, thought to be extinct for 100 million years, warn us to keep our minds open to such possibilities. Other no less dramatic discoveries have been made—for instance, the mollusc *Neopilina*, found in 1952 in the depths of the Pacific, belongs to a group previously supposed to have been extinct for 200 million years.

These are surprising survivals, but much more important is the great body of knowledge of the gradual appearance of new types, obtained by the study of fossils. As we look at the sequence of the rocks we see the gradual disappearance of whole groups of animals, and their replacement by others. This evidence is cumulative. We must always expect some

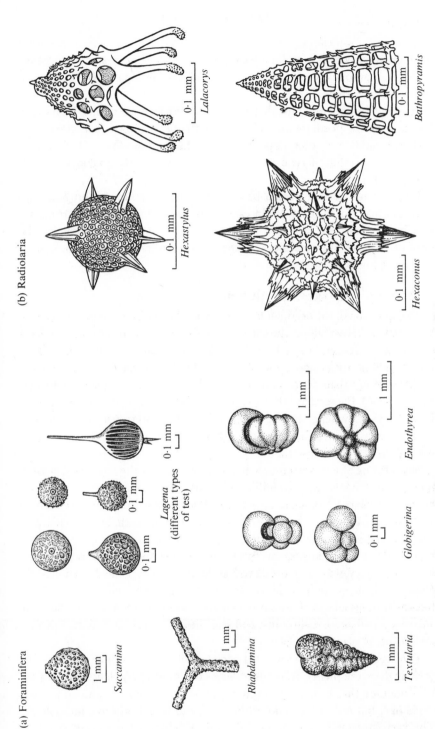

(a) Foraminifera

Saccamina

Rhabdamina

Textularia

Lagena
(different types
of test)

Globigerina

Endothyrea

(b) Radiolaria

Lalacorys

Bathropyramis

Hexastylus

Hexaconus

FIG. 29.2. Skeletons of various (a) Foraminifera and (b) Radiolaria. In the former the material is calcareous, in the latter siliceous.

surprises, but we can say, for example, that the evidence that there were no men on earth 100 million years ago is exceedingly strong, because the only mammals known from that time, or for long after, were little shrew-like creatures.

It is not quite so certain that there were no men 10 million years ago, but none have been found. The bones that *are* known from that time and later show a gradual approach to the human condition. The earliest skull of fully modern type was of a person living only 40 000 years ago (Chapter 33).

From such evidence we can be as certain as we can of anything that we have gradually arrived at our present condition. About other matters we remain less sure, for example whether we ever swung from boughs like apes or whether our ancestors of two million years ago would be recognizable as human.

2. The earliest stages of evolution

The question of the origin of life has already been discussed in Chapter 26. Very little is known about the early stages through which it passed. Objects that seem to resemble fossilized bacteria and blue-green algae have been found in flint rocks 2000 million years old in Canada and in sediments probably more than 3000 million years old in Swaziland (Banghoorn and Schopf 1966). Bacteria are thus the oldest as well as the simplest organisms. Little further evidence is available until the Cambrian period, about 500 million years ago. By that time the various groups of invertebrate animals were already well differentiated.

No remains of any vertebrates have been found in the rocks earlier than those of the Ordovician, 450 million years old. Before this there were plenty of fossil molluscs, crustaceans, and sea-lilies, stalked creatures related to sea-urchins. We may therefore reasonably conclude that no vertebrates had appeared before the Ordovician. Of course the ancestors of the vertebrates must have been present, but if they were without vertebrae or other hard parts they were not preserved as fossils. There is an ingenious and plausible theory as to how the vertebrates first arose by modification of the free-swimming larvae of a member of the group of echinoderms, familiar today as star-fishes, sea-urchins, and sea-lilies (for an account of this theory see *The life of vertebrates*, Chapter 3).

Throughout rocks of the Ordovician, Silurian, and early Devonian periods there are plenty of fossils of fishes but none of any land vertebrates. We conclude that in this 150 million years the fishes arose and continued to change, but only at the end of that time did they begin to come ashore. The earliest remains of undoubted land vertebrates have been found in

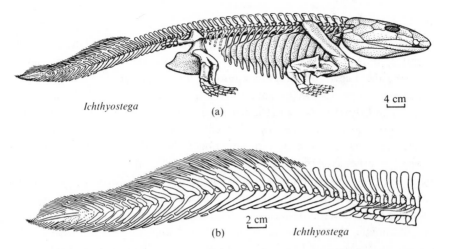

Ichthyostega   (a)   4 cm

(b)   *Ichthyostega*   2 cm

FIG. 29.3. (a) Reconstruction of the skeleton of *Ichthyostega*, an early fossil amphibian from the late Devonian rocks of Greenland, about 350 million years old. The body and tail were fish-like, about a metre long, and there were many small bones in the skull. The limbs already had the parts found in later land animals but were short and weak and perhaps could not raise the animal off the ground (after Jarvik 1960). (b) The tail of *Ichthyostega* retained the fish-like structure with dorsal fin rays. (After Jarvik 1952.)

late Devonian fresh-water deposits, about 350 million years old, in Greenland (Fig. 29.3). They were rather like large newts and probably evolved from creatures similar to the modern lung-fishes or the coelacanths (*Latimeria*). The lung-fishes have changed very little since the Devonian and we can regard them as 'living fossils', not very far from the line of our own descent. About 315 million years ago our ancestors were fishes quite like the existing *Neoceratodus* (Fig. 29.4). There is a direct father-and-son descent from such fishes to ourselves. They made the sperms and laid the eggs that carried sets of genes that have been modified to make us as we are today.

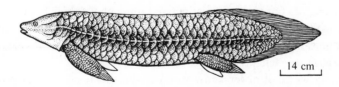

14 cm

FIG. 29.4. The Australian lung-fish *Neoceratodus*. This has changed very little from its ancestor *Ceratodus*, which was not very different from *Dipterus* 350 million years ago (see Fig. 29.5). (After Norman 1931.)

3. The origin of mammals

The earliest land animals gave rise in the Permian period to the first reptiles, known as the Cotylosaurs. These quite soon (as we judge evolutionary time) began to differentiate into the main types of reptile (Fig. 29.5). Thus we can recognize the ancestors of the great group of dinosaurs and lizards, and those of the aquatic ichthyosaurs and plesiosaurs. The line of the turtles and tortoises can be followed back to this early stage with relatively little change. Of course they acquired the specialized defence of the shell, but otherwise they have not altered much since the Permian. For example, they still have two equal aortic arches and in the brain there is a definite cerebral cortex. In the line that leads to the birds the left aortic arch has been lost and the cerebral cortex has been reduced. In our own line, the mammals, the right arch has disappeared and the cerebral cortex become greatly developed. It is useful to remember that our nearest relatives among the reptiles are the tortoises and turtles, while the crocodiles are quite remote cousins and the lizards are still further away. It is a mistake to speak as if there was an ascending series with all fishes at the bottom and all mammals at the top. We have to think of a branching bush, and try to recognize which creatures alive today have remained relatively less changed than others.

Among these early reptiles, the group ancestral to the mammals, the Therapsida was differentiated out quite early. It is often supposed that the mammalian stock flourished only recently, after the decline of the great group of reptiles. Actually these therapsids, the mammal-like reptiles, were among the earliest groups of reptiles to expand. They were numerous and of many different types 50 million years before the dinosaurs even began to be present in large numbers. A well-known example of these early mammal-like creatures is *Cynognathus* (= dog-jawed) (Fig. 29.6(a)). These animals did indeed have teeth differentiated into incisors, canines, and molars, which is one of the chief mammalian characters (Fig. 29.6(b)). They also walked or ran with the legs turned under to raise the body off the ground. There were, of course, many distinctive points about their bones, showing affinity with the mammals and difference from the groups that gave rise to the dinosaurs and survive today as crocodiles, lizards, and snakes (*The life of vertebrates*, Chapter 19).

Probably we shall never know whether the therapsid reptiles possessed the features of the soft parts that are so characteristic of mammals; whether they had warm blood and fur and good brains, or whether they laid eggs or retained the young in the uterus. The brain-case does not seem to be larger than that of other reptiles of the period, but brains do not always

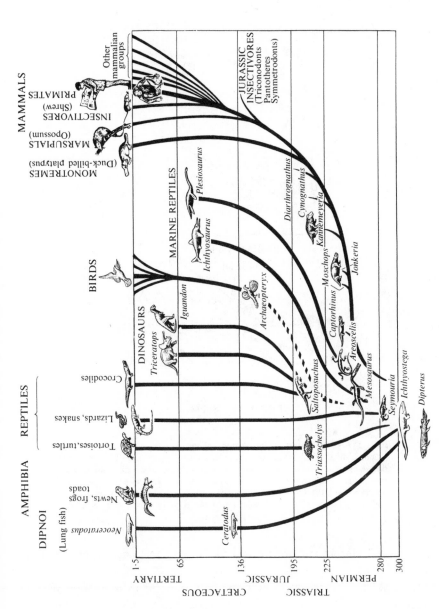

FIG. 29.5. The main lines of amphibian and reptilian descent, showing especially those leading to mammals and man.

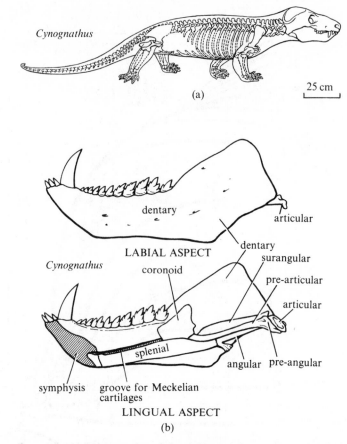

FIG. 29.6. (a) Reconstruction of the skeleton of *Cynognathus*, a therapsid (mammal-like) reptile that lived about 200 million years ago. The teeth are differentiated to some extent. Some are like incisors, others like canines and molars. The skull shows some mammalian features. The limbs raise the body off the ground. (b) The jaws of *Cynognathus*, showing the distinct types of teeth and the presence of a complicated set of bones to articulate with the skull. (After Romer 1956.)

fit the skull closely and we know little about the brains of any Permian reptiles.

It would be very satisfactory to be able to point to some animals alive today as representing survivors little changed from this period. The most plausible candidates are the monotremes, the duck-billed platypus and echidna, egg-laying mammals that still survive in Australasia. These have some characters so 'reptilian' that the animals must have separated very early from the rest of the mammalian stock. For example, the shoulder girdle is made up of a set of flattened plates, like that of some reptiles and

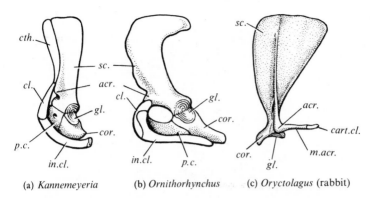

(a) *Kannemeyeria*   (b) *Ornithorhynchus*   (c) *Oryctolagus* (rabbit)

FIG. 29.7. The shoulder girdles of (a) a therapsid reptile, (b) the duck-billed platypus, (c) the rabbit (*Oryctolagus*). ((a) and (b) after Romer 1962.) *acr.*, acromion;
cl., clavicle; *cart.cl.*, cartilaginous clavicle; *cor.*, coracoid; *cth.*, cleithrum; *gl.*,
glenoid cavity for head of humerus; *in.cl.*, interclavicle; *m.acr.*, metachromion;
p.c., pre-coracoid; *sc.*, scapula.

quite unlike any other mammals (Fig. 29.7). From this and similar evidence
we may conclude that the monotremes left the mammalian stock not later
than, say, 200 million years ago. Perhaps, then, they tell us something of
what the mammal-like reptiles may have been like. They have fur and keep
their temperature well above that of the surroundings, but regulate it poorly,
with large fluctuations. They lay eggs, but provide a form of milk for the new-
born young. Their brains are relatively large, but lack many mammalian
features; for instance, there is no corpus callosum, the band of fibres that
joins the two sides of the cerebral hemispheres. The monotremes therefore
represent a very good link between the reptilian and mammalian condition.

The early mammal-like reptiles of the Permian radiated into a variety of
habitats. Some, for example, became quite large heavily built herbivores
(Fig. 29.8). Others were small shrew-like creatures. The interesting point
is that although these animals possessed many mammalian features these
characters did not enable most of them to continue beyond the Trias, even
if they included warm blood and good brains. Nearly all the varied Permian
and Triassic types became extinct, probably ousted by their dinosaur-like
cousins. The few that lived on were small, probably insectivorous and nocturnal. We have some fascinating fossils from the late Triassic, in which the
jaw is intermediate between the reptilian and mammalian conditions (Fig.
29.9). In reptiles there are several bones in the lower jaw, in the mammals
there remains only one, the mandible (dentary), the other jaw bones and
the quadrate bone of the reptilian upper jaw having moved backwards into
the middle ear. The articular bone of the lower jaw becomes the malleus
and the quadrate bone of the upper jaw the incus, providing the chain of

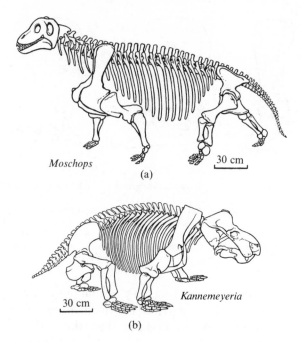

FIG. 29.8. Two herbivorous therapsid reptiles. (a) *Moschops*,
(from Gregory 1951); (b) *Kannemeyeria* (from Romer 1966).

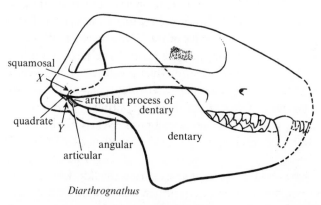

FIG. 29.9. Reconstruction of the skull and jaw of *Diarthrognathus* to show
the double articulation in which squamosal and quadrate of the upper jaw
make contact with dentary and articular of the lower. The quadrate and
articular in later evolution became bones of the middle ear. X = squamosal/
dentary articulation, Y = quadrate/articular. (After the account of Crompton
1958 and 1963 with the kind help of Dr. A. Bellairs.)

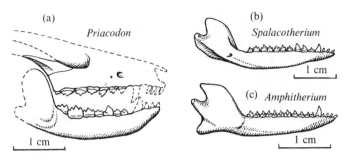

FIG. 29.10. The jaws and teeth of various Jurassic mammals. (a) *Priacodon*, a triconodont. (b) *Spalacotherium*, a symmetrodont. (c) *Amphitherium*, a pantothere. The first two represent extinct side-lines; the last has the triangular arrangement of the tooth cusps, which probably led to the condition in modern mammals. (From Romer 1945 after Simpson.)

ossicles by which airborne vibrations of large amplitude are given smaller amplitude but greater power to move the fluids of the inner ear. In one Triassic form both jaw articulations were still present. The squamosal (squamous temporal) meets the dentary (mandible), but the quadrate and articular also meet. This form is appropriately named *Diarthrognathus* ('two-jointed jaw'). It is a perfect link-form, showing that no sharp distinction can be made between reptiles and mammals. Once again we see that in an evolutionary continuum it is *impossible* to make clear classificatory divisions.

The next fossils as we ascend the series are of forms that have reached the full mammalian condition. In several strata of the Jurassic period 100–150 million years ago there are the jaws and teeth of very small shrew-like mammals (Fig. 29.10). The jaws consist each of only a single bone, that is, they are truly mammalian. The teeth are interesting, because they show the cusps sometimes arranged in a row from front to back ('triconodont'), but sometimes forming triangles facing opposite ways in the upper and lower teeth and so biting against each other (Figs. 29.11 and 29.12). This

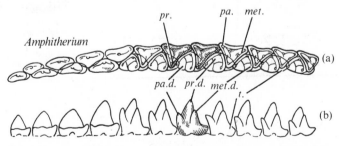

FIG. 29.11. (a) Attempted restoration of the triangular upper teeth of the Jurassic mammal *Amphitherium* by Gregory (1934) after the facts of Simpson about the lower teeth shown in (b). *met.*, metacone; *met.d.*, metaconid; *pr.*, protocone; *pa.*, paracone; *pa.d.*, paraconid; *pr.d.*, protoconid; *t.*, talonid.

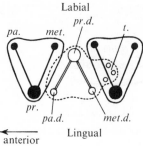

Labial

pa.　met.　pr.d.　t.

pr.

pa.d.　met.d.

anterior　Lingual

FIG. 29.12. Diagram to show the probable early arrangement of the cusps to provide grinding surfaces. Black cusps, upper molars; white, lower molars. The upper and lower patterns are essentially triangles. The lower molar has an added heel (talonid) posteriorly. The upper molars of later forms add a further cusp, the hypocone. Abbreviations as in Fig. 29.11.

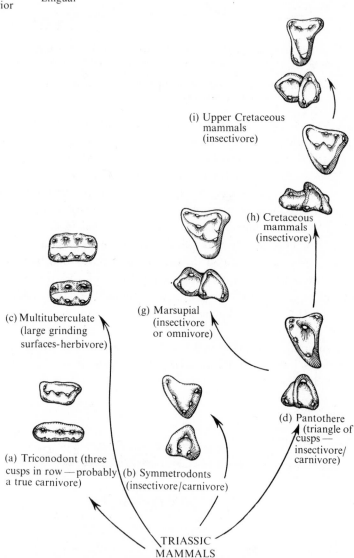

(i) Upper Cretaceous
mammals
(insectivore)

(h) Cretaceous
mammals
(insectivore)

(c) Multituberculate
(large grinding
surfaces-herbivore)

(g) Marsupial
(insectivore
or omnivore)

(d) Pantothere
(triangle of
cusps—
insectivore/
carnivore)

(a) Triconodont (three
cusps in row—probably
a true carnivore)

(b) Symmetrodonts
(insectivore/carnivore)

TRIASSIC
MAMMALS

FIG. 29.13. Some stages in the evolution of the mammalian cusp pattern; upper molars above, lower below. (a), (b), and (c) are early lines of mammals that died out before or during the Eocene. (Modified from Colbert 1955.)

condition is known as trituberculate and is the form from which the cusp pattern of all later mammalian teeth can be derived (Fig. 29.13). The over-lapping teeth provide, of course, the capacity to hold and crush food (Fig. 29.12). This may have been an important factor in allowing these early mammals to obtain enough nourishment to maintain their body temperature above that of the surroundings.

From our point of view it is interesting that all these mammals of the long Jurassic and Cretaceous periods, 150–70 million years ago, were small, insectivorous creatures. Judging by the teeth, they were not very different from the shrews today, which still have rather simple teeth with cusps in a triangular pattern (Fig. 29.15). Moreover, the earliest members of our own order of mammals, the primates, also have this simple cusp pattern. For this and other reasons we conclude that the primates were an early offshoot from the Insectivora. The shrews therefore are relatively unchanged descendants of the earliest mammalian forerunners of the primates. The proposition we have to face is that our ancestors of 100 million years ago were rather like the insectivores of today (Fig. 29.14).

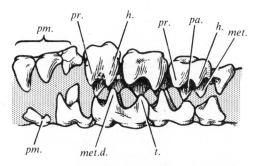

7 mm

Shrew

FIG. 29.14. The long-tailed shrew *Sorex cinereus*. The ancestors of man and the other mammals 100 million years ago may have been rather like this.

FIG. 29.15. Cheek teeth of an insectivore, the hedgehog (*Erinaceus*). Right-hand side seen from the inner (lingual) aspect. *pm.*, premolars; *h.*, hypocone. Other abbreviations as Fig. 29.11.

30

THE INFLUENCES OF ARBOREAL LIFE.
PROSIMIANS

1. Classification

THE classification in Table 30.1 lists most of the main genera now recognized among primates, but classification is continually changing and there is much disagreement, especially on points such as which genera should be admitted to the order Primates or to the family Hominidae. The sensitivity and disagreement among biologists and anthropologists about such questions provides an amusing insight into their humanity, though it leads to much confusion.

The number of living genera recognized in each group is given in parentheses, and also its range in geological time. The families and genera marked with a dagger are extinct.

TABLE 30.1

Classification of the primates
(partly after Buettner-Janusch 1963 and Simons 1963)

ORDER PRIMATES

Suborder 1 Prosimii
  Infra-order 1 Lemuriformes
    Superfamily 1 Tupaioidea
      Family 1   Tupaiidae. Recent (6). Tree shrews
                      Tupaia (tree shrew)
                      Ptilocercus (pen-tailed tree shrew)

    Superfamily 2 Lemuroidea
      Family 1   Plesiadapidae.† Palaeocene
                      Plesiadapis
      Family 2   Carpolestidae.† Palaeocene
                      Carpolestes
      Family 3   Phenacolemuridae.† Palaeocene
                      Phenacolemur
      Family 4   Adapidae.† Eocene
                      Adapis
                      Notharctus
      Family 5   Lemuridae. Recent (6). Lemurs
                      Lemur (lemur)
      Family 6   Indriidae. Pleistocene–Recent (3). Indrises
                      Indri (indris)
                      Propithecus (sifaka)

    Superfamily 3 Daubentonioidea
      Family 1   Daubentoniidae. Recent (1)
                      Daubentonia (aye-aye)

TABLE. 30.1 (*cont.*)

Infra-order 2 Lorisformes
　　Family 1　　　　Lorisidae. Pliocene–Recent (4). Lorises
　　　　　　　　　　Loris (slender loris)
　　　　　　　　　　Nycticebus (slow loris)
　　　　　　　　　　Perodicticus (potto)
　　Family 2　　　　Galagidae. Miocene–Recent (3). Galagos
　　　　　　　　　　Galago (bush baby)

Infra-order 3 Tarsiiformes
　　Family 1　　　　Anaptomorphidae.† Middle Palaeocene–Eocene
　　　　　　　　　　Tetonius
　　　　　　　　　　Necrolemur
　　Family 2　　　　Omomyidae.† Upper Palaeocene–Middle Eocene
　　　　　　　　　　Omomys
　　　　　　　　　　Hemiacodon
　　Family 3　　　　Tarsiidae. Recent (1). Tarsiers
　　　　　　　　　　Tarsius

Suborder 2 Anthropoidea
　　Superfamily 1　Ceboidea
　　Family 1　　　　Cebidae. Miocene–Recent (12). New World monkeys
　　　　　　　　　　Homunculus† (Miocene)
　　　　　　　　　　Cebus (capuchin monkey)
　　　　　　　　　　Alouatta (howler monkey)
　　　　　　　　　　Ateles (spider monkey)
　　Family 2　　　　Callithricidae. Recent (2). Marmosets and Tamarins
　　　　　　　　　　Callithrix (marmoset)

　　Superfamily 2　Cercopithecoidea
　　Family 1　　　　Parapithecidae.† Eocene–Oligocene
　　　　　　　　　　Amphipithecus (Eocene)
　　　　　　　　　　Parapithecus (Oligocene)
　　Family 2　　　　Cercopithecidae. Oligocene–Recent (14). Old World monkeys
　　　　　　　　　　Mesopithecus† (Pliocene)
　　　　　　　　　　Macaca (macacque)
　　　　　　　　　　Cercopithecus (guenon)
　　　　　　　　　　Cercocebus (mangabey)
　　　　　　　　　　Papio (baboon)
　　　　　　　　　　Colobus (guereza)
　　　　　　　　　　Presbytis (langur)

　　Superfamily 3　Hominoidea
　　Family 1　　　　Oreopithecidae.† Oligocene–Pliocene
　　　　　　　　　　Apidium (Oligocene)
　　　　　　　　　　Oreopithecus (Pliocene)
　　Family 2　　　　Pongidae. Oligocene–Recent (5). Apes
　　　　　　　　　　Propliopithecus (Oligocene)
　　　　　　　　　　Aeolopithecus† (Oligocene)
　　　　　　　　　　Pliopithecus† (Miocene)
　　　　　　　　　　Aegyptopithecus† (Oligocene)
　　　　　　　　　　Dryopithecus† (Miocene)
　　　　　　　　　　Hylobates (gibbon)
　　　　　　　　　　Symphalangus (siamang)
　　　　　　　　　　Pongo (orang-utan)
　　　　　　　　　　Pan (chimpanzee)
　　　　　　　　　　Gorilla (gorilla)
　　Family 3　　　　Hominidae. Pliocene–Recent (1). Men
　　　　　　　　　　Ramapithecus†
　　　　　　　　　　Australopithecus†
　　　　　　　　　　Homo

2. Life in the trees

The typical insectivores are animals that live on the ground (hedgehogs) or under it (moles). They are retiring creatures, active in the twilight or at night and therefore depending more on their noses than their eyes. Tree shrews, however, are insectivores that have left the ground and show the features necessary for tree life (Fig. 30.1). They climb and jump well, with

4 cm

FIG. 30.1. The tree-shrew, *Tupaia glis*.

a long tail for balance. Especially interesting for us is the large size of the eyes and of the parts of the brain primarily concerned with vision (Fig. 30.2). In the trees the sense of smell is of reduced value and the importance of sight is increased. In the tree shrews both senses are well developed, but as primate life evolved further, vision became increasingly important and the complexity of the nose and the parts of the brain connected with it were reduced. In the higher primates the eyes allow stereoscopic vision and have special central areas of cones, with a low sensitivity but high resolution, both between points near together and of wavelengths (colour vision). This central area (macula) has at its centre a pit (fovea) where the light reaches

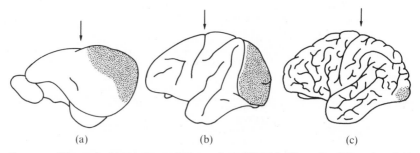

(a)   (b)   (c)

FIG. 30.2. The cerebral hemispheres of (a) tree-shrew (*Tupaia*), (b) monkey (*Macaca*), and (c) man (*Homo*) drawn to the same size to show the relative sizes of the primary visual cortex (striate area), which is stippled. (In man the visual cortex extends largely on the medial surface; comparing the lateral views in this way may give a wrong impression.) The arrows point to the region of the central sulcus, separating motor from sensory cortex. (Partly after Campbell 1966.)

directly to the cones without having first to pass through nerve cells as it does elsewhere in the retina. There are about 30 000 cones in the human fovea and with these we perform all our acts of finer visual discrimination, such as reading. Thus the primate eye has developed essentially into two receptor organs, both extremely efficient. With the central area we can discriminate between points a very small distance apart. With the peripheral part of the retina, after adaptation to the dark, we can detect spots of light of almost the minimum conceivable brightness (see *The life of mammals*, Chapter 26).

Together with the development of the eyes there was a change in methods of communication between individuals. In most mammals this takes place largely by smell, with the development of special scent glands whose secretions allow for recognition of the sexes and appropriate stimulation. These functions are not absent in monkeys or man but they are supplemented by the display of colours and patterns of movement, especially of the face. A shrew can hardly be said to show facial expression, and indeed lacks the musculature to do so. In the later primates the facial muscles have become highly differentiated and play an important part in the interpersonal communication system which is so characteristic of primates (Fig. 30.3). At the same time the whiskers (vibrissae) on the snout become smaller. As the face comes to be used for communication its sensory functions are reduced and taken over by the hand and tail.

3. The first primates. Prosimians

It is much debated whether the tree shrews should be classed as insectivores or as primates. The continuance of the debate shows that they lie almost exactly between the two; the non-specialist can be content to leave the argument to others. The order Primates constitutes one of the twenty or so orders into which living and extinct members of the class Mammalia may be divided. The order Insectivora is another, and others are the Chiroptera (bats), Carnivora (cats, dogs, and bears), and Cetacea (whales).

The primate order is itself subdivided into two suborders, the Prosimii and Anthropoidea. The former includes the fossil remains of the earliest primates to appear and some descendants that survive with relatively little change. The Anthropoidea include all the rest, that is to say, monkeys, apes, and man.

The prosimians alive today show us what our ancestors were like some 60–70 million years ago (Fig. 30.4). They include the lemurs, surviving isolated in the island of Madagascar and in a few other places, and the strange spectral tarsier of the Far East. Many of the lemurs show the incipient primate features in a fascinating way. They are, as it were, not quite

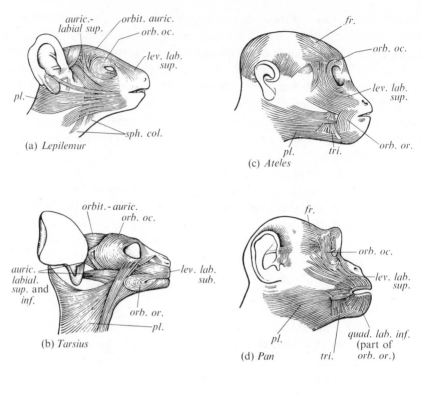

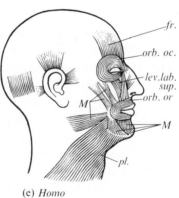

(e) *Homo*

FIG. 30.3. Stages in the differentiation of the muscles of the face. In lemurs (*Lepilemur*) there is no recognizable orbicularis oris, but this is present in *Tarsius*. In monkeys it is divided into several simple bundles (one of which is the triangularis). In apes the triangularis is powerful and the other facial muscles are further divided. In man this process of division produces numerous small distinct muscles. *auric.-labial.*, auriculo-labialis; *fr.*, frontalis; *lev. lab.*, levator labii; *orb. oc.*, orbicularis oculi; *orb. or.*, orbicularis oris; *orbit auric.*, orbito-auricularis; *pl.*, platysma; *quad. lab.*, quadratus labii; *sph. col.*, sphincter colli; *tri.*, triangularis; *inf.*, inferior; *sup.*, superior; *M.*, small muscles controlling shape of mouth. (After Grassé 1955.)

monkeys. Many are, of course, excellent performers in the trees and it is difficult to say that in this respect they are less efficient than monkeys. Every type of animal must be efficient in its habitat or it would become extinct. We can, however, recognize that only a few lemurs are able to venture into the habitats that require the fullest capacity for arboreal life, for example in the canopy of the tree-tops. On the other hand, many of them show adaptations that parallel those appearing later in monkeys and apes. Thus, *Lemur catta* sometimes exploits a ground-living habitat, living in small troops 'and has many of the temperamental characteristics of an unintelligent baboon' (Buettner-Janusch 1963). On the other hand another prosimian, *Indri*, lives among the tops of tall trees, swings with its arms, a little like a gibbon, and like the latter forms small family groups. Evidently parallel evolution has produced primates of somewhat similar types among both prosimians and monkeys—but where they are in competition the latter usually prevail.

It is interesting that some of these prosimians move with proverbial slowness (e.g. the slow loris, Fig. 30.4(c)) and many are nocturnal (the name lemur means 'ghost'). The central area of the retina varies, but in none, so far as is known, is there a fully developed cone fovea. The snout is still quite well developed, so that lemurs do not in general have quite the typical monkey face (Fig. 30.4(a)). Some of them have a variegated pelage and reasonably expressive face, but their sexual, social, and visual communicative patterns do not show the full primate developments. Some lemurs have scent-glands on the forelimbs; these are common among non-visual mammals and are used for recognition and to mark territory.

Several groups of prosimians have especially well-developed hind legs, so that they can make long jumps among the branches. This is a main attribute of the African bush-babies (*Galago*) (Fig. 30.4(b)) and the Oriental tarsier (*Tarsius*) (Fig. 30.4(d)). A result of this development is that the trunk is held vertically, and it has been suggested that this might be one of the features that has led to man's upright posture. *Tarsius* in particular is similar to the Anthropoidea in several ways, and it has even been supposed by some that the human line was derived from some tarsioid as long as 50 or 60 million years ago (Wood Jones 1929). This view of the early separation of our line has almost no adherents today, but the position of the tarsioids in relation to other prosimians remains uncertain.

The diet of most prosimians includes fruit and leaves as well as insects (lemurs) whereas a few, notably the aye-aye, retain the mainly insectivorous diet, which we presume to have been that of our earliest mammalian ancestors. Those rarely seen on the ground are probably more completely herbivorous (*Indri*). With various modifications all prosimians retain a

(a)

Ring-tailed
Lemur
9 cm

(b)

6 cm

Bush
baby

(c)
Slow
Loris

5 cm

(d)

Tarsius

4 cm

FIG. 30.4. (a) *Lemur catta*, from Madagascar, lives in woodland and although arboreal is clumsy in the trees and often adopts a terrestial habitat. The long tail is used in balancing while moving along horizontal branches. (b) *Galago senegalensis* (bush-baby). A nocturnal, jumping prosimian from the African mainland. (c) *Nycticebus coucang* (slow loris). (d) *Tarsius syrichta*, the Phillipine tarsier.

primitive condition of the molar teeth, especially the upper, which have a typical trigon. In the lower molars of *Tarsius* the primitive condition remains, but in lemurs the paraconid disappears and the talonid may have two cusps, giving square teeth, perhaps foreshadowing those of monkeys (p. 435).

The front part of the dentition is highly specialized in lemurs, the upper incisors being very small and the lower ones, with the canines, projecting forwards to make a comb (Fig. 30.5), which is used for cleaning the fur.

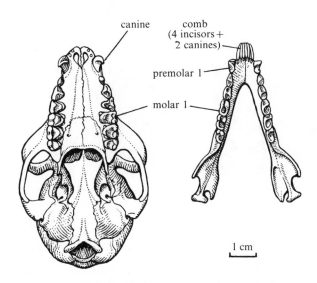

FIG. 30.5. Upper and lower jaws of *Lemur*. The incisors and canines of the lower jaw are modified to form a procumbent comb, possibly used in grooming. (After Grassé 1955.)

These procumbent teeth are a recent development, not found in the Eocene forms.

The sexual cycle and placentation of lemurs are interestingly different from those of other primates. Reproduction is seasonal, with several successive cycles ('polyoestrus'), whereas in some, but not all, monkeys cycles continue throughout the year. The placenta of lemurs is simple and primitive in that the uterine mucosal epithelium remains intact (hence 'epitheliochorial') (Fig. 30.6). It is vascularized by the apposition of the outer wall of the allantois against the chorion, again a very primitive character. The reproduction of *Tarsius* is strikingly different and much more like that of Anthropoidea, with a menstrual cycle continuing throughout the year and a placenta in which chorionic villi invade the uterine epithelium to make

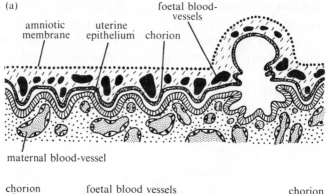

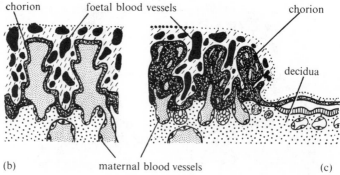

FIG. 30.6. *Placentation.* The relationship between the maternal and foetal tissues is shown in diagrammatic sections. (a) *Lemur*: epitheliochorial. The maternal tissue is bounded by an epithelial layer. (b) *Tarsius*: haemochorial. The chorionic villi of the foetus invade the uterine epithelium and come close to the maternal blood vessels. (c) Man: haemochorial. A similar situation to that in *Tarsius* which has probably evolved separately. (After O. Hill in Grassé 1955.)

contact with lakes of maternal blood (Fig. 30.6). This highly advanced 'haemochorial' placenta, essentially like that of monkeys, apes, and men, is one of the most puzzling features of *Tarsius*.

The prosimians are the earliest primates to be found as fossils; some are known as far back as the middle Palaeocene period, 60 million years ago. These very early forms were all rather rodent-like creatures, with protruding front teeth (Fig. 30.7 and 30.8). They may have been something like modern squirrels in their adaptation to tree life (but of course only in general, for squirrels are rodents, not primates). Many of these features show some similarity either to lemurs or to *Tarsius* (or to both) but it is not possible to identify more precisely ancestors of so very long ago.

At the beginning of the Eocene period, these rodent-like early primates all disappeared. No little-changed descendants of them remain today. However, some of them must have given rise to the later prosimians whose

(a)

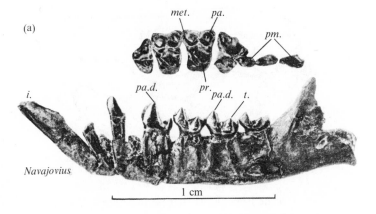

met.   pa.

pm.

i.

pa.d.   pr.
       pa.d.   t.

Navajovius

1 cm

(b)

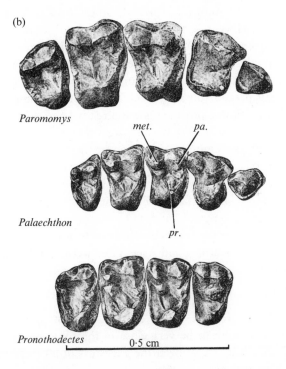

Paromomys

met.   pa.

Palaechthon

pr.

Pronothodectes   0·5 cm

FIG. 30.7. (a) Right upper teeth and left lower jaw of a Palaeocene prosimian, *Navajovius*, from Colorado. (b) Right upper teeth of three middle Palaeocene pro-simians from Montana, *i.*, incisor; *met.*, metacone; *pa.*, paracone; *pa.d.*, paraconid; *pm.*, premolar; *pr.*, protocone; *t.*, talonid. (From Simons 1963.)

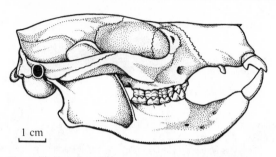

FIG. 30.8. Reconstruction of the skull of the Palaeocene prosimian *Plesiadapis*. (After Russell 1964.)

remains are found in the Eocene. At that period, from 50 to 40 million years
ago, the earth's climate was generally warmer than at present and the
widespread tropical forests housed many prosimians, some of which were
similar to modern Lemurs (*Notharctus*), others to Tarsiers (*Necrolemur*)
(Figs. 30.9–30.12). Twenty-eight species have been described from Europe
and forty-one from North America. These animals were probably quite
similar to the modern forms in some respects (Figs. 30.8 and 30.9). Thus
in *Necrolemur* the foramen magnum points downwards as it does in *Tarsius*
and the body was presumably held erect for much of the time. It is interesting that the brain of these prosimians was already large relative to the body
weight: 1/35 in *Necrolemur*. We may contrast this with the relatively small
brain (1/2000) of the contemporary Eocene herbivorous creatures, the
uintatheres, but relative weight is of course a poor criterion for a brain.

The ancestors of the Anthropoidea must have been derived from members of this great prosimian fauna. The actual ancestors were probably in
the large family of Omomyidae, such as *Hemiacodon*, which radiated widely
in the Eocene (Fig. 30.13). No less than eighteen genera are recognized
from North America, Europe, and Asia. They were therefore at least twice
as numerous and successful as the modern prosimians. They had a generalized tooth formula of $\dfrac{2.1.3.3.}{2.1.3.3.}$ similar to that of ceboids, although the
incisors were larger, relative to the canines, than in the latter. In many
other features they seem to be very close to the ceboids, cercopithecoids,
and hominids and could have been the ancestors of all these three groups
of modern higher primates.

Evidently the Anthropoidea later came to occupy most of the available
niches, for the prosimians disappear abruptly from the fossil records at the
end of the Eocene, about 40 million years ago, and are hardly found again
until the present. Their restricted distribution today itself indicates the
difficulty of survival in the presence of their descendants. It is therefore

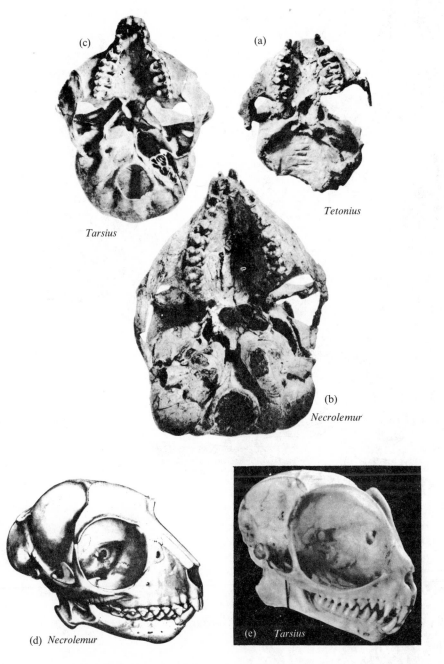

(c)

(a)

Tetonius

Tarsius

(b)
Necrolemur

(d) *Necrolemur*

(e) *Tarsius*

FIG. 30.9. Tarsioids from the Eocene (a), (b), and (d) were very similar to *Tarsius* alive today (c) and (e). Not to scale. ((a)–(c) from Gregory 1920, (d) from Buettner-Janusch 1966.)

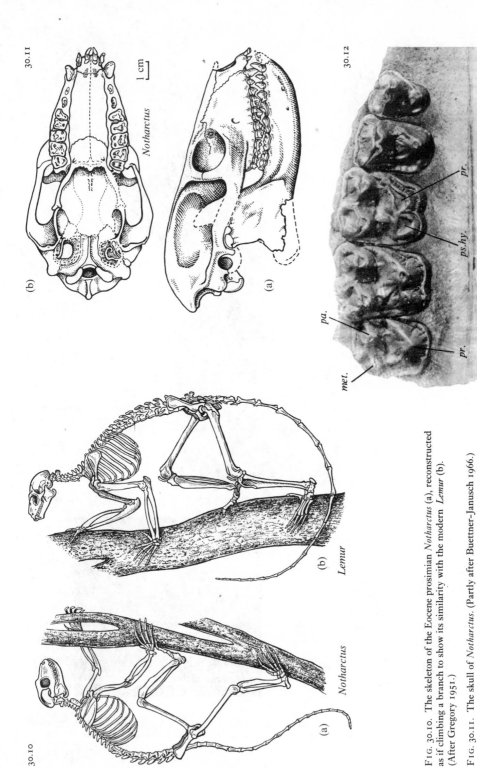

FIG. 30.10. The skeleton of the Eocene prosimian *Notharctus* (a), reconstructed as if climbing a branch to show its similarity with the modern *Lemur* (b). (After Gregory 1951.)

FIG. 30.11. The skull of *Notharctus*. (Partly after Buettner-Janusch 1966.)

FIG. 30.12. Upper-right molars of *Notharctus*. *met.*, metacone; *pa.*, paracone;

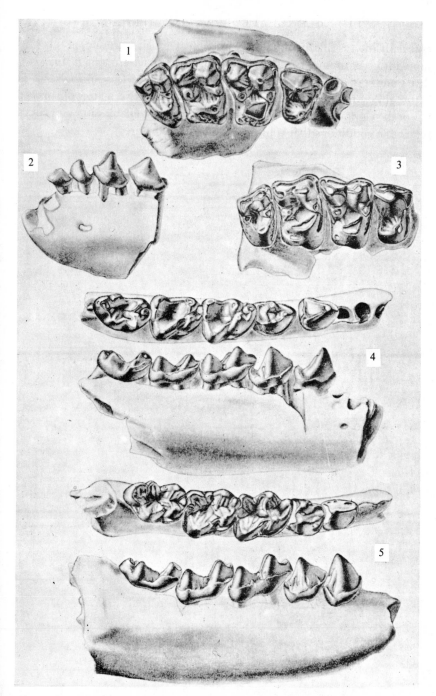

FIG. 30.13. Teeth of the eocene omomyid prosimian *Hemiacodon*, showing features that may be ancestral to the anthropoid primates, including man. 1, 2, 3, Right maxilla. The molars show basically a triangular cusp pattern but with the development of the posterointernal region they approach the more nearly square shape of monkeys, apes, and man. The third molar remains triangular. 4, 5, Right mandible. The molars are basically triangular, with a well-developed heel. (From Gazin 1958.)

especially interesting that they were previously much more successful. This supplanting of animal types by forms that appear later is one of the signs that some sort of progress is at work in evolution—at least in the sense of better ability to survive. Almost certainly it is not only a matter of survival but of development of new homeostatic devices that enable later animals to survive in conditions that could not be tolerated before.

31

ANTHROPOIDEA—MONKEYS AND APES

1. Oligocene primates, the earliest monkeys

IN spite of the abundance of prosimian fossils no remains of any monkeys or other undoubted Anthropoidea have been found in the Eocene. The reasonable assumption is that none existed, at least until the very end of that period. A fragment of a left mandible with parts of four teeth from the late Eocene from Burma (*Amphipithecus*) shows a cusp pattern that may be intermediate between that of the omomyid prosimians described in the last chapter and the few remains that are available of Oligocene primates (Fig. 31.1).

By the middle of the Oligocene, about 35 million years ago, fragments of several different anthropoidean types are found. Although we have not very much to go on it seems that the monkey and ape lines were already differentiated at that time. A form possibly somewhere near to the ancestor of the monkeys is *Parapithecus*, several of whose lower jaws have now been found in Egypt (Fig. 31.2) (Simons 1967a). The molar teeth no longer show the tricuspid pattern but have four main cusps arranged approximately in two rows. This is a plan that could have led to the characteristic type of tooth found in the monkeys of both Old and New Worlds, and also to the teeth of Hominoidea.

Probably from the Oligocene onwards the monkeys have evolved as a line (or lines) distinct from our own. The modern monkeys represent therefore a somewhat modified version of what our ancestors were like about 35 million years ago. This is a considerable time even by evolutionary standards and we must not expect that their structure and habits will greatly illuminate our own. In many respects wide divergence has occurred.

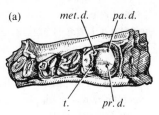

(a)

met.d.   *pa.d.*

t.   *pr.d.*

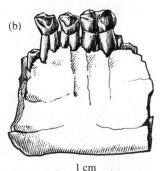

(b)

|__1 cm__|

FIG. 31.1. Drawing of late Eocene fossil *Amphipithecus*, a mandible whose molars show a pattern that may be intermediate between the tricuspid teeth of prosimians and quadrangular ones of anthropoids. (After Colbert 1938.) *met.d.*, metaconid; *pa.d.*, paraconid; *pr.d.*, protoconid; *t.*, talonid.

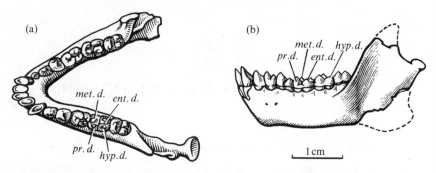

FIG. 31.2. *Parapithecus*, a mandible from the Oligocene of Egypt, with four-cusped molars that may well have belonged to a form near the ancestry of the monkeys. Of the original triangle only the proto-conid and metaconid remain. The heel has a well-developed hypoconid (*hyp.d.*) and medial to it an entoconid (*ent.d.*). (After Grassé 1955.) Other abbreviations as in Fig. 31.1.

2. Monkeys

The monkeys have greatly developed the arboreal capacities of the prosimians. They mostly climb and run along branches but the spider monkeys (*Ateles*) and woolly monkeys (*Lagothrix*) (Fig. 31.3(a)) of South America swing from branch to branch by the arms, a mechanism super-ficially similar to the brachiation adopted by gibbons. This tree life is so different from our own that it is difficult to suppose that many of the fea-tures later to develop specifically in humans had appeared at the Oligocene stage. But we really know so little of Oligocene primates that it is impossible to say what they were like or whether the ceboid, cercopithecoid, and hominoid lines had yet diverged. Indeed, there is very little further fossil information about the evolution of the two types of monkey. Fossils from the Miocene of South America show that by that period the ceboid type had already evolved there. For the cercopithecoids the evidence is even more scanty. This is strange, since the Old World monkeys have generally been considered to be a relatively primitive type, diverging early, perhaps in the Oligocene. They probably did this, but they may have remained unsuccessful for a long time, at least they have left few fossils. There are reasonably abundant remains of *Mesopithecus* of the late Miocene and Pliocene, and it is clear that these were already quite like modern monkeys (Fig. 31.4). The radiation of old world monkeys may therefore have occurred relatively late.

This leaves us ignorant as to how closely we are related to them, and hence how much we can learn of ourselves from their behaviour. Probably not very much, for both lines have changed greatly since they diverged. However, it is certain that we passed through a partly arboreal stage, though

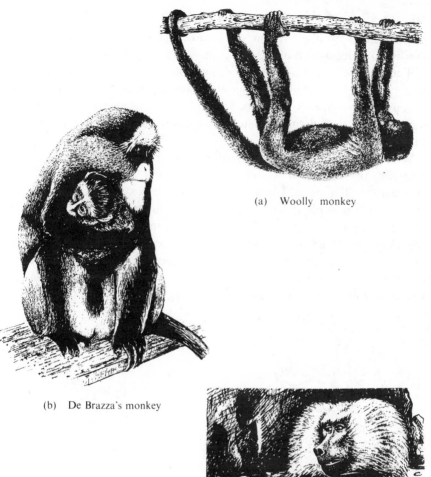

(a)   Woolly monkey

(b)   De Brazza's monkey

(c)   Baboon

FIG. 31.3. (a) Woolly monkey, *Lagothrix* (New World). (b) De Brazza's monkey, *Cercopithecus neglectus* (Old World). (c) Baboon, *Papio hamadryas* (N. Africa). (After Napier and Napier 1967.)

perhaps not very like any modern monkey and not including perfected brachiation such as that of the spider monkeys or gibbons.

The tree-life places large demands on motor co-ordination; the 'mechanical' side of human skills may therefore have begun here. More important, the environment puts a premium on vision at the expense of smell, which results in the typical rounded head and shortened face of both monkeys and higher primates.

With good vision the visual signalling systems become well developed, including the differentiation of coat colour (Fig. 31.3(b)) and of facial musculature (Fig. 30.3). Elaborate communication systems and social life thus became possible (Chapter 35). The development of the brain is, of course, an outstanding feature of primates and may well have followed the requirements of tree life and then made possible the developments of communication. In attempting to trace such sequences of cause and effect in evolution we are in fact isolating the populations from the conditions in which they lived. Primate brains became bigger and better because, being

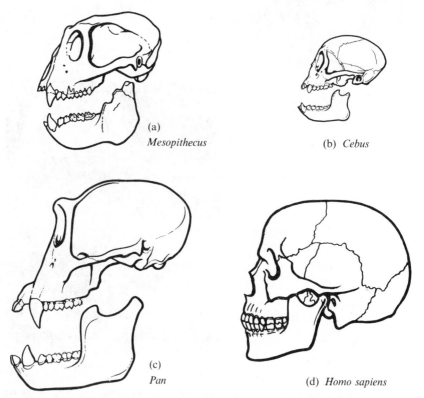

(a)
Mesopithecus

(b) *Cebus*

(c)
Pan

(d) *Homo sapiens*

FIG. 31.4. Skull of (a) *Mesopithecus* from the Miocene, compared with those of the modern (b) *Cebus* (New World monkey), (c) *Pan* (chimpanzee), and (d) *Homo*. (Partly after Le Gros Clark 1962.)

good already, they provided material that could be improved further by mutation and selection, which favoured them for life in the trees (pre-adaptation, see Chapter 34).

The patterns of reproductive life adopted in the trees have also remained in many higher primates. The small number of offspring, the pectoral position of the mammae, and the habit of carrying the young for a long period are all clearly suited to tree life and have no doubt played large parts in determining the later course of evolution. Indeed, the dependence of young on parents might be said to be one of the primary features of modern man. It may well have arisen in the common ancestors with monkeys, 35 million years ago.

3. The diet of primates

The diet of monkeys is mainly leaves and fruit, although most primates will eat meat and some do so regularly. The teeth of both groups of monkeys are rather specialized for a herbivorous diet (Fig. 31.5). The incisors are flattened, perhaps for cutting fruits. The canines are pointed and larger in the male, presumably a character of sexual and social significance, and perhaps defensive. The molars are of characteristic quadritubercular ('bilophodont') shape, especially in Old World monkeys. In the upper jaw this is achieved by adding a hypocone to the trigon. In the lower jaw the protoconid and paraconid form the anterior part of the square and the talonid has moved alongside them to make the posterior part carrying two cusps, hypoconid and entoconid. This forms a grinding arrangement, characteristic of monkey teeth, which distinguishes them from the low-cusped teeth of apes and men. Fruits and seeds provide especially rich sources of nourishment, not requiring the mastication of large quantities of siliceous grasses, upon which the grazing herbivore must spend so much time. The prime need is sharp eyes to find the fruit, hands and skill to pluck it, and taste to sample it. This form of diet may well have had much to do with the development of the quick-witted manipulating primate and its differences from the 'slower-brained' ungulate types (though such differences are hard to quantify).

The supply of fruits and seeds often changes and the primate has to resort to bark, shoots, and perhaps small animals, ants, termites, frogs, and lizards. Even the terrestrial baboons who live mainly on grass seeds and roots will eat meat (Fig. 31.3(c)). Most primates are thus catholic in their choice of diet and can digest meat. This is consonant with our own omnivorous diet. Knowledge about other animals does not really help us in deciding what is a 'good' diet, let alone a 'best' one. Indeed, man himself reflects the variety of diets. He makes do with what he can get. If there is nothing but rice he

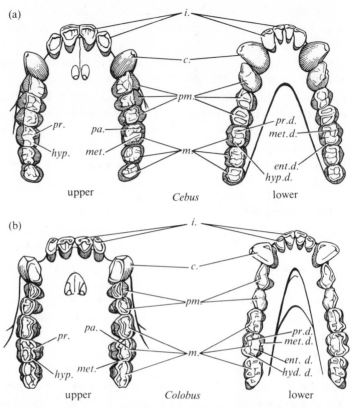

FIG. 31.5. Upper and lower teeth of (a) a New World monkey (*Cebus*) and (b) an Old World monkey (*Colobus*). (After Buettner-Janusch 1966.) *c.*, canine; *ent. d.*, entoconid; *hyp.*, hypocone; *hyp. d.*, hypoconid; *i.*, incisor; *m.*, molar; *met.*, metacone; *met. d.*, metaconid; *pa.*, paracone; *pm.*, premolar; *pr.*, protocone; *pr. d.*, protoconid.

will live on that, with little or no animal protein (though with, of course, the risk of malnutrition). Under conditions nearer the poles, where there is little vegetation, he becomes, as the Eskimos, almost wholly carnivorous. Others, such as Australian aborigines, bushmen, and the Hadza, eat a wide range of plants and animals (Barnicot 1969). Of course, these diets are not all equally adequate either in calories, particular amino-acids, or vitamins. It is curious that man seems to have relatively little capacity to seek out such foods as shall supplement the deficiencies. Perhaps the mechanisms for doing so have been developed by herbivores to search for a relatively narrow range of requirements. The primate method has been to develop an omnivorous habit and rely upon getting something of everything. There is little exact knowledge about these special capacities and tastes in different animals.

4. Early hominoids. Apes

TABLE 31.1
List of genera of hominoids
Age in years ago $\times 10^6$

Superfamily Hominoidea
  Family Oreopithecidae
     Apidium (30)
     Oreopithecus (13–7)
  Family Pongidae
     Pliopithecus (26–7) Europe and Africa
       including *Limnopithecus*
     Hylobates (gibbon). Recent
     Symphalangus (siamang). Recent
     Aegyptopithecus (? 30)
     Dryopithecus (25–10) Europe, Asia, Africa
       including *Sivapithecus, Proconsul, Bramapithecus*
     Pongo (orang-utan). Recent
     Pan (chimpanzee). Recent
     Gorilla (gorilla). Recent
  Family Hominidae
     Ramapithecus (14–7)
       including *Kenyapithecus*
     Australopithecus (5–1)
       including *Paranthropus, Plesianthropus*
     Homo (man). Recent

The ape-man stock probably diverged from that of monkeys during the Oligocene period 35–25 million years ago. We have little information about the earliest members of the stock and cannot therefore say very much about the adaptive features that may have been responsible. Of course at first the divergences were slight and our ancestors in the Oligocene period were probably quite like those of the monkeys. Teeth and skull of *Aegyptopithecus* recently found in Egypt could well have been near to the ancestry of the Miocene apes (Fig. 31.6(a)). The molars still show a distinct and rather compact trigon, recalling that of earlier primates. But the lingual (internal) part of the tooth is expanded to form a broad ridge. Such an expansion is known as a cingulum and it occurs similarly on the lingual side of some teeth of *Dryopithecus* (Fig. 31.8).

Of other Oligocene fossils *Aeolopithecus* (Fig. 31.6(c)) is quite like a gibbon, and *Propliopithecus* (Fig. 31.6(d)) could be fairly close to the lineage of the other modern apes and man.

The factors that had led to the initial separation of an ape-like line evidently became increasingly powerful, and remains of apes are relatively common in Miocene deposits from many parts of the world. We can tentatively correlate this appearance of the apes with climatic and other

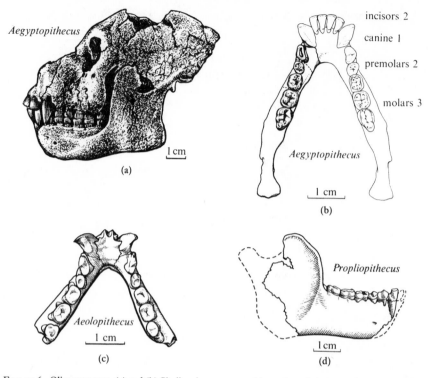

incisors 2

canine 1

premolars 2

molars 3

FIG. 31.6. Oligocene apes. (a) and (b) Skull and reconstructed lower jaw of *Aegyptopithecus*. (c) Lower jaw of *Aeolopithecus*. (d) Lower jaw of *Propliopithecus*. ((a) and (b) after Simons (1967a), (c) after Simons (1965), (d) after Grassé 1955.)

ecological features. During Miocene times the climate became cooler and drier and large areas of forest were replaced by open grassy plains and savannah. These were the conditions that stimulated the evolution of the horses and probably also of other running animals. Their relevance to the evolution of apes is less clear, for these are mostly partly arboreal animals and include some of the most agile performers in the treetops, the brachiating gibbons (*Hylobates*) and siamangs (*Symphalangus*). However, the other apes are all rather large animals, inhabiting mostly the lower regions of the trees rather than the canopy, though the orang goes high. Most apes spend some time on the ground. The earlier members of the group were probably not powerful brachiators. Thus *Pliopithecus* (Fig. 31.7) was definitely a Miocene gibbon, but without especially long arms (see Simons 1960).

Fossils of various Miocene apes have been known since 1856 but their affinities are still much debated. The remains are mostly teeth or jaws. More than 500 specimens have been found, from various parts of Europe, Asia, and Africa (no undoubted ones from America). They have been given

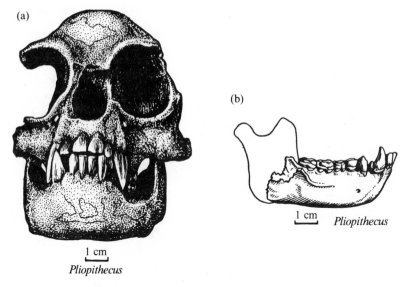

(a)

(b)

1 cm

Pliopithecus

1 cm *Pliopithecus*

F IG. 31.7. (a) Skull of *Pliopithecus*. (From Zapfe 1958.)
(b) Mandible of *Pliopithecus*. (After Grassé 1955.)

a great many names but we shall here assume that all those sufficiently well known to be relevant for us can be included as follows, though this involves more lumping together of genera than some anthropologists would wish (but see Simons 1963).

Pliopithecus = Limnopithecus
Dryopithecus = Proconsul = Sivapithecus = Bramapithecus
Ramapithecus = Kenyapithecus

Members of the first group were near to the ancestors of gibbons, those of the second to the other apes, and those of the third to man.

Fossils now referred to *Dryopithecus* are the most numerous and extend from early Miocene to Pliocene (25-10 million years ago). Many were large creatures, some as big as gorillas (but '*Proconsul nyanzae*' was a small form). Their characteristic is the large development of the incisors and canines (Fig. 31.8). The molars are large and rather square and increase in size backwards to the third. They have a crenellated surface pattern, a characteristic that is sometimes found in later primates and occasionally in man.

The post-cranial skeleton is reasonably well known in the form of Dryopithecine known as *Proconsul*. There were certainly no specializations for extreme brachiation or terrestrial life. In its limbs and its teeth *Dryopithecus* was close to the ancestors of the modern chimpanzee and gorilla.

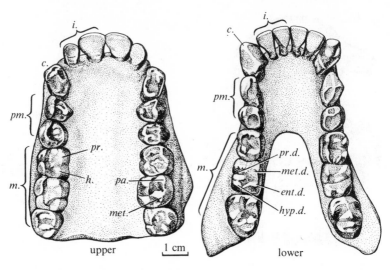

FIG. 31.8. Reconstruction of upper and lower teeth of *Dryopithecus* (= *Sivapithecus*) from the Miocene. (After Hellman, in Grassé 1955.) Note the rectangular plan of the tooth rows, and the large molars with a mainly quadrangular cusp pattern.

The fossils of *Ramapithecus* are less ape-like and more human. They were first named from specimens from the late Miocene of India, but the form known as *Kenyapithecus* from East Africa (14 million years K–Ar date) is similar. The most striking feature is that the arcade of the jaw was rounded, the canines small and, probably, the incisors small and spatulate (Fig. 31.9(a) and (b)). From these features it is deduced that the front teeth were

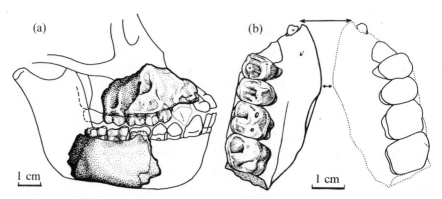

FIG. 31.9. (a) Hypothetical appearance of the skull and mandible of *Ramapithecus*, side view, reconstructed from the few known fossil fragments. The dotted canine is from '*Kenyapithecus*'. (After Simons 1964.) (b) Reconstruction of the palate of *Ramapithecus* using the fossil fragment of the right maxilla and its mirror image. This shows the rounded plan of the tooth rows. The arrows show the calculated space required for the incisors. (After Simons 1961.)

no longer used for tearing the food and that this was a function of the hands, freed by bipedalism for the task. These are obviously rather speculative conclusions, but *Ramapithecus* certainly provides a possible link between the definitely ape-like *Dryopithecus* and the later Pliocene and Pleistocene hominids (Fig. 31.10). The molar teeth of *Ramapithecus* are, of course,

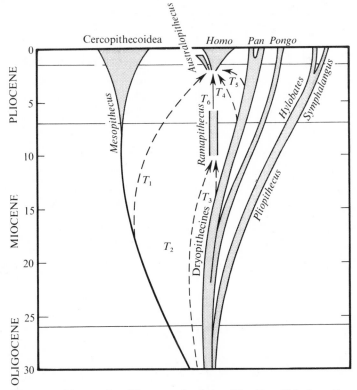

●FIG. 31.10. Diagram of possible courses of evolution of the old-world Anthropoidea. T_1-T_6 show possible origins of the Hominidae, in approximately increasing order of probability, according to the evidence. (Modified after Campbell 1966.)

relatively much larger than those of *Homo*, but are smaller than those of *Dryopithecus* and the third molar is smaller than the second. The whole animal was the size of a gibbon. *Ramapithecus* thus 'occurs in the proper time and place to represent a forerunner of Pleistocene Hominidae' (Simons 1961). As Simons remarks, it is illogical to treat *Ramapithecus* as a parallel development rather than close to our ancestral line.

The study of the Miocene and Pliocene apes thus serves to show us rather precisely our relationship to modern apes. We and they probably possessed a common ancestor in the Oligocene, such as *Propliopithecus*, some 30 million years ago. By 20 million years ago there were divergent lines.

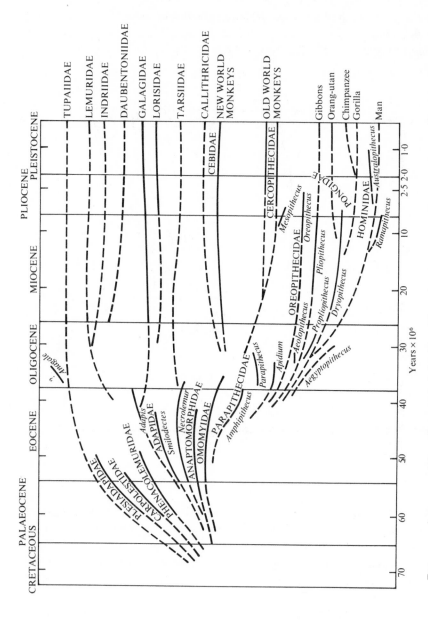

FIG. 31.11. A summary of the evolution and relationships of the main primate groups. The time scale changes at 2.5×10^6 years.

The gibbons became specialized first (*Pliopithecus*, Fig. 31.7(a) and (b)). The common stock of the other pongids and hominids were probably some pre-*Dryopithecus* of the early Miocene. By late Miocene, 10 million years ago, the hominid stock had probably diverged from the pongid as a *Ramapithecus*-like form.

The question of when the ape and human lines diverged is, however, still debated. Some of the possible alternatives are shown in Fig. 31.10. It has been traditional to suppose that the lines have been distinct since Miocene times, but some evidence suggests that the separation may have been much more recent. Studies of protein structure have emphasized the close similarity between man and the gorilla and chimpanzee. This has been shown both by immunological studies of serum proteins (Goodman 1964) and of haemoglobins (Zuckerkandl 1964). For example, there is only one established difference between the sequence of the 141 amino-acids in the α-chains of human and gorilla haemoglobins and one out of 146 in the β-chains. There are seventeen differences between human and horse haemoglobin, showing that quite large changes can be tolerated without loss of functional characteristics. From such data, and others such as the similarities in chromosome structure (Fig. 31.12), it is concluded by

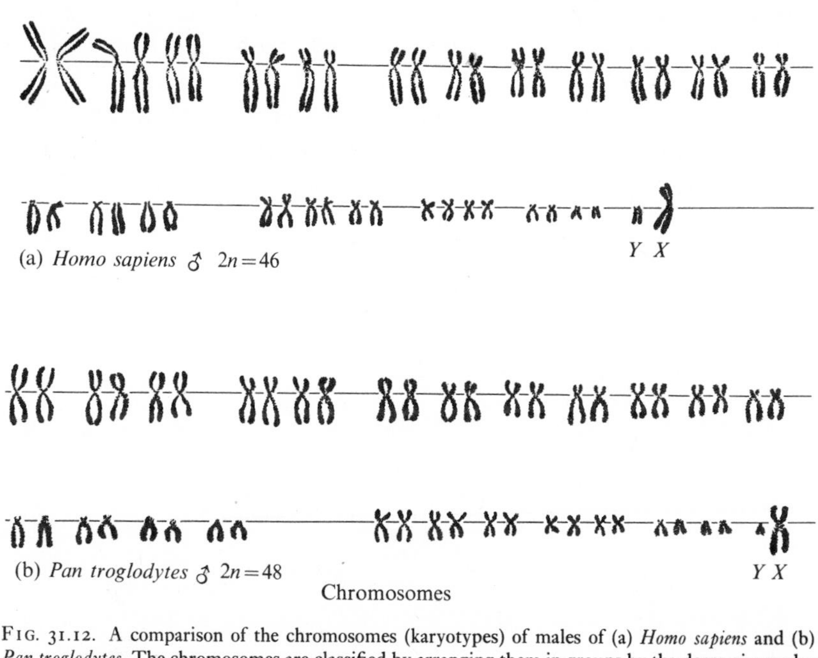

(a) *Homo sapiens* ♂ $2n=46$ Y X

(b) *Pan troglodytes* ♂ $2n=48$ Y X
                        Chromosomes

Fig. 31.12. A comparison of the chromosomes (karyotypes) of males of (a) *Homo sapiens* and (b) *Pan troglodytes*. The chromosomes are classified by arranging them in groups by the decreasing order of size. The first twelve pairs can usually be recognized individually and are very similar in man and chimpanzee. The remaining autosomes are placed in four groups, and here there may be some differences. (From Buettner-Janusch 1966 after Klinger.)

some people that the divergence of apes and man has been relatively recent (but see Barnicot *et al.* 1967). The fossil evidence does not decisively contradict this. The brain certainly remained ape-like for a long time. Further, 'In the lower Pleistocene the ischium is long and ape-like; the ilium and hand do not yet have the full characteristics of *Homo*. Most of the characteristics of *Homo* seem to have evolved well within the Pleistocene, and there is no need to postulate an early separation of man and ape' (Washburn 1964). This is one view; a different one is expressed in Chapter 33. Perhaps we have been too ready to emphasize the distance between ourselves and our cousin apes, by supposing that our common ancestors lived long ago. It is just possible that the common population existed not much more than two million years B.P., but evidence such as that of *Ramapithecus* is usually held by most anthropologists to put the date of divergence not later than the end of the Miocene, ten million years ago. The difference is considerable and emphasizes the extent of our ignorance about this period in our ancestry. However, with discoveries such as those of *Australopithecus* and *Ramapithecus* we have much more information today than was available twenty years ago. We may feel confident that future discoveries will narrow the area of uncertainty still further.

It is still not possible to say at what stage such human features as the upright posture appeared, let alone even more important human characteristics. *Ramapithecus* may have walked upright, as *Australopithecus* almost certainly did—but perhaps ten million years later. Uncertainty about these times of origin remains one of the weakest features of our knowledge of man's ancestry.

32

THE PENULTIMATE STAGE—
FELLOW HOMINIDS

1. The beginning of the Pleistocene

Ramapithecus may be close to the human line of evolution but if some of them were found alive should we regard them as human? Of course we know nothing of the post-cranial skeleton and cannot say anything about their brains nor even whether they walked on two legs. The problem of assessing both the intellectual status and the gait is somewhat less difficult for the next group of remains that are available, those of the *Australopithecines* of Africa, because we can estimate the size of their brains and associated with the fossils are found the earliest evidences of fabricated stone tools. Yet although these creatures made tools, almost certainly did stand upright, and showed many human features in their skeleton and teeth, the brain was no bigger than that of an ape. What were they like? It is obviously worth looking carefully at the evidence about them.

There is some difficulty about describing concisely either their characteristics or the dates when they lived. This is because discovery of the fossils is relatively recent and experts are still not agreed as to how to group and name the various types. Description is difficult without agreed names. Moreover, the effect of these discoveries is to show us that hominid creatures existed a good deal earlier than had previously been supposed. Some of the earliest remains from the Olduvai Gorge in Tanzania have some remarkably human features and are referred to by the discoverer, Leakey, and his co-workers as '*Homo habilis*'. It may be that ultimately some or all the forms now called *Australopithecus* will be referred to as various species of the genus *Homo* (see Robinson 1967). For the present we prefer to keep a somewhat more conservative (multigeneric) classification.

These hominid remains are associated with fossils marking the fauna known as Villafranchian. This includes in Europe members of the modern genus *Elephas*, zebras (*Equus stenonis*), and cattle (*Leptobos*). The Olduvai fauna includes *Elephas* and also the extinct *Mammuthus*, *Bos* (modern cattle), zebra-like horses, *Lycyaena* and other hyaenas, and sabre-toothed cats (*Machairodus*). The fact that the faunas are similar does not mean that they were contemporary in Europe and Africa. The change in fauna from

Pliocence to Pleistocene in Europe is supposed to have been associated with the onset of glacial conditions. The corresponding change in Africa was perhaps to a rainy climate (pluvial). The fact is that we still do not know precisely when (or why) either of these changes occurred, and our capacity to write a coherent history remains therefore weak—and this should be openly admitted.

2. Characters of the Australopithecines

There is much controversy over classification, but we shall refer all the early Pleistocene fossils so far found in Africa to one genus *Australopithecus* (Simons 1967). They seem to fall into two species as shown in Table 32.1.

TABLE 32.1
African Australopithecines

Species	Dates B.P.	Some synonyms	Localities
A. robustus	?4 000 000 to ?1 000 000	*Homo transvaalensis* *Paranthropus* *Zinjanthropus boisei* *A. boisei*	Kromdraai, South Africa Swartkrans, South Africa Olduvai, Tanzania
A. africanus	?5 000 000 to ?1 000 000	*Homo transvaalensis* *Homo habilis*	Taungs, South Africa Makapansgat, South Africa Garusi, Tanzania Olduvai, Tanzania
		Plesianthropus	Sterkfontein, South Africa

Among the earliest remains are those found in the lowest Bed I at Olduvai Gorge. This is now given a radiometric date of up to $2 \cdot 0 \times 10^6$ years (Oakley 1968); an earlier estimate was $1 \cdot 7 \times 10^6$ years (Leakey, Evernden, and Curtis 1961). On either estimate this is much earlier for the beginning of the Pleistocene than had previously been supposed. These specimens have been called *Homo habilis* by Leakey and his colleagues (1964), who gave for this purpose a new definition of the genus *Homo*. As we shall see, these fossils show many human characters but have only a small brain. The difficulty of classifying them shows *again that there are no sharp divisions*. It provides evidence that the characteristics of man emerged gradually, and not all at the same time. Further specimens of *Australopithecus* have recently been found in Ethiopia and may be as much as $3 \cdot 5 \times 10^6$ years old (Howell 1969), or even more (Pilbeam 1970).

We shall assume that the finds in Olduvai Bed I known as *Homo habilis* can reasonably be included in the species *Australopithecus africanus*, the name that was chosen by Dart in 1925 for the first Australopithecine skull found. This was discovered at Taungs in South Africa in a Lower Pleistocene deposit probably over 1 million years old. Other skulls found at Sterkfontein and Makapansgat, which are also in South Africa, and recently at Garusi in Tanzania can be placed in this species too. *A. africanus* thus seems to have lived from at least 2 to 1 million years ago, though the dating of the South African remains is very difficult.

There was another type of Australopithecine living in Africa for much of this time. In 1938 Broom found a heavily built skull and some other bones at Kromdraai, South Africa, and named them *Paranthropus robustus*. This genus is now often included in *Australopithecus*. It has been strongly argued, however, that its members stand so far apart that the genus *Paranthropus* should be retained (Robinson 1963, 1967). The creatures were probably a line of herbivores, existing parallel to the carnivorous or omnivorous *africanus* type. It is urged by Robinson that since the latter presumably went on to become *Homo* they should be included in that genus and that the genus *Australopithecus* should be dropped. This may well happen, but we shall follow the usual current practice of keeping *Australopithecus* and its two species. They certainly differ in many ways but both have very much smaller brains than the creatures usually placed in *Homo*. It must be admitted, however, that describing the characters of 'Australopithecines' in general is a rather superficial procedure. In *A. robustus* can be included also a more complete skull found at Swartkrans (South Africa). This, like the Kromdraai remains, is dated rather later than Taungs, perhaps 1×10^6 years B.P. We shall also include in *A. robustus* some much earlier remains from Olduvai, though this is more controversial. These fossils, found by Mrs. Leakey in 1959 in Olduvai Gorge, Bed I, at a level 2 ft above that of the '*H. habilis*' remains, were called *Zinjanthropus boisei* ('nutcracker man'). Few people would probably still wish to keep the genus distinct. Some would like to keep the species as *A. boisei*, but we shall follow Simons in putting these remains with *A. robustus*, and date them provisionally at 1.9×10^6 years B.P.

The characteristics of the genus *Australopithecus* as a whole may be seen from the original skull found at Taungs in South Africa, though it is of a juvenile (Fig. 32.1(a)). A similar skull was found at Sterkfontein in the Transvaal (Fig. 32.1(b)). The general appearance of the face is certainly not very human, with rather protuding jaws ('prognathous'). The skulls referred to the other species, *A. robustus*, are more heavily built, often with massive brow-ridges, and sometimes even a sagittal crest (Fig. 32.5). The foramen magnum of the Australopithecines is usually said to point forwards, which is consistent with an upright gait. This, however, was disputed

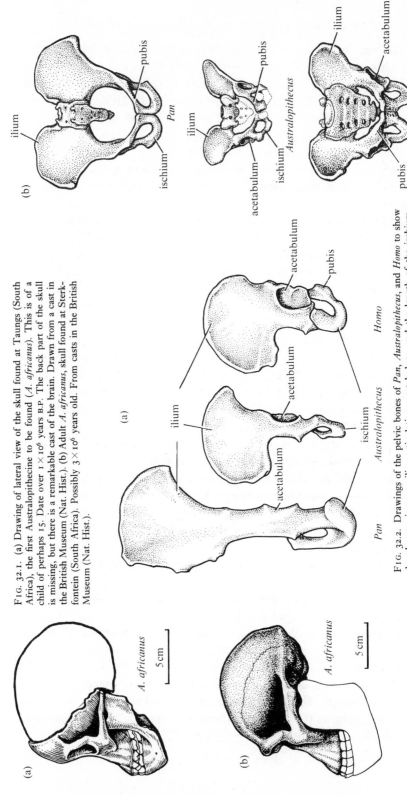

Fig. 32.1. (a) Drawing of lateral view of the skull found at Taungs (South Africa), the first Australopithecine to be found (*A. africanus*). This is of a child of perhaps 15. Date over 1×10^6 years B.P. The back part of the skull is missing, but there is a remarkable cast of the brain. Drawn from a cast in the British Museum (Nat. Hist.). (b) Adult *A. africanus*, skull found at Sterkfontein (South Africa). Possibly 3×10^6 years old. From casts in the British Museum (Nat. Hist.).

Fig. 32.2. Drawings of the pelvic bones of *Pan*, *Australopithecus*, and *Homo* to show the changes in sacro-iliac articulation, acetabulum, and the length of the ischium. (After Broom and Robinson in Grassé 1955.) The ilium of *Australopithecus* resembles that of man, but the ischium is much longer.

by Zuckerman and his colleagues at Birmingham, as were many other assertions of human affinities for these fossils (Zuckerman 1966). However, the evidence of some form of bipedalism is cumulatively rather strong, though this does not mean that the gait was identical with that of modern man.

The mastoid process is large (though smaller than in man). The ilium is known from Sterkfontein, Swartkrans, and Makapansgat and is short and broad, as in man, but with a small sacro-iliac articulation and an acetabulum different from that of man (Fig. 32.2). The ischium also differs from that of man quite markedly in being rather long, thus carrying the attachment of the hamstring muscles a long way from the acetabulum. This is a character of quadrupeds, giving a large mechanical advantage to the hamstring muscles for extension of the hip, drawing the leg backwards. In modern man, where these muscles have less part in propulsion, the ischium is short. It has been suggested that the Australopithecine gait was more a run than a walking stride (Washburn 1964, Napier 1964).

A foot is known from the remains in Olduvai Bed I referred to *H. habilis* (Fig. 32.3). Its general arrangement is very human. The first metatarsal is larger than the rest, but not as markedly as in *H. sapiens*. There is clear evidence that the foot was arched and the great toe not opposable.

The hand is also known from the remains in the bottom of Bed I and was very human, with a saddle-shaped joint on the trapezium, indicating an opposable thumb (Napier 1964). There were still some ape-like features, however, including curvature of the phalanges, and it is suggested that preceding the full bipedal habit, the weight may have rested on the knuckles (as in apes), while still allowing use of the hand for grasping (Washburn 1967). The opposable thumb was much shorter than in modern man, reaching little further than the base of the first phalanx of the index finger. The hand could exert a strong power grip, but not a precision grip (Figs. 34.4 and 34.5).

The dentition of *Australopithecus* provides features that are also interestingly suggestive

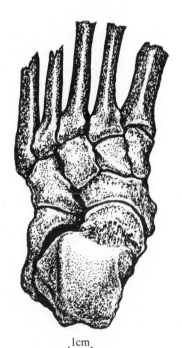

1cm

Australopithecus

FIG. 32.3. Foot of *A. africanus* from Olduvai Bed I, 2×10^6 years old. (After Day and Napier 1964.)

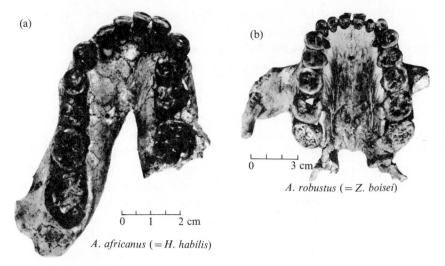

(a)

(b)

A. robustus (= Z. boisei)

```
0        3 cm
```

```
0    1    2 cm
```

A. africanus (= H. habilis)

FIG. 32.4. (a) Mandible of *A. africanus* (= *H. habilis* Olduvai Hominid 7). The jaw has been fractured on the right, before fossilization. Age: ?2×10^6 years. (From Day 1965.) (b) Palate and dentition of *A. robustus* (*Zinjanthropus*). Age: ?$1 \cdot 5 \times 10^6$ years. (From Day 1965.)

of man, yet not quite human. The dental arcade is rounded (Fig. 32.4), the canines are small and spatulate, and there is no diastema. The premolars and molars are much larger than in man and they increase in size to the third molar. These large teeth suggest a herbivorous diet, especially in *A. robustus* (Fig. 32.4(b)). In this connection, *A. robustus* teeth have many pits on the grinding surface, a typically herbivorous feature due to the grit on freshly dug roots (Robinson 1967). In this species there are very large jaws corresponding to the large brow-ridges and in some specimens there are quite prominent sagittal crests for the attachment of the temporalis muscles, which must have been powerful. The jugal bar is also thick, indicating a large masseter. On the other hand, the *A. africanus* teeth are smooth (like those of, say, a leopard), the jaws are lighter, and the skull has no crest (Fig. 32.1). These facts suggest that *A. africanus* was carnivorous and that the two species occurred in different habitats occupying different ecological niches from at least 2×10^6 years ago.

Further evidence for the carnivorous diet of *A. africanus* is furnished by the enormous piles of fossilized bones found in several caves investigated by Dart, such as one at Makapansgat, South Africa. Although it has been asserted that these bone collections were the work of hyaenas, it seems reasonably certain that they were made by *A. africanus*. (For a thorough summary of the evidence see Ardrey (1961).)

The question now arises, was *A. africanus* a scavenger, eating carrion and collecting bones for the marrow or did he *kill* animals? Two main lines

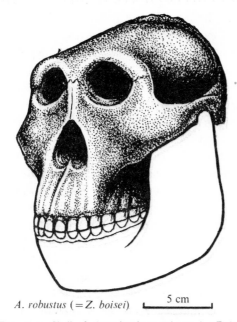

A. *robustus* (= Z. *boisei*) |——— 5 cm ———|

FIG. 32.5. Skull of *Australopithecus robustus* (= *Zinjan-thropus boisei*), from Olduvai Bed I. The jaw has been re-constructed from other specimens. Age about 1.5×10^6 years. From a cast in the British Museum (Nat. Hist.).

of evidence indicate that he did kill them, probably with weapons. The bone pile contained the fossilized bones and teeth of a wide range of animals from guineafowl and hares to baboons, hippopotami, and giraffes, and including *A. africanus* himself, a total of 4560 identifiable bones, portions of bone, and teeth (Dart 1957). First, there is very strong statistical evidence of systematic selection of bones *in the field* and their subsequent transport to the cave. The bones collected tended to be, with the exception of some whole heads, those that would either serve as knives (the mandible of a small antelope) or clubs (the distal portion of the humerus of a medium-sized antelope). The emphasis seemed to be on *functional* rather than *food* value—an example of foresight? The second line of evidence lies in the fact that of the crania collected the majority (including some belonging to *A. africanus*) appeared to have been struck with a heavy implement. It is not proved that this was the cause of death, but it is certain that the blow was not struck either after fossilization or well before death (i.e. there was no healing). Some outstanding examples were found (Dart 1949): the skull of a baboon with an antelope humerus bone (distal end) jammed through the open mouth and lodged in the base of the skull; a skull of *A. africanus* with a rock still embedded in it; another *africanus* skull with two small

holes in it, close together, entering at different angles. Of forty-two examin-
able baboon skulls, every one showed damage to the muzzle or cranium.
Moreover, on many specimens there was a double depression at the impact
point that exactly fitted the protuberances on the distal end of an antelope
humerus bone, which was the commonest bone in the Makapansgat pile.
Likewise it is interesting that most of these baboons received their (presumably fatal) injuries from the front. However it has also been suggested
that the depressions on the skull were made by leopards (Brain 1970).

In summary, it has been argued (especially by Dart and Ardrey) that
A. africanus was a carnivore, killed his prey, and killed his own kind. It is also
agreed that the Australopithecines are somewhere near to the line leading to
Homo. It does not follow that men have a 'need' to fight (Chapter 43).

The size of the brain of all Australopithecines was probably in the ape
range of 400-600 ml. Higher estimates (up to 700 ml) have been given (i.e.
for '*H. habilis*'), but are based on reconstruction of fragments and must be
regarded as uncertain at present. Attempts are made to stretch the range of
brain size of modern man in order to show that the Australopithecines
'nearly get there'. An immense range of modern human material is available, extending from 1000 to 2000 ml, but a useful mean is 1400 ml, with a
standard deviation of perhaps 150 ml. The Australopithecines may have
reached the *H. erectus* level of brain but do not come within the range of
H. sapiens, and this is one of their most interesting features (Tobias 1964).

It is clear that the interpretation of the '*habilis*' remains as 'human' rather
than Australopithecine is a question open to some doubt, especially as some
of the specimens may be of juveniles. The controversy serves only to suggest
that we are nearer than is often realized to having complete evidence of the
gradual transition from an ape-like form to man. Since some decision has
to be made as to how to name these fossils we shall include them with
Australopithecus africanus (following Simons 1967), but others would keep
A. boisei (Oakley 1968).

A further special interest of the *habilis* remains (and those of '*Zinjan-
thropus*') is that they were associated with chipped stone instruments
(Chapter 36). In addition there were the bones of numerous tortoises, cat-
fishes, and aquatic birds and the jaw of a sabre-toothed tiger. One of the
bones had probably been fashioned into a tool. There is thus some further
evidence of a carnivorous diet and it seems that these are the remains of a
population that used tools for hunting.

To debate whether they were 'really men' is to miss the point. The whole
interest of these creatures is that they were like, but not quite like, modern
man. What would be interesting would be evidence whether they were
or were not on the line leading directly to ourselves, but this we cannot

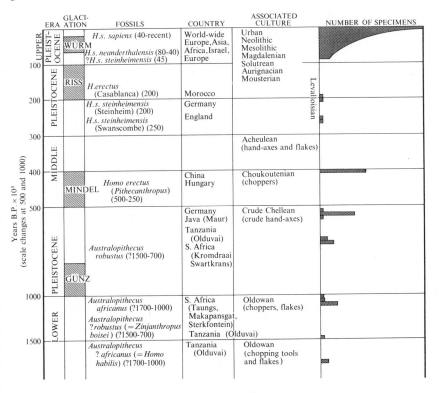

F I G. 32.6. Scheme showing relation of some Australopithecine finds to each other and to more recent hominid fossils. The last column gives the approximate number of individuals represented by the various finds; the smallest squares indicate one specimen. Notice the small number of specimens available and that they are widely scattered in time. Dating is still very tentative, especially for the Australopithecines of South Africa, which were fossilized in a limestone breccia that does not allow radiometric dating, see Table 32.2. (Partly after Campbell 1964.)

decide. If they did indeed make the primitive Oldowan flints then this shows that tool-making does not depend upon a large brain—but we know already that children make 'tools'.

Some important conclusions from these most interesting discoveries seem to be:

1. That human evolution has been 'mosaic'; hand and foot reached the human stage before brain size.

2. That creatures with ape-size brains could make and use tools.

3. That this stage was reached at least between 2·0 and 1·7 million years ago, much earlier than had been supposed.

4. That gradual changes proceeded along several related lines. It may well be that the *A. africanus* line went on to produce *Homo* while *A. robustus* remained herbivorous and became extinct.

TABLE 32.2

Summary of some data on hominid evolution

Approx. age (years) $\times 10^6$	Site	Authority	Possible name (and specimen number)	Estimated average cranial capacity (ml)
>9	Baringo, Kenya (Ngorora Beds)	Bishop and Chapman	(?) *Australopithecus*	
5	Lothagam, Kenya	Patterson	(?) *Australopithecus africanus*	
4	Kanapoi, Kenya	Patterson and Howells	(?) *A. africanus*	
3·5–3	Baringo, Kenya (Chemeron Beds)	King; Tobias	(?) *Australopithecus*	
3	Garusi, Tanzania	Kohl-Larsen; Robinson	(?) *A. africanus* (*Meganthropus*)	
4–1·75	Omo, Ethiopia	Howells; R. Leakey	(?) *A. robustus* (? *Zinjanthropus boisei*) (L7–125) *A. africanus* (W.23)	
?3	Sterkfontein, S.A.	Broom; Robinson	*A. africanus*	440
?2	Taungs, S.A.	Dart	*A. africanus*	440
1·9	Olduvai, Tanzania (Lower Bed I)	Leakey; Tobias; Napier; Oxnard	*A. robustus* (*Z. boisei*) (hominid 5) *A. africanus* (*Homo habilis*) (hominids 6, 7, and 8)	530 >600
2–?1·5	Makapansgat, S.A.	Dart	*A. africanus*	435
?1·25	Olduvai, Tanzania (Lower Bed II)	Leakey and Leakey; Tobias; Day	*A. robustus* (*Z. boisei*) (hominid 20) *A. africanus* (*H. habilis*) (hominids 10 and 16)	>600
1·5–?1	Swartkrans, S.A.	Broom; Robinson	*A. robustus* (*Paranthropus*) (?) *A. africanus* (*Telanthropus*)	530
1·5–1	Kromdraai, S.A.	Broom	*A. robustus* (*Paranthropus*)	475
1·0	Olduvai, Tanzania (Upper Bed II)	Tobias	*A. africanus* (*H. habilis*) (hominids 13 and 14) *A. robustus* (*Z. boisei*) (hominid 3)	590
?1·0	Peninj, Tanzania	Isaac and R. Leakey; Tobias	*A. robustus*	
?1·0	Olduvai, Tanzania	Leakey	*Homo erectus* (hominid 9)	1000
1·0	Lantien, China		(?) *H. erectus*	780
1·0	Djetis, Java	von Koenigswald	*H. erectus*	750
0·7–0·5	Trinil, Java	Dubois	*H. erectus*	775–975
0·5	Pekin, China	Black; Weidenreich	*H. erectus*	1050 (850–1300)
0·4	Vértesszöllös, Hungary		*H. erectus*	1400
0·2	Steinheim, Germany Swanscombe, England		*H. sapiens steinheimensis*	1200
0·07–0·04	Dusseldorf, Germany Mt. Carmel, Israel Shanidor, Iraq Broken Hill, Zambia		*H. s. neanderthalensis*	1600
0·04–0·00	Niah, Borneo Cro-Magnon, France, etc.		*H. s. sapiens*	1400

There has recently been a rapid increase in knowledge of the African Pliocene and Pleistocene deposits, necessitating caution over dates mentioned in the text (Pilbeam 1970 and personal communication, Bishop and Chapman 1970, Patterson, Behrensmeyer, and Sill 1970). Table 32.2 attempts to summarize new and old data and to present a view of current knowledge of hominid evolution.

There is new evidence from Omo of numerous teeth of hominids existing up to 4 million years ago and a mandible at Lothagam about 5 million years ago. A single molar crown at Ngorora is more than 9 million years old. There is now evidence of tools as much as 2·6 million years old (R. Leakey 1970).

On the other hand the date of Upper Bed II at Olduvai and of the Peninj deposits is now uncertain and may be not later than 1 million years. In that case it may be that the Australopithecines did not continue, as such, much beyond that time. However there is also evidence that some of them may have then transformed into early types of *H. erectus*. Further facts about these questions can be expected shortly (see Clark 1970 for recent data).

33

THE APPEARANCE OF *HOMO*

FAMILY HOMINIDAE. Ages $\times 10^6$ years ago

Ramapithecus (14–6)	Asia, Africa
including *Kenyapithecus*	

Australopithecus (?3·5–?0·7)	Africa,
A. africanus (?3·5–?0·7)	Olduvai, Taungs, Sterk-
including *Homo habilis, Plesianthropus*	fontein, Makapansgat
A. robustus (?3·5–?0·7)	Kromdraai, Swartkrans,
including *Paranthropus, Zinjanthropus*	Olduvai

Homo (?0·5–Recent)	World-wide
H. erectus	Asia, Africa
including *Pithecanthropus, Sinathropus,*	
Atlanthropus	
H. erectus erectus (0·5–0·4)	Java, Heidelberg,
	?Olduvai
H. erectus sinensis (0·4–0·25)	Pekin
H. sapiens (0·25–Recent)	
including *Javanthropus, Palaeoanthropus,*	
Cyphanthropus, Protanthropus,	
H. sapiens steinheimensis	Swanscombe, Steinheim
(0·25–0·20)	
H. sapiens neanderthalensis	La Chapelle, Tabun,
(0·07–0·045)	Skūhl, Krapina
including *soloensis, rhodesiensis*	Fontéchevade, Broken
	Hill, Saldanha
H. sapiens sapiens	Cro-Magnon, Chance-
(0·04–Recent)	lade, Grimaldi

Unplaced: *Gigantopithecus, Telanthropus, Meganthropus*

1. The gradual appearance of man

BIOLOGISTS probably mostly agree that the question of which fossils are truly those of a man cannot ever be settled. If evolutionary change is gradual it is not simply difficult to solve such questions, it is *impossible* in principle. Apart from the difficulty of the gradualness of change there is the question of definition, which is bound to be to some extent arbitrary. A sudden beginning for man might be imagined as the result of the operation of some creative process, not found elsewhere. The endowment of the race by some outside force, agent, or God with a new entity 'the soul' would be such a process, and of course it is not to be ruled out arbitrarily that this is what happened. Again there might, conceivably, have been a sudden genetic mutation, in one person, leading his descendants to be not only highly successful but also fertile only among themselves. We could then say that he was the first man. A possible suggestion of this sort is that the size of the brain was suddenly doubled by the addition of one more cell division before the end of multiplication of neurons. Such suggestions are not likely to be made by anyone who has studied evolutionary problems closely. He will be much more ready to suppose that some interbreeding but varied population gradually changed until it reached the condition we recognize as that of *Homo sapiens*, itself a collection of very distinct people today.

But the fact that other organisms have been shown to evolve in this way must not prejudice us. What we need is not speculation as to how man might conceivably have arisen, but evidence as to how he did. This can only come from fossils, and the facts we have described already show that up to the stage that may be called pre-man (*Australopithecus*) the changes were gradual. *Ramapithecus* was more like man than were the Dryopithecines, *Australopithecus* was more like a man than *Ramapithecus*, and so on. The series is very incomplete and the existence of sudden small jumps cannot be ruled out, but the evidence is compatible with gradual change. Moreover the human character appears in some features (the gait) before others (size of brain); this is the phenomenon called mosaic evolution.

Perhaps it is at the last stage of all that we should be most prepared to expect the occurrence of some sudden change. Man is indeed very different from all other animals, even from such fossils as those of *Australopithecus*. We feel that we must be in some way widely divergent from them, the product of some special and perhaps sudden process. This feeling is egocentric but cannot be dismissed as wholly irrational. Modern man *is* very different. Can we believe that there has been a gradual evolution of his habits of co-operation, of his language, of his self-consciousness and conscience, of his religion, his art, and his artefacts? The answer in the one case where we have data is *yes*, for the artefacts. There is a continuous series from the first African pebble tools of perhaps 2 million years or more ago, to the flying machines and rockets of today. The development of language is certainly related to that of tools, but we do not know how closely, especially in the early stages.

Man's special features are mostly directed to the habit of co-operation in the business of life, especially perhaps in the use of artefacts. Self-awareness and individuality also have a place in this pattern of co-operation, and we shall have to consider these matters separately later (Chapters 34-6). For the present we are concerned to provide an outline of the time-scale of human origin. It was apparently surprisingly rapid, especially considering the magnitude of the change. Of course there may conceivably have been humans alive during the 20 million years of the Miocene and Pliocene, or even earlier. It is impossible to prove a negative. But the fact that quite numerous ape fossils have been found in that period, but men fossils *only* later makes us conclude provisionally that men have appeared within the last two million years. Assuming rather more than four generations to a century this allows for some 100 000 generations. This certainly gives some margin for gradual change when we think that there have been only perhaps 500 generations since man emerged from the last ice age.

The decisive evidence, however, is that such fossils as have been found show that there have existed creatures who were anatomically intermediate between the Australopithecine types and modern man. The series is not complete and interpretation is difficult, but these early forms are indisputably not quite modern man as we know him today. Taken with the evidence of the evolution of tools the finding of these fossils makes us adopt the hypothesis of continuous steady change. The possibility of sudden jumps will perhaps never be rigorously excluded, but this must not of course be read to mean that the evidence in any way suggests that such jumps occurred.

These intermediate forms are the remains of populations referred to three further taxonomic groups before the appearance of modern man (*Homo sapiens sapiens*). The first of these, the Java and Pekin men, used to be placed in a separate genus *Pithecanthropus erectus*, now usually referred to as a distinct species of the genus *Homo*, *H. erectus*. They lived from perhaps 1 000 000 (Upper Bed II, Olduvai) to 250 000 years ago (Casablanca). The other groups antecedent to modern man include the Neanderthalers, previously also given specific status (*H. neanderthalensis*) but now usually treated as a distinct early subspecies *H. sapiens neanderthalensis*, and two skulls of an earlier date classed as *H. s. steinheimensis*. Besides these three reasonably well-defined forms of hominid there are isolated fossil fragments of some twenty further types that had not reached the stage of modern man. We shall not describe them in detail but the existence of these fragments strengthens the suggestion that human evolution was gradual, with many different branches (Fig. 33.1). Moreover, as we should expect, as further fossils are found it becomes increasingly difficult to fit them into

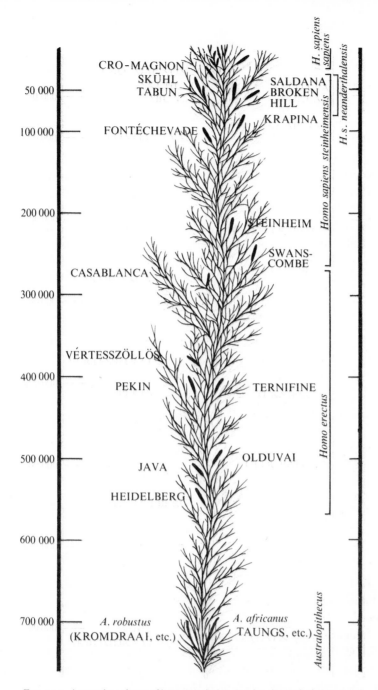

FIG. 33.1. A tentative scheme of human evolution showing the gradual change and that there must have been many different branches and anastomoses of slightly separated lines. Note that there is no main 'trunk'. Some known fossil remains are shown in their relative positions but the dating of the early forms is uncertain. *H. s. steinheimensis* is shown surviving till 45 000 years ago to include such skulls as those of Fontéchevade and Skūhl, but this is doubtfully correct (p. 465).

clear-cut categories. This is irritating for the systematically minded 'typo-logists', but for the evolutionist the existence of this difficulty is itself the best evidence that gradual change occurred.

2. *Homo erectus*

The first fossils of *H. erectus* were found in Java in 1891 and the species is often called 'Java man'. Other specimens have been found there since and still others in China ('*Sinanthropus*') (Fig. 33.2). More recently remains of similar creatures have been found in East Africa (Olduvai Upper Bed II, hominid 9 'Chellean man'), South Africa ('*Telanthropus*') and at Ternifine and Casablanca in North Africa ('*Atlanthropus*'). The single jaw of '*H. heidelbergensis*' is a similar type from Germany. Not all are contemporary,

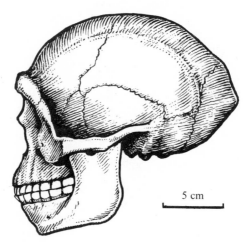

5 cm

FIG. 33.2. Lateral view of skull of female 'Pekin man' (*H. erectus*). The possessor lived about 400 000 years ago. Note massive jaw and low forehead. From cast in the British Museum (Nat. Hist.).

the Olduvai specimens being among the earlier and in some respects less advanced. All the remains, however, are of creatures quite close to man (many modern anthropologists wish to include *H. erectus* within *H. sapiens*). The foramen magnum is further forward than in *Australopithecus* and the upright gait is confirmed by remains of several femora, which are very human. No pelves, hands, or feet are known.

The skull of *H. erectus* was massive and thick, with cranial capacities from 775 to 1200 ml (see below). The shape of the skull differed from that of *H. sapiens* in the low forehead, perhaps a significant sign that the frontal lobes were poorly developed and hence these were people of not quite human character (p. 487). On the other hand, the occipital region was well developed. The jaw was much heavier than in modern man, but less so than in *Australopithecus* (Fig. 33.3). Correspondingly there are never special temporal crests (as in *A. robustus*) and the zygoma is thinner than in the Australopithecine fossils but still thicker than in *H. sapiens*. The teeth are of typically human cusp-pattern and the third molar is smaller than the second. Yet, once again the teeth are larger than in most modern men (Fig. 33.3) (Howell 1960, Day 1965). These people were probably omnivorous.

One of the most important of the many results of investigations by the Leakeys at Olduvai has been to show the possibility of a gradual evolution from *Australopithecus* to *H. erectus*. Specimens that can reasonably be referred to the former genus occur in the lowest beds of the series, now dated up to 2 million years before the present. Maxillae and mandibles found in the lower-middle Bed II at Olduvai have been referred to as a more hominid version of '*H. habilis*' (Tobias 1965). These are about 1 million years old and may represent intermediates between *Australopithecus* and *H. erectus*. The latter also occurs at Olduvai, from the top of

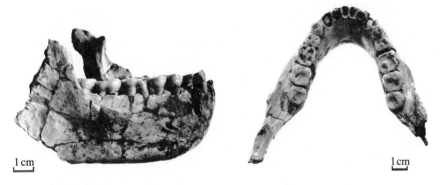

FIG. 33.3. Mandibles of *H. erectus* from Ternifine, Algeria, North Africa. Lived about 400 000 years ago. Note massive jaw and large teeth. Third molar smaller than second. (From Day 1965.)

Bed II, dated at perhaps 500 000 years B.P. (Tobias *et al.* 1965, Hay 1963). These remains are very like those of some of the early Asian *H. erectus*, skulls from Modjokerto and Sangiran in Java, the former an infant. The age of these Javan fossils is uncertain, but is probably greater than 500 000 years and perhaps as much as 700 000. Though fragmentary, they have been judged to have cranial capacities of only 780 ml and 900 ml, while the estimate for the African form is 900–1000 ml. These specimens together thus suggest that by the middle Pleistocene period more nearly human creatures had evolved, perhaps from some Australopithecine stock, possibly represented by *A. africanus*.

The remaining specimens of *H. erectus* include the more complete ones from Trinil, in Java, and those from China. They are probably of a rather later date, 550 000–350 000 years B.P., and some had larger brains (range of cranial capacities 915–1225 ml). It is interesting that the distribution of these finds extends much further north than that of any hominid of earlier date (41° in China, 49° in Germany). Correlated with this there is evidence, from ash heaps and charcoal in the cave in which the remains were found near Peking, that *H. erectus* not only sought shelter in caves but used fire. The date for the cave is about 400 000 years B.P. and this is the earliest evidence of the use of fire. Remains of various mammals were also found, including large carnivores, a deer, and rhinoceros. Cores and flakes of a crude chopper industry were found ('Choukoutienian') and were presumably used to cut up the prey. The *H. erectus* skull at Olduvai is also accompanied by tools, of Chellean type (Chapter 36). Fragments of jaws found at Casablanca in Morocco are similar to the other remains of *Homo erectus* and perhaps show that this type survived until 250 000 years ago, but the dating is uncertain. Thus the *Homo erectus* populations, although distinctly different from modern man, had already developed some important features of culture. Their brain size was intermediate between that of *Australopithecus* and modern man. All we know of them suggests that they were truly an intermediate stage of primitive man and they lived throughout Europe, Asia, and Africa from about 1 000 000 to 250 000 years ago.

3. The appearance of *Homo sapiens*

The fact that some modern anthropologists would like to include *H. erectus* within *H. sapiens*, though confusing, confirms us in the supposition that our species arose gradually. The earliest fossils referred to *H. sapiens* are the skulls from Swanscombe in the Lower Thames Valley and Steinheim in Germany, dated *c*. 250 000 and *c*. 200 000 years B.P. respectively (Fig. 33.4). They were people we should almost certainly recognize as human, though with thick skulls. Of course we do not know whether they had all the characters we expect in a human today, particularly speech. It is convenient therefore to place them in a distinct subspecies of *H. sapiens steinheimensis*. There is then an unfortunate gap in the record until about 50 000 B.P. After that time, remains are abundant and there is a gratifying confusion of opinions as to how they should be classified. Indeed the next population to be mentioned, Neanderthal man, is still often referred to as a distinct species, *H. neanderthalensis*. The name comes from the first fossil skull to be scientifically studied, found in the Neander valley near Dusseldorf in 1856. Before describing the Neanderthalers we meet again the familiar difficulty that they were not all alike! The 'Classic

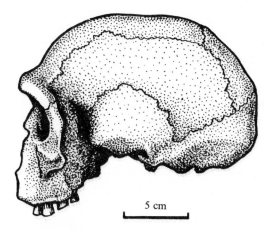

F I G. 33.4. *Homo sapiens steinheimensis.* Age: 200 000 years.
From a cast of the Steinheim skull in the British Museum
(Nat. Hist.).

Neanderthalers' were somewhat different from modern man, the 'Progressive Neanderthalers' much more like him.

In the classic Neanderthal type (*H. s. neanderthalensis*) the face was narrow, long, and prognathous. The brow ridges were quite prominent and formed a continuous supraorbital torus or ridge above the eyes (Fig. 33.5). This character suggests somewhat powerful jaw muscles, and the

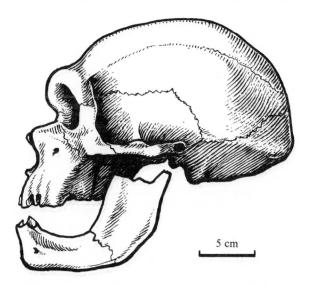

F I G. 33.5. *H. sapiens neanderthalensis.* The 'classic' Neanderthal skull from La Chapelle aux Saints. Age: 40 000 years. From a cast in the British Museum (Nat. Hist.).

jaws and teeth were indeed generally heavier than today. The teeth sometimes show a rather enlarged pulp cavity and small roots (taurodontism).
The chin was small. The cranial capacity was as large as today, indeed many
skulls are very large, about 1600 ml. Characteristically the forehead appeared
low, perhaps because the torus was large, and the occipital region was well
developed, both being of course also features of *H. erectus*. The post-
cranial skeleton is well known and shows no major differences from that
of today. Neanderthalers are often shown as if walking with a bent back
and shuffling gait, but there is no justification for this (Straus and Cave
1957). These classic Neanderthalers are found at some of the best known
sites, including Spy (Belgium), Le Moustier and La Chapelle (France),
Neanderthal (Germany), Gibraltar and eastwards to the Crimea, Palestine,
and Iraq. There are indications that similar types existed in Africa (at
Broken Hill in Zambia, 'Rhodesian Man', Fig. 33.8, and at Saldanha Bay,
South Africa). Eleven skulls found at Solo in Java show the existence of
'tropical Neanderthalers'.

In the progressive Neanderthalers living at the same time the brain
case was short and narrow, with a high forehead and reduced occiput
(Fig. 33.6). These are in fact nearly typical skulls of modern *H. sapiens
sapiens*. A difference is in the thickness of the bones of the vault and weight
of the jaw. These seem to be the skulls of people like modern man except
for the fact that they had to work harder with their jaws to obtain nourishment. Such skulls have been found at many places, Ehringsdorf in Germany, Fontéchevade (France), Saccopastore (Italy), Krapina (Jugoslavia),
and at Skūhl (Israel) and in Uzbekistan (U.S.S.R.). With the exception
of the last two these progressive Neanderthalers are all from Europe. This
may be only an accident of preservation and discovery.

The existence of the two types has led many people to suppose that
the classic Neanderthalers were an aberrant line, not leading to modern
man, and that they were exterminated by invaders of the progressive
type. The incomplete skull at Fontéchevade and a mandible found at
Montmaurin in France were associated with bones indicating a warm
climate, probably of the Riss-Würm or Last Interglacial period, that is,
more than 70 000 years ago. They provide almost the only link between
the Swanscombe and Steinheim skulls and the progressive neanderthalers,
such as those at Skūhl.

On Mount Carmel in Israel there are two nearby caves, one containing
classical Neanderthalers (Tabun) and the other those of a more progressive
type (Skūhl). Carbon dating gives 45 000 ± 2000 years B.P. for both caves
(but Skūhl may be 10 000 years later). These finds show dramatically the
problem of analysing the relationships of these remains of the peoples who

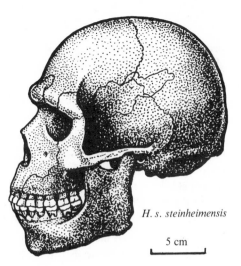

FIG. 33.6. *H. sapiens steinheimensis.* Progressive Neanderthal skull from Skūhl. Age: 45 000 years. From a reconstituted cast in the British Museum (Nat. Hist.).

H. s. steinheimensis

5 cm

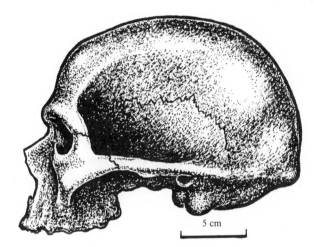

FIG. 33.7. Cro-Magnon skull, an early specimen of *H. sapiens sapiens.* Age: 25 000 years. From photo in Day 1965 and British Museum (Nat. Hist.) cast.

H. s. sapiens

5 cm

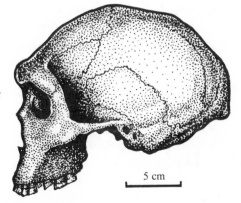

H.s. neanderthalensis

FIG. 33.8. Rhodesian skull (*H. sapiens neanderthalensis*). Age: about 40 000 years. From cast in British Museum (Nat. Hist.).

5 cm

presumably included our immediate ancestors. From as long ago as 250 000 years there were people with brains fully as large as ours, but with rather heavier jaws and thick skulls. In the classic Neanderthalers living very much later, these primitive features were especially marked and these characteristics remained clear in some populations until 40 000 years ago. But long before that the progressive Neanderthalers were in existence throughout Europe and it was probably from them that undoubtedly human peoples arose (*H. sapiens sapiens*), sometime after 40 000 years ago. For this reason skulls of the progressive Neanderthalers are often said to be of 'pre-sapiens' type. But we really do not know whether they represent a single group persisting over the very long period between the skulls at Swanscombe (250 000 B.P.) and Skūhl (45 000 B.P.). At any rate, this last date corresponds approximately in time with the earliest undoubted remains of *H. sapiens sapiens*, found in Borneo (Niah) aged 40 000 years. Fully human remains of somewhat later date have been found in France (Combe-Chapelle, 34 000, and Cro-Magnon, 25 000 years old respectively Fig. 33.7), and Zambia (Mumbwai, 23 000 years old).

We have to admit, therefore, that in spite of the relatively large number of fossils available the evidence is still not adequate to say much about the subdivisions of these early human populations with any scientific precision. We can make statistical distinctions that will refer specimens to one of the two groups, and methods for estimating the degree of similarity, based upon a number of measurements, have recently been applied to these early human populations (Campbell 1964). The statistical technique derives from Fisher's discriminant function and it expresses the morphological distance between specimens on a basis of all the characters that can be quantified, thus avoiding the problem of selection of features to measure. Five hundred *H. sapiens sapiens* skulls of Bronze Age were taken as a basis, and the divergence of the Swanscombe, Skūhl, and La Chapelle skulls from these is shown in Fig. 33.9. Different figures are given according to whether the Swanscombe skull is considered to be male or female. In addition the position of eighteen skulls taken from all the major modern 'races' of man are shown. The values express only the degree of divergence from the reference population, not the direction of divergence. It is clear that the 'progressive Neanderthalers' differed strongly from the classical ones (e.g. La Chapelle) and that they also differ from all modern populations, but not by very much. It seems probable that all the Neanderthalers were variants within one interbreeding population, from some part or parts of which modern man evolved. The culture of Neanderthal man is discussed on p. 506.

No doubt there was a great deal of variation in the human population then, as there is today. Probably there were cultural differences, some

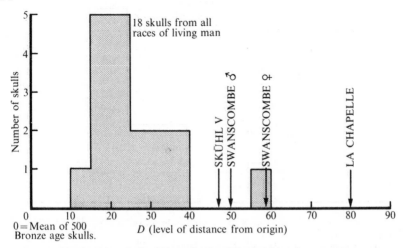

F I G. 33.9. Measurements of a discriminant function ('D² values') based on seventeen measurements of parietal and occipital bones of modern and fossil men. The ordinate shows the number of skulls that show each level of departure from the mean dimensions of a modern population (at the origin). The Swanscombe and Skūhl skulls are nearer to the modern condition than is a 'classical' Neanderthaler (La Chapelle). Two values for Swanscombe are given, one assuming it is a male, the other female. (From Campbell 1964.)

associated with physical differences. Both the physique and the culture of each group was presumably suited to particular conditions—as also today (Chapter 38). There is, however, no more justification for dividing these populations of our ancestors into distinct races, if by that is meant groups that could not mix either genetically or culturally, than there is for man today. No more justification and no less. Difference in physique and culture has meant different ways of life, in the past as today. Mixing of the genes and the cultures seems to go on extensively at present and there is no reason to think that it has not done so for a very long time. Nevertheless the variation remains. The fact that it was already present among our ancestors 50 000 or more years ago suggests that variation may be one of the main secrets of the success of man, as it is of many other species. Polymorphic hereditary characteristics only remain side by side in a population if each of them has some special advantage to confer, at least under certain circumstances. Such polymorphism allows the species to maintain itself in a number of slightly different habitats and it is correspondingly ready to become changed if there are large changes in the environment.

   It is an interesting question whether human evolution has proceeded especially fast (p. 400). Using Haldane's (1949) unit of increase or decrease of a character by 1/1000 per 1000 years (=1 darwin) it is calculated from the shape of the skull that from 'Pekin man' to modern man the rate has been 620 millidarwins (md). This is fast compared with maxima of 78 md

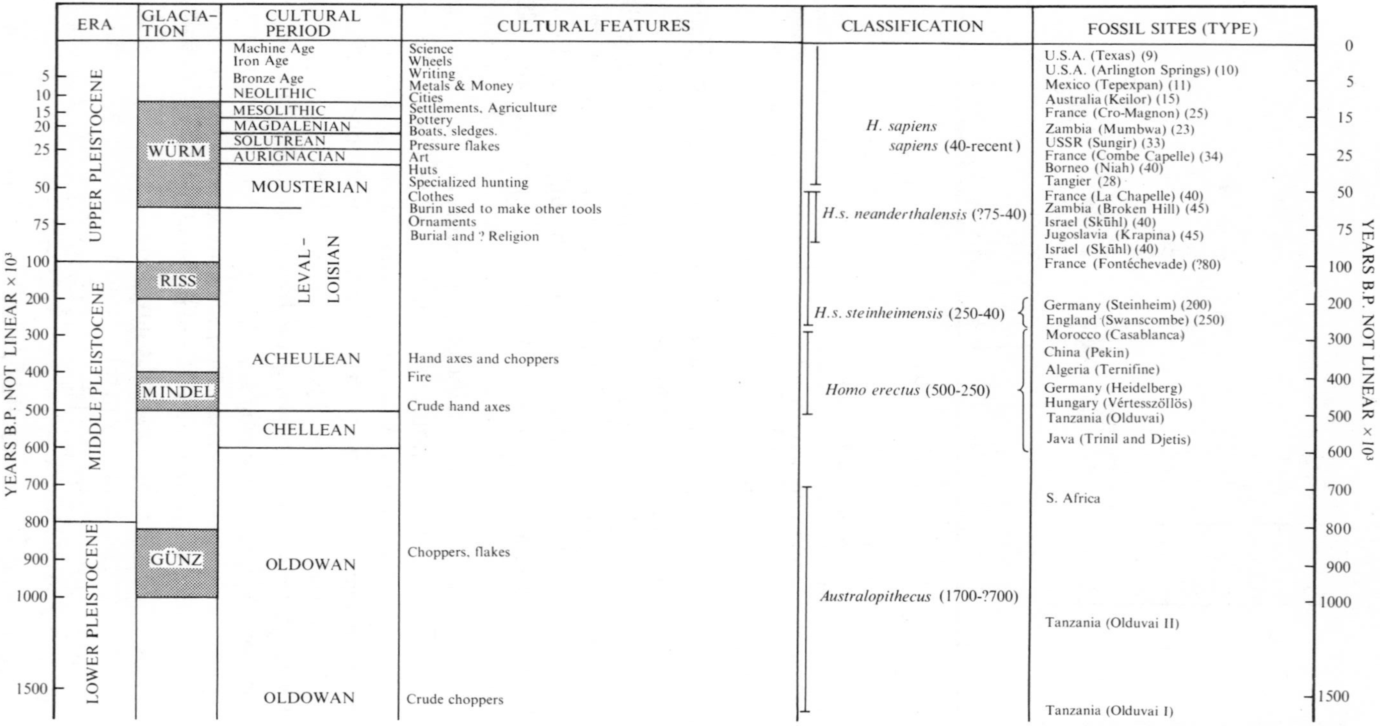

ERA
GLACIATION
CULTURAL PERIOD
CULTURAL FEATURES
CLASSIFICATION
FOSSIL SITES (TYPE)
YEARS B.P. NOT LINEAR × 10³
0
5
10
15
20
25
50
75
100
200
300
400
500
600
700
800
900
1000
1500
UPPER PLEISTOCENE
MIDDLE PLEISTOCENE
LOWER PLEISTOCENE
WÜRM
RISS
MINDEL
GÜNZ
Machine Age
Iron Age
Bronze Age
NEOLITHIC
MESOLITHIC
MAGDALENIAN
SOLUTREAN
AURIGNACIAN
MOUSTERIAN
LEVAL-LOISIAN
ACHEULEAN
CHELLEAN
OLDOWAN
OLDOWAN
Science
Wheels
Writing
Metals & Money
Cities
Settlements, Agriculture
Pottery
Boats, sledges.
Pressure flakes
Art
Huts
Specialized hunting
Clothes
Burin used to make other tools
Ornaments
Burial and ? Religion
Hand axes and choppers
Fire
Crude hand axes
Choppers, flakes
Crude choppers
H. sapiens sapiens (40-recent)
H.s. neanderthalensis (?75-40)
H.s. steinheimensis (250-40)
Homo erectus (500-250)
Australopithecus (1700-?700)
U.S.A. (Texas) (9)
U.S.A. (Arlington Springs) (10)
Mexico (Tepexpan) (11)
Australia (Keilor) (15)
France (Cro-Magnon) (25)
Zambia (Mumbwa) (23)
USSR (Sungir) (33)
France (Combe Capelle) (34)
Borneo (Niah) (40)
Tangier (28)
France (La Chapelle) (40)
Zambia (Broken Hill) (45)
Israel (Skūhl) (40)
Jugoslavia (Krapina) (45)
Israel (Skūhl) (40)
France (Fontéchevade) (?80)
Germany (Steinheim) (200)
England (Swanscombe) (250)
Morocco (Casablanca)
China (Pekin)
Algeria (Ternifine)
Germany (Heidelberg)
Hungary (Vértesszöllös)
Tanzania (Olduvai)
Java (Trinil and Djetis)
S. Africa
Tanzania (Olduvai II)
Tanzania (Olduvai I)

FIG. 33.10. Scheme to show fossils of early man and the various approximate dates and associated cultures. The scale is not linear. (*H. s. steinheimensis* is shown surviving to 45 000 years ago. See Fig. 33.1 and p. 466.)

for the teeth of horses throughout the Tertiary and 60 md for size of dinosaurs. Brain volume seems to have increased very rapidly before and at the time of appearance of modern man, but little since (Table 33.1). Indeed some Neanderthalers had larger brains than ourselves. It will be seen that the estimated rate differs somewhat with the character used (620 md for skull shape, 732 md for cranial capacity).

TABLE 33.1

*Rate of evolution of man. Change of 1/1000 part per 1000 years=
1 darwin. (After Campbell 1964.) Some of the dates used in this
table differ from those adopted elsewhere in this chapter*

	Date B.P. $\times 10^6$	Cranial capacity (ml)	Rate in md
Australopithecus	1·2	500	..
to			
H. erectus (Java)	0·5	900	280
to			
H. erectus (Pekin)	0·4	1000	351
to			
H. sapiens steinheimensis	0·15	1325	375
to (Swanscombe)			
H. sapiens sapiens (modern)	0·0	1375	6

34

SOME DETERMINANTS OF HUMAN
EVOLUTION

1. What is meant by the causes of evolution?

BEFORE trying to find what has 'caused' man to emerge we should have to inquire into the meaning of 'causation' and the question whether evolution can be said to have causes. Evolution is our name for the series of changes that occur as populations adapt to their changing surroundings. Mankind at any given moment of time is one of the populations that have resulted. In so far as the achievement of that state can be said to have causes, they are to be found in the past history of the populations and of the environmental changes that occurred. The nature of the populations will, of course, include those tendencies to strive to survive, to add to living matter, and to find new environments, that together provide the basis for the purposive activities that man, like other organisms, presents by his aspirations (p. 606).

The prime factors that have caused our evolution must thus be sought in the natures of our ancestors, that is to say, in primate life in general. This in turn is to be sought in the way of life of mammals, of tetrapods, of vertebrates, of their ancestors, and ultimately in the character of life. These are all technically proximate causes and it is questionable whether we can attach any exact significance to the concept of a final cause (p. 635). We have seen how all the adaptive changes can be considered as a sequence of selections made among rather limited sets of elements, molecules, organelles, and cell-types. As the selection proceeds, under the pressure of environmental stress and competition, new types of living systems are continually emerging. Our present task is to try to identify the factors that have been especially responsible for *human* life.

2. The influence of tree life

The basic determinant of the primate system of life has been life in the trees. Therefore a prime determinant of human life was the evolution of trees from the Permian period onwards (Fig. 27.2). Presumably the development of luxuriant tropical forests in the Eocene and Oligocene gave an especially large premium to the development of monkeys and apes. Tree life is often associated with rapid and agile movement, good senses, and a good brain. All of these were essentials as a basis for the human achievements of manipulating, tool-making, observation, and, finally, speaking, thinking, and reasoning. Vision is especially useful in the trees, where olfactory tracks and signs are more difficult to place and recognize than on the ground (though lemurs use marking with scent). Accordingly the olfactory organ and the part of the brain associated with it becomes relatively smaller passing up the primate series (Fig. 34.1). In the trees

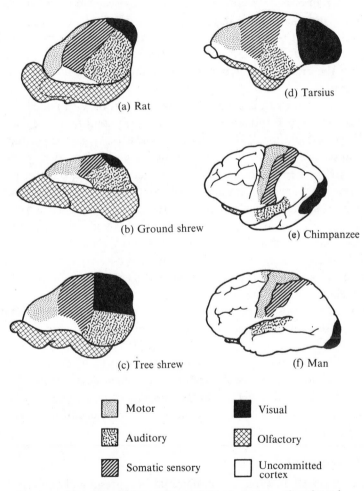

(a) Rat

(d) Tarsius

(b) Ground shrew

(e) Chimpanzee

(c) Tree shrew

(f) Man

☐ Motor   ■ Visual

▦ Auditory   ▨ Olfactory

▨ Somatic sensory   ☐ Uncommitted cortex

FIG. 34.1. Mammalian brains, to show variations in the proportions devoted to different activities. The comparison can only be rough because important parts are often concealed. The area devoted to olfaction is much reduced in primates. The area marked 'uncommitted cortex' is not related to particular sensory or motor functions. It includes the parietal association areas and much of the frontal and pre-frontal lobes (see Fig. 35.1). (After Penfield, in Eccles 1966.)

communication between individuals by smell is also not very effective. Hence visual and auditory methods of signalling are developed by primates, as they are also in birds. Communication by visual and auditory signals provides the base for much more precise statements than can be achieved by depositing scents. The latter are admirable as signs widely addressed, 'to whom it may concern', by which an animal signals its condition, whether it be the fear substances released by fishes or the sex stimulants of mammals. But scents do not seem to provide an alphabet of signs useful for objective description of outside events (though this may seem so to us only because we do not use them in this way).

Another effect of tree life is that the primate mother can carry only a small number of young and must look after them well. This feature made possible the emergence of the human condition of prolonged childhood and learning.

These are some of the aspects of primates that have provided the background from which human life emerged. Such conditions are sometimes called 'pre-adaptations', but it is not clear what is gained by this label. Adaptation is a process of change to meet a particular existing condition in the environment. It has a future reference, it is true, but this is on the basis that the particular condition will continue to exist. The word 'pre-adaptation' suggests that a particular living state has been developed in anticipation that it will be useful for homeostasis under some conditions that have not yet existed. It is doubtful whether even man can be said to make forecasts in this sense. If we speak of pre-adaptation it should only be in the sense of noting that the existence of one condition made possible the development of some others.

Perhaps the most important of all these characteristics of primate life for the development of man was the tendency to investigate and observe, and then to remember the results and so to plan each individual life, and if necessary to seek out new and diverse environments. These activities were certainly stimulated by tree life and the consequent developments of senses and brain. They led, together, to the appearance of the phenomenon that we call mentality or thinking, dependent upon the use of internal models in the brain.

3. The return to the ground

The particular features of the hominid line presumably emerged when populations endowed with these arboreal gifts were forced to leave the trees. There is much evidence that during the Miocene period many forest areas turned into open plains or tundra. This was the stimulus that led to the evolution of the horses and fast-moving ungulates. Although no undoubted fossil hominids are known from the Miocene there is evidence that types such as *Ramapithecus* were beginning to show human characters, but unfortunately we are ignorant of their method of locomotion.

There has been debate as to whether the bipedal gait emerged from animals that were strictly quadrupedal, or from those that jumped, or from semi-brachiators. The jumping habit produces an upright posture of a sort, and may lead to efficient bipedal locomotion (as seen for example in the Indrid lemurs such as *Propithecus*). There are some similarities between hominids and the jumping tarsioid prosimians (Chapter 30). Wood Jones (1943) went so far as to suggest that the human stock arose in this way in the Eocene, and has remained separate from that of monkeys and apes ever since. The evidence that has been reviewed certainly suggests divergence of man from a stock previously related to the tarsioids.

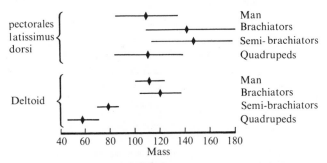

F I G. 34.2. Relative masses of arm muscles in man and various brachiators, semi-brachiators, and quadrupeds among primates. The pectorales and latissimus dorsi are propulsive muscles; the deltoid is an arm-raiser (abductor). Man is nearer to the quadrupeds in respect to the first group but to the brachiators in the second. (After Campbell 1966, data from Oxnard 1963.)

It is more likely, however, that the bipedal gait of man emerged from creatures that were at least semi-brachiators, often swinging from their arms, but frequently walking and standing on their hind legs while supported by their arms. The habit of brachiation demands great mobility of the upper limb, especially at the shoulder joint and also by movements of pronation and supination at the forearms and flexion of the long phalanges of the hands. All these features are characteristic of man although he does not use them for brachiation. Man is more similar to the apes than to monkeys in the muscles that move the arms (Fig. 34.2). In respect of the angle of the glenoid cavity of the scapula, man definitely departs from the apes (Fig. 34.3) and also, incidentally, from *Australopithecus* (Chapter 32). The apes other than gibbons in any case live much of their lives on the ground. They mainly go on all fours, using the knuckles of the hands, but walking on two legs is quite common. The fossil evidence, such as it is,

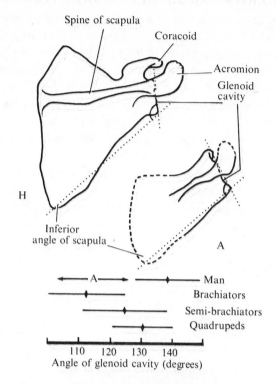

Spine of scapula

Coracoid

Acromion

Glenoid cavity

H

Inferior angle of scapula

A

←——A——→ ————+———— Man

————————+———————— Brachiators

————————————+———— Semi-brachiators

————————————+—— Quadrupeds

110   120   130   140
Angle of glenoid cavity (degrees)

FIG. 34.3. Estimates of the angle of the plane of the glenoid cavity (in degrees) with respect to the scapula (see dotted lines). In this angle man (H) is closer to the quadrupeds than to the brachiators. The angle in *Australopithecus* (A) is much nearer that of the brachiators than of man. (After Campbell 1966, after Broom *et al*, 1950, and Oxnard 1963.)

suggests that the hominid line arose from some semi-brachiating pre-ape such as *Dryopithecus* (Proconsul) (Fig. 34.4), and we can reasonably conclude that the features of the arms originated in this way.

It is less easy to see signs that the foot of such an animal could readily give rise to the human one. Very drastic changes are required in the whole lower limb to produce the full striding bipedal gait. The gluteus maximus muscle is turned from an abductor into an extensor of the hip, to provide the lift that raises the trunk into the upright position. The propulsive thrust is no longer produced by the hamstring muscles acting as retractors of the hip, as they do in quadrupeds, but by the extensors of the knee (quadriceps) and ankle (calf muscles). In fact the whole rhythmic system for balancing and unbalancing by moving the legs seems to be different in quadrupedal and bipedal gaits. Perhaps the similarities are greater than they appear.

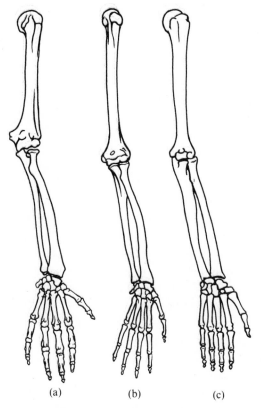

(a)   (b)   (c)

FIG. 34.4. Skeleton of the forelimb of (a) chimpanzee,
(b) *Dryopithecus*, and (c) man, reduced to same length. Man
resembles the (presumed) semi-brachiator. (After Campbell
1966 and Le Gros Clark 1962.)

The basic neurological mechanism producing the rhythmic movements of
locomotion is probably essentially similar throughout the mammals (perhaps with some exceptions, such as whales). Yet these movements themselves differ very greatly. A gallop is very different from a trot. Bipedalism
means something quite different according to whether it consists of a short
rushing run, or prolonged striding, or standing. Probably the earlier bipedal
efforts consisted of short runs, which can be achieved by many monkeys
and apes, though they are incapable of striding or long standing (Chapter 32, Napier 1964*a*). In the Australopithecines the ischium was relatively
longer than in modern man (p. 449) so that the leg could not have been fully
extended backwards in a long stride. Moreover the gluteus medius and
minimus muscles, which in man act to prevent the body falling when one
foot is off the ground, in Australopithecines probably acted as extensors

(Napier 1964*b*, 1967). Equally large changes were needed to convert the prehensile ape foot into the sprung arches of man, one of his most specialized features.

Bipedal locomotion must have produced some substantial advantage over the older, more stable, quadruped gait. Of course semi-brachiation would become less useful in the absence of trees, but apes often revert to a quadrupedal gait on the knuckles. Bipedalism brings the advantage of a greater range of vision and frees the hands for the use of tools and for carrying food. Presumably it was adopted because it provided a complex of these and other advantages.

4. From herbivore to hunter

Undoubtedly the assumption of a bipedal gait proved a key change in initiating a new form of life. The change was almost certainly gradual, beginning in the Miocene perhaps 20 million years ago. As the hands became freed from locomotion they were available for the using and then the making of tools. We do not know for certain when this began, but the oldest definitely known stone culture, the Oldowan, is associated with *Australopithecus* in Africa, dating from perhaps 2 million years ago or more. Evidence for the use of tools in much earlier times is claimed from the finding of skulls of Miocene animals with depressed fractures (Leakey 1968). Stones found near by are said to show signs that they were the weapons or tools that were used, perhaps by a *Dryopithecus*-like creature (see Chapter 32). Presumably, even before this, suitable stones were used for throwing or hitting.

The descent to the plains may well have been associated with a marked change of diet, from mainly herbivorous, as are the apes, to truly omnivorous, with killing first of small animals, lizards, and birds, and later of the increasingly large mammals of the plains. The bones associated with the remains of *Australopithecus* at Olduvai include small animals, birds, lizards, and rodents, as well as large ones. Presumably *A. africanus* ate some of these animals as well as vegetable food (see Clark 1970 and Chapter 32).

5. Some physical requirements for hunting

Co-operative hunting requires many special characteristics both of the individual and of society. In the following sections we shall consider some of these, beginning with the more obvious physical features and proceeding to the social, sexual, and intellectual characters that resulted from less obvious physical changes in brain and glands.

The capture of large prey no doubt depended greatly upon cunning, but swiftness, endurance, and power were probably also important. Bipedal walking and running do not provide the speed of the ungulates or the sudden

dash of the cats, but were perhaps suitable for sustained tracking, particularly over rough and varied terrain. The foot is one of man's most
remarkable organs, allowing sustained locomotion over irregular ground.
It seems to have been already evolved by the Australopithecine stage, and
the freedom of movement allowed would have been a necessary feature for
capturing large ungulates.

In primates the hand, instead of bearing claws for tearing the prey, has
developed nails, allowing fine movements and ultimately the holding of
tools. The lengthening and opposability of the thumb had perhaps preceded
the hunting habit, but were essential for it. Napier has distinguished between
a power grip, with the whole hand, and a precision grip, by the thumb and
fingers (Fig. 34.5). Selection for hands of the appropriate structure, and

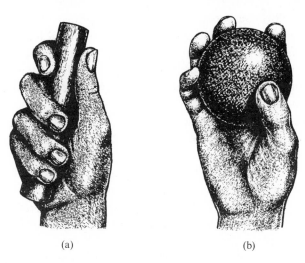

(a)   (b)

FIG. 34.5. Demonstrating the difference between (a) the power grip,
largely with the long flexors, and (b) the precision grip using also the
small muscles within the hand. (After Napier 1956.)

brains to use them, would have proceeded if it gave advantage to the individual and to his group. No doubt precision was of special importance, but
the load-carrying capacities of the arm and hand are also among man's
special features. The great mobility at the shoulder joint is perhaps an
inheritance from partial brachiation. It allows the hand to be brought into
almost any position in relation to the body. The joints at the elbow ensure
that the hand is held away from the body by a 'carrying angle' during walking. Other relevant features of the fore limb are the great capacity for pronation and supination and the arrangement at the wrist that allows the hand
to be deviated through wide angles in both the radial and ulnar directions.

All these, together with the structures of the fingers and thumb, make possible the working hand of man and all have their beginnings in adaptation to arboreal life. The great power of the deltoid muscle allows man to lift and carry weights that are large in relation to himself. In fact, besides his intellect and skill, man is outstanding among all creatures as a great load-carrier and worker. These characteristics must have been developed for some special purposes. We do not know for certain what they were, but it is reasonable to suppose that they included trapping and killing large prey and carrying it home for the women and children.

Tools must have been important from an early stage for killing the prey and also for skinning it and cutting up the meat. Man's largely vegetarian primate ancestry had left him poorly equipped physically for this purpose. The claws were already reduced to nails, in the interests of gripping and manipulation during arboreal life. The teeth of primates have none of the specializations for tearing and cutting that are so useful for the carnivore both before and after the death of the prey. The large canines of some male apes are not used in this way (their true use is, indeed, unknown; it may be for display in social situations) and the canines have become *reduced* during hominid evolution.

Among the physical features characteristic of man few are more striking than his nakedness. It would be satisfactory to find that this condition was also in some way related to the hunting habit. Perhaps the best suggestion is that the exertions involved, in a hot climate, required the maximum development of the cooling system by evaporation of sweat. This is ensured by reduction of the layers of hair, lying outside the epidermis, while the insulation needed at other times against heat loss is provided by the fatty layer of the dermis, which does not interfere with water evaporation. The explanation is not very convincing for such a very striking condition. The only other mammals of comparable nudity are elephants, pigs, a few rodents that live underground, and numerous aquatic forms. Comparison with the latter has led to the suggestion that man passed through an aquatic, or at least a wading phase (Hardy 1960). Many human features are compatible with this possibility but it is difficult to find direct evidence for it (or indeed against it!).

The need to hunt large animals may have been a main stimulus in the development not only of many physical features but also of social life and language. There is little evidence to go on but it is easy to imagine that the populations that survived contained genes ensuring co-operation among individuals, as well as efficient tool-making and tool-using. Hunting may well have been difficult for females and young and this would have led to the formation of stable social groups, with specialization of functions and sharing the results of the chase. This could be achieved by development of tendencies to co-operate, of which there are considerable signs already in monkeys and apes, though not usually for the purpose of getting food. Co-operation to drive, trap, and kill large prey such as antelopes or even elephants requires a reduction of competitive and aggressive behaviour between individuals. In a sense this could be said to involve in man the continuation throughout life of the characteristic features found among juveniles of monkey and other animal communities. There are indeed several signs that the evolution of man has involved a process of 'juveniliza-tion' or even 'foetalization'. Such a change, technically called neoteny (or paedomorphosis), has in fact occurred often in the course of the evolution of diverse animals (de Beer 1958). It is not difficult to understand how a delay in the rate of development of the reproductive system relative to the rest of the body could be produced by even a small genetic change; for instance, one affecting the pituitary gland. The result might be a striking alteration in the age structure of the population and hence in the psychology of its members. With a long period before puberty the young would be more readily restrained and taught by their elders, to the benefit of the whole community. Moreover some of the physical determinants of aggressiveness and non-co-operation might well be eliminated from the population al-together by neoteny. We know that stimulation of some regions of the brain will release aggressive behaviour and of others will prevent it. We do not fully understand how these centres are normally controlled, but evidently what we regard as 'emotional' responses have very definite and localized physical determinants. There is every reason to think that hereditary influences must operate to modify the operations of either the centres that increase or those that decrease the tendencies that we call 'aggression' (Chapter 43).

How far these changes can be regarded as neoteny is perhaps immaterial. Some alterations of conduct of this sort must have occurred even to allow for the elementary co-operation involved in Palaeolithic hunting life. The later progress of humanity seems to have involved still further co-operation, and it is a good guess that the physical changes in man since the middle Pleistocene have included alterations in glands, brains, and perhaps repro-ductive functions. Increased co-operation was especially in evidence in the change from Palaeolithic hunting to Neolithic culture and further to agriculture and the development of cities and states. Although we are still cursed by our mutual aggressions today, they are probably gradually becoming less and less manifested as individual fights, for which increas-ingly people have no stomach. Such changes are, of course, deeply in-fluenced by social customs, but it would not be unreasonable to conclude that physical alterations in the relevant parts of the brains and glands of our populations are continuing day by day. The type of aggressiveness required to make a successful business man, politician, or even soldier is no longer that of the bruiser. Ferocity and loss of temper may pay in the underworld but will land most men in the unskilled labour market or lower. And this is true of more and more parts of the world and its societies, though not all. It will indeed be interesting to see what sort of man will prevail and survive.

This is obviously not to say that the problems of human aggressiveness are well on the way to solution. It is all too easy to find evidence of the persistence of gross insensitivity, brutality, and indeed mass murder on the part of the peoples of almost every country of the world. This tendency to human strife has been widely discussed as a strange biological phenomenon (Lorenz 1966 and Chapter 43). It is probably best to admit that the biologist does not understand it. He can say that physical aggressive reaction almost certainly involves the excitation of centres in the hypothalamus such as those whose electrical stimulation can produce rage or stop it in an animal. We presumably have such centres, and they can probably be activated to produce rage either by physical stimuli (pain) or by 'psychological' ones, such as insult. They are brought into action in many conflict situations, whether between individuals (as in family quarrels) or between gangs, or armies in the field. In this sense they are involved in some acts of warfare, but it seems difficult to hold that the arousal of rage responses is the 'cause' of war or is even a necessary part of it under modern conditions. The struggles between groups of peoples may have biological roots in whatever were the original factors that led to human differentiation. We know only little about these factors, and certainly not enough to disentangle them as causes of conflict from the economic, political, and social forces that are involved in the origin of wars. The biologist is as interested in this problem as anyone else. He sees that for the first time there is a possibility that men will exterminate themselves, and perhaps all life on earth. If he is wise he will deny all those who bring only simple biological arguments to this most serious of all debates, whether they are introduced to prove that war is inevitable ('nature's pruning-hook') or as claims to methods of preventing it.

What the biologist can perhaps do is to encourage people to realize that continued maintenance and homeostasis are not necessarily served by pursuit of the immediate ends of separate individuals. Indeed, the equipment man receives from his past history is especially designed to ensure communication and co-operation. We have seen how our growth patterns seem to be planned to these ends (Chapter 18) and that we are endowed with a brain from which speech springs naturally as we mature (Chapter 19). These and many other pieces of evidence suggest that the full realization of man's inherited capabilities is to be found in co-operation with others and that in this way also he will find the fullest personal satisfaction. This is no great new discovery and in any case it needs to be tempered with the recognition that the human process of finding a means of survival by skill in thinking requires the maximum creative effort by every individual brain (Chapter 42). The problem of how people are best motivated to optimize plans for survival is indeed a difficult one. The biologist, with present knowledge, can make only some contribution to the discussion; he is in no position to claim that he has any technical knowledge that will provide a solution.

This is not to say that inquiry into the origins of the basic cerebral characteristics of man is without importance. We shall consider further features that may have evolved as man turned into a co-operative hunter of large animals.

6. Some social effects of co-operative hunting, caves, and fire

If the females and infants were to be left behind during the hunt all sorts of developments of the social system may have been required. In our nearest relatives among the surviving apes, the chimpanzees and gorillas, the social systems are rather loose, with variable associations of a male and a group of females and juveniles. Sometimes there are small family groups; in other situations quite large bands may be formed, presumably affording protection. There are only very rare records among apes of any sort of co-operation in collecting food or of food-sharing. Large changes in behaviour must have been necessary to make greater co-operation effective as man evolved. The association of individuals must have become reasonably stable; some kind of home base, even if temporary, was required, to which the food could be brought back. This, as well as the need for shelter, may have been a factor in the development of cave life. The very fact of carrying food to other individuals was a new development among primates, though of course common in carnivorous mammals and in birds. It required the development of a built-in system for assuring attention to the needs of others as well as oneself. The fact that man has such tendencies to altruism is as much a fact of nature as is his selfishness. We need to find out as much as we can about the origins of the habits and drives that lie behind some of our deepest emotions.

It is perhaps unwise to speculate too much about the influence of the development of a 'home' on the origin of the form of life that we call human. The conception is so powerful among peoples today (though not universal) that any clues as to its origin may be important. That the cave is not only for protection against cold is suggested by the fact of early cave occupation in central Africa. It may be that its first importance was as a central site for the group as well as for protection from other carnivores.

The capacity to obtain protection against the weather must have played a large part in the success of man further north in surviving the glacial and pluvial periods. The first signs of the use of fire come during a cold period (the second glacial (Mindel)) about 450 000 years B.P. and from rather northerly sites, in Hungary and at Pekin. In both places there are hearths associated with remains of *H. erectus* (p. 462). No traces of fire have been found in African open living-floors or rock-shelters.

Presumably, as with stone tools, some use of natural fire preceded man's discovery of how to make it. If the first use was for warmth its value for cooking may have been discovered by accident. As a process of external digestion cooking has no doubt played an important part in the final stages of the development of the human face by reduction of the jaws. One of the most striking characteristics that differentiate all the early hominid fossils, Australopithecines (particularly *A. robustus*) and *H. erectus*, from modern man is the size of the teeth and of the parts of the skull that bear the muscles that move the jaws. The reduction of the teeth and jaws proceeded rapidly after the discovery of cooking, in the middle Pleistocene, and is still proceeding today. The pre-digestion of the food by cooking may have been one of the factors leading to a greater economy of time, with consequent release of capacity to make not only further tools but also statues and other artistic artefacts. The presence of these in turn may have helped to unify societies, to promote communication, and stimulate ideas for further invention (Chapter 36).

The capacity to make and control fire we can rank as man's second great technological jump, the first being the manufacture of stone tools, at least a million years earlier. No doubt fire was put to many uses such as splitting stones or hardening wood. But it was only after a further 400 000 years that it led to the next really great technical revolution with the discovery of the smelting of ores to obtain metal. Meanwhile man had made many other discoveries, above all in language and communication (Chapter 35).

7. The origins of human sexual and mating habits

One of the very striking characteristics of modern man is to form pairs who remain together for relatively long periods. Such pairing is said to occur in gibbons but is not general in primates. The organized hunting by middle Pleistocene hominids would obviously have required some adjustments if the sexes were separated for long periods. It can be argued that these separations were at least part of the reason for the socialization of mating as marriage and also the particularly intense human interest in sex, even without relation to reproduction. If the sexes are often to be separated, and yet the mother and offspring cared for, there must be strong bonds between individual males and females. This may be the basis for the various features of heightened sexuality that are characteristic of man. Most important of these is the occurrence in the female of an orgasm comparable to that of the male ejaculation. This is accompanied by (or has produced) an almost uniform reciprocal acceptability of males and females throughout the menstrual cycle. There has been an almost complete disappearance of the changes that occur in many primates at the time of ovulation at the middle of the cycle, which serve, for instance in baboons, to advertise the condition of the female and to excite the male, so that copulation occurs only at that time. Some women are regularly aware of the time of ovulation by pains and even slight bleeding at the middle of the month. There are also characteristic slight rises in temperature but data on frequency of copulation do not show clear signs of greater receptivity or attractiveness at this time (Chapter 15) (Kinsey et al. 1953).

Mating face to face is another characteristic almost unique to man. In nearly all primates the male mounts the female from behind. In gorillas and chimpanzees the female may lie on her back, with the male squatting between her legs rather than lying on her body. The characteristic human position may well have resulted simply from the resting prostrate position of a terrestrial bipedal creature. No doubt, however, it contributed to the formation of a closer communication between the individuals, with corresponding advantage for the family and for the young. Presumably at the same time many mating signs were transferred from the back of the female to the front. The characteristic sexual sign of primates is the sexual skin, a special area around the genitalia and buttocks, which becomes swollen and often bright red at the time of oestrus (corresponding to the mid-month ovulation of human menstrual cycles). In humans the characteristic features of the female are on the ventral side, especially the delicate features of face and lips, rounded breasts with coloured and sensitive skin around the nipples, and the distribution of the pubic hair. Correspondingly the male has beard and distinct distributions of hair on the body.

These and other physical features make the sexual life of hominids more continuous and richer between the members of a pair than in any other primates. In many animals stimulation of the clitoris by the penis of the male serves to ensure entrance at the moment of maximum female response, although a high blood-pressure may persist for a long time in the female (for instance in the bitch). The human response, after penetration, is waves of high blood-pressure producing the orgasm in the female, as in the male. The physical responses are of course the culmination of processes of love-making of a much more subtle character by which the pair maintain their interest in each other and support the lives of themselves and their family. We shall probably never know at what stage of evolution the family emerged from the promiscuous troop. Apparently in baboons and even chimpanzees and gorillas there is no long-lasting pair formation. However, the gibbon is monogamous and the family holds a pair territory (Schaller 1965). It may be that the earlier Palaeolithic hunters lived in small troops. But it is not unlikely that the really successful co-operation began in those populations where the genital and cerebral aspects of sex were such that pairs stayed together long enough to raise families.

THE EVOLUTION OF THE POWERS OF THE
HUMAN BRAIN AND OF SPEECH

1. The receptors of early man

THESE physical and social characteristics that we have been considering found their expression in creatures able to obtain a living from some new ecological niche in the Middle Pleistocene, when man first appeared approximately as we know him today. We are suggesting that this habit was the hunting of large ungulates. The special conditions of reproduction, growth of the brain, and delayed maturity produced people with sufficient intelligence to be able to adopt this way of life, without the usual carnivore's equipment of teeth and claws. The actual finding and tracking of the prey probably depended more on the use that was made of the information of the senses rather than on their refined sensitivity. A man has neither the eyes of a hawk nor the nose of a dog. But his brain makes very good use of what he does see and hear and smell.

Sight in particular was already the basis of his life as a primate. With the terrestrial habit and upright posture the head and eyes are free to survey the surroundings. Most mammalian carnivores hunt mainly by smell. As Campbell (1966) points out, man was 'something novel among land animals: a carnivore that hunted by sight'. Unfortunately we know very little of the way in which each animal species selects for attention certain features of the changes in the world around. There can be no doubt that whatever the perceptual world of a monkey may be it is something very different from our own, and that of a dog is more different still. Probably the brain of each species contains what may be called classifying cells, ready to detect specific changes in certain features of the world around (Young 1964). The remarkable work of Hubel and Wiesel (p. 619) shows that each cell of the visual cortex of a cat or monkey responds especially to a contour of illumination that has a particular orientation. Some cells respond to simple rectangles, others, especially in the parts of the cortex around the primary visual area, to figures of increasing complexity. We do not yet know how the responses to these simple features are integrated to provide a 'perception' of the whole complex scene, nor indeed what scenes are attended to by a cat (Sutherland 1968). Probably the limitations and possibilities are partly determined by heredity, partly by experience, building connections between the simpler units so that they can detect certain complex patterns (Hebb 1966). In man, for example, we know that experience largely determines the way we see. Those who live in western-type houses and cities have an experience of vertical and horizontal lines that is different from an inhabitant of the jungle, who, it is said, does not experience the same spatial illusions (Gregory 1966).

Perhaps one of the most important influences in improving the perceptual powers of early man was his manipulation of objects, a capacity already well developed in lower primates. To a creature that picks things up and examines them it may be that the world has an altogether more complex nature than for the one who only moves around within an environment that remains mostly static. For the latter, there are scenes, but the only entities in them that are separately distinguishable may be other animals, which alone change their places relative to each other. We are too ignorant to say more but it may be that with handling came the beginning of recognition of other classes of objects, and their classification. With using and then actually shaping them came further development of whatever groupings of cells and activities in the brain provide the internal representations that allow 'thinking' about them and, either before or after this, naming.

It may seem idle to speculate about stages that we shall perhaps never know. But since it was changes of this type that really made man what he is, it is important at least to discuss them. It is sad that the facts of fossilization lead us to know so much less about the brains of our ancestors than of their teeth. At least we need not be misled into thinking that changes in the teeth were the more important.

2. Motivation, goal-seeking, and restraint

A further unique feature of man among primates is his capacity to concentrate for a long time on one goal. In this he resembles carnivores such as tigers, who may wait and follow one prey for hours or even days. In man we can identify from fossil evidence at least one of the changes that was probably related to this capacity for attention. The development of the frontal lobes of the brain, and hence of the high forehead, is one of the most striking features by which members of the genus *Homo* differ from earlier genera, and indeed in this respect *H. sapiens* differs from *H. erectus*. We cannot measure the development of the frontal lobes in phylogeny accurately, but it must have occurred very fast in the Middle Pleistocene, which is the time when we suppose so many of the characteristic features of man to have emerged.

The functions of the frontal lobe are now reasonably well known, though not easy to summarize. They may be described in man as the maintenance of the proper balance between action and restraint, and the capacity to perform actions for which the reward is delayed. The extreme front part (prefrontal lobes), in particular, is responsible for the maintenance of sustained attention and initiative. People without these lobes are less able to concentrate for long periods on demanding tasks. Other effects of removals of parts of the frontal lobe are to weaken the restraints on which social life depends. Indeed, surgical disconnection is adopted as a means to remove the excessive inhibition that leads to some forms of chronic depression. After frontal leucotomy a person may make tactless, indiscreet, or unduly frank remarks. Sometimes he may show dangerously aggressive behaviour. We do not understand precisely how the frontal lobes function, but undoubtedly they play an important part in producing the balanced personality that is so characteristic of man. Experiments in dogs have shown that after removal of the frontal lobes the animals cannot make a delayed response, for instance, to proceed to the right one of several boxes one minute after they had seen food put in it. In monkeys also there is evidence that the frontal lobes are concerned with delayed responses.

3. Learning

Man is evidently a very good learner, though quantitative comparative estimates of this power are not easy to make. To do so would require a more thorough analysis of learning and memory than is possible here. One outstanding feature is our capacity to recall and act upon individual items of information, stored sometimes even from the distant past. There are anecdotal claims of this power in animals, but it is almost certainly accentuated in man, who can take actions that are appropriate in the light of what happened on single occasions, either recently or long ago. This seems to involve the making of a record of individual occasions, which of course would be useful only if provided with an addressing system that allows it to be readily consulted.

This capacity is especially connected with the functioning of what Penfield calls the interpretive cortex. This is an area distinct from the fields that are mainly associated with vision, hearing, and touch sensation (Fig. 35.1). Electrical stimulation in this area in conscious patients arouses memories of single past occasions, often those in which the person was looking at some scene or otherwise paying attention to something. The recalls are like flashes, and can be repeatedly evoked from a given spot. There is therefore some evidence that this region is especially involved in the capacity to call up a record of events of the past (Chapter 42).

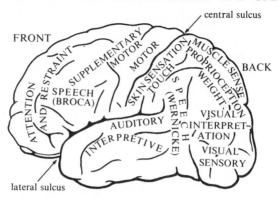

FIG. 35.1. The left (dominant) hemisphere of man showing various areas. Complex memories ('flashbacks') are evoked by electrical stimulation of the area marked 'interpretive'. There are two areas concerned with speech, one more anterior (Broca) and the other lying between the areas connected with the main receptor systems (Wernicke's area). (Partly after Penfield and Roberts 1959.)

4. Concept-formation

Another characteristic of man's memory is in a sense the opposite, that it allows recognition and abstraction of features that a number of objects have in common. This may be expressed as the naming and use of concepts, such as 'food' or 'wet', that are attributes of objects and situations that can be recognized in various ways and by different senses. Moreover some of the more elaborate concepts, for example 'cause' or 'space', involve abstraction from the data that are provided by several of the senses. Almost nothing is known about the neurological basis for the achievement of such abstractions. It may, however, be connected with the development of the areas of the parietal cortex that lie between the association areas for vision, hearing, and touch (Fig. 34.1). This has been called the association area of association areas, and is so greatly developed in man that it partly covers the others. Thus the primary visual cortex of man no longer appears on the lateral surface of the brain as it does in monkeys.

5. Speech centres

Some evidence about the brain areas involved in speech comes from the defects (aphasias) that result from injuries (Geschwind 1967, Newcombe 1969, Critchley 1970). Unfortunately the damage is rarely restricted to a small area and there is seldom anatomical evidence to confirm exactly what has been destroyed. Further, it is unrealistic to try to divide the process of communication by speech or writing into separate activities with distinct localizations. Many parts of the brain enter into the performance of any one activity and conversely each part affects many activities. Nevertheless it is agreed that after damage to a region in the inferior frontal convolution on the left side (Broca's area, Fig. 35.1) patients have difficulty in producing effective speech (motor aphasia). They may be able to articulate individual sounds but cannot combine them properly to produce words. They suffer 'a disturbance of the serial organization of phonemic articulatory processes' (Luria 1966). Such patients may also have difficulties with writing, but their comprehension of the speech of others may remain quite good.

On the other hand with more posterior lesions (Wernicke's area, Fig. 35.1) there may be difficulty mainly in hearing or comprehending speech (sensory or semantic aphasia). The superior temporal gyrus contains the primary auditory cortex and it is understandable that lesions here would influence the recognition of sounds and hence also of the patient's own speech production. But a considerable area posterior to this was also found to be involved in speech by Penfield and Roberts (1959). During electrical stimulation of the brain anywhere in either the anterior or posterior areas marked SPEECH in Fig. 35.1 the patients showed interference with their ability to speak. The more posterior region includes of course the association area of association areas already mentioned. It is an area difficult to define anatomically. The region behind the superior temporal gyrus is sometimes called the angular gyrus and has been held to be characteristically well developed in man (Geschwind and Levitsky 1968). It has also been called the 'area of ideational speech' or indeed 'word store'. Lying in a region between the sensory areas it is well suited to allow operations for recognition of the significance of objects and speaking about them. Study of the effects of various lesions is only just beginning to give clues as to the distinct stages of these processes. We need to know far more of the neuronal mechanisms that are involved in the production of elaborately patterned sequences of muscular action such as are involved in speech. A suggested hypothesis of how this may involve selection between alternative pathways is given in Chapter 42.

Unfortunately cranial casts of fossils do not show when these speech areas first developed to their present state. It can, however, reasonably be assumed that it was during the time of most rapid expansion of the brain, somewhere between the Australopithecine stage, with about 550 ml cerebral capacity, say between 2 000 000 and 500 000 years ago, and the appearance of *Homo sapiens sapiens* 40 000 years ago (1400 ml). *Homo erectus* stands almost exactly halfway in time and in cerebral capacity.

6. The origin of language

Perhaps we shall never know when speech began. The question of the origin of language has indeed produced so much loose talk that even to discuss the subject was taboo at one time among some linguists. Recently there has been a revival of interest in this problem, accompanying the greater awareness that language is a phenomenon with a biological background (Lenneberg 1967). There is much to suggest that the human brain has an innate capacity to learn to use speech (Chapter 19). It is reasonable to suppose that this power did not appear fully formed, but evolved gradually, like any other physical trait. It is too early yet to make useful speculations about what such an early language might have been like. Probably any power to transmit information or utter instructions would give advantage to the demes possessing it, especially in co-operative hunting. It is not clear how the capacity for creative speech arose from the transmission of signs of emotional states, which is common among animals. Presumably the early 'conceptual' words were in some way associated with the previous emotional signs. This may incidentally be part of the reason for the entanglement that still exists between objective description and subjective emotion (Chapter 10).

Communication between individuals is of course widespread in primates, using olfactory, tactile, visual, or auditory signals (see Hall and de Vore 1965). During primate evolution there has evidently been selection for the various characters that allow the formation of stable social groups. These include the nervous and muscular mechanisms for emitting and receiving finely graded signals and the disposition to react appropriately. Thus signs of greeting such as the kiss with the lips or the hand-shake are used by apes, as by man, to establish the contact that is needed for communication to be effective. These signs may be derived from the handling and suckling procedures of infancy; we have already seen that the growth-patterns of apes and men suggest that our communications system involves a sort of prolonged childhood (Chapter 34). The habit of grooming each other and the search for fleas is another social activity widespread among primates.

Further signals that we share with apes are the threat by making a loud noise, accompanied by a snarl, baring the teeth as a signal for biting. The fixed stare and frown are another form of threat. But all these signals are a long way from language. Even the range of calls made by chimpanzees and baboons to provide information about where they are, where the food is, and other matters, constitute only a fixed system in which each sign has one meaning.

There is a sharp distinction between such non-linguistic and truly linguistic signalling systems. The former are 'closed' in that they consist of a finite, and small, number of basic signs. Linguistic signals are 'open', in the sense that there is an infinite (or very large) possibility for combining them in such ways as to produce new messages. Moreover new uses are continually evolving by semantic shift or invention. The question how and when these capacities arose has not been settled. There is no anatomical feature of the skull by which we can decide whether its possessor could speak.

7. Visual communication

Communication by speech is connected with visual communication, which in many species of monkeys and apes includes a set of ten or more signs, often graded and recombined in various ways. The face is often elaborately patterned, especially around the eyes, and it is clear that facial communication is a very important element in the organization of the social life of all species (see Marler in de Vore 1965). Temporal patterning plays a large part in determining the meanings. A direct gaze will displace a subordinate individual, whose looking away is itself a sign of submission. The open-mouth threat (Figs. 35.2 and 35.3) is another sign of dominance and the grimace or frightened grin is the corresponding sign of submission (Fig. 35.2). Further pacificatory signs are the smacking of the lips (Fig. 35.4(b)).

Similar signs are used by different species and this prompts the suggestion that the visual signalling system of man may contain similar elements. Visual signals are still of great importance in man. In spite of the similarities it is certainly unsafe to interpret the animals' expression by 'humanizing' them. The use of each sign needs to be studied as it appears in the animal in its natural situation. (For evolution of threat display see Guthrie 1970.)

The monkey's grin and our smile are alike in that they are gestures of reconciliation (p. 490). Obviously there are wide differences in the equipment available. Man has largely lost the power of raising his hair as a sign (Fig. 35.5), but he has added winking and blushing and other signs of embarrassment. These are perhaps submission signs developed as a protection system against false communication, which becomes an increasing danger as men become better at influencing each other's behaviour by words. We may yet have a long way to go in developing such signs. The men who cannot lie may be the ones to survive, if their less scrupulous fellows destroy each other. Blushing and other signs of social sensitivity and incapacity for falsehood are perhaps among our most recent evolutionary acquisitions and truest signs of humanity, though they may all too readily be misused or perverted.

8. Non-linguistic vocal communication

Systems of non-linguistic vocal communication are also very well developed from prosimians upwards (Marler 1965). Most species have about ten to fifteen distinct signal sounds, the greatest number yet found being

FIG. 35.3: Male baboon (in wild) showing typical threat. The exposed canines are of obvious universal and 'primitive' threatening value, while the pale, lowered eyelids are perhaps more highly evolved, conventionalized gestures of conspecific, social threat. (After de Vore in Campbell 1966.)

FIG. 35.2. Facial expressions of crab-eating macaques (in captivity). (a) Open mouth threat. (b) Subordinate animal on right is showing a typical grimace of submission or appeasement (grin). (From Marler in de Vore 1965.)

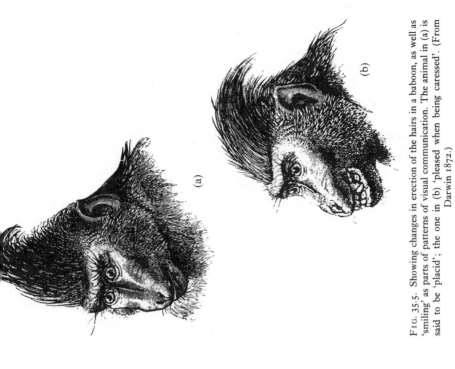

(a)

(b)

FIG. 35.5. Showing changes in erection of the hairs in a baboon, as well as 'smiling' as parts of patterns of visual communication. The animal in (a) is said to be 'placid'; the one in (b) 'pleased when being caressed'. (From Darwin 1872.)

(a)

(b)

FIG. 35.4. (a) Crab-eating macacque, mildly threatening, with eye-lids exposed. (b) Animal lip-smacking in a fairly neutral or mildly pacificatory situation. (From Marler in de Vore 1965.)

twenty-five in the Japanese Macacque. Of course many of the signs intergrade and there are difficulties of classification. These sounds mostly indicate a condition or emotion of the sender, perhaps also his location, age, sex, social status, and species. As Marler puts it, the sounds may act as 'identifiors, appraisors, prescriptors, or designators'.

Humans, of course, also emit a range of non-linguistic sounds such as laughs, moans, shrieks, cheers, and the cries of children. In both animals and man the use of these signals is largely the result of an inherited pattern of action, but obviously it is not wholly so. They are mostly rather loud and sustained and many but not all are produced, like those of other primates, by alterations in the larynx or lower, or at the very front of the airway (lips).

9. Speech sounds

True linguistic sounds are produced by rapid concurrent alterations of several different parts of the upper vocal tract. These produce the consonants, which are interspersed with vowel sounds that are possibly more nearly similar to the steady open resonances of some non-linguistic signals. It is characteristic of speech that the sounds are emitted and recognized in varied sequences. This is possible only by structuring the utterance according to well-marked phonetic and grammatical rules. Without this device we should have to learn to say and to recognize all communicable messages, which would be possible only for a small number. As it is, we learn a relatively small vocabulary and use it with the set of formations and transformations that are permitted in the language.

Recent studies suggest that all languages share certain features (Chomsky 1968, Lyons 1970). It is astonishing that they are so readily learned by the child (p. 274). In all cultures children quickly come to recognize correct grammatical form and divide up the sounds they produce in appropriate ways. Another feature is that languages do not depend upon the use of a few fixed sets of signals but allow the individual to produce an unending set of original sentences mostly never spoken before. Chomsky believes that certain phonological, syntactic, and semantic units are universal, not in the sense of occurring in all languages but of being definable within a general theory. Thus Jakobson has recognized twenty distinctive phonological features of speech (Fig. 35.6). At the level of syntax categories such as noun or verb or tense are found in all languages, allowing the production of sentences that are relevant to the fulfilment of human needs. Semantic categories such as 'male', 'physical object', 'movement', 'food', or 'desire' are universals needed to describe the world and human reaction to it. Further, Chomsky lays much emphasis on the formal universals or general principles determining the rules and operations in the grammar of various languages. It therefore seems that in spite of the Babel of tongues, human language may be a unitary phenomenon, with a specific genetic basis.

There is some evidence that the capacity to transmit and receive messages in this way is an inherited feature of the human brain. At least, the power of speech comes 'naturally' as the child grows and does not strictly have to be 'taught' (Chapter 19). The changes needed for the initiation of speech would in any case be in the brain and in the muscular system controlling the relevant points along the airway. Like other evolutionary changes it is probable that this was gradual, and that the new equipment and way of operating arose out of the old. Perhaps one faint clue is that vowel sounds resemble some non-linguistic signs. It can be imagined how the increasing control of the airway would add variety to the signals. But this does not touch the fundamental problem of how speech signals come to be sent and recognized in richly varied combinations. However, although with speech we can send an infinite variety of messages, in practice what any known speaker says in a given social context shows less than infinite variety. In fact we can receive speech only because we pick up some of the signals and synthesize the presumed message from our knowledge of the language, speaker, and context. The communication is usually effective only because it is one item of a rather restricted set. This perhaps helps us to imagine how language might have originated in a simpler form than we find in any modern languages. Introduction of consonantal sounds into the non-linguistic utterances could have increased their variety and information content. But we still have to explain how the lexical items came to be usable in varied combinations. The basic question is how did the generative rules of grammatical formation and transformation arise? Presumably it must have been by gradual change of existing brain processes.

Undoubtedly particular developments must have occurred in the brain to make even simple speech possible. We have already discussed the two special areas involved. Significantly, one of them (Broca's) is in the frontal (motor) region and the other (Wernicke's) is near the 'association area of association areas' (Fig. 35.1). Moreover, they are on one side of the brain only (usually the left), indicating perhaps that a special method of memory storing, addressing, and retrieval is involved, a system more precise than the bilateral (redundant?) stores elsewhere in the brain.

We can get some idea of the phonetic problem from the scheme used by linguists, following Roman Jakobson, for the binary description of phonemes (see Lyons 1968). Twelve distinctive features are more than sufficient to describe all the phonemes of all languages, and nine are enough for English

(Fig. 35.6). Each phoneme is characterized by whether it does or does not contain each feature, but some features are irrelevant for some phonemes and are left blank.

1. Vocalic/non-vocalic
2. Consonantal/non-consonantal
3. Compact/diffuse
4. Grave/acute
5. Flat/plain
6. Nasal/oral
7. Tense/lax
8. Continuant/interrupted
9. Strident/mellow

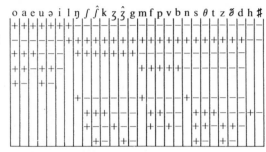

FIG. 35.6. The phoneme pattern of English, according to Jakobson. All language sounds can be characterized by nine distinctive features or binary oppositions, such as vocalic/non-vocalic, nasal/oral, etc. Any pair of phonemes is distinguished by at least one feature opposition. Thus (b) and (d) differ only in grave/acute, (b) and (t) differ in two features and (t) and (u) in three.

Key to phonemic transcription: /o/-pot, /a/-pat, /e/-pet, /u/-put, /ə/-putt, /i/-pit, /l/-lull, /ŋ/-lung, /ʃ/-ship, /ʃ̂/-chip, /k/-kip, /ʒ/-azure, /ʒ̂/-juice, /g/-goose, /m/-mill, /f/-fill, /p/-pill, /v/-vim, /b/-bill, /n/-nil, /s/-sill, /θ/-thill, /t/, -till, /z/-zip, /ð/-this, /d/-dill, /h/-hill, ‖-termination. The prosodic opposition, stressed vs. unstressed, splits each of the vowel phonemes into two. (After Cherry 1966.)

Evidently with twelve features the number of possible combinations is $2^{12} = 4096$. Yet most languages use very much fewer. English uses only forty of them. The point is that this arbitrary system used by the linguists gives us an insight into the sort of rules that the speaker must obey and hence to the number of binary selections that must be made by his brain. The number is not large for each phoneme, but we have no idea of how the sequential selection is made in such a way as to transmit complete effective messages, consisting of sequences of phonemes, syllables, morphemes, and sentences. There are certain underlying regularities in these units that may possibly even be 'built-in'. Most native speakers of a language will agree as to whether an utterance is grammatical, non-grammatical, agrammatical, or ambiguous (see Menyuk in Salzinger and Salzinger 1967). As a child begins to speak he produces constructs that are approximations to well-formed structures. He may say 'I know what is that' but never says 'know what is I that'. The surprising thing is that such grammatical, semantic, and phono-logical·rules are learned so very quickly. We do not yet know whether this capacity depends upon any particular brain structure.

The origin of language must have involved a great increase in the capacity to make sequences of selections between distinctive features. The selections would have to correspond to the occurrence of particular events both inside the person and without, as well as to the sounds made by other people in similar situations. This may have been made less complicated by the very early development of the restrictions of grammar. Only certain combinations of sounds are 'allowed' in the language. We do not know how this restriction is arrived at, but it is possible that it may include limitations imposed by the inherited organization of patterns of brain action, presumably ultimately of brain structure (see Chapter 19). Some part, at least, of the power to use language must depend simply upon the capacity to learn the conventions. This is no doubt extremely complicated, but there are signs that we may be able to understand it in terms of the learning of choices between alternatives, on the model suggested by the mnemon hypothesis (Chapter 42).

The meagre evidence, mainly of brain size, suggests that this emergence of language may have begun less than a million years ago, perhaps less than half a million. If so, it must have proceeded with startling rapidity for such a large change. But of course it constituted in effect the invention of a wholly new biological phenomenon, the transmission of detailed forecasts by codes other than genetic (Huxley 1942, Waddington 1960). A greatly increased rate of further change was to be expected with the development of such a new form of inheritance (p. 516). Perfection of the brain mechanisms that were responsible would have proceeded rapidly by the advantage of the more intelligent demes and individuals over others. It has been suggested that at some stage the brain may have become doubled in size by the addition of one further cell division to the sequence of some thirty mitoses that exist between the first cleavage and the cessation of division in the nervous system. But the significance of the number of cells in a brain is complicated by the fact that it is affected by the absolute size of the animal, as well as by what might be called the adaptive function of the brain. In relation to this Jerison (1963) has made estimates that show a *gradual* increase in the numbers of what he calls 'adaptive' or 'extra' brain cells during hominid evolution (Table 35.1). Though doubling is still not completely ruled out, the selective advantage of developing communication through language may well have been sufficient without any such sudden jump.

If we are right in concluding (a) that language depends upon the particular structure and activities of the brain and (b) that these have changed very rapidly, then it seems that further changes in the same direction are likely. The acceleration of improvement in communication in the later Pleistocene led to the further biologically revolutionary advance of *storing information outside the body altogether*, in the form of writing. This happened less than 10 000 years ago (p. 516) and has produced what most people probably regard as all the major technological advances (treating the discoveries of how to make stone tools and fire with undeserved contempt!) Indeed, the inventions that many modern people would consider really important have been made in the last few hundred years, mostly in the last fifty.

TABLE 35.1

Estimates of adaptive cortical neurons in mammals of different brain and body sizes (after Jerison 1963)

Animal	Brain weight (g)	Body weight (g)	Number of adaptive neurons ($\times 10^9$)
Macaca mulatta	100	10 000	1·2
Papio sp.	200	20 000	2·1
Pan troglodytes	400	45 000	3·4
Gorilla gorilla	600	250 000	3·6
Australopithecus africanus	500	20 000	4·4
Homo erectus	900	50 000	6·4
Homo sapiens	1300	60 000	8·5
Elephant	6000	7 000 000	18·0
Porpoise	1750	150 000	10·0

10. Man's accelerating evolution

It is hard for individuals who live less than 100 years to see such accelerated change in perspective. How ridiculous that we ask whether man is still evolving! He is changing faster than any other species has ever done before. It is true that we do not know what changes are going on in his genetic constitution (though changes there certainly are). What has happened in man's evolution is that non-genetic information-transfer has become more important than genetic change. It may well be that brains have altered a lot in the last few thousand years, but the information stored in brains has changed still more, and new information stores have grown, made neither of proteins nor of nucleic acids, but of clay tablets, papyrus, paper, and now magnetic tape. It is often asked whether computers will replace human beings. The answer is that in a sense they have been doing so since writing was invented, and at a generally increasing rate. It may be that only those individuals and groups of people whose brains are good enough to make use of and compete with computers will be able to survive the further impacts of this same change. The population that emerges will almost certainly be very different from our own. They may look much like us; goodness knows, with our huge heads we are very odd creatures already. But they will probably talk about quite different and more interesting matters than do most of us. Almost certainly they will behave more sensibly and react less violently to each other. Each person and group will be too powerful for any that undertake aggression to survive the impact. The meek may indeed inherit the earth—if they are also clever enough to keep out of the way while the proud are destroying each other.

36

THE EVOLUTION OF CULTURE

1. Culture and tool-making

THE concept of culture is widely used by anthropologists to cover all those skills and ways of life that are transmitted by interpersonal communication and tradition rather than by genetical means. Although each culture is supposed to be a 'whole' it includes many different aspects of the life of a people, their knowledge and language, their religion, beliefs and laws, their customs, rituals and arts, their tools, foods, utensils, and other means of getting a living. No doubt all these matters react upon each other and in that sense each culture *is* a whole, but there must also be many situations in which items vary independently and incorporate aspects of other cultures.

For the earlier part of man's history our knowledge of his culture is almost entirely restricted to the stone or bone tools that have been preserved. The fabrication of tools is sometimes regarded as a sign of the achievement of human status. The logical foundations for making this a landmark are supposed to be (1) that tool-making involves foresight as to the use of the tool; but all organisms show 'foresight' or prediction in much of what they do. (2) That tools are made by a technique that is learned from others and involves symbolic communication, presumably by language. But the manufacture and use of tools is already seen in other animals, for instance among apes, which will peel a stick and dig it into an ants' nest to collect food. Birds make nests with standard techniques, though these are not learned from others, but tits learn to open milk bottles by imitation. Monkeys are said to learn to swim from others. Many other instances of animals using tools are given by Hall (1963). It cannot therefore be assumed dogmatically that any creatures that learn to make tools are men.

2. The earliest pebble tools

Even if the earliest tools were made by individuals on their own initiative there is evidence that traditions as to how it should be done became established at least by the later Australopithecines (perhaps nearly 2 million years ago) (Chapter 32). These earliest known human artefacts are called pebble tools. They were made from various lumps and pieces of lava or quartz, crudely flaked by a few strokes on one side to make a cutting edge

(a)

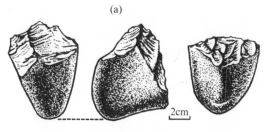

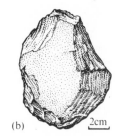

(b)

FIG. 36.1. (a) Pebble tools made of lava from Olduvai, Bed I, about 1 700 000 years old. These are the oldest known human artefacts. They are crudely chipped along one edge. (After Oakley 1969.) (b) More developed pebble tool (Chellean hand-axe) from Olduvai, Bed II, more than 500 000 years old. The tool is a 'biface' core-tool, more fully worked than those of (a), by percussion around the periphery.

(Fig. 36.1(a)). There were chopping tools and flakes but no axes. There is little evidence that the tools were made according to a convention or 'industry'. In the very earliest (Olduvai, Bed I), only a few flakes had been removed on one side. Later, in Bed II they were more fully worked, often all round the edge and on both faces, hence the name 'biface' (Fig. 36.1(b)). The technique was probably either to strike the parent stone ('core') with another used as a hammer, or to strike the core on an anvil stone. In either case a piece is removed, called a 'flake' and a depression left on the core. In later industries the flake was itself further worked. The fact that tools were made according to an evolving convention suggests that the social system of *Australopithecus* was already more highly developed than that of the modern apes, even though the transmission and improvement of traditions of tool-making does not necessarily imply the presence of an elaborate symbolic language. It seems possible that even 2 million years ago the human social system was such as to allow some degree of specialization of activities and freedom from the crudest forms of aggression and competition between individuals or family groups (see M. D. Leakey 1967).

We know nothing more about the social life of *Australopithecus*. There is no evidence of the use of fire or of burial of the dead, and probably enough sites have now been studied to reveal signs of those if they were present. It may therefore provisionally be supposed that during the enormous period between at least 2 million and 500 000 years ago, the Australopithecines possessed some elementary means of communication of detailed facts, such as those about chipping flints, and a social organization at least somewhat different from that of apes.

3. The evolutionary sequence of tool-making

By study of the tools found at a series of levels the further gradual evolution of toolmaking has been traced by archaeologists. There is a certain degree of correspondence between the sequence in different parts of the world but cultures quite commonly persist in one area long after they have been replaced in others. A long sequence has been studied at Olduvai in Tanzania, and in Europe by Breuil and many other workers (see Oakley 1969, Clark and Piggott 1970). There has been much discussion as to how cultures originate, evolve, and migrate. In particular it would be very interesting to know whether innovations are made in one place and then spread by diffusion, or whether they evolve in parallel in different peoples. The data are at present too uncertain to allow us to summarize this important question. We cannot specify with precision the conditions that promote human creativity.

The sequence of industries was first worked out by archaeologists in Europe, and the most widely used names for the stages are derived from the places at which the industries were first discovered. The nomenclature is confusing and names are often involved in controversies as to whether one culture has been derived from another. Moreover there is a wide divergence in use of the names between archaeologists of different modern cultures. Recommendations for standardization are being made (see Bishop and Clark 1967). Here attempts will be made to relate archaeological data to knowledge about the brain, but the difficulties will be all too obvious.

With these qualifications we may use a series of names mainly from the sequence studied in the Somme valley in France as our source of reference (Fig. 36.2). The sequence of industries is called Palaeolithic ('old stone') to cover the whole period during which instruments were made by chipping and the people were hunters and food-gatherers. A Mesolithic period from about 11 000 years ago then leads to the Neolithic period, in which instruments were more varied, agriculture developed, and settlement progressively led to urban civilization. The Palaeolithic can be divided into a Lower Palaeolithic, from the earliest times to 100 000 years B.P., a Middle Palaeolithic ('evolved Lower Palaeolithic') until 30 000 B.P., and an Upper Palaeolithic lasting until 11 000 B.P. The stages of culture were not reached everywhere at the same time, which makes difficulties of nomenclature and dating. We can recognize relative dates (or stages) as distinct from absolute or 'chronometric' dating (see Oakley 1969). It is important again to remember that cultures have never been uniform all over the world at any one time. This is still obvious today, when, for example, Australian aborigines are living much as did Upper Palaeolithic hunters. Indeed, the last few thousand years of human history have seen a continuous change everywhere from hunting to farming, and then to urban and industrial life. People all over the world are to be found today in various stages of this progression.

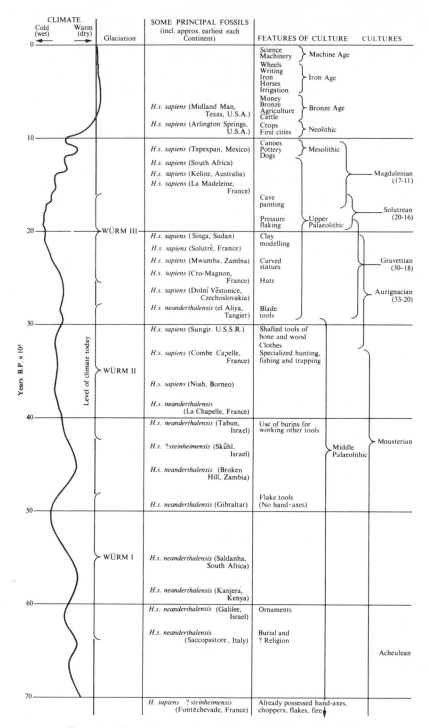

CLIMATE			SOME PRINCIPAL FOSSILS (incl. approx. earliest each Continent)	FEATURES OF CULTURE		CULTURES
Cold (wet) ←	Warm (dry) →	Glaciation				

FIG. 36.2. Chart of the evolution of cultures in the Upper Palaeolithic.

4. Classification of Palaeolithic cultures

It is convenient to recognize five modes of old stone age work as follows (see Clark 1969).

TABLE 36.1

A broad classification of Palaeolithic cultures.
(Partly after Clark 1969.)

Mode	Tools	Approx. earliest date (B.P.)	Culture	Species
1	Choppers, scrapers, unworked bones	2 000 000	Lower Palaeolithic	*Australopithecus ? africanus*
2	Hand-axes, picks, choppers, scrapers, bone flakes	500 000	Lower Palaeolithic	*H. erectus*
3	Narrow flakes from prepared cores, awls, sharp scrapers	70 000	Middle Palaeolithic	*H. sapiens neanderthalensis*
4	Sharp blades steeply retouched with a punch, knives, burins, needles, harpoons, many other tools of bone and wood	35 000	Advanced Palaeolithic	*H. sapiens sapiens*
5	Microliths, bows and arrow heads, fish hooks, knives, adzes with handles	11 000	Mesolithic	*H. s. sapiens*

For more than a million years no progress was made beyond the production of very crude choppers, cleavers, and picks (see M. D. Leakey 1970). These have been found in many parts of the world, in Africa (Oldowan culture), Europe (Clactonian), India (Soan), and China (Choukoutienian). The men who colonized Australia carried this culture with them and the aborigines still use it today.

Stratigraphical sequences such as that at Olduvai in Tanzania show that the chopper tools slowly improved by two-way chipping of the edge. Later the hand-axe was gradually evolved by extending the flaking on to the surface (Figs. 36.3 to 36.5). The flakes removed were further shaped and the hand-axe culture made use of a range of sharp picks, scrapers, and cleavers.

FIG. 36.3. A hand-axe made by chipping a flint core, showing how it was probably used.

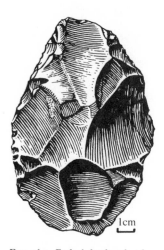

FIG. 36.4. Early Acheulean hand-axe from Chelles-sur-Marne. A roughly chipped core-tool, of perhaps 400 000 years ago. (After Oakley 1969.)

The conception of carefully preparing the flint first and then striking off the flake at one blow appears still later and may be used to define the third mode or Levalloisian technique, used especially by the Neanderthal people (Fig. 36.6). All these were however relatively small changes and throughout the Middle Palaeolithic culture evolved only very slowly. There had been relatively only a small advance from the earliest chopper industry. The really rapid change began only some 35 000 years ago with the appearance of the modern form of man, *Homo sapiens sapiens*. The associated change in tool-making was the use of a very steep, almost vertical, touch to produce very thin blades that were both sharp and strong. They were in great variety. Some were cutting knives, others the chisels (burins) were used for shaping and engraving bone or wood. From this point on a wide range of instruments was developed.

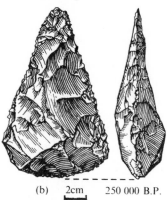
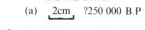

(a)   2cm   ?250 000 B.P   (b)   2cm   250 000 B.P.

FIG. 36.5. Acheulean hand-axes. These are core tools, more extensively chipped than the earlier ones of Fig. 36.4. (a) from St. Acheul in the Somme Valley. (b) from Swanscombe Middle Gravels, Kent. (After Oakley 1969.)

5. The cultures of *Homo erectus*. Chellean and Acheulean hand axes

No tools anything like as old as the earliest at Olduvai have been reliably identified in Europe, where the earliest are the flint industry often known as 'early Acheulean' or Chellean. These hand-axe industries may very well have arisen in Africa and migrated thence all over Europe and much of

FIG. 36.6. Levalloisian flints: (a), (a¹), (a²) cores, showing where the flakes have been struck off (above); (b) flake whose surface was chipped before being struck from the core; its underside is smooth; (c) pointed tool; and (d) knife, made in the same way. About 100 000 years old. (After Oakley 1969.)

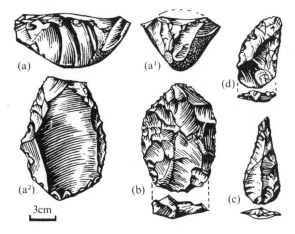

3cm

Asia. In the earliest flints found in Europe the chipping is rough but extensive, and the products included hand-axes, probably used to kill the prey, and cleavers with which it was cut up (Figs. 36.3 and 36.4). Possibly the early tools may have been used for digging roots, for skinning animals and other purposes. Tools of age similar in Britain are known as Clactonian, and date from the beginning of the Mindel-Riss interglacial period 400 000 years B.P. (Fig. 36.2), but include no hand-axes.

The primitive Chellean phase of tool-making seems to have lasted in Europe from about 500 000 to 400 000 B.P. The succeeding cultural phases known as Acheulean lasted until about 100 000 years ago or later, with three major and many minor stages. The Acheulean flints are much more extensively worked, including special chipping to make thinner tools with a sharp edge and shaping to a point (Fig. 36.5). The flakes removed from the core were also secondarily chipped. These seem to be better tools than the earlier ones (or than natural flints), but not very much better. It had taken 1·5 million years or more for man to progress this short distance, whether by change in the structure of his brain or of the information he had learned to put in it.

The people who used the Chellean- and Acheulean-type tools were probably of the *Homo erectus* type. The remains of Pekin man were found associated with Choukoutienian culture, rather similar to the Clactonian, including crude chopper tools, points, and scrapers but no hand-axes. The jaw found at Casablanca, the latest known fragment that is referred to *H. erectus* (250 000 years B.P.) was associated with bifaced Acheulean hand-axes.

These tools are somewhat in advance of even the better Oldowan ones and there is other evidence that *Homo erectus* possessed the elements of a truly human culture. With his weapons and tools, his intelligence and his organization he was able to kill deer, horses, wild pig, bison, elephants, rhinoceros, baboons, and other monkeys, all of them animals that are not easy to catch and most of them extremely dangerous. Some of the bones were also perhaps made into simple tools. There is convincing evidence at Pekin and at Vértesszöllös in Hungary that fire was used in hearths, and charred bones show that cooking had begun. There is evidence suggestive of cannibalism, for some of the bones and skulls had been split open but whether for the contents or by accident remains uncertain.

Probably even 400 000 years ago man had developed some of his basic features, characterized by the power of undertaking actions abstracted from immediate ends, in order ultimately to achieve further goals. This is indeed an additional justification for including the Java, Pekin, and other remains of *erectus* type in the genus *Homo*.

6. Mousterian culture. Neanderthal man

At the end of the third glacial period (Riss) the variant of Acheulean tool-making technique called Levalloisian can be recognized (Fig. 36.6). In this the flake was worked upon before detaching it from the core. From here onwards various industries known as Mousterian (from Le Moustier in France) used more and more delicate chipping, with or without the Levalloisian technique (Fig. 36.7). These industries were contemporary with the Neanderthal people (50 000 to 30 000 B.P.) (*H. sapiens neanderthalensis*).

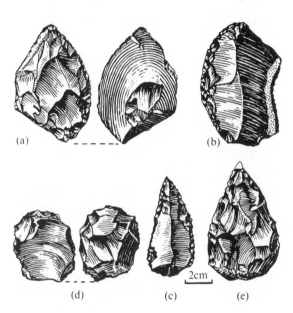

FIG. 36.7. Flint artefacts from the type-site of Mousterian culture (a rock-shelter at Le Moustier in the Dordogne). Perhaps 50 000 years old. (a) and (b) are side scrapers, (c) a point, (d) a disc-core, and (e) a biface hand-axe, not very different from the Acheulean ones of several hundreds of thousands of years before. (After Oakley 1969.)

They may have existed much earlier; we have little exact evidence about man between 200 000 and 50 000 years ago. Dating is very difficult for that period (p. 462).

There was great variation in the Mousterian industries in different areas. For example, hand-axes were common in lowlands in Europe but absent in the mountains, though the significance of the difference is not clear. The Mousterian tools were more standardized but still not very different from those used before. They do not suggest any very subtle culture other than hunting. Besides hand-axes there were also more pointed tools, perhaps used for killing the prey. In others the working edge was along one side; these were perhaps used for skinning and cutting up ('side scrapers'). The bones found with the Neanderthals show that these people could kill the largest animals (mammoths and woolly rhinoceroses), perhaps after trapping them in pits armed with spiked stakes. They made little use of worked bone, and had no ornaments or art. Some Neanderthalers were cannibals. At Monte Circeo a skull was found that had been opened at the base, perhaps for extraction of the brain. At Krapina in Jugoslavia the remains of numerous humans of all ages have been found mixed with those of animals and many had been cooked and broken for the marrow.

On the other hand burials appear and provide evidence that there was already a system of beliefs some 50 000 years ago (see Chapter 37). At several sites of Last Interglacial times the body is in a hole shaped to receive it. In a cave in Uzbekistan a child's grave is surrounded by a ring of ibex horns. Late Mousterian sites show complex burial rites, including mounds and rings of stones (at Monte Circeo, Italy). These are certainly the remains of ritual procedures, though their significance is not known. They surely show that these people would be recognized by us as human, with language, some social customs, and signs of thinking about themselves as well as their tools.

7. Upper Palaeolithic industries. *Homo sapiens sapiens*

The Mousterian industries (Middle Palaeolithic) disappeared in Europe and Western Asia about 35 000 years ago and were then succeeded by a series of Upper Palaeolithic industries, making smaller and finer tools (Aurignacian, Gravettian, Solutrean, and Magdalenian). It has been debated whether this change was due to invasion by the new *Homo sapiens sapiens* type, perhaps exterminating the Neanderthals, but there is really no evidence for any sudden break and indeed changes that take thousands of years are hardly 'sudden' (see Chapter 33).

The characteristic new tools of the Upper Palaeolithic were narrow blades, struck from cores by use of a hammer and punch. Some of them

1cm

FIG. 36.8. Mag-
dalenian burin, a
tool for working
wood or bone,
c. 15 000 B.P. (After
Oakley 1969.)

were cut at one end to make a narrow chisel, known as
a burin, used for working softer materials such as bone,
ivory, or wood (Fig. 36.8). Clearly these peoples had progressed considerably. The achievement of a goal was
sought by increasingly indirect methods. The flint was
not simply struck upon an anvil or with a hammer. The
hammer was now used to strike an intermediate tool,
used as a punch. The burin is itself a tool to make tools
out of other materials. Evidently the brain of these early
Homo sapiens sapiens was at work much as it is today. The
people now increasingly rapidly gathered information as
to the nature of the materials and events around them to
which they could apply their intelligence.

The analysis of the Upper Palaeolithic cultures is a
complicated problem of dates and migrations (see Hawkes
and Woolley 1963). The simple concept, held until recently, was that the
Aurignacian succeeded the Mousterian and was in turn replaced by the
Gravettian and Solutrean and these by the Magdalenian. Probably there
was no such simple evolution in any one part of the world of one type of
industry into another. Migrations, mixtures, and also extinctions were
perhaps almost continuous. It is unfortunately unlikely that we shall ever
be able to follow the story in detail. Indeed, as we have seen with other
aspects of evolution, it is inevitable that the more we learn of the details of
continuous sequences the more confused we become. All that we can do
here is to mention some of the industries that show the nature of Upper
Palaeolithic cultures. The sequence shown in Fig. 36.2 is certainly over-
simplified.

However, radiocarbon dating shows that the succession of stages long
recognized in France did in fact follow each other (Fig. 36.9). The new
techniques appeared in S.W. Asia before they did in Europe. The French
Châtelperronian was transitional from the Mousterian and included sharp
knives, steeply re-touched. In the following Aurignacian there were greater
changes. The characteristic tool was a blade, made by parallel flaking of a
core (Fig. 36.9). These people also made bone points for attachment to a
shaft, which were the earliest bone tools of standard created form. The
Aurignacians still showed no great advance over Mousterian culture. Their
successors, the Gravettians (27–20 000 B.P.) progressed rapidly. They had
simple huts made by scooping a hole and roofing it with branches upon
pillars supported by uprights placed in postholes or wedged by stones.
Huts may indeed have been made long before this. There is some evidence
of rings of stones even in Bed I at Olduvai and at some Acheulean sites.

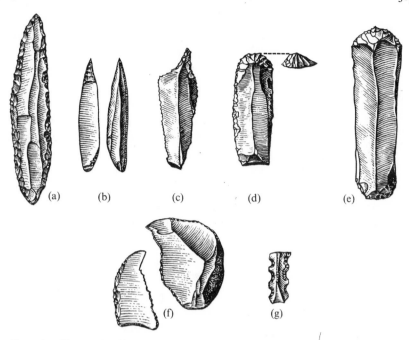

F IG. 36.9. Upper Palaeolithic tools in approximate order of age: (a) Aurignacian blade, the oldest; (b) Gravettian points; (c) Solutrean piercer; (d) Solutrean scraper (*c.* 20 000); (e) Magdalenian scraper (*c.* 15 000); (f) Magdalenian 'parrot-beak' burins; (g) Magdalenian saw. (a), (b), and (f) after Rosenfeld, the rest after Oakley 1969.)

The Gravettians certainly lived in settlements, at least for part of the year. They were, of course, still hunters, working along the rivers and over the plains of central Europe and southern Russia. They lived in the interval between the second and third (last) phases of the Würm glaciation (the Paudorf Interstadial), a time when the climate was somewhat less severe than earlier or later, though still much colder than today. They hunted mammoth and other large game, probably in open tundra, with a climate like that of northern Canada today, but perhaps with finer summer weather. At around 20 000 years ago the climate again became colder (Fig. 36.2). Thus although we cannot closely relate the relatively rapid outburst of human development by the Gravettians to climatic factors, conditions were relatively mild when it occurred. These peoples showed the first signs of the rapid changes of technique and culture that have continued ever since. Their flints were small and shaped by longitudinal chipping (Fig. 36.9). They were often placed in shafts or handles. Bone and ivory were frequently used, including as tools for working skins (awls and bodkins), showing that these people wore clothes. They made ornaments and beads, often of mammoth ivory, decorated with simple patterns. Most interesting of all

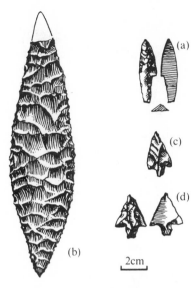

are the carved human and animal figures in ivory or a mixture of bone and clay (Chapter 37). They buried the dead with clothes and ornaments and sprinkled them with red ochre.

The various phases of Gravettian culture thus show signs that by this time there had appeared many of the characteristic features that we call human. There were evidently some relatively very rapid advances during the period 30 000–20 000 years ago. From the first use of fire, perhaps 400 000 years before, to the Aurignacian period, there is slight evidence of change. It is very difficult, however, to evaluate this *absence* of evidence. It is in the nature of things that remains should become scantier as we pass backwards.

FIG. 36.10. Solutrean tools produced by pressure flaking: (a) shouldered point (?lance or spear); (b) 'Laurel-leaf' blade; (c) and (d) arrow heads. *c.* 20 000 B.P. (After Oakley 1969.)

Objects made of wood are unlikely to survive for hundreds of thousands of years. The fact that only stone lasts so long does not mean that earlier men used stone and nothing else.

Further developments of the culture of nomadic hunters can be traced in the Upper Palaeolithic. In the type of industry known as Solutrean the characteristic was the use of pressure flaking, in which one tool is pressed against the core and struck by another, producing finely grooved and sharp 'laurel-leaf' spearheads (Fig. 36.10). The last phase of Palaeolithic culture in Europe shows further progress in the making of burins and of artefacts produced by them (Fig. 36.11). These Magdalenian peoples of about 17 000 to 11 000 B.P., produced a large variety of fine instruments for hunting, including harpoons, fish hooks, arrowheads, hammers, spears, and needles. Some were elaborately decorated. Indeed, many of their products were purely decorative bracelets, pendants, and ritual batons and maces (Fig. 36.11(a)).

If the evidence can be trusted, it may be that after the advent of *Homo sapiens sapiens* the use of abstract symbols began to reach a much higher level than before. The faculties that enabled men to learn to make tools perhaps also generated the need for progressively more elaborate decoration. Yet these were still food-gathering peoples, probably without settled homes. It is not too much to suppose that their religions, symbolism, and decoration survived and developed because they were useful in various ways for

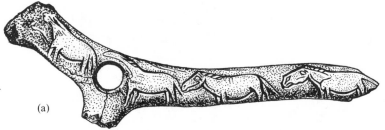

FIG. 36.11. Magdalenian artefacts made from reindeer antlers: (a) ceremonial baton, engraved with animal figures; (b) and (c) barbed harpoon-heads. From the type-site La Madeleine rock-shelter, Dordogne. *c.* 15 000 B.P. (After Oakley 1969.)

maintaining the delicate balance of personal initiative and satisfaction and social benefit that was needed for the hunting life to be successful.

8. Mesolithic culture. The retreat of the ice-sheet

During the period between about 15 000 and 5000 B.P. mankind expanded greatly and underwent changes almost as large as those that have occurred since. This was a period in which the climate became in general warmer and the ice-sheets retreated. Perhaps because of this the late Palaeo-lithic hunters were able to spread from the central areas of Africa and Eurasia over almost the whole world.

The dating of the retreat of the ice-sheet has been well worked out in northern Europe and is seen in Fig. 36.2, with the dates as given by carbon-14 measurements, and the main cultural stages. From about 14 000 B.P. on-wards the sea level has risen by 500 ft in the North Sea, owing to melting of the ice.

The effect of the retreat of the ice in Europe was that the open steppe and tundra were replaced by forests. Instead of the large herds of reindeer there were varied animal types, perhaps less abundant and more difficult to catch. For whatever reasons, the result seems to have been to concentrate the humans of this Mesolithic period in northern Europe into small groups, often along rivers, They fished and hunted small game, often with the small hafted weapons known as microliths. Conditions in general were evidently more favourable for men than before, and the culture became richer and more varied. Aesthetically some Mesolithic designs make a less immediate appeal to us than the large works of the late Palaeolithic cave painters. They include relatively simple abstract designs upon stones, but also many fine hunting scenes. Whatever their significance they certainly suggest a further

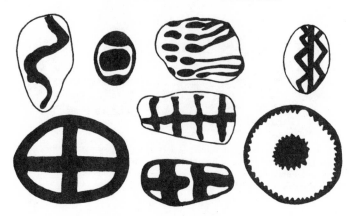

F1G. 36.12. Mesolithic painted pebbles (Azilian culture). *c.* 12 000 B.P. (After
Marringer 1960, from Carrington 1963.)

advance in symbolic thought and presumably language (see Chapter 37).
Some give a curious impression of a sort of 'pre-writing'. The human faculty
of isolating, abstracting, and symbolizing was developing relatively fast at
this time, though no doubt still slowly by the standards of recent centuries.
Corresponding to the level of abstraction the life was evidently increasingly
complex and 'remote from nature' in the sense that tools were becoming
continually more varied.

Some evidence about Mesolithic dwellings is known, but it is not clear to
what extent individuals and groups led a settled life in one place. Remains
from Danish bogs show huts made of branches pushed into the ground and
then pulled together at the top, and with bark floors. These Maglemosians
left no pieces of pottery, they cultivated no crops, and kept no animals
except dogs. On the other hand hunting and fishing became increasingly
refined. They made canoes, with paddles, and a whole array of fishing and
hunting gear including bows and arrows, harpoons (Figs. 36.11(b) and
(c)), netting needles and awls, spearheads, and axes. Their sledges are the
first known land vehicles. Many of their tools were made from antlers and
bones as well as wood and they were elaborately decorated. Some objects were
purely decorative, including charms and amulets and carved pieces of amber.

Of course it is really a mistake to try to describe the peoples and culture
of such an immense period as 4000 years as if they were the same all the time
or in different places. Throughout this period, from, say, 12 000 B.P. onwards, men were in general taking advantage of the warmer conditions and
were spreading over the earth. During this time they occupied the whole
of America, the Pacific islands, and Australia and spread northwards on
the Eurasian land mass where they were already established.

9. The first farming. Neolithic culture

The transition from the Mesolithic hunting to the Neolithic farming way of life took place gradually (see Hawkes and Woolley 1963). It began in south-west Asia about 9000 years B.P. and spread outwards. The ancestors of man's barley and wheat, sheep, goats, cattle, and pigs can be found around the deserts in Anatolia, Iraq, and Jordan. The change reached western Europe and Britain only about 5000 B.P. (3000 B.C.) as the 'Windmill Hill' culture. It spread gradually through Asia to China. It reached east Africa 3000 years ago and south Africa 1000 years later. Only today is it changing the way of life of the remaining hunter-fisher-gatherers in the Arctic, in Australia, and among the Bushmen, pygmies, and Bantu of Africa. The change seems to have occurred in America independently (p. 514).

The process may have begun by the specialization of later Palaeolithic hunters, some of whom became almost symbiotic with particular game species (Clark 1969). Thus the late Magdalenians found in a cave at Peters-fels in South Germany obtained four-fifths of their meat from reindeer. But such herds probably disappeared as the forests encroached and the people developed a more mixed economy, which gradually evolved into a settled way of life. There is evidence from Mureybit in Syria that wild barley was harvested about 9000 B.P. by people who also hunted wild oxen and gazelle.

Of course the transition happened in different ways at various times and places (see Childe 1942, 1966). There is ethnographic evidence that hunters and food-gatherers today may take some steps to conserve their stocks. They may avoid killing pregnant female animals or they may bury hoards of seeds. Archaeological evidence suggests that wild plants were reaped with sickles before true agriculture began. The domestication of animals perhaps sometimes occurred independently of that of plants.

The remains left by the people known as Natufians, living in Jordan and Israel about 10 000 years ago, provide evidence of the transition from hunting to agriculture. They lived in rock shelters, chiefly on fish and gazelle, but they used flint sickles, which clearly show signs that they were used to cut straw, or perhaps the wild emmer wheat. Some of their picks may have been used for digging the earth, for the planting of wheat and barley (rye, oats, and rice were cultivated only much later).

These people resembled the Maglemosians in many ways, and from such cultures there developed the first farming settlements. The remains show that the bones of wild animals account for only 5 per cent of the meat eaten, the rest were of sheep and goats. Barley, emmer wheat, and peas were planted, and flint microliths used to cut them. Mats were made but there was at first no pottery, though this appears in later levels. From such earliest farmers there gradually developed the full Neolithic culture with its characteristic polished stone axe-blades and pottery. An early Neolithic settlement is at Catal Hüyük in Anatolia (8000 years B.P.), which was a large community of closely packed houses, without doors, probably entered through a hole in the roof.

These Neolithic peoples could smelt copper and lead and used them for beads and ornaments, but not for tools. They made carvings and paintings, sometimes as decoration for small shrines. The first large temples are those of the Ubaid peoples of the Euphrates Valley. In the Tigris and Euphrates valleys, about 6500 years B.P., there developed the first full urban civilization, the Sumerian. Metallurgy grew from the making of a few copper axes and silver vessels to the addition of tin to copper to produce the full Bronze Age technology of tools and weapons (from 5000 B.P.). The Sumerians developed the first pictographic writing and wheeled vehicles. At about this time the beginnings of modern human social organization appeared in the great river valleys, including city states led by kings with armies. They were often at war with each other, and with marauding pastoral highlanders attracted by the wealth of the cities. Large parts of S.W. Asia were united under the First Dynasty of Babylon about 4000 B.P.

From 9000 to 5000 B.P. the Neolithic culture spread north over Europe. The gradation in frequency of blood-group genes across Europe probably shows the extent to which these new people intermixed with the existing hunters (Chapter 41). In the west of Europe there are still some pronounced signs of distinct populations, for example the Basques and Lapps, and in Sardinia. The Basques have a very high frequency of O and Rh genes and low of B genes (but their fingerprint patterns are similar to those of the populations around them). The increasing body size passing west and north in Europe may also show the remains of the long-continued presence of hunters under arduous conditions (p. 593).

There is no evidence that the transition from hunting to farming in America depended upon Neolithic colonization from the Old World, but it is hard to be sure that it was entirely independent. The first people to reach America were Palaeolithic hunters, and their descendants the Aleuts and Eskimos retain much of this culture today. Others migrating over the continent seem to have subsisted at first on wild plants and small game. The change to farming began somewhere in the centre, perhaps in Mexico, about 6000 B.P. From this time on there are signs of the cultivation of the local maize (not wheat or barley). The spread may have been slow because of the difficulties that agriculture meets in tropical forest areas (Chapter 25).

Cut and burn was (and is) the method in many places. In a few parts of America where there were valleys highly suitable for cultivation, like those of S.W. Asia, large-scale agriculture was developed. As a result civilization advanced faster, for example, in Peruvian valleys and on the coasts below the Andes than elsewhere.

10. The human explosion

The history of man's development after the Neolithic is too complicated to be followed here. After the discovery of the smelting of ores and making bronze, which probably occurred in south-west Asia about 5000 B.P., the agricultural instruments and weapons that were produced made it easier not only to till the soil and kill animals but also to fight other men. The discovery of iron some 2000 years later accelerated the processes of change that metal produced. With these new materials the inventive capacity of the human brain soon began to release the stream of new aids to life that has increased until today. The essential features that we have seen already in the changes of man in his early history continued and became greatly accentuated. New sorts of tools were invented, just as the stone hand-axes had been, to assist with living by substitution of some function that men previously performed with their unaided powers, and to do this with increasing efficiency. As the tools were perfected, symbolic communication about them was developed. New language forms such as those of logic and mathematics were invented and more and more subtle religious and philosophical concepts appeared. The communities that were able to take advantage of such developments survived at the expense of their neighbours. Education, conformity, and restraint must have been important factors, as well as inventiveness and physical strength. The power to discover and use new tools with which to get a living and to fight were increasingly necessities for success. All such capacities involve subtle features of the brain and glands, which are necessary for the 'cultural' factors to be transmitted. Unfortunately we know almost nothing about the inheritance of such capacities and can at present only speculate as to how it operates to determine human history, past, present, and future (see Darlington 1969).

It would be absurdly superficial to try to follow out the course of the development of modern man in simple biological terms. Yet it is fascinating to us to wonder what it was that led to our present developments and whether we can thus find any clue to the future. The changes in human life in the last 10 000 years have certainly been tremendous, both in quantity (more people) and quality (more variety of techniques and cultures). This explosion can reasonably be ascribed to the exploitation of the new favourable climatic conditions by people who had achieved the power of communication by symbolic means. Words confer the ability to discuss the properties of objects and events that are not present, and so to extend immensely the range of actions to meet the future, which we have seen to be the property of all life. Although we do not know when man acquired what we should call 'language' it was almost certainly long before 10 000 B.P. (p. 497). Language provides the opportunity for information to be passed between many individuals and not merely from two parents to their offspring as in the usual method of heredity. This constitutes what we may call multi-parental inheritance, and must have provided an enormous acceleration in the speed of evolutionary change. Culture had indeed been evolving rapidly before 10 000 B.P., but the 'explosion' must have been stimulated by some further change. Perhaps it was the climate. But it seems equally likely that some feature of human organization, perhaps in his pituitary gland, his hypothalamus, or his frontal lobes, made possible a still greater degree of co-operation and hence the settled community life of agricultural peoples.

11. Writing. The extra-somatic information store

The invention of writing seems to have occurred only after the beginnings of settlement and perhaps as a result of the social pressures set up (see Hawkes and Woolley 1963). There is some evidence of symbolic code-signs scratched on bones at Palaeolithic sites (Marschak), but the first undoubted tablets are from the Sumerians, about 3500 B.C. (5500 B.P.). The capacity to embody information in records outside the body provides an even further means of accelerating the rate of evolutionary change. With language and writing we have not only multiparental inheritance but an extra-corporeal information store. Written records are, like all other tools, an artificial substitute for a function that was previously performed in the body—in this case by the chromosomes of the germ cells. As has happened with other tools the invention of the capacity to make extra-somatic memory records in written codes has led eventually to an understanding of the code in the body. But it has taken men some 5000 years to do it (Chapter 3). Geneticists and biochemists now use the language of linguists to speak about the alphabet of the genes, just as physiologists speak of muscular work in terms of the concepts of energy that they have derived from engineers.

The inventions of language and writing were presumably the essential tools, if we may so call them, with which all the others were produced, and led to Bronze, Iron, and Machine ages. Yet the acquisition of a store of information has not been by any means uninterrupted. Periods of advance, such as those of the Chinese, Sumerians, Minoans, and Greeks have been followed by stagnation in the increase of knowledge, or its loss, as in

Barbarian Europe after the fall of the Romans. Over most parts of the world the process of gathering new information has in any case been slow and in some areas not apparent at all. The factors that have been responsible for the changes of some peoples may again be seen partly to come from without, in the climate, and partly from within, in the inherited capacities for social organization. Moderate climates stimulate invention and hinder diseases, especially those borne by parasites. Of course many civilizations have flourished in warm climates, but it is those of the temperate regions that have left long lasting information, notably China, Arabia, and Greece, leaving aside the more recent.

12. The biological basis of modern societies

The capacity to organize coherent and developing societies has been investigated intensively by anthropologists, but its biological basis is still not known, nor indeed whether it has any special basis (see Ardrey 1967). The different forms of symbolism, institutions, and laws must have varying degrees of effectiveness, even granted the variety of conditions. Family organization may have been inherited from pre-human ancestors or been evolved relatively early as a response to the needs of the Palaeolithic hunters (Chapter 34). Social groups seem to have become large relatively very rapidly after the beginning of the neothermal period. The biologist is naturally prone to suppose that there were particular biological features in the groups that gave rise to huge societies, with kings, priests, and slaves, religion, ritual, and war. It seems certain that there are hereditary differences in the constitution of individuals, making them more or less able to act effectively as members of large communities, whether as rulers or ruled. It is less certain how far such differences are important today, when the transmission of culture by language is relatively efficient. Our culture is inclined to believe that schemes of social organization are the result of cerebration and not of special inherited powers. But we have seen at various points in this inquiry how important is the underlying capacity that makes human performance possible. For example, the powers of speech as well as those of social co-operation certainly depend upon inherited nervous and glandular conditions. Selection for such features was probably the basis for the emergence of the unique organism Man. The selection involved some changes in outward visible structure, especially in the size and shape of the head. But the really important changes were invisible ones within. There is no reason to think that such selection has stopped. Little is known about differential reproduction today, but it certainly occurs (Chapters 38–41). Some types of men and women will prove to be more viable than others, and not only in the long run. It is likely that our successors a few hundred years from now will laugh at our childish methods of thought and co-operation. If they do not it will be because we have no successors.

It is interesting to consider whether the transition from the late Palaeolithic societies of 12 000 B.P. to the cities of 8000 B.P. was accompanied by a genetic change. Ecologically and socially the change was enormous—from carnivore to herbivore, from relatively small communities to large societies with complex hierarchical organization, from the technology of slaughter of wild animals to that of cultivation of crops and herds, and so on. All these seem to require great biological alteration in the species, yet could there have been enough genetic changes in a mere 4000 years, perhaps 160 generations? The biologist's answer must surely be that he would not expect them *unless man had evolved some special mechanism of selection and evolution*. It is by no means implausible that with the development of transfer of information by means other than genetic—by speech—the selection of those individuals who were competent in such skills became unusually severe at the expense of the non-speakers. The very power of speech, and the social organization that it made possible, may have led to the extinction by slaughter or by starvation of the groups that were less able to communicate and to organize. Similar replacements have proceeded in the subsequent 10 000 years and are still at work today. The fate of the Tasmanians and American Indians is not encouraging to any of the relatively less intelligent or less well-organized communities of the world.

EVIDENCE OF EARLY ART FORMS
AND RELIGION

1. The importance of art and ideology for survival

THERE is no body of facts that yet enables us to understand the origins of aesthetic creation or religious beliefs and practices. Presumably both sorts of activity were somehow of assistance to Palaeolithic man in the business of getting a living. This does not mean that carving, or painting, or offering prayers for the dead were crudely of 'practical' value, for instance, by improving hunting technique. Yet there is a case for saying that creation of new aesthetic forms, including those of worship, has been the most fundamentally productive of all forms of human activity. Whoever creates new artistic conventions has found methods of interchange between people about matters that were incommunicable before. The capacity to do this has been the basis of the whole of human history. It remains so today, and has taken many new shapes, including the creative discoveries of science and the inventions of engineering, as well as new forms of visual, literary, and musical artistic invention. Similarly, fresh and deeper religious, political, and other ideologies continually provide more and more convincing means of helping individuals to live together in effective societies, and also helping them with their separate lives. We are all aware how far from perfect our societies are today. The deficiencies make it hard to see that communication and creation are more advanced and helpful than ever before. Indeed, the very fact that they are so makes the deficiencies more obvious, because so much more publicized.

Man has produced a set of techniques for communication that enables individuals to co-operate to obtain a living. These techniques are highly varied and complicated and we still do not know how each of them contributes to the maintenance of society. How much does the transfer of information depend upon the developments that we call Art? Can there be Law and sufficient conformity of individuals without the beliefs and rituals that we call Religion? Can there be Peace without War?

It is beyond the young science of human biology to provide answers to these questions. But we can begin to see some of the factors that have been and are still at work at determining human conduct. In particular we can survey some of the most characteristic human activities of people in the past. We can even very tentatively relate them to the probable human needs at that time. Apart from the scarcity of evidence there is a serious danger of pomposity in interpreting the evidence that is available, such as by labelling sexy statues as symbols of fertility myths, or wounded animals as signs of hunting cults and so on. At first sight it seems that these activities present no problem; most humans (and animals) are interested in sex and in food. Therefore, it is said, 'Of course people *enjoy* talking about them or making symbols of them. What more explanation do we need for representations?' But chimpanzees do not make sex symbols, either sensuous and aphrodisiac or abstract and symbolic. What we have to ask is whether there is any evidence about when and why human beings began to do such things.

2. The art of making tools and weapons

We have to think back to the time, say, 3 000 000 years ago, when our still ape-like ancestors had no art and no religion at all. Their 'law' was probably the product of instinctive attack and threat by the strong, and retreat and submission by the weaker (Chapter 43). Their language was perhaps a series of grimaces and sounds expressing the reactions of the individual to each particular situation as it occurred and calling for the appropriate reaction of his fellows.

It is surely significant that the first evidence of what we may call nearly human behaviour is of the making of tools, and in particular weapons. A stone chipped to make a chopper is pre-eminently practical and is directly useful for helping in survival. It is a startling fact that making of tools of stone and bone remained the sum of man's creative achievement that left any material trace for perhaps 2 million years. Of course flint is durable, whereas artefacts in wood or other material are unlikely to survive for such long periods. We have continually to remember that the evidence that we have is biased by its very capacity to survive.

Looking at the stone tools, however, it seems that creative efforts for nearly 2 million years were devoted to relatively small improvements in the techniques of napping. We do not know whether changes were gradual or in jumps, but in the aggregate they were exceedingly slow. Human generations succeeded each other for tens of thousands upon tens of thousands of years, leaving hardly any signs of change in way of life. Of course, there were certainly some changes that have left no trace. Yet stability over such a long time suggests that the early techniques for making and using weapons may have proceeded in an almost stereotyped way, depending little on the vagaries of individual creation. Nevertheless, the very slow changes in methods of flint chipping may have contained the first elements of creative art. To make something for future use already argues a capacity for abstraction from the present. To make it so that it is sharper or otherwise does its job better than before is creative even if not 'artistic'. To chip it in such a way that it shows patterns of symmetry or rhythm may make it a pleasure to see, to hold, and to use, and the result may therefore be *more practical because it is more 'beautiful'*.

Some animals as well as humans are said to show responses to rhythms of visual pattern as well as of action. It is claimed that apes, monkeys, and birds choose visual patterns that show rhythm rather than disorder (Rensch 1957). Many young animals perform rhythmical jumps and gymnastic feats in their play. Juvenile play may be in itself an education for life and could be the basis, with juvenile curiosity, for feats of creativeness. Capacity to develop new and individual action patterns is characteristic of the brains of mammals, and especially of primates, and is of course most evident in the young. One may not think much of chimpanzee painting, but at least the young ones do it. When they get older they can no longer be bothered to be creative (Morris 1962).

Rhythm and balance are features of action patterns, and visual art translates them into symbols. It is not impossible that the chipping of a flint to make it better to handle may have been the earliest manifestation of art, as it certainly was of craft. It may have been the parent of many other arts or, indeed, of all of them.

It is worth speculating in this way because the prevalence of stone tools for such a very long preliminary period of human history is our chief source of data on the subject. Of course, there may have been other artefacts that have perished (there were certainly some of bone) and there may have been rhythmical dances before religion, and simple language long before that, all of which left no enduring remains. But the signs that *were* left were of stone, and stone tools are above all *useful*. They may also have been 'beautiful', and the makers may have enjoyed making them, in the sense at least that their life was much improved when they made good ones, easy on the hand as well as the eye, and more effective in the hunt. Those societies in which the young were good learners would be provided with good craftsmen, able by good language to pass on their skills. The earliest consumers of the products of both art and education may well have been the leaders of the hunt, who would have also been the first art critics!

3. The use of fire

The next innovation of which we have evidence is the use of fire, first found in the lower cave near Pekin, with the remains of *Homo erectus*, perhaps 500 000 years ago, and also at Vértesszöllös in Hungary. Fire was no doubt important in many different ways, for keeping away carnivores as well as for keeping people warm. By assisting digestion cooking may have made more food available (and made it more palatable). One of the advantages of a carnivorous way of life is that the time spent eating is reduced. Large herbivores must eat for many hours a day. The technology of making and keeping fires no doubt also provided further stimulus to language and co-operation.

4. The earliest burials and evidence of religious beliefs

A further major sign of cultural advance that is left to us is burial, first without additions and then with the accompaniment of decorative ornaments and beads and their arrangement in designed patterns. All these are tremendous advances and the signs of them come only after a long interval, with the Mousterian culture, probably of *H. s. neanderthalensis*. At La Ferrassie in France more than 35 000 years ago, two adults were buried in recesses, one natural and one excavated. There were also two child burials, one in a ditch containing animal bones, which were plausibly left as offerings. The other child was buried under a stone decorated on its lower side with a simple pattern of pairs of pits. Such 'cup marks' are often found in later burials, though their symbolism is obscure. Other Neanderthal burials have been found at La Chapelle (35 000–45 000 years old) and Mount Carmel (*c.* 41 000 years old). They are few and simple. But at both sites there are some signs that offerings had been buried, including at La Chapelle the bones of a whole animal still articulated. At Monte Circeo in Italy there was a ring of stones around the skull, whose base was fractured as if (perhaps) the brain had been eaten.

These evidences of offerings are the best signs that we have of the beginnings of religious practices. The fact of burial itself is often difficult to prove and in any case might have involved simply disposal of the body. More complex burials begin to appear some 10 000 years later, in the flourishing Gravettian period of the warmer times of the Paudorf oscillation, around 25 000 years ago. The woman buried near the carving of Fig. 37.1 was crouched and facing west at Dolní Věstonice in Czechoslovakia. With her were placed tools, also the paws and tail of an arctic fox in one hand and its teeth in the other. Her body and head had been painted with red ochre and were covered by two large mammoth scapulae, one scratched with lines. Evidently a whole series of symbols are involved, though we can only guess at their meaning. People with such developed symbolism must have had a language with already a long history and possibly not fundamentally different from language today.

The origins of religious practices may have been very much earlier, and have left no trace. Possibly they may have begun simply as patterns of movement or sound. It is likely that such activities were parts of the system of intercommunication that enabled individuals to co-operate to obtain a living. The enforcement of morality and co-operation is a prominent feature of religions today. It is possible to imagine that those groups of early men in which individuals were united by common ceremonies, and enjoyed satisfying rhythmic experiences, whether of visual pattern or dance, would have been more coherent and successful than less 'cultured' neighbours. The linking of such ceremonies with sexual practices may have had a basis in their aphrodisiac effects. The sexual practices would in any case be subject to restrictions to ensure adequate numbers and care of the young, as they are in all primates and, indeed, other animals.

More abstract conceptions of gods, spirits, and magic may have come later (though still long before the Gravettian burials), with the further development of language and especially with the descriptive analysis of self and not-self in terms of person language (Chapter 10). One can speculate indefinitely about possible origins for the elaborate web of beliefs and practices that mankind has constructed. They are compounded of fears and hopes and of methods for obtaining a whole variety of biologically practical results, including the proper distribution of territory and of genes. It would be offensive as well as unscientific to attempt to give any superficial general account of these cherished and often socially central practices. The biologist must recognize the fact of the belief of many people in the existence of a transcendent Spirit. To make such a generalization has been one of the most astonishing feats of human brains. Such beliefs are held and stated as a result of cerebral action. We may therefore hope that better

FIG. 37.1. Woman's head carved in ivory from Dolní Věstonice (Czechoslovakia). Gravettian, c. 25 000 years B.P. (Moravian Museum, Brno.) (After Sandars 1968.)

knowledge of the brain will give us still better beliefs, or at least better insight into those that we have. The purpose of the study of man is to *enlarge* his capacities and his understanding, including his faculties of wonder and worship, and his appreciation of beauty. This is the process of growth of culture in the widest sense, which has been going on at least for the last 25 000 years, during which men have certainly held some sort of view of the agents at work in the world. Probably the process began long before that, but if so it left no enduring mark until men began to bury their dead.

The recognition of death is probably very ancient. Baboons in zoos give a characteristic bark when surrounding a dead individual (Zuckerman 1932). After a chorus of these barks have been heard at night in the wild a dead baboon may be found the next morning (Marais 1939). A possible sign of interest in the dead is that the remains of *Australopithecus* in the Makapansgat caves seemed to be placed against the wall, away from the main pile of animal bones.

The solution to the problems of the origins of religion would be of great value, but no one has yet found a way of using the earliest known burials and ornaments to solve them. Burial suggests a developed system of description of the self and its endurance, but other religious forms may have existed before belief in soul and spirit. Rituals and dances, like fears of devils or aspirations towards gods, leave few or no remains.

Apart from burials there are few signs of religious activity until the beginnings of Neolithic life in the Middle East, less than 10 000 years ago. From then onwards shrines and temples and their accompanying images and symbols become increasingly common. There must have been religious gatherings before this, and perhaps particular places were treated as sacred long before temples were built. It may be that these were often hills of striking shape and even that artificial hills were constructed as convenient meeting-places, the first cathedrals (Fig. 37.2). Indeed Canterbury and other cathedrals rest on henge megalithic monuments (Borst 1969, Young 1950).

5. Upper Palaeolithic carving—the first symbolic art forms

The first evidence that is left of the capacity to make representations of men and animals comes from the Upper Palaeolithic. Aesthetic endeavour may have begun much earlier in improvement of the symmetry of weapons of stone, in carvings of bark or wood, and especially in production of ornaments. In a cave at Brno in Czechoslovakia the figure shown in Fig. 37.3 was buried with a necklace (or head-dress) of hundreds of pieces of mother-of-pearl from the shells of the mollusc *Dentalium*. Ornaments were no doubt used before this, perhaps originally to increase the attractiveness or impressiveness of the individual to his fellow men (or women). The function of

FIG. 37.2. Photograph of Silbury Hill (England). This is the largest man-made mound in Europe. Its date and function are unknown. (Aerofilms Ltd.)

trinkets is rather simply to excite attention, even today. The making of representations is a much more complex activity. A carved or painted figure can serve to excite emotion, but it also transmits a message indicating a particular creature *that is not present when the object is seen.* This is the essence of abstract symbolism.

The earliest of these representations that have survived were carved figures, either on cave walls or as small statues. The small figurines may have been carried by the hunters on their wanderings. However, nearly all of them come from huts at Aurignacian or E. Gravettian sites in eastern Europe, from the somewhat warmer period (though the climate was still as hostile as, say, that of much of northern Canada today). There were some signs of settled life in simple houses with clay walls and stone floors. Mammoth and reindeer were main items of food, no doubt along with smaller animals and plants. It seems likely that these people had largely abandoned the nomadic life, which was continued much longer by the Magdalenians of western Europe, but these, although they painted much in caves, left no figurines.

The carvings show a preponderance of animals, but human figures are not rare. Among the oldest is a large statue of a man, carved in mammoth ivory, from a burial in Brno, probably 25 000–30 000 years old (Fig. 37.3). This is a highly naturalistic carving, showing rather heavy brows, as there were indeed also on the skull that was found with the figure. Equally natural- istic are the animals of bone and ivory of about the same date found at

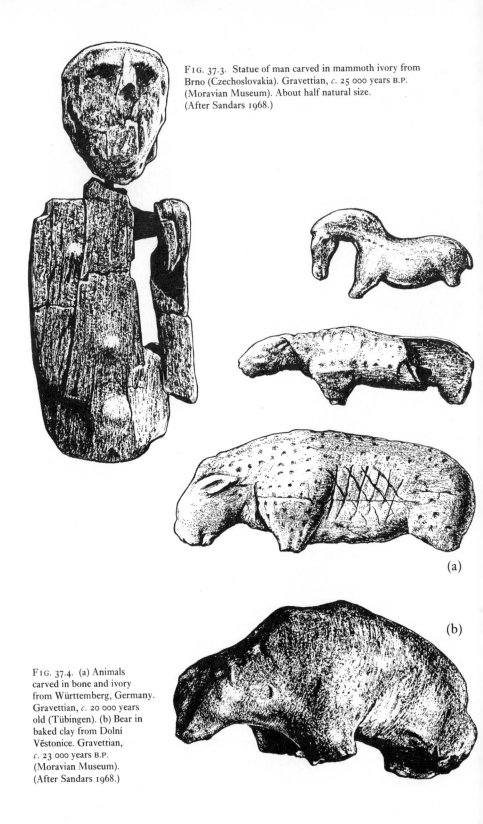

FIG. 37.3. Statue of man carved in mammoth ivory from Brno (Czechoslovakia). Gravettian, *c.* 25 000 years B.P. (Moravian Museum). About half natural size. (After Sandars 1968.)

(a)

(b)

FIG. 37.4. (a) Animals carved in bone and ivory from Württemberg, Germany. Gravettian, *c.* 20 000 years old (Tübingen). (b) Bear in baked clay from Dolní Věstonice. Gravettian, *c.* 23 000 years B.P. (Moravian Museum). (After Sandars 1968.)

FIG. 37.5. Woman's torso carved in haematite from Ostrava Petřkovice (Czechoslovakia). Gravettian, *c.* 25 000 years B.P. (Brno, Academy of Sciences). (After Sandars 1968.)

FIG. 37.6. Limestone statue of a woman from Willendorf (Austria). Late Gravettian-Solutrean, *c.* 18 000 years B.P. (Vienna).

Württemberg (Germany) and the remarkable woman's torso from Ostrava Petřkovice (Czechoslovakia) (Figs. 37.4 and 37.5).

The Venus of Willendorf, a limestone figure of roughly the same date (from Austria, Fig. 37.6) shows no facial features, but is still not strongly formalized or idealized. We have few samples of this early art of carving to judge from, and dates are approximate, since they are near the limit of the usefulness of the carbon-14 method. But many of the earliest were naturalistic representations of men and animals. Some, indeed, may even be portraits of individuals. The carved face of Fig. 37.1 shows a crooked mouth and brow such as might perhaps have been due to an injury to the left facial nerve ('Bell's palsy'). Curiously enough there was found near by the skeleton of an old woman of 40, buried with elaborate ritual, and showing damage on the left of the skull. Was she a famous leader 25 000 years ago? Even more curiously there is another face with similar features roughly sketched in a dwelling near by (Fig. 37.7) (Sandars 1968).

We understand about as much and as little of the significance of these early signs of human artistic creation as we do of the

FIG. 37.7. Drawing of two of the ivory heads from Dolní Věstonice, showing possibly similar facial deformity. (After Sandars 1968.)

basic social significance of the efforts of artists today. To make the figurines the Palaeolithic sculptors must have required good tools, physical skill, much observation, and also thought, leisure, and some motivation. From the earliest times art involved the double task of making something and of matching it with natural objects. It is interesting that the earliest works of art that have been found include several representations of the human face and figure. This may perhaps be no more than an accident, but it agrees with our suggestion that communication among humans centres on recognition of facial signs and that learning of these is the first task of the child's brain. The earliest communication by symbols may well have included indication of facts about people when they were absent. It is quite possible that the deficiencies of the earliest verbal communications were assisted by the use of visible symbols. Such communications may at first have been only about matters of overwhelming importance, such as the unity and discipline of the group. The name of the leader would be among the verbal signs to demand the greatest attention, and an image would help.

Of course, we know from the prevalence of burials that religion was already well developed much earlier than these signs of art from about 25 000 years ago. The continuation of the name and image of the leader as a symbol of unity may have been as much a cause as a result of the development of religious burial. It is all too easy to speculate—yet perhaps the exercise has some value in making us think about why men act as they do. As we have seen, it is not possible to reconstruct the origins of either art or religion. Yet origins they must have had, in the truest sense, for they are not there in apes. Almost certainly they arose gradually, at a much earlier period, first in some elementary form in which we should hardly recognize them today. They were of value for the powers of co-operation and communication that they conferred on the groups that practised them. Their practices possibly included emphasis on the human face and figure. These may have served as symbols of the dawning consciousness of the individual as an entity able to discourse of himself, others, and the world.

Other pressing subjects of discourse were of course sex, food, and enemies. Besides the human figures the earliest representations include animals and various sex symbols (Fig. 37.8). Some of these may have served quite simply as salacious objects to arouse or appease sexual desire; pornography has a long and honourable history in the genesis of art. The rich literature of psychological studies today tells us much of the significance of the representations that humans make, and the early propensity to sexual symbolism provides some useful data in forming a realistic view of Man.

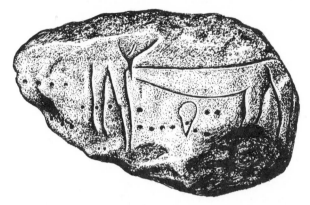

FIG. 37.8. Female signs (vulvae) and an animal engraved on rock at La Ferrassie, Dordogne, France. Aurignacian, *c.* 30 000 years B.P. (After Sandars 1968.)

6. Palaeolithic cave art

Palaeolithic cave-painting was largely restricted to a limited area in southern France and the Pyrenees, with a few outlying examples elsewhere in western Europe (Ucko and Rosenfeld 1967). Thus there were evidently great geographical differences between various Upper Palaeolithic cultures. In eastern Europe there was no cave art but many animal and human figurines carved in ivory or stone; in the west there were fewer figurines and fewer representations of man, but many caves with animal paintings. Even allowing for the accidents of survival these differences suggest that from its earliest appearance the making of representations, one of the most distinctive characters of man, was culturally conditioned and used varied conventions. But of course these earliest *surviving* evidences of art forms do not tell us when or how it began. Nor can we tell whether there was any steady progression such as from chipping flints to carving figures, to making of low relief, and so to drawing and painting. Some of the earliest representations are of animal heads engraved on small stones from the early Aurignacian cultures of perhaps more than 30 000 years ago at La Ferrassie (Fig. 37.8). From the later Aurignacian (known as Perigordian) at Labatut there are securely dated painted deer (Fig. 37.10), as well as an engraved horse. The well-known bas-relief figures at Laussel also probably belong to this period (Fig. 37.11).

Few cave-paintings can be referred with certainty to the Solutrean and early Magdalenian periods, but this does not prove that none then existed. The great majority of the work is usually referred to the latter part of the Magdalenian, say 15 000–11 000 years B.P., but much of it cannot be securely dated and may be from a long time earlier.

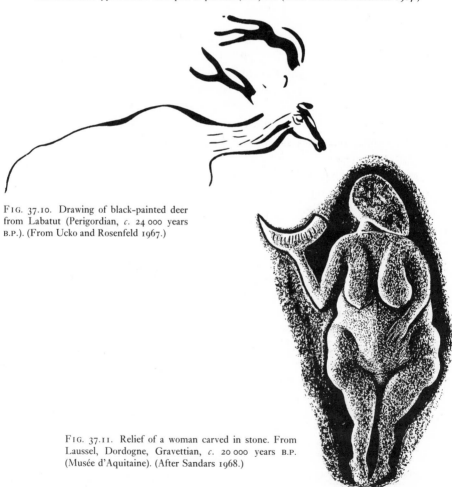

Year B.C.	Culture	Tools and Weapons		Parietal art
10 000		Late		
15 000	Magdalenian	Middle		
		Early		
20 000	Solutrean Proto-Magdalenian Perigordian	Late		
25 000	Aurignacian	Middle		
30 000	Châtelperronian	Early		

FIG. 37.9. Time chart of the Upper Palaeolithic in western Europe, with carbon-14 determinations and some typical dated examples of parietal (wall) art. (After Ucko and Rosenfeld 1967.)

FIG. 37.10. Drawing of black-painted deer from Labatut (Perigordian, *c.* 24 000 years B.P.). (From Ucko and Rosenfeld 1967.)

FIG. 37.11. Relief of a woman carved in stone. From Laussel, Dordogne, Gravettian, *c.* 20 000 years B.P. (Musée d'Aquitaine). (After Sandars 1968.)

7. Techniques of cave-painting

Painting was practised in a variety of situations, sometimes in caves that were occupied, but more often deep within long tortuous passages, far from the light. In some places the remains of the torches used have been found. When the paintings are high up, as at Lascaux, they must have required either a pole or else some kind of scaffolding, and evidence of the remains of this has been claimed. Bas-relief sculpting, engraving, and painting were often combined, especially the last two. The paints were earth pigments of various shades of red, brown, and yellow, obtained from ochre, native or burnt. Manganese oxides provided violet and black, which were also made from soot and burnt animal substances. No blues or greens are known.

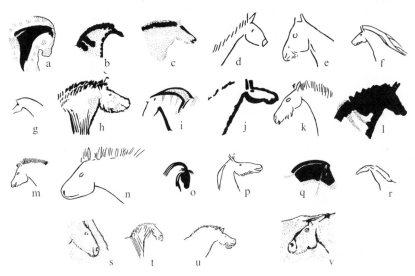

FIG. 37.12. The variety of styles used by Palaeolithic artists to show horses' heads.
(From Ucko and Rosenfeld 1967.)

The animals are shown by a great variety of clever abstractions and techniques, used to show characteristic details (Fig. 37.12). The styles are so varied that it is hard to identify any specific conventions characteristic of 'Palaeolithic art' as a whole. Moreover the attempt to trace the evolution of styles has so far ended mainly in controversy. Using securely dated works Laming (1959) has modified the original scheme produced by Breuil. Roughly there can be recognized an early Aurignacian–Perigordian period in which there are stencils of hands, rows of dots, large red signs, and meandering lines of clay and simple outlines of animals—in one colour.

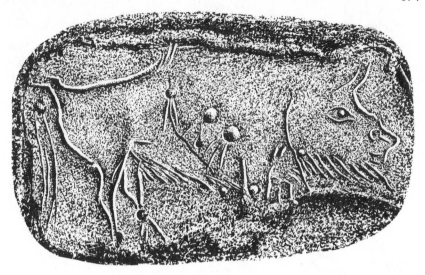

F IG. 37.13. Figure of bison engraved in floor with natural hollows. Niaux, France. Magdalenian *c.* 13 000 years B.P. (After Sandars 1968.)

These are naturalistic but with either stiff legs or none, the horns shown full face in twisted perspective.

In the second 'stage' there are many low-relief sculptures, black animal outlines in blotted or dotted lines, and flat-work figures in red, black, or sepia, sometimes bichromes. The twisted perspective is more elaborately used.

In Laming's third stage we have the fully developed Magdalenian polychrome paintings and black engraved animals, shown in true perspective (Fig. 37.13).

These attempts at classification are very attractive but must be looked at cautiously since they make many assumptions, especially that the styles were the same everywhere at any one time, whereas variety is one of the characteristics of Palaeolithic art, as it is of art today (Ucko and Rosenfeld 1967).

The animals shown are mostly horses, cattle, mammoth, woolly rhinoceros, cave lion, red deer, and reindeer. The individual animals are often drawn with striking skill, though with stereotyped techniques. Sometimes the paintings are of groups but there is little composition as we know it, which would indeed be difficult with the limitations of the caves. The figures may be superposed on each other, perhaps to represent herds, perhaps simply because drawn by successive visitors (Fig. 37.14). Human figures bearing animal heads sometimes appear. In other 'compositions' there are strange collections of figures presumably symbolic—but of what? (Fig. 37.15).

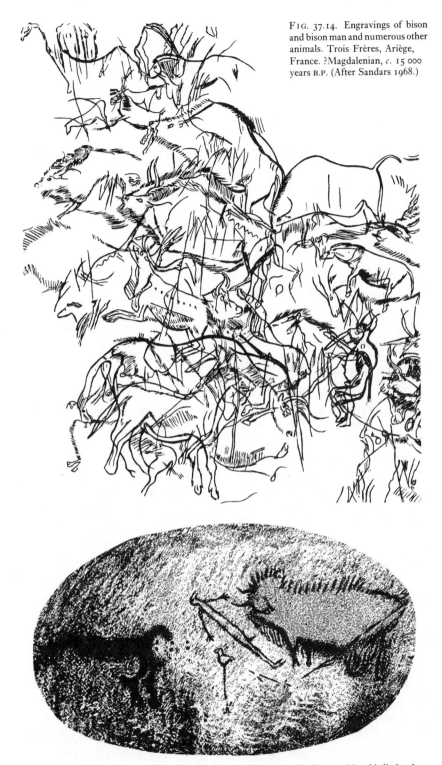

FIG. 37.14. Engravings of bison and bison man and numerous other animals. Trois Frères, Ariège, France. ?Magdalenian, c. 15 000 years B.P. (After Sandars 1968.)

FIG. 37.15. Wall painting said to include a wounded bison, a dead man with a bird's head, a bird on a stick, and a rhinoceros. The scene is in a shaft of the cave and is hard to view. Lascaux, Dordogne, France. Early Magdalenian c. 17 000 years B.P. (After Sandars 1968.)

8. Composition and placing of paintings

Recently, discussion about interpretation of cave-painting has centred around the fact that the representations of various animals are not scattered at random but are grouped more or less systematically. There is often a rather regular sequence, proceeding from the entrance of the cave. First are signs classed by some archaeologists as male and with them animals said to be symbolic of masculinity, horses, deer, and ibex. There follow signs alleged to be female and animals supposed symbolic of that sex— cattle, bison, and mammoth—often forming the main pictures at the centre of the system. Still further in there may be other male symbols (Leroi-Gourhan 1965).

If the arrangement of the figures and signs is correctly interpreted, it seems to have some sexual symbolic significance. But Leroi-Gourhan, who has analysed the paintings extensively, seems not to be prepared to say much more about the significance than that it was in some way religious. Moreover, the identification and classification of the figures is by no means easy or certain (see Ucko and Rosenfeld 1967).

9. The 'meaning' of cave-paintings

The fact is that in spite of all the analysis we do not know why the Upper Palaeolithic peoples did these paintings. Their reasons may, indeed, have been as varied as those that are given by Australian aborigines, who also do cave painting.

The paintings may have been connected with a system of fertility magic or with a cult of food magic, the representation supposedly serving to increase the probability of finding game. A few of the animals are apparently pierced with spears and this has also suggested that they are enactments of hunting scenes. They could indeed have served as pictorial adjuncts to verbal communication in something of the way suggested above for early sculpture. Pictures are a great help to communication even today and would have been even more so if talking itself was a laborious and perhaps boring task, as writing is for young children now. But such explanations are much too simple. For one thing the caves were dark and inaccessible—not at all the place to teach the young to hunt.

Probably by the Upper Palaeolithic period of man's history ideas had already developed on to much more subtle planes. The pictures almost certainly have some kind of magical or mystical purpose, directed to influencing events, perhaps with rituals to pacify spirits, postulated as likely to be inimical if not placated. It is a pity that we have not yet been able to interpret them well enough to understand how men spoke and thought in those days. Probably the motivation to paint was complex then, as it is

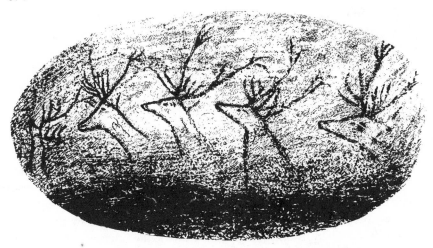

FIG. 37.16. Row of heads of deer tossing as if running or swimming in a herd. Magdalenian, Lascaux. *c.* 15 000 years B.P. (After Sandars 1968.)

today. The urge to represent seems strong in creatures like humans who are steeped in symbolism. The annual migrations of masses of animals upon which the men depended must have powerfully aroused this tendency to represent the objects of interest, their multiplicity, their movement (Fig. 37.16), and their death at the hands of the hunters. Perhaps it was this very tendency to represent that provided the capacity for communication upon which co-operative hunting depended. It may have spilled over from dance form and ritual into sounds and words, and as these became more abstract, into signs and pictures, conserved deep in the caves and added to by generation after generation of hunters on their regular migrations. The three main theories that have been put forward to 'explain' cave painting may perhaps be summarized as follows (see Ucko and Rosenfeld 1967).

1. *Art for art's sake*

The paintings may have been done simply for the pleasure of the painter or to decorate the living space of the group. This motivation cannot be ignored, but neither can it be accepted as the whole answer. Everyday experience tells us that *H. sapiens sapiens* likes drawing and painting. Ethnological studies tell us that food-gathering peoples, such as Australians who decorate caves today, give this as part of their motive. As evidence that the matter is more complex than this is the inconvenience of the placing of many Palaeolithic paintings and the fact that they show only a limited subject-matter—nearly always large food animals, rarely humans, carnivores, or birds, and never plants or inanimate objects.

On the other hand, some paintings are at accessible sites, which were used for occupation; these in fact include more representations of humans than are found in the caves. It may well be that these were done for purposes of decoration or as erotic stimulants, or perhaps just as 'doodles', even by children. Many of the obscure signs may perhaps have no 'meaning' at all; and the superposition of one drawing on another may have no more significance than imitative repetition.

2. *Sympathetic magic*

With all possible allowance for the artistic and casual reasons there remain strong indications that the paintings have an element of symbolism. The choice of subject suggests that this was concerned with the hunt, serving to make more prey available either by magic or instruction, or by a mixture of both these. There is still disagreement about the interpretation of the marks on the animals that are classified as spears or wounds, and not all carry them. One observer who is himself a hunter has suggested that many of the representations seem to be drawings of *dead* animals (Leason 1939). The extent of belly revealed, the perspective of the legs, projecting tongue, and prominent jaw suggest that they were drawn from prostrate corpses, not standing animals. Yet another interpretation is that the large bellies sometimes shown indicate pregnant animals, presumably as part of a fertility cult. Difficulties with all such suggestions are that they generalize from a few instances and take insufficient account of the possibility that the features shown are stylistic conventions. The artist may draw animals as if from the side because that was the accepted way to do it; this was the way animals were thought of and that was how you showed them. The concept may have come originally from seeing dead animals, without the artist meaning to represent dead ones in his picture.

3. *The pictures as symbols of religion or totemism*

The Abbé Breuil, who made a comprehensive study of the paintings, insisted that the caves were in essence 'sanctuaries'. There is certainly much to show that they were indeed connected with some kind of ritual. The very fact of difficulty of access points to some secret ceremonial purpose. An obvious suggestion is that the animal signs were somehow connected with totemism, that is the division of society into a number of groups each connected with an animal. The art of modern hunting communities sometimes has some such connection (but by no means always!). There are some suggestions that the caves may have been used for initiation ceremonies; for example, there may be numerous small foot-marks, said to be those of children (but how big were the Palaeolithic feet anyway?).

Perhaps the strongest evidence of ritual significance is the fact of the varying proportions of the various animals in different parts of the caves. Counts have been made by Leroi-Gourhan to substantiate this plan, but the identifications of the animals are bound to be difficult and the percentages in different parts of the caves are not very convincing (Ucko and Rosenfeld 1967).

Ucko and Rosenfeld conclude that the truth is that we do not understand the paintings. 'It is possible . . . that some representations were the work of children (perhaps some of the floor engravings), that some were used in acts of sympathetic magic (perhaps some of the representations pierced with holes), that some were placed in particular situations in order to please (perhaps some of the open-air low-reliefs), and that some were illustrations of myths and traditions (perhaps those which contain imaginary creatures, anthropomorphs and unexpected combinations of animal species). It is very possible, however, that some and perhaps many Palaeolithic representations were made for reasons which still totally escape the modern observer.'

10. The origins of abstraction

The evidence suggests that already by the Upper Palaeolithic the human brain had begun to see objects in a new way, which we can describe as 'abstract'. Men began to 'take-away' parts of descriptions of things from their context and to use them in other connections to make forecasts. Characteristic of this is the use of tools to make other tools, as mentioned already. Again, although many of the figures were naturalistic representations of detail, others were highly abstract (Fig. 37.17). We do not know

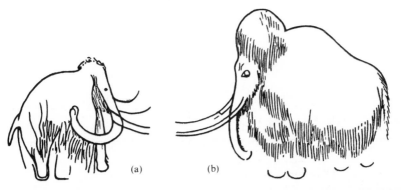

FIG. 37.17. To show how painting may have become more abstract. The Aurignacian drawing (a) (c. 25 000 years B.P.) is clumsy, but naturalistic and complete. The Magdalenian mammoth (b) (c. 15 000 years B.P.) concentrates on essentials ('a general impression of tusky woolliness. The eye is conventionalised and out of drawing. The legs and feet . . . are suggested by incomplete ellipses'). (After Pumphrey 1953, and Burkitt 1925.)

FIG. 37.18. Gravettian–Solutrean sculpture of a woman (*c.* 20 000 years B.P.). (After Pumphrey 1953, and Burkitt 1925.)

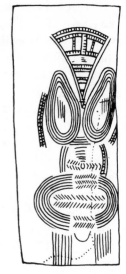

FIG. 37.19. Gravettian engraving representing womanhood, ?*c.* 20 000 years B.P. (After Pumphrey 1953, and Burkitt 1925.)

when this capacity for abstraction began but it may have become progressively more prominent. The early artists showed human figures and faces in full detail very effectively (Fig. 37.18). But in other works and especially later, they tended to emphasize particular features (femininity, Fig. 37.19) and finally produced purely abstract patterns (Fig. 37.20).

It has been suggested by Pumphrey (1953) that this power of abstraction is related to the development of the power of planning several stages of action in the future, and so to the development of language. He pointed out that sounds constitute an exchange both of general information about the

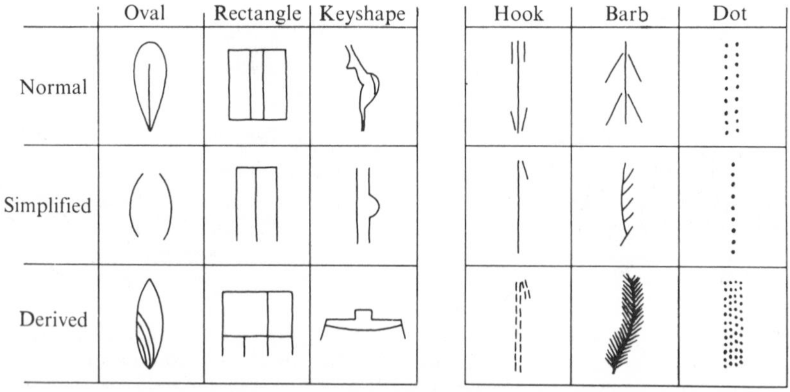

	Oval	Rectangle	Keyshape		Hook	Barb	Dot
Normal							
Simplified							
Derived							

FIG. 37.20. Signs from Upper Palaeolithic cave paintings and their suggested interpretations. Those on the left are female; those on the right, male. (After Leroi-Gourhan 1968.)

state of.two or more communicators, and of detailed factual information (which he calls 'intelligence').

For example, studies by telephone engineers of the possibility of limiting the waveband used in speech have shown that if the normal wide band (between 10 and 10 000 cycles per second) is gated so as to pass through ten narrow gates each 32 cycles wide (using a device known as a 'vocoder') then the 'intelligence' gets through, but all the 'personality' and 'emotion' of the speaker is lost.

The lesson that this teaches is that the total amount of information over a wide bandwidth provides us with clues about how to react to situations, but the detailed information is carried in a much more abstract and limited *code*. Indeed, to discard the emotional information is an *advantage*. As Pumphrey pointed out, if the word 'lion' began as some kind of imitative expression and it at first aroused all the responses appropriate to the animal, then its use would have been limited if all the hearers gave the right escape reactions! Speech becomes really useful only when the brain learns to attach a core of meaning to abstract conventional symbols used to talk about the animal or object when it is not there, and so to be able to combine word signals to communicate detailed forecasts about the future. We shall probably never know exactly when this first became possible (as Pumphrey said, 'Nothing leaves less trace in history than sound waves'). The early existence of abstract art suggests that it may have occurred already by the Upper Palaeolithic. No doubt long before that time a complex vocabulary of useful sounds had been built up. But it was only when they became abstract, and hence could become brief, that language acquired its flexibility. Even today we see proceeding a continuing tendency to simplify the formal structure of language and to reduce redundancy.

Unfortunately our understanding of Upper Palaeolithic art is still too imperfect to allow us to read from it much about the evolution of brain processes. The interpretation given by Pumphrey would be challenged by others, who have seen in the sequence of styles increasing skill in naturalistic reproduction (Fig. 37.21) (Leroi-Gourhan 1968). No doubt with further analysis we shall learn how to judge these styles better. They provide one of our best hopes of solving the great problem of the origins of our own culture.

Certainly the power of abstraction was highly developed even in the Upper Palaeolithic. The more naturalistic figures were often accompanied by abstract signs, even in the earliest Aurignacian times. Many, perhaps most, of the signs are interpreted as human figures—either female if 'wide' or male if 'narrow' (Fig. 37.20). The tendency to draw representations of human sexual organs upon walls is strong even today, and perhaps we understand the significance of modern graffiti little better than we do those of the Aurignacians.

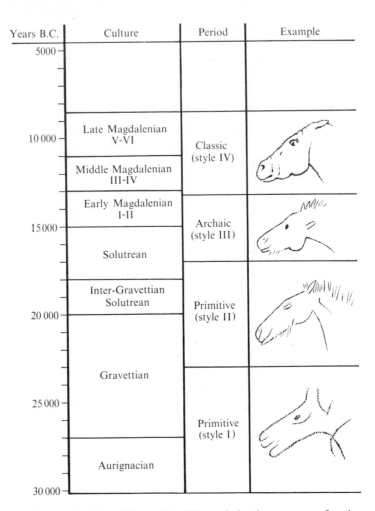

Years B.C.	Culture	Period	Example
5000			
10 000	Late Magdalenian V-VI	Classic (style IV)	
	Middle Magdalenian III-IV		
15000	Early Magdalenian I-II	Archaic (style III)	
	Solutrean		
20 000	Inter-Gravettian Solutrean	Primitive (style II)	
25 000	Gravettian	Primitive (style I)	
30 000	Aurignacian		

FIG. 37.21. Styles of Upper Palaeolithic art during the 20 000 years from its appearance with the Aurignacians about 30 000 B.P. (After Leroi-Gourhan 1968.)

HUMAN VARIETY TODAY

1. Is human variety useful?

THE evidence of previous chapters shows that the species *H. sapiens*, like others, has included sub-populations with differing characteristics. It has been claimed that man is especially variable and that this very variety has been a part of the secret of the success of the species, but other primates are probably equally variable (Schultz 1964). At the present time men are still very varied. It may be that with the spread of communications of all sorts they are becoming more alike, but there is no clear evidence of this one way or the other. It is therefore important to inquire into the value of human variety for our well-being and homeostasis. Moreover, a chief reason for our concern with variety is that the differences between us, whether large or small, influence the decisions we make about each other almost every minute of the day. We might conduct our affairs better if we understood more of the reasons behind these differences in behaviour. Unfortunately the subject is so enormous that we can only touch upon some general aspects of it here (see Darlington 1969).

The differences between people come from many sources, and are broadly divided into those that are hereditary, that is genetic, on the one hand and those due to environment on the other. But of course these two factors interact, in that the degree of manifestation of genetic factors depends on environment. Such interaction may be important in producing differences between people that are useful, in the sense that they allow human life to exist in a wider range of environments than would be possible if we were all the same (see Baker and Weiner 1966).

The question of the significance of the persistence of variety in animal and plant populations has been much debated. It has been argued that if natural selection operates fully it will ensure that all members of the species conform to one type—the best. But this is a very superficial view of the 'best', and completely fails to consider the complexity of environments and of the relation of organisms to them. For example, there is now good field evidence that genes producing shells of several different colours and bands are maintained in some populations of snails (*Cepaea*). Darker shells are less conspicuous to predators on some backgrounds and lighter ones on others, and this is especially important as the background changes throughout the year (see Sheppard 1967). This is an example of the phenomenon of *polymorphism*, the persistence in a population of several genes and phenotypes because each has some different selective advantage (p. 397).

Man is clearly a polymorphic species, but it is not easy to prove rigorously that the persistence of various genes confers advantages. Some have maintained that their presence is due simply to the chance of 'random drift', due to genes maintained in small isolated populations (p. 398, Morton *et al.* 1966). However, as we shall see, some genes whose manifestations seem deleterious are so numerous in the population that we must assume that they give some advantage (e.g. the Rhesus negative gene, p. 586, see Hertzog and Johnston 1968 and Workman 1968). It is rarely that we can see the advantage as clearly as for the sickle-cell gene and malaria (p. 595). We can, however, examine various situations in which the occurrence of a gene for an apparently superficial character has been shown to be correlated with some other particular bodily condition or liability to disease.

It is gradually becoming apparent that the facts of heredity are very complicated, in the sense that a gene may influence many characters and a character may be influenced by many genes. Nevertheless, the recent understanding that each gene consists of a particular sequence of nucleotides, and allows for the production of a particular protein, should allow progressive clarification even of the difficult problems of human genetics.

Man is a world-wide species, having spread probably from Africa (Chapter 32). It is very unlikely that, under the conditions that have determined survival in the past, people of one single genotype would be equally suited to live in all the climates from the tropics to Greenland. Surely the original roots of human racial diversity must have been partly in the production of types suited to particular conditions? We shall inquire into this aspect of human ecology later. But man being a particular sort of social animal has tended to maintain, and perhaps to magnify for social or economic reasons, superficial differences in features such as skin colour, even if they are basically adaptive, calling them 'racial differences' (Chapter 41).

If we are to consider properly how the force of selection has operated to determine the hereditary characteristics of mankind we should need to know something about differential fertility and the numbers of children born and their survival rates (Chapter 24). These figures soon show that the risks of death at all ages were until quite recently enormously greater than they are in the western world today. It is curious that it is fashionable to emphasize the 'insecurity' of modern people, referring to atomic risks or the pervasiveness of unwanted change in all aspects of life. Yet individuals in the western world enjoy the prospect of an expectation of life far greater than their forebears did a hundred years ago, or than exists still in many parts of the world today. They are more secure than people have ever been before. It is useful before thinking about human genetics and human variety to remember the very heavy mortality that was prevalent everywhere until quite recently. Even where mortality is reduced, selection still operates (Chapter 39). It is probable that the genotypes of human populations *will* change, and that people even a few hundred years hence will be rather different from those today, and a few thousand years hence quite markedly different.

We know too little to forecast the selective forces that will operate, or to foresee how the human genotype will change in the future. The selective forces may be applied consciously, as well as more directly by the environment, and changes may then be rapid. Selection will not necessarily lead to uniformity, though it may do so. Human communities remain distinct today partly because they contain individuals whose genes give them very different physical capacities. Moreover, the diversity of human beings within a community may well itself constitute a polymorphism that is maintained by ongoing selection. The pattern of human life is not based upon communities composed of identical individuals. Rather, we depend upon the presence of varied capacities, motivations, satisfactions, and hence opinions. The outstanding example of polymorphism is the difference between men and women. To recognize the importance of variety for homeostasis is fundamental for human welfare. *One implication is that the varied types are in principle equally valuable and that societies will be stable only if they treat them so.*

These are some of the general considerations we may have in mind in considering human variety, and especially its inheritance. The details of human genetics are so well treated by textbooks that we shall look only at the outlines of a few genetic conditions, to illustrate some of the problems of the interacting effects of heredity and environment.

With man's habits of controlling the conditions around himself the whole question of what constitutes his 'environment' assumes a new aspect. Some anthropological inquiries evade this by discussing either historical questions or the characteristics of 'primitive' peoples today, who are often more directly exposed to the unmodified surroundings than is modern man. The subject is more complicated than it appears, since the very fact of the actions by which men insulate themselves may itself place a premium on particular types. Thus the extremes of some climates stimulate the inhabitants to find ways to isolate themselves from heat or cold and the more clever succeed better in doing so. It has been claimed that the need to find ways to meet the rigours of a cold climate in the last Ice Age was the stimulus that elicited the developments of the brain that produced *Homo sapiens sapiens*. But the Neolithic revolution started after the conditions had recently become warmer (Chapter 36).

Living in the centrally heated and air-conditioned microclimates of North American buildings has its own hazards for the pharynx and respiratory system and presumably sets up selection pressures that are at least marginally different from those to which the British are subjected as they move with less protection in their damp but equable macroclimate.

Although it may be true that man can to a considerable extent isolate himself from some of the conditions around him, infectious disease has been until recently an environmental factor that he could not easily evade. Some of the most important differences between people are in the pattern of their resistance to infection. But now it is rapidly becoming clear that *inventiveness and intelligence are man's chief defence even against disease*. The factors that above all others are likely to influence man's future are in his brain and the actions it controls, especially the social actions. A modern inquiry will evidently be especially concerned to discuss the value of diversity among human beings in their brains, and in the social behaviour and cultures that the brains generate.

2. The sources of human variety

We may accordingly try to arrange our ideas on these matters by identifying the influences that differentiate men as either (*a*) genetic or (*b*) environmental. Both factors are likely to influence every character. We may perhaps recognize as further categories, including both hereditary and environmental elements:

1. differences due to accident,
2. differences due to adaptive response during the lifetime of the individual,
3. differences due to cultural influences.

It would be impossible here to discuss any of these causes of difference fully. For good books on human genetics see Stern (1960), Roberts (1970), Harris (1970), McKusick (1969), Kalmus (1957). In this and the following chapters we shall attempt only to outline some of the principles that may be used in trying to think about the origins of human variety. Use of sound principles about the reasons for the differences between people is essential for a whole range of human activities. For example, it is important when we try to estimate the degree of responsibility of people for their actions (as in the law) or to decide how best to assist them, for example by education, medical care, or legislation. Our judgements on particular matters in a whole host of practical affairs will be sound only if we have some understanding of the influences of heredity and environment that have affected each individual.

We may begin by a short study of the known facts about the similarities and differences between twins. We can then discuss shortly some obvious environmental influences and proceed to examine something of what is known about the inheritance of various characteristics. Finally we shall look briefly at the distribution of different heritable characters among human populations, the much-debated question of race. The distribution of social, cultural, and economic factors is, of course, at least as important as hereditary factors in determining the divisions of men that we call racial. Indeed, *Homo sapiens* is pre-eminently a species in which the behaviour of each individual is determined by learning, that is, by the environment in which he lives. The capacity to learn is his especial biological characteristic and we must be continually cautious to emphasize this, rather than to regard human biology as the study of those hereditary and other characteristics in which man does not stand so widely apart from other animals.

3. The differences between twins

Fortunately there is one situation in which the relative contributions of heredity and environment can be studied. Monozygotic twins (MZ) are the products of the separation of the first two cells after division of the fertilized zygote, and they are therefore genetically identical. Their characteristics have been compared, in various situations, with those of fraternal or dizygotic (DZ) twins of the same sex, reared either together or apart, whose hereditary likeness is no greater than that between non-twin sibs. Rather than trying to summarize the very numerous twin studies we may extract the relatively simple facts from studies of pairs of identical twins reared apart, compared with a corresponding set reared together, and with fraternal twins. These were investigated in a classical study by the biologist Newman, the psychologist Freeman, and the statistician Holzinger (1937), and since then by several other groups (see Huntley 1966, Bulmer 1970).

Identical twins are not in all respects more alike than fraternal ones. The MZ foetuses share a common chorionic blood supply and this usually puts one of them at a disadvantage. They actually differ more in size as embryos than do DZ twins, and incidentally have a mortality rate several times higher. These differences in pre-natal environment are probably responsible for much of the difference between MZ twins reared together. In many characteristics the MZ get *more* alike as they get older, the DZ less alike.

Comparison of fifty pairs of identical twins with fifty pairs of fraternal twins (in both cases reared together) showed much greater similarity between the MZ than the DZ in physical dimensions. In intelligence the two kinds of twins were much more similar, and even more so in educational achievement. They were also alike in 'personality'. There is thus no doubt that heredity enters largely into all these characteristics, including the last, but the contribution, as we should expect, is least for the characters controlled by the brain, whose speciality is its responsiveness to the environment.

This was fully borne out by the study of nineteen pairs of MZ twins reared apart and brought together by the investigators (sometimes in dramatic circumstances). They were found to differ no more than MZ twins reared together in height, head measure, or certain 'neurotic traits'. But they differed much more than those reared together in weight, intelligence-test score, and educational achievement. Even more interesting, although the differences in some physical characteristics of the MZ pairs reared apart were less than those of DZ pairs, in others, such as weight and in intelligence and educational achievement, *the separated MZs were as different as the DZs*. We cannot, of course, conclude from this that heredity has *no* effect on these fundamental aspects of human life, but its effects can be masked and over-ridden by environment. As the biologist Jennings put it 'what heredity can do environment can do also'. This is not truly a general principle, but it certainly applies to some aspects of development of the capacity of the brain.

Newman and his colleagues in their study tried to correlate the amount of separation of the MZ twins in physical, social, educational, and other respects with the degree of difference observed (p. 557). The correlation between differences in physical conditions (food, etc.) and differences in weight, was 0·60, but with differences in temperament only 0·47. Differences in schooling correlated between 0·46 and 0·79 with intelligence test score but 0·91 with educational achievement. On the other hand, social environmental differences correlated with intelligence score only 0·32–0·53. Obviously differences in schooling are likely to produce maximal differences in educational achievement, but these findings are a remarkable demonstration of the adaptability of the human brain to its surroundings. Even so, the authors conclude that the degree of environmental influence on the variance in intelligence test scores of fraternal twins is only 25–30 per cent. But in this estimate the doubts about the validity of such tests again intrude (Chapter 20).

A further careful study of identical twins was made by Burt (1955). These results compared with those already discussed are shown in Table 38.1. In this study the correlations between identical twins reared apart and those reared together were more alike than in the study by Newman and his colleagues (1937). Perhaps this difference includes an element due to varying degrees of divergence in the circumstances of adoption;

if so, it is, paradoxically, evidence for an environmental influence. It is impossible to decide. The evidence from both studies together gives for correlation in intelligence-test scores:

(*a*) identical twins reared together   0·92,
(*b*) identical twins reared apart   0·78,
(*c*) non-identical twins reared together   0·58.

TABLE 38.1

Correlations (y) between intelligence test scores for monozygotic and dizygotic twins (after Burt 1966)

	Burt and Conway		Newman, Freeman, and Holzinger		
	N Pairs	r	N Pairs	r Group test	r Individual test
Identical twins reared together	95	0·925	50	0·922	0·881
Identical twins reared apart	53	0·874	19	0·727	0·767
Non-identical twins reared together	127	0·534	52	0·621	0·631
Siblings reared together	264	0·531	..	..	..
Siblings reared apart	151	0·438	..	..	..
Unrelated children reared together	136	0·267	..	..	..

The evidence for a hereditary influence is thus very strong. Burt puts it that 'at least 75 per cent of the entire variance must be due to genetic influences'. It is not clear precisely what this phrase implies, and others would feel that this estimate is too high. After a still more recent study the summary was: 'It would seem, then, that certainly well over half the variability of this predominantly verbal kind of intelligence in the population is due to genetic differences between people. It is probably fair to suggest that for general operational intelligence genetic differences will be responsible for something nearer three-quarters, perhaps 70 per cent, of the total variability' (Huntley 1966). This is an expert opinion, but again the same doubts about the influence of the methods on the results arise. Moreover, in all these studies it is important to remember that populations and classes differ in the extent of the environmental differences between individuals, as presumably also in the genetic differences. Thus, if a sample is taken from a group of people who all have similar educational and other opportunities, of course the differences between them will be mainly those of heredity. Moreover, IQ tests have been shown sometimes to be inconstant for individuals and in any case far from culture-free. Adopted children resemble their foster-parents in IQ more closely than their real parents (p. 558) and yet the correlations were lower than those of normal children with their parents.

No one supposes that children actually inherit detailed factual information about the outside world from their parents. The question is to what extent the capacity to acquire such information in the brain is inherited. This leads us to the whole question of the inheritance of the power to adjust to circumstances, that is, to learn.

4. Differences in powers of adaptation

These twin studies thus show us that some characteristics such as height are subject to a very high degree of hereditary control, which is not easily altered by environment. Conversely, the development of the brain, though subject to hereditary influences, is greatly affected by the environment. No doubt a whole range of characteristics, such as those of the endocrine and exocrine glands, muscles, or blood, are intermediate between these extremes, some features having greater, others less capacity to adapt to circumstances during development (Baker and Weiner 1966). Little is known about the inheritance of the powers of 'adaptation' by which the various organs respond to environmental influences. It would be interesting, for example, to know whether there are hereditary differences in the adrenal cortex in the capacity to respond to stress. In wild rats the adrenal cortex is as much as one-third larger than in those reared in the laboratory (Richter 1954), but how much of the difference is due to heredity? The capacity of the nervous and endocrine systems to respond to stress may perhaps be one of the major selective factors in human evolution today.

5. Human differences due to accident

In contrast to these differences in responsiveness of the tissues are those differences due to circumstances over which the individual has no control and to which he can give no adequate compensatory response. These may be of little importance for homeostasis but it is important to know about them to avoid them. Few, if any, differences between people could be said to be *wholly* due to accident. Presumably some people are born a little wiser than others in avoiding even the effects of earthquakes or atom bombs, as they are born more likely to be cautious in traffic or resistant to infection.

Children whose mothers catch German measles (rubella) during the early months of pregnancy commonly suffer serious defects in the heart, brain, bones, and elsewhere. The detailed nature of the pathological process is obscure. There may be hereditary differences in susceptibility by the foetus, but the risk is 50 per cent or more if the rubella is in the first month, and so the responses of the child have little chance to be effective (Cooper 1966).

Among the conditions over which the individual has unusually little control are the time of his conception and the place of residence of his mother, yet both of these may affect the chance that he will diverge from the 'normal'. Study of mentally defective children admitted to hospital in Columbus, Ohio, between 1943 and 1948 showed that significantly more of them were born in the first quarter, January to March. This was due to their conception and hence early embryonic development in the hot weather, as was shown by the fact that years when the summer temperature was above the median produced rates of admission of mentally deficient children significantly above those in the years when it was below (1·658 per 1000 against 1·206). The explanation is probably that in hot weather not only is there special liability to infection but mothers tend to take a diet that is inadequate during the critical period of the first twelve weeks of foetal life. Of course, such statistical correlations may be misleading, but there is much supporting evidence that complications of pregnancy are especially prevalent in lower socio-economic groups and lead to a variety of clinical conditions 'ranging from cerebral palsy through epilepsy, mental deficiency, behaviour disturbances, reading disturbances and tics' (Knobloch and Pasamanick 1958 in Bresler 1966). These effects are not necessarily limited only to children of the poorest. It is reported that in Cincinnati children conceived in the summer months have only half the chance of entering college of those conceived in winter. And it is certainly a fact that only four of the thirty-three Presidents of the United States were conceived in the third quarter of the year (Mills 1949).

6. Some accidental effects of geographical location

All men depend ultimately on the environment for their food, water, air, warmth, and many other factors. It is in a sense absurd to try to specify effects that are so numerous. Even among advanced urbanized populations all the individuals are still greatly influenced by the climate. Here we can only call attention to a few examples of environmental effects, choosing especially some that influence the whole developmental processes.

For example, it has been shown that congenital malformations are higher in some areas of New York State than in others. The areas with high incidence contain igneous rocks or black shale with a relatively high radioactivity. Various other factors can be ruled out and it is suggested that the malformations were produced by the external radiation. Results from study of the effects of atomic radiation in Japan and from experimental animals have, of course, already shown that massive radiation doses have such effects. But the radiation levels in the 'high' areas of New York State corresponded only to 2·1–3·2 rads per 30-year period (Gentry *et al.* 1966). This is not a high rate compared, for instance, to the estimated total radiation dose from generally occurring sources of about 0·12 rads per year (3–4 rads/30 years, 7 rads in a standard lifetime of 70 years, see Chapter 28). So the evidence that these relatively low rates produce malformations is not conclusive but the effects of relatively weak sources must be seriously considered, since they are cumulative. Radiation from medical treatment is the main artificial source of exposure, with fall-out from atomic explosions at present a long way behind. Thus, it is estimated that of 150 000 cases of leukaemia a year in the world, 1500 result from background radiation and 75 from atomic testing (figures for 1958, falling later).

7. Climate and disease

The relationship of climate and disease is an enormous subject and no systematic treatment will be attempted (see Burnet 1962). Diseases due to the prevalence of parasites and intermediate hosts in certain areas are among the major problems of human homeostasis. In the past malaria has been perhaps the chief and it is still important. Hook-worm reduces the effectiveness of countless millions as do bilharzia, eye-worm, yellow fever, dysentery, sleeping sickness, and many other tropical conditions.

Resistance to all of these no doubt depends largely on hereditary factors. Indeed, the capacity to survive at all when riddled with worms or parasitic protozoans must depend upon the presence of special conditions in many parts of the body—including a brain that can allow the individual to tolerate his diseased state. Although physiological defence-mechanisms depend on heredity, resistance also depends in practice on environmental circumstances such as how big a dose a person gets and thus whether he can develop adequate immunity. However, selection must certainly operate and the peoples of tropical countries must for these reasons alone differ from those of temperate zones, where these diseases are not prevalent because their intermediate hosts do not flourish. There is very little information about the genetics of any such differences.

The problem of removing these scourges is not one of genetics but of economics, hygiene, and chemotherapy. The more strictly biological effects of such measures are, of course, profound in allowing increase of population and removal of selection for the genes that confer immunity.

8. Variations in susceptibility to infection

Some of the differences between human beings are undoubtedly due to the fact that survival depends largely on capacity to resist infection. The classical instance is the condition produced by the sickle-cell gene, which changes one amino-acid in the haemoglobin, reducing its value as an oxygen carrier (p. 60). This is fatal for the human carrier when homozygous, but when heterozygous allows life to continue and confers some protection against the malaria parasite (p. 595).

Presumably there are variations in capacity to resist all infective diseases, for instance by production of antibodies. Very little is known about this in detail. For tuberculosis it was shown in one study of identical twins that in 30 per cent of those affected the other twin was too, whereas for fraternal twins the figure was 13 per cent. Of course, identical twins are especially liable to go about together and infect each other, but the figure is suggestive.

Resistance to infection by diphtheria bacilli is partly the result of the presence of a hereditary factor, and the familial distribution of poliomyelitis and other diseases in the United States suggests that hereditary factors are involved.

For conditions of whose causes we are unsure the genetical situation is even less clear. Cancer, for example, is a malignant growth that may be produced by many different stimuli. Inherited differences of susceptibility presumably influence most of them, but we cannot speak of a general 'heredity of cancer'. Yet in special cases the hereditary factor may be strong. One form of cancer of the intestine is preceded by formation of a series of polyps (small growths) produced by a dominant gene. Development of this form of cancer in one individual of a family makes it very likely that sibs will be affected and appropriate operations can remove the polyps (Dukes 1952). For most cancers the genetical situation is very obscure.

The capacity to resist the more 'ordinary' infections is little understood. Almost all children get streptococcal infections of the throat, but about 2 per cent develop the serious consequences known as rheumatic fever (in northern Europe and America). In this condition there is inflammation of various tissues including joints and the valves of the heart, and as a result the heart valves may be permanently scarred. There is evidence that there is a hereditary factor involved but the detailed mechanism is not known.

9. Some striking metabolic variations

In recent years many 'abnormalities' of metabolism have been discovered. Where they are due to single genes those presenting them stand out markedly from the rest of the population. Presumably there is hereditary control and variation of almost every aspect of metabolism but its results are too complicated to strike us.

Numerous single genes produce enzyme deficiency, and the classical case is the gene for *alkaptonuria*, described long ago by Garrod in the *Lancet*

(1908) and in his pioneering book *Inborn errors of metabolism* (1909). Sufferers lack the normal power to break down the products of phenylalanine and tyrosine and they excrete them as homogentisic acid, which turns the urine black. This ultimately produces blackening and degeneration of the teeth and bone tissue.

In a related condition, phenylketonuria (also due to a gene whose manifestation is recessive), the amino-acid phenylalanine is not converted to tyrosine and accumulates in the blood. Its effects on the brain produce mental deficiency. This result can be prevented (with difficulty) by a diet that is almost free of phenylalanine. The condition affects about one child in 40 000 (in northern Europe and North America) and one in 100 of those in hospitals for mentally retarded children. It can be recognized early by testing the urine. Equally important is to test for heterozygotes, who can be recognized by giving a large dose of phenylalanine. Some of the genetic risks of cousin marriage can be estimated in this way, provided the information is obtained.

Other metabolic abnormalities are more complex. One of the commonest is that known as fibrocystic disease of the pancreas. This is in fact an abnormality of the actions of the mucous glands and sweat glands, where accumulation of an excess of viscid mucus blocks the pancreatic duct and the lungs. The gene manifests as a recessive, but is so common that one child in 2000 is homozygous and therefore affected (in northern Europe and North America). This means that the gene is carried in one person in 23. This rate is much too high to be maintained by mutation; so presumably the heterozygous carriers must have some advantage (or at least have had one in the past), keeping the gene in the population.

10. Diabetes

The two distinct sorts of diabetes have hereditary backgrounds. Water diabetes (diabetes insipidus) may be due either to failure to produce enough anti-diuretic hormone from the pituitary or to failure of the kidney tubules to concentrate the urine. The pituitary type may be produced by either of two genes, one acting as a dominant and the other as a sex-linked recessive. Again in this case the heterozygote (females) can often be recognized because the effect of the gene shows in their need to drink abnormally large amounts of water.

Diabetes mellitus (sugar diabetes) is due (usually) to the failure of the pancreas to produce enough insulin and has a large hereditary component. About 50 per cent of identical twins share the condition, as against 10 per cent of fraternal twins and 5 per cent for non-twin sibs. The true figures are probably all higher than this, since the condition usually manifests itself after age 40 and it is hard to follow the cases late in life. The precise means of inheritance are not known and there is as yet no way to identify carriers.

11. Hereditary variations of the nervous system

1. *Variations in the sensory system*

A large range of extreme and mild variations of the nervous system have been shown to have a genetic basis. A minimal yet striking example is the inheritance of the capacity to taste the substance phenylthiourea. For about 70 per cent of English and North Americans this substance is unpleasant, whereas 30 per cent can taste it only in strong solutions if at all. The tasters carry a gene manifesting as dominant (i.e. their genotype is Tt or TT). The selective reason for the continued polymorphism of the gene is not known but substances of this type inhibit thyroid secretion and there is some connection between the phenylthiourea-taster phenotype and liability to certain kinds of thyroid disease (Kalmus 1963).

Colour perception is another nervous function whose heredity is partly understood. Total colour-blindness may be produced by a rare autosomal recessive. Abnormalities of each of the individual capacities to detect red, green, and blue are known, but blue-blindness is rare. Colour-blindness for red and green is produced by rather common sex-linked recessives and the various forms are manifest in 1–5 per cent of males, though only rarely in females because female homozygotes are rare. It has been suggested that male colour-blindness might have had a selective advantage among hunters in that it defeats the camouflage schemes of animals when these are based on the assumption of colour vision by their predators. Such evidence as there is about the eyesight of contemporary hunting tribes unfortunately does not support this hypothesis (Post 1962); the frequency of colour-blindness today is said to be least among hunters and food-gatherers (0·020), greater in those who are partly agricultural (0·033), and greater still in wholly agricultural communities (0·051). Those who are red-green blind cannot identify ripe or rotten fruit or even see red berries among the leaves! We do not know the significance of the continued polymorphism for colour-blindness.

2. *Variations in complex brain functions*

When we come to consider the inheritance of variations in higher nervous functions we meet with very serious difficulties. Man depends so much upon his brain that variations in its operations profoundly affect the treatment he receives by his fellows at almost all stages of his life—at least after the age of about 2 years. 'The chief predisposing cause of social failure in early life is low intelligence level' (Penrose 1963). This social treatment in turn reacts upon the development of his brain, for good or ill. Any of the many various sorts of inadequacy may lead to his being labelled as 'mentally deficient', just as an equally numerous and varied set of conditions may lead him to success and fame. The brain is so complex that both heredity and environment affect it in many different ways. To ask for simple answers about the inheritance of either intelligence or mental defect is to show a serious misunderstanding of the complexity of the biological problem. Yet we all do tend to ask these questions, and what is surprising, genetical science does proffer some answers to them. Perhaps we should suspect these answers more than we do. Nearly all of them have been based on the use of intelligence tests and other tests, whose limitations we have already discussed. Perhaps, in the future, investigation of the inheritance of particular cerebral capacities will provide a firmer basis.

Proper treatment of the subject must depend upon proper means of definition. Thus if mental defect is characterized by the number of inmates of institutions, there were 3·75 per 1000 in England and Wales (in 1935), 1·63 in Finland, and only 0·16 in Japan. Clearly what is measured by such figures is not some condition of the brain but social attitudes, natural wealth, etc. Unfortunately this is also true of means of measurement that are at first sight more attractive. Thus, if intelligence-test scores are normally distributed (which is not strictly true) then we might make an arbitrary decision and take twice the normal standard deviations as 'abnormal', which would give 2·27 per cent at either end. But, even apart from their rather inhuman arbitrariness, it is by no means clear what is measured in intelligence tests. Undoubtedly they are very useful, but are also heavily loaded with reference to cultural patterns. It seems, again, that we should be able to assess the inheritance of some feature(s) of general cerebral capacity. But reflection may make us doubt whether it is even sensible to ask whether the brain has any such 'general' capacities. Some psychologists still believe that they can measure a general factor of intelligence, 'g', but this is partly a question of methods of testing and statistical treatment (Chapter 20). Probably most psychologists now prefer to recognize that all tests are mainly of special capacities and that individuals will vary in different directions with the various tests. Unfortunately nearly all genetical studies have been made with classical intelligence tests and can be interpreted only within their inherent limitations.

Actually the intelligence-test scores of children otherwise rated defective overlap with those called normal (Fig. 38.1). The level of 'intelligence' in the whole population thus displays a continuous and nearly normal distribution. There is abundant evidence that a large hereditary influence

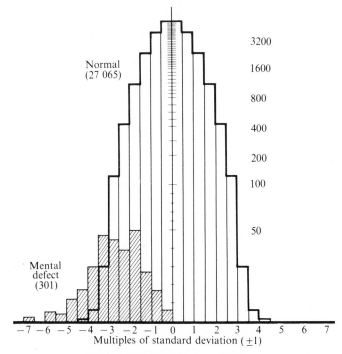

F IG. 38.1. Distribution of intelligence based on Binet tests of 301 defective (shaded area) and 27 000 normal children (expressed as multiples of the standard deviation ± 1). (After Pearson 1931.)

enters into this variation in intelligence-test rating. Comparisons of adult and child test scores are difficult, but to obtain a general view of the situation Penrose used a rating scale in which mental hospital patients and their parents and sibs were classified into five grades (Table 38.2). The difficulty of evaluating all such data is to disentangle the influences of heredity and environment. Many studies have shown a clear correlation between estimates of the intelligence of parents and offspring, and of sibs (Table 38.3). This would, however, be expected in any case, since not only is the correlation between the intelligence of parents high, but also relatives are highly correlated for environment as well as heredity. If perfectly additive hereditary factors were responsible for the intelligence scores then the high correlation between parents should lead to correlation as high as 0·75 between parents and children and sibs. The fact that few of the figures approach this level shows that a great deal of the variance on intelligence-test scores is not due to heredity. About one-half is an appropriate estimate according to Penrose (1963), quoting Willoughby. As we have seen, Burt and others would put the hereditary influences higher (p. 547).

TABLE 38.2

Mental grades of parents and sibs of 1148 patients of mental hospitals
(from Penrose 1963)

Grades of parents		Patients and sibs: number in each grade					
		S Superior	N Normal or average	D Dull or borderline	F Feeble-minded	Imbecile	Idiot
S×S	Patients	..	..	..	..	I	..
	Sibs	..	..	..	..	..	..
S×N	Patients	..	..	I	3	2	3
	Sibs	8	15	..	..	..	..
N×N	Patients	..	..	100	216	303	178
	Sibs	59	2753	174	56	47	23
N×D	Patients	..	..	40	86	51	19
	Sibs	I	552	173	79	28	12
N×F or D×D	Patients	..	..	11	62	26	14
	Sibs	..	196	97	65	17	9
N×Imbe-cile or D×F	Patients	..	..	6	32	13	3
	Sibs	..	60	33	39	13	5
D×Imbe-cile or F×F	Patients	..	..	2	9	12	I
	Sibs	..	17	11	28	9	I

TABLE 38.3

Correlation coefficients for intelligence (from Penrose 1963)

Source	Type of related pairs		
	Parent-child	Sib-Sib	Parent-parent
Burt (1946)	0·34†	0·48	..
Thorndike (1928)	..	0·60	..
Willoughby (1928)	0·35	0·42	0·44
Jones (1928)	0·53	0·49	0·60
Herrmann *et al.* (1933)	..	0·32	..
Matthews *et al.* (1937)	..	0·30	..
Penrose (1938)	..	..	0·39
Cattell *et al.* (1938)	0·84	0·77	0·81
Roberts (1940)	..	0·54	..
Halperin (1945, 1946)	0·37	..	0·65
Alström (1961)	0·54 ⎱ 0·55 ⎰	0·47 ⎱ 0·58 ⎰	0·50

† Estimated from parental occupations.

This difficulty of estimating the influence of environment enters all studies of the problem. In his famous study, *Hereditary genius*, Galton (1869) showed that about one-quarter of the fathers, sons, and brothers of eminent men were also eminent. This is a much higher proportion than is found in unrelated men of similar status. Moreover the proportion fell sharply in relations of second degree (grandfathers, uncles, etc.) and disappeared by the fourth degree. This thesis assumes that there is some quality of 'general ability' responsible for success of the individuals bearing it in their different fields, which as we have seen is itself a doubtful proposition. The data about eminent persons provide a suggestion that heredity may strongly influence mental capacity, but without showing the extent of the effect.

Rather more precise results have been obtained by twin studies, though they still leave many doubts. The best series of cases are those of Newman, Freeman, and Holzinger (1937) and of Burt (1955), which have already been discussed. Table 38.4 shows some further details of the effects of environmental differences.

Clearly monozygotic twins reared together are more like each other than are dizygotic twins. But if they are reared apart they may differ greatly and some would not assess the hereditary contribution to their intelligence score as more than one-half. It is interesting that great differences in educational

TABLE 38.4

A comparison of differences in IQ scores in identical twins reared apart. Differences in educational and social advantages were rated empirically by the decision of a number of judges studying the data (from Carter 1962, data from Newman et al. 1937)

Case No.	Sex	Age at separation	Age when tested	In years of schooling	In estimated educational advantages	In estimated social advantages	IQ differences
				Environmental differences			
11	F	18 months	35	14	37	25	24
2	F	18 months	27	15	32	14	12
18	M	1 year	27	4	28	31	19
4	F	5 months	29	4	22	15	17
12	F	18 months	29	5	19	13	7
1	F	18 months	19	1	15	27	12
17	M	2 years	14	0	15	15	10
8	F	3 months	15	1	14	32	15
3	M	2 months	23	1	12	15	− 2
14	F	6 months	39	0	12	15	− 1
5	F	14 months	38	1	11	26	4
13	M	1 month	19	0	11	13	1
10	F	1 year	12	1	10	15	5
15	M	1 year	26	2	9	7	1
7	M	1 month	13	0	9	27	1
19	F	6 years	41	0	9	14	9
16	F	2 years	11	0	8	12	2
6	F	3 years	59	0	7	10	8
9	M	1 month	19	0	7	14	6

advantages produce wide differences in IQ scores, but differences in social advantages do not.

A suggestion of rather greater hereditary influence is given by comparison of IQ scores of adopted and non-adopted children (Table 38.5). There is a much wider spread for the latter. But obviously there are other problems of interpretation here, including pre-natal influences. Another approach, through adoption, compared the IQ of mothers (86) with that of their children adopted by other parents (112 at age 6 and 106 at 13). Here the influence of environment is very clear (in spite of some regression).

TABLE 38.5

A comparison between father's occupation and intelligence-test score of natural and adopted children (from Carter 1962, after Leahy 1935)

Father's occupation	Adopted children		Own children	
	No.	Average score	No.	Average score
Professional	43	112·6	40	118·6
Managerial	38	111·6	42	117·6
Clerical and skilled manual	44	110·6	43	106·9
Semi-skilled	45	109·4	46	101·1
Unskilled	24	107·8	23	102·1

In summary, there is no doubt that heredity has much influence upon intelligence as measured by IQ scores. We cannot say how great that influence is, and there is evidence that it can be partly masked by appropriate environmental influence, particularly by education. We know even less about the detailed mechanism of the inheritance of cerebral capacity. A few clearly segregating genes for gross disorders are known. Presumably much of the inheritance is polygenic. Of course, hereditary factors with relatively minor effects on the working of the brain are not likely to be detected.

3. *Fertility and rising intelligence*

There is a clear negative correlation in school-children between the number of sibs of a child and its intelligence-test score. Various surveys have shown this correlation to reach levels as great as $-0·33$. If intelligence is entirely governed by additive genes then this correlation would lead us to expect a continual fall in intelligence, especially as fertility is highest in the groups with low intelligence scores. The fall expected was calculated by Burt

(1946) as two points per generation. Well-known studies in Scotland (Maxwell 1953, Thompson 1949) showed that between 1932 and 1947 there was in fact a *rise* from a mean test score of 34·46 (S.D.±15·5) to 36·74 (S.D.± 16·1) points out of 76. Family size correlated −0·28 with intelligence score. These surveys were based on very large numbers (87 498 and 70 805). The differences are significant and again clearly show that environmental influences can overcome at least many of the hereditary factors that contribute to intelligence, since these factors could have led only to a decline.

Further studies will no doubt tell us more about long-term changes in mental capacity. Obviously intelligence has not been steadily declining and yet the lower fertility of very able people is probably no new phenomenon. Data on this are poor but Penrose quotes Bacon: 'The Noblest workes, and Foundations have proceeded from Childlesse Men' (1625). Penrose suggests (following Gorer 1947) that it is not impossible that there is a biological explanation for this negative association between intelligence and fertility. It may be that the supply of genes for mental ability is maintained by the greater fertility of the pool of heterozygotes of lesser ability. The question is unsolved, but is clearly important and intriguing, since manifestations of increased cerebral power have been man's outstanding biological development, especially over the past 10 000 years.

4. *Inheritance of cerebral deficiencies*

Numerous conditions produced by single gene differences associated with cerebral defects are known. There is also a range of conditions produced by chromosome duplications or other abnormalities of either an autosome (e.g. mongolism) or of sex chromosomes (Klinefelter's syndrome). In the latter condition various abnormalities of sexual development are produced, and there has been much study of these since methods of examining the chromosomes in cultures of human tissues were developed.

Most of these conditions due to single genes or chromosome abnormalities are very rare and are the concern mainly of specialists. It would be of more general interest to be able to define the genetic background of the much more common and less severe, but still serious, 'mental diseases'. Here there is certainly some evidence of heredity. There is a concordance of 80 per cent in the incidence of schizophrenia between identical twins as against only 13 per cent for non-identical (Kallmann 1953). We have, of course, to bear in mind the effect of the disease in one twin on the other, but there are a few cases in twins reared apart. There is some evidence of a higher incidence of schizophrenia than manic-depressive psychosis in relatives of schizophrenics and vice versa. No one would question that there is *some* hereditary factor in such conditions, but when we try to determine what genetic factors are involved, and the extent of their influence, then the data are less satisfactory. Schizophrenia has been claimed to be produced by one major recessive gene, when supported by some other minor ones.

For manic-depressive illness there is a 77 per cent concordance between identical twins against only 19 per cent for fraternal. Identification of the genetic background is even more difficult than for schizophrenia. These affective manic-depressive conditions are especially subject to environment, they vary in manifestation from day to day, and are often not very serious. A few cases of transmission in families suggest a simple genetic mechanism but perhaps at most a general predisposition is all that can be recognized genetically.

Epilepsy is the manifestation of cerebral disorder in the form of convulsions, and may have very varied origins. Sometimes it is a result of other disease processes ('symptomatic epilepsy') and these may have a genetic origin (e.g. phenylketonuria, p. 552). The greater majority of epilepsy is due to a slightly abnormal threshold in some part of the brain, leading to seizures. The condition may be accompanied by a low IQ, but not necessarily. In one group studied the incidence in relatives of epileptics was only $1\frac{1}{2}$ times that of relatives of other patients (Penrose 1963). There is therefore some genetic influence, but it is not very strong.

VARIATION IN HEIGHT, BODILY FORM, AND OTHER POLYGENIC CHARACTERISTICS

1. On proportions

HUMAN beings vary a good deal in details but it is striking that, like other animal species, they are all *about* the same size and shape. Swift's biology was wrong in *Gulliver's Travels* when he described the Lilliputians. There could not be human beings even as small as 1 ft high or as large as 10 ft. Yet we know that other mammals can be of these and other sizes. Evidently there must be selective factors that have kept men of about the size and shape that they are. There must be many different influences at work. If the body becomes larger its weight increases as the cube of the linear dimensions, but the strength of the legs increases with the cross-section; that is, only as the square. Elephants have relatively larger limbs than mice. The femur of a young adult human is said to have a safety factor of six times the stresses that are put upon it when running, yet it may break, and especially in old people (*The life of mammals*, Chapter 5). Thus people could not be much bigger than they are while keeping their present proportions. Man is already a rather slow animal, though skilful over rough ground. Presumably with relatively much larger limbs he would be slower still. It is interesting that there are no bipedal creatures today that are much larger than men. The bipedal birds have roughly the same maximum size, ostriches weighing up to 155 kg. The only much larger bipedal creatures that have existed were giant carnivorous reptiles of the Jurassic and Cretaceous periods such as *Tyrannosaurus*, but these had a large tail and may perhaps have been 'tripedal'. In any case, speed was perhaps not at such a premium in those days.

At the other end of the scale people could not be very much smaller than they are. A dwarf only a few inches high would, among other things, have a head too small to accommodate the neural equipment that is needed to be a man. The head and brain are already quite absurdly large relative to the body in normal humans. No doubt if we ever have visitors from space one of their first comments will be on the extraordinary size of our heads, the reason for which they will presumably well understand and commend— they wouldn't get here at all unless they were clever themselves.

Selection still operates today to keep our build within limits. Extreme genotypes mainly die as foetuses or at birth or soon after. This is not to say that there may not be striking changes in human form in the future, but the prospect is not very close (see Huber 1968). Although machines do much of our working and travelling for us it is hard to see how creatures with hands or legs much feebler would be at a selective advantage—unless this somehow made their brains much better. Perhaps this will happen some time. Certainly the jaws have become reduced from considerably more massive structures over the last million years or less (Chapter 34). For the immediate future we are more interested in the differences of height and bodily form within the human population today. Are they of hereditary or environmental origin and are they adaptive?

2. Selection of birth weight

There is direct evidence of the operation of selection at birth for size (Fig. 39.1). Of the babies in a survey covering 13 730 births 4·47 per cent were stillborn or died in the first 4 weeks. The very small and very large failed to survive. The mortality is shown in the figure as the percentage of each

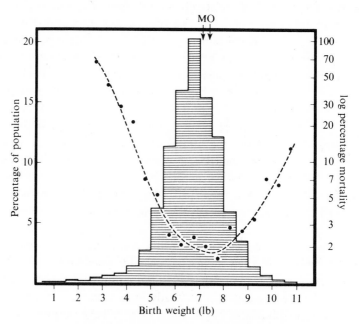

FIG. 39.1. Distribution of birth weights of children born in University College Hospital 1935–46. The points indicating the perinatal mortality for each group are shown on a logarithmic scale. *M* is the mean birth weight and *O* the weight with minimum mortality. (From Mather 1964, after Karn and Penrose 1952.)

size class, plotted on a logarithmic scale because of the high values at the extremes. Selection is thus tending to stabilize the character near its average. It must, however, be noted that there is not a close correlation between birth weight and adult size, the former being largely influenced by the size of the mother (p. 208).

3. Inheritance of height

Height is controlled by many genes. This may be partly because there are in the population many alleles (A_1 A_2 A_3 A_4 ... A_n) at a locus, any two of which can be present; e.g. (A_1 A_4) or (A_3 A_6), etc. More important is that the total height is influenced by many distinct physiological and growth processes, for instance, the amount of pituitary growth hormone, the efficiency of the stomach, the rate of ossification of the femur, and so on. Each of these is the result of the operation of many distinct enzymes, whose production is regulated by one or more pairs of genes. As a result, every individual will have some genes that tend to increase and others to decrease the character 'height'. If the alleles P_i P_d, $Q_i Q_d$, R_i R_d, etc. are those that increase (i) and decrease (d) height then individuals will be, say (P_i P_d, $Q_d Q_d$, R_i R_i ...), or (P_d P_d, $Q_i Q_d$, R_i R_d ...), and so on. The net result of such polygenic inheritance (if the effects of the genes are approximately equal and additive) is to produce a population in which the characteristic is distributed in a normal (Gaussian) curve, with the largest number in the mean class (Fig. 39.2). Of course, the operation of random environmental influences will work with the many genes to produce a continuous distribution of the character. Conversely, sharply distinct environments will divide a population into separate groups in spite of its genetical homogeneity. For example, in a famine the larger starve before the others (p. 397).

Such polygenic inheritance probably controls many characteristics, including some that have been previously considered to be controlled by single or few gene pairs. This fallacy (of supposing inheritance to be simple) is usually the result of arbitrary classification. Thus blood pressure is often classified as 'high' or 'low', but Pickering and his colleagues (Hamilton *et al.* 1954) showed that in fact it is normally distributed (Fig. 39.3). Hereditary factors are involved, since high pressures are more frequent in relatives of those with higher pressures. The inheritance is probably polygenic, but here, as so often, there is no detailed information.

4. Polygenes and selection

A character affected by many genes is, as it were, selectively sensitive to selection pressure. Selection may eliminate any mutations that produce extreme variants (such as giants or dwarfs). It will also remove individuals

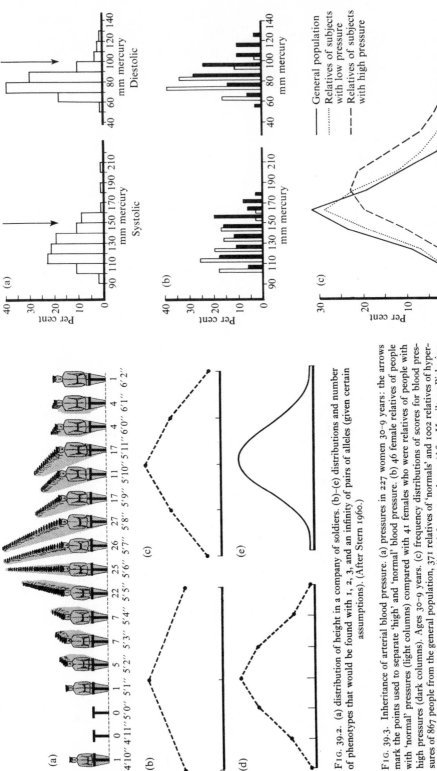

FIG. 39.2. (a) distribution of height in a company of soldiers. (b)–(e) distributions and number of phenotypes that would be found with 1, 2, 3, and an infinity of pairs of alleles (given certain assumptions). (After Stern 1960.)

FIG. 39.3. Inheritance of arterial blood pressure. (a) pressures in 227 women 30–9 years: the arrows mark the points used to separate 'high' and 'normal' blood pressure. (b) 46 female relatives of people with 'high' pressures (light columns) compared with 41 females who were relatives of people with high pressures (dark columns). Ages 30–9 years. (c) frequency distributions of scores for blood pressures of 867 people from the general population, 371 relatives of 'normals' and 1002 relatives of hypertensives. Males and females, 10–79 years but adjusted for age and sex. (After Hamilton, Pickering, Roberts, and Sowry 1954. From *Principles of Human Genetics*, 2nd edn., by Curt Stern. W. H. Freeman and Co. Copyright © 1960.)

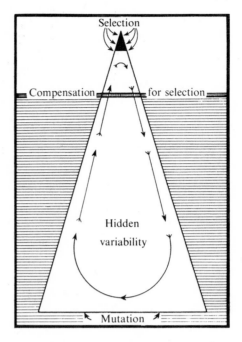

who have a fortuitous combination that produces extremes. But this will still leave an immense reservoir of the same genes in other individuals where they are balanced or counteracted (unless there is dominance) by genes working in the opposite direction. 'Thus the variability mediated by a polygenic system is like an iceberg: only a small fraction of it is displayed as differences observable between the individuals, by far the greater part lying hidden below the surface in the form of genic differences between individuals who, because of the way the genes balance out one another's effects, do not display the full effects of their genes' (Mather 1964) (Fig. 39.4). Investigation of this situation in animals and plants has shown that selection can work upon this variation (Mather 1964).

A further result of additive polygenic inheritance is that effects of many new mutants are masked and they accumulate in the population, for example, as a result of radiation, without their effects appearing, because they are counteracted by genes at other loci and all have effects of similar magnitude.

5. Selective advantages of differences in bodily form

If there is evidence that the genotype is so sensitive to selection we must seriously consider whether the differences in body form of various human populations are of assistance to homeostasis. There is good evidence that much of the difference is hereditary. Thus, although the better nutrition of California increases the height of Japanese immigrants it does not alter their final bodily proportions (Greulich 1957). Dwarfs who are made to catch up (with pituitary hormone) by growth at as much as four times the usual rate maintain normal proportions (Tanner 1967).

It is widely held that human beings follow the same rule as other animals in that in hot climates they are smaller and show a larger ratio of surface area to weight than in cooler conditions (Bergmann's rule). Further, warm-blooded animals in cold climates have the extremities of the body reduced, presumably, to minimize heat loss (Allen's rule). Not all mammals obey these rules strictly, nor do all human populations; for example those in Africa south of the Sahara. But data such as those of Table 39.1 show such gradated characters ('clines') strikingly over considerable areas.

TABLE 39.1

Ratio of body weight (kg) *to surface area* (m²). *The surface area was not measured directly, but calculated from size and weight according to a formula* (after Schreider 1951)

Frenchmen	38
Albanians	37
Arabs	36
Somalis	35
Mexicans	35
Andamanese	32

Again, among the American aborigines (Indians) and in Eurasia and Malaysia there are gradations in the expected directions (Fig. 39.5) (Newman 1953). Such clines are common in animal populations, and are presumed to have adaptive significance. They are seen also in many other human features; for example, the elongation and narrowing of the face and reduction of the nose in people of colder regions (Figs. 39.6 and 39.7). All these features can be related to heat loss. They presumably all have a genetic component, but may be affected directly by environment. Thus North American children born in Panama were found to be shorter and lighter than those born in the U.S.A. (Mills 1942). The effects of temperature and other climatic conditions on growth are considerable, but are not understood. Moreover marked 'physiological' adaptation to cold and hot conditions can take place. The hands of Eskimos who have been much exposed to cold become 'adapted' and remain functional where non-adapted hands would be useless (see Scholander 1955). Added to this is the very

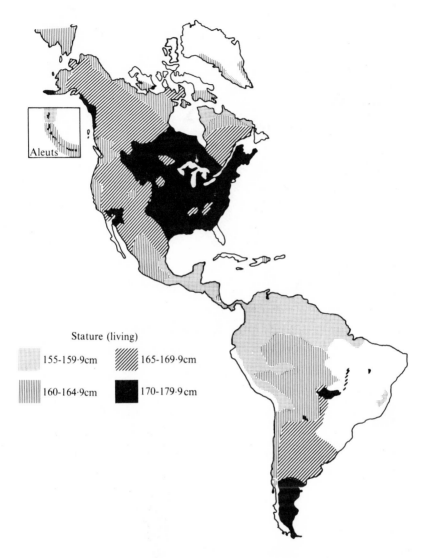

Stature (living)

155-159·9cm   165-169·9cm

160-164·9cm   170-179·9 cm

FIG. 39.5. Height of male 'Indians' in North and South America. (After Newman 1953.)

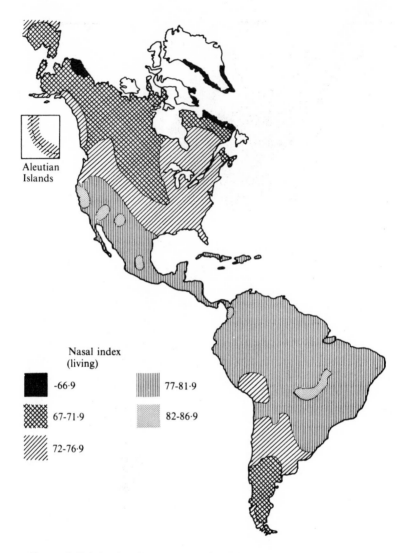

Aleutian
Islands

Nasal index
(living)

-66·9

67-71·9

72-76·9

77-81·9

82-86·9

FIG. 39.6. Relative size of nose as measured on living people. (After Biasutti 1953.)

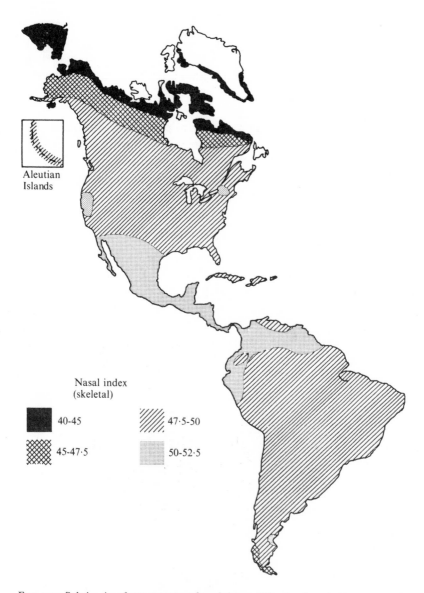

Aleutian
Islands

Nasal index
(skeletal)

40-45   47·5-50

45-47·5   50-52·5

FIG. 39.7. Relative size of nose as measured on skeletons. (After Lundman in Newman 1953.)

obvious fact that man has other ways of 'adapting': for instance, wearing fur coats and gloves and lighting fires. In any case, the facts often require careful examination. Australian aborigines (supposed to have a body form adapted to a hot climate), are often at night in the desert or in winter exposed naked at near-freezing temperatures in conditions that no Eskimo or European could stand!

There are undoubtedly 'clines' in human populations and some of them may be the residues of earlier human history. Some may even be of adaptive advantage today. But it is likely that such bodily features are becoming increasingly irrelevant to homeostasis, and human biology should not place too much emphasis upon them.

6. Inheritance of fingerprints (dermatoglyphs)

The patterns of ridges on the fingers and toes are unusual characters in that (1) they are unique to each individual, but are alike in identical twins, (2) they do not change from the fourth month of foetal life onwards under the influence of either age or environment. The patterns are determined by heredity in a complex way. The usual means of classifying finger-prints is into arches, loops, and whorls (Fig. 39.8). For genetic analysis counts are made of the ridges from the triradius to the centre of the pattern (Holt 1961). An arch, being without a triradius, scores as 0; in a loop there is one count, and in a whorl two, the higher count being then used. The

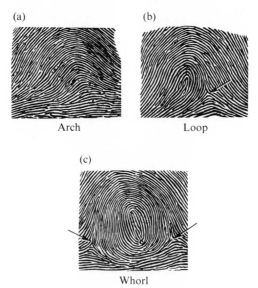

(a)   (b)

Arch   Loop

(c)

Whorl

FIG. 39.8. Typical human fingerprints of the three main types. The arrows indicate the triradii. (After Holt 1961.)

TABLE 39.2

Correlations for total finger ridge count between relatives (from Holt 1961)

	Correlation coefficient	No. of pairs
Parent–child	0·48	810 (200 families)
Midparent–child	0·66±0·03	405 ,,
Mother–child	0·48±0·04	405 ,,
Father–child	0·49±0·04	405 ,,
Parent–parent	0·05±0·07	200 ,,
Sib–sib	0·50±0·04	642 (290 sibships)
Monozygotic twin–twin	0·95±0·01	80
Dizygotic twin–twin	0·49±0·08	92

ridge counts on all ten fingers are added together. Correlations between relatives show the effects of heredity (Table 39.2).

The parent–child and sib–sib correlations are near to 0·5, indicating the action of additive genes with independent effects but no dominance (Fisher 1918). The very high correlation for monozygotic twins shows that the ridge number is almost completely determined by heredity, only about 5 per cent of the variability being due to some intrauterine influence.

Fingerprint counts should be nearly ideal for the study of genetic differences between populations. So far as is known, they are not affected by selective factors, though this has not been proved, and abnormalities of finger- and palm-prints are associated with mongolism. Unfortunately, no large numbers of measurements have been made. Data from various European countries have not shown significant differences in total counts; perhaps these will appear with larger samples. There are differences between populations in the proportions of the various patterns (Fig. 39.9).

The patterns of ridges on the palms of the hands do not correspond precisely to the creases formed by use (Figs. 39.10 and 39.11). The latter are the signs used by fortune-tellers. Since the creases are a product both of hereditary influence and use it is not wholly unreasonable to suppose that their pattern should be correlated with the 'character' of the individual.

7. Body types

We are so used to the fact that human populations consist of individuals who differ widely in physical shape as well as in physiological and psychological characteristics that we seldom stop to ask why these differences persist. It is not known to what extent they are due to environmental influences during development, but certainly they have a large hereditary component.

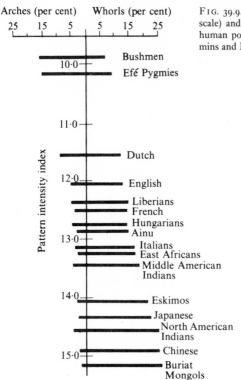

Arches (per cent)   Whorls (per cent)

25   15   5   5   15   25

Pattern intensity index

10·0 — Bushmen
Efé Pygmies

11·0 —

Dutch

12·0 — English

Liberians
French
Hungarians
Ainu

13·0 — Italians
East Africans
Middle American
Indians

14·0 — Eskimos

Japanese
North American
Indians

15·0 — Chinese

Buriat
Mongols

FIG. 39.9. Percentage of arches and whorls (horizontal scale) and pattern intensity index (vertical) for various human populations. (After Holt 1961; data from Cummins and Midlo 1943.)

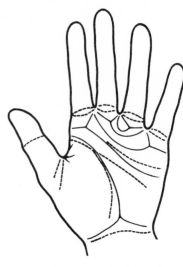

FIG. 39.10. The main lines and triradii of the palm. The palmar creases are shown as dotted lines. (After Harrison *et al.* 1964.)

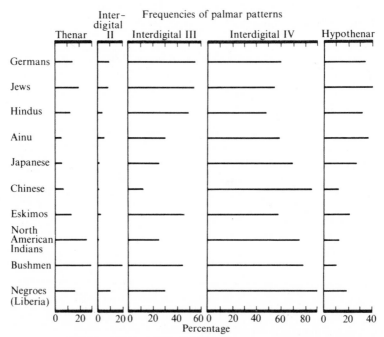

Frequencies of palmar patterns

	Thenar	Inter-digital II	Interdigital III	Interdigital IV	Hypothenar

Germans
Jews
Hindus
Ainu
Japanese
Chinese
Eskimos
North American Indians
Bushmen
Negroes (Liberia)

0   20   0   20 0   20   40   60 0   20   40   60   80 0   20   40

Percentage

FIG. 39.11. Frequency patterns of the five areas of the palm in ten different populations. (After Holt 1961; data from Cummins and Midlo 1943.)

Probably the polygenes that produce them are maintained in polymorphic form in the population because it is an advantage to society that these various types should exist. It is hard to prove this, but it is reasonable to think that even today for each of the different functions of society there will be a different optimum in bodily form, physiological capacity, intelligence, and emotional make-up. It takes a different sort of man to make a politician or a policeman, a farm labourer or a mechanic, a pedagogue or a poet, though it would be hard to specify the characteristics of any of them. It is possible that the diversity of types is more conspicuous among men than women.

Recognition of the significance and value of differences between people is important if we are all to live together effectively. It is important for the individual and society in many situations that he should find the place best suited to his abilities. This is well recognized by those who have to choose people suitable for any form of occupation. Much selection is still done empirically, and better systems of analysis and classification of human types are badly needed. It is difficult to believe that those already invented are the best possible, but some of them will be briefly described. Very important also is the fact that people of different constitutions have different patterns of liability to disease. This is so marked that an experienced physician can sometimes hazard a guess at the patient's complaint after seeing his build as he enters the consulting room.

These differences have been recognized since classical times. Hippocratic medicine identified a *status phthisicus*, liable to respiratory complaints, and *status epilepticus*, prone to vascular disease. The best-known modern classifications are those of Kretschmer and of Sheldon (see Harrison, Weiner, Tanner, and Barnicot 1964). Kretschmer tried to force everyone into one of three classes, *pyknic* (round and fat), *leptosome* (long and thin), and *athletic* (broad and strong). Sheldon's system of 'somatotyping' recognizes not three classes but three 'components' of physique, variously combined in each individual. He invented a way of measuring these by photographing the subjects and using trained observers to make comparison with standard photographs. Each 'component' was then rated on a seven-point scale. Thus the endomorph is round and fat and supposed to have large liver, gut, and lungs. He is relaxed, amiable, and sociable (a state that Sheldon calls viscerotonia).

In mesomorphs muscle and bone predominate, the heart is large and they are adventurous, aggressive, extroverted, and dominating (somatotonia). Ectomorphs are long and thin, with narrow chest but large brain. They are inhibited, secretive, introverted but often intelligent (cerebrotonia).

The degree of manifestation of each feature is given a number (1–7) and these are listed in the order endomorphy, mesomorphy, ectomorphy. In practice individuals of course have a moderate amount of each component, and common types are 3.4.4., 4.3.3., and 3.5.2. The three components are named from the supposed prevalence of each of the three germ layers in development. Although this connection cannot seriously be maintained, Sheldon's system has found some supporters and uses. The classifications are said to be made consistently by observers, without the need for long training. But the system has several severe statistical defects, particularly in that the items are not independent but are negatively correlated with each other. You cannot be 7.7.7. Further, the system as it stands does not allow for differing trends in various parts of the body ('dysplasia'), though more complicated regional somatotyping has been attempted.

8. Sex differences in body form

Somatotyping has hardly been applied to women. Some attempts have been made but no reference atlas of types has been published. There are great physical, physiological, and psychological differences among women, but it is possible that in the past human populations have had to make use of more types of men than of women. Of course, the differences in body form between the two sexes itself presents us with a differentiation of human bodily types so fundamental and familiar that we forget to notice it scientifically! Yet human life depends absolutely for its continuance on this differentiation of functions. Apart from the primary sex differences in the gonads and genital ducts we can recognize 'secondary sexual characters', less directly connected with reproduction; and we might add 'tertiary sexual characters', differences important for the person's place in society but not directly connected with reproduction. Of course these categories are not sharply distinct. A man's beard and a woman's beauty are clearly secondary sexual characters more directly related to mating than are the man's strength or the woman's capacity to cook. But these last are mating attractions too.

Sex differences are found in almost every part of the body and it would be impossible to list them here. As we have seen, males show a greater acceleration of growth at puberty than females, in other primates besides man. We must assume that this faster growth was advantageous in Palaeolithic man in providing a group of particularly strong individuals capable both of hunting and of dominating in social groups. This advantage was perhaps even accentuated in Neolithic and in later farming and urban communities. The most advanced urban societies today still use groups of strong males for the construction of their skyscrapers. The introduction of power-activated tools has not removed the need for a large supply of such labour, often provided by social groups that could be said to be specialized for it (London's newer buildings are largely the work of Irish labour). Other obvious essential uses of male physique are in the police for the maintenance of order and in the armed services for defence. Here again mechanization has not yet altogether re-moved the need for physical power, though it is rapidly doing so.

In the extraction of raw materials the greater male strength is obviously useful. It cannot be an accident that in few places in the world are there women miners or foresters (though women went down the Cornish tin mines). In agriculture, on the other hand, both sexes participate, the women usually (but not always!) taking the less arduous roles. Similarly, in indus-trial production there are jobs for which each sex is the more suited. The woman's advantage is sometimes in dexterity, but especially in patience, and perhaps also in persistence.

Trying to make such absurdly wide generalizations emphasizes the great diversity of functions that enter into the life of human societies, whether primitive or advanced. At present, as in the past, these require people with very different ranges of capacity. Women, besides those bodily and emo-tional features needed strictly for child-bearing, have obviously developed other specialized features essential to human conservation. They have the temperament and attitudes for looking after the children (and also often the men) and providing much of the education. Probably they have been responsible for preparing food since the introduction of fire (although cooking was presumably at first a crude affair). Their more conservative, cautious, and perhaps further-seeing qualities may have been responsible for organizing the laying-in of stocks for the winter. But the problem of which sex arranges for direction and organization of human affairs has become in-creasingly difficult. Perhaps at some early Palaeolithic stage the males were completely dominant (though not all higher primate societies form family groupings with a dominant male as some baboons do). As mankind has evolved women have come to play an increasing part in the direction of affairs, and this tendency continues today. In fact, the differentiation of mankind into physically and psychologically different groups with specialized functions is undoubtedly becoming less marked. Even the secondary sex characters are minimized (men with long hair, women with small breasts). One can imagine that if ectogenesis ever becomes practicable mankind might cease to be dif-ferentiated into two sexes at all. The selected gonads could be maintained either in a few nurse individuals, or actually *in vitro*. The 'nurses' might well become mere nutritive individuals, as queen bees have done, nourished by the asexual workers and serving only to produce gametes (see p. 197).

This is more than a mere fantasy. If man is to build a society in which altruism is truly the dominant behaviour-pattern it may be biologically *necessary* to have some such form of reproduction (Chapter 43). If genes that promote altruism are to be successful, the self-denying behaviour of individuals must ensure a greater chance for survival of their genes than for those of more 'selfish' individuals. This is achieved in other altruistic animal societies such as bees, ants, and termites because all members of the community are genetically alike, being produced by one queen. Indeed in some species (bees) there is a special precaution to ensure genetic uniformity, because the males come from haploid eggs. It is not impossible that human communities that discovered some technique for ensuring genetic homogeneity would be able to gather the full fruits of self-denial and social actions by their members. It is hard to see whether this would compensate for the disadvantages of genetic uniformity. Creatures as intelligent as man should be able to arrange to have the advantages both of altruism and of genetic and other variety.

It is probable that the development of gonad-banks will at least come to be considered for man, especially as they are already found to be effective for farm animals. Meanwhile it is more important that mankind is still highly differentiated, and whatever it becomes will be by gradual evolution from the present polymorphic population (see Darlington 1969).

9. Body form and disease

There are certainly correlations between physique and the liability to disease. Men high in mesomorphy are especially liable to coronary disease. But it is not clear whether this is because they put themselves under great stress or have particularly vulnerable hearts or even whether it is that having much muscle they need much exercise and often do not get enough of it.

Endomorphs are said to be especially liable to diabetes and ectomorphs to pulmonary tuberculosis. An association of bodily type with liability to mental illness was noticed by Kretschmer, who found that his pyknics tended to be what Jung calls extroverted while leptosomes were introverted. In Sheldon's terminology we can say that mesomorphs are liable to become paranoid, ectomorphs tend to schizophrenia. Manic depressives are high in endomorphy. Ectomorphs are liable to conditions of anxiety; mesomorphs and ectomorphs to hysterical conditions and depression.

These rather simple and broad correlations are well established and fairly obvious. Indeed, when we think about it we find that this system is only a refinement on the sort of common-sense classifications of people that we all make. The very fact that we do so suggests that such classifications may have a real biological basis in that a number of features tend to vary together, producing a relatively limited number of types, perhaps such as are valuable for the survival of the population. This is a proposition that cannot be proved or disproved at present but it is important at least to think about it if we wish to have well-balanced and effective societies.

Different sections of society come to have their own somatotypes

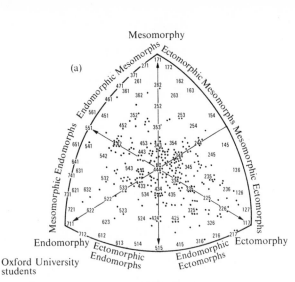

(a)

Mesomorphy

Oxford University
students

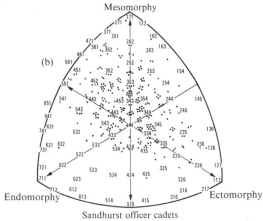

(b)

Mesomorphy

Sandhurst officer cadets

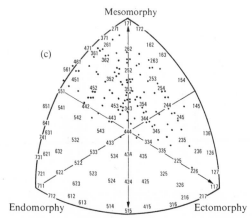

(c)

Mesomorphy

Physical Education students-Loughborough Training College

FIG. 39.12. Distributions of somatotypes for three groups of
students. (After Tanner, in Harrison *et al.* 1964.)

(Fig. 39.12). Thus whereas Oxford University students were found to be of various types, military cadets and physical education trainees were conspicuously high in mesomorphy. This again is an obvious finding, but there has been a considerable range of less expected observations, as that physics and chemistry students are more ectomorphic than those of engineering and medicine (at Harvard) and that boys who become classified as 'delinquent' are unusually mesomorphic.

It is almost certain that much more subtle ways will be found for measuring bodily form and physiological, biochemical, and psychological personality. Indeed, one that has been found useful for some purposes is shown in Fig. 39.13. The point about this system is that it depends upon the actual measurements of distinct features. When separate measurements are made of different parts of the skeleton it is found that many vary independently:

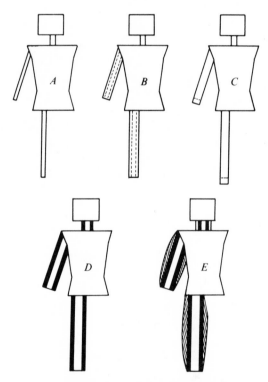

FIG. 39.13. Diagram to show technique of defining shape by five factors. *A–C* represent skeletal size and shape, *D* and *E* soft tissues. Thus *A* shows an individual defined by his score in the frame size factor, other skeletal factors being given of average values. *B* shows his limb-bone width factor, *C* his limb-bone length factor, *D* his muscle factor, and *E* his fat factor. (After Tanner, in Harrison *et al.* 1964.)

for instance, length of the head and neck; thorax and pelvis. Sizes of hands and feet are related to each other, but are independent of other features, and so on. Evidently we have only just begun to examine the problem of variation of human body form. There is very much to be done by discovery of the various genetical and developmental factors involved and correlating them with the different ways in which humans contribute to the lives of their societies.

40

VARIATION IN SKIN COLOUR AND IN BLOOD GROUP

1. Clines of skin colour

SURFACE pigmentation is another characteristic that shows many gradations and in some places clines, and for which an adaptive value has been claimed. Although environmental influence plays a part, skin colour is highly determined genetically. It is this that provides racialist overtones to the subject. Skin colour is made to serve as a marker, indicating the population from which the individual has come.

The measurement of skin colour is not easy. Colours can be graded by matching against cards or by spinning on the skin a colour top, which can be adjusted until a match is obtained. A much better method is to use a reflectometer with standard lighting. Steady clines of pigmentation have been found in Africa and elsewhere, corresponding in general to the amount of solar radiation (Fig. 40.1). But in American Indians and Mongolians differences proceeding north and south are slight. There is undoubtedly a correlation between skin colour and solar radiation, especially in the ultraviolet, but the actual levels of exposure in particular climates and cultures have seldom been determined and measurement of solar U.V. actually received is technically difficult. There may be less for some tropical forest dwellers than for those living on snow.

2. Skin colour and vitamin D

The experience of any light-skinned person over-exposed to sun is sufficient to show that some protection is needed. There is evidence that in the southern U.S.A., Australia, and South Africa there is more skin cancer on hands and feet among white than pigmented people. If man arose in Africa it may be that the less pigmented people have secondarily lost the colour, and it has been plausibly suggested that this is determined by the need to synthesize vitamin D in the skin. This substance is not really comparable to other vitamins, since it is almost absent from all foods except the liver of some fishes (Table 40.1).

The only source for populations without access to the sea is by synthesis from the waxy substance 7-dehydrocholesterol, which takes place in the

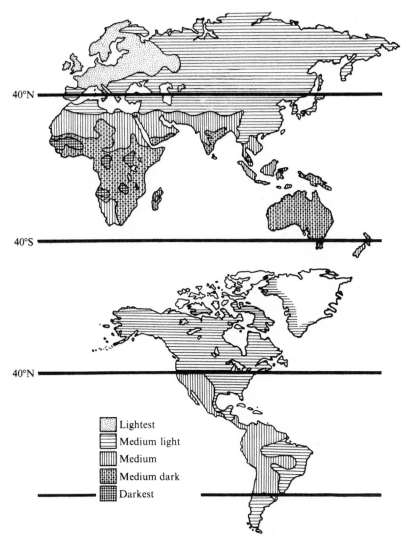

FIG. 40.1. Distribution of human skin colour before A.D. 1492. (After Brace and Montagu 1965.)

TABLE 40.1

Vitamin D content of various foods (from Loomis 1967)

	Vitamin D Int. unit/g		Vitamin D Int. unit/g
Halibut-liver oil	2000–4000	Cream	0·5
Cod-liver oil	60–300	Egg yolk	1·5–5·0
Milk	0·1	Calf liver	0·0
Butter	0·0–4·0	Olive oil	0·0

deeper layers of the skin under the influence of ultraviolet light. Yet vitamin D is essential for proper calcium metabolism and health of bony tissue. In its absence there is rickets in children and the corresponding weakening of the bones (osteomalacia) in adults. It is especially important for pregnant women, and vitamin D deficiency is said to be common in Indian women in purdah, who get little sun.

The amount needed is 400 international units ($=$ 10 μg) per day and it is synthesized at the rate of 6 units per cm^2 per hour by white human skin. This means that the necessary 400 units would be made in the pink cheeks of a baby in its pram in the latitude of Great Britain exposed for 3 hours daily to reasonably bright sunlight (not necessarily direct).

Vitamin D, like vitamin A, has the characteristic that too much of it is as bad as too little. Doses above 100 000 I.U. (2·5 mg) per day can produce calcification in various parts of the body, possibly even ending in death from kidney stones. At the rate given above a European would produce up to 800 000 I.U. per day in the tropics and might therefore suffer from hypervitaminosis, for the body has no way of detoxicating any excess. But pigmentation of the skin reduces the access of ultraviolet light by up to 95 per cent and limits the synthesis to between 5 and 10 per cent of the above, leaving an acceptable amount.

The obvious interpretation, first suggested by Murray in 1934, is that pigmentation of the skin was a necessity for early man in tropical Africa, but had to be lost before man could colonize northern regions where the winter sun is 20° or less above the horizon, and much of the ultraviolet light is filtered out by the long passage through the atmosphere. The incidence of rickets has long been recognized as characteristic of cities in northern latitudes. It has been especially prominent in Great Britain, which has an unusually warm and damp climate in relation to the amount of sunlight, because of the Gulf Stream (Glasgow is at about the same latitude as the Aleutian Islands). There is almost no rickets in the tropics, for instance in the West Indies. On the other hand, coloured people are specially liable to rickets in northern cities. (Of course, their economic circumstances may tend to aggravate the situation.)

An added piece of evidence for this analysis of the colour situation is that tanning of white skin is produced by the effect of ultraviolet radiation of the same wavelength that is needed for vitamin D synthesis. It is difficult to avoid the conclusion that men lost their skin pigmentation as an adaption to living in northerly latitudes, while the capacity to change colour by tanning the skin in summer may have developed at the same time. The Eskimos are the only northerly people with dark skins, and they have access to abundant supplies of the only rich dietary source of vitamin D. Mongoloid people are said to gain protection from excess sunlight by accumulation of keratin granules in the skin as well as some melanin. This may have certain advantages in increasing the reflection. The black Yoruba skin has been shown to reflect only 24 per cent of light, whereas untanned European skin reflects 64 per cent. This heat factor alone would produce light skins in the tropics and dark in northern climates. The fact of the opposite gradient again emphasizes the importance of vitamin D synthesis and its control.

3. Inheritance of skin colour

In spite of the capacity for tanning, the main factor regulating skin colour is heredity. Several genes are involved, but perhaps not more than about five major genes. Fig. 40.2 shows the frequency of various degrees of pigmentation of American negroes as determined with the colour top. Assuming that this population has 70 per cent African and 30 per cent Caucasian

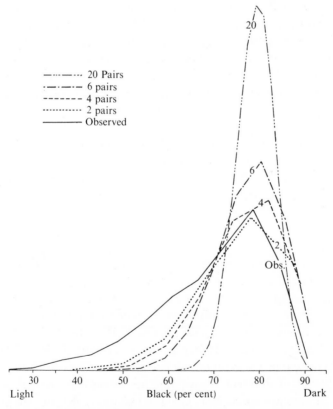

FIG. 40.2. Distribution of actual skin pigmentation in American Negroes and the distribution that would be expected if genes acting at 2, 4, 6, and 20 loci were acting additively. (After Stern personal communication.)

ancestry, the dotted lines show the expected distributions with various numbers of pairs of genes. Evidently the number of gene pairs involved is not large.

Although the genetic mechanisms are not fully known, they agree with the well-established observation that inheritance is polygenic and children show a degree of pigmentation intermediate between that of the parents and never at any great distance away in either extreme direction. Contrary to popular myth, there is no evidence that there is ever a sudden reappearance of extremes of pigmentation in the later generations after crossing.

Whatever the detailed genetical and physiological mechanisms may be, there is no doubt that human populations are highly polymorphic for skin colour. The fact that such different genes are retained must mean that they have some selective advantages (or have had them until recently). These need not necessarily be actually in the colour itself. Pigmentation might be linked with other metabolic features that provide the advantage, but the simplest explanation is the connection with vitamin D synthesis discussed above. It is tragic that, partly because of the circumstances of the exploitation of the work-power of pigmented people in the tropics, colour should have come to have such terribly strong emotional and political importance. Some of the other factors involved in setting up the barriers between populations are discussed later. As far as relation to sunlight goes it is useful to be pigmented in the tropics and useful to be white farther north or south. It is possible to compensate either way, but perhaps the coloured person has the greater potential range, since it is easier to take vitamin D than to keep out of the sun. It is interesting that no large fully unpigmented populations have yet become established in the tropics. The nearest to this state of affairs is perhaps Brazil, where there is a free mixture that may yet provide an example that is followed by all mankind.

4. Blood groups

A large part of our knowledge of the distribution of genes in Man depends upon the fact that there is polymorphic variation in certain mucopolysaccharide constituents of the red cells of the blood. These differences may have significant functional effects in the blood itself and elsewhere in the body (see below). Their special interest is that the various mucopolysaccharides act as antigens. If they are introduced into the blood of a person of different genetic constitution the latter will produce antibodies to them. When bloods of different constitution are mixed the antibodies present will cause agglutination. For blood transfusion, determination of the 'blood group' of patients and donors is therefore essential.

For this reason vast numbers of people have been 'typed'. Fourteen different systems of blood antigen genes are known (Race and Sanger 1962). The most familiar of them are three multiple alleles known as G^A, G^B, and G, the first two being both dominant to G. These genes are often called simply *A*, *B*, and *O*. The genes G^A and G^B cause the red cells (and other cells) of the person carrying them to produce antigens capable when injected into another individual of inducing the formation of specific antibodies. Blood cells from a person with constitution G^A G^A or G^A G will therefore be agglutinated if they are injected into a person whose serum contains anti-A. Among peculiar features of the arrangement is the fact that usually people who carry the G^A G^A genes have anti-B in their serum and vice versa. Those with G^A G^B have neither antibody and are thus 'universal acceptors'. GG people carry no antigens on their cells and have both antibodies in the serum, and are thus 'universal donors'.

Phenotype	Genotype	Cell antigens	Serum antibodies
Group A	$G^A G^A$ or $G^A G$	A	anti-B
Group B	$G^B G^B$ or $G^B G$	B	anti-A
Group AB	$G^A G^B$	A+B	neither
Group O	GG	none	anti-A and anti-B

The ABO 'antigen' system is obviously different from antigen–antibody systems elsewhere, if only because of the widespread 'natural' occurrence of the antibodies. It is not clear at present whether people without G^A come to make anti-A because they have been immunized at some stage by contact with the G^A tissue of their mother or someone else. One view is that they are antibodies to bacteria with A-like antigens, which are of very wide distribution. The antigens are present in nearly all cells in the young foetus, but after the twelfth week they become more restricted (Szulman 1964). However, in about 75 per cent of the population (England) they are secreted in saliva and other body fluids, due to the presence of a further distinct gene with dominant manifestation, that is they are *Se Se* or *Se se*, while non-secretors are *se se*. These secretor genes are quite independent of the ABO genes.

Because of the importance of these genes for blood transfusion enormous numbers of people have been typed for their ABO groups all over the world. The distribution of the genes is known better than that of any others in man, better perhaps than of any genes in any animal. The frequencies of G^A, G^B, and G vary in different parts of the world and this gives some indication of the affinities between populations (Chapter 41). The situation is complicated by the fact that not only do we not understand the biological significance of these antigens but also that it is beginning to appear that they are associated with some conditions that may have selective effects.

Thus it has been noticed that fewer A-group children are produced by B mothers than would be expected. It may be that the A child induces the mother to produce anti-A antibodies of some special sort, which kill the foetus. Moreover, there are some associations between the ABO group and diseases for which there is no known immune response. Thus, in various parts of the world it has been found that those who get duodenal ulcers include more group O than would be expected. Non-secretors are more liable to the disease than secretors. People of Group A are 20 per cent more likely to develop cancer of the stomach than those of O or B. Other probable associations are of A with pernicious anaemia and with diabetes mellitus.

Evidently these genes produce multiple effects (pleiotropy) and some of these effects are adverse. Presumably there are other effects that are advantageous under some circumstances, for it is by such varied advantages that the polymorphic condition is maintained in the population (Chapter 28). Unfortunately there are fewer opportunities for correlating genes with useful conditions than harmful ones.

Besides the ABO blood groups as many as thirteen further sets of genes are known that control the production of antigens on red cells. In most of these other systems of blood groups the antibodies are not found naturally, and the genes are discovered after noting that two bloods supposed to be compatible produce agglutination. The situation is then investigated by testing the unknown serum against a panel of cells of different known genetic constitution to see if it is really a previously recorded antibody or not. One of the better-known of these is the MN system, controlled by a simple pair of alleles with no dominance, Ag^M and Ag^N, with about equal frequency (in Europe).

A very important system was discovered when after injecting red cells of Rhesus monkeys into rabbits the serum of the latter was found to agglutinate about 85 per cent of caucasoid human bloods. This is called the 'Rhesus-positive' condition, the other 15 per cent being 'Rhesus-negative'. The Rh^+ appears as a dominant, but the condition is probably really controlled by three allelic pairs of genes (known as Cc, Dd, and Ee), closely linked. If a Rhesus-negative mother carries a positive child owing to a Rh^+ gene (nearly always D) from the father, she may, if foetal cells get into the maternal circulation, produce antibodies that will damage or destroy the red cells of this child or of the next that she bears. The child is born with agglutinated corpuscles (haemolytic disease of the newborn). Fortunately, ways of countering the condition have been found, essentially by removing most of the child's blood and replacing it with Rhesus-negative blood of the same ABO group. In the majority of pregnancies

Rhesus-negative women do not, however, become immunized by a Rhesus-positive foetus. Even in those that do so, the condition does not develop equally in every pregnancy but tends to increase in severity in later pregnancies, with an increase in the mother's titre of antibodies. There are various connections with the ABO system, in that the Rhesus immunization of the mother is less likely to happen if the parents are ABO incompatible, presumably because the foetal cells are destroyed if they reach the mother's bloodstream.

Populations differ greatly in the proportions of the various members of the CDE Rhesus system. Presumably the genes produce adverse effects on foetal mortality and they are maintained in a polymorphic state because they have other compensating advantages. A strong selection pressure for the Rh-negative gene has been found in populations of New World Negroes but it is not yet clear what advantage the gene confers (Hertzog and Johnston 1968).

41

THE DIFFERENTIAL DISTRIBUTION OF
GENES. 'RACES'

1. Difficulties in the concept of race

In the last analysis every feature by which homeostasis is maintained is influenced partly by heredity. The life of man, like that of every other species, is what it is by virtue of its past history. However much we change ourselves by changing our environment or upbringing we remain human because our genes make us so. Moreover, as we have seen, many of the large differences between people in their homeostatic capacities are the result of inheritance alone. The fact that these are not uniformly distributed throughout the species is painfully familiar to us as the phenomenon of racial differences. We are apt to experience these as an insistent social phenomenon, and perhaps therefore overlook that they are basically nothing more than local differences in the distribution of genes.

The differences strike us because the genes are not at present randomly distributed about the world, though they may well be more nearly so in the future. Groups of genes tend to occur together, basically for the reason that human beings are not infinitely mobile. Even today there are great limitations in the choice of mates. An example of how limited mobility was in the past was given recently by a survey of the marriage registers of a village in Oxfordshire (Küchemann *et al.* 1967) (Fig. 41.1). Attempts have been made to estimate the choice open to people today using the frequency of first-cousin marriages and assuming that these are at random (which they often are not). It seems that each western European man or woman has in practice a choice among only about 500 of the opposite sex.

The limitations are, of course, partly the chances of geography, partly of social custom and language. Perhaps because of the importance of symbolic communication, man is a species in which like is especially liable to mate with like. Similarity, whether genetic, social, or linguistic, has obvious advantages in a mate although undue emphasis on it is one cause of perpetuating social divergence. That mating systems are involved in 'race' is suggested by the fact that some of the most marked and clearly heritable differences are in characters involved in mating. These include hair structure and distribution, conformation of the lips and face, and bodily odours.

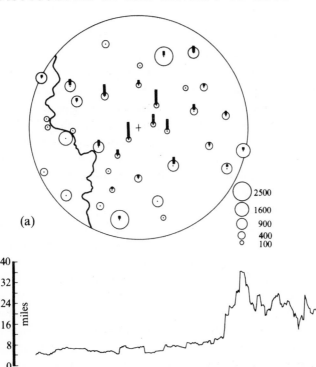

FIG. 41.1. (a) Limitations on mobility in Oxfordshire in 1861. The village of Charlton-on-Otmoor, pop. 375, is marked with a cross. The bars mark the contribution to the breeding population of Charlton from each of the surrounding villages. The size of each circle indicates the population of the village. The line on the left is the course of the river Cherwell, evidently acting as a barrier though only 10 ft wide! (b) Marriage distance from Charlton where one partner was outside the parish. (After Küchemann *et al.* 1967.)

It used to be the belief of some anthropologists that these facial and other features were 'non-adaptive' characters, but as every ordinary individual knows, they are the first to be noticed on meeting any other human being and are among the factors that influence mating.

Many features, then, social, sexual, and linguistic, along with geography and genetics, constitute the basis for the alleged concept that mankind is divided into races. The various sources claimed for the concept are hopelessly interwoven and confused. Moreover, we cannot overstress that there is continual gradation in all these respects, between minor local differences and major 'racial' groupings. We shall have to inquire also whether any of these distributions and groupings rests upon the fact that the genes or the customs are adapted to the climates where they occur.

2. Minor differences in gene distribution

To some extent everyone is aware of the presence of distinct physical types of people within the more immediate surroundings. One cannot at once say for certain that a given man is English, Scottish, or Welsh, but inhabitants of these countries often show characteristic features of build, face shape, colour of hair and eyes, as well of course as in speech and habits. The ABO blood groups of people in Wales with Welsh names like Jones or Edwards include significantly more O and B individuals and fewer A and AB than those with English names like Smith (Roberts 1942).

From minor local differences there is an infinite series of further grada-tions. Walking in the streets first of Stockholm then of Rome, it is obvious that most of the people in the two cities are physically distinct (but not all), and most of the difference is hereditary. All these people are distinct again from the inhabitants of central Africa. But proceeding from Stockholm through Rome and Athens and on to Cairo and Nairobi we should find a whole series of gradations. Where sharper discontinuities are found they are often connected with geographical barriers; for example between Europe and Africa, or Africa and Asia, though even here intermediates are present. The sharper discontinuities are not geographical but social, where a new group has entered an area and mixed relatively little with the indigenous population, as in South Africa and North America. But even here there are infinite gradations.

The fact that the distribution of genes usually changes gradually with distance can be studied most precisely by means of the blood groups (p. 584). This gradation of distribution makes it impossible to divide mankind into any set of sharply distinct 'races', though some anthropologists continue to try to do so (e.g. Coon 1962, 1966). The attempt has been a major feature of man's naïve study of himself and still is so in spite of the demonstration that it is scientifically impossible and socially dangerous. Classifications were probably first built up when human mobility was slight and local rivalry great. The identification of members of alien groups, especially when they are liable to invade his territory, seems to have been a prominent feature of the biology of *Homo sapiens* as it is in many animals (Chapter 33). It may be partly a survival from his more primitive ancestors but today is closely linked with language and culture. Biologists have no satisfactory explanation for this emphasis by mankind on the distinctness of his groups. It is partly 'territorial', but there is more to it than this (Chapter 43). The Tower of Babel phenomenon is indeed so characteristic of man as to be outside the reach of the ordinary disciplines of biology as we understand it at present. We can only hope that knowledge will provide enlightenment in the future.

The geographical differences in the distributions of genes are often graded in a regular manner so that people at one extreme of each cline can be readily recognized as distinct from those at the other (Mourant *et al.* 1958). In this sense only can we recognize races, whether major or minor. Their characters are those of the extremes of large or small ranges. The 'races' are worthy of names only in so far as these enable us to discuss the adaptive features of the various groups of genes or the liability to disease or other features represented by each extreme (see Darlington 1969).

Three major poles of differences among peoples have long been recognized. At the negroid pole are genes for dark skin, kinky hair, broad nose, and thick everted lips. At the caucasoid extreme are fair skin, much long wavy hair, thin nose, and thin lips. Thirdly, the mongoloid genes produce yellow to reddish skin, the characteristic slanted eyelids, and straight black hair, sparse on the body. A fourth, smaller, population grouping of genes may be called australoid, characteristic not only of the Australian aborigines but of other people in the East Indies and parts of India. Their genes produce a dark skin but other characters of the body form and hair resemble those produced by caucasoid genes, so that these people have been regarded as survivors of groups that in the north acquired the genes for light skin colour.

These are only the roughest outlines of the gene groupings that have become the traditional stereotypes by which we speak of races. The anthropologist finds it increasingly difficult as knowledge grows to draw up clear-cut schemes for the division of mankind. Certainly genes are not distributed uniformly; but neither, in general, are they distributed in sharply distinct groups. Rather than trying to name and characterize races we do better to look at the distribution of some known genetic factors, and to consider whether there is evidence that they have become predominant in particular parts of the world because of some advantage that they confer.

3. Distribution of blood groups

Our best information about the distribution of genes is for the ABO blood groups. The over-all world frequencies of these genes are estimated to be G 62·3 per cent, G^A 21·5 per cent, and G^B 16·2 per cent, but frequencies in different parts of the world are very unequal. The simplest condition is that of the American Indians, who in some areas have almost wholly G with little or no G^A or G^B (Fig. 41.2). G is very common throughout the indigenous 'Amerindians', including the Eskimos (but the latter contain more A and B). G is common in western Europe but falls to its lowest, around 40–50 per cent, in central Asia. Yet Asiatics, with Amerindians, are grouped in more classical terms as 'mongoloid'. This shows the sort of problem that we meet if we try to make clear-cut divisions of people

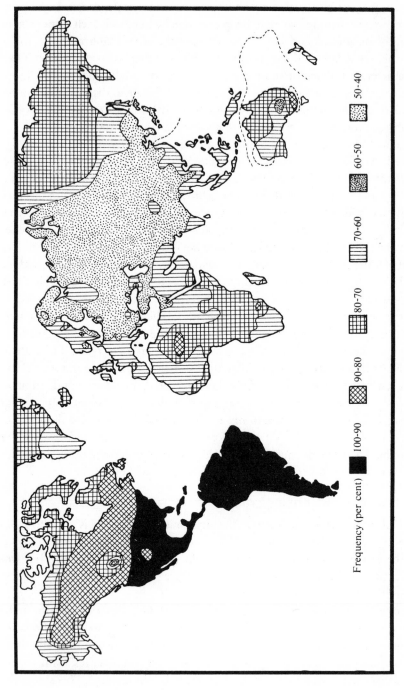

Frequency (per cent)

100-90   90-80   80-70   70-60   60-50   50-40

FIG. 41.2. Distribution of frequencies of the gene G° (for the blood group O in the aboriginal populations of the world). (After Mourant et al. 1958.)

into 'races'. This example is not, however, typical. There is in general some correlation between the distribution of blood-group alleles and the major racial groupings.

The distribution of the G^B gene is the inverse of G, being relatively common in central Asia, but rare in indigenous populations of America (Fig. 41.3). This gene shows a steadily decreasing frequency (cline) passing from central Asia to western Europe and falling to its lowest value in the Basque population, where the frequency of O is very high and there is also (incidentally?) a highly distinctive language, not of the Indo-European type. Other populations with low G^B and high O are found around western Europe (e.g. in Ireland). There are also high frequencies of Rhesus-negative genes among the Basques.

The interpretation of the significance of such gene differences is very difficult. They strongly suggest the invasion and partial mixing of populations. For instance, the populations round the edge of western Europe may show some genetic characteristics of an earlier European population, which was pushed westwards by invasions from Asia (p. 514). There are such suggestions from the distributions of blood-group genes all over the world. They carry us further in understanding what we may mean by race only in emphasizing that whatever the 'invasions' may have been like politically or socially, from a genetic point of view they generally represented a gradual infusion of one population into another, the new genes partly replacing the old (Darlington 1969).

4. Are there selective values in racial characters?

The difficulty in interpreting the significance of blood-group distributions is that we do not know how far the genes confer selective advantage. Indeed, it was for long supposed that their distribution was 'accidental'. Chance, or 'genetic drift', is still often put forward as the explanation for aberrant gene frequencies, if the groups are geographically separate (see Chapter 28). Such explanations may sometimes be correct (especially for small isolated populations), but invoking 'chance' as an explanation is often simply a mask for ignorance. The general principle enunciated by Fisher and Ford (see Ford 1965) is that few if any genes are precisely neutral, that is, have no good or bad effects upon survival. This is probably true, but it may take a long time for gene frequencies to change.

It is now known that some blood-group genes are associated with conditions that are, indeed, likely to increase mortality (p. 585). Their persistence therefore suggests that they must also confer some corresponding advantage. This reason for the persistence of a balanced polymorphism has in fact been found to be true for the distribution of the sickle-cell gene

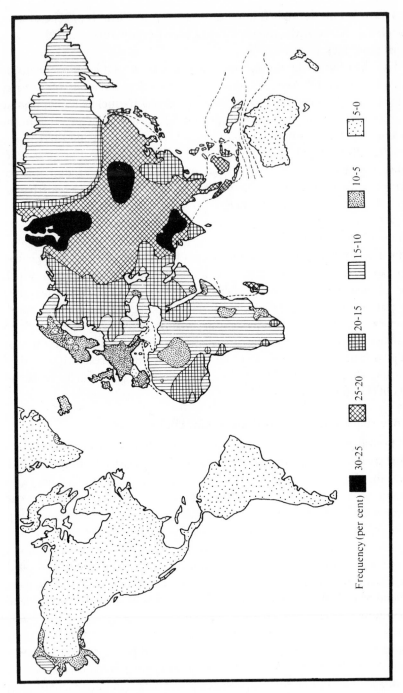

Frequency (per cent)

| 30-25 | 25-20 | 20-15 | 15-10 | 10-5 | 5-0 |

FIG. 41.3. Distribution of gene G^B (blood group B). (After Mourant *et al.* 1958.)

(p. 60). Children homozygous for the gene die of anaemia, but the hetero-zygotes survive. Their haemoglobin is impaired and this hinders the growth of malaria parasites, giving them some protection against malaria, especially when young. The sickling gene would become eliminated in perhaps 10–20 generations if it did not confer some advantage, and it is in fact commonest in malarial areas (Fig. 41.4). It exists in 20 per cent of individuals in central African tribes but only in 9 per cent of the Negro population of the U.S.A.

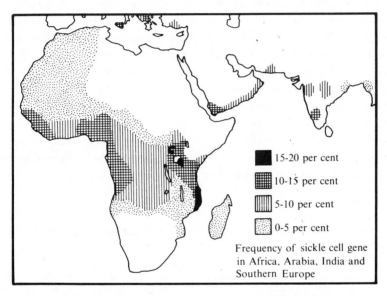

15-20 per cent

10-15 per cent

5-10 per cent

0-5 per cent

Frequency of sickle cell gene in Africa, Arabia, India and Southern Europe

FIG. 41.4. Frequencies of sickle cell genes. (After Allison 1961.)

Other genes producing haemoglobin of reduced efficiency cause the vari-ous conditions known as thalassemia. The genes may be fatal in the homo-zygous condition but nevertheless are prevalent in various Mediterranean areas and several other places that have been subject to malaria, for example Thailand and New Guinea.

5. Distribution of skin colour

The distributions of blood groups and haemoglobin genes do not at first strike us as 'racial characteristics'. This is probably because we cannot *see* them, and therefore they have not been seized upon as a basis of social divisions. Yet some at least of the features that we regard more commonly as 'racial' may be or have been basically adaptive characters, in essentially the same sense as the characteristics of the blood. The pigmentation of the skin, the basis of 'colour problems', is almost certainly adapted to suit the amount of incident sunlight (Chapter 40). The dark pigment protects against too much ultraviolet light penetration; its absence allows penetration and promotes the synthesis of vitamin D.

Some of the facial and bodily features commonly associated with race have also been held to be 'climatic' adaptations. Thus the broad nose, long body, and large limbs of some Africans are contrasted with the thin faces, smaller body, and smaller limbs of more northern peoples (p. 566). There are, however, many exceptions to these climatic 'rules' of Bergmann and Allen. Moreover, bodily conformation can undergo quite striking changes as a result of nutritional and other environmental conditions. Similarly it is held that some races are especially suited to meet extreme conditions. Eskimos undoubtedly resist frostbite especially well and Negroes badly (e.g. American Negroes suffered very severely in the Korean war). But there is considerable adaptation to cold as a result of prolonged experience of it, and no one knows how far this capacity to adapt has a genetic basis.

Similarly, capacity to tolerate hot conditions is undoubtedly greater in some populations than others (Table 41.1). But we do not know how far this is a result of acclimatization to a lifetime in these conditions.

TABLE 41.1

Comparison of heat and sweat loss in Asians and Europeans exposed to similar hot conditions (from Harrison, Weiner, Tanner, and Barnicot 1964)

	Mean wt (kg)	Calorie cost per kg/h	Calorie cost (total body wt/h)	Mean surface area (m²)	Heat produced (cal m⁻² h⁻¹)	Heat loss by evaporation (cal m⁻² h⁻¹)	Total sweat loss (g/h)
Asian group	55	4	220	1·6	137	165	440
European group	80	4	320	2·0	160	195	650

The suggestion that particular 'races' have special climatic adaptations meets the especial difficulty that people with superficially similar features may live in extremely different conditions. Thus the American Indians in the extreme north (Canada) and south (Tierra del Fuego) live in very cold conditions, while in central America peoples similar to these superficially and in blood groups live in the tropics.

6. Racial characteristics and communication

It seems, then, that although there are many hereditary characters that are useful under some circumstances, such as sickling or skin colour, yet *Homo sapiens* is not greatly dependent on a large variety of particular hereditary characters for the range of habitats that the species occupies. The fact remains that human populations differ considerably in superficial features, which they themselves recognize and to which they attach great importance. As we have seen, these include facial characters, which are used for communication, and it is not surprising that, in a species depending as much as we do upon information transfer between individuals, the systems by which it is conveyed should be subject to selection.

It is clear that such facial features as the lips and muscles of expression are part of the mechanism of communication. It may be that differences in such respects make communication somewhat more difficult, though it is quite clear that if there is such a barrier it can readily be overcome. There is evidence of some hereditary correlation with features of language (Darlington 1947, Brosnahan 1961). The peoples in Europe who use the sound 'th' live at the periphery, have a high level of O blood group, and may be survivors of an earlier group displaced by invaders from the East (p. 593). Obviously the structure of the airways is largely controlled by heredity, but it does not seem at all likely that hereditary differences in this respect are the basis for the variety of human language.

It is curious that man, who is the most co-operative of creatures with those that he 'knows', finds it so difficult to share his humanity with others who differ slightly in certain facial features and in the surface structure of their speech. It arouses the suspicion that in the past it may have been advantageous to keep breeding units small. There are other reasons for thinking that division of the population into small subunits, partly isolated genetically, may have provided suitable conditions for rapid evolution (Chapter 28). But it is hard to believe that the tendency of man to separate into small groups is mainly based upon this factor. We have the curious paradox that man's special capacities for co-operation seem to have evolved in a system that restricts this co-operation to relatively small groups. Biologists have not found the answer that explains this, but they are moving towards it by mathematical investigation of the conditions under which various forms of selection would operate (see, for example, Hamilton 1963).

7. Can there be selection for altruism?

Study of the ecology of many types of animals has led to the concept that many species have developed behaviour-patterns by which the population density is limited (Chapter 43) (Wynne-Edwards 1962, 1964). This may be by formal competitive fights for breeding territory (as in grouse on moorland) or by ceremonies of assembly in which dominance relations are established and accepted (as in the roosts of starlings). Formalized behaviour of this sort may well have been of importance for man in the past, as it is for many primates and, indeed, for man today. Such behaviour, of course, favours the group rather than the individual and has evolved by some form of group selection, but individuals who are too aggressive or too timid would fail to leave offspring (Maynard-Smith 1964).

Genes for altruism will be selected if they increase the chances only of relatives who carry them (p. 575). Undoubtedly some forms of behaviour favour the survival of close relatives of the affected individual; for example alarm notes or injury-feigning by birds and, indeed, parental care in general. This has been called 'kin selection' and may extend to more distant relatives, particularly if they live together in family groups, partly isolated from each other. Selection could operate in favour of altruism in such a group, once the situation that all members carry the relevant genes has been established. This might have been a result of genetic drift, which in turn is more likely in isolated populations.

There is thus something to suggest that the evolution of altruistic behaviour and, indeed, of powers of communication and co-operation, has somehow been connected with the division of man into small groups. The fact that so much of tribal formal behaviour is related to totemism and marriage customs also strikes the biologist very strongly. It is to be hoped that we may soon begin to understand these questions better.

There is no doubt that the genetics of co-operative behaviour is a most fundamental question. As Wynne-Edwards puts it: 'The hereditary compulsion to comply, for example, in lemmings doomed to emigrate or sticklebacks inhibited from maturing by the inescapable domination of an α male, is the real keystone of social adaptation. Individuals submitting to total deprivation are eliminated altogether, most often before they have produced any offspring, yet the tendency to comply is renewed in every subsequent generation, and is not bred out. One is bound to conclude that it is very securely buffered from "ordinary" selection acting against submissive individuals and at the same time promoting their more dominant sibs....' (1964).

The relevance of this problem to the human situation now, as well as in the past, is obvious enough. Human society today depends upon the acceptance of appropriate roles of submission of the individual, at least at some times of his life. Somehow we need to solve the paradox of producing numerous people of great ability, and indeed energy and initiative, who yet remain co-operative. At present we do not even know whether any current mating or social systems are better than others in these respects, and most 'eugenic' prescriptions that propose to advance such ends look suspiciously as if they were aimed simply at the maintenance of existing orders of dominance.

8. Mixture of gene pools

Certainly today there is no evidence that mixture of gene pools has any biological disadvantage, though in some communities it may produce social difficulties. The example of the greater height of Swiss children whose parents come from different villages (p. 250) shows that mixture of highly inbred gene pools may produce the phenomenon of heterosis or hybrid vigour. But it is not really clear that greater height should be a sign of 'vigour' in man, and there are other difficulties in interpreting this example, such as the fact that the more enterprising individuals are obviously selected for mobility. In inbred populations, such as the isolated colony of a Christian sect in Southern Dakota, studied by Mange (1964), it was found that the sons of first-cousin marriages were an average of 2 cm shorter than non-inbred males, and the daughters 5 cm shorter on average than non-inbred females.

The gene pools of most human populations contain such a variety of genes that it is not really possible to make any very general statements about the results of mixing them. The factors responsible for particular features combine in various ways according to their particular genetic characteristics. The hair of first-generation caucasoid/negroid crosses shows mainly the negroid genes, but the skin colour is usually intermediate. The particular condition of inheritance of each characteristic depends upon the number of genes involved and their dominance relations. In later generations there is seldom complete simple segregation of the original characters, because usually so many genes are involved.

In experimental animal genetics 'interracial' crosses (between distinct populations) may produce increased 'fitness' due to heterozygosity (Dobzhansky 1955). This 'heterosis' is perhaps due to dominance or even 'overdominance', in which the heterozygote excels both homozygotes. Search for signs of heterosis in man has been complicated by the difficulty of finding clear situations, but the general conclusion is that 'hybrid populations are intermediate for metrical traits, without detectable heterosis or recombination effects' (Chung et al. 1966, Trevor 1953). Among the difficulties, however, have been (1) that the studies have been on long-established hybrid populations, either containing many individuals, as Anglo-Indians or American Negroes, or few, for example Norfolk Islanders; (2) the parental groups are now represented only by descendants of remote relatives; (3) the parental and hybrid groups occupy dissimilar environments; (4) measurements are made by different observers. Such difficulties are worth noting, for they are likely to make general conclusions suspect. Nevertheless, Trevor found that the hybrid mean was intermediate between those of the

600 DIFFERENTIAL DISTRIBUTION OF GENES. 'RACES' 41.8

parents in all but one of thirty-six characters in nine interracial crosses (American Negroes, Jamaican 'Browns', half-blood Sioux, Ojibwa-whites, Yucatans, Reheboth Bastards, Kisar Mestizos, Norfolk Islanders, and Anglo-Indians). A very thorough study in Hawaii, where there are seven major racial groups, reached the same conclusion for characters such as birth weight, congenital malformation, or any of the metrical characters studied in some 180 000 observations (Chung et al. 1966). A somewhat less thorough study in Brazil gave similar results (Saldanha 1964).

It is an interesting question whether particular gene combinations may have been selected because either they are in some way internally balanced or, more simply, that they produce biologically effective individuals. Obviously for each variable of human physiology there are suitable levels of other variables. Each person must have heart, lungs, stomach, bladder, and legs of the appropriate size: disproportions would be inefficient. There is no clear evidence, medical or otherwise, that unfortunate results ('negative heterosis') may occur from the mixing of widely diverse gene pools in man (see Chung et al. 1966). If selection has operated to produce such distinct 'co-adapted' or 'homeostatic' groups, then there might be harm in breaking them up, but the studies have not shown signs that this happens.

A situation where obvious incompatibilities may arise is in matings between people with different proportions of the Rhesus genes (p. 586). Mongoloid populations have very few Rhesus-negative genes and therefore little or no haemolytic disease of the newborn. Matings of men with caucasoid-type genes with women with mongoloid-type will also produce no erythroblastosis (in the first generation). But in matings of mongoloid-group men and caucasoid-group women about 16 per cent of the latter (the Rhesus-negative) will be at a risk slightly greater than they would be with caucasoid-group husbands. The introduction of Rhesus-negative genes into mongoloid populations can thus evidently be said to have a 'bad' effect, but the dilution of the Rhesus-negative gene caucasoid populations by the pure positive complement of mongoloid gene pools would reduce the incidence of Rhesus disease.

No doubt there are all sorts of major and minor differences between the capacities developed by different gene pools. In malarial regions it is good to carry the sickle gene, but elsewhere it is a disadvantage. Caucasoid genes seem to go with susceptibility to scarlet fever, tuberculosis is relatively rare among Jews but they are subject to amaurotic idiocy, and so on. However, for the great majority of disease conditions there is no known group gene background—though it does not follow that none exists.

It is even harder to evaluate the positive physical and mental advantages conferred by the genes of particular geographic or national groups. An ingenious method has been to study the physical characteristics of Olympic athletes. These people are highly selected for the capacity to perform particular tasks, and the degree to which the relevant physique is present in different gene pools can be assessed. All hurdlers have long legs, but African hurdlers have longer legs than Asian hurdlers, and so on (Tanner 1964).

These athletic capacities no doubt have their specialized usefulness, but we have no comparable data for the part of the body about which we should like to know most, the brain. It is axiomatic that different gene pools produce somewhat different brains, but there are no reliable data even about brain weights (given comparable environment), let alone cell number or structure (statements are sometimes made about these, but are not supported by reliable evidence). In any case we do not know how to assess the significances, if any, of variations in such features. Once again the problem of assessing cerebral capacity arises when we ask whether different gene pools produce people of greater or less mental ability or intelligence. The effects of environmental and especially cultural differences are so enormous that we cannot say how great or small may be the underlying genetic differences.

9. The divisions of mankind

The whole subject of the division of Man into races is thus exceedingly complicated and it is hard indeed to make generalizations about it. It is doubtful whether strictly 'biological' factors in the simple sense are major influences in maintaining the separation of races today. Some genotypes are better adapted to one climate, others to another, but it is not these differences that cause people to be hostile to each other. There may be difficulties of communication or differences in mutual physical acceptability; if so they can be readily overcome. Interracial unions abound in all parts of the world. The divisions of man today are certainly mainly those that anthropologists classify as 'cultural', but this gives the word a sinister significance. There seems still to be a definite tendency to separate into groups that are diverse in religion, habits, laws, and language. This may in the past possibly have had its basis in the evolution of behaviour suitable for the acquisition and holding of territory, habits that are widespread among mammals. Possibly the aggressiveness that plays some part in maintaining the human divisions is a trait surviving from the time when territory for food-getting was all-important. Further, the division of a population into numerous partly isolated subpopulations seems to be one of the conditions for rapid evolution (Chapter 28). It is even possible that the partial isolation of populations by geography, reinforced by man's social divisiveness, has been a factor in promoting the rapid development of the brain that has produced language and the use of tools.

It is a pity that we cannot be more precise, or pretend to be of much use in forecasting the future or how it may be improved. After the enthusiasm for the effects of science and knowledge in such fields in the past 100 years, and optimism about their powers, the present is a time of doubt and anxiety for the future. Certainly there are very grave difficulties in store for man. But our study of human history seems to show that over the last ten thousand years there has been in general an enormous and accelerating increase, not only in human numbers, but in what we can call the quality of human life. There is no reason to expect any sudden change in these tendencies.

Numbers will almost certainly continue to increase and while this will bring great problems it may also, as in the past, enforce and liberate tendencies for common action, creativity, and productiveness. Indeed, if there is any lesson to be read from the long-term view of human evolution it is that individuals and populations without these capacities are likely to be replaced by those that have them.

Whatever may have been the origins of the present human social and national groupings it would be unrealistic to deny that they remain among the most powerful forces in the determination of our affairs today. It may be that it is not rationally necessary with modern knowledge for us to remain divided into groups, but it seems unlikely that in practice we shall soon cease to be so. This situation undoubtedly has great dangers, but perhaps also some advantages. It is doubtful whether even with much more information than we have today we should know how to regulate rationally a single common human population. Possibly that day will come, but it is not seriously in the immediate political prospect. What we can and do need to do is to ensure that the aggressiveness that goes with our divisions does not lead us to massive nuclear contests or biological warfare, which would help no one. The increasing populations that are made possible by medical science will produce demands and situations in which it will be hard to keep the peace. The biologist can help by studying the springs both of aggression and of population increase. He can help in making it possible for populations to regulate themselves, and also in producing the food that is needed. But the question of how to ensure social and political co-operation is beyond current scientific knowledge.

42

THE SPRINGS OF HUMAN ACTION

1. What can we know of causes?

WHAT makes us act as we do? This is perhaps the question to which we should most like human biology to help to give an answer, yet to start a discussion in this way is obviously so drastic a simplification as to be almost ludicrous. People act in immensely various ways, and for equally varied reasons. It would be absurd to try to give anything like a survey of human actions. What we can do is to look at some of the principles that may be used to talk sensibly about the difficult questions that centre around the concepts of choice and decision to act.

Many people, when asked of something, 'Why did you do that?' will find it sufficient to answer, 'Because I wanted to'. Can we usefully improve upon this answer? As usual with questions about causes there is a whole series of answers from 'efficient' or proximate causes, extending out towards final causes, if we can be said to have any information about these. The position we have adopted here is that human beings act as they do because of their properties as homeostatic or self-maintaining systems. Each of us is provided with certain equipment for detecting changes in the surrounding conditions and then taking such corrective action as is indicated to be appropriate by internal receptors signalling 'needs'. The most immediate, proximate causes for what we do are thus the changing conditions around and within us. If food is in front of a child he will put out his hand to eat it if he is hungry, or push it away if sated.

The reactions that can be given are dependent of course on more remote causes, events that happened in the past, some recently, some a very long time ago. Each organism has received from heredity and experience an organization that constitutes a source of information as to the lines of conduct that are likely to prevent it from merging with its surroundings. These more remote causes of our behaviour include the genes given us by our parents and the records written during our individual lives into the memory-systems of our brains.

Still more remote causes are the long sequences of selections that have produced our evolution from the earliest organisms to the present day. These selections must have depended upon the conditions prevailing at the time, and in this sense we could say that our actions today literally depend upon the past history of the earth. We have been able to make some inquiry into these and still more remote causes, as to how this power of continued maintenance arose and how it has evolved to its present state in our own selves (Chapters 26–33). We have not been able to find any answer to the question whether a 'final cause' could be found in the pattern of the universe that produced the situation on earth that led to the appearance of life (Chapter 26). Yet there has undoubtedly been considerable progress on many fronts in this search for antecedents or causes.

By means of such an analysis we can begin to give answers of one sort to the questions about why people act as they do. We may find reasons in their immediate circumstances, or in their education, or in their heredity, or in the simple facts of their humanity, such as that they have capacities both for aggression and co-operation (Chapter 43). Such an analysis is not strikingly novel, but nevertheless is useful and, indeed, important in helping us to arrange our lives. For example, in deciding the best course of action in relation to those who threaten society, say by theft, or worse by killing, we are likely to do well to consider whether the activity that hurts arises in the immediate circumstances of the individual or far back in the chain of causation. If it is the latter we may not be able to do much about it, but at least we shall avoid deluding ourselves by applying remedies directed only to immediate conditions, whether by punishment or encouragement to reform. Man is above all else a learning creature and it may be that we shall find much of the 'cause' of a person's actions in what he has learnt in the past, and the 'cure', if any is needed, in further learning in the future. But this is not to deny that there are large and intractable effects of individual heredity and fundamental human and, indeed, animal nature in the determination of what we do.

2. Choice

But answers of this sort to the question why we act as we do will immediately be challenged as leaving out what some would call the essential feature, namely the decision by the will of the individual. If what we do is all determined, either by immediate or past circumstances, how is it that, if asked, we should all say that we can choose whether to drink the glass of water on the table or not? As with other questions about consciousness, we have to admit that we do not yet know enough about ourselves fully to resolve this apparent paradox (Chapter 10). Yet there are indications that it need not really present us with the dilemma that somehow each of us consists of two people, a body and a mind. The outlines of a possible solution may become clear if we consider first the processes that are involved in the brain when we make a choice.

The human organism, like every other, is provided with a repertoire of possible reactions, out of which selection is made of acts suitable to ensure continued maintenance. The particular characteristic of the human reaction system is that we can do such a wide range of different things. Although animal actions are very varied it is generally possible to forecast fairly accurately which of a limited number of things an animal will do. This of course can be done for a person who one knows well, but the range of possibilities is much greater than in any animal. The act that we call willing is the exercise of choice between these alternatives. Many of them have only very slight differences; for example, which words to use in speech or writing. The making of such minute decisions lies at the basis of all the outstanding human achievements. In particular, it is by means of fine distinctions of communication that we have built up our vast extra-corporeal store of information about the sequence of events in the world. It is this corpus of knowledge that enables us not only to predict the course of events but to invent ways of influencing them in our favour. This surely is the basis of modern civilization, which, whether we like it or not, alters the very course of nature.

Presumably there is some 'reason' or 'cause' behind even the making of the fine choices between abstractions that lead, along with much else, to the discoveries of an Einstein or an Edison. But it is a truism that the causes even of ordinary human choice are complicated and difficult to discover. The basic needs such as for food, warmth, and sex are of course there even in the motivation of the most abstract creation. But they are supplemented and largely overlain by the social needs, such as the need for approval, and indeed by the drive to seek knowledge and understanding for its own sake. When I say that I did something 'because I wanted to' it is the expression of the operation of this whole complex of needs in reaching a decision. The neurologist is a very long way from being able to present a picture of how the brain reaches such decisions. The psychologist and psychiatrist step in here and provide, with moderate success, models that allow forecasts of behaviour, with little consideration of what goes on in the head. Nevertheless it cannot seriously be doubted that the 'decision' is in fact preceded by a brain process and that this could in principle be observed, say, by study of the electrical activities of the brain. It is important to admit that this cannot yet be done precisely, but it is equally important that we can now recognize some of the factors that are involved in the making of choices by the brain. There is no doubt that more will be known in future. Decision-making is not the act of some private creature, 'the mind', operating upon the brain. This, of course, does not dispose of the question of how best to describe that entity which each of us calls 'myself'. It merely emphasizes that our language for doing so is inadequate because it makes use of the same terms as are used to describe the behaviour of other people, postulating, reasonably enough, the presence of an agent within the body. This 'person language', as we have so often stressed, develops from the earliest communications of the child. Although it seems to describe inner events it is essentially using the language of public description, and perhaps must always do so (p. 125).

That choice and decision are accompanied by brain action does not in any way reduce the responsibility of the individual for them. This may seem paradoxical until we remember that what we call the act of choosing or willing is our description of the decision process that is going on within. To live as human beings we must continually make such decisions, and the bigger and better the decision the more valuable is the person making it. Individuals and groups who make bad decisions suffer and may perish. We are driven by our very natures to continue to try as best we can. (For discussion and literature on free will see Lucas 1970.)

Informed people would probably agree that in all decisions, whether voluntary or involuntary, important or trivial, some physical process is involved. There must be some corresponding change in the brain. This physical change is presumably the result of the balancing of the various factors that are influencing the operation of the neurons concerned. Few, if any, physiologists now seriously maintain that the 'mind' is an entity able to interfere physically with these neuronal activities (see, however, Eccles 1953). This being so, it is easy to ask, 'Are all choices then physically determined?' The orthodox scientific answer would be that they must be, but it is wiser to be empirical and to admit that we cannot attach exact meaning to the question, and therefore should refuse to answer it. We do not yet know the limits of precision with which we can in practice define the operations of complicated physical systems such as a human being. Nor do we know how the brain operates when decisions are made. This refusal to answer what seems a straight question will be judged evasive by some. Others may be stimulated to try to determine the limits of forecastibility more clearly. We need fundamental scientific principles that are based upon the study of complex systems, to supplement the precise principles such as quantum theory developed by physical science from study of simple systems (see Pantin 1968 and for brain and mind Harré 1970).

We are not justified therefore in saying dogmatically that it is meaningful to assert that human beings either are or are not 'fully determined' in all that they do. One of the most characteristic features of their organization is that they can choose between many slightly different actions (for example by speech) in response to the stimulus of current input, using a large amount of stored information. This process of deciding between different, often almost equiprobable actions we call free choice. The decisions depend particularly upon information individually acquired (rather than on inherited information), and this makes the process that we call free individual choice outstandingly important. Indeed, it is the means by which human beings have been able to take actions that give them much greater control of the environment than is exerted by any other species. This importance of the individual is not obscured by the fact that the actions that he takes to control the earth are mainly social actions, involving co-operation with others, largely through words. Effective social action by the individual therefore depends upon a high degree of conformity to the group; for instance, he must speak the common language. Yet the provision of a wide range of information to individuals and insistence on their privilege and duty of choice is essential if the group is to maintain the flexibility and variety of action that are needed for effective adaptation to circumstances.

3. Parapsychology

Among the possible factors influencing human conduct we must discuss those commonly referred to as extra-sensory perception (ESP). Many reports have appeared of experiments that claim to show the existence of *telepathy*, the capacity of a person to be aware of another's thoughts without any communication through usual sensory channels. Other similar alleged capacities are *clairvoyance*, knowledge of an object or event acquired without the senses, and *precognition* of another's future thoughts, or of future events. We may also include *psychokinesis*, the supposed influencing of physical events at a distance by thought alone.

These reports raise fundamental questions and it is not surprising that they elicit strong reactions of belief or disbelief, summarized for instance by Rao (1966) and Hansel (1966). There have been statements of belief by a few scientists, and there is a widespread if vague conviction that 'there must be something in ESP'. However it is impossible not to be impressed by the fact that even the allegedly most convincing experiments, such as those of Soal, were conducted only with a few subjects and with few variations of technique. It is hard to be satisfied by the control of the conditions under which they were done, even allowing generously for the possibility that the ESP faculty might be impaired by the imposition of unfavourable restrictions. It is also true that the results even of successful subjects are variable. To evaluate the claim properly one must give full consideration to the numerous occasions when they failed to demonstrate the phenomenon. It is possible that these failures were due to the fact that on those occasions there was no opportunity for transfer of information by *ordinary* sensory channels, voluntary or involuntary. Further it is not unduly sceptical to note that a greater proportion of fraud and deception has been unmasked in these experiments than is usual for scientific investigations.

It is probably true that most scientists do not find the evidence for parapsychological phenomena convincing. In spite of human variety there are close similarities between many of us. The reporting of common experiences, especially between relatives, is not really strange or unexpected. People are easily influenced to think alike, even when they are far apart. Full investigation of the reasons for shared experiences requires further knowledge about how our brains operate. Investigation of this is likely to be more profitable than further attempts to show that people can guess unseen cards or influence the fall of dice.

4. The brain as a deductive/inductive inference computer

The chief new additions to biological knowledge in this century have been the increased understanding of the control systems of living things, in general by their polynucleotides and of man in particular by his brain. The study of how control by the brain is operated occupies the whole of neurology and psychology, and obviously cannot reasonably be summarized here. We are concerned now with the principles of the systems by which we regulate our conduct. We may obtain some insights by looking at some features of these systems. But the brain is extremely complicated and we should not expect to be able to describe in a few pages even its general plan, let alone the detailed operations by which it produces the finer shades of behaviour. There is no place here to tell all that has been found out about how the brain discriminates between patterns, whether recognized by eye, ear, or touch, though extensive data are now available about this (see Sutherland 1961). Nor can we even try to follow all the elaborate processes by which effective sequences of behaviour are produced throughout the daily life of any animal or man. All we can do is to describe some aspects of recent work on certain themes, as illustrations of the insight that can be hoped for as studies of the brain become more complete.

The brain can be regarded roughly as an instrument for answering the question 'What is it best to do under these circumstances in order to promote the continuity of life?' It does not do this by consulting a record in which the answer to every likely question is written. This would mean having a fantastically large memory store and a complicated system for finding the 'addresses' of the right answers. The brain *has* a very good memory record, and can retrieve from it single items such as the name of a person heard perhaps only once ten years ago. We do not know how its system operates to find the answers, but it is interesting to think of possible analogies, even if they are imperfect. One useful suggestion emphasizes that the brain is not a precise logical device but works towards its answers by running through a series of sequences of operations that approximately match the situation under review. There are no man-made machines that work in this way, though computer programmes could be written to investigate how such approximations may be achieved. But the brain does not work like a computer by running through all possibilities. It somehow manipulates its information, inherited and acquired, so as to produce a match to the input pattern. We cannot say how this is done, but at least the concept of working for the answer can be seen by thinking how an aircraft collision radar obtains the answer to the question, 'Am I likely to collide with anything?' The machine is designed to sense the two relevant data, the presence of a moving object and the relative vectorial velocities, and to ignore all the irrelevant data such as actual position, actual velocity, type of aircraft, etc. The data are not compared with a table of all possible situations, but are coded and computed according to a general rule that gives a *yes* or *no* answer to the question. The brain might be said to be in one respect like this in that it produces the answers by manipulating its own coded version of the facts of the problem (for discussion see Young 1964). We do not know what this code may be, or how it is used. No doubt in time we shall do so and presumably we shall then be able to think a lot better. All that we can do at present is to identify the source of the organization and some of the working parts of the system.

As von Foerster puts it (1965), we can look upon the brain 'as if it were a computer whose internal organization changes as a result of its interaction with an environment that possesses some order. The changes of the internal organization of this computer take place in such a way that some constraints in the environment which are responsible for its orderliness are mapped into the computer's structure. This homomorphic "environment-system" reveals itself as "memory" and permits the system to function as an inductive inference computer.'

We may add that the brain has certain constraints built into it as a result of natural selection due to experiences of its ancestors. These have, as it were, 'taught' that life is possible only if a certain selection is made for attention from all the changes around, and only certain types of action are adopted. In other words, each organism has only *limited* receptor, central, and effector systems. It functions as a deductive/inductive inference computer. It does not build up its action pattern only from its own experience (induction) but makes 'deductions', with built-in 'assumptions' as to what the world is like.

5. Arousal

In order to get to work at all the brain must be aroused and kept operating, otherwise it lapses into the condition of sleep. The EEG (electroencephalogram) is a record of the activity of the brain, taken by placing electrodes on the scalp (Fig. 42.1). When a person is sitting with closed eyes and not thinking, there are often regular waves at about 10 per sec—the alpha rhythm. When he is deeply asleep there are low-voltage low-frequency waves or even a flat record. When he wakes up, or begins to look around or to solve a problem, then the waves become much more irregular. Unfortunately it has not yet been possible to identify the source of these electrical

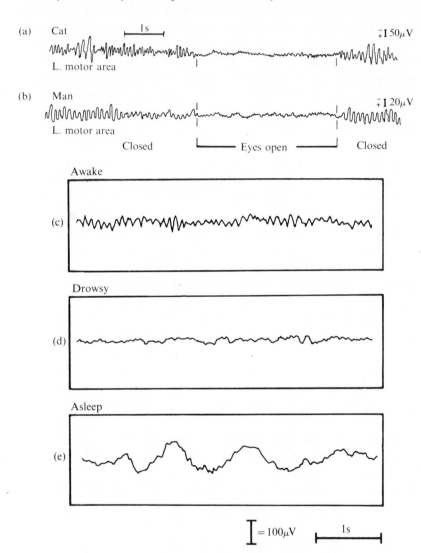

FIG. 42.1. Records of the electroencephalogram recorded by electrodes attached to the scalp in a cat (a) and man (b) with eyes open and closed. (c), (d), and (e): as a man goes to sleep, the irregular changes are replaced by a regular slow rhythm. (After Brazier 1968.)

potentials. There is no doubt that synchronous beating of numerous neurons occurs in brains—it can be recorded in a frog's brain removed altogether from the head (Gerard and Young 1937). The more irregular oscillations produced with the eyes open may eventually tell us much about brain functioning. They are already used for various forms of clinical diagnosis. In a sleeping person the times of dreaming can be identified in the EEG (p. 133).

Changes in the state of arousal can, of course, be produced by external stimuli: a loud noise will awaken and dreamy music may send to sleep. But the maintenance of the calculating activity of the brain does not depend only upon the flow of peripheral stimuli. The reticular system is a set of nerve cells and fibres running down the centre of the brain, whose activities probably play an important part in maintaining the action pattern (Moruzzi and Magoun 1949). There are both ascending and descending pathways in it, and the former are open to stimulation from a wide range of peripheral sources (Fig. 42.2). In this sense the brain is dependent on stimulation for

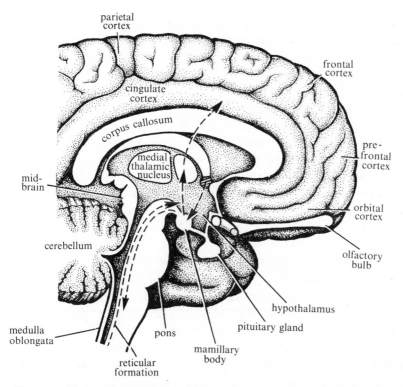

FIG. 42.2. Diagram of a section through the human brain, showing the ascending and descending reticular formations and their connections with the circuit between hippocampus, hypothalamus (mamillary body), thalamus, and cingulate cortex.

its continued activity, and complete sensory deprival, by isolation so far as possible from all external stimuli, leads to serious disturbance.

Besides this general arousal system there are, of course, stimuli that produce more specific tendencies to action, sometimes described as *drives* or *motivations*. The classification of these is very difficult, especially for man, whose 'needs' seem to extend far beyond those of simple bodily maintenance. To put it otherwise, he achieves homeostasis by actions that are directed not only to the solution of immediate problems but also to the solution of other more remote ones. The motivations for these longer-term actions are therefore complex and obscure and do not seem at first to depend upon the activation of any particular afferent systems. Nevertheless it is probable that the 'needs' at all levels are at least partly linked up together.

Some of the simpler homeostatic actions are operated by groups of nerve cells in the hypothalamus, a region at the base of the forebrain (Fig. 42.2). It contains numerous centres for regulating activities such as eating, drinking, sleeping or waking, retreat or aggressive attack, sexual rhythm, and maternal behaviour (Cross 1964). For many of these activities there are paired centres, one increasing the action (say food intake), the other reducing it. (For the hunger centres see below and for aggression p. 615.)

The fact that such 'centres' exist begins to provide some insight into the question of the immediate causes of our actions. We are each provided by heredity with a set of possible action patterns, ranging from eating to rage, which can be turned on under appropriate circumstances. This is interesting but upon reflection takes us only a little further than the knowledge that we have legs for walking or stomachs for digestion. The answer to the question of what determines the pattern to be switched on remains unstated. Nevertheless we should not minimize the importance of the discovery of the hypothalamic centres (for which the Swiss physiologist Hess received the Nobel Prize in 1949). Knowing that the centres are there we can search for the sources from which they are activated.

6. Centres for short-term homeostatic actions

The shortest-term regulations are those of such essential activities as respiration and the heart rate, which are controlled mainly from the medulla oblongata (Fig. 42.2). The hypothalamus also influences these basic functions, but is especially concerned with those such as hunger and thirst, which though not changing from moment to moment, must obviously be used every day in the interests of short-term homeostasis. Hunger and thirst are regulated partly by receptors in the stomach and throat, indicating that these are empty or dry, partly by the response of cells in the brain to changes in the composition of the blood (such as its degree of dilution or content of sugar). These signals express the level of *need* of the individual and can sometimes be quite specific for particular components that are lacking. We recognize them subjectively as appetites. The *achievement* of the required situation is also signalled by receptors, which set off the consummatory response. Thus when food is found, the nerve impulses of taste activate the hypothalamic centre for eating (a response that can also be evoked by electrical stimulation of the centre). These nerve impulses can be called signals of the results of action, or more simply signals of reward, as we also name them in the subjective language. Besides producing the consummatory responses these reward signals have the further function of teaching the memory system what is good (or bad) to eat (see Young 1964). This result is perhaps achieved through the circuital connections of some of the hypothalamic centres with the parts of the brain immediately below the cerebral cortex, the 'limbic system' (Figs. 42.2 and 42.3). Such a circuit

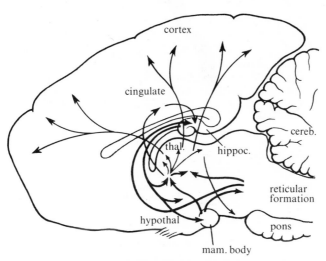

F IG. 42.3. Diagram of a section through the cat's brain showing the reticular formation and the circuit that is shown also in Fig. 42.2. (Partly after Parmeggiani 1967.)

from hippocampus to hypothalamus (mamillary body) to anterior thalamus to cingulate cortex has been called the 'circuit of emotion' by the American neurologist Papez. Injury to some of these basic circuits leads to disorders of emotion (that is of the reward system and the results of activating it) and also to loss of the power of recording in the memory. The suggestion is that these circuits serve to hold a short-lasting record of immediately preceding events (short memory) and then to allow whatever reward signals may come along to produce transfer from the short-term to a long-term (permanent) record. The latter presumably involves the cerebral cortex, but how the record is made remains speculative (see Young 1965 and p. 621).

It is significant that the sensory association areas of the visual cortex (such as the secondary visual area, area 18) have their largest connections with the lateral and basal parts of the temporal lobes (Fig. 42.4). These in turn are closely connected with the limbic system. It is probably by this route that the signals of 'reward' come to be associated with those given by the 'distance receptors' indicating events in the external world (see Magoun 1963).

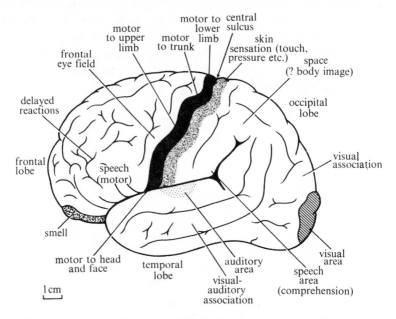

FIG. 42.4. Left side of the human brain showing the main sensory and motor areas heavily shaded or stippled. Some of the functions that can be referred to other areas are also indicated.

This relationship between the limbic system and hypothalamic centres that regulate consummatory actions such as eating and the higher parts of the brain is one of the most powerful clues that can be used in trying to discover the springs of our actions. It has been plain at least since the work of Freud that many of our most complex activities have somehow an underlying spring (or 'unconscious motivation') in simpler activities, for instance sex. The physiologist can begin to see how such connections arise, but he will need much more information before he can seriously attempt to understand the physiological foundation of the entities such as ego, super-ego, and id, which the psycho-analyst identifies inside us with his version of the person language.

7. Reactions of defence and attack

Many of the response patterns initiated from the hypothalamus are not used to provide materials for daily homeostasis, but function only intermittently, when some emergency arises. In this respect the response patterns of flight and fight obviously resemble the emergency mechanism of repair (Chapters 11 and 12). The simpler stimuli initiating these defensive actions are the signals that arise when tissue is traumatized, signals that we identify subjectively as pain. There is still uncertainty as to whether these always involve impulses carried in a specific set of pain fibres (Melzack and Wall 1965). The simplest response to the pain signals is obviously withdrawal of the injured part, if this is possible. Indeed the 'flexor reflex', by which a limb is withdrawn from, say, a pinprick or a burn has been one of the most fully studied of all responses (Sherrington 1906, 1952). This response will occur even in a 'spinal animal', that is one with the brain separated from the spinal cord. More complex responses to pain are mediated by the hypothalamus ('rage'). The still more complex ones involve the cerebral cortex, which may initiate and pursue a whole sequence of offensive or defensive actions.

Stimulation by electrodes implanted in certain parts of the hypothalamus of a cat produces phenomena of rage (see Magoun 1963). This is called 'sham rage', because it is incomplete and presumably because our language habits demand that 'true rage' is something generated by the 'mind' of the animal or man. The narrowness of the distinction will again raise suspicions of the efficiency of description that is based upon a mind–body dualism.

After a lesion in some parts of the hypothalamus a cat that formerly responded kindly to petting will turn upon anyone who touches it. Conversely after lesions in other near-by regions (the amygdala) monkeys do not show the phenomena of caution, including retreat and warning chatter, with which strangers are normally greeted. After lesions in the temporal lobe they will pick up and examine snakes, of which all normal monkeys show 'fear' (Klüver and Bucy 1939).

The signals of pain, like those of hunger, reach also to the higher centres, and serve to make a record in the memory such that actions producing pain are not repeated. A rat placed in a box whose floor is partly electrified will quickly learn to find any part where the shock is avoided. Placed again in the box it will show signs of fear, which might be roughly defined as a learned response to the prospect of pain. Further responses such as pressing a lever to escape from the dangerous box can be learned under the motivation of the fear.

The responses given in face of a dangerous situation were among the first to be investigated by Cannon in his pioneer work on homeostasis, *Bodily changes in hunger, fear and rage*, first published in 1915. They involve the activation of the sympathetic nervous system, which is itself influenced from the hypothalamus, and has such actions as accelerating the heart and raising blood pressure, stopping digestion, increasing blood sugar, lowering the clotting time of the blood, and releasing adrenalin, a hormone that itself contributes to these and other 'sympathetic' actions. This *emergency reaction* contributes to homeostasis by preparing the body for fight or flight. Incidentally, the parasympathetic nervous system has the opposite effects, promoting digestion and other conservative functions.

8. Control of reproduction by the brain

The hypothalamic centres evidently work at various time-scales: those for hunger and thirst are in regular use; those for flight or defence have to operate only intermittently. The most far-reaching homeostatic reactions of all, those of reproduction, are also controlled by the hypothalamus and other basal forebrain regions. Lesions in various centres have been shown to produce excessive or reduced sexual or maternal responses. The activation of these centres involves a complex of hormonal influences and nerve impulses, after stimulation of the genitalia and other parts of the body. In immature animals and boys and girls up to the age of puberty these centres do not produce the full drive to sexual activity. They are not, however, completely inactive and there is much still to be learned about the sexual responses that occur before puberty, and especially those of humans, where puberty is so long delayed.

The increase in sex-hormone levels at maturity somehow sensitizes these sexual centres of the brain (Chapter 18). Some of the effects of such sensitization can be seen in female rats, where the hormone levels change throughout the 4-day oestrus cycles (Fig. 42.5). At the time of oestrus the female not only actively seeks copulation but shows a maximum of exploration and other activity. It is not known precisely how the hormones produce these patterns of behaviour. In women the changes in hormone levels do not produce such striking variations in behaviour, but there are certainly some changes with the menstrual cycle, and of course more dramatically at puberty (menarche) and at the menopause, when menstrual cycles stop. It is characteristic of the human condition that patterns of sexual behaviour, though influenced by simpler biological factors, such as hormones, are finally and decisively controlled by the cortical parts of the brain. Thus, not only does sexual activity occur at all times in the menstrual cycle, but continues after menopause and on into old age in both sexes, though with declining intensity.

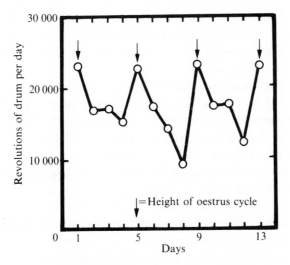

FIG. 42.5. The effect of the oestrus cycle upon activity in a female rat. The ordinate shows the revolutions of a drum per day. The unmated rat ovulates once every four days at the points of the cycle marked with arrows. (After Wang 1923.)

The signals of the results or rewards of sexual activity have the effect of releasing in orgasm the tension set up by the activation of the cerebral sex centres (Chapter 15). The physiological nature of this release is not yet understood and might prove to be very relevant to explaining the influence of sex upon the higher nervous centres. The reward signals of sex, like those of taste or of pain, not only elicit consummatory reactions (orgasm) but also have effects in the setting-up of records in the higher memory centres. The details of this process are very obscure, but the result is the striking fact that human sexual responses may be aroused by a wide range of stimuli besides the presence of a member of the other sex. Psychologists and anthropologists and, indeed, all of us devote much attention to such compulsive 'fetishes'. Particular words, garments, sounds, smells, or memories become associated with sexual arousal, presumably by a process of conditioning.

Complicated oedipus responses are produced by the early sexual reactions to the parents, and play a large part in determining later sexual response. Reactions of guilt and jealousy are a result of the family situation in which conformity is required, and are perhaps furthered by a built-in capacity for submission, which yet involves suppressing other responses. The result may be to canalize sexual response so that it is elicited especially by either aggression (sadism) or submission (masochism) or is directed to the same sex (homosexuality). Understanding of the biological basis of these trans-ferences is still imperfect and will no doubt improve as we learn more of the operation of the sexual centres in the brain. Such knowledge cannot by itself provide complete answers to these serious problems but may be of substantial help in enabling us to understand the reactions and conduct of ourselves and of others.

It is relevant that the differences between maleness and femaleness depend upon a balance of genes in the chromosomes, and that there are elements of each sex in the other. Thus in the fruit fly *Drosophila melanogaster* both sexes have three pairs of similar chromosomes (autosomes) and a single pair of sex chromosomes, which differ in the two sexes. The female karyotype has two X chromosomes and the male one X and a different chromosome, known as the Y, which carries no sex genes. The sex genes for femaleness are carried on the X chromosomes, those for maleness on the autosomes. Thus in a normal male the ratio of autosomes to sex chromosomes in 6A:X and in a female 6A:2X, i.e. 3A:X. Individual flies with three sets of autosomes and two X chromosomes can be produced and they are intersexes, with some male and some female characters, because they have 9A:2X, i.e. 4·5:1X.

In humans the female is also XX and the male XY. The X carries genes for femaleness but the male genes are in the Y. Proper development of sex depends on the correct chromosomal balance. In the condition known as Turner's syndrome the person has only an X and no Y; although outwardly a female she has no ovaries and is sterile. Another chromosome abnormality is the basis of Klinefelter's syndrome, where sex chromosomes are XXY. Such individuals have male external genitalia but small testes and some breast development; they are usually very long-legged. About one person in 500 carries this condition and unfortunately they tend to have a liability to social delinquency. This has raised the important question of whether the presence of such a condition should be regarded as in any way to be considered in mitigation of sentence of those carrying this karyotype who are found guilty of crime. The doctrine of 'diminished responsibility' is already accepted for certain forms of mental defect. The whole question of what constitutes 'responsibility' is obviously in need of constant examination in the light of current knowledge (see Glover 1970).

The balance of maleness and femaleness within the individual is, of course, reproduced also at the hormonal level, where oestrogens and androgens are present in both sexes, but in different proportions. No doubt some bisexual pattern exists in the organization of the brain cells, and in their connection patterns and chemical sensitivities, but of this unfortunately we as yet know very little.

9. Centres for maternal behaviour

These are activated by the pituitary hormone prolactin. When this is injected into female rats they begin to make nests, and so do injected male rats. The full maternal drive that leads to retrieving the young and nursing them presumably depends upon further responses by the same system. Once again in humans complicated cortical influences control the rearing of the young, in addition to the immediate hormonal effects upon the mother during lactation.

10. Memory and higher levels of motivation

In animals with well-developed brains the 'causes' of their actions are obviously likely to be found largely in the things that they have learned to do. As we do not know what changes take place when the brain learns we cannot say very much that is exact about this, even in lower animals. We may begin to provide an account of the process by saying that the brain of each species is so designed that it can acquire information about those details of its surroundings that are relevant to produce behaviour adequate for its life. The brain is thus deductive in the sense that it starts with certain presuppositions; its very structure is such that it can acquire information and make inductive forecasts only about *certain types* of situation. Receptors indicate occurrence of relevant events and records of these are somehow assembled to form a model which the brain can later use to make comparison with events as they occur and forecast the best line of action to adopt (Craik 1943).

These concepts of built-in restrictions and capacity for model-making are still very vague and crude. There is, however, much solid evidence about the limitations imposed upon the acquisition of information by animals by the very nature of their receptor organs and brain structure. Thus the classic experiments of Hubel and Wiesel (1968) have shown by recording the responses of cells in the visual cortex of cats and monkeys that each cell is pre-set to respond to a particular configuration of contour (Fig. 42.6). Anatomical and behavioural evidence suggests that there are similar cells in octopuses (Young 1960, Sutherland 1960).

It is not clear how the responses of such 'classifying cells' become combined to provide reactions to complex configurations, such as a face or a scene. This presumably involves learning, and a particular suggestion is that the formation of the model depends upon limitation, during learning, of the possible outputs that can follow when particular classifying cells are

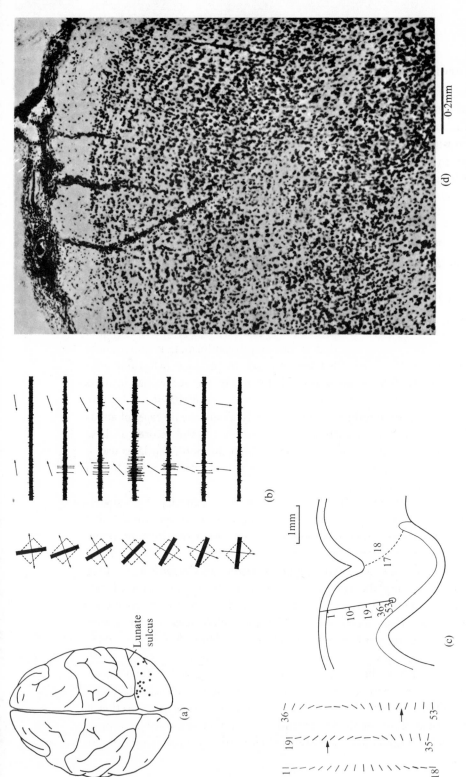

FIG. 42.6. Extracellular recordings from a microelectrode in single cells of the monkey's striate cortex in response to a black bar moving in the opposite visual field. (Hubel and Wiesel 1968.) (a) Diagram of monkey brain from above to show the sites of electrode penetration. (b) Responses of a 'complex' cell in the right striate cortex. The receptive field in the left eye is indicated by dashed rectangles. The cell fires only when a bar is moved across the field at a certain angle and in one direction. (c) On the right a reconstruction of a penetration near the borders of the 1st and 2nd visual areas (striate and peristriate). On the left are the orientations at which a bar produces a response in the numbered cells. Each line represents one

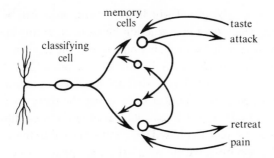

FIG. 42.7. The components of a single memory unit or mnemon. This has been postulated to explain experiments on the visual memory of an octopus. The brain is supposed to contain classifying cells each recording the occurrence of a particular type of visual contour (see Fig. 42.6). Each of these cells can initially make the octopus either attack or retreat. Following an attack, signals indicating its results arrive; these signals may be, say, either of food or pain. These signals produce the appropriate reaction—swallowing food or retreat, but they also reach to the memory system and 'teach' it that the action was 'correct' or 'incorrect'. The hypothesis is that they do this through collaterals, which activate small cells causing them to produce an inhibitory substance that blocks the unwanted pathway. Thus if, say, an attack at a vertical rectangle was punished with a shock the pain impulses would cause retreat, and through the collateral would switch on the upper of the two small cells, blocking the 'attack' pathway. The classifying cell would thereafter always tend to produce 'retreat' when a vertical rectangle appeared. (Young 1965.)

stimulated (Fig. 42.7). To have the capacity to learn implies that initially an organism can make more than one response to stimulation of any given cell or set of cells. It is therefore not unlikely that learning consists in the blocking of the pathways that are *not* needed (Young 1965). It is suggested that this is done by turning on the production of an inhibitory transmitter substance, this being the specific function of certain small cells with short axons. Such cells are abundant in the higher nervous centres. They are present also in lower ones, where they serve for the short-lasting inhibition of reciprocally antagonistic reflexes. Learning may thus have arisen by prolongation of such inhibitory actions by the 'microneurons'.

If this sort of system is correct learning consists in the 'switching' of a series of units, probably hierarchically arranged. Each such unit (mnemon) stores one bit of information, in the sense that it records whether the action taken as a result of activating it was good or bad for the animal, and therefore should or should not be repeated. This hypothesis has been suggested in detail only in relation to simple learning situations (in octopuses) and is far from proved even there. The fact that in mammals circuits activated by signals of need and reward (such as those of the limbic system) are also involved in memory-recording encourages us to think that the scheme is on the right lines. Perhaps it may be used in its most general form, namely that in learning we build up a model in the brain, by use of which correct responses can be computed in the future, the principle of construction being to close unwanted channels.

Even if it is correct this is probably only one of the ways in which changes in patterns of connectivity in the brain can take place. Yet if we knew for certain the mechanisms of change that are involved in memory we should still have the much greater task of unravelling the patterns that constitute the model in the brain. Even this would leave the yet more difficult question of how impulses circulate in phased time-patterns within the system. Hebb's concept of a cell assembly within which there are phase sequences of activity gives some idea of the problems involved (1949, see also John 1967).

We are a very long way from being able to specify the characteristics of brain models in any precise way. Many people will say that it is misleading even to talk about them, or at least that it is a waste of time. The future will show whether the hope of understanding the brain in this or any other way, is unrealistic. If we could describe the operations of the model in a brain we should know how its programmes are organized, which in a sense is what we mean by the 'mind' of the individual, as when we say 'that is the way his mind works'.

The question of the channels by which rewards reinforce learning in man is itself extremely complicated. The simplest view would be that a child begins with rewards for only certain simple primary needs such as satisfaction of hunger and avoidance of pain, and then gradually builds up an adequate operating system. Certainly many complicating factors play a part as the brain matures. The power of speech apparently depends upon the development of appropriately organized brain centres, partly by hereditary maturation, partly by learning (Chapter 19). No doubt many faculties depend upon the same sort of co-operation of heredity and environment, and development can proceed wrongly either from some fault in unfolding of the cerebral pattern, or from failure to receive the appropriate input. Thus the powers of co-operation and of altruistic behaviour may well have a background of inherited cerebral organization, though unfortunately there is no clear evidence of what this organization might be.

The human situation, so far as we understand it neurologically, is dominated by the two capacities, those for speech and for co-operation. Neither is strictly 'localized' in the brain, but there are two areas especially involved in speech, and the frontal lobes have a rather obscure relationship to social life (Fig. 42.4).

The whole brain system of man is regulated by the fact that he is as much influenced by language and concepts as by the cruder inputs of hunger or sex. Secondly, man must submit to a large degree of conformity to those around him. His overriding needs and rewards are to be recognized by others and to receive the security and fulfilment of moral and social approval. Achievement of the full expression of his faculties depends upon proper cerebral equipment and proper stimulus and opportunity to use it. If we understood better how the parts of the brain concerned with such rewards operate we might be better able to assist their development.

11. Man's capacity for generalization

The most comprehensive of all forms of cerebral operation is that which leads to investigation and the attempt to make *general* forecasts. Man is not the only animal who can be said to explore, but he certainly does it much more fully and systematically than any of the others. Moreover he has the tendency to organize the results of his inquiries into systems of explanation and forecasting, such as the religious and scientific. These powers of producing logical deductive/inductive conceptual systems presumably depend largely on the operations of the parts of the brain that produce language. There may perhaps be special properties of these regions, built-in during development following inherited instructions, so that, when appropriately activated, they allow the production of such generalizations. The speculative suggestion has been made that one basis of communication by speech is the use of the idiom that all objects are occupied by entities that have some of the appearances and qualities of persons (Chapter 19). If this is so, then the most natural means of expression of the general properties of the world would be that they depend upon a God who has some of the attributes of a person. It is certainly very difficult for most of us to think beyond this position. We should not be surprised that this is so if in a real sense it is 'natural' for us. Thus our exploration of the world in recent centuries has led us back to explore ourselves. We begin to see, very imperfectly, the reasons why we think as we do, using this 'person language'. This may make us look once again, as we all should do from time to time, beyond proximate causes to final causes. The question is not really 'Why do we act as we do?' but 'What can we know of why the world is as it is?' It is no longer necessary to dismiss such questions as 'metaphysics'. There are already some *facts* available about the nature and limitations of our knowledge, determined in the end by the structure of our brains as well as by the nature of the world around. Biologists, psychologists, and linguists are beginning to show how we come to think as we do about the world, from the minute world revealed by physicists and chemists to the immense one of the astronomers. By appropriate combination of the essential features of all these techniques it should be possible in future to produce a truly general science of Man and his World. But we shall have to be very clever or very lucky, or very privileged, if we are to 'understand' the Universe.

HUMAN CO-OPERATION AND
HUMAN AGGRESSION

1. Animal territories

THE dangers threatened by men's capacity to destroy each other are of such importance today that no discussion of human biology could ignore them. Indeed, one reaction to the fear of nuclear war has been the renewed attention given to naturalists who have studied the similarities and differences between animals and men in their aggressive reactions, especially in relation to territory and population (Wynne-Edwards 1962, Lorenz 1966, Tinbergen 1968, Ardrey 1967). One must, of course, remember that human beings live in societies of a very special sort and it is not wise to expect to learn how to regulate these by study of animal life alone. However, the human societies have grown out of animal ones and physiological mechanisms for both aggression and co-operation are widespread. We can learn at least a little about ourselves by studying the situation in other species. Something has been said about this already in Chapter 34 but the subject is so important that we here inquire further into some of the factors that may promote or allay aggression.

It is widely held that in man, as in animals, the defence of a 'territory' is the basis of much conflict. We may therefore first look at some of the facts about the ways animals acquire and keep their territories. In many species there is competition between individuals for the right to own a portion of land or space, on which to feed and mate and rear the young. It is the 'drive' to gain and retain this particular bit of space that leads to much of the intraspecific combat in animals. Ornithologists were the first to realize the importance of territory, since in the life of birds it is a very obvious feature (Fig. 43.1). The system of defence of a territory in a number of different bird species was studied long ago by the amateur naturalist Eliot Howard (1920). Similar territorial behaviour has since been found in a great many animals and shown to serve a variety of functions.

In many species of birds and mammals territory is a necessary factor in obtaining a mate. Male birds arrive first after migration and establish territories. They not only defend these but assert their occupation by singing, for instance from a prominent tree in the territory. The song serves as a claim and a warning to invaders, and as an attraction to females. Males without territory do not mate. In many animals the boundaries between territories are monitored by fighting, though this seldom leads to death. Often there is a built-in hereditary system of signs by which the loser shows his admission of defeat by submission. When an individual crosses the boundary of another's territory the occupier will adopt a position of threat, and the intruder will usually submit and retreat. The possession of its own area gives the individual some appearance of strength, which is recognized by the intruder (see Ardrey 1967).

Displays involving the actual tenure of territory have in many species developed into ritualized displays serving also (according to Wynne-Edwards) to regulate the population density. If there were no such mechanisms the excess production of individuals would lead to constant conflict and undernutrition for all. In fact this does not happen because the conflicts are largely ritualized, often as massed movements. They range from 'the dancing of midges, the milling of whirligig beetles to the manœuvres of birds and bats at roosting time, the choruses of birds, bats, frogs, fish, insects, and shrimps . . .'. These displays are commonly synchronized at dawn and dusk by the rapid change of light intensity. 'Then for some minutes at least there is generally a chorus in which the rival members of the local society

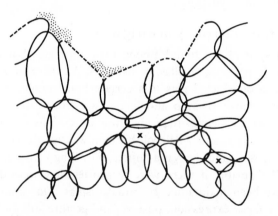

FIG. 43.1. The red grouse of Scotland are controlled by a territorial system. They feed on heather and in the autumn the males, by threat and display in the dawn hours, establish territorial patches containing sufficient food to raise a family. These were the areas for 140 acres of moorland in 1961. In February the females join them to breed. Weaker males and unmated females are kept outside the area, forming a reserve that does not breed, is a surplus for predators, and is diminished by poor food and disease. Territories vary ultimately with the quality of the heather: the population adjusts itself to the food available. (From Watson 1961.)

take part. Nothing could be more perfectly adapted to indicate the population density than such a synchronized vocal display' (Wynne-Edwards 1962).

We are here concerned with more strictly territorial systems. It seems probable that these are maintained chiefly by the fact that the *intruder* responds to the song and threat gestures of the occupant by going away. Only rarely does he persist, and then it may be the owner who goes, also without fighting. The system thus depends for its present functioning on a signalling system rather than on competitive struggle. The selective advantage of this is obvious in increasing the prospect of colonizing all possible habitats and avoiding fighting to death over the best (Lack 1954). As an example, Great Tits find more food (caterpillars) in broad-leaved than in pine woods, but they nest in both, the former woods being more crowded. By means of these territorial habits the area available for feeding is partitioned in such a manner that the successful individuals can feed themselves and their families adequately. There is the additional advantage that they do not have to waste energy in searching for food far from the home or nest (Carpenter 1942, Ardrey 1961). Individuals left over, for whom there is no really suitable territory, will establish themselves as best they can in the surrounding areas. They do not find mates and are liable to perish from undernutrition and predation.

2. The question of territory in early man

Territorial systems are found among many primates but are not conspicuous in chimpanzees, gorillas, or baboons. All these three species live in groups, each of which keeps to a certain home range. The ranges of different groups often overlap and when two groups meet they do not usually fight (see Carpenter 1942, de Vore 1965). There is of course no direct evidence as to whether Palaeolithic man was 'territorial', but it seems possible that he was, since he was a hunter, returning with some of the prey to a home. Presumably if there were territories they were defended but may well have been maintained by ritual display. Our systems of communication by facial expression, posture, and gesture still include signs of threat and others of submission, the frown, and snarl, or the smile (Chapter 35). Moreover, these signs transcend the boundaries of language. In some early Palaeolithic fossils there is said to be direct evidence of fighting (Chapter 33). The oldest known skull of *Australopithecus* ('*Homo habilis*') had been broken, but not necessarily in conflict. The remains of *H. erectus* at Pekin show that the marrow of the bones had been removed. Many Palaeolithic skulls are broken and the brain may have been eaten. Even if proved, neither fighting nor cannibalism necessarily indicate territorial behaviour. We may concede that there is some evidence that these early men warred among themselves, unlike most primates, which usually maintain their distributions by ritualized threats. Possibly the warlike behaviour came with the transition from vegetarian to carnivorous diet.

It is suggested that the improvement of the equipment for killing was not equalled by appropriate changes in ritual behaviour. The need for appeasement varies according to the reality of the threat. Natural fighters such as ravens or wolves can hurt each other seriously in fighting, and in these species inhibition is reliably generated by adoption of the appropriate submissive posture (Lorenz 1966). The responses of both parties are presumably inborn. In contrast, it seems that those animals that do not habitually kill prey or fight do not usually need any significant appeasement behaviour, because even if they fight they do not hurt each other much. The absence of an inhibition on fighting to death is also found where an animal's way of life promotes easy escape, both from its own kind and from predators; for instance, an arboreal or aerial habit as against ground living. A caged dove will beat another dove to death; there seems to be absolutely no inhibition against killing.

It may be that man at first belonged to the appeasement class. Although, like chimpanzees, he may have been irascible and even aggressive he could not quickly kill his opponent, who had time to make the slower pleas of submission that were necessary. The invention of weapons, according to this thesis, introduced the danger of quick killing and also killing at a distance, while any existing gestures and words of submission were of insufficient effect. Even more is this true of remote-control weapons. 'The man who presses the releasing button is so completely screened against seeing, hearing or otherwise emotionally realising the consequences of his action, that he can commit it with impunity' (Lorenz 1966).

It therefore seems probable that the defence of territory by families, or groups of them, has been a feature of human life for a long time but that observance of ritual responses has also long been followed. As the new agricultural and urban societies developed, the need to defend crops and dwellings from others was no less pressing than defence of the hunter's territory. From the emphasis on martial pursuits in many civilizations it is evident that this need was a primary factor in the organization of societies from the first and has remained so ever since. Whether one likes it or not, the importance of military power in politics is still increasing in almost all parts of the world. Nevertheless, the ritual responses, of showing respect for the claims of the occupier, may provide for man, as for many animals, a more satisfactory means of ensuring distribution than naked conflict. It is entirely in agreement with biological principles that law, morals, and the military should collaborate to ensure the maximum possible opportunity for life in any human community or set of communities.

3. Can we compare modern human and animal territories?

Societies of the present day are mostly much too complicated for it to be appropriate to compare their wars with the defence of territory by animals, as this is usually understood. Animal territories are associated either with families or with groups of a few hundred. We cannot safely extrapolate to the behaviour of communities of millions. The system works in 'nature' because the defeated individuals, having shown the signs of submission, retire to the periphery to die or at least remain low in the hierarchy with correspondingly reduced prospects of survival and reproduction. It is not to be expected that nations will act in this way; men increasingly refuse to accept a hierarchy of dominance. Yet so long as populations increase there is an intractable problem of how to arrange the distribution of resources. There is no easy solution to this, but the animal analogy cannot be taken literally because men have developed quite considerable altruistic tendencies; we seldom let others die of starvation, at least in 'civilized' communities. Again, some would say it is every person's *right* to have children. The problem is actually made harder *because in man there is no set limit to the resources.* This gives hope of the possibility of solutions, but it also adds complications to the problem of determining optimum numbers. Certainly there is no necessity for the added millions to be condemned to death or a marginal existence. Even if active steps are taken to limit population there is certain to be a great increase in the near future. It should be possible to channel the resulting pressures into increased production. But it will require a wide measure of good sense and good will as well as ingenuity. It is impossible to say how far these will be forthcoming (Chapter 25).

There are certainly many reasons for being pessimistic. On the other hand man has succeeded in maintaining very rapid increases in the past, and now has a much greater fund of knowledge available. But the future increases are likely to be even larger than any before. It is in the interest of every individual alive today to feel that this is a personal problem for him or her. We may all become hungry almost any year now if we fail to show greater adaptability, skill, and above all social sense, restraint, and concern for our neighbours.

In any case it is exceedingly doubtful whether such matters can be determined by master plans. They certainly never have been in the past. Each society has developed effective customs and practices, though they may not always be easy to recognize and may change faster than formerly.

4. Is there an instinct for aggression?

It is frequently held that people have an 'instinct' for aggression which must find some outlet. The capacity for rage when appropriately aroused is undoubtedly a 'physiological' response, including activation of specific hypothalamic and other centres (Chapters 34 and 42) and is a 'defence' instinct. It is less clear that there is in man an inborn 'need' for aggressive or cruel behaviour. This is certainly present in some carnivores (e.g. felines), though even here it is shown only when awakened by a stimulus. A cat is not ferocious until it sees a mouse or bird or something simulating these. Presumably a hypothalamic mechanism allows a pattern of rage to appear in man, as in the cat. But to have this capacity is not the same as to have a higher cortical mechanism that is especially apt to learn to switch on the hypothalamic rage system. It could be argued that such is present, selected in past times when both individuals and groups needed to be aggressive. The question is unanswered, and cannot be settled by reference to other species. Carnivorous mammals are said to secrete large amounts of noradrenalin, which makes them aggressive, whereas adrenalin alone produces fear and retreat. This may possibly be true, and tigers may have brains especially prone to learn to hunt and kill. But even if true, it proves nothing about human brains. In any case, carnivores can be trained to live with other species without conflict. Men may well inherit a capacity for a fierce defensive behaviour that was necessary for defence of territory, and perhaps one for aggressive behaviour to obtain prey. In the expression of aggression against an enemy men certainly easily find a stimulus and a group identification. These facts are the stock-in-trade of those who have an interest in promoting war. They are dangerous facts. It does not follow that man has an 'instinct' for war which *'must'* be satisfied, a manifestation of the alleged 'aggressive', carnivorous, instinct. It is a matter for debate whether it is wise to elicit the manifestations of aggression by 'sublimation' through sports, especially if these are bloody. It is not good biology to look only at the behaviour patterns whose adaptiveness has largely departed, leaving them as relics. We should not ignore aggression, which certainly has a place in human affairs, but should look also at the biological features that have enabled men to co-operate in such startlingly successful ways. Humans have the capacity, even propensity, to become fierce, often habitually so, and this is the source of much suffering. But certainly the initiation of aggressive behaviour is often a result of the stresses and conflicts that can hardly be avoided in the long period of parental and social conditioning.

5. Human restraint

We cannot emphasize too often that this long period of learning is one of the most characteristic of human attributes. What we learn to do is of course superimposed on biological needs, for example to breathe, to eat, and to reproduce, and biological capacities, including those for both fighting and for love. But comparison of ourselves with other primates chiefly draws attention to our unique capacity to *restrain* both our aggressive and our sexual capacities in order to perform co-operative actions. No individual or group of monkeys or apes will sit still and attend to one task as even children will do and the reader is doing now. So it is reasonable to hope and, indeed, to expect that co-operative behaviour in the future will enable even an enlarged population to maintain itself with the aid of the multitude of new tools now at our disposal.

If this occurs it will be because of the success of the characteristically human system of late maturation and hence restrained behaviour and depth of learning of the young (Chapters 18–21). As these are among the features in which man differs most profoundly from other primates, so the first presumption is that they will increasingly control his behaviour.

6. The necessity of co-operation

So far as we can plan, we should do so on the basis that man's special genius is for co-operation. This is not simply optimism, as some people seem to wish to show, but a rational forecast based upon the evidence. Men and women have tendencies to love and help much more than to hate each other: we are not fallen angels but risen apes, getting better! The conflict between good and evil has been the focus of human interest at least since cultures began. We learn more about this conflict and the means of resolving it every day, from literature and life as well as from psychologists and anthropologists. It has often been hinted that perhaps the line between good and evil has been too sharply drawn and the Devil in us is not wholly useless. At least he must have had an adaptive function or he would have been selected out long ago. There are, of course, many features of human behaviour that point in both directions. Men and women are certainly not going suddenly to become perfectly submissive and conditionable. It is not likely that they would build stable societies if they did. Hammering out a steady course for the vast populations of the future may well require at least some part of the capacity for aggressiveness that we carry, perhaps from a more crudely territorial past. But there is obviously a need for all people to be on their guard against the traps into which arousal of their aggression by demagogues can lead them (see Tinbergen 1968).

There is presumably in the human brain a centre whose activation arouses the symptoms of rage. This can be serious without reaching the point of open aggression. Everyone feels a rising of anger sometimes, perhaps especially when there is a threat that he will be deprived of possessions or rights. This may well be a residue of rather simple territorial behaviour. Indeed, it is marked that people will show a rudely aggressive attitude to anyone trespassing on their property, whether it be a secretary with her desk, or a farmer with his fields.

In such forms aggression does little harm, but when aroused in large masses of people it can lead to war. Hitler raised his masses to enthusiasm by calling up their feelings of lost territory and imposition by aliens (Jews). What has happened with demagogues before will probably happen again. People will be aroused by them and will act collectively in ways that are not likely to lead to stability either for themselves, their friends, or their enemies. The aggressive response may have been appropriate for small territorial claims but when aroused in masses it is likely to damage attackers and attacked alike. With nuclear and biological weapons it could be fatal to all life on earth.

We all have built-in tendencies to co-operate as well as to contest. Individually and collectively we shall be wise to plan in expectation of seeing both sorts of tendencies at work in ourselves as well as others. As Lorenz points out, 'we can feel the full, warm emotion of friendship and love only for individuals, and the utmost exertion of will power cannot alter this fact'. We cannot love all our brothers indiscriminately. Nevertheless, he continues, the powers of reason and natural selection together may well be sufficient to produce a selection pressure that 'in the not too distant future will endow our descendants with the faculty of fulfilling the greatest and most beautiful of all commandments'. We might add that the commandment to 'love thy neighbour' is great and beautiful because it is the expression of the most intricately balanced form of life that has yet appeared on earth, namely, human co-operation to increase life and improve it.

44

A SUMMARY OF OUR KNOWLEDGE OF
LIFE AND ITS EXPANSION

1. The satisfactions and dissatisfactions of twentieth-century thinking

PEOPLE in many parts of the world now have more reliable information by which to guide their lives than ever before. By the use of this knowledge, and by the technical products that flow from it, many millions of people live at levels of health and happiness that 100 years ago were achieved by at most a few thousands. But neither knowledge nor standards are equally distributed. At least half of the world's population lives still in the old conditions of ignorance and insecurity. Moreover, even where knowledge abounds there is discontent because it is not unified to make a complete and satisfactory system around which thinking can safely and easily proceed. In the old systems completeness was achieved, in effect, by the assumption that the brain's operations provided a full and correct view of God and man and their respective ways. If we are right in supposing that the model in the brain is built around the images of persons and what they do, then we can see why thinking of the image of a powerful Father as the controller of all provides a satisfactory answer to fundamental questions. It explains 'naturally' because it is based upon our 'natural' ways of cerebral functioning. Each religion has its own way of building upon this basic mode of human thinking (p. 623).

The 'certainty' that derives from religious belief is in fact only an assertion that our own way of thinking provides a 'correct' view of the universe and its causes. In a sense, of course, this *must* be true, since all facts about which we can discourse have been collected by human brains. The only sort of knowledge we can have must therefore have passed through this filter.

This question of the status of biological studies in relation to others has worried us throughout our search (Chapters 1 and 10). It is one aspect of the old question of the limits of language. Is there some essential difference between the factual (corrigible) propositions of scientific knowledge and the *a priori* propositions of logic? What is the status of the proposition that logical propositions owe their truth to our brain structure? Can we recognize 'elementary propositions', individual units of discourse, as Wittgenstein at one time tried to demonstrate? In the light of what we know about the operations of the brain this does not seem to be a very profitable approach. Yet before we can begin to produce a truly general theory of biology we must have a general theory of logic. What does it mean to make statements of factual observation? We must agree about this before we can discourse systematically about the brain or anything else (see Quine 1969).

These are old difficulties of epistemology and metaphysics and they are far too big to be discussed properly here, much less answered. It must be recognized that with this omission our study does not provide the necessary introduction to a system for the study of man. At most it can present an 'approach' to that study. What it may perhaps do is to show that modern studies of the brain and of linguistics may be able to produce a genuinely new approach to these old problems. The usages here suggested do not 'answer' the old questions about fact and logic, body and mind, freedom and determinism, science and value. They do suggest that usages can with advantage be changed in the light of new knowledge. We may be able to talk more interestingly and usefully about ourselves and the world in the light of the many facts that have been discovered about how life goes on and in particular how the brain works.

Until now all systems of knowledge (epistemology) have had to assume the essential characteristics of human logic as an unexamined postulate. Perhaps there is a sense in which this must always remain so. But investigation of brain processes can, as it were, allow us to study ourselves from the outside. We may be able before long to use our knowledge of the physical properties of the world to explain why we speak and act as we do. Of course, it may be asked what is meant by 'explain' in this context. Descartes 'explained' the mechanisms of the brain as due to movement of the pineal body controlling the flow of vital spirits. We say he was wrong in detail but perhaps right in principle. What we need to do is to examine in what sense our present model of the operations of the brain is 'truer' than that of Descartes. The answer would surely be that it allows us to make more accurate and effective forecasts about how our brains will operate under various conditions and how their actions can be assisted. It is of course true that the making of forecasts is a task that is for ever incomplete. Nothing will prove that we have any right to rely upon the continued success of induction. Yet what we are now saying is that by our inductive studies it has been found that the brain is a system operating with certain intrinsic deductive principles (e.g. grammar) to make inductive forecasts. This is indeed a circular study, which clearly needs clarifying. The certainties of deduction need examination as much as the uncertainties of induction.

It has been held that deductive arguments can be 'validated' whereas inductive ones can only be 'vindicated' because they work (Reichenbach, see Katz 1956). But the 'validity' of our logic is only that it is the system that we must use to allow communication among us. Knowledge of the neurological basis of this system of logic and language is still only fragmentary. There can be little doubt that as it grows it will help to clarify our ideas. What changes in operation of the brain are involved in scientific revolutions? (Kuhn 1963, Popper 1970). At present it seems absurd even to look for them. But this is because we are not used to speaking of brain actions. The systems of description of each epoch must, indeed, bear a relation to biological knowledge, and will change with it. Whatever system we use now will be little used after 100 years, will seem completely antiquated in 500, and will probably be forgotten altogether in 1000 or less. This does not matter; what is important is to find the best possible scheme to promote life *now*.

2. The order of life and its origin

We have tried throughout our analysis to reach a general scheme that will describe and explain human life, and allow us to see it in a consistent general framework. The investigation of various aspects of our existence has shown that the outlines of such a scheme are visible. We are still lamentably ignorant, and our concepts will no doubt seem very weak to our successors. But they are an advance on those that have been available in all the centuries that people have been trying to read the riddles of the universe.

We now know something about origins. All animals and plants are composed of approximately the same small selection of elements from the ninety-two that occur naturally on earth (Chapter 2). These few elements are combined to form systems, such as our own bodies, which are of greater complexity than any others found in inorganic nature (at least there are no others as complex on earth). The order of these lives is maintained by the continual expenditure of energy in elaborate ways that counteract tendencies to degradation and disorder. All these actions are directed by the highly selected molecules of the polynucleotides, which ensure the synthesis of proteins appropriate to prevent dissolution (Chapter 3).

The question arises of where this order comes from and when it began to be apparent. We cannot answer this in full, but we have overwhelming evidence that the present high degree of order has been arrived at gradually, by the changes that we call evolution (Chapters 27 and 28). The later animals and plants to arise are, in general, more complex than the earlier. The DNA has come to carry more and more information, and in animals an increasing part of its programme has been concerned with directing subsystems that themselves acquire further information, culminating in the human brain.

Enormous amounts of information are involved in the control of living organisms (i.e. they are very highly ordered). As evolution has proceeded creatures depending upon more and more information have appeared. This is to say that life has been becoming increasingly complex and has invaded habitats where it can survive only by more elaborate life processes (see Young 1938, 1951).

The information is carried by the sequence of nucleotide pairs in the DNA, very much as information is conveyed by the sequence of letters in a book (Chapter 3). If we assume 2000 letters to a page, then the instructions for a virus would occupy 100 pages (2×10^5 nucleotide pairs), those for a bacterium a book of 2500 pages (5×10^6 pairs), and those for a man 1700 books of 1000 pages each ($3 \cdot 5 \times 10^9$). This gives an idea of the tremendous complexity of life and also warns us of the enormous difficulty that faces us if we wish to know the human genetic instructions fully. We already understand the principles of the language in which they are written, but reading in it is hard, and to get through the 1700 books is a huge task. One wonders if it will ever be completed. Of course we read now only haltingly, like young children. Our successors may laugh at us as they skim through the descriptions of the genotypes, visualizing the effects of the enzymes.

The earliest known fossils of some 3000 million years ago were apparently little more complex than bacteria. The knowledge of the gradual increase in complexity since then does not tell us how life arose, but it gives us at least a possibility of finding out (Chapter 26). We do not have to ask, as our ancestors did, how man was made, but 'How did the first self-maintaining system arise?' This is hard enough to answer, but the making of some simple life system by 'artificial' means has become a serious scientific possibility.

Until we know more about the first stages of life it is little use asking questions about still more remote 'causes'. It seems likely that it will be found that life first arose 'spontaneously' from the operation of the conditions prevalent upon the early earth. If so, these conditions *contained the antecedents of the order that we see in our lives today*. It is for astronomers to tell us about the source from which this order in turn was derived. The rest of us can only speculate, with them, about the meaning of the patterns of the stars. There, if anywhere, we may find the still more distant origins of order, perhaps even signs of a Final Cause, and its relevance for the significance of our own lives.

3. What can knowledge of the brain tell us?

Here the weakness of our concepts becomes glaring, and they will no doubt seem childishly ridiculous to our successors. Even today to look for God among the stars will seem as impious and old-fashioned to some people as it may seem imaginative to others. 'The kingdom of God is within you', might be the response of the religious. And the biologist might not greatly disagree with him. For instead of beginning our account as we did, with the elements and molecules that men are made of, we might better have begun by emphasizing our knowledge of the brain, by which all knowledge comes to us, including that of atoms, astronomy, and Final Cause. To discuss brain function adequately we must consider operations commonly called 'mental' (Harré 1970). Yet we do begin to see how each brain is the centre of a very special type of deductive/inductive forecasting system (Chapter 42). Here again, our concepts remain primitive and incomplete, but what we know about the brain already gives us understanding far beyond anything our predecessors had. We do not fully understand the dilemma of our awareness of self and otherness, but there are enough facts known about aberrations of consciousness to make us very suspicious of the apparently self-evident dualist propositions of ordinary language on this subject. The categories of mind and body are not, as they seem at first, simple or easy to contrast (Chapter 10).

Again, it is not known in detail how the cerebral system forms representations of the world and uses them for forecasting. We have used the concept of a 'model in the brain', but it is little more than a general metaphor (Craik 1943). It is a useful way of referring to an entity whose existence we can recognize but whose properties we cannot yet define. To use such a phrase at all may seem not merely irritating but specious and even unscrupulous to those psychologists and others who appreciate the complexities of the operating system that is involved. The neurologist is the first to agree with these doubts, for he knows only too well how complicated the brain is. No one who has tried to discover the connection patterns and operations of even a small part of it can fail to appreciate that we do not know how to describe what is involved in such a multichannel system. These very difficulties may have led neurologists to be overcautious in their attempts to understand the mechanisms responsible for animal and human actions. Yet in some respects we can begin to give real meaning to the concept of a model in the brain (Chapter 42).

It is certainly a further large step to our suggestion that the model in its early stages in each of us is built around the use of symbolic representations of persons and their communications (Chapter 19). Knowledge about this may, however, provide light on the reasons why we cannot help thinking 'anthropomorphically' about all sorts of matters, from personal ones such as our own references to ourselves, our egos, ids, and superegos, to searches for ultimates in physics, metaphysics, or religion. It is certain that attitudes to all these great questions will be fundamentally changed as we come to know how it is that our brains deal with them as they do. We can only reap the meagre first fruits of such knowledge in practical matters yet. The facts of its existence and yet feebleness warn us not to be 'simple-minded' and yet to be humble in our ignorance. We may be encouraged by the thought that perhaps we are of a generation that first *begins* to understand the cerebral basis of thinking.

What has been found out has already revolutionized treatment of some aberrations of brain functioning. Anyone who has had to deal with the problems of depression or psychosis, for example, knows what has been achieved by pharmacological means—and how much remains to be done. We have not dealt here with pathology, nor with the equally important topic of the impact of understanding of the brain upon our management of child development and especially of education. The long period of learning has been one of the chief features that have led to human dominance. Indeed, man's 'explosion' was probably initiated by the selection of those hormonal and cerebral characteristics that were necessary to exploit this delayed development (Chapter 35). But even today we have little detailed understanding of how best to use this period of learning. Nearly all educational theory is empirical, in the sense that it takes no account of brain processes. We do not know how to improve the model in the brain. How could we, since we know so little about it and how it operates? The studies of child development are beginning to provide some foundations, though as yet with little relation to cerebral physiology (Chapters 19–21). Failing proper scientific knowledge of the brain we have to make do with empirical 'intelligence tests' as measures of cerebral capacity (Chapter 20).

4. A summary of homeostatic reactions on various time-scales

1. *Short-term adjustments*

What goes on in the brain is of such supreme importance to each of us that it is right that it should be treated first and separately, as the central part of our understanding of life. Yet perhaps it is because all knowledge comes through the brain that the knowledge we have about the brain itself is very poor. We know far more about physics and chemistry, or about other parts of the body, than we do about the mechanism that acquires this knowledge. It is this detailed knowledge of physical science that gives to modern man his great powers of control. By the application of such knowledge also to biological problems we now have some insight into the details of the system by which life is controlled, on various time-scales.

For the short term there are all the detailed physiological adjustments that the body makes to preserve its integrity. The maintenance of a steady state necessarily involves a system for signalling departures from standards of reference (Chapter 7). Organisms remain alive because the actions that they take are appropriate to ensure their continuity according to the circumstances. Every individual has a repertoire of actions, varying from switching on the production of an enzyme in a bacterium to the discussions of politicians at a peace conference.

The full definition of the principles of operation of all these elaborate systems of control constitutes much of the science of biology; no short summary can be adequate. For higher animals, however, we have a system of description of the 'motivations' and 'drives' by which the organism is activated to take the actions that are appropriate to fulfil its 'needs' (Chapter 42). If the need continues the organism is in a state of want, stress, and perhaps pain: when the need is met it is 'pleased' or 'satisfied'. Description here is heavily confused by the subjective (person) language and we find it difficult, if not impossible, to dispense with it perhaps simply because we are made that way (Chapter 10). We shall in practice continue to use person language for much of our daily communication (Chapter 19). It is the direct and 'simple' way to which we are accustomed. But the scientific language for describing what we do in terms of what is known about the brain is much more powerful and detailed and should help us to understand and allow for any minor or major deviations from 'normal' behaviour. To know something of the existence of the driving forces within at least helps to explain our problems, though knowledge may not yet be sufficient to heal our neuroses.

2. Medium-term adjustment. Replacement and repair

One of the most striking features of the system of thought provided by biology is the concept of turnover (Chapter 5). The old static mechanistic concept was of a body with 'structure' and 'functions'. The analogy is linked closely with the technology of machines. But it has been made clear by the use of radioisotopes that many of the molecules of the body remain there for only a short time. There is some enduring structural framework, but most of the more important parts of the living material are continually changing, under the control of the instructions of the DNA. This turnover itself provides one of the main guarantees of the continuity of the system. It allows continual adjustment, and especially replacement of parts that have suffered from 'wear' at all levels, from molecules upwards. To put it in another way, the body has found means of continually monitoring its moving parts and replacing them as they wear—techniques that might well be envied by industry (and copied?).

Special processes are programmed in the instruction book for correcting faults that occur only sporadically. These are, of course, what we usually call the mechanisms of healing, repair, and regeneration (Chapter 12). It is especially useful for medicine to be able to see them in their proper context, as special procedures to ensure maintenance, kept in readiness to correct events that occur less often and less regularly than those that are met by the daily physiological adjustments.

3. *Long-term adjustment. Ageing, death, and reproduction*

But there are accidents and defects that occur still more rarely, or accumulate more slowly. The question of the place of senescence and death in the scheme of life is obviously central for every man. In spite of the controversies discussed in Chapter 22 it is not too much to claim that we begin to understand this too. The self-maintaining systems of the body are remarkably efficient, but accidents will happen, and no hierarchy of repair systems can correct them all: 'What repairs the repairer of the repairer?' and so on (p. 288). It would be wrong to say that this regress 'explains' the inevitability of death. Indeed, in a sense the paradox makes the continuity of life seem impossible. How do living things defeat the regress? Life continues for millions of years in spite of the impossibility of correcting all defects, while the conditions around change profoundly.

The 'secret' of this continuity is precisely that no living system remains unchanged. Not only does it continually turn over and adapt, but from time to time it reduces itself to the minimum and starts again. By this act of reproduction the system reduces to little more than the instructions of its DNA, and the attendant polymerase enzymes by which they are 'read'. From these a new individual is built. Moreover, in all sexual organisms the new instructions are the combination of those of two parents, and thus provide a new phenotype, perhaps able to meet changed conditions. So, by continual production of an excess of individuals, it is ensured that the system remains adequate for survival as conditions change (Chapter 28).

4. *Evolution*

The effect of the continual adjustment of the instructions of living systems has been to produce the slow changes of evolution (Chapter 27). These are as much part of the mechanisms of homeostasis as are the second-by-second adjustments of, say, respiration and heart rate. Evolution is simply a very long-term physiological 'mechanism', selected because it keeps living matter alive. Thus many of our own characteristics are specifically adapted to ensure evolution. The division into two sexes is perhaps the most conspicuous example. The particular mechanisms of evolution have, however, produced the further effect of steadily creating more complicated organisms, able to survive in conditions ever more remote from those in which life first arose. For example, the earliest organisms were probably salty, watery systems living in a salty sea. Some then came to live in fresh water, using special pumps to prevent themselves from being flooded (Chapter 6). Later some came on land and acquired suitable mechanisms to prevent dehydration and so to maintain a salty, watery system, where there was no water. This invasion of new habitats continues today. Birds, bats, and men have come to be able to live in the air, and now man even lives in space. All vertebrates require oxygen, but man can arrange to live where there is none—if he takes it with him.

This expansion of living powers must have been one of the features inherent in the replicative characteristics of the earliest forms of life (Chapter 26). It would be very interesting to understand more of the origin of this urge to expand, since it is the prototype of our own ambitions. This is not, of course, to say in any mystical sense that the need to strive, as we know it, was developed in the proto-amoeba. There is abundant evidence that the capacity to seek for distant goals has itself grown throughout evolution (*The life of vertebrates*). It is indeed the corollary of the increasing capacity to collect and store information that the organism shall find ways to use it in the future. Man learns and teaches more than any other creature and therefore has the greatest possibility and opportunity to direct the course of events in the world. It is his nature and his biological function or duty to do so. Looking at the whole sequence of the living world there is no doubt of this special position of man. Organisms depend upon collection and transmission of information, and man does this better than any of them. There is no need for this pre-eminence to make us arrogant, still less heedless of the significant parts that are played by other organisms. We certainly cannot afford to do so, for we depend upon them—are indeed all one with them together. Everything we find about living things emphasizes our unity. All of us use the same genetic code to make the same amino-acids into proteins of similar types. All of us, animals, plants, and bacteria, form one closely interlocked network of ecological relationships (p. 115). All use a means for producing genetic variability so that, after selection, forecasts are made that certain structures or reactions will be useful in the future.

It is easy to elevate these facts into a pretentious scheme of the whole living world as one 'organism'. Yet there is a sense in which this is true.

It is difficult to exaggerate our interdependence. We need plants, animals, and bacteria just as they need us. Man, by the invention of language, and later writing, has found ways of making forecasts much more efficiently than is possible by bi-parental inheritance. Each of us obtains the information for his life not merely from two parents but compounded from as many sources as he can hear or read. With this great capacity for processing information, men have the power to direct many of the operations of the whole natural system of which all organisms are a part. It is the business of each of us to make sure that it is directed wisely and well.

APPENDIX

Table of the elements

Atomic number	Element	Symbol	Atomic weight
1	Hydrogen	H	1·00797
2	Helium	He	4·0026
3	Lithium	Li	6·939
4	Beryllium	Be	9·0122
5	Boron	B	10·811
6	Carbon	C	12·01115
7	Nitrogen	N	14·0067
8	Oxygen	O	15·9994
9	Fluorine	F	18·9984
10	Neon	Ne	20·183
11	Sodium	Na	22·9898
12	Magnesium	Mg	24·312
13	Aluminium	Al	26·9815
14	Silicon	Si	28·086
15	Phosphorus	P	30·9738
16	Sulphur	S	32·064
17	Chlorine	Cl	35·453
18	Argon	Ar	39·942
19	Potassium	K	39·102
20	Calcium	Ca	40·08
21	Scandium	Sc	44·956
22	Titanium	Ti	47·90
23	Vanadium	V	50·942
24	Chromium	Cr	51·996
25	Manganese	Mn	54·9380
26	Iron	Fe	55·847
27	Cobalt	Co	58·9332
28	Nickel	Ni	58·71
29	Copper	Cu	63·54
30	Zinc	Zn	65·37
31	Gallium	Ga	69·72
32	Germanium	Ge	72·59
33	Arsenic	As	74·9216
34	Selenium	Se	78·96
35	Bromine	Br	79·909
36	Krypton	Kr	83·80
37	Rubidium	Rb	85·47
38	Strontium	Sr	87·62
39	Yttrium	Y	88·905
40	Zirconium	Zr	91·22
41	Niobium	Nb	92·906
42	Molybdenum	Mo	95·94
43	Technetium	Tc	..
44	Ruthenium	Ru	101·07
45	Rhodium	Rh	102·905
46	Palladium	Pd	106·4
47	Silver	Ag	107·870
48	Cadmium	Cd	112·40

Atomic number	Element	Symbol	Atomic weight
49	Indium	In	114·82
50	Tin	Sn	118·69
51	Antimony	Sb	121·75
52	Tellurium	Te	127·60
53	Iodine	I	126·9044
54	Xenon	Xe	131·30
55	Caesium	Cs	132·905
56	Barium	Ba	137·34
57	Lanthanum	La	138·91
58	Cerium	Ce	140·12
59	Praseodymium	Pr	140·907
60	Neodymium	Nd	144·24
61	Promethium	Pm	..
62	Samarium	Sm	150·35
63	Europium	Eu	151·96
64	Gadolinium	Gd	157·25
65	Terbium	Tb	158·924
66	Dysprosium	Dy	162·50
67	Holmium	Ho	164·930
68	Erbium	Er	167·26
69	Thulium	Tm	168·934
70	Ytterbium	Yb	173·04
71	Lutetium	Lu	174·97
72	Hafnium	Hf	178·49
73	Tantalum	Ta	180·948
74	Tungsten	W	183·85
75	Rhenium	Re	186·2
76	Osmium	Os	190·2
77	Iridium	Ir	192·2
78	Platinum	Pt	195·09
79	Gold	Au	196·967
80	Mercury	Hg	200·59
81	Thallium	Tl	204·37
82	Lead	Pb	207·19
83	Bismuth	Bi	208·980
84	Polonium	Po	..
85	Astatine	At	..
86	Radon	Rn	..
87	Francium	Fr	..
88	Radium	Ra	..
89	Actinium	Ac	..
90	Thorium	Th	232·038
91	Protactinium	Pa	..
92	Uranium	U	238·03
93	Neptunium	Np	..
94	Plutonium	Pu	..

International Atomic Weights 1961. (From I.U.P.A.C. Bulletin No. 14B, Butterworth's Scientific Publications.)

APPENDIX

Metric conversion tables

Length

kilometre	(km)	=	10^3 metre = 0·62137 miles
metre	(m)	=	1 metre = 3·2808 feet
centimetre	(cm)	=	10^{-2} metre = 0·3937 inches
millimetre	(mm)	=	10^{-3} metre
micron	(μm)	=	10^{-6} metre
nanometre	(nm)	=	10^{-9} metre

Area

square kilometre	(km²)	=	0·3861 square miles
square hectometre	(hm²)	=	hectare (ha) = 10^4m² = 2·471 acres
square centimetre	(cm²)	=	0·1550 square inches

Volume

litre	(l)	=	1 litre = 0·21998 gallons
millilitre	(ml)	=	10^{-3} litre = 16·894 minims
microlitre	(μl)	=	10^{-6} litre

Mass

kilogramme	(kg)	=	10^3 gramme = 2·2046 pounds
gramme	(g)	=	1 gramme = 0·035274 ounces
milligramme	(mg)	=	10^{-3} gramme = 0·015432 grains
microgramme	(μg)	=	10^{-6} gramme
nanogramme	(ng)	=	10^{-9} gramme
picogramme	(pg)	=	10^{-12} gramme

Temperature

degrees Celsius (Centigrade) (°C) = (°F − 32) $\times \frac{5}{9}$

degrees Fahrenheit (°F) = (°C $\times \frac{9}{5}$) + 32

degrees Kelvin (absolute temperature) (°K) = (°C + 273)

Atmospheric Pressure

1 atmosphere = 760 mm mercury = 29·921 inches mercury

GLOSSARY

Abiogenesis. The supposed spontaneous generation of life.

Actomyosin. A combination of two proteins, actin and myosin, responsible for the shortening of muscle fibrils.

Adaptation. The processes of physiological and evolutionary changes that make organisms able to survive in their environments.

Adrenal. An endocrine gland whose outer part (cortex) is concerned with growth, sex, responses to stress, and many metabolic matters. The central medulla produces adrenalin and noradrenalin, which prepare the body for defence or attack. Adrenal cortical hormones include corticosteroids, progesterone, androgens, and oestrogens.

Adrenocorticotropic hormone, ACTH. The secretion of the pituitary that stimulates the adrenal cortex.

Aerobic. Dependent upon oxygen for life.

Agglutination. The clumping together of cells or viruses when they come into contact with an antigen specific to them.

Albumins. Blood proteins that are soluble both in water and in salt solutions (cf. *Globulins*).

Aldosterone. A hormone of the adrenal cortex controlling salt balance.

Allantois. The foetal bladder. In placental mammals contributes blood vessels to and from the placenta.

Allele. One member of the set of genes that can occur at a given locus on a chromosome.

Allopatric. Species occupying distinct geographic ranges (cf. *Sympatric*).

Allosteric. Of an enzyme with two receptor sites, one of which binds to a substrate the other, reversibly, to a low molecular allosteric effector molecule. This produces conformational changes modifying the activity of the catalytic site. Allosteric effects thus function as control points for metabolic paths.

Amino acid. Contains basic (NH_2) and acidic groups (COOH). Amino acids can combine with each other to make protein chains.

Amnion. A two-walled sack enclosing a cavity in which the embryo of land vertebrates develops.

Amniotes. Animals producing an amniotic sack around the embryo, which can thus develop on dry land. Reptiles, birds, and mammals.

Amylase. An enzyme that splits starch, e.g. the ptyalin of the saliva.

Anaerobic. Living without oxygen (certain bacteria).

Androgen. Hormone with masculinizing action, e.g. testosterone.

Animal pole. The end of an egg that contains the nucleus, often has rather little yolk.

Anthropomorphism. Ascription of human characteristics to animals, physical events, or gods.

Antibiotic. Substance that kills bacteria, produced by bacteria or fungi.

Antibody. A specific protein (globulin) produced when a particular antigen enters the body.

Anticodon. A nucleotide triplet of transfer RNA complementary to a codon triplet of mRNA. The tRNA is thus able to attach its amino acid at the correct place in a growing polypeptide.

Antigen. Substance that promotes the formation in the body of an antibody that will react with it.

Aphasia. A disorder of speech. Loss of the power to speak or to understand speech.

Archaeology. The study of remains left by former human cultures.

Atom. The smallest portion of an element that can take part in a chemical reaction. Consists of a positively charged nucleus surrounded by one or more negative electrons. Nearly all the mass is in the nucleus, which consists of a charged proton and one or more neutrons. The chemical behaviour depends upon the number of electrons (atomic number) which equals that of the protons. Most elements have *isotopes*, with differing numbers of neutrons.

Autoimmune disease. One in which the patient produces antibodies against certain of his own tissues.

Autolysis. The process of solution of cells by their own enzymes.

Autosome. A chromosome that is not a sex chromosome. In man there are twenty-two pairs.

Axilla. Armpit.

Axoplasm. The contents of an axon.

Axon. The long part of a nerve cell, conducting signals (usually) away from the nerve cell body (see Fig. 12.1).

Bandwidth. The range of frequencies required to transmit a signal, expressed as cycles per second (hertz). Any communication system requires an optimum bandwidth.

B.P. Before the present time (usually taken as A.D. 2000).

Biopoiesis. The original formation of living matter.

Black-box experiment. One in which the performance of a system is described without consideration of its contents.

Blastoderm. The disc of cells formed during cleavage of a bird or mammal. The central part forms the embryo.

Blastopore. The aperture of the inner cavity (archenteron) of a developing embryo (gastrula). Cells move over the lips of this aperture in the morphogenetic movements by which the embryo differentiates.

Blastula. The ball of cells produced by cleavage of the egg.

Boltzmann's constant. $k = \dfrac{R}{N} = 1\cdot38054 \times 10^{-16}$ erg $^\circ$K^{-1} where R is the gas constant and N Avogadro's number (i.e. number of molecules (or atoms) in a gramme–molecule (gramme–atom) $= 6\cdot02252 \times 10^{23}$).

Bond (= *valency bond*). The link by which one atom is attached to another in a chemical compound. The bond energy is that required to separate the atoms

and bond length is the distance between their nuclei.

Breccia. A rock composed of fragments of stone, often also with bone.

Bronze Age. The first period of the use of metal. From about 4000 B.C. in the Middle East.

Catalysis. The alteration of the rate of a reaction by a substance (catalyst) that brings the reagents together but remains unchanged at the end. Enzymes are catalysts.

Chemistry. Study of the composition of substances and their effects on each other.

Chorion. The outer layer of the amniotic sack.

Chromosomes. Threads of DNA, protein (histone), and RNA. Occur in pairs in somatic cells of higher animals and plants. The members replicate before mitosis but separate in meiosis so that each gamete has one of each pair.

Cilia. Fine hairs, usually motile, as in those that keep the epithelia of the nose and mouth clean. Have in all organisms the same pattern of a ring of nine outer double fibres with two at the centre.

Ciliates. Protozoa characterized by numerous cilia which they use for moving and feeding, e.g. *Paramecium.*

Cistron. A section of DNA specifying a particular polypeptide chain.

Cleavage. The division of the fertilized egg into a number of blastomeres, ultimately forming a blastula.

Cline. A gradual change with distance in a phenotypic characteristic of a population of organisms.

Clitoris. The sensitive and erectile tissue of the vulva whose stimulation produces erotic responses. The penis is the male homologue of the clitoris.

Clone. The descendants produced asexually from a single individual. All have the same genetic constitution.

Code. A regular relationship between the members of two sets. Hence any system of arbitrary signals used to convey information in a communication channel is a code.

Codon. The triplet of contiguous nucleotides in DNA or RNA which determines that a particular amino acid shall be inserted at a particular place in a polypeptide chain.

Co-enzyme. An essential substance in many sequential enzyme reactions, is changed by one enzyme and then changed back by the next.

Cohort. The term used by demographers for all the individuals born in a given place and period (usually 1 year).

Collagen. A fibrous protein of connective tissue.

Concept. A generalization about qualities, aspects, relations, or other attributes. Normally expressed by a word. Thus the concept of truth, or of weight.

Condom. Contraceptive or prophylactic sheath, usually of rubber, worn by the male.

Conservation of mass and energy. It used to be supposed that neither can be created or destroyed. Einstein's theory shows this is not true for nuclear reactions or near the velocity of light. However the sum of mass and energy always remains constant.

Continental drift. The theory that the land masses of the earth were once united and are drifting apart.

Contraceptive. An agent preventing fertilization, either by physical means such as male sheaths or female caps, or by chemicals that kill sperms, or by hormones that prevent ovulation ('the pill').

Control. The process of regulation of the actions of a system.

Co-repressor. A metabolic product which combines with a repressor to inhibit the formation of the enzymes that produce it.

Correlation. The tendency of two sets of values to vary together. Measured statistically as the correlation coefficient (r), running from -1 to $+1$.

Cortex. Strictly the outer crust of anything. The sheet of tissue covering the cerebral hemispheres of the brain. Receives information from many or all receptors and controls many actions.

Corticosteroid ($=$ *corticoid*). One of the adrenal cortical steroid hormones (see *Adrenal*).

Cortisone. One of the adrenal cortical hormones, influencing carbohydrate metabolism (see *Adrenal*).

Cosmos ($=$ *universe*). Vague terms for all that is.

Covalent bonds. Strong links formed by sharing pairs of electrons, one provided by each atom. Found in non-ionizable organic compounds.

Cretaceous period. From about 135 to 65 million years ago. The time of the chalk Downs.

Crossing over. The exchange of genetic material between homologous chromosomes during meiosis.

Cryptobiosis. The state of an organism when it shows no visible signs of life and when its metabolic activity becomes hardly measurable, or comes reversibly to a standstill.

Culture. The sum of the technology, arts, science, and customs of a people.

Cybernetics. The study of control.

DDT. An insecticide (dichloro-diphenyl-trichlorethane).

Degenerative diseases. Those in which the repair and replacement processes are no longer able to maintain normal structure and function.

Deme. A group of individuals with certain characteristics, e.g. genetical, cytological, etc. Often used for a gamodeme or group of interbreeding individuals.

Demography. The study of human populations.

Dermis. The layer of the skin lying deep to the epidermis. Largely connective tissue; leather is made from it.

Diapause. Period of spontaneous dormancy with very reduced metabolism, independent of environmental conditions, in insects.

Diploid. The state in which each set of chromosomes is represented twice.

Discriminant function. A statistical measure of the degree of difference between two sets of variables.

Dizygotic twins. Siblings derived from two (or more) separate fertilized ova.

Dominance (genetics). The condition in which the effects of one allele mask those of another (see *Recessive*).

Dominant side of brain. In man, but no other animal, one side, usually the left, differs from the other in containing areas essential for speech.

Drive. Used in psychology for the motive force that initiates and sustains particular types of behaviour, e.g. hunger drive, sex drive.

Echolalia. Reiteration of words or phrases heard.

Ectoderm. The outer layer of an embryo, includes future skin and nervous system.

Ectogenesis. The rearing of the young of a normally viviparous species outside the body.

Ectoloph. The outer ridge on a horse's molar tooth.

Electron. Negatively charged elementary particle. Has rest mass of $9 \cdot 1091 \times 10^{-28}$ g.

Element. A substance consisting of atoms with the same atomic number. May have several isotopes with differing numbers of neutrons. Eighty-three stable natural elements are known, uranium having the highest atomic number (92). Some others have been made artificially and are unstable. See appendix, p. 642.

Empirical. Strictly means knowledge based on experience. Often used for knowledge based on experience only of the outward performance, without an understanding of the internal operations of a system.

Endocrine organs. Glands of internal secretion. They produce specific substances (hormones) to act as signals. These are released into the blood and influence the specific target organs elsewhere in the body. Examples are pituitary, adrenal, pancreatic islets, etc.

Endoderm. The inner layer of an embryo; includes the future lining of the gut.

Energy. Capacity of matter or radiation to produce an effect, i.e. to do work. One joule is the work done by a force of 1 newton acting through 1 metre, p. 90 (see *Force*).

Entropy. A measure of the disorder of an isolated system. The ratio of the amount of heat taken up to the absolute temperature. The entropy of an isolated system never decreases, that is to say it tends to become less well ordered.

Enucleate. With the nucleus removed.

Enzyme. A protein that catalyses a particular reaction.

Eocene period. From about 55 to 40 million years ago.

Epidermis. The outer layer of the skin; continually renewed by addition of cells from beneath.

Epilepsy. A condition of the nervous system in which the patient has paroxysms (fits) and may fall and become unconscious.

Epistemology. The study of the validity of knowledge. Usually considered a branch of metaphysics, but must depend upon the brain.

Equilibrium. State of balance between opposing forces.

Erectile tissue. A special system of blood vessels of the penis and clitoris, which become enlarged with erotic stimulation and released in orgasm.

Erogenous. Producing erotic, i.e. sexual, effects.

Escherichia coli (E. coli). Bacterium living in the colon of man.

Ethology. The study of animal behaviour, especially in natural habitats.

Eugenics. The study of the possibility of racial improvement in man by control of mating, encouraging the spread of some genes in preference to others.

Eukaryote. Organisms having a nucleus with a membrane (i.e. not bacteria).

Evolution. The long-term maintenance of homeostasis by change in the characters of populations in successive generations descended from each other.

Exocrine gland. One that pours out its secretion through a duct, e.g. the salivary glands.

Exponential. Changing according to some power function, e.g. exponential growth, p. 141.

Extrovert. Person whose interests are directed outwards to others and to nature rather than to himself.

Fecundity. The probability that a woman will conceive, p. 318.

Fertility. The number of live offspring produced by a woman throughout her life, p. 318.

Fibrin. The protein of a blood clot. Formed, when tissues are damaged, from the fibrinogen in solution in the blood.

Fibroblasts. The cells of connective tissue that produce the protein collagen (= fibrocytes).

Foramen magnum. The hole at the back of the skull through which the spinal cord passes.

Foraminifera. Protozoans with chambered calcareous shells, hence preserved as fossils, making chalk.

Force. External agency capable of altering the state of rest or motion of a body. One newton is the force required to accelerate 1 kilogramme by 1 metre per second.

Fossil. Remains of an organism preserved in the earth's crust.

Frontal lobes. The anterior part of the brain (originally the motor part) responsible for controlling action. Especially developed in man, where the most anterior part (pre-frontal) is responsible for producing restraint, e.g. social behaviour.

Galaxy. A cluster of stars, e.g. the Milky Way, which has 10^{11} stars, of which one is the sun.

Gas constant. R in gas equation $pv = RT$, where p is pressure, v volume, and T absolute temperature ($^\circ$K).

Gastrula. The two-layered embryo produced by moving in of some cells of a blastula to make an inner layer of endoderm.

Gastrulation. The process in development that converts a single-layered ball of cells into a two-layered system. In higher animals includes more complex processes.

Geiger counter. Instrument for detecting and counting ionizing radiation (alpha, beta, and gamma rays).

Gene. A hereditary unit at a given chromosome locus, which can mutate to various allelic forms, producing different results.

Gene complex. The set of genes in an individual.

Genetic drift. A chance change in gene frequencies, which may be noticeable in very small populations.

Genetics. The study of heredity.

Genotype. The genetic constitution of an organism, as compared with its outward appearance (see *Phenotype*).

Genus. A number of similar species arbitrarily grouped together as being sufficiently different from those in another genus.

Globulins. Proteins of the blood. They are insoluble in pure water but soluble in salt solutions (cf. *Albumins*).

Glucose. Grape sugar, dextrose, $C_6H_{12}O_6$.

Gonadotropic hormones. The secretions of the pituitary that regulate the sex organs.

Haploid. The number of chromosomes in a gamete ($= n$) as compared with the diploid number in a zygote ($= 2n$).

Heterochronic grafts. Grafts of tissue between individuals of different ages.

Heterokaryon. A cell with two or more nuclei of different constitution. Occurs in fungi, and by artificial introduction of nuclei from one cell to another.

Heterosis. The greater vigour of growth, survival, and fertility of hybrid over inbred lines. Probably due to heterozygosity.

Heterozygous. Carrying different genes at a locus.

Histone. A type of basic protein associated with the DNA of nuclei, combining with the phosphoric acid residues.

Homeostasis. The condition of maintaining a constant organization in spite of continuous interchange with the surroundings.

Homologous chromosomes. Two that pair during meiosis and then proceed one to each gamete.

Homozygous. Carrying two identical genes at a given locus on homologous chromosomes.

Hormones. Chemical messengers (signals). Produced by endocrine glands and have specific effects on sensitive target organs. Are often of relatively low molecular weight.

Hybrid. Offspring of a cross between unlike parents.

Hydrocarbons. Organic compounds containing only carbon and hydrogen.

Hydrogen bond. The weak attraction between a hydrogen atom covalently bonded to an O or N atom and an atom with an unshared electron pair.

Hydrophobic. Having a lack of affinity for water, e.g. the fatty acids or the fatty end of a phosphatide molecule.

Hyperplasia. Abnormal increase in cell number.

Hypertrophy. Abnormal increased development of an organ.

Hypothalamo-hypophysial system. The centres of the brain that control the pituitary gland (hypophysis) and so regulate much of growth, development, and homeostasis in general.

Hypothalamus. A region at the base of the brain containing centres controlling many activities essential to homeostasis (e.g. feeding, reproduction). Controls the pituitary gland. Concerned also in memory.

Ice Ages. A series of periods of colder climate. Usually refers to those of the Pleistocene but others had occurred earlier.

Ilium. The most dorsal bone of the pelvic (hip) girdle. Short and broad in man, larger and narrower in quadrupeds.

Immune reaction. The reaction between a specific antigen and antibody.

Immunization. Stimulation by an antigen to produce antibodies.

Inducer (effector). A metabolite of low molecular weight which inactivates a repressor molecule and thereby allows the synthesis of the enzyme producing the metabolite.

Information. The amount of order in a system. Can be defined in relation to that in other systems. One bit (binary digit) is the amount of information that decides between two equiprobable alternatives.

Intelligence quotient (IQ). A child's mental age, divided by his chronological age and multiplied by 100 (p. 268).

Introvert. A person whose interests are in his own thoughts and feelings.

Invagination. During embryological development the movement of cells over the lips of a blastopore to make an inner sac (enteron). One of the movements that converts a blastula into a gastrula.

Invertebrate. Member of one of the many groups of animals that have no backbone.

Ion. Electrically charged atom (or group of atoms). Cations are positively charged (due to loss of electrons), anions negatively charged.

Iron Age. From about 2000 B.C.

Ischium. The posterior bone of the pelvic (hip) girdle. Long in quadrupedal, short in bipedal animals.

Isomers. Chemical compounds with the same molecular composition but different arrangement of the atoms.

Isomorphic. Having the same form or structure.

Isostasy. The equilibrium condition in the earth's crust. Continents rise and fall, e.g. when denuded or under ice.

Isotopes. Most atoms exist in nature as mixtures of isotopes having the same number of protons (p) but different numbers of neutrons (n). The isotope is designated by its mass number ($n+p$). Thus ordinary hydrogen is ^1H, deuterium ^2H, and tritium ^3H. The last is radioactive, with half-life 12·26 y and emits low-energy β-rays.

Jurassic period. From about 190 to 135 million years ago. The time of the formation of the Cotswold Hills.

Karyotype. The chromosome complement of an individual or species.

Keratin. The characteristic protein of skin and hair. Contains sulphur. Is very inert and insoluble and hence gives good protection.

Lactose. Milk sugar, $C_{12}H_{22}O_{11}$, on hydrolysis gives glucose and galactose.

Lamarckism. The theory that characteristics acquired during the lifetimes of individuals are passed through the gametes to their offspring (untrue).

Leucine. An amino acid.

Leucotomy. Cutting the connections of the prefrontal lobes of the brain as a cure for depression.

Leukaemia. A disease in which there is overproduction of white blood cells (or production of imperfect ones).

Life table. Shows the expectation of life of members of a cohort as they age.

Limbic system. A series of interconnected centres below the cerebral cortex, including the hippocampus.

Linkage. Tendency for characters to be associated because the controlling genes are carried on the same chromosome.

Locus (genetics). The linear position of a gene in a chromosome.

Macrophages. Large phagocytic white cells. They enter a clot and remove debris after a wound.

Magma. One of the semi-fluid strata beneath the earth's crust; the molten rock-material from which igneous rock results by cooling and crystallization.

Malignant tumours. Growths of cells that invade neighbouring tissues and then spread along lymph and blood vessels to produce secondary growths (metastases).

Maltose. Malt sugar $C_{12}H_{22}O_{11}$, formed from starch by the enzyme diastase.

Manic-depressive psychosis. A disorder in which periods of excitement alternate with those of depression.

Masochism. Obtaining sexual pleasure in suffering physical pain.

Mass. The constant of proportionality between the force applied to a body and the acceleration that results. The mass varies with the velocity. The rest mass is the mass of a body relative to the observer.

Mastoid. A swelling on the periotic bone, behind the ear. Contains air spaces and may become infected. The muscles attached to it help to hold up the head in man.

Masturbation. The production of orgasm by manual or other artificial stimulation of the sex organs.

Maturation. The completion of inherited growth processes, as contrasted with effects of the environment.

Medium. A nutrient broth used for the artificial cultivation of cells outside the body.

Meiosis. The two nuclear divisions by which the gametes are formed, with one member only of each pair of homologous chromosomes. During meiosis there is interchange of material between homologous chromosomes (*crossing over*), which increases the variability of the species.

Menarche. The onset of puberty in the female, as marked by the first menstrual period.

Menstrual cycle. The alternate growth and shedding of the lining of the uterus. An ovarian follicle grows for about 14 days, secreting oestrogen. The ovum is then discharged and the follicle becomes a corpus luteum and produces progesterone, which makes the uterine wall thicken further. If no pregnancy occurs the luteum stops secreting and the uterine wall breaks down, producing the menstrual flow.

Menstruation. The monthly discharge of blood and tissue of the uterine wall at the end of the luteal phase of the menstrual cycle.

Mental age. The average age at which children achieve a given intelligence test score.

Mesaxon. The fold of Schwann cell surface that surrounds a myelinating axon (Fig. 12.1).

Mesoderm. The middle layers of an embryo. Includes future blood vessels, muscles, skeleton, and much else.

Mesolithic. The period, after the end of the Palaeolithic, when men lived largely in small waterside communities by fishing and hunting and the beginnings of agriculture. From about 12 000 to 10 000 years ago.

Metabolism. The chemical processes ensuring the continuity of life. Includes anabolism or synthesis, with storage of energy, and catabolism or breakdown, with its release for the organism's activities. The enzymes producing metabolism are similar throughout plant and animal kingdoms.

Metaphysics. The branch of speculation that deals with the first principles of things.

Meteorite. The remains of a meteor that falls to earth.

Microvilli. Minute hairs, shown by electron-microscopy on many cells (p. 212).

Millimole. One-thousandth of the molecular weight.

Miocene period. From about 25 to 7 million years ago.

Mitochondria. Organelles present in all cells (except bacteria and blue-green algae). Contain the enzymes of the phosphorylation cycle by which the energy-yielding

ATP is formed. Hence 'the power-houses of the cell'.

Mitosis. Division of a nucleus such that the daughter nuclei each contain a full (diploid) set of chromosomes.

Molecular weight. The sum of all the atomic weights of elements in a molecule.

Molecule. The smallest piece of a substance that can exist alone and keep its properties.

Monozygotic twins. Siblings derived by division of a single fertilized ovum.

Morphogenesis. The process of translation of the instructions in the DNA into the various different functioning cells and tissues.

Mucopolysaccharide. A combination of protein (mucin) and polymerized carbohydrate. Characteristic of connective tissues.

Mucoprotein. A combination of polysaccharide and protein, found especially in connective tissues.

Mutation. A change in a gene, as by change of one of the bases in it. Caused by radiation or the action of some chemicals (mutagens). Average frequency about 1 in 10^5 per gene in the individuals of human populations.

Myelin sheath. The fatty layers around some nerve fibres. Serves to increase the speed of conduction.

Neolithic. The period, after the Mesolithic, in which settled agricultural communities began and before the use of metal (Bronze). Began about 10 000 years ago. Lasted in Britain until 4000 years ago or later (2000 B.C.).

Neoteny. Process by which a larval form continues to the adult phase and sexual maturity without metamorphosis. For possible neoteny in man, see p. 479.

Neural plate. The thickened ectoderm of the dorsal midline of an early vertebrate embryo. It will roll up to form the nervous system.

Neurology. The study of the nervous system, in particular that of man by experts in nervous disease.

Neurosis. A vague term. Covers abnormalities in which a person gives exaggerated reactions to stresses but does not lose all contact with reality. Condition may be transient and curable but patient may cling to neurotic behaviour patterns (cf. *Psychosis*).

Neutron. Constituent of the nucleus of all atoms except hydrogen (^{1}H). Mass slightly greater than proton but no charge. Outside a nucleus a neutron decays with half-life 12 minutes into a proton, an electron, and an anti-neutrino.

Neutrophils. White blood corpuscles whose granules stain only with neutral stains.

Nucleoside. A purine or pyrimidine base attached to a sugar (ribose or deoxyribose), e.g. thymidine, cytidine, etc.

Nucleotide. A complex of a nucleoside with phosphoric acid, e.g. thymidilic acid, cytidilic acid, etc. Are incorporated into DNA and RNA.

Objective. In psychology means relating to things or events in the world that are observable, e.g. an objective description is one using terms that can be understood by all (cf. *Subjective*).

Oestrogen. Steroid hormone liberated by the maturing follicle during the first phase of the menstrual cycle.

Oestrous cycle. Cycle of changes in female mammals. In a follicular phase the ripening ovarian follicle produces oestrogen. When the follicle ruptures discharging the egg the female is in 'full oestrus' (heat) and will accept the male. If there is no fertilization the empty follicle forms a corpus luteum producing progesterone but ultimately regressing so that the thickened uterine wall breaks down. The cycle is controlled by the pituitary. Cycles may follow regularly (rodents) or occur once or twice a year (carnivores) or in a breeding season. The human menstrual cycle is a modified oestrous cycle.

Oligocene period. From about 40 to 25 million years ago.

Open system. In thermodynamics a system in and out of which matter and energy can flow and be changed in the process.

Operon. A set of cistrons lying close together, producing proteins that regulate a single function and are controlled by a single operator gene, which can be repressed or de-repressed.

Opposable. A first digit of hand or foot that

can be moved to meet the other digits and so grasp branches or other objects.

Organelle. One of the formed units of the cell, e.g. mitochondria, Golgi bodies.

Orgasm. The culminating response to sexual stimulation.

Osmosis. The flow of a solvent from a weaker to a stronger solution across a membrane through which the solute cannot pass ('semi-permeable membrane').

Ovary. The female gonad. Contains many unripe ova (oocytes) and much other tissue. In a woman one ovum usually develops each month and is discharged at the middle of the menstrual cycle. The ovary also produces hormones (*oestrogens* and *progesterone*).

Ovulation. Discharge of an ovum from the ovary. Occurs in women about 14 days after the beginning of the previous menstrual flow.

Ozone. The form of oxygen having three atoms in the molecule, O_3.

Palaeocene period. From about 65 to 55 million years ago.

Palaeolithic period. The old Stone Age, when men were hunters, using flints. Lasted from perhaps 2 million to 12 000 years ago.

Palaeontology. The study of fossils.

Panmictic unit. A population where mating is random.

Parameter. A term for a variable quantity (used in several different senses in geometry and statistics).

Parasympathetic nerves. A system of motor nerves running mainly to internal organs, e.g. the muscles of the viscera. Has actions opposite to those of the sympathetic, e.g. promotes recovery, by digestion, etc.

Parenchymatous tissue. Composed of cells fitted closely together, e.g. liver.

Parietal cortex. The part of the cerebral cortex at the side. Includes important association areas.

Pathogen. An agent producing disease, e.g. a virus or bacterium.

Penis. The male sexual and urinary organ. Becomes distended when the sensitive tip is stimulated, producing the orgasm at which semen is emitted.

Peptide. A compound of two or more amino acids, joined by the peptide linkage -NH-CO-.

Periodic system. Arrangement of the elements according to the law that their properties are in periodic relation to their atomic weights, i.e. the elements form a series of families.

Peristalsis. Contraction of the muscles of the walls of a tube, such as the intestine or oviduct, propelling the contents forwards.

Permian period. From about 280 to 225 million years ago.

pH. A measure of acidity or alkalinity measured in terms of the hydrogen ion concentration of a solution.

Phage (=bacteriophage). A virus whose host is a bacterium. *Escherichia coli* is the host to a series of phages T_1-T_7.

Phenotype. The observable properties of an individual after development as a result of the interaction of its genotype with the surroundings.

Pheromone. A substance produced by one individual to send signals to others of the same species (e.g. sex stimulants, fear substances in fishes).

Phoneme. One of the sounds recognized by linguists as the units of speech.

Phonetics. The study of the sounds that make up speech.

Photosynthesis. Formation of organic compounds from water and carbon dioxide using the energy of the sun and chlorophyll as catalyst.

Physics. The study of the properties of matter and energy.

Pilocarpine. A drug that imitates the action of parasympathetic nerves, e.g. by producing secretion of the pancreas.

Pituitary. A gland below the brain whose many secretions regulate nearly all aspects of homeostasis. Hence 'the leader of the endocrine orchestra'. Is itself regulated by the hypothalamus, lying above it.

Placenta. The organ elaborated in the uterus by embryonic and maternal tissue where the foetal and maternal blood are brought close together to allow exchange of oxygen and nutrients.

Plasma. The liquid part of the blood, contains proteins, etc. in solution. (Has other meanings in physics.)

Pleiotropic genes. Those with many effects.

Pleistocene period. From about 2 million to 10 000 years ago. Contained three major Ice Ages.

Pliocene period. From about 7 to 2 million years ago.

Ploidy. The multiple of the chromosome set present in an organism (e.g. haploid (one set), 6-ploid, etc.).

Polygenes (= *multiple factors*). Genes with small effects that combine to produce graded phenotypes (e.g. stature in man).

Polymer. A macromolecule formed by covalent bonding of repeating simpler molecules (monomers), in life by the action of a polymerase enzyme.

Polymerase. An enzyme producing formation of a polymer from monomers.

Polymorphism. The existence of two or more genetically different classes in a population because each has some selective advantage under particular circumstances.

Polymorphs. White cells of the blood, having lobed nuclei. The first cells to enter a clot after injury.

Polyoestrous. A condition in which there are several oestrus cycles each year.

Polyploid. An individual with more than two sets of chromosomes.

Population. A group of individuals of the same species.

Post-mitotic tissues. Those whose cells never divide after differentiation, e.g. nerves and striated muscle.

Pottery. First made in Neolithic times, about 6000 B.C.

Progesterone. The steroid hormone produced by the ovary during the post-ovulatory (luteal) phase of the menstrual cycle in pregnancy.

Prognathous. With protruding jaws.

Prosodic variations. Changes of stress in pronunciation of vowel sounds.

Protein. A molecule made of hundreds or thousands of amino acids joined to make a chain, which may be elaborately folded.

Proton. Stable elementary particle with charge equal to an electron (but opposite) and mass 1836·12 times the latter.

Protozoa (*Protophyta*). Single-celled animals (plants).

Psychosis. A vague term. Covers severe abnormalities in which the patient's behaviour is detached from reality and is unlikely to be restored to normal. Includes conditions due to a variety of abnormalities of brain functioning (cf. *Neurosis*).

Puberty. The maturing of the sex organs and functions.

Pubis. The most ventral bones of the pelvic (hip) girdle. The two meet in the midline, above the penis or clitoris. Wider in females to allow birth of the young.

Pulsars. Sources of radio-frequency emission fluctuating with various frequencies.

Quantum. One of the discrete units of energy, e.g. photon for electromagnetic radiation, meson for nuclear forces (usually). The energy emitted depends upon the frequency of radiation and Planck's constant ($h = 6 \cdot 625 \times 10^{-27}$ erg seconds) $E = h\nu$.

Quantum mechanics. The method of describing the distribution of quanta of energy within atoms. See *Wave mechanics*.

Quasar. Quasi-stellar radio source outside our galaxy.

Race. A term used loosely for a geographically distinct portion of a species having certain distinctive genes.

Rad. The unit of ionizing radiation. The energy absorption of 100 ergs per gramme.

Radical (chem.). A grouping of atoms present in a series of compounds and giving them characteristic properties, e.g. ammonium NH_4, methyl CH_3.

Radioactivity. The spontaneous disintegration of unstable atomic nuclei with emission of either alpha, beta, or gamma rays.

Radiolaria. Protozoans with siliceous shells.

Recessive. A gene whose effects are not manifested in the presence of a contrasting gene, but only in the homozygous state.

Representation. A system represents another if it carries a likeness or similarity to it that will be recognized by a suitable observer. The likeness may be conveyed by a convention or code.

Repressor molecule. Protein produced by a regulator gene and able to react allosterically with a particular metabolite (effector or inducer) and with the operator gene of the operon that controls its production, so that this is blocked.

Rhesus factor. A set of antigens on blood corpuscles, first found in rhesus monkeys. A Rhesus-negative mother carrying a Rhesus-positive child may produce antibodies that destroy the child's red cells.

Sadism. Obtaining sexual pleasure from cruelty to others.

Savanna. A tropical or subtropical plain with few or no trees.

Schizophrenia. A mental disorder in which the rational intellectual processes are dissociated from emotional ones.

Schwann cells. The supporting cells of peripheral nerves. They wrap round axons to produce the myelin sheaths (Fig. 154).

Scrotum. The sack containing the testes.

Semantics. The study of the meaning of words.

Semen. The male ejaculate, including spermatozoa, produced by the testis, and a volume of fluid produced by the vesicula seminalis and prostate gland (Fig. 15.1).

Serum. The liquid pressed out from clotted blood, therefore the plasma without the substances that make it clot.

Sex chromosomes. Those that differ in the two sexes. In man there are two X chromosomes in the female, and an X and a Y in the male.

Sex hormones. Masculinizing or feminizing substances produced by tissues in ovary or testis other than those that form the gametes. Control the secondary sex characters. Are steroids (e.g. *oestrogen* in female, *testosterone* in male). Production stimulated by the pituitary, which itself in turn is stimulated by these hormones.

Sexual skin. The region around the genitalia and anus that becomes swollen and coloured at the time of ovulation in some primates (e.g. baboons).

Sib(ling)s. Brothers and or sisters who are children of the same parents.

Sign or signal. The element in a communication channel that carries information.

Somatic. Belonging to the body, e.g. somatic mutation, one occurring in the body, not in the germ cells.

Species. The basic unit of classification. A group of individuals able to breed among themselves but not with other species.

Sporozoa. A group of parasitic protozoans reproducing by spores, e.g. malaria parasite.

Static electricity. Electricity at rest, producing an electrostatic field. Contrasted with current or dynamic electricity.

Steady state. Condition maintained by a continuous process.

Steroid. A family of lipids including many hormones and vitamin D. They contain at least seventeen carbon atoms, in four rings.

Streptococcus. A pathogenic bacterium.

Subjective. Pertaining only to the individual, e.g. a subjective description is one given by someone including only his own particular sensations (cf. *Objective*).

Svedberg (s). Unit used to indicate the speed at which a particle sediments under standard conditions and related to the weight and size of the particle.

Symbol. An object or action that stands for or represents something else.

Sympathetic nerves. A system of motor nerves running mainly to internal organs, especially blood-vessels. They operate by secreting adrenalin-like transmitters in the tissues. In the main they prepare the body for attack or defence (cf. *Parasympathetic nerves*).

Sympatric. Species whose areas of distribution overlap.

Syncytia. Cells with many nuclei.

Synthesis. The formation of a substance from its usually simpler components.

System. A set of interdependent entities connected to form a unity.

Systemic factors. Those affecting the whole organism, such as substances secreted into the blood.

Taboo. A prohibition imposed by society in connection with dress, speech, sex, etc., usually associated with some magical or religious explanation.

Template. A mould for the synthesis of a similar entity. A strand of DNA is the template either for a complementary one of DNA or of mRNA.

Territory. In ethology indicates the area

defended by an animal or pair and from which others of the same species are expelled.

Testis. The male gonad, consists of long coiled tubes in which spermatozoa are produced. Between the tubes are groups of glandular cells which produce the male sex hormones that cause the secondary sex characters to appear (beard, deep voice, etc.).

Testosterone. A steroid hormone produced by the interstitial cells of the testis and having masculinizing actions.

Tetrapods. Vertebrates that walk on four legs. Chiefly land animals.

Thermodynamic equilibrium. The state of a system in which there is mechanical, chemical, and thermal equilibrium so that no further changes can occur.

Thermodynamics. The study of the laws governing processes involving heat-changes and the conservation of energy. *First Law.* Conservation of energy. In a system of constant mass energy can be neither created nor destroyed. *Second Law.* The entropy of a closed system increases with time.

Tissue. An aggregate of cells of one or several kinds having a particular function, e.g. muscle, skin.

Tissue culture. The growing of cells in a culture medium outside the organism.

Totipotent. Of an undifferentiated cell, able to develop into any cell-type of the species.

Tracer. In radioactive tracing stable radioactive isotopes are introduced to the body and serve to show how long that element remains in any given molecule or part and hence the speed of turnover (p. 82).

Transcription. The formation of mRNA against a DNA template.

Translation (genetics). The reading of the genetic code of mRNA molecules to produce specific proteins. Occurs at a ribosome.

Transneuronal degeneration. Death of a nerve cell that has been deprived of its normal source of stimulation.

Trapezium. The bone of the wrist upon which the thumb rotates.

Triassic period. From about 225 to 190 million years ago.

Tritiated thymidine. The nucleotide thymidine labelled with the isotope of hydrogen ^{3}H (*tritium*).

Tritium. Radioactive isotope of hydrogen (^{3}H) with half-life 12·26 years. Used to label compounds so that they can be traced in the body.

Trophoblast. Ectodermal part of embryonic vesicle responsible for penetration of uterus at region of contact.

Tundra. A tree-less region with frozen subsoil.

Ulcer. An erosion of the continuity of a membrane, forming a sore.

Ultraviolet. Light of wavelength shorter than that we see as violet.

Universe see *Cosmos.*

Uterus. The womb, which receives fertilized ova from the uterine tubes and nourishes them by the placenta. Opens below into the vagina (Fig. 15.2).

Vagina. The passage opening from the uterus to the exterior (*vulva*). Receives the penis in copulation and allows passage of the young at birth (Fig. 15.2).

Valency. The combining power of an atom, the number of hydrogen atoms with which it will unite (or replace). An atom with valency 2 or more may make double or triple bonds with another. The valency is due to rearrangement of the outer shells (octets) of electrons either by loss and gain (as in electrolytes to form ions) or by sharing electrons (covalent bonds).

Variance. The amount of diversity in a population. Usually measured as the mean of the squared deviation of all the values from the mean.

Variations. The differences between individuals.

Vegetal pole. The pole of an egg away from that containing the nucleus (*animal pole*). Usually contains much yolk.

Vertebrates. Animals with backbones—from fishes to mammals.

Vitamin. A substance necessary for health that cannot be synthesized in the body and must therefore be taken in the food.

Vulva. The opening of the vagina between the labia minora, whose stimulation has erotic effects.

Wave mechanics. The modern form of quantum mechanics in which the energy distribution is treated as a system of waves whose frequency and amplitude are determined by rules partly by analogy with light waves and partly *ad hoc*. Orbital electrons are represented by three-dimensional wave functions, whose magnitude represents the amplitude of the wave system at various points around the nucleus, thus specifying the probability that the electron (as a particle) will be at a certain point. Its precise position and velocity cannot both be determined (uncertainty principle).

Weight. The force of attraction of the earth on a given mass (q.v.).

X-rays. Radiation of wavelength much shorter than light, produced when cathode rays strike an object.

Zygoma. The bar of bone below the eyes to which the masseter muscle of the jaw is attached.

BIBLIOGRAPHY

GENERAL

BAYLISS, L. E. (1959). *Principles of general physiology.* Vol. I. *The physico-chemical background.* Vol. II. *General physiology.* Longmans, London.
BELL, G. H., DAVIDSON, J. N., and SCARBOROUGH, H. (1968). *Textbook of physiology and biochemistry.* 7th edn. Livingstone, Edinburgh.
BUETTNER-JANUSCH, H. (editor) (1963). *Evolutionary and genetic biology of the primates.* Vols. I and II. Academic Press, New York.
CAMPBELL, B. G. (1966). *Human evolution: an introduction to man's adaptations.* Aldine, Chicago.
CLARK, G. (1969). *World prehistory: a new outline.* 2nd edn. Cambridge University Press.
CLARK, W. E. LE GROS (1962). *The antecedents of man.* 2nd edn. Edinburgh University Press.
—— (1971). *The tissues of the body.* 6th edn. Clarendon Press, Oxford.
DARWIN, C. (1879). *The descent of man: and selection in relation to sex.* Murray, London.
DAVIES, D. V., and COUPLAND, R. E. (editors) (1967). *Gray's anatomy: descriptive and applied.* 34th edn. Longmans, London.
GRASSÉ, P-P. (editor) (1955). *Traité de zoologie. Anatomie, systématique, biologie.* Tome XVII, *Mammifères. Les ordres: Anatomie, éthologie, systématique.* Second fasc. Masson, Paris.
HANDLER, P. (1970). *Biology and the future of man.* Oxford University Press, New York.
HARRIS, H. (1970). *The principles of human biochemical genetics.* North-Holland Publishing Co., Amsterdam.
HARRISON, G. A., WEINER, J. S., TANNER, J. M., and BARNICOT, N. A. (1964). *Human biology: an introduction to human evolution, variation and growth.* Clarendon Press, Oxford.
HEBB, D. O. (1966). *A textbook of psychology.* Saunders, Philadelphia.
KALMUS, H. (1957). *Variation and heredity.* Routledge and Kegan Paul, London.
PASSMORE, R., and ROBSON, J. S. (editors) (1968). *A companion to medical studies in three volumes.* Vol. I. *Anatomy, biochemistry, physiology, and related subjects.* Blackwell, Oxford.
QUINE, W. V. O. (1960). *Word and object.* M.I.T. Press, Cambridge, Massachusetts.
RIEGER, R., MICHAELIS, A., and GREEN, M. M. (1968). *A glossary of genetics and cytogenetics.* Springer-Verlag, Berlin.
ROBERTS, J. A. F. (1970). *An introduction to medical genetics.* 5th edn. Oxford University Press, London.
ROMER, A. S. (1966). *Vertebrate paleontology.* 3rd edn. University of Chicago Press.
SAUVY, A. (1969). *General theory of population.* Weidenfeld and Nicolson, London.
YOUNG, J. Z. (1950). *The life of vertebrates* (2nd edn. 1962). Clarendon Press, Oxford.
—— (1951). *Doubt and certainty in science.* Clarendon Press, Oxford.
—— (1957). *The life of mammals.* Clarendon Press, Oxford.
—— (1964). *A model of the brain.* Clarendon Press, Oxford.

CHAPTER I. POSSIBILITIES AND DIFFICULTIES FOR A SCIENCE OF MAN

BRAITHWAITE, R. B. (1953). *Scientific explanation.* Cambridge University Press.
CANNON, W. B. (1929). *Bodily changes in pain, hunger, fear and rage.* Appleton, New York.
DOBZHANSKY, T. (1969). *The biology of ultimate concern.* Rapp and Whiting, London.

ECCLES, J. C. (1953). *The neurophysiological basis of mind: the principles of neurophysiology.* Waynflete Lectures, 1952. Clarendon Press, Oxford.

FONG, P. (1968). Phenomenological theory of life. *J. theor. Biol.* **21**, 133-52.

POPPER, K. R. (1965). *Conjectures and refutations. The growth of scientific knowledge.* Routledge and Kegan Paul, London.

ROCKEFELLER FOUNDATION (1967). *The President's Review and Annual Report 1967.*

SAUVY, A. (1969). *General theory of population.* Weidenfeld and Nicolson, London.

SHERRINGTON, C. S (1940). *Man on his nature.* Cambridge University Press.

YOUNG, J. Z. (1950). *The life of vertebrates* (2nd edn. 1962). Clarendon Press, Oxford.

—— (1951). *Doubt and certainty in science.* Clarendon Press, Oxford.

—— (1964). *A model of the brain.* Clarendon Press, Oxford.

CHAPTER 2. WHAT ARE MEN MADE OF?

CONWAY, E. J. (1943). The chemical evolution of the ocean. *Proc. R. Ir. Acad.* **B48**, 161-212.

DYSON, F. J. (1954). What is heat? *Scient. Am.* **191** (Sept.), 58-63.

FAIRBRIDGE, R. W. (editor) (1967). *The encyclopedia of atmospheric sciences and astrogeology. Encyclopedia of earth sciences series.* Vol. II. Reinhold, New York.

GALBRAITH, W. (1967). How elementary are elementary particles? Inaugural lecture, University of Sheffield.

LERMAN, L., WATANABE, A., and TASAKI, I. (1969). Intracellular perfusion of giant squid axons: recent findings and interpretations. In *Neurosciences Research,* **2**, 71-106 (editors S. Ehrenpreis and O. C. Solnitzky). Academic Press, New York.

MOROWITZ, H. J. (1968). *Energy flow in biology.* Academic Press, New York.

NEEDHAM, A. E. (1965). *The uniqueness of biological materials.* Pergamon Press, Oxford.

PULLMAN, A., and PULLMAN, B. (1962). From quantum chemistry to quantum biochemistry. *Horizons in biochemistry* (editors M. Kasha and B. Pullman). Academic Press, London.

SCHÜTTE, K. H. (1964). *The biology of the trace elements. Their role in nutrition.* Crosby Lockwood, London.

SCHWEIGART, H. A. (1962). *Vitalstoff-lehre Vitalstoff-Tabellarium.* Verlag Hans Zauner jr., Dachau-München.

WALD, G. (1964). The origins of life. *Proc. natn. Acad. Sci. U.S.A.* **52**, 595-611.

WATSON, J. D. (1965). *Molecular biology of the gene.* Benjamin, New York.

CHAPTER 3. LIVING ORGANIZATION

BELL, E. (1969). *I*-DNA: Its packaging into *I*-somes and its relation to protein synthesis during differentiation. *Nature, Lond.* **224**, 326-8.

BLAKE, C. C. F., MAIR, G. A., NORTH, A. C. T., PHILLIPS, D. C., and SARMA, V. R. (1967). On the conformation of the hen egg-white lysozyme molecule. *Proc. R. Soc.* **B167**, 365-77.

BODO, G., DINTZIS, H. M., KENDREW, J. C., and WYCKOFF, H. W. (1959). The crystal structure of myoglobin. V. A low-resolution three-dimensional Fourier synthesis of sperm-whale myoglobin crystals. *Proc. R. Soc.* **A253**, 70-102.

BRETSCHER, M. S. (1968). How repressor molecules function. *Nature, Lond.* **217**, 509-11.

BULLOUGH, W. S. (1967). *The evolution of differentiation.* Academic Press, London.

CAIRNS, J. (1963). The chromosome of *Escherichia coli. Cold Spring Harb. Symp. quant. Biol.* **28**, 43-6.

CRICK, F. H. C. (1968). The origin of the genetic code. *J. molec. Biol.* **38**, 367-79.

CULLIS, A. F., MUIRHEAD, H., PERUTZ, M. F., ROSSMAN, M. G., and NORTH, A. C. T. (1962). The structure of haemoglobin. IX. A three-dimensional Fourier synthesis at 5·5Å resolution: description of the structure. *Proc. R. Soc.* **A265**, 161-87.

DINGLE, J. T., and FELL, H. B. (editors) (1969). *Lysosomes in biology and pathology*. Vols. I and II. North-Holland Publishing Co., Amsterdam.

EDGAR, R. S., and LIELAUSIS, I. (1968). Some steps in the assembly of bacteriophage T4. *J. molec. Biol.* **32**, 263-76.

GILBERT, W., and MÜLLER-HILL, B. (1967). The lac operator is DNA. *Proc. natn. Acad. Sci. U.S.A.* **58**, 2415-21.

GLAUERT, A. M. (1962). The fine structure of bacteria. *Br. med. Bull.* **18**, 245-50.

HAGGIS, G. H. (editors G. H. Haggis, D. Michie, A. R. Muir, K. B. Roberts, and P. M. B. Walker) (1964). The structure of small protein molecules. *Introduction to molecular biology*. Longmans, London.

HARRIS, H. (1967). The reactivation of the red cell nucleus. *J. Cell. Sci.* **2**, 23-32.

—— (1968). *Nucleus and cytoplasm*. Clarendon Press, Oxford.

HORNE, R. W., and WILDY, P. (1962). Recent studies on the fine structure of viruses by electron microscopy, using negative-staining techniques. *Br. med. Bull.* **18**, 199-204.

JACOB, F. (1966). Génétique de la cellule bactérienne. *Les Prix Nobel en 1965*. Imprimerie Royale P. A. Norstedt & Söner, Stockholm.

—— and MONOD, J. (1961). Genetic regulating mechanisms in the synthesis of proteins. *J. molec. Biol.* **3**, 318-56.

KENDREW, J. C. (1966). *The thread of life, an introduction to molecular biology*. Bell, London.

KING, J. (1968). Assembly of the tail of bacteriophage T4. *J. molec. Biol.* **32**, 231-62.

KING, R. C. (1968). *A dictionary of genetics*. Oxford University Press, New York.

KLEINSCHMIDT, A. K., LANG, D., JACHERTS, D., and ZAHN, R. K. (1962). Darstellung und Längenmessungen des Gesamten Desoxyribonucleinsäure-Inhaltes von T2 Bakteriophagen. *Biochim. biophys. Acta* **61**, 857-64.

KORNBERG, A. (1968). The synthesis of DNA. *Scient. Am.* **219** (Oct.), 64-78.

LURIA, S. E. (1960). The bacterial protoplasm: composition and organization. In *The bacteria*, Vol. I (editors I. C. Gunsalus and R. Y. Stanier). Academic Press, London.

MICHIE, D. (1964). The gene. *Introduction to molecular biology* (editors G. H. Haggis, D. Michie, A. R. Muir, K. B. Roberts, and P. M. B. Walker). Longmans, London.

MIRSKY, A. E. (1968). The discovery of DNA. *Scient. Am.* **218** (June), 78-88.

MONOD, J., CHANGEUX, J.-P., and JACOB, F. (1963). Allosteric proteins and cellular control systems. *J. molec. Biol.* **6**, 306-29.

MORSE, D. E., BAKER, R. F., and YANOFSKY, C. (1968). Translation of the tryptophan messenger RNA of *Escherichia coli*. *Proc. natn. Acad. Sci. U.S.A.* **60**, 1428-35.

NIRENBERG, M. W., and MATTHAEI, J. H. (1961). The dependence of cell-free protein synthesis in *E. coli* upon naturally occurring or synthetic polyribonucleotides. *Proc. natn. Acad. Sci. U.S.A.* **47**, 1588-602.

ORGEL, L. E. (1968). Evolution of the genetic apparatus. *J. molec. Biol.* **38**, 381-93.

PAULING, L., ITANO, H. A., SINGER, S. J., and WELLS, I. C. (1949). Sickle-cell anemia, a molecular disease. *Science, N.Y.* **110**, 543-8.

PERUTZ, M. F. (1967). Some molecular controls in biology. *Endeavour* **26**, 3-8.

—— ROSSMAN, M. G., CULLIS, A. F., MUIRHEAD, H., WILL, G., and NORTH, A. C. T. (1960). Structure of haemoglobin. *Nature, Lond.* **185**, 416-22.

PORTER, K. R. (1961). The ground substance: observations from electron microscopy. In *The cell* II (editors J. Brachet and A. E. Mirsky). Academic Press, New York.

QUASTLER, H. (1965). General principles of systems analysis. In *Theoretical and mathematical biology* (editors T. H. Waterman and H. J. Morowitz). Blaisdell, New York.

RICHARDSON, C. C., SCHILDKRAUT, C. L., APOSHIAN, H. V., and KORNBERG, A. (1964). Enzymatic synthesis of deoxyribonucleic acid polymerase of *Escherichia coli*. *J. biol. Chem.* **239**, 222-32.

SPEYER, J. F. (1967). The genetic code. In *Molecular genetics*. Pt. II (editor J. H. Taylor). Academic Press, New York.

Sueoka, N. (1967). Mechanisms of replication and repair of nucleic acid. In *Molecular genetics*. Pt. II (editor J. H. Taylor). Academic Press, New York.

Watson, J. D. (1965). *Molecular biology of the gene*. Benjamin, New York.

Wood, W. B., and Edgar, R. S. (1967). Building a bacterial virus. *Scient. Am.* **217** (July), 60–74.

CHAPTER 4. CELLS, ORGANS, AND ORGANISMS

Britten, R. J., and Davidson, E. H. (1969). Gene regulation for higher cells: a theory. *Science, N.Y.* **165**, 349–57.

Brown, D. D., Dawid, I. B., and Reeder, R. (1969). Nucleic acid and protein synthesis during oogenesis and development. In Annual report of the Director, Department of Embryology, *Carnegie Institution Year Book 1967*.

Dawid, I. B. (1970). The nature of mitochondrial RNA in oocytes of *Xenopus laevis* and its relation to mitochondrial DNA. *Symp. Soc. exp. Biol.* **24**, 227–46.

Goodwin, B. C. (1964). A statistical mechanics of temporal organization in cells. *Symp. Soc. exp. Biol.* **18**, 301–26.

Gurdon, J. B. (1962). Adult frogs derived from the nuclei of single somatic cells. *Develop. Biol.* **4**, 256–73.

—— (1970). The autonomy of nuclear activity in multicellular organisms. *Symp. Soc. exp. Biol.* **24**, 369–78.

—— and Woodland, H. R. (1969). The influence of the cytoplasm on the nucleus during cell differentiation, with special reference to RNA synthesis during amphibian cleavage. *Proc. S. Soc.* B**173**, 99–111.

Kit, S. (1963). Coding by purine and pyrimidine moieties in animals, plants, and bacteria. In *Information storage and neural control* (editors W. S. Fields and W. Abbott). Thomas, Springfield.

Kroon, A. M. (1969). DNA and RNA from mitochondria and chloroplasts (biochemistry). In *Handbook of molecular cytology* (editor A. Lima-de-Faria). North-Holland Publishing Co., Amsterdam.

Loening, U. E. (1968). Molecular weights of ribosomal RNA in relation to evolution. *J. molec. Biol.* **38**, 355–65.

Marinos, N. G. (1960). The nuclear envelope of plant cells. *J. Ultrastruct. Res.* **3**, 328–33.

Noll, H. (1970). Organelle integration and the evolution of ribosome structure and function. *Symp. Soc. exp. Biol.* **24**, 419–47.

Steward, F. C. (1970). From cultured cells to whole plants: the induction and control of their growth and morphogenesis. *Proc. R. Soc.* B**175**, 1–30.

Vickerman, K. (1962). Patterns of cellular organisation in *Limax* amoebae. An electron microscope study. *Expl. Cell Res.* **26**, 497–519.

—— (1966). Genetic systems in unicellular animals. *Sci. Prog., Lond.* **54**, 13–26.

—— and Cox, F. E. G. (1967). *The Protozoa*. Murray, London.

Young, J. Z. (1950). *The life of vertebrates* (2nd edn. 1962). Clarendon Press, Oxford.

CHAPTER 5. LIVING ACTIVITIES, TURNOVER

Khan, A. A., and Wilson, J. E. (1965). Studies of turnover in mammalian subcellular particles: brain nuclei, mitochondria and microsomes. *J. Neurochem.* **12**, 81–6.

McEwen, B. S., and Hydén, H. (1966). A study of specific brain proteins on the semi-micro scale. *J. Neurochem.* **13**, 823–33.

Rogers, A. W. (1967). *Techniques of autoradiography*. Elsevier, Amsterdam.

Schoenheimer, R. (1946). *The dynamic state of body constituents*. Harvard University Press, Cambridge, Massachusetts.

THOMPSON, R. C., and BALLOU, J. E. (1956). Studies of metabolic turnover with tritium as a tracer. V. The predominantly nondynamic state of body constituents in the rat. *J. biol. Chem.* **223**, 795-809.

WRIGHT, G. PAYLING (1961). The metabolism of myelin. *Proc. R. Soc. Med.* **54**, 26-30.

CHAPTER 6. THE DIRECTION OF LIVING ACTIVITY. HOMEOSTASIS

CANNON, W. B. (1932). *The wisdom of the body.* Norton, New York.

DENNETT, D. C. (1969). *Content and consciousness.* Routledge and Kegan Paul, London.

KITCHING, J. A. (1951). The physiology of contractile vacuoles. VII. Osmotic relations in a suctorian, with special reference to the mechanism of control of vacuolar output. *J. exp. Biol.* **28**, 203-14.

MOROWITZ, H. J. (1968). *Energy flow in biology.* Academic Press, New York.

TAYLOR, C. (1964). *The explanation of behaviour.* Routledge and Kegan Paul, London.

VICKERMAN, K., and COX, F. E. G. (1967). *The Protozoa.* Murray, London.

CHAPTER 7. THE CONTROL OF LIVING ACTIVITIES

ADOLPH, E. F. (1968). *Origins of physiological regulations.* Academic Press, New York.

DARWIN, C. (1859). *The origin of species by means of natural selection.* Murray, London.

EULER, C. VON (1964). The physiology and pharmacology of temperature regulation with particular reference to the chemical mediators. *Proc. second int. pharmac. Meet., Prague, 1963. Biochemical and neurophysiological correlation of centrally acting drugs.* Pergamon Press, Oxford.

FISHER, R. A. (1930). *The genetical theory of natural selection.* Clarendon Press, Oxford.

FORD, E. B. (1964). *Ecological genetics.* Methuen, London.

HALDANE, J. B. S. (1932). *The causes of evolution.* Longmans, Green, London.

LEHNINGER, A. L. (1965). *Bioenergetics.* Benjamin, New York.

METTLER, L. E., and GREGG, G. (1969). *Population genetics and evolution.* Prentice-Hall, New Jersey.

PLATT, J. R. (1958). Functional geometry and the determination of pattern in mosaic receptors. In *Symposium on information theory in biology* (editor. H. P. Yockey). Pergamon Press, London.

QUASTLER, H. (1965). General principles of systems analysis. In *Theoretical and mathematical biology* (editors T. H. Waterman and H. J. Morowitz). Blaisdell, New York.

SCHRÖDINGER, E. (1944). *What is life? The physical aspect of the living cell.* Cambridge University Press.

SHAKESPEARE, W. (1600). *Midsummer night's dream.* First folio. Thomas Fisher, London.

SHANNON, C. E., and WEAVER, W. (1949). *The mathematical theory of communication.* University of Illinois Press, Urbana.

WATERMAN, T. H. (1968). Systems theory and biology—view of a biologist. In *Systems theory and biology.* Proceedings of the III Systems Symposium at Case Institute of Technology (editor M. D. Mesarović). Springer-Verlag, New York.

WIENER, N. (1949). *Cybernetics or control and communication in the animal and the machine.* Wiley, New York.

WRIGHT, S. (1949). Adaptation and selection. In *Genetics, paleontology and evolution* (editors G. L. Jepsen, E. Mayr, and G. G. Simpson). Princeton University Press.

CHAPTER 8. PERSONAL ADAPTATION. IMPROVEMENT OF THE REPRESENTATION ON DIFFERENT TIME SCALES

KRANTZ, S. B., and JACOBSON, O. (1970). *Erythropoietin and the regulation of erythropoiesis.* University of Chicago Press.

YOUNG, J. Z. (1964). *A model of the brain.* Clarendon Press, Oxford.

CHAPTER 10. CONSCIOUSNESS

ADRIAN, LORD (1966). Consciousness. In *Brain and conscious experience* (editor J. C. Eccles). Springer-Verlag, Berlin.
AKERT, K., BALLY, C., and SCHADÉ, J. P. (editors) (1965). *Sleep mechanisms. Progress in brain research* **18**. Elsevier, Amsterdam.
ASHBY, W. R. (1960). *Design for a brain*. Chapman and Hall, London.
AYER, A. J. (1963). Can there be a private language? In *The concept of a person and other essays*. Macmillan, London.
BERGER, R. J. (1963). Experimental modification of dream content by meaningful verbal stimuli. *Br. J. Psychiat.* **109**, 722-40.
BRAITHWAITE, R. B. (1953). *Scientific explanation*. Cambridge University Press.
BROADBENT, D. E. (1970). Psychological aspects of short-term and long-term memory. *Proc. R. Soc.* B175, 333-50.
CASTAÑEDA, H-N. (1967). *Intentionality, minds, and perception*. Wayne State University Press, Detroit.
CRAIK, K. J. W. (1943). *The nature of explanation*. Cambridge University Press.
DENNETT, D. C. (1969). *Content and consciousness*. Routledge and Kegan Paul, London.
EMMONS, W. H., and SIMON, C. W. (1956). The non-recall of material presented during sleep. *Am. J. Psychol.* **69**, 76-81.
FREUD, S. (1927). *The interpretation of dreams* (translated by A. A. Powell). George Allen and Unwin, London.
GOSSE, E. (1907). *Father and son*. Heinemann, London. (Penguin Books, 1970.)
HEAD, H. (1920). *Studies in neurology*. Vol. II. Oxford University Press, London.
HENSEL, H., and BOMAN, K. K. A. (1960). Afferent impulses in cutaneous sensory nerves in human subjects. *J. Neurophysiol.* **23**, 564-78.
HINSHELWOOD, C. (1959). Anniversary address. *Proc. R. Soc.* A253, 442-9.
HOLLOWAY, R. L., JR. (1966). Cranial capacity, neural reorganisation and Hominid evolution: A search for more suitable parameters. *Am. Anthrop.* **68**, 103-21.
LENNEBERG, E. H. (1967). *Biological foundations of language*. Wiley, New York.
LIBET, B. (1966). Brain stimulation and the threshold of conscious experience. In *Brain and conscious experience* (editor J. C. Eccles). Springer-Verlag, Berlin.
LUCE, G. G., and SEGAL, J. (1967). *Sleep*. Heinemann, London.
MCINTYRE, A. K., HOLMAN, M. E., and VEALE, J. L. (1967). Cortical responses to impulses from single Pacinian corpuscles in the cat's hind limb. *Expl. Brain Res.* **4**, 243-55.
MILLER, N. E. (1965). Chemical coding of behaviour in the brain. *Science, N.Y.* **148**, 328-38.
MORUZZI, G., and MAGOUN, H. W. (1949). Brain stem reticular formation and activation of the EEG. *Electronenceph. clin. Neurophysiol.* **1**, 455-73.
OSGOOD, C. E. (1964). *Method and theory in experimental psychology*. Oxford University Press, New York.
OSWALD, IAN (1962). *Sleeping and waking*. Elsevier, Amsterdam.
—— (1965). Some psycho-physiological features of human sleep. In *Sleep mechanisms. Progress in brain research* **18**, 160-9 (editors K. Akert, C. Bally, and J. P. Schadé). Elsevier, Amsterdam.
PENFIELD, W. (1968). Engrams in the human brain. *Proc. R. Soc. Med.* **61**, 831-40.
—— and PEROT, P. (1963). The brain's record of auditory and visual experience—a final summary and discussion. *Brain* **86**, 595-696.
QUINE, W. V. O. (1960). *Word and object*. The Technology Press of the Massachusetts Institute of Technology.
—— (1969). *Ontological relativity and other essays*. Columbia University Press, New York.
QUINTON, A. M. (1968). Excerpt from 'Contemporary British philosophy'. In *Wittgenstein—the philosophical investigations* (editor George Pitcher). Macmillan, London.

RHEES, R. (1968). Can there be a private language? In *Wittgenstein—the philosophical investigations* (editor George Pitcher). Macmillan, London.

RYLE, G. (1949). *The concept of mind*. Hutchinson, London.

SCHILDER, P. (1935). *The image and appearance of the human body*. Kegan Paul, Trench, Trubner, and Co., London.

SPERRY, R. W. (1966). Brain bisection and mechanisms of consciousness. In *Brain and conscious experience* (editor J. C. Eccles). Springer-Verlag, Berlin.

SPRAGUE, J. M., LEVITT, M., ROBSON, K., LIU, C. N., STELLAR, E., and CHAMBERS, W. W. (1963). A neuroanatomical and behavioral analysis of the syndromes resulting from mid-brain lemniscal and reticular lesions in the cat. *Archs ital. Biol.* **101**, 225–95.

STRAWSON, P. F. (1968). Review of Wittgenstein's *Philosophical investigations*. In *Wittgenstein—the philosophical investigations* (editor George Pitcher). Macmillan, London.

TURING, A. M. (1950). Computing machinery and intelligence. *Mind* **59**, 433–60.

WITTGENSTEIN, LUDWIG (1953). *Philosophical investigations* (translated by G. E. M. Anscombe). Blackwell, Oxford.

YOUNG, J. Z. (1964). *A model of the brain*. Clarendon Press, Oxford.

CHAPTER 11. GROWTH, TURNOVER, AND THE RISKS OF DAMAGE

BIZZOZERO, G. (1894). An address on the growth and regeneration of the organism. *Br. med. J.* **1**, 728–32.

COWDRY, E. V. (1952). Ageing of individual cells. In *Problems of ageing* (editor A. I. Lansing). Williams and Wilkins, Baltimore.

DEAN, A. C. R., and HINSHELWOOD, SIR C. (1966). *Growth, function, and regulation in bacterial cells*. Clarendon Press, Oxford.

MÁLEK, I., and FENCL, Z. (editors) (1966). *Theoretical and methodological basis of continuous culture of microorganisms*. Academic Press, New York.

MANDELSTAM, J., and McQUILLEN, K. (1968). *Biochemistry of bacterial growth*. Blackwell, Oxford.

MITCHISON, J. M. (1957) The growth of single cells: I. *Schizosaccharomyces pombe*. *Expl. Cell Res.* **13**, 244–62.

OCHS, S. (1966). Axoplasmic flow in neurons. In *Macromolecules and behavior* (editor J. Gaito). Appleton Century Crofts, New York.

WEISS, P., and KAVANAU, J. L. (1957). A model of growth and growth control in mathematical terms. *J. gen. Physiol.* **41**, 1–47.

YOUNG, J. Z. (1950). *The life of vertebrates* (2nd edn. 1962). Clarendon Press, Oxford.

CHAPTER 12. REPAIR OF THE INDIVIDUAL

ABERCROMBIE, M. (1964). Behavior of cells toward one another. In *Advances in biology of skin*. **5**. *Wound healing* (editors W. Montagna and R. E. Billingham). Pergamon Press, Oxford.

ARGYRIS, T. S., and ARGYRIS, B. F. (1959). Stimulation of hair growth during skin regeneration. *Devl. Biol.* **1**, 269–80.

BULLOUGH, W. S., and LAURENCE, E. B. (1960). The control of epidermal mitotic activity in the mouse. *Proc. R. Soc.* **B151**, 517–36.

FAWCETT, D. W. (1966). *An atlas of fine structure. The cell. Its organelles and inclusions*. Saunders, Philadelphia.

GOSS, R. J. (1964). *Adaptive growth*. Logos Press, London.

—— (1969). *Principles of regeneration*. Academic Press, New York.

HALDANE, J. B. S. (1954). *The biochemistry of genetics*. Allen and Unwin, London.

HARDING, C. V., and SRINIVASAN, B. D. (1961). A propagated stimulation of DNA synthesis and cell division. *Expl. Cell Res.* **25**, 326–40.

JAMES, D. W. (1964). Wound contraction—a synthesis. In *Advances in biology of skin*. 5. *Wound healing* (editors W. Montagna and R. E. Billingham). Pergamon Press, Oxford.

KUTSKY, R. J. (1959). Nucleoprotein constituents stimulating growth in tissue culture: active protein fraction. *Science, N.Y.* **129**, 1486-7.

LEVI-MONTALCINI, R. (1964). Growth control of nerve cells by a protein factor and its antiserum. *Science, N.Y.* **143**, 105-10.

—— and ANGELETTI, P. U. (1968). Nerve growth factor. *Physiol. Rev.* **48**, 534-69.

ODLAND, G., and ROSS, R. (1968). Human wound repair. I. Epidermal regeneration. *J. Cell Biol.* **39**, 135-51.

ROBERTSON, J. D. (1966). *See* FAWCETT, D. W. (1966).

ROSS, R. (1968). The fibroblast and wound repair. *Biol. Rev.* **43**, 51-94.

SCHILLING, J. A. (1968). Wound healing. *Physiol. Rev.* **48**, 374-423.

VERNON, C. A., BANKS, B. E. C., BANTHORPE, D. V., BERRY, A. R., DAVIES, H. ff. S., LAMONT, D. M., PEARCE, F. L., and REDDING, K. A. (1969). Nerve growth and epithelial growth factors. In *Homeostatic Regulators* (editors G. E. W. Wolstenholme and J. Knight). Churchill, London.

WIGGLESWORTH, V. B. (1937). Wound healing in an insect (*Rhodnius prolixus* Hemiptera). *J. exp. Biol.* **14**, 364-81.

YOUNG, J. Z. (1946). Effects of use and disuse on nerve and muscle. *Lancet* **251**, 109-13.

—— (1949). Factors influencing the regeneration of nerves. *Adv. Surg.* **1**, 165-220.

—— (1957). *The life of mammals*. Clarendon Press, Oxford.

CHAPTER 13. REPLACEMENT AND REGENERATION OF PARTS AFTER LOSS

BUCHER, N. L. R. (1963). Regeneration of mammalian liver. *Int. Rev. Cytol.* **15**, 245-300.

GOSS, R. J. (1964). *Adaptive growth*. Logos Press, London.

JACOBSON, M., and GAZE, R. M. (1965). Selection of appropriate tectal connections by regenerating optic nerve fibers in adult goldfish. *Expl. Neurol.* **13**, 418-30.

LIEBERMAN, A. R. (1971). The axon reaction. *Int. Rev. Neurobiol.* **14**.

NEEDHAM, A. E. (1964). *The growth process in animals*. Pitman, London.

—— (1964). Biological considerations of wound healing. In *Advances in biology of skin*. 5. *Wound healing* (editors W. Montagna and R. E. Billingham). Pergamon Press, Oxford.

TEIR, H., and RYTÖMAA, T. (editors) (1967). *Control of cellular growth in adult organisms*. Academic Press, London.

WATSON, W. E. (1968). Observations on nucleolar and total cell body nucleic acid of injured nerve cells. *J. Physiol., Lond.* **196**, 655-76.

YOUNG, J. Z. (1949). Factors influencing the regeneration of nerves. *Adv. Surg.* **1**, 165-220.

CHAPTER 14. REPRODUCTION AND DEVELOPMENT AS GUARANTEES OF HOMEOSTASIS

ABERCROMBIE, M. (1967). General review of the nature of differentiation. In *Cell differentiation*, a CIBA Foundation Symposium (editors A. V. S. de Reuck and J. Knight). Churchill, London.

BALTZER, F., CHEN, P. S., and WHITELEY, A. H. (1958). Biochemical studies on sea urchin hybrids. *Expl. Cell Res.* Suppl. **6**, 192-209.

BRACHET, J. (1967). Biochemical changes during fertilization and early embryonic development. In *Cell differentiation*, a CIBA Foundation Symposium (editors A. V. S. de Reuck and J. Knight). Churchill, London.

CONKLIN, E. G. (1905). Organization and cell lineage of the ascidian egg. *J. Acad. nat. Sci. Philad.* **13**, 1-119.

CURTIS, A. S. G. (1960). Cortical grafting in *Xenopus laevis*. *J. Embryol. exp. Morph.* **8**, 163–73.

DALCQ, A. (1952). *Initiation à l'embryologie générale*. Masson, Paris. (1957) *Introduction to general embryology* (translated by J. Medawar). Oxford University Press.

GOODWIN, B. C. (1963). *Temporal organization in cells. A dynamic theory of cellular control processes*. Academic Press, London.

—— (1968). The division of cells and the fusion of ideas. In *Towards a theoretical biology*. I. *Prolegomena*, an IUBS symposium (editor C. H. Waddington). Edinburgh University Press.

GURDON, J. B. (1970). The autonomy of nuclear activity in multicellular organisms. *Symp. Soc. exp. Biol.* **24**, 369–78.

—— and WOODLAND, H. R. (1968). The cytoplasmic control of nuclear activity in animal development. *Biol. Rev.* **43**, 233–67.

HARRIS, M. (1964). *Cell culture and somatic variation*. Holt, Rinehart, and Winston, New York.

SCHMIDT, A. J. (1968). *Cellular biology of vertebrate regeneration and repair*. University of Chicago Press.

WADDINGTON, C. H. (1966). Fields and gradients. In *Major problems in developmental biology* (editor M. Locke). Academic Press, New York.

YOUNG, J. Z. (1957). *The life of mammals*. Clarendon Press, Oxford.

CHAPTER 15. MATING AND FERTILIZATION

ALEXANDER, D. P., BRITTON, H. G., and NIXON, D. A. (1968). Maintenance of sheep fetuses by an extracorporeal circuit for periods up to 24 hours. *Am. J. Obst. Gynec.* **102**, 969–75.

ARON, C., ASCH, G., and ROOS, J. (1966). Triggering of ovulation by coitus in the rat. *Int. Rev. Cytol.* **20**, 139–72.

BASTOCK, M. (1967). The physiology of courtship and mating behaviour. *Adv. reprod. Physiol.* **2**, 9–51.

BLANDAU, R. J. (1969). Gamete transplant—comparative aspects. In *The mammalian oviduct: comparative biology and methodology* (editors E. S. E. Hafez and R. J. Blandau). University of Chicago Press.

CROSS, B. A. (1964). The hypothalamus in mammalian homeostasis. *Symp. Soc. exp. Biol.* **18**, 157–93.

DICKINSON, R. L. (1933). *A topographical hand atlas. Human sex anatomy*. Baillière, Tindall, and Cox, London.

ECKSTEIN, P. (1970). Mechanisms of action of intrauterine contraceptive devices in women and other mammals. *Br. med. Bull.* **26**, 52–9.

EDWARDS, R. G., BAVISTER, B. D., and STEPTOE, P. C. (1969). Early stages of fertilization *in vitro* of human oocytes matured *in vitro*. *Nature, Lond.* **221**, 632–5.

FORD, C. S., and BEACH, F. A. (1951). *Patterns of sexual behaviour*. Harper, New York; Hoeber, New York.

GORER, G. (1971). *Sex and marriage in England today*. Nelson, London.

HARRIS, G. W. (1959). The nervous system—follicular ripening, ovulation, and estrus behavior. In *Recent progress in the endocrinology of reproduction* (editor C. W. Lloyd). Academic Press, New York.

KINSEY, A. C., POMEROY, W. B., and MARTIN, C. E. (1948). *Sexual behavior in the human male*. Saunders, Philadelphia.

—— —— —— and GEBHARD, P. H. (1953). *Sexual behavior in the human female*. Saunders, Philadelphia.

MANN, T. (1964). *The biochemistry of semen and of the male reproductive tract*. Methuen, London.

MANN, T. (1969). The science of reproduction. *Nature, Lond.* **224**, 649-54.

MATSUNGA, E., and MARUYAMA, T. (1969). Human sexual behaviour, delayed fertilization, and Down's syndrome. *Nature, Lond.* **221**, 642-4.

MENKIN, M. F., and ROCK, J. (1948). *In vitro* fertilization and cleavage of human ovarian eggs. *Am. J. Obstet. Gynec.* **55**, 440-52.

MICHAEL, R. P., and KEVERNE, E. B. (1968). Pheromones in the communication of sexual status in the primates. *Nature, Lond.* **218**, 746-9.

NELSON, L. (1967). Sperm motility. In *Fertilization.* Vol. I (editors C. B. Metz and A. Monroy). Academic Press, New York.

NEW, D. A. T. (1967). Development of explanted rat embryos in circulating medium. *J. Embryol. exp. Morph.* **17**, 513-25.

PARKES, A. S. (editor) (1965). *Marshall's Physiology of reproduction.* Vol. I, Part 2. Longmans, London.

PENROSE, L. S., and BERG, J. M. (1968). Mongolism and duration of marriage. *Nature, Lond.* **218**, 300.

RESTALL, B. J. (1967). The biochemical and physiological relationships between the gametes and the female reproductive tract. *Adv. reprod. Physiol.* **2**, 181-212.

STEPTOE, P. C., EDWARDS, R. G., and PORDY, J. M. (1971). Human blastocysts grown in culture. *Nature, Lond.* **229**, 132-3.

SWYER, G. I. M. (editor) (1970). Control of human fertility. *Br. med. Bull.* **26**, No. 1, 91 pp.

UDRY, J. R., and MORRIS, N. M. (1968). Distribution of coitus in the menstrual cycle. *Nature, Lond.* **220**, 593-6.

WAITES, G. M. H., and SETCHELL, B. P. (1969). Physiology of the testis, epididymis, and scrotum. *Adv. reprod. Physiol.* **4**, 1-63.

CHAPTER 16. HUMAN GROWTH

CHEEK, D. B. (1968). *Human growth. Body composition, cell growth, energy and intelligence.* Lea and Febiger, Philadelphia.

FALKNER, F. (1962). The physical development of children. A guide to interpretation of growth-charts and development assessments; and a commentary on contemporary and future problems. *Pediatrics* **29**, 448-66.

—— (1966). General considerations in human development. In *Human development* (editor F. Falkner). Saunders, Philadelphia.

GRUENWALD, P. (1967). Growth of the human foetus. *Adv. reprod. Physiol.* **2**, 279-309.

JOST, A. (1968). Full or partial maturation of fetal endocrine systems under pituitary control. *Perspect. Biol. Med.* **11**, 371-5.

—— and PICON, L. (1957). Hormonal factors in the growth of the foetus. *Symp. Soc. exp. Biol.* **11**, 228-34.

MEDAWAR, P. B. (1940). The growth, growth energy and ageing of the chicken's heart. *Proc. R. Soc.* B**129**, 332-55.

NEEDHAM, J. (1931). *Chemical embryology.* Cambridge University Press.

OUNSTED, M., and OUNSTED, C. (1966). Maternal regulation of intra-uterine growth. *Nature, Lond.* **212**, 995-7.

POMEROY, R. W. (1955). Live-weight growth. In *Progress in the physiology of farm animals.* Vol. II (editor J. Hammond). Butterworths, London.

TANNER, J. M. (1962). *Growth at adolescence.* Blackwell, Oxford.

—— WHITEHOUSE, R. H., and TAKAISHI, M. (1966). Standards from birth to maturity for height, weight, height velocity and weight velocity: British children, 1965, Parts I and II. *Archs Dis. Childh.* **41**, 454-71 and 613-35.

WIDDOWSON, E. M. (1968). Growth and composition of the fetus and newborn. In *Biology of gestation.* Vol. II. *The fetus and neonate* (editor N. S. Assali). Academic Press, London.

CHAPTER 17. RELATIVE RATES OF GROWTH

ABERCROMBIE, M. (1957). Localized formation of new tissue in an adult mammal. *Symp. Soc. exp. Biol.* **11**, 235-54.

AITKEN, J. T., SHARMAN, M., and YOUNG, J. Z. (1947). Maturation of regenerating nerve fibres with various peripheral connexions. *J. Anat.* **81**, 1-22.

BAUDEY, J., and LAVAL-JEANTET, M. (1963). Microradiographies et moulages des impressions digitales chez le nouveau-né. *Annls. Radiol.* **6**, 126-31.

BLINKOV, S. M., and GLEZER, I. I. (1968). *The human brain in figures and tables.* Basic Books, New York; Plenum Press, New York.

CRAGG, B. G. (1967). Changes in visual cortex on first exposure of rats to light. Effect on synaptic dimensions. *Nature, Lond.* **215**, 251-3.

EBERT, J. D. (1954). Some aspects of protein biosynthesis in development. In *Aspects of synthesis and order in growth.* 13th Growth Symposium (editor D. Rudnick). Princeton University Press.

FAWCETT, D. W. (1966). *An atlas of fine structure. The cell. Its organelles and inclusions.* Saunders, Philadelphia.

GYLLENSTEN, L., MALMFORS, T., and NORRLIN, M. L. (1965). Effect of visual deprivation on the optic centers of growing and adult mice. *J. comp. Neurol.* **124**, 149-60.

HAMILTON, W. J., BOYD, J. D., and MOSSMAN, H. W. (1964). *Human embryology.* Heffer, Cambridge.

HIERNAUX, J. (1968). Bodily shape differentiation of ethnic groups and of the sexes through growth. *Hum. Biol.* **40**, 44-62.

LARROCHE, J.-C. (1968). Développement des hémisphères au cours de la vie fœtale. *Le Médical*, Janvier. Éditions de la Tournelle, Paris. (Chapter—Paediatry.)

LEVI-MONTALCINI, R. (1964). Growth control of nerve cells by a protein factor and its antiserum. *Science*, **143**, 105-10.

MONTAGNA, W., and SCOTT, E. J. VAN (1958). The anatomy of the hair follicle. In *The biology of hair growth* (editors W. Montagna and R. A. Ellis). Academic Press, New York.

NEEDHAM, A. E. (1964). *The growth process in animals.* Pitman, London.

REEVE, E. C. R., and HUXLEY, J. S. (1945). Some problems in the study of allometric growth. In *Essays on growth and form presented to D'Arcy Wentworth Thompson* (editors W. E. Le Gros Clark and P. B. Medawar). Clarendon Press, Oxford.

SAVARA, B. S. (1965). Application of photogrammetry for quantitative study of tooth and face morphology. *Am. J. phys. Anthrop.* **23**, 427-34.

SCAMMON, R. E., and CALKINS, L. A. (1929). *The development and growth of the external dimensions of the human body in the fetal period.* University of Minnesota Press, Minneapolis.

SHEPHERD, R. H., SHOLL, D. A., and VIZOSO, A. (1949). The size relationships subsisting between body length, limbs and jaws in man. *J. Anat.* **83**, 296-302.

TANNER, J. M. (1962). *Growth at adolescence.* Blackwell, Oxford.

TWITTY, V. (1955). Eye. In *Analysis of development* (editors B. H. Willier, P. A. Weiss, and V. Hamburger). Saunders, Philadelphia.

WEISS, P. (1941). Self-differentiation of the basic patterns of co-ordination. *Comp. Psychol. Monogr.* **17**, 1-96.

WISLOCKI, G. B. (1956). The growth cycle of deer antlers. In *CIBA Foundation Colloquia on Ageing.* Vol. II (editors G. E. W. Wolstenholme and E. C. P. Millar). Churchill, London.

YOUNG, J. Z. (1957). *The life of mammals.* Clarendon Press, Oxford.

—— (1950). *The life of vertebrates* (2nd edn. 1962). Clarendon Press, Oxford.

CHAPTER 18. LATER STAGES OF HUMAN GROWTH

AMBROSE, A. (editor) (1969). *Stimulation in early infancy.* Academic Press, London.
BLAKEMORE, C., and COOPER, G. F. (1970). Development of the brain depends on the visual environment. *Nature, Lond.* **228**, 477–8.
CHEEK, D. B. (1968). *Human growth. Body composition, cell growth, energy and intelligence.* Lea and Febiger, Philadelphia.
GREGORY, R. L. (1966). *Eye and brain.* Weidenfeld and Nicolson, London.
GREULICH, W. W., CRISMON, C. S., and TURNER, M. L. (1953). The physical growth and development of children who survived the atomic bombing of Hiroshima or Nagasaki. *J. Pediat.* **43**, 121–45.
HARLOW, H. F. (1962). Development of affection in primates. In *Roots of behavior* (editor E. L. Bliss). Harper, New York.
HARRIS, G. W., and JACOBSOHN, D. (1952). Functional grafts of the anterior pituitary gland. *Proc. R. Soc.* B**139**, 263–76.
HULSE, F. S. (1957). Exogamie et hétérosis. *Archs suisses Anthrop. gén.* **22**, 103–25.
KINSEY, A. C., POMEROY, W. B., and MARTIN, C. E. (1948). *Sexual behavior in the human male.* Saunders, Philadelphia.
MEDAWAR, P. B. (1960). *The future of man.* Methuen, London.
MILICER, H. (1968). Age at menarche of girls in Wrocław, Poland, in 1966. *Hum. Biol.* **40**, 249–59.
REISEN, A. H. (1947). The development of perception in man and chimpanzee. *Science, N.Y.* **106**, 107–8.
ROBINOW, M. (1942). The variability of weight and height increments from birth to six years. *Child Dev.* **13**, 159–64.
SIMMONS, K. (1944). The Brush Foundation study of child growth and development. II. Physical growth and development. *Monogr. Soc. Res. Child Dev.* **9**, No. 1, 87 pp.
—— and TODD, T. W. (1938). Growth of well children: analysis of stature and weight, 3 months to 13 years. *Growth* **2**, 93–134.
STREETER, G. L. (1920). Weight, sitting height, head size, foot length and menstrual age of the human embryo. *Contr. Embryol.* **11**, No. 55, 143–70.
TANNER, J. M. (1962). *Growth at adolescence.* Blackwell, Oxford.
—— (1966). Galtonian eugenics and the study of growth. *Eugen. Rev.* **58**, 122–35.
—— (1968). Earlier maturation in man. *Scient. Am.* **218** (Jan.), 21–7.
—— (1969). Growth and endocrinology of the adolescent. In *Endocrine and genetic disease of childhood* (editor L. Gardner). Saunders, Philadelphia.
—— (1970). Postnatal growth. In *Child life and health* (editor R. Mitchell). Churchill, London.
THOMSON, A. M. (1959). Maternal stature and reproductive efficiency. *Eugen. Rev.* **51**, 157–62.
WELLS, M. J., and WELLS, J. (1959). Hormonal control of sexual maturity in *Octopus. J. exp. Biol.* **36**, 1–33.
WIDDOWSON, E. M. (1951). Mental contentment and physical growth. *Lancet* **260**, 1316–18.
WIGGLESWORTH, V. B. (1964). The hormonal regulation of growth and reproduction in insects. In *Adv. Insect Physiol.* **2**, 247–336.
WILSON, D. C., and SUTHERLAND, I. (1950). Age at menarche. *Br. med. J.* **1**, 1267.
—— —— (1953). The age of the menarche in the tropics. *Br. med. J.* **2**, 607–8.
YOUNG, J. Z. (1964). *A model of the brain.* Clarendon Press, Oxford.

CHAPTER 19. MATURATION OF THE BRAIN AND THE STUDY OF THINKING

AMBROSE, A. (editor) (1969). *Stimulation in early infancy.* Academic Press, London.
BARTLETT, F. (1964). *Thinking. An experimental and social study.* Unwin University Books, London.

CHEEK, D. B. (1968). *Human growth. Body composition, cell growth, energy and intelligence.* Lea and Febiger, Philadelphia.

EAYRS, J. T., and GOODHEAD, B. (1959). Postnatal development of the cerebral cortex in the rat. *J. Anat.* **93**, 385-402.

FANTZ, R. L. (1965). Visual perception from birth as shown by pattern selectivity. *Ann. N.Y. Acad. Sci.* **118** (Art. 21), 793-814.

HUBEL, D. H., and WIESEL, T. N. (1970). The period of susceptibility to the physiological effects of unilateral eye closure in kittens. *J. Physiol. Lond.* **206**, 419-36.

INHELDER, B., and MATALON, B. (1960). The study of problem solving and thinking. In *Handbook of research methods in child development* (editor P. H. Mussen). Wiley, New York.

LENNEBERG, E. H. (1965). The capacity for language acquisition. In *The structure of language. Readings in the philosophy of language* (editors J. A. Fodor and J. J. Katz). Prentice-Hall, New Jersey.

—— (1969). On explaining language. *Science, N.Y.* **164**, 635-43.

NEWELL, A., SHAW, J. C., and SIMON, H. A. (1963). Chess-playing programs and the problem of complexity. In *Computers and thought* (editors E. A. Feigenbaum and J. Feldman). McGraw-Hill, New York.

NORMAN, D. A. (1970). *Models of human memory.* Academic Press, New York.

POPPER, K. R. (1965). *The logic of scientific discovery.* Hutchinson, London.

PURPURA, D. P., SHOFER, R. J., HOUSEPIAN, E. M., and NOBACK, C. R. (1964). Comparative ontogenesis of structure-function relations in cerebral and cerebellar cortex. In *Growth and maturation of the brain. Progress in brain research.* **4** (editors D. P. Purpura and J. P. Schadé). Elsevier, Amsterdam.

ROBINSON, R. J. (editor) (1969). *Brain and early behaviour: development in the fetus and infant.* Academic Press, London.

SHOLL, D. A. (1956). *The organization of the cerebral cortex.* Methuen, London.

SPERRY, R. W. (1968). Plasticity of neural maturation. *Devl. Biol. Suppl.* **2**, 306-27 (editor M. Locke). Academic Press, New York.

WASON, P. C. (1968). 'On the failure to eliminate hypotheses . . .', a second look. In *Thinking and reasoning* (editors P. C. Wason and P. N. Johnson-Laird). Penguin Books, Harmondsworth.

YOUNG, J. Z. (1951). *Doubt and certainty in science.* Clarendon Press, Oxford.

CHAPTER 20. THE MEASUREMENT OF INTELLIGENCE

AMBROSE, A. (editor) (1969). *Stimulation in early infancy.* Academic Press, London.

BAYLEY, N. (1955). On the growth of intelligence. *Am. Psychol.* **10**, 805-18.

—— and ODEN, M. H. (1955). The maintenance of intellectual ability in gifted adults. *J. Gerontol.* **10**, 91-107.

BINET, A., and SIMON, TH. (1905). Méthodes nouvelles pour le diagnostic du niveau intellectuel des anormaux. *Année psychol.* **11**, 191-244.

BURT, C. (1940). *The factors of the mind.* University of London Press.

—— (1955). The evidence for the concept of intelligence. *Br. J. educ. Psychol.* **25**, 158-77.

CAMERON, J., LIVSON, N., and BAYLEY, N. (1967). Infant vocalisations and their relationship to mature intelligence. *Science* **157**, 331-3.

CHOMSKY, N. (1957). *Syntactic structures.* Mouton, The Hague.

EYSENCK, H. J. (1962). *The scientific basis of personality.* Routledge and Kegan Paul, London.

—— and EYSENCK, S. B. G. (1969). *Personality structure and measurement.* Routledge and Kegan Paul, London.

GUILFORD, J. P. (1959). Three faces of intellect. *Am. Psychol.* **14**, 469-79.

HEBB, D. O. (1949). *The organization of behavior.* Wiley, New York.

HOFSTAETTER, P. R. (1954). The changing composition of 'intelligence': a study in T-technique. *J. genet. Psychol.* **85**, 159-64.

HUDSON, L. (1966). Selection and the problem of conformity. In *Genetic and environmental factors in human ability* (editors J. E. Meade and A. S. Parkes). Oliver and Boyd, London.

JONES, H. E., and CONRAD, H. S. (1933). The growth and decline of intelligence: a study of a homogeneous group between the ages of ten and sixty. *Genet. Psychol. Monogr.* **13** (No. 3), 223-98.

KANT, I. (1798). *Anthropologie in pragmatischer Hinsicht abgefasst.* Königsberg.

LENNEBERG, E. H. (1967). *Biological foundations of language.* Wiley, New York.

MACKINNON, D. W. (1962). The nature and nurture of creative talent. *Am. Psychol.* **17**, 484-95.

MCNEMAR, Q. (1964). Lost: our intelligence? Why? *Am. Psychol.* **19**, 871-83.

MEADE, J. E., and PARKES, A. S. (editors) (1966). *Genetic and environmental factors in human ability.* Oliver and Boyd, London.

PIDGEON, D. (1966). Intelligence testing and comprehensive education. In *Genetic and environmental factors in human ability* (editors J. E. Meade and A. S. Parkes). Oliver and Boyd, London.

SCHAEFFER, E. S., and BAYLEY, N. (1963). Maternal behavior, child behavior and their intercorrelations from infancy through adolescence. *Monogr. soc. Res. Child Develop.* **28**, No. 3, 127 pp.

SPEARMAN, C. E. (1932). *The abilities of man: their nature and measurement.* Macmillan, London.

TERMAN, L. M., and MERRILL, M. A. (1961). *Stanford-Binet intelligence scale—manual for the third revision form L-M.* Harrap, London.

—— and ODEN, M. H. (1962). The gifted group at mid-life. In *Readings on the exceptional child* (editors E. P. Trapp and P. Himelstein). Methuen, London.

VERNON, P. E. (1964). *Personality assessment: a critical survey.* Methuen, London.

—— (1966). Development of current ideas about intelligence tests. In *Genetic and environmental factors in human ability* (editors J. E. Meade and A. S. Parkes). Oliver and Boyd, London.

—— (1969). *Intelligence and cultural environment.* Methuen's Manuals of Modern Psychology, London.

WECHSLER, D. (1958). *The measurement and appraisal of adult intelligence.* Williams and Wilkins, Baltimore.

CHAPTER 21. THE DEVELOPMENT OF THE CHILD AS SEEN BY PIAGET

FANTZ, R. L. (1965). Visual perception from birth as shown by pattern selectivity. *Ann. N.Y. Acad. Sci.* **118** (Art. 21), 793-814.

FLAVELL, J. H. (1963). *The development psychology of Jean Piaget.* Van Nostrand, Princeton, New Jersey.

PIAGET, J. (1967). *Biologie et connaissance.* Editions Gallimard, Paris.

RUSSELL, R. W., and DENNIS, W. (1939). Studies in animism. I. A standardized procedure for the investigation of animism. *J. genet. Psychol.* **55**, 389-400.

VERNON, P. E. (1965). Environmental handicaps and intellectual development, Parts I and II. *Br. J. educ. Psychol.* **35**, 9-20, 117-26.

CHAPTERS 22 AND 23. AGEING AND LIFE TABLES AND THE
PATTERN OF SENESCENCE

ALEXANDER, P. (1967). The role of DNA lesions in the processes leading to ageing in mice. *Symp. Soc. exp. Biol.* **21**, 29-50.

ANDERSEN, A. C., and ROSENBLATT, L. S. (1965). Survival of beagles under natural and laboratory conditions. *Expl. Geront.* **1**, 193-9.

BENJAMIN, B. (1959). Actuarial aspects of human life-spans. In *CIBA Foundation Colloquia on Ageing.* 5. *The life-span of animals* (editors G. E. W. Wolstenholme and M. O'Connor). Churchill, London.

BEVERTON, R. J. H., and HOLT, S. J. (1959). A review of the life-spans and mortality rates of fish in nature and their relation to growth and other physiological characteristics. In *CIBA Foundation Colloquia on Ageing.* 5. *The life-span of animals* (editors G. E. W. Wolstenholme and M. O'Connor). Churchill, London.

BIDDER, G. P. (1932). Senescence. *Br. med. J.* (1932), **2**, 583-5.

BODENHEIMER, F. S. (1938). *Problems of animal ecology.* Oxford University Press.

BOURLIÈRE, F. (1957). Ageing and metabolism. In *Symposia of the Institute of Biology.* Vol. 6, *The biology of ageing* (editors W. B. Yapp and G. H. Bourne). The Institute of Biology, London.

BURNET, M. (1965). Somatic mutation and chronic disease. *Br. med. J.* (1965) **1**, 338-42.

CALLAN, H. G. (1967). The organization of genetic units in chromosomes. *J. Cell. Sci.* **2**, 1-7.

CARREL, A. (1924). Tissue culture and cell physiology. *Phys. Rev.* **4**, 1-20.

COMFORT, A. (1964). *Ageing. The biology of senescence.* Routledge and Kegan Paul, London.

—— (1966). Models of aging. Mammals. In *Perspectives in experimental gerontology* (editor N. W. Shock). Thomas, Springfield.

COON, H. G., and WILLIAMS, I. (1967). An established cell line of fibroblasts from goose cells. *Yb. Carnegie Inst. Wash.* **67**, 421-3.

CURTIS, H. J. (1966). A composite theory of ageing. *Gerontologist* **6**, 143-9.

—— (1967). Radiation and ageing. *Symp. Soc. exp. Biol.* **21**, 51-63.

DANIELLI, J. F., and MUGGLETON, A. (1959). Some alternative states of *Amoeba* with special reference to life-span. *Gerontologia* **3**, 76-90.

DEVI, A., LINDSAY, P., RAINA, P. L., and SARKAR, N. K. (1966). Effect of age on some aspects of the synthesis of ribonucleic acid. *Nature, Lond.* **212**, 474-5.

GLINOS, A. D., and BARTLETT, E. G. (1951). The effect of regeneration on the growth potentialities *in vitro* of rat liver at different ages. *Cancer Res.* **11**, 164-8.

GLUCKSMANN, A. (1964). Mitosis and degeneration in the morphogenesis of the human foetal lung *in vitro. Z. Zellforsch. mikrosk. Anat.* **64**, 101-10.

GURDON, J. B., and WOODLAND, H. R. (1968). The cytoplasmic control of nuclear activity in animal development. *Biol. Rev.* **43**, 233-66.

HAHN, H. P. VON (1966). Aging in molecules—DNA. In *Perspectives in experimental gerontology* (editor N. W. Shock). Thomas, Springfield.

—— and VERZÁR, F. (1963). Age-dependent thermal denaturation of DNA from bovine thymus. *Gerontologia* **7**, 105-8.

HALDANE, J. B. S. (1953). Some animal life tables. *J. Inst. Actuaries* **79**, 83-9.

HAMERTON, J. L., TAYLOR, A. I., ANGELL, R., and McGUIRE, V. M. (1965). Chromosome investigations of a small isolated human population: chromosome abnormalities and distribution of chromosome counts according to age and sex among the population of Tristan da Cunha. *Nature, Lond.* **206**, 1232-4.

HAMILTON, W. D. (1966). The moulding of senescence by natural selection. *J. theor. Biol.* **12**, 12-45.

HAYFLICK, L. (1965). The limited *in vitro* lifetime of human diploid cell strains. *Expl. Cell Res.* **37**, 614-36.

HINTON, H. E. (1968). Reversible suspension of metabolism and the origin of life. *Proc. R. Soc.* B**171**, 43-57.

JARVIK, L. F., and FALEK, A. (1963). Intellectual stability and survival in the aged. *J. Geront.* **18**, 173-6.

KÄLLÉN, B. (1955). Cell degeneration during normal ontogenesis of the rabbit brain. *J. Anat.* **89**, 153–60.

KROHN, P. L. (1962). Review lectures on senescence. II. Heterochronic transplantation in the study of ageing. *Proc. R. Soc.* B**157**, 128–47.

LANSING, A. I. (1947). A transmissible, cumulative and reversible factor in aging. *J. Geront.* **2**, 228–39.

LEFFORD, F. (1964). The effect of donor age on the emigration of cells from chick embryo explants *in vitro. Expl. Cell Res.* **35**, 557–71.

LINHART, S. B., and KNOWLTON, F. F. (1967). Determining age of Coyotes by tooth cementum layers. *J. Wildl. Mgmt.* **31**, 362–5.

LIU, R. K., and WALFORD, R. L. (1966). Increased growth and life-span with lowered ambient temperature in the annual fish *Cynolebias adloffi. Nature, Lond.* **212**, 1277–8.

MAYNARD SMITH, J. (1962). The causes of ageing. *Proc. R. Soc.* B**157**, 115–27.

McCAY, C. M., MAYNARD, L. A., SPERLING, G., and BARNES, L. L. (1939). Retarded growth, life span, ultimate body size and age changes in the albino rat after feeding diets restricted in calories. *J. Nutr.* **18**, 1–13.

MEDAWAR, P. B. (1952). *An unsolved problem of biology.* An inaugural lecture delivered at University College, London, 6 December 1951. Lewis, London.

MEDVEDEV, ZH. A. (1967). Molecular aspects of ageing. *Symp. Soc. exp. Biol.* **21**, 1–28.

METCHNIKOFF, E. (1907). *The prolongation of life; optimistic studies.* Heinemann, London.

MUGGLETON, A., and DANIELLI, J. F. (1968). Inheritance of the 'life-spanning' phenomenon in *Amoeba proteus. Expl. Cell Res.* **49**, 116–20.

ORGEL, L. E. (1963). The maintenance of the accuracy of protein synthesis and its relevance to ageing. *Proc. natn. Acad. Sci. U.S.A.* **49**, 517–21.

PEARL, R. (1940). *Introduction to medical biometry and statistics.* Saunders, Philadelphia.

—— and MINER, J. R. (1935). Experimental studies on the duration of life. XIV. The comparative mortality of certain lower organisms. *Q. Rev. Biol.* **10**, 60–79.

PORSILD, A. E., HARINGTON, C. R., and MULLIGAN, G. A. (1967). *Lupinus arcticus* Wats. grown from seeds of Pleistocene Age. *Science, N.Y.* **158**, 113–14.

PYHTILÄ, M. J., and SHERMAN, F. G. (1968). Age-associated studies on thermal stability and template effectiveness of DNA and nucleoproteins from beef thymus. *Biochem. biophys. Res. Commun.* **31**, 340–4.

RICHARD, A. (1967). Rôle de la photopériode dans le déterminisme de la maturation génitale femelle du Céphalopode *Sepia officinalis* L. *C.r. hebd. Seanc. Acad. Sci., Paris* **264**, 1315–18.

SAMIS, H. V., JR., FALZONE, J. A., JR., and WULFF, V. J. (1966). H³—Thymidine incorporation and mitotic activity in liver of rats of various ages. *Gerontologia* **12**, 79–88.

SCHLETTWEIN-GSELL, D. (1966). Nutrition as a factor in aging. In *Perspectives in experimental gerontology* (editor N. W. Shock). Thomas, Springfield.

SELYE, H. (1962). *Calciphylaxis.* University of Chicago Press.

SIKES, S. K. (1966). The African elephant, *Loxodonta africana*: a field method for the estimation of age. *J. Zool. Lond.* **150**, 279–95.

SMITH, A. U. (1961). *Biological effects of freezing and supercooling.* Arnold, London.

SPEYER, J. F. (1965). Mutagenic DNA polymerase. *Biochem. biophys. Res. Common.* **21**, 6–8.

STREHLER, B. L. (1967). The nature of cellular age changes. *Symp. Soc. exp. Biol.* **21**, 149–77.

TODARO, G. J., and GREEN, H. (1963). Quantitative studies of the growth of mouse embryo cells in culture and their development into established lines. *J. Cell Biol.* **17**, 299–313.

UNITED NATIONS (1967). *Demographic Yearbook 1966.* 18th Issue. United Nations, New York.

VEVERS, H. G. (1961). Observations on the laying and hatching of octopus eggs in the society's aquarium. *Proc. zool. Soc. Lond.* **137**, 311–15.

WADDINGTON, C. H. (1968). The basic ideas of biology. In *Towards a theoretical biology*. I. *Prolegomena*, an IUBS symposium (editor C. H. Waddington). Edinburgh University Press.

WELLS, M. J., and WELLS, J. (1959). Hormonal control of sexual maturity in *Octopus*. *J. exp. Biol.* **36**, 1–33.

WILLIAMS, G. C. (1957). Pleiotropy, natural selection, and the evolution of senescence. *Evolution* **11**, 398–411.

WOODS, J. (1965). Octopus-watching off Capri. *Animals* **7**, 324–7.

WOOLHOUSE, H. W. (1967). The nature of senescence in plants. *Symp. Soc. exp. Biol.* **21**, 179–213.

CHAPTERS 24 AND 25. HUMAN FERTILITY AND MORTALITY AND
THE GROWTH OF THE HUMAN POPULATION

BARCLAY, G. W. (1958). *Techniques of population analysis*. Wiley, New York.

BEAUJEU-GARNIER, J. (1966). *Geography of population*. Longmans, London.

BERELSON, B., and FREEDMAN, R. (1964). A study in fertility control. *Scient. Am.* **210** (May), 29–37.

BOREHAM, A. J. (1970). Economics and population in Britain. In *The optimum population for Britain* (editor L. R. Taylor). Symposia of the Institute of Biology No. 19. Academic Press, London.

BRASS, W., COALE, A. J., DEMENY, P., HEISEL, D. F., LORIMER, F., ROMANIUK, A., and WALLE, A. VAN DE (1968). *The demography of tropical Africa*. Princeton University Press.

BURNET, M. (1953). *Natural history of infectious disease*. (3rd edn. 1962.) Cambridge University Press.

CARR-SAUNDERS, A. M. (1936). *World population. Past growth and present trends*. Clarendon Press, Oxford.

CENTRAL STATISTICAL OFFICE, LONDON (1968). *Annual abstract of statistics No. 105*. H.M.S.O., London.

CLARK, COLIN (1967). *Population growth and land use*. Macmillan, London.

DARLING, F. FRASER (1970). *Wilderness and plenty*. British Broadcasting Corporation, London.

DAVIS, J. S. (1949). Our amazing population upsurge. *J. Fm. Econ.* **31**, 765–78.

DORN, H. F. (1966). World population growth: an international dilemma. In *Human ecology* (editor J. B. Bresler). Addison-Wesley, Massachusetts.

DRAKE, M. (1969). *Population and society in Norway 1735–1865*. Cambridge University Press.

EVERSLEY, D. E. C. (1970). The special case—managing human population growth. In *The optimum population for Britain* (editor L. R. Taylor). Symposia of the Institute of Biology No. 19. Academic Press, London.

FOOD AND AGRICULTURAL ORGANIZATION OF THE UNITED NATIONS (1969). *The state of food and agriculture 1969*. F.A.O., Rome.

GENERAL REGISTER OFFICE (1967). *The Registrar General's statistical review of England and Wales for the year 1966*. Pt. I. Tables, medical. H.M.S.O., London.

—— (1968). *The Registrar General's statistical review of England and Wales for the year 1966*. Pt. II. Tables, population. H.M.S.O., London.

—— (1970). *The Registrar General's statistical review of England and Wales for the year 1968*. Pt. II. Tables, population. H.M.S.O., London.

GLASS, D. V. (1967). Demographic prediction. *Proc. R. Soc.* **B168**, 119–39.

HOSTETLER, J. A., and HUNTINGTON, G. E. (1968). Communal socialization patterns in Hutterite society. *Ethnology* **7**, 331–55.

HUTCHINSON, J. (1969). *Population and food supply*. Cambridge University Press.

JANSSENS, P. A. (1970). *Palaeopathology. Diseases and injuries of prehistoric man.* John Baker, London.

KEYFITZ, N., and FLIEGER, W. (1968). *World population. An analysis of vital data.* University of Chicago Press, Chicago and London.

LANGER, W. L. (1964). The black death. *Scient. Am.* **210** (Feb.), 114-21.

MALTHUS, T. R. (1798). *An essay on the principle of population, as it affects the future improvement of society.* Johnson, London. (1967) *Essays on the principle of population.* Everyman Library, Dent, London.

NICHOLSON, M. (1970). *The environmental revolution.* Hodder and Stoughton, London.

PEARSON, F. A., and HARPER, F. A. (1945). *The world's hunger.* Cornell University Press, New York.

PINCUS, G. (1965). *The control of fertility.* Academic Press, London.

REGISTRAR GENERAL'S REPORT (1900). *Annual report.* H.M.S.O., London.

RESTALL, B. J. (1967). The biochemical and physiological relationships between the gametes and the female reproductive tract. *Adv. reprod. Physiol.* **2**, 181-212.

ROCKEFELLER FOUNDATION. Toward the conquest of hunger. *The President's Review and Annual Report 1967.* Rockefeller Foundation, New York.

SAUVY, A. (1969). *General theory of population.* Weidenfeld and Nicolson, London.

SHREWSBURY, J. F. D. (1970). *A history of bubonic plague in the British Isles.* Cambridge University Press.

STAMP, L. D. (1960). *Our developing world.* Faber and Faber, London.

SUITTERS, B. (prepared by) (1967). The history of contraceptives. *8th Int. Conf. plann. Parent.* Santiago, Chile.

TAYLOR, L. R. (editor) (1970). *The optimum population for Britain.* Institute of Biology Symposium No. 19. Academic Press, London.

UNITED NATIONS (1958). *The future growth of world population. Population studies No. 28.* United Nations, New York.

—— (1968). *Demographic Yearbook 1967.* 19th Issue. United Nations, New York.

ZIEGLER, P. (1969). *The black death.* Collins, London.

CHAPTER 26. THE ORIGIN OF LIFE

BERNAL, J. D. (1960). The problem of stages in biopoesis. In *Aspects of the origin of life* (editor M. Florkin). Pergamon Press, Oxford.

—— (1967). *The origin of life.* Weidenfeld and Nicolson, London.

BRYSON, V., and VOGEL, H. J. (1965). *Evolving genes and proteins.* Academic Press, New York.

CALVIN, M. (1969). *Chemical evolution.* Clarendon Press, Oxford.

—— and VAUGHN, S. K. (1960). Extraterrestrial life: some organic constituents of meteorites and their significance for possible extraterrestrial biological evolution. *Space research* **1**, 1171-91. Proceedings of the First International Space Science Symposium (editor H. Kallmann Bijl). North-Holland Publishing Co., Amsterdam.

DIXON, M., and WEBB, E. C. (1958). *Enzymes.* Longmans, London.

FISHER, R. L., and HESS, H. H. (1963). Trenches. In *The Sea. The earth beneath the sea. History.* Vol. III, 411-36 (editor M. N. Hill). Interscience, New York.

FOWLER, W. A. (1964). The origin of the elements. *Proc. natn. Acad. Sci. U.S.A.* **52**, 524-48.

GREENSTEIN, J. L. (1964). The history of stars and galaxies. *Proc. natn. Acad. Sci. U.S.A.* **52**, 549-65.

HALDANE, J. B. S. (1929). The origin of life. *Rationalist Annual.* In *The origin of life* by J. D. Bernal (1967). Weidenfeld and Nicolson, London.

—— (1965). Data needed for a blueprint of the first organism. In *The origins of prebiological systems* (editor S. W. Fox). Academic Press, New York.

HINTON, H. E. (1968). Reversible suspension of metabolism and the origin of life. *Proc. R. Soc.* B**171**, 43–56.

KVENVOLDEN, K. A., PETERSON, E., and POLLOCK, G. E. (1969). Optical configuration of amino-acids in Pre-Cambrian Fig Tree Chert. *Nature, Lond.* **221**, 141–3.

MCKENZIE, D. P. (1970). Plate tectonics and continental drift. *Endeavour* **29**, 39–44.

MORGAN, W. J., VOGT, P. R., and FALLS, D. F. (1969). Magnetic anomalies and sea floor spreading on the Chile Rise. *Nature, Lond.* **222**, 137–42.

OPARIN, A. I. (1924). *Proiskhozhdenie zhizni.* Moscow: Izd. Moskovskii Rabochii. (1957) *The origin of life on the earth* (trans. A. Synge). 3rd edn. Oliver and Boyd, Edinburgh.

—— (1964). *The chemical origin of life.* Thomas, Springfield, Illinois.

—— (1968). *Genesis and evolutionary development of life.* Academic Press, New York and London.

ORÓ, J., and KIMBALL, A. P. (1961). Synthesis of purines under possible primitive earth conditions: I. Adenine from hydrogen cyanide. *Archs Biochem. Biophys.* **94**, 217–27.

—— —— (1962). Synthesis of purines under possible primitive earth conditions: II. Purine intermediates from hydrogen cyanide. *Archs Biochem. Biophys.* **96**, 293–313.

PAVLOVSKAYA, T. E., and PASYNSKII, A. G. (1959). The original formation of amino acids under the action of ultra violet rays and electric discharges. In *The origin of life on earth* (editors A. I. Oparin *et al.*). Pergamon Press, London.

REVELLE, R. (1964). History of the universe: introduction. *Proc. natn. Acad. Sci. U.S.A.* **52**, 517–23.

SCHRAMM, G. (1965). Synthesis of nucleosides and polynucleotides with metaphosphate esters. In *The origins of prebiological systems and of their molecular matrices* (editor S. W. Fox). Academic Press, New York.

YOUNG, J. Z. (1950). *The life of vertebrates* (2nd edn. 1962). Clarendon Press, Oxford.

CHAPTER 27. THE EVOLUTION OF POPULATIONS

CALVIN, M. (1967). Chemical evolution. In *Evolutionary biology.* Vol. I (editors T. Dobzhansky, M. K. Hecht, and W. C. Steere). Appleton-Century-Crofts, New York.

FORD, E. B. (1964). *Ecological genetics.* Methuen, London.

—— (1965). *Genetic polymorphism.* Faber and Faber, London.

FORD, H. D., and FORD, E. B. (1930). Fluctuation in numbers, and its influence on variation, in *Melitaea auriria*, Rott (Lepidoptera). *Trans. R. ent. Soc. Lond.* **78**, 345–51.

MAYR, E. (1963). *Animal species and evolution.* Belknap Press of Harvard University Press, Massachusetts.

ROMER, A. S. (1966). *Vertebrate paleontology.* 3rd edn. University of Chicago Press.

SIMPSON, G. G. (1953). *The major features of evolution.* Columbia University Press, New York.

YOUNG, J. Z. (1950). *The life of vertebrates* (2nd edn. 1962). Clarendon Press, Oxford.

CHAPTER 28. VARIATION AND SELECTION AS THE AGENTS OF EVOLUTION

DUBININ, N. P. (1964). *Problems of radiation genetics.* Oliver and Boyd, Edinburgh and London.

FISHER, R. A. (1930). *The genetical theory of natural selection.* Clarendon Press, Oxford.

GRÜNEBERG, H. (1952). *The genetics of the mouse.* Martinus Nijhoff, The Hague.

HALDANE, J. B. S. (1949). Suggestions as to quantitative measurement of rates of evolution. *Evolution, Lancaster, Pa.* **3**, 51–6.

—— (1956). The theory of selection for melanism in Lepidoptera. *Proc. R. Soc.* B**145**, 303–6.

KETTLEWELL, H. B. D. (1961). The phenomenon of industrial melanism in the Lepidoptera. *Ann. Rev. Ent.* **6**, 245–62.

LACK, D. (1956). *Swifts in a tower*. Methuen, London.

MALTHUS, T. R. (1798). *An essay on the principles of population, as it affects the future improvement of society*. Johnson, London. (1967) *Essays on the principle of population*. Everyman Library, Dent, London.

MAYR, E. (1963). *Animal species and evolution*. Belknap Press of Harvard University Press, Massachusetts.

PURDOM, C. E. (1963). *Genetic effects of radiations*. Newnes, London.

SHEPPARD, P. M. (1951). Fluctuations in the selective value of certain phenotypes in the polymorphic land snail *Cepaea nemoralis* (L). *Heredity, Lond.* **5**, 125-34.

SIMPSON, G. G. (1944). *Tempo and mode in evolution*. Columbia University Press, New York.

—— (1949). Rates of evolution in animals. In *Genetics, paleontology and evolution* (editors G. L. Jepson, E. Mayr, and G. G. Simpson). Princeton University Press.

WADDINGTON, C. H. (1953). Genetic assimilation of an acquired character. *Evolution, Lancaster, Pa.* **7**, 118-26.

WRIGHT, S. (1951). The genetical structure of populations. *Ann. Eugen.* **15**, 323-54.

CHAPTER 29. MAN'S PREMAMMALIAN ANCESTORS

BANGHOORN, E. S., and SCHOPF, J. W. (1966). Micro-organisms three billion years old from the Precambrian of South Africa. *Science, N.Y.* **152**, 758-63.

COLBERT, E. H. (1955). *Evolution of the vertebrates*. Wiley, New York; Chapman Hall, London.

CROMPTON, A. W. (1958). The cranial morphology of a new genus and species of ictidosauran. *Proc. zool. Soc. Lond.* **130**, 183-216.

—— (1963). The evolution of the mammalian jaw. *Evolution, Lancaster, Pa.* **17**, 431-9.

GEOLOGICAL SOCIETY OF LONDON (1964). The Phanerozoic time-scale. A symposium dedicated to Professor Arthur Holmes. *Q. Jl geol. Soc. Lond.* **120**, S, 260-2.

GREGORY, W. K. (1934). A half-century of trituberculy, the Cope-Osborn theory of dental evolution. *Proc. Am. phil. Soc.* **73**, 169-317.

—— (1951). *Evolution emerging*. Vol. II. Macmillan, New York.

JARVIK, E. (1952). On the fish-like tail in the ichthyostegid stegocephalians. *Meddr. Grønland* **114** (12), 1-90.

—— (1960). *Théories de l'évolution des vertébrés*. Masson, Paris.

NORMAN, J. R. (1931). *A history of fishes*. Benn, London.

ROMER, A. S. (1945). *Vertebrate paleontology*. 2nd edn. (3rd edn. 1966). University of Chicago Press.

—— (1956). *Osteology of the reptiles*. University of Chicago Press.

—— (1966). *The vertebrate body*. 3rd edn. (4th edn. 1970). Saunders, Philadelphia and London.

YOUNG, J. Z. (1950). *The life of vertebrates* (2nd edn. 1962). Clarendon Press, Oxford.

CHAPTER 30. THE INFLUENCES OF ARBOREAL LIFE. PROSIMIANS

BUETTNER-JANUSCH, J. (1963). An introduction to the primates. In *Evolutionary and genetic biology of primates*. Vol. I (editor J. Buettner-Janusch). Academic Press, New York.

—— (1966). *Origins of man*. Wiley, New York.

CAMPBELL, B. G. (1966). *Human evolution: an introduction to man's adaptation*. Aldine, Chicago.

GAZIN, C. L. (1958). A review of the Middle and Upper Eocene primates of North America. *Smithson misc. Collns* **136**, 1-112.

GRASSÉ, P.-P. (editor) (1955). *Traité de zoologie. Anatomie, systématique, biologie*. Tome XVII. *Mammifères. Les ordres: Anatomie, ethologie, systématique*. Second fasc. Masson, Paris.

GREGORY, W. K. (1920). On the structure and relations of *Notharctus*, an American Eocene primate. *Memoirs of the American Museum of Natural History: New Series.* **3**, pt. 2, 51–243.
—— (1951). *Evolution emerging.* Vol. II. Macmillan, New York.
JONES, F. WOOD (1929). *Man's place among the mammals.* Arnold, London.
RUSSELL, D. E. (1964). Les mammifères paléocènes d'Europe. *Mem. Mus. natn. Hist. nat Paris*, Série C, **13**, 1–324.
SIMONS, E. L. (1963). A critical reappraisal of tertiary primates. In *Evolutionary and genetic biology of primates.* Vol. I (editor J. Buettner-Janusch). Academic Press, New York.
YOUNG, J. Z. (1950). *The life of vertebrates* (2nd edn. 1962). Clarendon Press, Oxford.
—— (1957). *The life of mammals.* Clarendon Press, Oxford.

CHAPTER 31. ANTHROPOIDEA—MONKEYS AND APES

BARNICOT, N. A. (1969). Human nutrition: evolutionary aspects. In *The domestication and exploitation of plants and animals* (editors P. J. Ucko and G. W. Dimbleby). Duckworth, London.
—— JOLLY, C. J., and WADE, P. T. (1967). Protein variations and primatology. *Am. J. phys. Anthrop.* N.S. **27**, 343–56.
BUETTNER-JANUSCH, J. (1966). *Origins of man.* Wiley, New York.
CAMPBELL, B. G. (1966). *Human evolution: an introduction to man's adaptations.* Aldine, Chicago.
CLARK, W. E. LE GROS (1962). *The antecedents of man.* 2nd edn. Edinburgh University Press.
COLBERT, E. H. (1938). Fossil mammals from Burma in the American Museum of Natural History. *Bull. Am. Mus. nat. Hist.* **74**, 255–434.
GOODMAN, M. (1964). Man's place in the phylogeny of the primates as reflected in serum proteins. In *Classification and human evolution* (editor S. L. Washburn), Methuen, London.
GRASSÉ, P.-P. (editor) (1955). *Traité de zoologie. Anatomie, systématique, biologie.* Tome XVII. *Mammifères. Les ordres: Anatomie, ethologie, systématique.* Second fasc. Masson, Paris.
NAPIER, J. R., and NAPIER, P. H. (1967). *A handbook of living primates.* Academic Press, London.
SIMONS, E. L. (1960). New fossil primates: a review of the past decade. *Am. Scient.* **48**, 179–92.
—— (1961). The phyletic position of *Ramapithecus. Postilla* No. **57**, 1–9.
—— (1963). A critical reappraisal of tertiary primates. In *Evolutionary and genetic biology of primates.* Vol. I (editor J. Buettner-Janusch). Academic Press, New York.
—— (1964). On the mandible of *Ramapithecus. Proc. natn. Acad. Sci. U.S.A.* **51**, 528–35.
—— (1965). New fossil apes from Egypt and the initial differentiation of Hominoidea. *Nature, Lond.* **205**, 135–9.
—— (1967a). The earliest apes. *Scient. Am.* **217** (Dec.), 28–35.
WASHBURN, S. L. (1964). Behaviour and human evolution. In *Classification and human evolution* (editor S. L. Washburn), pp. 190–203. Methuen, London.
YOUNG, J. Z. (1957). *The life of mammals.* Clarendon Press, Oxford.
ZAPFE, H. (1958). The skeleton of *Pliopithecus* (*Epipliopithecus*) *vindobonensis* Zapfe and Hürzeler. *Am. J. Phys. Anthrop.* N.S. **16**, 441–55.
ZUCKERKANDL, E. (1964). Perspectives in molecular anthropology. In *Classification and human evolution* (editor S. L. Washburn), pp. 243–72. Methuen, London.

CHAPTER 32. THE PENULTIMATE STAGE—FELLOW HOMINIDS

ARDREY, R. (1961). *African genesis*. Collins, London.

BISHOP, W. W., and CHAPMAN, G. R. (1970). Early Pliocene sediments and fossils from the Northern Kenya Rift Valley. *Nature, Lond.* **226**, 914-18.

BRAIN, C. K. (1970). New finds at the Swartkrans australopithecine site. *Nature, Lond.* **225**, 1112-19.

BROOM, R. (1938). The Pleistocene anthropoid apes of South Africa. *Nature, Lond.* **142**, 377-9.

—— ROBINSON, J. T., and SCHEPERS, G. W. H. (1950). Sterkfontein Ape-Man, *Plesianthropus*. *Transv. Mus. Mem.* No. 4.

BUETTNER-JANUSCH, J. (1966). *Origins of man*. Wiley, New York.

CAMPBELL, B. G. (1964). Quantitative taxonomy and human evolution. In *Classification and human evolution* (editor S. L. Washburn), pp. 50-74. Methuen, London.

CLARK, J. D. (1970). *The prehistory of Africa*. Thames and Hudson, London.

DART, R. A. (1925). *Australopithecus africanus*: the man-ape of South Africa. *Nature, Lond.* **115**, 195-9.

—— (1949). The predatory implemental technique of Australopithecus. *Am. J. phys. Anthrop.* N.S. **7**, 1-38.

—— (1957). The Osteodontokeratic culture of *A. prometheus*. *Transv. Mus. Mem.* No. 10.

DAY, M. H. (1965). *Guide to fossil man. A handbook of human palaeontology*. Cassell, London.

—— and NAPIER, J. R. (1964). Hominid fossils from Bed I, Olduvai Gorge, Tanganyika. *Nature, Lond.* **201**, 967-70.

HOWELL, F. C. (1969). Remains of Hominidae from Pliocene/Pleistocene formations in the lower Omo basin. *Nature, Lond.* **223**, 1234-9.

LEAKEY, L. S. B. (1959). A new fossil skull from Olduvai. *Nature, Lond.* **184**, 491-3.

—— EVERNDEN, J. F., and CURTIS, G. H. (1961). Age of Bed I, Olduvai Gorge, Tanganyika. *Nature, Lond.* **191**, 478-9.

—— TOBIAS, P. V., and NAPIER, J. R. (1964). A new species of the genus *Homo* from Olduvai Gorge. *Nature, Lond.* **202**, 7-9.

LEAKEY, R. E. F. (1970). Fauna and artefacts from a new Plio-Pleistocene locality near Lake Rudolf in Keyna. *Nature, Lond.* **226**, 223-4.

NAPIER, J. (1964). The locomotor functions of hominids. In *Classification and human evolution* (editor S. L. Washburn), pp. 178-89. Methuen, London.

OAKLEY, K. P. (1968). The earliest tool-makers. In *Evolution und hominisation*. 2nd edn. (editor G. Kurth). (1962) *Evolution and hominization: Contributions in honour of Gerhard Heberer on the occasion of his 60th birthday*. Gustave Fischer Verlag, Stuttgart.

PATTERSON, B., BEHRENSMEYER, A. K., and SILL, W. D. (1970). Geology and fauna of a new Pliocene locality in North-western Kenya. *Nature, Lond.* **226**, 918-21.

PILBEAM, D. (1970). *The evolution of man*. Thames and Hudson, London.

ROBINSON, J. T. (1963). Adaptive radiation in the australopithecines and the origin of man. In *African ecology and human evolution* (editors F. C. Howell and F. Boulière). Methuen, London. *Viking Fund Publications for Anthropology*. No. 36. Wenner-Gren Foundation for Anthropological Research Incorporated, New York.

—— (1967). Variation and the taxonomy of the early hominids. In *Evolutionary biology*. Vol. I (editors T. Dobzhansky, M. K. Hecht, and W. C. Steere). Appleton-Century-Crofts, New York.

SIMONS, E. L. (1967). The significance of primate paleontology for anthropological studies. *Am. J. phys. Anthrop.* N.S. **27**, 307-32.

TOBIAS, P. V. (1964). The Olduvai Bed I hominine with special reference to its cranial capacity. *Nature, London*. **202**, 3-4.

—— (1967). *Olduvai Gorge*. Vol. II (editor L. S. B. Leakey). Cambridge University Press.

—— (1968). The taxonomy and phylogeny of the australopithecines. In *Taxonomy and phylogeny of old world primates with references to the origin of man* (editor B. Chiarelli). Rosenberg and Sellier, Torino.

WASHBURN, S. L. (1960). Tools and human evolution. *Scient. Am.* **203** (Sept.), 62–75.

—— (1964). Behaviour and human evolution. In *Classification and human evolution* (editor S. L. Washburn), pp. 190–203. Methuen, London.

—— (1967). Behaviour and the origin of man (Huxley memorial lecture 1967). *Proc. R. anthrop. Inst. for 1967*, pp. 21–7.

YOUNG, L. B. (editor) (1970). *Evolution of man.* Oxford University Press, New York.

ZUCKERMAN, S. (1966). Myths and methods in anatomy (Struther's lecture). *Jl R. Coll. Surg. Edinb.* **11**, 87–114.

CHAPTER 33. THE APPEARANCE OF *HOMO*

CAMPBELL, B. G. (1964). Quantitative taxonomy and human evolution. In *Classification and human evolution* (editor S. L. Washburn), pp. 50–74. Methuen, London.

DAY, M. H. (1965). *Guide to fossil man. A handbook of human palaeontology.* Cassell, London.

HALDANE, J. B. S. (1949). Suggestions as to quantitative measurement of rates of evolution. *Evolution, Lancaster, Pa.* **3**, 51–6.

HAY, R. L. (1963). Stratigraphy of Beds I through IV, Olduvai Gorge, Tanganyika. *Science, N.Y.* **139**, 829–33.

HOWELL, F. C. (1960). European and northwest African Middle Pleistocene hominids. *Curr. Anthrop.* **1**, 195–232.

LEAKEY, L. S. B., and GOODALL, V. M. (1969). *Unveiling man's origins.* Methuen, London.

STRAUS, W. L., and CAVE, A. J. E. (1957). Pathology and the posture of Neanderthal man. *Q. Rev. Biol.* **32**, 348–63.

TOBIAS, P. V. (1965). New discoveries in Tanganyika: their bearing on hominid evolution. *Curr. Anthrop.* **6**, 391–411.

CHAPTER 34. SOME DETERMINANTS OF HUMAN EVOLUTION

DE BEER, G. R. (1958). *Embryos and ancestors.* Clarendon Press, Oxford.

CAMPBELL, B. G. (1966). *Human evolution: an introduction to man's adaptations.* Aldine, Chicago.

CLARK, J. D. (1970). *The prehistory of Africa.* Thames and Hudson, London.

CLARK, W. E. LE GROS (1962). *The antecedents of man.* 2nd edn. Edinburgh University Press.

HARDY, A. C. (1960). Was man more aquatic in the past? *New Scient.* **7**, 642–5.

JONES, F. WOOD (1943). *Habit and heritage.* Kegan Paul, Trench, Trubner and Co., London.

KINSEY, A. C., POMEROY, W. B., MARTIN, C. E., and GEBHARD, P. H. (1953). *Sexual behavior in the human female.* Saunders, Philadelphia.

LEAKEY, L. S. B. (1968). Bone smashing by late Miocene Hominidae. *Nature, Lond.* **218**, 528–30.

LORENZ, K. (1966). *On aggression* (translated by M. Latzke). Methuen, London.

NAPIER, J. R. (1956). The prehensile movements of the human hand. *J. Bone Jt Surg.* **38**, Series B, 902–13.

—— (1964*a*). The locomotor function of hominids. In *Classification and human evolution* (editor S. L. Washburn), pp. 178–89. Methuen, London.

—— (1964*b*). The evolution of bipedal walking in the hominids. *Archs Biol., Liège* **75**, Suppl. 673–708.

—— (1967). The antiquity of human walking. *Scient. Am.* **216** (April), 56–66.

OXNARD, C. E. (1963). Locomotor adaptations in the primate fore-limb. *Symp. zool. Soc. Lond.* **10**, 165–82.

PENFIELD, W. (1966). Speech, perception and the uncommitted cortex. In *Brain and conscious experience* (editor J. C. Eccles). Springer, Berlin.

SCHALLER, G. B. (1965). Behavioural comparisons of the apes. In *Primate behavior: field studies of monkeys and apes* (editor I. de Vore). Holt, Rinehart, and Winston, New York.

CHAPTER 35. THE EVOLUTION OF THE POWERS OF THE HUMAN BRAIN AND
OF SPEECH

CAMPBELL, B. G. (1966). *Human evolution.* Aldine, Chicago.

CHERRY, C. (1966). *On human communication.* M.I.T. Press, Massachusetts.

CHOMSKY, N. (1968). *Language and mind.* Harcourt, Brace, and World, New York.

CRITCHLEY, M. (1970). *Aphasiology and other aspects of language.* Arnold, London.

DARWIN, C. (1872). *The expression of the emotions in man and animals.* Murray, London.

GESCHWIND, N. (1967). The neural basis of language. In *Research in verbal behavior and some neurophysiological implications* (editors K. and S. Salzinger). Academic Press, New York.

—— and LEVITSKY, W. (1968). Human brain: left-right asymmetries in temporal speech region. *Science, N.Y.* **161**, 186-7.

GREGORY, R. (1966). *Eye and brain: the psychology of seeing.* Weidenfeld and Nicolson, London.

GUTHRIE, R. D. (1970). Evolution of human threat display. In *Evolutionary biology.* Vol. IV (editors T. Dobzhansky, M. K. Hecht, and W. C. Steere). Appleton-Century-Crofts, New York.

HALL, K. R. L., and DE VORE, I. (1965). Baboon social behaviour. In *Primate behavior: field studies of monkeys and apes* (editor I. de Vore). Holt, Rinehart, and Winston, New York.

HEBB, D. O. (1966). *A text book of psychology.* Saunders, Philadelphia.

HUBEL, D. H., and WIESEL, T. N. (1968). Receptive fields and functional architecture of monkey striate cortex. *J. Physiol. Lond.* **195**, 215-43.

HUXLEY, J. S. (1942). *Evolution, the modern synthesis.* Allen and Unwin, London.

JERISON, H. J. (1963). Interpreting the evolution of the brain. *Hum. Biol.* **35**, 263-91.

LENNEBERG, E. H. (1967). *Biological foundations of language.* Wiley, New York.

LURIA, A. R. (1966). *The human brain and psychological processes.* Harper and Row, New York.

LYONS, J. (1968). *Introduction to theoretical linguistics.* Cambridge University Press.

—— (1970). *Chomsky.* Fontana Modern Masters (editor F. Kermode). Collins, London.

MARLER, P. (1965). Communication in monkeys and apes. In *Primate behavior: field studies of monkeys and apes* (editor I. de Vore). Holt, Rinehart, and Winston, New York.

MENYUK, P. (1967). Acquisition of grammar by children. In *Research in verbal behavior and some neurophysiological implications* (editors K. and S. Salzinger). Academic Press, New York.

NEWCOMBE, F. (1969). *Missile wounds of the brain.* Oxford University Press.

PENFIELD, W., and ROBERTS, L. (1959). *Speech and brain-mechanisms.* Princeton University Press.

SUTHERLAND, N. S. (1968). Outlines of a theory of visual pattern recognition in animals. *Proc. R. Soc.* **B171**, 297-317.

WADDINGTON, C. H. (1960). *The ethical animal.* George Allen and Unwin, London.

YOUNG, J. Z. (1964). *A model of the brain.* Clarendon Press, Oxford.

CHAPTER 36. THE EVOLUTION OF CULTURE

ARDREY, R. (1967). *The territorial imperative.* Collins, London.

BISHOP, W. W., and CLARK, J. D. (editors) (1967). *Background to evolution in Africa.* University of Chicago Press.

CARRINGTON, R. (1963). *A million years of man*. Weidenfeld and Nicolson, London.

CHILDE, V. GORDON (1942). *What happened in history*. Penguin Books, Harmondsworth.

—— (1966). *Man makes himself*. 4th edn. Fontana Library. Collins, London.

CLARK, G. (1969). *World prehistory: a new outline*. 2nd edn. Cambridge University Press.

—— and PIGGOTT, S. (1970). *Prehistoric societies*. Penguin Books, Harmondsworth. Hutchinson, London.

DARLINGTON, C. D. (1969). *The evolution of man and society*. Allen and Unwin, London.

HALL, K. R. L. (1963). Tool using performances as indicatory of behavioural ability. *Curr. Anthrop.* 4, 479-94.

HAWKES, J. (1954). *Man on earth*. The Cresset Press, London.

—— and WOOLLEY, L. (1963). *History of mankind. Cultural and scientific development.* Vol. I. *Prehistory and the beginnings of civilization*. Allen and Unwin, London.

LEAKEY, M. D. (1966). Review of the Oldowan culture from Olduvai Gorge, Tanzania. *Nature, Lond.* 210, 462-6.

—— (1967). Preliminary survey of the cultural material from Beds I and II, Olduvai Gorge, Tanzania. In *Background to evolution in Africa* (editors W. W. Bishop and J. D. Clark). University of Chicago Press.

—— (1970). Stone artefacts from Swartkrans. *Nature, Lond.* 225, 1222-5.

MARINGER, J. (1960). *The gods of prehistoric man* (trans. from German by M. Ilford). Weidenfeld and Nicolson, London.

OAKLEY, K. P. (1969). *Framework for dating fossil man*. 3rd edn. Weidenfeld and Nicolson, London.

CHAPTER 37. EVIDENCE OF EARLY ART FORMS AND RELIGION

BORST, L. B. (1969). English henge cathedrals. *Nature, Lond.* 224, 335-42.

BURKITT, M. C. (1925). *Prehistory: A study of early culture in Europe and the Mediterranean*. 2nd edn. Cambridge University Press.

LAMING, A. (1959). *Lascaux*. Penguin Books, Harmondsworth.

LEASON, P. A. (1939). A new view of the western European group of Quaternary cave art. *Proc. prehist. Soc.* 5, 51-60.

LEROI-GOURHAN, A. (1968). The evolution of Paleolithic art. *Scient. Am.* 218 (Feb.), 58-70.

MARAIS, E. N. (1939). *My friends the baboons*. Methuen, London.

MORRIS, D. (1962). *The biology of art: A study of the picture-making behaviour of the great apes and its relationship to human art*. Methuen, London.

PUMPHREY, R. J. (1953). The origin of language. *Acta psychol.* 9, 219-39.

RENSCH, B. (1957). Ästhetische Faktoren bei Farb-und Formbevorzugungen von Affen. *Z. Tierpsychol.* 14, 71-99.

SANDARS, N. K. (1968). *Prehistoric art in Europe*. Penguin Books, Harmondsworth.

UCKO, P. J., and DIMBLEBY, G. W. (editors) (1969). *The domestication and exploitation of plants and animals*. Duckworth, London.

—— and ROSENFELD, A. (1967). *Palaeolithic cave art*. Weidenfeld and Nicolson, London.

YOUNG, J. Z. (1950). B.B.C. Reith Lectures (1951). *Doubt and certainty in science*. Clarendon Press, Oxford.

ZUCKERMAN, S. (1932). *The social life of monkeys and apes*. Routledge and Kegan Paul, Trench, Trubner and Co., London.

CHAPTER 38. HUMAN VARIETY TODAY

BACON, F. (1625). *Essayes on Counsels Civill and Morall VII: of Parents and Children*. In *The Philosophical works of Francis Bacon* (1905) (editor J. M. Robertson). Routledge and Kegan Paul, London.

BAKER, P. T., and WEINER, J. S. (editors) (1966). *The biology of human adaptability*. Clarendon Press, Oxford.

BULMER, M. G. (1970). *The biology of twinning in man.* Clarendon Press, Oxford.
BURNET, M. (1962). *Natural history of infectious disease.* 3rd edn. Cambridge University Press.
BURT, C. L. (1946). Intelligence and fertility. *Occ. Pap. Eugen.* **2.** Hamish Hamilton, London.
—— (1955). The evidence for the concept of intelligence. *Br. J. educ. Pyscol.* **25,** 158–77.
—— (1966). The genetic determination of differences in intelligence: a study of mono-zygotic twins reared together and apart. *Br. J. Psychol.* **57,** 137–53.
CARTER, C. O. (1962). *Human heredity.* Penguin Books, Harmondsworth.
COOPER, L. Z. (1966). German measles. *Scient. Am.* **215** (July), 30–7.
DARLINGTON, C. D. (1969). *The evolution of man and society.* Allen and Unwin, London.
DUKES, C. E. (1952). Familial intestinal polyposis. *Ann. Eugen.* **17,** 1–29.
GALTON, F. (1869). *Hereditary genius.* Macmillan, London. (1962) Fontana Library, Collins, London.
GARROD, A. E. (1908). The Croonian lectures on inborn errors of metabolism. *Lancet* **2,** 1–7, 73–9, 142–8, 214–20.
—— (1909). *Inborn errors of metabolism.* Frowde, Hodder, and Stoughton, London.
GENTRY, J. T., PARKHURST, E., and BULIN, G. V., JR. (1966). An epidemiological study of congenital malformations in New York State. In *Human ecology* (editor J. B. Bresler). Addison-Wesley, Massachusetts.
GORER, P. A. (1947). Genetic factors and population. In *Child health and development* (editor R. W. B. Ellis). Churchill, London.
HARRIS, H. (1970). *The principles of human biochemical genetics.* North-Holland Publishing Co., Amsterdam.
HERTZOG, K. P., and JOHNSTON, F. E. (1968). Selection and the Rh polymorphism. *Hum. Biol.* **40,** 86–97.
HUNTLEY, R. M. C. (1966). Heritability of intelligence. In *Genetic and environmental factors in human ability* (editors J. E. Meade and A. S. Parkes), pp. 201–18. Oliver and Boyd, Edinburgh and London.
KALLMANN, F. J. (1953). *Heredity in health and mental disorder.* Norton, New York.
KALMUS, H. (1957). *Variation and heredity.* Routledge and Kegan Paul, London.
—— (1963). Genetical taste polymorphism and thyroid disease. *Proc. 2nd int. Congr. hum. Genet.* Instituto Gregorio Mendel, Rome.
KNOBLOCH, H., and PASAMANICK, B. (1958). Seasonal variation in the births of the mentally deficient. *Am. J. publ. Hlth.* **48,** 1201–8, in *Human ecology* (editor J. B. Bresler) 1966. Addison-Wesley, Reading, Massachusetts.
LEAHY, A. M. (1935). Nature-nurture and intelligence. *Genet. Psychol. Monogr.* **17,** 236–308.
MAXWELL, J. (1953). *See* Scottish Council for research in education.
—— (1961). *The level and trend of national intelligence: The contribution of the Scottish mental surveys.* University of London Press, London.
McKUSICK, V. A. (1969). *Human genetics.* 2nd edn. Prentice-Hall, Englewood Cliffs, New Jersey.
MILLS, C. A. (1949). Temperature dominance over human life. *Science, N.Y.* **110,** 267–71.
MORTON, N. E., KRIEGER, H., and MI, M. P. (1966). Natural selection on polymorphisms in north-eastern Brazil. *Am. J. hum. Genet.* **18,** 153–71.
NEWMAN, H. H., FREEMAN, F. N., and HOLZINGER, K. J. (1937). *Twins: a study of heredity and environment.* University of Chicago Press.
PEARSON, K. (1931). On the inheritance of mental disease. *Ann. Eugen.* **4,** 362–80.
PENROSE, L. S. (1963). *The biology of mental defect.* 3rd edn. Sidgwick and Jackson, London.
POST, R. H. (1962). Population differences in red and green colour vision deficiency. *Eugen. Q.* **9,** 131–46.
RICHTER, C. P. (1954). The effects of domestication and selection on the behaviour of the Norway rat. *J. natn. Cancer Inst.* **15,** 727–38.

ROBERTS, J. A. F. (1970). *An introduction to medical genetics.* 5th edn. Oxford University Press.

SCHULTZ, A. H. (1964). Age changes, sex differences, and variability as factors in the classification of primates. In *Classification and human evolution* (editor S. L. Washburn), pp. 85-115. Methuen, London.

SCOTTISH COUNCIL FOR RESEARCH IN EDUCATION (THOMSON, G. M.) (1949). *The trend of Scottish intelligence.* University of London Press.

—— (MAXWELL, J.) (1953). *Social implications of the 1947 Scottish mental survey.* University of London Press.

SHEPPARD, P. M. (1967). *Natural selection and heredity.* 3rd edn. Hutchinson, London.

STERN, C. (1960). *Principles of human genetics.* 2nd edn. W. H. Freeman and Co., San Francisco and London.

THOMSON, G. M. (1949). *See* Scottish Council for research in education.

WILLOUGHBY, R. R. (1928). Family similarities in mental test abilities. *Twenty-seventh yearbook of the National Society for the Study of Education, Nature and Nurture.* Part I: *Their influence upon intelligence,* p. 55. Public School Publishing Co., Bloomington, Ill.

WORKMAN, P. L. (1968). Gene flow and the search for natural selection in man. *Hum. Biol.* **40,** 260-79.

CHAPTER 39. VARIATION IN HEIGHT, BODILY FORM, AND OTHER POLYGENIC CHARACTERISTICS

BIASUTTI, R. (1953). *Le Razze e i Popoli della Terra.* Vol. I, 2nd edn. Unione Tipografico-Editrice Torinese, Turin.

CUMMINS, H., and MIDLO, C. (1943). *Finger prints, palms and soles.* Blakiston, Philadelphia.

DARLINGTON, C. D. (1969). *The evolution of man and society.* Allen and Unwin, London.

FISHER, R. A. (1918). The correlation between relatives on the supposition of Mendelian inheritance. *Trans. R. Soc. Edinb.* **52,** 399-433.

GREULICH, W. W. (1957). A comparison of the physical growth and development of American born and native Japanese children. *Am. J. phys. Anthrop.* N.S. **15,** 489-515.

HAMILTON, M., PICKERING, G. W., ROBERTS, J. A. F., and SOWRY, G. S. C. (1954). The aetiology of essential hypertension. 1. The arterial pressure in the general population. 2. Scores for arterial blood pressures adjusted for differences in age and sex. 4. The role of inheritance. *Clin. Sci.* **13,** 11-35, 37-49, 273-304.

HARRISON, G. A., WEINER, J. S., TANNER, J. M., and BARNICOT, N. A. (1964). *Human biology: an introduction to human evolution, variation and growth.* Clarendon Press, Oxford.

HOLT, S. B. (1961). Dermatoglyphic patterns. In *Genetical variation in human populations.* Vol. IV (editor G. A. Harrison), pp. 79-98. Pergamon Press, Oxford.

HUBER, N. M. (1968). The problem of stature increase: looking from the past to the present. In *The skeletal biology of earlier human populations* (editor D. R. Brothwell). Symp. Soc. Study of Human Biology No. 7. Pergamon Press, Oxford.

KARN, M. N., and PENROSE, L. S. (1952). Birth weight and gestation time in relation to maternal age, parity and infant survival. *Ann. Eugen.* **16,** 147-64.

MASON, A. S., and TANNER, J. M. (1967). Human growth hormone in the treatment of dwarfism. In *Modern trends in endocrinology.* Vol. III (editor H. Gardiner-Hill). Butterworths, London.

MATHER, K. (1964). *Human diversity.* Oliver and Boyd, Edinburgh and London.

MILLS, C. A. (1942). Climatic effects on growth and development with particular reference to the effects of tropical residence. *Am. Anthrop.* **44,** 1-13.

NEWMAN, M. T. (1953). The application of ecological rules to the racial anthropology of the aboriginal New World. *Am. Anthrop.* **55,** 311-27; in *Human ecology* (editor J. B. Bresler), 1966. Addison-Wesley, Massachusetts.

SCHOLANDER, P. F. (1955). Evolution of climatic adaptation in homoiotherms. *Evolution*, Lancaster, Pa. **9**, 15-26; in *Human ecology* (editor J. B. Bresler), 1966. Addison-Wesley, Massachusetts.

SCHREIDER, E. (1951). Race, constitution, thermolyse. *Revue scient.*, Paris **89**, 110-19. See also (1950) Geographical distribution of the body weight/body surface ratio. *Nature, Lond.* **165**, 286.

SHELDON, W. H., STEVENS, S. S., and TUCKER, W. B. (1940). *The varieties of human physique.* Harper, New York.

TANNER, J. M., and WHITEHOUSE, R. (1967). Growth response of twenty-six children with short stature given human growth hormone. *Brit. med. J.* **2**, 69-75.

YOUNG, J. Z. (1957). *The life of mammals.* Clarendon Press, Oxford.

CHAPTER 40. VARIATIONS IN SKIN COLOUR AND IN BLOOD GROUP

BRACE, C. L., and MONTAGU, M. F. ASHLEY (1965). *Man's evolution.* Macmillan, New York.

HERTZOG, K. P., and JOHNSTON, F. E. (1968). Selection and the Rh polymorphism. *Hum. Biol.* **40**, 86-98.

LEHMANN, H., and HUNTSMAN, R. G. (1966). *Man's haemoglobins, including the haemoglobinopathies and their investigation.* North-Holland Publishing Co., Amsterdam.

LOOMIS, W. F. (1967). Skin-pigment regulation of vitamin-D biosynthesis in man. *Science, N.Y.* **157**, 501-6.

MURRAY, F. G. (1934). Pigmentation, sunlight and nutritional disease. *Am. Anthrop.* **36**, 438-45.

RACE, R. R., and SANGER, R. (1962). *Blood groups in man.* 4th edn. Blackwell, Oxford.

SZULMAN, A. E. (1964). The histological distribution of the blood group substances in man as disclosed by immunofluorescence. III. The A, B, and H antigens in embryos and fetuses from 18 mm in length. *J. exp. Med.* **119**, 503-15.

CHAPTER 41. THE DIFFERENTIAL DISTRIBUTION OF GENES. 'RACES'

ALLISON, A. C. (1961). Abnormal haemoglobins and erythrocyte enzyme-deficiency traits. In *Genetical variation in human populations.* Vol. IV (editor G. A. Harrison), pp. 16-40. Pergamon Press, Oxford.

BROSNAHAN, L. F. (1961). *The sounds of language. A inquiry into the role of genetic factors in the development of sound systems.* Heffer, Cambridge.

CHUNG, C. S., MORTON, N. E., and YASUDA, N. (1966). Genetics of interracial crosses. *Ann. N.Y. Acad. Sci.* **134** (2), 666-87.

COON, C. S. (1962). *The origin of races.* Knopf, New York.

—— (1966). The taxonomy of human variation. *Ann. N.Y. Acad. Sci.* **134** (2), 516-23.

DARLINGTON, C. D. (1947). The genetic component of language. *Heredity, Lond.* **1**, 269-86.

—— (1969). *The evolution of man and society.* Allen and Unwin, London.

DOBZHANSKY, T. (1955). A review of some fundamental concepts and problems of population genetics. *Cold Spring Harb. Symp. quant. Biol.* **20**, 1-15.

FORD, E. B. (1965). *Genetic polymorphism.* All Souls Studies V. Faber and Faber, London.

HAMILTON, W. D. (1963). The evolution of altruistic behaviour. *Am. Nat.* **97**, 354-6.

HARRISON, G. A., WEINER, J. S., TANNER, J. M., and BARNICOT, N. A. (1964). *Human biology: an introduction to human evolution, variation and growth.* Clarendon Press, Oxford.

KÜCHEMANN, C. F., BOYCE, A. J., and HARRISON, G. A. (1967). A demographic and genetic study of a group of Oxfordshire villages. *Hum. Biol.* **39**, 251-76.

MANGE, A. P. (1964). Growth and inbreeding of a human isolate. *Hum. Biol.* **36**, 104-33.

MAYNARD SMITH, J. (1964). Group selection and kin selection. *Nature, Lond.* **201**, 1145-7.

MOURANT, A. E., KOPEĆ, A. C., and DOMANIEWSKA-SOBCZAK, K. (1958). *The ABO blood groups.* Blackwell, Oxford.

ROBERTS, J. A. FRASER (1942). Blood group frequencies in North Wales. *Ann. Eugen.* **11**, 260-71.

SALDANHA, P. H. (1964). Frequency of congenital malformations in mixed populations of southern Brazil. In *Second International Conference on congenital malformations.* New York 1963. International Medical Congress Ltd., New York.

TANNER, J. M. (1964). *The physique of the Olympic athlete.* George Allen and Unwin, London.

TREVOR, J. C. (1953). Race crossing in man. The analysis of metrical characters. *Eugen. Lab. Mem.* **36**.

WYNNE-EDWARDS, V. C. (1962). *Animal dispersion in relation to social behaviour.* Oliver and Boyd, London and Edinburgh.

—— (1964). Group selection and kin selection. *Nature, Lond.* **201**, 1147.

CHAPTER 42. THE SPRINGS OF HUMAN ACTION

BAJUSZ, E. and collaborators (1969). *Physiology and pathology of adaptation mechanisms: neural-neuroendocrine-humoral.* Pergamon Press, Oxford.

BRAZIER, M. A. B. (1968). *The electrical activity of the nervous system. A text book for students.* Pitman, London.

CANNON, W. B. (1915). *Bodily changes in pain, hunger, fear and rage.* (1929) 2nd edn. Appleton, New York and London.

CRAIK, K. J. W. (1943). *The nature of explanation.* Cambridge University Press.

CROSS, B. A. (1964). The hypothalamus in mammalian homeostasis. *Symp. Soc. exp. Biol.* **18**, 157-93.

ECCLES, J. C. (1953). *The neurophysiological basis of mind: the principles of neurophysiology.* Clarendon Press, Oxford.

GERARD, R. W., and YOUNG, J. Z. (1937). Electrical activity of the central nervous system of the frog. *Proc. R. Soc.* B**122**, 343-52.

GLOVER, J. (1970). *Responsibility.* (International Library of Philosophy and Scientific Method, editor T. Honderich). Routledge and Kegan Paul, London.

HANSEL, C. E. M. (1966). *E.S.P.—a scientific evaluation.* Scribners, New York.

HARRÉ, R. (1970). *The principles of scientific thinking.* Macmillan, London.

HEBB, D. O. (1949). *The organization of behavior.* Wiley, New York.

HUBEL, D. H., and WIESEL, T. N. (1968). Receptive fields and functional architecture of monkey striate cortex. *J. Physiol. Lond.* **195**, 215-43.

JOHN, E. R. (1967). *Mechanisms of memory.* Academic Press, New York.

KLÜVER, H., and BUCY, P. C. (1939). Preliminary analysis of functions of the temporal lobes in monkeys. *Archs. Neurol. Psychiat., Chicago* **42**, 979-1000.

LUCAS, J. R. (1970). *The freedom of the will.* Clarendon Press, Oxford.

MAGOUN, H. W. (1963). *The waking brain.* 2nd edn. Thomas, Springfield.

MELZACK, R., and WALL, P. D. (1965). Pain mechanisms: a new theory. *Science, N.Y.* **150**, 971-9.

MORUZZI, G., and MAGOUN, H. W. (1949). Brain stem reticular formation and activation of the EEG. *Electroenceph. clin. Neurophysiol.* **1**, 455-73.

PAKKENBERG, H. (1966). The number of nerve cells in the cerebral cortex of man. *J. comp. Neurol.* **128**, 17-20.

PANTIN, C. F. A. (1968). *The relations between the sciences.* Cambridge University Press.

PARMEGGIANI, P. L. (1967). On the functional significance of the hippocampal θ-rhythm. In *Progress in brain research.* Vol. XXVII (editors W. R. Adey and T. Tokizane). Elsevier, Amsterdam.

RAO, K.-R. (1966). *Experimental parapsychology.* Thomas, Springfield.

SHERRINGTON, C. S. (1906, 1952). *The integrative action of the nervous system.* Constable, London.

SUTHERLAND, N. S. (1960). Theories of shape discrimination in *Octopus*. *Nature, Lond.* **186**, 840-4.

—— (1961). The methods and findings of experiments in the visual discrimination of shape by animals. *Exp. Psychol. Monogr.* No. 1. 68 pp.

VON FOERSTER, H. (1965). Memory without record. In *Conference on learning, remembering and forgetting, Vol. I. Anatomy of memory* (editor D. P. Kimble). Science and Behaviour Books, California.

WANG, G. H. (1923). The relation between 'spontaneous' activity and oestrous cycle in the white rat. *Comp. Psychol. Monogr.* **2**, No. 6.

YOUNG, J. Z. (1960). The visual system of *Octopus*. 1. Regularities in the retina and optic lobes of *Octopus* in relation to form discrimination. *Nature, Lond.* **186**, 836-9.

—— (1964). *A model of the brain.* Clarendon Press, Oxford.

—— (1965). The organisation of a memory system. The Croonian lecture 1965. *Proc. R. Soc.* B**163**, 285-320.

CHAPTER 43. HUMAN CO-OPERATION AND HUMAN AGGRESSION

ARDREY, R. (1961). *African genesis.* Collins, London.

—— (1967). *The territorial imperative.* Collins, London.

CARPENTER, C. R. (1942). Societies of monkeys and apes. *Biol. Symp.* **8**, 77-204.

DE VORE, I. (editor) (1965). *Primate behaviour: field studies of monkeys and apes.* Holt, Rinehart, and Winston, New York.

HOWARD, H. E. (1920). *Territory in bird life.* Murray, London.

LACK, D. (1954). *The natural regulation of animal numbers.* Clarendon Press, Oxford.

LORENZ, K. (1966). *On aggression* (trans. M. Latzke). Methuen, London.

MONTAGU, ASHLEY (editor) (1968). *Man and aggression.* Oxford University Press, New York.

TINBERGEN, N. (1968). On war and peace in animals and man. *Science, N.Y.* **160**, 1411-18.

TROTTER, W. (1917). *Instincts of the herd in war and peace.* Fisher Unwin, London.

WATSON, A. (1961). Seventh Progress Report, Nature Conservancy Unit of Grouse and Moorland Ecology (Fig. 4). See Wynne-Edwards (1962).

WYNNE-EDWARDS, V. C. (1962). *Animal dispersion in relation to social behaviour.* Oliver and Boyd, Edinburgh.

CHAPTER 44. SUMMARY OF OUR KNOWLEDGE OF LIFE AND ITS EXPANSION

CRAIK, K. J. W. (1943). *The nature of explanation.* Cambridge University Press.

KATZ, J. J. (1962). *The problem of induction and its solution.* University of Chicago Press.

KUHN, T. S. (1963). *The structure of scientific revolutions.* University of Chicago Press.

POPPER, K. R. (1970). Normal science and its dangers. In *Criticism and the growth of knowledge* (editors I. Lakatos and A. Musgrave). *Proceedings of the International Colloquium in the Philosophy of Science, London, 1965, Vol. 4.* Cambridge University Press.

YOUNG, J. Z. (1938). The evolution of the nervous system and of the relationship of organism and environment. In *Evolution. Essays presented to E. S. Goodrich* (editor G. R. de Beer). Clarendon Press, Oxford.

—— (1950). *The life of vertebrates* (2nd edn. 1962). Clarendon Press, Oxford.

—— (1951). *Doubt and certainty in science.* Clarendon Press, Oxford.

AUTHOR INDEX

Italics show references cited only in the bibliography and indicate the relevant chapter or the general section (*Gen.*).

The names of all authors are given in this index although only the first one of a citation may appear in the text.

Abercrombie, M. (1957), 211
  (1964), 160-1
  (1967), 178
Adolph, E. F. (1968), 103
Adrian, E. D. (1966), 123, 136
Aitken, J. T. (1947), 210
Akert, K. (1965), 133
Alexander, D. P. (1968), 197
Alexander, P. (1967), 288, 299
Allison, A. C. (1961), 595
Ambrose, A. (1969), 247, 267
Andersen, A. C. (1965), 289
Angel, R. (1965), 297
Angeletti, P. U. (1968), 156
Aposhian, H. V. (1964), 51
Ardrey, R. (1961), 450, 626
  (1967), 517, 624-5
Argyris, B. F. (1959), 161
Argyris, T. S. (1959), 161
Aron, C. (1966), 194
Asch, G. (1966), 194
Ashby, W. R. (1960), 129
Ayer, A. J. (1963), 126-7

Bacon, F. (1625), 559
Bajusz, E. (1969), *42*
Baker, P. T. (1966), 541, 548
Baker, R. F. (1968), 58
Ballou, J. E. (1956), 84
Bally, C. (1965), 133
Baltzer, F. (1958), 176
Banghoorn, E. S. (1966), 406
Banks, B. E. C. (1969), 156
Banthorpe, D. V. (1969), 156
Barclay, G. W. (1958), 323
Barnes, L. L. (1939), 315
Barnicot, N. A. (1964), 572-3, 577-8, 596, *Gen.*
  (1967), 444
  (1969), 436
Bartlett, E. G. (1951), 299
Bartlett, F. (1964), 254
Bastock, M. (1967), 185
Baudey, J. (1963), 218
Bavister, B. D. (1969), 197
Bayley, N. (1955), 266-72
  (1963), 271
  (1967), 267

Bayliss, L. E. (1959), *Gen.*
Beach, F. A. (1951), 182
Beaujeu-Garnier, J. (1966), 322, 325, 349, 351
Behrensmeyer, A. K. (1970), 455
Bell, E. (1969), 55
Bell, G. H. (1968), *Gen.*
Benjamin, B. (1959), 307, 309
Berelson, G. (1964), 338
Berg, J. M. (1968), 195
Berger, R. J. (1963), 135
Bernal, J. D. (1960), 373
  (1967), 371
Bernard, C., 93
Berry, A. R. (1969), 156
Beverton, R. J. H. (1959), 310
Biasutti, R. (1953), 568
Bidder, G. P. (1932), 312
Binet, A., 264
  (1905), 260
Bishop, W. W. (1967), 501
  (1970), 455
Bizzozero, G. (1894), 145
Blake, C. C. F. (1967), 66
Blakemore, C. (1970), 244
Blandau, R. J. (1969), 189
Blinkov, S. M. (1968), 222
Bodenheimer, F. S. (1938), 311
Bodo, G. (1959), 62
Boman, K. K. A. (1960), 133
Boreham, A. J. (1970), 353
Borst, L. B. (1969), 524
Boswell, J., 337
Bourgeois-Pichat, J., 319
Bourlière, F. (1957), 314
Boyce, A. J. (1967), 588-9
Boyd, J. D. (1964), 220
Brace, C. L. (1965), 581
Brachet, J. (1967), 178
Bradley, D. J., 216
Brain, C. K. (1970), 452
Braithwaite, R. B. (1953), 2, 124
Brass, W. (1968), 322
Brazier, M. A. B. (1968), 610
Bretscher, M. S. (1968), 59
Breuil, H. E. P., 536
Britten, R. J. (1969), 75, 77
Britton, H. G. (1968), 197

SUBJECT INDEX